PUBLIC LAND POLICIES

This is a volume in the Arno Press collection

THE MANAGEMENT OF PUBLIC LANDS IN THE UNITED STATES

Advisory Editor
Stuart Bruchey

Research Associate
Eleanor Bruchey

Editorial Board
Marion Clawson
Paul W. Gates

*See last pages of this volume
for a complete list of titles*

PUBLIC LAND POLICIES

Management and Disposal

Edited with an Introduction by

Paul Wallace Gates

ARNO PRESS
A New York Times Company
New York • 1979

Editorial Supervision: JOSEPH CELLINI

———◆———

Reprint Edition 1979 by Arno Press Inc.

Arrangement and Compilation Copyright © 1979
by Paul Wallace Gates

Introduction Copyright © 1979 by Paul Wallace Gates

THE MANAGEMENT OF PUBLIC LANDS IN THE UNITED STATES
ISBN for complete set: 0-405-11315-3
See last pages of this volume for titles.

Manufactured in the United States of America

———◆———

Library of Congress Cataloging in Publication Data

Main entry under title:

Public land policies.

   (The Management of public lands in the United States)
   1. United States--Public lands--History--Addresses,
essays, lectures. I. Gates, Paul Wallace, 1901-
II. Series.
HD191.P8   333.1'0973   78-56714
ISBN 0-405-11360-9

ACKNOWLEDGEMENTS

"Private Land Claims in the South" by Paul W. Gates from *Journal of Southern History,* Vol. XXII, No. 2, May, 1956. Copyright 1956 by the Southern Historical Association. Reprinted by permission of the Managing Editor.

"The Forfeiture of Railroad Land Grants, 1867-1894" by David Maldwyn Ellis and "Timber Empire from the Public Domain" by Roy E. Appleman have been reprinted from *Mississippi Valley Historical Review* by permission of the Organization of American Historians.

"The Northern Pacific Railroad and Montana's Mineral Lands" by Thomas A. Clinch, Copyright © 1965 by the Pacific Coast Branch, American Historical Association. Reprinted from *Pacific Historical Review,* Vol. 34, No. 3, pp. 323-335 by permission of the Branch.

"Public Lands, Politics, and Progressives: The Oregon Land Fraud Trials, 1903-1910" by John Messing, Copyright © 1966 by the Pacific Coast Branch, American Historical Association. Reprinted from *Pacific Historical Review,* Vol. 35, No. 1, pp. 35-66 by permission of the Branch.

"The Homestead Act: Free Land Policy in Operation, 1862-1935" by Paul Wallace Gates and "The Homestead Act in Perspective" by Mari Sandoz have been reprinted from *Land Use Policy and Problems in the United States* by Howard W. Ottoson by permission of the University of Nebraska Press. Copyright © 1963 by the University of Nebraska Press.

"Land Disposal in Nebraska, 1854-1906: The Homestead Story" by Homer Socolofsky has been reprinted from *Nebraska History,* Vol. 48, No. 3, Autumn, 1967 by permission of the Nebraska State Historical Society. Copyright © 1967 by the Nebraska State Historical Society.

CONTENTS

Clinch, Thomas A.
THE NORTHERN PACIFIC RAILROAD AND MONTANA'S
MINERAL LANDS (Reprinted from *Pacific Historical Review,* Vol.
XXXIV, No. 3), Berkeley, California, August, 1965

Appleman, Roy E.
TIMBER EMPIRE FROM THE PUBLIC DOMAIN (Reprinted from
The Mississippi Valley Historical Review, Vol. XXVI, No. 2),
September, 1939

Gates, Paul W[allace]
 THE HOMESTEAD ACT: Free Land Policy in Operation, 1862-1935
(Reprinted from *Land Use Policy and Problems in the United States*)
Lincoln, Nebraska, 1963

Sandoz, Mari, THE HOMESTEAD IN PERSPECTIVE (Reprinted
from *Land Use Policy and Problems in the United States*) Lincoln,
Nebraska, 1963

Gates, Paul Wallace
FEDERAL LAND POLICY IN THE SOUTH, 1866-1888 (Reprinted
from *The Journal of Southern History,* Vol. VI, No. 3) University,
La., August, 1940

Anderson, George L.
THE ADMINISTRATION OF FEDERAL LAND LAWS IN
WESTERN KANSAS, 1880—1890: A Factor in Adjustment to a New
Environment (Reprinted from *The Kansas Historical Quarterly,* Vol.
XX, No. 4), Topeka, Kansas, November, 1952

Socolofsky, Homer
LAND DISPOSAL IN NEBRASKA, 1854-1906; The Homestead
Story (Reprinted from *Nebraska History,* Vol. 48, No. 3), Lincoln,
Nebraska, Autumn, 1967

Ganoe, John T.
THE DESERT LAND ACT IN OPERATION, 1877-1891 (Reprinted
from *Agricultural History,* Vol. 11, No. 2), April, 1937

Larson, Gustave O.
LAND CONTEST IN EARLY UTAH (Reprinted from *Utah
Historical Quarterly,* Vol. XXIX, No. 4), Salt Lake City, Utah,
October, 1961

Mosk, Sanford A.
LAND TENURE PROBLEMS IN THE SANTA FE RAILROAD
GRANT AREA, Berkeley, Cal., 1944

Messing, John
PUBLIC LANDS, POLITICS, AND PROGRESSIVES: The Oregon
Land Fraud Trials, 1903-1910 (Reprinted from *Pacific Historical
Review,* Vol. XXXV, No. 1), Berkeley, Ca., February, 1966

Williams, R. Hal
GEORGE W. JULIAN AND LAND REFORM IN NEW MEXICO,
1885-1889 (Reprinted from *Agricultural History,* Vol. XLI, No. 1),
January, 1967

Lee, Robert
VALENTINE SCRIP: The Saga of Land Locations in Southern
Dakota Territory Originating from a Mexican Land Grant (Reprinted
from *South Dakota History,* Vol. 2, No. 3), Pierre, South Dakota,
Summer, 1972

Le Duc, Thomas
THE DISPOSAL OF THE PUBLIC DOMAIN ON THE TRANS-
MISSISSIPPI PLAINS: Some Opportunities for Investigation
(Reprinted from *Agricultural History,* Vol. 24, No. 4), October, 1950

INTRODUCTION

The more deeply historians carry their researches into the sources of public land history, the more they realize how infinitely complex the system became with its numerous mutually irreconcilable features and objectives and with many conflicting economic groups trying to shape policy in Congress, in the administration, in the states and in the courts. To the usual sources used by early writers historians must now delve into federal and state land entry and tract books, original census schedules, deed, mortgage, tax and probate records, court records, private manuscript collections, papers of credit institutions and the great volume of correspondence of the land administering agencies. Long accepted generalizations may appear still acceptable, but the wide variety of influences—geographic, economic and political, make reconsideration necessary on many points. Modern computerized studies can achieve much, but practitioners must be careful to ask the correct questions. The tendency to concentrate upon contributions to the Gross National Product has tended to limit the usefulness of such studies.

Because of the complexity and variety of state and national history, even the best general syntheses of public land policies fail to discuss fine points and distinctions that specialized researchers have grasped. Some of these intensive investigations have appeared only as articles in historical journals. They are not exactly buried, but they have been too frequently overlooked by generalists. An illustration is a thoughtfully researched and brilliant analytical study by George L. Anderson on "The Board of Equitable Adjudication, 1846-1930," in *Agricultural History* for 1955. Many settlers, who on equitable grounds, deserved to receive patents found their applications suspended because they had failed to conform fully to the requirements of the laws and the administrative decrees. Probably some consideration was given to exceptional cases before 1845, but in that year Congress created the Board of Equitable Adjudication consisting of the Secretary of the Treasury, the Attorney General and the Commissioner of the Land Office to decide such cases in equity. As statutory and administrative law became increasingly complex, the Board's activities became familiar to many who through ignorance or inattention had not satisfied the exact requirements for title to the land on which they had invested their labor. As Anderson says: "However much...the picture of land administration may be painted in dark colors of fraud, corruption and unscrupulous self-seeking, here is a small segment that stands out in bold relief: an agency...whose only purpose was to confirm the title to a particular tract of land to a person who tried to comply with the law, but had failed...through ignorance, error, or obstacle over which he had no control."

The first serious problem the United States had to deal with when it took control of areas previously a part of British, French, Spanish and Mexican territory was that of adjudicating the land grants given by the predecessor governments. In most instances the records of the private land claims were in poor shape, some were totally missing. More than a few claims were mere occupancy rights or were conditional. Included in these claims were the sites of major cities of today such as New Orleans, St. Louis, San Francisco, Detroit and Mobile. They also included much of the best cotton and sugar cane growing land in Louisiana, Mississippi and Alabama and much of the richest vegetable and fruit growing land in Florida and California. If the grants proved legitimate and if the grantees had fulfilled the requirements they were confirmed by commissions and courts and ordered to patent by Congress. At every step in the judicial process serious problems were encountered in eliminating the fraudulent claims and resolving those with overlapping boundaries. R.S. Cotterill, in a brief but thoughtful article on "The National Land System in the South," brings out the complexities faced by government commissioners who commonly were not well versed in Spanish or French and were even less familiar with Spanish and French law. Cotterill shows that residents in areas settled when American control was established in the Louisiana Purchase were each given 640 acres, whether or not they had legal grants, and that Americans who moved into the Natchez and Tombigbee areas between 1798 and 1803 were allowed pre-emption rights.

Lemont K. Richardson provides a setting for the 3,748 Spanish claims amounting to well over a million acres in eastern Missouri, and Paul Gates treats the larger claims in the five southern public land states. The land commissions were somewhat less demanding of proof on the smaller claims if there was evidence that they had been improved, but were more discriminating in considering the larger claims that ran up into hundreds of thousands of acres.

Paul Gates shows how influential Americans grabbed up many of the southern claims, even those which were questionable on their face and over and over again tried to secure confirmation by congressional action. A number of very large claims that were clearly not worthy of confirmation, when sold to others in small tracts and improved, the settlers on them were allowed to purchase them at the government minimum price of $1.25 an acre. The Spanish grants contributed largely to the concentration of ownership of highly fertile land in the richest sugar cane and cotton producing areas of Mississippi and Louisiana.

One of the earliest government officials dispatched to a new frontier was the surveyor. He generally, though by no means always, preceded the squatter, established his base lines and principal meridians, divided the land into 640 acre sections and quarter sections, and attempted to leave marks as guides for land lookers. Dwight L. Agnew concentrates on the surveyors in early Michigan. They were remote from civilization, suspiciously watched by Indians, harassed by mosquitoes, plagued by floods and uncertain about completing their work with profit. Some were later to capitalize upon their knowledge of the land by selling their information to speculators for a share in the land.

Congress early began sharing its land with the states, giving them grants for education, for the establishment of universities, for the building of canals and railroads and for other public institutions. It also made large grants direct to railroad companies to assist them in building their lines through undeveloped territory. Altogether some 340,000,000 acres was thus granted to states and railroads. The biggest corporate beneficiary of this largesse was the Northern Pacific Railroad which was given alternate sections for a distance of 40 miles on each side of its line in the territories through which it was projected, and for 20 miles on each side within states. This grant amounted to 39,000,000 acres, or an area larger than all New England. The Union and Central Pacific received large financial loans in addition to their land grants. Every public land state but Ohio, Indiana and South Dakota benefitted from these grants. The West was almost solidly for the grants at the outset, but after the railroads were built and the smaller lines integrated into systems, their rates became increasingly heavy, or so the shippers felt, and they turned against the principal companies demanding government regulation, maximum rates and better services. If the railroads had not built all the mileage specified in the grants or were withholding land for high prices contrary to the $2.50 maximum specified in some grants, westerners demanded forfeiture of the land. David M. Ellis's study of the move for the forfeiture of unearned grants, or grants whose other requirements had not been fulfilled, and of the demand for the return to public land status of 37,000,000 acres of railroad land reveals the depth of the anti-railroad sentiment.

Ellis's second article centers on the grant to the Oregon & California Railroad Co., a subsidiary of the Southern Pacific, which had failed to make its lands available to settlers at $2.50 an acre and finally had withdrawn them from sale. The evasion of the granting act and the company's obvious intention of retaining the richly endowed timber lands created a strong demand for the forfeiture of this grant. Congress, ordinarily less susceptible to demands for forfeiture, yielded. The United States thereby recovered ownership of what is today the most valuable timbered areas in public ownership.

The political lobbying leading to the enactment of railroad land grants and the sale policies and emigration promotion activities of some leading railroad companies have been well described in book length studies, but the grant or selection of mineral lands by the railroads and the enormous amounts of oil, gas and coal deposits these lands contain are topics about which little is known. Thomas A. Clinch's, "The Northern Pacific Railroad and Montana's Mineral Lands," shows that the Northern Pacific officials tried to select, as part of its grant, lands that were presumably suitable for agriculture but were known to have valuable mineral deposits. Congress was belatedly induced to enact a measure to halt the "wholesale depredations by a land-hungry railroad" on mineral lands, though the Northern Pacific was still able "to acquire timber lands with mine works located on them through obvious corruption...."

From early days economic forces have tended to assure that the better timber lands, save where they were also suitable for farming, were early acquired in large blocks by lumber interests or speculators. Some railroad land grants, especially those of the Southern Pacific and the Northern Pacific which contained great acreages of commercial stands of softwoods, were either sold to lumbermen or retained by the railroads. Equally important is the fact that the settlement laws which were designed to make easy the road to ownership of farm land were extensively used by timber companies to acquire billions of board feet of Sugar Pine, Redwood, and Douglas Fir timber. The favored procedure was for land dealers to employ people as dummies to enter land for them under the Pre-emption, Homestead or Timber and Stone Act and to transfer the land to them when they had satisfied the minimum requirements. Roy E. Appleman's, "Timber Empire from the Public Domain" shows how great holdings were established by the lumber companies "through circumvention of the laws," a fact that subsidized historians have either glossed over or excused with the argument that though the land fell to the big companies, the illegal activities or circumvention of the laws was the responsibility of others.

After the Revolution, the United States needing revenue to refinance and retire its war debt and being disinclined to tax heavily, turned to the public lands for the necessary income. By the eighteen-thirties the debt was retired; henceforth, the public lands were thought of as property that should be available to those who would make farms upon them. The price of public land was gradually reduced, until in 1862 Congress adopted the Homestead Act, which promised every citizen or intended citizen of 21 years of age or over, a quarter section of land provided he would settle upon it and farm it for five years. Henceforth, the public lands, or at least lands suitable for farming, were increasingly spoken of as planned for the settlers who were pouring into the new states and territories.

Paul Gates shows that the Homestead Act was made a part of a land system that included numerous features in conflict with the idea of free land for the landless. The first twenty years of its operation was its heyday, during which the Act was most effective in fulfilling its purpose: the creation of family farms. In later years the Act was subject to growing abuse, as was the Pre-emption law before its repeal in 1891 and the Desert Land Act. Part of that abuse resulted from settlers using these laws to gain an extra quarter section they might sell to raise capital needed to purchase farm machinery and to improve their land. Though the Great Plains was the area where homesteading was most widely pursued, everywhere there still remained public lands, it was resorted to as the best means of gaining ownership of land. We will not know what proportion of these entries under the settlement laws were legitimate entries for the creation of single family farms and what proportion were for the benefit of mining, lumbering and livestock interests, until intensive investigation into the records of public land entries, original census schedules and county deeds have been made.

In her impressionistic account of homesteading in the Sand Hills of western Nebraska, much of it based on stories told her by her father, Mari Sandoz describes the experiences of the pioneers building their sod houses, digging their wells and suffering from meager diets, isolation, blizzards, drought, and prairie fires. Miss Sandoz concentrates on the coming of the settlers to the dry and sandy part of Nebraska, their search for suitable land with the aid of the landlooker whose charge was $25, the advantage the Homestead Law had over the Pre-emption Act for those lacking capital, the sod plowing and the sod crop, and the benefits of the Kinkaid Act to dry land farmers. Her account is so charming that readers will want to go back to *Old Jules* for a fuller story.

The Southern Homestead Act of 1866 was intended to retain the remaining public lands in Arkansas, Alabama, Florida, Louisiana and Mississippi for homesteaders and to deny them to speculative purchasers. Its principal author, George W. Julian, an ardent land reformer, who not knowing the south well, thought these heavily timbered, long leaf pine and sandy barren lands might make good farms for the freedmen. Lacking capital, it was almost impossible for the freedmen to farm them and the Act failed of its objective. It came to be thought of by southerners as discriminatory, as one of the punitive reconstruction measures. Paul Gates shows how southerners joined with lumbermen of the Lake States in an effort to secure its repeal. This was accomplished in 1876. Thereafter, northern lumbermen grabbed up much of the best of the standing long leaf pine and cyprus land remaining in government hands in these five states. Years later Mississippi and Louisiana had good reason to regret the repeal of the Act, as did Walter Webb when he wrote his classic polemic, *Divided We Stand,* against northern capital which had made the South its economic fief.

Two in depth studies of the functioning of the land system in the Great Plains during the homestead era, one by George L. Anderson and one by Homer Socolofsky bring out the importance of getting to the grass roots of entries and early transfers. Anderson on Kansas starts out by scoffing at the charges of fraud in public land entries by speculators, cattlemen, land agents and actual settlers made by Commissioner Sparks. Then, by a careful reading of correspondence of the land office with western settlers, land agents, attorneys, and others, Anderson amasses evidence to show that the fraud Sparks charged was widespread and that false swearing in support of fraud was almost universal. It is in the intimate analysis of cases, especially in the footnotes, that Anderson adds much to our understanding of pioneering and the struggle for land west of the 98th meridian in Kansas. Socolofsky provides details about pioneering in Nebraska, the cost of farm making, the type of cases brought before the Board of Equitable Adjudication, and reports of instances of outright hostility to the Homestead law in a state that was one most benefitted by it.

The Desert Land Act was designed, so its framers stated, to aid people of limited resources to bring under cultivation the semi-arid lands of the West that needed irrigation. John T. Ganoe shows the failure of the Act to create the relatively small irrigated farms that its sponsors had predicted it would. The measure was fathered in the Senate by Aaron A. Sargent of California who was closely linked with Haggin & Tevis in their effort to accumulate great stretches of land and monopolistic water rights in the San Joaquin Valley. Unlike the Pre-emption Law, the Homestead Act and the Timber Culture Act which all carried a limitation of 160 acres on the amount individuals could acquire with each of them, the Desert Land Act allowed a full section. Speculators, livestock men and lumbermen utilized dummy entrymen to acquire extensive areas of dry land. Indeed, within three years of its adoption, the Desert Land Act was declared by Thomas Donaldson in *The Public Domain* to be "an aid to land-grabbing." Large holdings thus established created much controversy and led to a demand that the act should either be repealed or more carefully safeguarded so that its original purpose—the creation of small irrigated holdings—might be realized.

Gustave O. Larson in "Land Contest in Early Utah," brings out the long delay before land in Utah was surveyed, and the even longer delay before the first land office was established where settlers could file their applications and establish their rights to land. He shows the difficulties met in attempting to reconcile the Mormon system which was in operation for as much as 20 years with that of the United States when it was finally instituted in the territory.

Sanford A. Mosk describes in "Land Tenure Problems in the Santa Fe Railroad Grant Area," how there developed a pattern of ownership that in its worst period was more complicated than anywhere else in the public domain states. The state of Arizona was allowed to select four sections in each township. Two railroads shared the Atlantic & Pacific grant of alternate odd numbered sections for a distance of 40 miles on each side of its route. The even sections, not selected by the state, were subject to homestead or to be grazed by anyone's flocks or herds. The Navaho Indians, attempting to preserve their rights in a portion of the area, established their allotments wherever they found water or deemed the land useful for their tribe. In addition, portions of the public lands were placed in National Forest status, and to block up areas Congress allowed persons who had bought from the railroads, or who had acquired other rights, to surrender their land after they had cut off the timber, for scrip that could be located elsewhere, for example on rich Douglas Fir land in Washington. Much of Arizona was an area whose grass cover was so thin that thousands of acres were essential for an efficient cattle ranch. The complex ownership pattern prevented the establishment of controls on the range lands with the result that the grass cover was nearly destroyed. The rate of depletion ranged from 30% on the National Forest lands to 67% on the public domain lands. Comparable circumstances elsewhere contributed to the move for the adoption of the Taylor Grazing Act to place the best of the remaining public lands in organized grazing districts over which controls could be provided to restore the forage resources. Mosk's land ownership maps illustrate the complicated pattern.

John Messing takes up the story of land frauds in the timbered regions of Oregon which he found it difficult to exaggerate. In "Public Lands, Politics and Progressives, The Oregon Land Fraud Trials, 1903-1910," he maintains that the studies of fraud should be traced to their ultimate conclusion, no matter whose reputation is blasted. His account of the well-known Oregon land frauds brings out the frustrations honest bureaucrats met in attempting to unearth the truth, that personal as well as honest convictions drove people to take public positions, and that high officials in the Republican party were involved. Though small men were used to aiding the dealers in timber lands the small men found themselves facing prison terms while the persons for whom they were working too often got off scot free.

Land reform was persistently before the public eye from the days of George Henry Evans in the eighteen-thirties to Horace Greeley in the forties and fifties, George W. Julian in the sixties and seventies and Henry George throughout the remainder of the Nineteenth Century. R. Hal Williams' story of Julian's career in New Mexico as Surveyor General is one of frustration and vilification. Earlier as Indian Congressman, Julian was a fiery abolitionist, bitter radical reconstructionist, an outstanding leader of the movement for free homesteads to actual settlers and advocate of restricted titles to prevent land from accumulating in the hands of large owners. Author of the Southern Homestead Act of 1866, he tried to extend its provisions to all the arable lands remaining in government hands so that none but actual settlers could acquire them. He deplored the powers the railroads were acquiring in Congress where he fought their efforts to gain control of Indian reservations through the use of treaty-making powers. When Julian was appointed Surveyor General for New Mexico by President Cleveland in 1885 he questioned the legality of some of the huge Mexican grants in which influential politicians had shares. He also became convinced that the settlement laws were being badly abused in New Mexico and uncompromisingly sought to hold up titles until sufficient investigation could be made. In this way he brought down upon himself bitter denunciation by most elements in the territory and many of his reforms were promptly undone by his Harrison appointed successor in 1889.

Early in the development of the public land system Congress provided forms of land office money, warrants and scrip, which were accepted at district offices in lieu of cash. Best known and the largest in amount were the military bounty land warrants of 40 to 160 acres given to veterans of past wars by various acts of 1847 to 1855. Land scrip was issued for other purposes but in more restricted amounts. Some forms of scrip, notably Porterfield, Soldier's Additional Homestead, and Valentine, became much sought after and more valuable than other kinds because there were fewer restrictions on their use. For example, Valentine scrip could be entered on any unclaimed and unreserved public domain land which was non-mineral. Its value grew with the increasing restrictions on land entries, reaching in the twentieth century as high as $4,000 an acre. Robert Lee tells the story of the "Valentine Scrip: The Saga of Land Locations in Southern Dakota Territory Originating from a Mexican Land Grant" in California.

These articles all add materially to an understanding of the role of public land policies in shaping the settlement, ownership and land use patterns of the public land states. There remain many aspects of land policies and problems that have not received adequate attention. Thomas Le Duc's "The Disposal of the Public Domain in the Trans-Mississippi Plains," suggests lines of inquiry that should be followed. Perhaps the most significant of his suggestions is that to study the disposal of the public lands effectively one must follow further the first transfer of title "examining actual land use and searching for the date when ownership became stabilized."

Paul W. Gates

THE BOARD OF EQUITABLE ADJUDICATION

George L. Anderson

THE BOARD OF EQUITABLE ADJUDICATION, 1846-1930

GEORGE L. ANDERSON

University of Kansas

Although there has been marked improvement during recent years in the attention that is being given by historians to questions concerning the public lands, it will be conceded by some that the administrative practices, regulations, and decisions of the General Land Office have been passed over too lightly. The agency that is the subject of the present study has not received mention, much less adequate treatment, in any published historical work. It is not considered in any of the general histories of the public lands.[1] Donaldson did not find room for it in his ponderous volume.[2] Monographic studies do not deal with it.[3] Even the annual reports of the Commissioner of the General Land Office contain very little information concerning it. Some will hasten to conclude that such obscurity must be deserved. The present writer does not believe that it is. Mere longevity of an institution does not in itself justify historical study, yet the fact that the active life of an administrative agency spans the years from James K. Polk to Harry S. Truman suggests that it merits attention.[4]

During its lifetime the Board of Equitable Adjudication functioned in connection with every major land law. The powers and prerogatives of the General Land Office were extended by it. In 1890 it was asserted that the legality of the titles to thousands of entries depended upon its rulings.[5] Following the enactment of the Three-Year Homestead act in 1912 which provided, among other things, for the reduction of the statutory life of an entry from seven to five years the Board was threatened with an inundation of appeals. It was asserted that the greater part of the 300,000 homestead entries then outstanding would have to pass through its hands for confirmation.[6] Fortunately it was possible to reconcile the new requirements with established procedures in such a way as to protect existing entries without Board action. If this had not been done the historians of the public lands, whose principal index of importance is the number of acres involved, would have had a first rate problem on their hands. Earlier in the career of the Board a section of the general land act of 1891 providing for the automatic confirmation of certain classes of suspended entries that had been regularly processed by it, reduced its jurisdiction at a time when its work for

[1] Benjamin H. Hibbard, *A History of Public Land Policies* (New York, 1924); Roy M. Robbins, *Our Landed Heritage* (Princeton, 1942).

[2] Thomas Donaldson, *The Public Domain, its History with Statistics* (Washington, 1884).

[3] Harold H. Dunham, *Government Handout, A Study in the Administration of the Public Lands, 1875–1891* (Ann Arbor, 1941); Paul Wallace Gates, *Fifty Million Acres: Conflicts over Kansas Land Policy, 1854–1890* (Ithaca, 1954); Charles Lowell Green, *The Administration of the Public Domain in South Dakota* (Pierre, S. D., 1939); Addison E. Sheldon, *Land Systems and Land Policies in Nebraska* (*Publications of the Nebraska State Historical Society*, vol. 22, Lincoln, 1936).

[4] The most recent decision that has come to the attention of the present writer was written by Oscar L. Chapman, Under Secretary of the Interior, April 4, 1947, re Carl F. Reynolds, *Decisions of the Department of the Interior Relating to the Public Lands*, 59: 486 (Hereafter cited as L.D.).

[5] Secretary William F. Vilas to Commissioner Strother M. Stockslager in the Irwin Eveleth case, January 21, 1889, *ibid.*, 8: 88–93, especially page 91. This letter contains an exhaustive review of the legal aspects of the Board's jurisdiction. This case and *Pecard v. Camens*, *ibid.*, 4: 152, involve the highly complex problem of lands offered for public sale being withdrawn because they were located within the bounds of a grant, then offered at the double minimum price and entries permitted by local officials without the formality of reoffering after the price was reduced. Strictly speaking, these cash entries on unoffered public lands were void.

[6] Instructions prepared by First Assistant Secretary of the Interior, Andreus A. Jones, to General Land Office, December 23, 1913, *ibid.*, 42: 579–580.

a single year had amounted to action on 8,841 entries involving a total of nearly a million and a half acres.[7]

The justification for a careful study of the Board of Equitable Adjudication does not rest entirely on the fact that it confirmed the titles to a significant number of entries every year. It lies partly in providing one feasible line of approach to the study of the larger problem of land administration in Washington as well as in the local offices. In Board cases the primary concern of the officials seems to have been with the *bona fide* settler who was trying to comply with the law. However much the broad canvas that is the picture of land administration may be painted in the dark colors of fraud, corruption, and unscrupulous self-seeking, here is a small segment that stands out in bold relief: an agency of public land administration whose only purpose was to confirm the title to a particular tract of land to a person who had tried to comply with the law, but had failed in some particular through ignorance, error, or obstacle over which he had no control. Even granted that on some occasions title was confirmed to an entry-man whose honest purpose might have been questioned, this type of perspective on the operation of governmental administrative machinery provides a healthful corrective.

Another aspect of the study of the cases that came before the Board has even greater possibilities. They provide the "control" data that are essential to a detailed study of land entries, particularly those entries that became involved in contest cases. In the administrative mind there was a great gulf fixed between a "Board" case and a contest case. An essential ingredient of the former was that the only parties in interest were the government and an entryman who did not have a legal leg to stand on. Indeed in most instances his entry was vulnerable to contest prior to its suspension. If perchance a valid contest were filed it could not be a "Board" case, but followed the regular channels for handling contests. If contesting was as well-nigh universal as it appears to have been in the early phases of settlement; and if every new community was burdened with an over-supply of professional contestors who blackmailed entrymen

into buying them off, land locators who searched out the entries liable to contest, land lawyers who specialized in contest cases, loan-sharks who traded in contested entries and relinquishments, and just ordinary shysters who sought to harvest the fruits of the labors of other men—if all these were present in a new community, why were there any Board cases at all? When the present writer first became interested in the Board of Equitable Adjudication more than fifteen years ago, it was with the purpose of seeking an answer to this question. Although this broader objective has not been attained, it is possible at this time to present a reasonably complete history of the agency.

The establishment of the Board of Equitable Adjudication may be traced to the following passage contained in the report of the Commissioner of the General Land Office for 1845,

Cases of suspension (of land entries) for various causes exist in all the States and Territories in which the public lands are situated. These have been accumulating since the commencement of the present public land system, and give rise at the present time to an amount of correspondence very embarrassing to the operations of this office. In many instances patents are withheld from claimants for causes wholly irremovable under existing legislation; and yet, on principles of substantial justice, the purchasers are entitled to their patents. As it is utterly impracticable to provide by law for each particular case, and as it is necessary that these suspensions, which are increasing from year to year, be finally disposed of, I would suggest that the Secretary of the Treasury, the Attorney-General, and the Commissioner of the General Land Office be authorized by law to act together as a board, and examine and determine all cases of suspension upon principles of equity and justice. In this way, honest and *bona fide* purchasers will be able to obtain their patents, and claims that are unjust and inequitable can be finally rejected. Some measure of this kind is indispensable to relieve this office from embarrassment and remove the doubt and uncertainty which hang over the titles of some of our citizens to the very farms on which they have resided for years.[8]

---

[7] *U.S. Statutes at Large*, 26: 1095–1097, as interpreted in Instructions dated July 1, 1891, L.D., 13: 1–3, and April 29, 1930, *ibid.*, 53: 101. A law passed on March 2, 1889, *U. S. Statutes at Large*, 25: 896, provided for the automatic confirmation of a type of suspended entry that had been referred to the Board in large numbers.

[8] *Annual Report of the Commissioner of the General Land Office for 1845* (29 Cong., 1 Sess., Executive Document no. 12), 6. Hereafter cited as L.O.R. James Shields as Commissioner addressed his report to R. J. Walker, Secretary of the Treasury. The purpose of Congress in creating the Board was well stated by Secretary Lucius Q. C. Lamar to Commissioner William A. J. Sparks in *Pecard v. Camens*, September 17, 1885. After reviewing the several laws the Secretary said, "The necessity for this law was occasioned by the fact that through inadvertence or ignorance it was found

On August 3, 1846, the law establishing the Board of Equitable Adjudication, fixing its jurisdiction, and requiring it to report to Congress was enacted.[9]

The meager bits of information that are available indicate that the Board functioned as planned and the accumulated suspensions were confirmed or cancelled. The act of August 3, 1846, which expired by limitation in two years, was renewed on July 17, 1848. By December of the following year under its new lease on life the Board had processed 3,495 cases.[10] As a result of persistent pressure by the General Land Office legislation reviving the Board for a period of ten years and authorizing it to deal with both accumulated and current cases was enacted on March 3, 1853.[11] With the exception of an important modification of the jurisdiction of the Board made in June, 1856, and a few scattered decisions published in Lester's *Land Cases*, there is a gap of nearly fifteen years in its history.[12] In 1871 the Commissioner of the General Land Office reported that he had submitted a number of cases "to the board constituted under the act of August 3, 1846, as amended . . . to confirm certain equitable cases. . . ."[13] Two years later the provisions of the several acts plus an additional section extending jurisdiction over all cases that had arisen since June 26, 1856, and all that might arise under the several land laws in the future appeared as sections 2450 through 2457 of the *Revised Statutes of the United States*.[14] A curious feature of these sections was the perpetuation of the Secretary of the Treasury as a member of the Board in spite of the legislation of August 3, 1849, which had transferred all duties relating to the General Land Office from the

Treasury to the Interior Department. On February 27, 1877, this error was corrected.[15] The last modification in the membership of the Board occurred in 1922 when the Attorney-General was dropped.[16] It appears that the agency had some sort of special staff. At least one of the printed lists of suspended entries confirmed by the Board bears the names of two clerks who processed these cases. On the envelopes which contain the materials relating to the cases there appears a stamp confirming the action of the Board of Equitable Adjudication which bears the name of C. A. Lawrence, who is designated as the Secretary of the Board.[17]

Just as the general land administration was operated on the basis of the "Rules of Practice" so the Board of Equitable Adjudication functioned within the framework of a set of rules. These were prepared by the Commissioner of the General Land Office and approved by the other members. Every case that was submitted to the Board had to be placed under a rule or designated as a "Special" case. Although the Land Office attached a great deal of importance to the principle of *stare decisis* the practice of submitting new cases by citing decisions in earlier ones of a similar character was specifically prohibited.[18] The procedure seemed to be that each separate case had to stand on its individual merits within the framework of a general rule.

Prior to 1922 the Board had adopted thirty-four rules for the guidance of the Commissioner of the General Land Office in submitting cases. A complete set of these rules has not come to the attention of the present writer.[19] In spite of the cheerful comment made by Secretary George Chandler

---

that many instances occurred in which, without any fault of the purchaser, in the administration of the land laws, some essential step demanded by law or departmental regulation had not been observed, and Congress was frequently called upon by special acts to supply the broken threads in the title. To this Board was committed the supplying of these broken threads, whenever the purchaser on his part had conformed to law and the neglect or breach had been on the part of the officers of the government." L.D., 4: 156.

[9] *U. S. Statutes at Large*, 9: 51; L.O.R., 1846, p. 5.

[10] L.O.R., 1849, p. 30.

[11] L.O.R., 1850, p. 17; 1852, p. 68, and 1855, p. 156.

[12] W. W. Lester, *Public Land Cases and Land Laws* (Philadelphia, 1860), 484-490.

[13] L.O.R., 1871, pp. 31-32.

[14] 1873-1874 edition, 1: 452.

[15] L.O.R., 1875, p. 20; 1876, p. 10.

[16] C. G. Fisher, comp., *Circulars and Regulations of the General Land Office* (Washington, 1930), 311.

[17] All of this material is in the National Archives. Particular cases may be found by ascertaining from the Tract Books (also in the Archives) the final certificate number assigned to a given entry by the local land office.

[18] Acting Secretary George Chandler to Commissioner Lewis A. Groff, March 13, 1890, L.D., 10: 299; Secretary Noble to Attorney-General W. H. H. Miller, March 6, 1890, *ibid.*, 10: 299-300.

[19] Rules 1-16, adopted October 3, 1846, March 13, 1847, and March 16, 1854, are contained in Lester, *Public Land Cases and Land Laws*, 482; Rules 17-27, approved May 8, 1877, are in L.O.R., 1877, pp. 100-101; Rules 28, 29, 30, adopted April 28, 1888, may be found in L.D., 6: 799-800; Rules 31, 32, and 33, adopted April 28, 1890, may be found *ibid.*, 10: 502-503.

that the rules were "simple and relatively few in number" a mere reading of them would consume a substantial amount of time. Perhaps their flavor can best be conveyed by quoting the general statement that was promulgated in 1922 when all of the previous rules were revoked. On that occasion the jurisdiction of the Board was defined to include,

All classes of entries in connection with which the law has been substantially complied with and legal notice given, but the necessary citizenship status not acquired, sufficient proof not submitted, or full compliance with the law not effected within the period authorized by law, or where the final proof, testimony, or affidavits of the entrymen or claimants were executed before an officer duly authorized to administer oaths but outside the county or land district in which the land is situated, and special cases deemed proper by the Commissioner of the General Land Office for submission to the Board, where the error or informality is satisfactorily explained as being the result of ignorance, mistake, or some obstacle over which the party had no control, or any other sufficient reason not indicating bad faith, there being no lawful adverse claim.[20]

From one point of view the thirty-four rules taken as a whole give an insight into the mechanics of an administrative agency which had become bogged down in minutia and detail of its own creation. The regulations for final proof required six publications of the official notice, but many proofs were accepted by the local officials wherein it was clear that only five publications had occurred. The regulations designated certain officials as proper ones to take proof, but entrymen frequently made their proof before other kinds of officials. The printed notices would specify that the final proof would be made by a given entryman on a particular date at a specified place, but frequently the proof was made and accepted a day or two early or late,[21] or at a different place,[22] perhaps in a

[20] Fisher, *Circulars and Regulations of General Land Office*, 311.

[21] The most complete account of the problem of proof that was not made on the day advertised is contained in a discussion of the Martin Gleeson case by Secretary Chandler in a letter to Acting Commissioner William H. Stone, August 16, 1889, L.D., 9: 283–284. The effect of the law of March 2, 1889, upon the jurisdiction of the Board is discussed. The 7th section provided for automatic confirmation if proof was made within ten days of date advertised provided the delay was due to "accidents or unavoidable delays." See application of this new procedure in a Dakota case,

different town. More serious was the failure to begin residence on the land within six months after entering it or to prove up during the statutory lifetime of the entry.[23] A blizzard, a washout on the railroad, illness in the family, or any one of the many vicissitudes of life could cause a delay that would render the final proof of an entryman liable to suspension.

In addition to providing the means of curing reasonably trivial defects in the final proof process, the body of rules adopted by the Board established definite procedures for regularizing exceptions to the regulations which formed the basis of administering the public land laws. It is in this connection that an analysis of the jurisdiction of the Board as revealed in the published decisions and statements of its members will be of some value. Beyond doubt the most definite statement concerning the powers of the Board of Equitable Adjudication is contained in a letter from Secretary of the Interior Henry Teller to Commissioner of the General Land Office N. C. McFarland on December 8, 1882. In part the Secretary said,

This Board is a tribunal of special and limited jurisdiction. Its powers are conferred and defined by statute. Outside of these it has no authority, but within the sphere thereof they are exclusive, and no other person, officer, or tribunal may control its doings.... Hence no appeal lies from the decisions of this Board, nor are they subject to review in any other tribunal, because the statute is silent in respect to these matters. When, therefore, a case is referred to the Board, it becomes invested with its statutory rights, it acquires exclusive jurisdiction thereof, and your office and this Department lose all control over it.[24]

May 23, 1890, L.D., 10: 596–597. The leading case on this point is the Geraghty case, Acting Secretary Henry L. Muldrow to Acting Commissioner Stockslager, January 16, 1888, *ibid.*, 6: 460–461. See circular, July 17, 1889, *ibid.*, 9: 123–124. A case of early proof is described *ibid.*, 6: 695.

[22] Secretary Chandler to Commissioner Thomas H. Carter of General Land Office, January 29, 1891, *ibid.*, 12: 102–103.

[23] The cases of dereliction in these respects are too numerous and the materials too voluminous for specific citation. A large proportion of the cases listed in the abstracts of suspended entries involve one or the other of these *laches*. The leading case so far as the failure to reside in six months is concerned is the Frank W. Hewit case first reported *ibid.*, 7: 488–490 and again on review *ibid.*, 8: 566–570.

[24] *Conlin v. Yarwood*, *ibid.*, 1: 411–413. The exclusive

The "special and limited-jurisdiction" to which Secretary Teller referred included "all suspended entries and locations" arising under any of the land laws wherein,

... the law has been substantially complied with, and the error or informality arose from ignorance, accident, or mistake which is satisfactorily explained; and where the rights of no other claimant or pre-emptor are prejudiced, or where there is no adverse claim.[25]

In another portion of the statutory basis of the Board it is explicitly stated that it could operate only "to divest the title of the United States" to the entries referred to it for confirmation. As has been pointed out earlier the absolute condition for consideration by the Board was the absence of an adverse claim to the land.[26] If, as happened in many instances, a contest had been brought against an entry, it had to be disposed of in some formal fashion before the Commissioner could refer the case to the Board.[27] Quite frequently this took the form of a ruling that an entry under suspension could not be contested on the basis of facts already known to the government.[28]

In a sense the frequently quoted phrase "voidable but not void" most briefly describes a Board case. The key words in this phrase fix the narrow limits within which the principles of equity and

justice could be applied.[29] If an entry was not voidable it could be passed to patent without action of the Board; if it was void it was fraudulent or defective to such a degree that the Board could do nothing to cure it.[30]

The third phrase that is characteristic of the decisions to refer cases for equitable adjudication is "good faith." This was regarded as an essential ingredient of a Board case. The pages of supplemental proof together with accompanying affidavits and documents which form the record in each case seem to have been assembled for the purposes of determining good faith and deciding the question of substantial compliance.[31]

Another limitation on the jurisdiction of the Board is contained in the oft-repeated admonition that "... its province is confined to entries so far complete in themselves, that, when the defects on which they are submitted have been cured by its favorable action, they pass at once to patent."[32] The restricted jurisdiction of the Board was reflected in the sparing use of its powers.[33] On many occasions the Commissioner of the General Land Office would be reminded that "equity cannot

---

jurisdiction of the Board in settling equities is emphasized by Secretary Hoke Smith in the Gage case, December 28, 1895, *ibid.*, 21: 549–550. It is relevant to recall that "The Commissioner of the General Land Office under the direction of the Secretary of the Interior is authorized to enforce and carry into execution by appropriate regulations every part of the provisions of this title not otherwise provided for." Sec. 2478, *Revised Statutes of the United States*, quoted by Secretary Vilas in the Eveleth case, L.D., 8: 91.

[25] Sec. 2457, *Revised Statutes of the United States*, 1873–1874, p. 452.

[26] Secretary Henry M. Teller to Commissioner Noah C. McFarland in *McCarthy v. Darcy*, October 20, 1882, L.D., 1: 78–79; see also *Florida Railway and Navigation Company v. Hawley, ibid.*, 18: 236–241; and *Cooke v. Villa, ibid.*, 17: 210–212.

[27] Decision in *Rice v. Simmons*, July 22, 1914, *ibid.*, 43: 344–346.

[28] Secretary Smith to Commissioner Silas W. Lamoreux of the General Land Office, September 26, 1895, in *Gage v. Atwater, ibid.*, 21: 211; see also *Walker v. Snider, ibid.*, 19: 467–469; *Cooke v. Villa, ibid.*, 19: 443–446; and for earlier cases see, *ibid.*, 17: 255 and 14: 83–85.

[29] The most complete discussion of this question is in a letter by Secretary Smith to the Commissioner of the General Land Office, March 21, 1894. The case under consideration was *Florida Railway and Navigation Company v. Hawley, ibid.*, 18: 236–241.

[30] Secretary Carl Shurz to Attorney General Charles Devens, May 28, 1880, *Copp's Land Owner*, 7: 91 (September, 1880). An earlier case had been discussed by Acting Commissioner U. J. Baxter, July 6, 1877, *ibid.*, 4: 68 (August, 1877). See also Graham case, L.D., 6: 767–769; and Blank case, *ibid.*, 17: 506–507.

[31] Secretary Lamar in writing to the Commissioner of the General Land Office on January 25, 1886, emphasized substantial compliance as determinative of jurisdiction, *ibid.*, 4: 350. See also Acting Secretary Chandler to Commissioner Groff, March 13, 1890, *ibid.*, 10: 299, and Acting Secretary Campbell to the Commissioner of the General Land Office, July 10, 1905, *ibid.*, 34: 40–41.

[32] Secretary Chandler to Commissioner Stone, August 9, 1889, *ibid.*, 9: 230–231; quoted in Richter case, *ibid.*, 25: 2. It should be observed that if an entry had passed to patent the outstanding patent had to be canceled before the case could go to the Board. Secretary Lamar to Attorney General Augustus H. Garland, November 9, 1887, *ibid.*, 6: 314. See also decision in the Hagerman case, *ibid.*, 8: 183.

[33] Acting Secretary Thomas Ryan to Commissioner Binger Hermann of the General Land Office, July 22, 1898, *re* Patrick A. Quealy, *ibid.*, 27: 218.

create a right which the law denies. . .";[34] that the express provisions of law could not be circumvented by referring cases to the Board, thus permitting the Land Department to do indirectly what it could not do directly;[35] that it must deal with the record of a case as it was and not as it should have been; and that it could not change statutory requirements.[36] The Commissioner was never permitted to forget that the Board operated on the basis of equitable considerations. In appropriate cases the Secretary of the Interior would remind him that, "It is a familiar principle of equity jurisprudence that equity considers as done that which should have been done."[37] This comment obviously refers to cases under suspension because of dereliction in duty by local officials. In another case reference was made to, "The well established equitable maxim that what has already been done need not be again performed. . . ."[38]

Finally, no entryman could claim reference of his case to the Board as a matter of right.[39] Such action was completely within the discretion of the Land Department. This particular point forms the basis of the only case decided by the Supreme Court of the United States with reference to the Board of Equitable Adjudication. An entry under the Timber and Stone act had passed through the hands of several transferees on the basis of the final receipt of the local land office before it was suspended for fraud and cancelled. The land subsequently passed to patent to another party under the homestead law. The disgruntled purchasers under the original entry, citing a decision by a Circuit Court Justice in a comparable case, asserted that the cancellation of the entry by the Commissioner of the General Land Office should have been referred to the Board of Equitable Adjudica-

tion prior to such action. After reviewing the entire history of the Board and all of the relevant statutory provisions Justice Harlan speaking for the Court said,

The purpose of the legislation was not to limit or restrict the general or ordinary jurisdiction of the land officers. It was rather to supplement that jurisdiction by authorizing them to apply the principles of equity for the purpose of saving from rejection and cancellation a class of entries deemed meritorious by Congress, but which could not be sustained and carried to patent under existing land laws.

Emphasizing the key words in the statutes that adjudications "shall operate only to divest the United States of the title to the lands embraced thereby" the Justice concluded that "it follows that only decisions sustaining irregular entries are required to be submitted to the Board for its approval."[40]

Quite apart from the light shed upon purely legal and administrative problems the materials relating to cases referred to the Board of Equitable Adjudication whether published in the *Decisions* or contained in the Land Office section of the National Archives, are full of information concerning the problems and conditions of settlement.[41] After

---

[34] Secretary Teller to Commissioner McFarland in *Bray v. Colby*, January 29, 1884, *ibid.*, 2: 79–80.

[35] *Ibid.*, 37: 287.

[36] Secretary Smith to the Commissioner of the General Land Office in the Lockwood case, April 18, 1895, *ibid.*, 20: 361; Secretary Chandler to Commissioner Stone, August 19, 1889, *ibid.*, 9: 291–293.

[37] Secretary Chandler to Commissioner Stockslager, April 25, 1889, *re* Melissa Cunningham, *ibid.*, 8: 435.

[38] Secretary Carl Schurz to Commissioner James A. Williamson of the General Land Office, December 20, 1880, *Copp's Land Owner*, 9: 35 (May, 1882).

[39] In a long opinion dated April 16, 1892, Secretary John W. Noble refused to refer forty timber and stone entries to the Board. This was one of many such cases. *United States v. Allard et al.*, L.D., 14: 395–407.

[40] *Hawley v. Diller, U. S. Supreme Court Decisions*, 178: 479–495, especially 493–494. First Assistant Secretary of the Interior Edward C. Finney discussed this matter at length in the Ben McLendon case, June 7, 1923, L.D., 49: 562–563. In addition to dealing with the main point, Finney held that there was no appeal from the decision of the Secretary to the Board.

[41] The present writer has studied a large number of cases on the basis of the individual packages of material presently housed in the National Archives. In order to locate a case, one must secure the exact description of the land from the published list of suspended entries and then ascertain the Final Certificate number issued to the entry by the local land office. In some offices this seems to be the same as the Register's and Receiver's number. The filing envelopes are arranged in numerical sequence on the basis of the final certificate numbers. The information contained in the Henry Meverden case is reasonably typical. This entryman was born in Prussia and came to Kansas by way of Wisconsin. A carpenter by trade, he did not own either horses or implements when he made his entry, but continued to work at his trade until he could establish himself. The information given is detailed even to the inclusion of the statement that he planted two acres of pumpkins one season. F. H. 2729, Kirwin Series, National Archives.

All National Archives cases will be cited by final

making substantial allowance for the obvious fact that the entrymen tried to place their cases in the most favorable light, there is significant data in the case files that cannot be obtained from any other source. The number, depth, and value of wells, the cost of breaking the land, and the kinds and cost of fencing are given. The types of housing, whether sod, stone, or frame, and whether floored, plastered and ceiled, are listed, together with the alleged value of each size and type. The number and kinds of farm buildings and their value, the numbers and kinds of livestock, the kinds of crops with estimated yields, the various types of farm machinery, and even the character of the home furnishings are contained in the documents.[42] The historian who has an antiquarian interest in primitive plumbing facilities will be intrigued by the frequent references to "out-houses," "commodes," and "thunder-mugs."[43] Something of the social life of the community is revealed in the references to exchanging work and visiting with the neighbors.

The particular cases of settlers whose entries were in a state of suspension range from the tragic to the comic. The abandoned wife with the inevitable brood of four to nine children who could not prove up on her husband's entry appears frequently.[44] In connection with one such case in

Kansas it was alleged that the woman's husband sent her on a visit to Missouri, relinquished his entry for a price, and used the money to elope with his neighbor's wife.[45] In another Kansas case, Wilhelm and Wilhelmina thoughtfully entered adjoining tracts of land, but married too soon thus sacrificing Wilhelmina's status as a qualified entrywoman.[46] The cases of immigrant entrymen who died before making final proof or becoming naturalized and the unfortunate settlers who became insane prior to proof add another type of variety to the study of Board cases.[47] The frequency with which "ignorance of the law" is alleged as an excuse for failure to comply with it raises some important questions concerning the early settlers; whereas the information concerning storms, droughts, floods, health conditions, crop failures, grasshopper invasions, and transportation facilities has obvious relevance to basic studies of frontier conditions.[48] The principal point that is being

---

certificate number, the name of the local office, and the initials N.A.

[42] Mrs. M. M. Hurlbutt valued a twenty foot well at $20, 65 acres of breaking at $130, and a 12 x 18 frame house at $100. She had no farm implements and only one cow. Her list of home furnishings is impressive. F. C., 10,696, Kirwin, N. A. The A. Smith case is even more informative. He claimed a total of $1,775 in improvements, including an eight room house ($1,000), 3 wells ($100), 70 acres in cultivation ($150), and 64 acres fenced ($125). Even the outhouse and a one-half interest in a lister are mentioned. F. C. 10,724, Kirwin, N. A. The Silvanous Palin case is concerned largely with financial problems. The crux of the matter seems to have been that the entryman refused to make new proof for submission to the Board of Equitable Adjudication and thus relieve his entry of suspension unless the mortgage company which had already loaned him a substantial sum would loan him an additional $500. F. H. 9,576, Kirwin, N. A. John Van Dyke even included his "swill pail" in his long and impressive list of improvements. F. C., 13,757, Kirwin, N. A.

[43] A. T. Dwinelle mentions the "thundermug" along with swill pails, crocks, washtubs, looking glass, etc. F. C. 13,933, Kirwin, N. A.

[44] The problem involved in this type of case was mentioned as early as 1871, L.O.R., 1871, p. 31.

It was discussed in considerable detail by Secretary Teller in *Bray v. Colby* under date of January 29, 1884, L.D., 2: 78–82. The individual cases that were referred to the Board are too numerous for citation. A particularly pathetic case occurred in Kansas when the husband of Sarah Fordyce threw her out of the door onto a plow, injuring her so seriously that she was rendered bedfast, and then abandoned her. F. H. 3087, Kirwin, N. A.

[45] *Copp's Land Owner*, 7: 38 (June, 1880).

[46] Secretary Smith to the General Land Office *re* Wilhelmina [(Huber)] Roth, May 13, 1896, L.D., 22: 528–529. She was allowed to prove up on the principle that "she should not be made to suffer by the mistake of her husband . . . ." In the Susan Herre case, *ibid.*, 10: 166–167, under date of February 13, 1890, Secretary Chandler summarized a typical case, emphasized the absence of an adverse claim (Funk case, *ibid.*, 9: 215), and said: "It strikes me that it would be a harsh rule, one which does not commend itself to the equitable side of our nature and judgment to hold that when this woman had fully satisfied the laws and the rules of the Department except remaining sole until after she had submitted her final proof, that she has forfeited her right to enter this tract. Such a rule is in restraint of marriage which neither law nor equity favors."

[47] An Oxford, Idaho, case involved both an absence of citizenship proof and insanity, *ibid.*, 11:3–5. The Margaret Sinder case contains a great deal of information. She was a 66 year old widow who had not become naturalized. F. C. 4781, Kirwin, N. A.

[48] The filing packages contain affidavits by doctors as to illnesses, operations, general infirmities and the like; naturalization papers and certificates; affidavits

stressed here is that an almost infinite variety of problems and conditions seem to have been characteristic of the cases presented to the Board of Equitable Adjudication.

If one turns from the Washington scene as represented by the origin and location of data to the physical characteristics of particular entries, variety is again the keynote. In seeking information concerning individual tracts of land the present writer has used original survey notes, early atlases, the Plat and Tract Books, maps indicating ground water resources, and a series of maps prepared by the Soil Conservation Service of the United States Department of Agriculture indicating the kinds of soil and the drainage patterns. This phase of the study has been confined to the Board cases involving land entries located west of the Sixth Principal Meridian in Kansas. Only a meagre beginning has been made. The only conclusion that can be stated with any assurance is that any generalization would be extremely vulnerable. In some counties there are as many as fifty Board cases whereas in nearby counties there are as few as two. In some counties Board and contest cases occupy adjoining tracts, in others they seem to fall in different parts of the county. In one county the fifty-four Board cases are scattered indiscriminately in stream valleys, along projected railroad routes, and adjacent to the town-sites, as well as in the more remote sections of the area. In each of the nearly fifty counties the pattern of distribution seems to be different. The writer is well aware of the fact that locations within a county have very little significance apart from proximity to towns, especially county-seats, but the important fact is that on the basis of

present knowledge no generalization can be made which will be valid. Moreover the diversity covers such a wide spectrum of possibilities that no sampling process can be devised that will provide an adequate answer to the question as to why one group of vulnerable entries passed to patent without contest and others were not only contested once, but several times. Certainly the reasonably complete analysis of the administrative principles and practices of the Board did not yield the answer. It is clear that individual cases were handled on their merits within a framework of rules as interpreted in explicit decisions.

There are bits of evidence to indicate that some important factors in determining the location of Board cases were at work. The most important of these is the contrast in the number of times that a tract, which was to become the subject of equitable adjudication, was entered and the number of entries on adjoining tracts. The Plat Books reveal that in a significant number of instances the Board tracts were entered only once or twice whereas the surrounding tracts were entered and relinquished so many times that the officials ran out of space on the plat.

In making this study the writer has not been unmindful of the fact that all sorts and conditions of men made the entries; that they had a great variety of objectives in mind; that the prevailing weather conditions whether of drought or abundant rainfall must have exerted an influence as did the general economic conditions at the time settlement took place; and that the views and policies of particular Commissioners of the General Land Office must have played an extremely important role in determining the number and distribution of the suspended entries. But having said these things merely serves to emphasize the complexity of the influences that were at work in the settlement of the public lands.

describing particular crop conditions; and some reasonably complete descriptions of weather conditions.

THE NATIONAL LAND SYSTEM IN THE SOUTH:
1803-1812

R. S. Cotterill

THE NATIONAL LAND SYSTEM IN THE SOUTH:
1803-1812

By R. S. COTTERILL

The United States established its first territorial government in the South in 1790, but it was seventeen years later that it began the sale of its public land. In the Territory South of the River Ohio, as the North Carolina cession was officially styled, the lands were reserved for the satisfaction of North Carolina grants, and these proved insatiable.[1] The erection of Mississippi Territory, in 1798, was accompanied by the assurance that the act was not to be construed as a disparagement of the claims of Georgia. The Georgia sense of humor, however, proved inadequate to the proper appreciation of this Pickwickian statement, and the United States refrained from straining it further by the sale of lands. Not until Georgia ceded its western lands (for a consideration), in 1802, was the United States in a position to begin the sale of lands in the South. A further delay of five years was brought about by conditions in Mississippi.

As a matter of fact, the establishment of the national land system in Mississippi Territory was not only made possible by the Georgia Compact, but was made imperative by it, inasmuch as the Compact specified that the United States should establish land offices there within a year. As a consequence of this positive injunction, supplemented by petitions from the Mississippi people, Congress passed the Act of March 3, 1803, "regulating the grants of lands, and providing for the disposal of the land of the United States south of the State of Tennessee."[2] In this

[1] Technically, the Territory South of the Ohio River included not only the North Carolina cession, but also the South Carolina cession of 1787. I have tried to show that the land ceded by South Carolina had no terrestial existence. R. S. Cotterill, "The South Carolina Land Session," MISSISSIPPI VALLEY HISTORICAL REVIEW, XII, 376.

[2] *Debates and Proceedings of Congress*, 7 Cong., 2 sess., 1594. The cumbrous title of this act was probably due to the fact that the land betweeen Tennessee and 32° 30′ had not yet been annexed to Mississippi Territory. Even after 1804, however, Congress continued to use the phraseology, "south of the State of Tennessee," to indicate the land of Mississippi Territory.

Act, cognizance was taken of the fact that there would be three different classes of people seeking land titles in Mississippi. First, there would be those claiming land by virtue of grants from Spain, Great Britain, or Georgia (under the Bourbon County Act); commissions were to be established for adjudging their claims. Second, there would be the "actual settlers" without pretense of title; those who had come in before 1798 were to be given a section each, and those coming in between 1798 and 1803 were to be given preëmption rights to the land occupied. Third, there would be the prospective immigrants after 1803; for these land offices were to be opened and the land sold.[3]

The first step in carrying out the provisions of the Act of 1803 had to be that of locating and adjudging the claims of those holding grants from Spain, Great Britain, and Georgia. Until this was done, no land could be consigned to others. In each of the two land districts created by the Act, a commission was set up composed of the register of the land office and two other persons named by the President.[4] The Georgia grants gave no trouble, since there were only some 130 of them, and the judging of their validity presented no difficulty.[5] But in dealing with the British and Spanish grants, the two commissions found themselves involved in a wild tangle of doubtful, overlapping, and contradictory claims without parallel in the entire history of the public domain. It was estimated that there were 23 different classifications of these claims. It is only by a ruthless and self-denying sacrifice of details that any intelligible account of them can be given.

The grants made by the French before 1763 had been taken over by the British, and re-issued as British grants. In addition to these, the British had issued some 300 grants (comprising about 250,000 acres) to Englishmen and colonials before the Spanish put an ungentle stop to their activities by capturing

---

[3] Both the Georgia Compact and the Act of 1803 made provision for the Yazoo claims, in addition to those mentioned above; but the Yazoo claims have been so exhaustively treated elsewhere that it seems superfluous to discuss them further.

[4] The commissioners in the district west of the Pearl were Thomas H. Williams, register, Robert Williams, and Thomas Rodney; east of the Pearl were Joseph Chambers, register, Ephraim Kirby, and R. C. Nicholas.

[5] Dunbar Rowland (ed.), *Mississippi Territorial Archives, 1798-1803* (Jackson, 1905), I, 544.

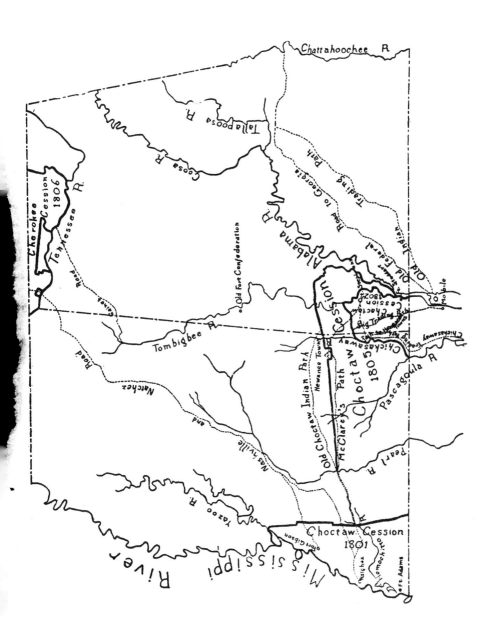

West Florida in 1779.[6] These British grants had been made in the two widely separated regions ceded to them by the Choctaw in March, 1765. For the most part, they lay along the Mississippi from the mouth of the Yazoo, south to the 31 parallel, but there were a few along the lower Tombigbee. In a majority of cases, the titles to these lands were technically imperfect because the provisions of the grants had not been carried out, such as settlement, residence, and cultivation, although the grantees could say (and did not omit saying), that under the easy-going British rule in West Florida, a close observance of such technicalities had not been required. A considerable portion, probably the greater number, of these grants were in the hands of speculators who had never lived on them and never intended to live on them. The confusion of these British grants was rendered worse, confounded by the action of the Spanish government after 1783. I called upon the British grantees to have their titles confirmed by the Spanish authorities. To this invitation the British grantees gave scant consideration. alleging that Spain had no right under the treaty of 1783, to question British grants. There was something to be said for this contention, but it is difficult to escape the belief that the refusal of the British grantees was based less on a devotion to international law, than on the possession of a firm conviction that their claims would not bear inspection of a critical nature. After giving the British a liberal time to submit their titles, the Spanish began the re-granting of these lands to other people. They displayed such enthusiasm in this that, by 1795, nine-tenths of the land in Mississippi Territory that was claimed at all, was claimed on grants from at least two different authorities, with the chances strongly in favor of both grants being invalid, for the Spanish grantees had been as neglectful in perfecting their titles as had the British. There was also a strong suspicion, later developing into a certainty, that a goodly portion of the Spanish grants had been made after 1795 and thoughtfully ante-dated. Most of these Spanish re-grants had been made to speculators who, like the original British grantees, preferred functioning as absentee landlords; the

---

6 The number of British grants with acreage, year by year, is given by Dunbar Rowland, *History of Mississippi: the Heart of the South* (Chicago, 1925), I, 275.

actual settlers were mostly "squatters," having no legal rights except that nine points of the law that consists of possession.

Into this slough of despond, the two commissions waded valiantly and, after long delay and eminent exertions, emerged with a verdict. They confirmed British and Spanish grants to the amount of some 450,000 acres, the rejections being due chiefly to non-residence and ante-dating.[7] On the whole, the commissions gave the grantees — the British especially — the benefit of a very extensive doubt, and Congress, by subsequent legislation, was more liberal still. By the Act of June 30, 1812, the claims were confirmed (up to 640 acres each) of every British and Spanish grantee actually residing in Mississippi on the date of the Treaty of San Lorenzo, and, by an act of five days later, all non-resident British grantees had their claims validated.

The two commissions had the task, also, of adjudging the claims of the actual settlers without grants, and the confirmation of these claims added 100,000 acres to the total of private claims in Mississippi Territory. The commissions also granted preëmption certificates. By the Act of 1803, these certificates were limited to the settlers coming in before that date. But on the last day of March, 1807, Congress decreed that all actual settlers at that date might have permission to remain on their land, and, January 19, 1808, authorized the giving of preëmption certificates to them.

Altogether, something like a half-million acres of land had been disposed of in Mississippi Territory before the United States began the sale of its public domain. While the commissions had been wrestling with foreign grants, identifying old settlers for donation rights, and granting preëmption certificates, the United States had taken the two necessary steps preliminary to the sales; it had negotiated cessions of land from the Indians and it had started the surveys. Between 1798 and the time when the commissioners rested from their conflict, four cessions of land had been obtained from the Indians. In 1801

[7] The commission west of the Pearl began its work, Dec. 1, 1804, and finished in June, 1807; the commission east of the Pearl began, Feb. 2, 1804, and finished, Sept. 21, 1805. As has been explained, the overwhelming majority of the claims was west of the Pearl. The final reports of the commissions are found in *American State Papers, Public Lands*, I, 598, 699 ff.

and 1802, the Choctaw confirmed to the United States the land they had ceded to the British in 1765. The first of these cessions was a triangular strip along the Mississippi, with its base on the 31 parallel and its apex at the mouth of the Yazoo; the second was the region between the Chickasawhay and Tombigbee rivers. In 1805, the Choctaw made their third cession, consisting, for the most part, of the region between the former cession and that south of the trading path from Natchez to St. Stephens. In 1806, the Cherokee ceded their land in the present Alabama north of the Tennessee River.[8] In these cessions, the surveyors went to work as soon as the boundaries were established, dividing the land into townships and sections as in the Northwest.[9] But, by 1807, only the land inherited from the British was ready for sale.

By the Act of 1803, two land districts were created in Mississippi Territory: the district west of the Pearl, and the district east of the Pearl. It was left to the President to locate a land office in each district, and he selected St. Stephens, on the Tombigbee, for the eastern district and Washington, near Natchez, for the western. Up to 1807, the land offices had been open only for the filing of claims; in 1807, the long-anticipated sale of lands finally got under way.

Yet, notwithstanding the long delay and the constant clamor for the sales to begin, the record for the first two years was very disappointing. Less than 75,000 acres were sold in 1807, while in 1808 the sales fell to the low level of 18,000 acres.[10] It is quite probable that the sales of the first two years were chiefly to those holding preëmption certificates and this class exhausted itself the first year. Then, too, the most desirable land in Mississippi Territory was in the hands of British and Spanish speculators or taken up by old settlers on donation rights. Squatters were

---

[8] The texts of the treaties by which these cessions were made are given in A. J. Keppler, *Indian Affairs, Laws and Treaties* (Washington, 1904), Part II, 56, 63, 87, 90. The Cherokee cession of 1806 overlapped a Chickasaw concession of the preceding year.

[9] From 1803 to 1807, Isaac Briggs was surveyor of Mississippi Territory; from 1807 to 1820, Seth Pease.

[10] *Am. St. Paps., Finance*, II, 253, 315. For 1807, the sales west of the Pearl were 70,067 acres; east of the Pearl, 4,125; for 1808, west of the Pearl, 13,820; east of the Pearl, 4,073. In 1807, the eastern office reported in February, and the western in July; both reports in 1808 were made in July.

numerous and were in no hurry to buy, thinking, perhaps, that the government would eventually give them donation rights if they exercised a rigid self-control in the matter of avoiding the land auctions. In both years, practically no sales at all were made east of the Pearl, where the squatters were chiefly located.

The reports for 1809 show a pronounced reaction from the depression of the preceding year, the sales amounting to 87,000 acres. The explanation of this marked increase over the preceding year is found in the fact that new lands were being opened, and a new land office was being established. The new lands were those of the Choctaw cession of 1805, the sale of which was authorized, March 31, 1808, and those of the Cherokee cession of 1806 which were put on sale by an act of the following June.[11] The Cherokee cession included some of the best land then at the disposal of the government. It was the Muscle Shoals region, which had been ardently sought by speculators even in the Confederation period, and had been the scene of the evanescent Houston County, created by Georgia in 1784.[12] Attracted by the reports of the rich lands here and of the big spring, where Huntsville now is, settlers had begun to come into the region as early as 1805, and by the end of 1808, a government census reveals that there were 2,545 between the Tennessee River and the Tennessee state line. All these were squatters and most of them were evidently of the poorer class, since there were only 322 slaves among them. They intended to buy land of the government whenever the sales began, and while they were waiting they proceeded to put out their crops — chiefly corn — and to erect their houses. This done, they built themselves a mill where they could grind their corn, and constructed a distillery where the surplus product might be put into shape suitable either for distribution or consumption. They were so orderly and so evidently of good intent, that the government, under the Act of 1807, gave them official permission to remain on the land until the sales should begin — a proceeding which practically amounted to giving them preëmption. There was an element of

[11] *Laws of the United States. . . . Having Operation and Respect to the Public Lands* (Washington, 1817), 152.

[12] A. P. Whitaker, ''The Muscle Shoals Speculation,'' MISS. VAL. HIST. REV., XIII, 365.

trouble present, however, in the person of one Michael Harrison, who held a huge tract of land under the Tennessee Company and busied himself selling to the newcomers. In December, 1808, the Governor of Mississippi Territory created Madison County in the Shoals country and appointed a sheriff and magistrates to deal with the anticipated disorder.[13] This action was taken none too soon, for, although the old settlers were law abiding, there came into the county, in the first half of 1809, some 300 new families who were by no means so well disposed. Many of these were apparently brought in by Harrison, and an appreciable number of them were planters who brought their slaves with them from Virginia and Georgia. Meanwhile, in March, 1807, Congress had authorized a land office in the Cherokee cession, but the President, in anticipation of disorder in Madison County, located it, April, 1809, in Nashville.[14] The surveys were completed in June, 1809, and the sales finally began in August. In 1809, the land sales in Madison County, for the two months the land office was open, were more than that of the entire territory the preceding year; and the price of land was around $3 per acre, while at the other offices, both in 1809 and before, it had, with strict sobriety, held to the minimum. In Washington in 1809, the sales were five times as great as in 1808, but in St. Stephens, the sales were even fewer than in the preceding year.[15]

In neither of the next two years, did the land sales in Mississippi Territory equal those of 1809. In some small measure, this was due to the fact that east of the Pearl the steadily decreasing sales had reached an irreducible minimum and disap-

[13] E. C. Betts, *Early History of Huntsville* (Montgomery, 1916), chaps. i, ii.

[14] The most valuable contemporary account of the conditions in the Muscle Shoals region in 1808 and 1809, is the *Letter from the Secretary of the Treasury* (Washington, 1809). This is a report by Gallatin to the House of Representatives, Dec. 15, 1809, concerning intruders upon the public lands. Betts, *op. cit.*, gives much useful information. William Dixon was register of the land office in Nashville, and John Brahan was receiver. *Am. St. Paps., Pub. Lands*, II, 251. Brahan's commission was given, April 10, 1809. *Ibid.*, III, 553. Feb. 25, 1811, Congress authorized the President to remove the land office from Nashville, "to such place within the district for which it was established as he may judge most proper." Notwithstanding this, the office remained in Nashville until 1817, in which year it was removed to Huntsville.

[15] *Ibid., Finance*, II, 381, the figures are: east of the Pearl, 3,613 acres; west of the Pearl, 60,063; Madison County, 23,960.

peared altogether — at least no sales were reported there either in 1810 or in 1811. Partly, it was caused by a tremendous falling-off in the district west of the Pearl, due, probably, to the perils and pleasures of that "revolution" in West Florida in which the people of Mississippi Territory took such a neighborly, and even proprietary, interest. Madison County, alone, showed an increase, the sales in each year being double those of 1809.[16] Even in Madison County, there was a falling-off from 1810 to 1811, due to the fears of the people aroused by the Fletcher *v.* Peck decision and to their apprehension over losing their land on account of the heavy land tax. Both these fears, of course, played directly into the hands of Harrison and the Cox agents. It required a personal visit from the Nashville receiver to re-assure the people.[17] Since the government had no military force in the region and none that could be sent thither, its agents had to rely entirely upon threats and moral suasion, neither of which ordinarily had any affect on the frontiersman.

The best year of the land sales in the South was the last one. In 1812, the sales were practically double those of the best of the preceding years, reaching a high total of 145,000 acres. An analysis of the figures shows that the sales were still falling off in Madison County, but almost doubling west of the Pearl. The most astonishing part of the record, however, was the showing of the eastern district, which sold 64,000 acres in 1812, as compared to 12,000 in the preceding five years and in the last two nothing at all.[18] It is not easy to explain the phenomenon. Apparently, a very considerable migration was getting under way toward the Mobile and Tombigbee regions, and this migration was overflowing into the western district. The new Federal Road, from eastern Georgia through the Creek country, was coming into use as an immigrant trail; and the old McClary Path, between Natchez and St. Stephens, had recently been improved into the Three-Notch Road. Madison County had apparently shot its bolt for the time being, but lower Mississippi seemed on the verge of a great immigration when the War of

16 *Ibid.*, 446, 502, the figures are: 1810, Madison County, 53,612 acres; west of the Pearl, 23,424; 1811, Madison County, 48,464; west of the Pearl, 33,449.

17 *Ibid., Pub. Lands,* II, 249.

18 *Ibid., Finance,* II, 586, the figures are: Madison County, 22,209 acres; west of the Pearl, 58,362; east of the Pearl, 64,301.

1812 abruptly checked it. In that war, the Creeks, to their subsequent undoing, went on the war path and effectually put an end to travel through their territory. Madison County sales held up during the war, but in the two lower districts the sales practically stopped.[19] The Great Migration had to wait for the coming of peace and, perhaps, for the publicity of war.

The total of the land sales in Mississippi Territory, prior to the War of 1812, was less than 500,000 acres. On the face of it, this would indicate less than 1,500 sales in the six years the land offices were open, and at most an immigration of some 7,500 people. As a matter of fact, there is reason to believe that the sales were much fewer than 1,500, since we know that much of the land, especially in Madison County, was bought in large tracts by the planters and by speculators. A comparison of the census of 1800 with that of 1810 shows, it is true, that in these ten years the population increased from 8,850 to 40,352; but in each year nearly half of the population was slave.[20] From this we may infer two things: that the number of immigrant families was probably in the neighborhood of 3,500; and that a considerable proportion of them were planters. While it is impossible to be exact, there is no doubt that a goodly percentage of the incoming people was securing its land from other sources than the government sales, or else simply squatting on the land and waiting in Micawber-fashion for something to turn up. It is not merely a matter of conjecture that squatters were present; we know that the federal government made repeated efforts to remove them and that they flourished with special vigor in the Tombigbee region.[21]

During this entire period, the land offices of Mississippi Territory had to encounter vigorous competition from Kentucky, Tennessee, and Georgia. Kentucky, under its general land law of 1800, was selling land in 400-acre tracts at twenty cents an acre, payable in six and twelve installments, and with an obliging legislature always willing to extend the time of payment. In Georgia, the land was being disposed of under the lottery

[19] The land sales in Mississippi Territory amounted to only 30,261 acres in 1813, and to 41,272 in 1814.

[20] There were 3,489 slaves in 1800, and 17,088 in 1810. The free colored population increased from 182 to 240.

[21] *Am. St. Paps., Pub. Lands*, II, 242-51.

system at a nominal price of six or eight cents an acre. In Tennessee, as has already been explained, the land was reserved for the satisfying of North Carolina military warrants with the result that emigration from that state was directed almost wholly toward Tennessee. With such competition north and east, the wonder is not that the land sales were so few, but that they were so many.

Isolation, as well as competition, accounts for the lack of immigration and the consequent lack of land sales. Mississippi Territory was all but inaccessible. From the north the Natchez country could be reached only by a long roundabout voyage down the Mississippi or overland by way of the Natchez Trace. It may be taken for granted that there was no considerable immigration over the Trace, since such a journey involved a passage of several hundred miles through Indian country. The population of the Natchez district was partly composed of flatboatmen who preferred staying in Mississippi to walking home over the Trace. Madison County was the most accessible district of the territory, easily reached from Nashville, by the Tennessee River and by the trading paths from Georgia. Until the Federal Road was opened through the Creek country, the district east of the Pearl could be reached only over the McClary Path from Natchez or down Gaines Trace and the Tombigbee from Madison County. But as for this district east of the Pearl, one is tempted to adopt the conclusion of Tacitus about ancient Germany: no one would voluntarily go thither unless he were already there.

Such land as was sold in Mississippi Territory before 1812, was sold to Southern people, and their principal motive in buying it was for the raising of cotton. Cotton was king in Mississippi Territory as early as 1808, and had been the leading crop for many years previous. There are evidences that the Embargo was severely felt in Mississippi Territory and that one of its effects was to discourage immigration.[22] Even the Indians made some progress in changing their ways to a more even tenor by raising cotton, and the federal government encouraged them by the erection of a cotton gin at Cotton Gin Port on the upper Tombigbee in 1801.[23]

[22] *Ibid.*, I, 597.

[23] G. J. Leftwich, ''Cotton Gin Port and Gaines' Trace,'' Mississippi Historical Society, *Publications*, VII, 263 ff.

Prior to 1812, the United States gained two accessions of territory in the South, the Louisiana Purchase and West Florida. But in neither section were any land offices opened nor any land sold until after the war. In both sections, commissions were appointed to adjust the land claims, and in both sections this validating of titles was still going on when the war came. Nor did the United States gain any revenue from the sales in Mississippi Territory. By the Compact of 1802, the first $1,250,000 from the Mississippi sales was to go to Georgia, and at the time of the outbreak of the war, the collections were far below this figure. Georgia held its mortgage, so to speak, until after the war.

PRIVATE LAND CLAIMS IN MISSOURI

Lemont K. Richardson

PRIVATE LAND CLAIMS IN MISSOURI

BY LEMONT K. RICHARDSON*

SPANISH COLONIAL LAND POLICY, 1763-1800

From 1763 to 1800, the Spanish occupation of the Mississippi Valley reflected a keen interest in immigration and settlement.[1] Governor Don Antonio de Ulloa in 1768 predicted that soon the Valley would be "thickly settled with people who are irreconcilable enemies of England"[2] and advised his expeditions to the Illinois Country that "at the same time one sets about the founding of a fort, that he is aiming also at the creation of a settlement; for a settlement will be of great aid and help in maintaining the fort."[3] A decade later, in 1778, to bolster the shaky defenses of the Upper Mississippi River, the officials in Upper Louisiana were instructed to do anything in their power to attract Acadians, Roman Catholics, Irish, or Germans.[4] Special inducements were tendered to the emigrants in an attempt to negate the hardships of the pioneering experience. A fund of 40,000 pesos was set aside to defray their transportation expenses. A tract of land five arpents in width (an arpent is a French measure of land equivalent to six-sevenths of an acre), necessary tools, and a barrel of maize for every individual twelve years or older were presented to arriving families to stake them through the first year in the Spanish wilderness.[5]

With the cessation of the American Revolution, Spanish colonizing activities were accelerated to checkmate the American expansion

*Lemont K. Richardson was born in Wisconsin, attended Reed College, received his A.B. degree from the University of Wisconsin, his M.A. from Cornell University, and returned to the University of Wisconsin to complete his Ph.D. The research for this series of articles was done at Cornell under the direction of Professor Paul Gates.

[1]Standard works on this period are Arthur Preston Whitaker, *The Spanish-American Frontier, 1783-1795* (Boston, 1927); Whitaker, *The Mississippi Question* (New York, 1934); Elijah Wilson Lyons, *Louisiana in French Diplomacy, 1759-1804* (Norman, Okla., 1934); Louis Houck, *A History of Missouri* (3 vols., Chicago, 1908). Pertinent documents may be found in Houck, *The Spanish Regime in Missouri* (2 vols., Chicago, 1909). Lawrence Kinnaird (ed.), *Spain in the Mississippi Valley, 1765-1795*, 3 vols., in the *Annual Report of the American Historical Association, 1945*; James Robertson, *Louisiana Under the Rule of Spain, France, and the United States, 1785-1807* (2 vols., Cleveland, 1911).

[2]Kinnaird, *Spain in the Mississippi Valley*, II, 40-42, Ulloa to Grimaldi, February 11, 1768.

[3]Houck, *Spanish Regime in Missouri*, I, 8-10, Instructions of Ulloa to the Expedition into the Illinois Country, 1767.

[4]Kinnaird, *Spain in the Mississipi Valley*, II, 258-60, Special Instructions of Galvez, March 9, 1778.

[5]Houck, *Spanish Regime*, I, 152, Galvez to the Prime Minister of Spain, January 27, 1778; *Ibid.*, 155-57, Decree of Galvez, February 19, 1778.

that was rolling down the Tennessee and Ohio Rivers. Upper Louisiana was in grave danger of being over-run, and Spain tried to puncture the advancing phalanx of American settlement by enticing Catholic priests to come over to the west bank. The Kaskaskia settlement, Illinois, bore the brunt of this good will offensive losing three priests as well as whole congregations to New Madrid, Ste. Genevieve, and St. Louis. To the Kaskaskians, alarmed at the high price of public lands and the remoteness of the land offices, the lure of free lands across the river was irresistible. And in addition, the Spanish colonial government supported the price of tobacco.[6]

On the other hand, it has been argued that Spain's colonial land policy could not possibly have been an inducement to immigration and settlement because of the severity of the conditions of settlement and forfeiture.[7] A quick review of the regulations of Governors Alexander O'Reilly, Manuel de Lemos Gayoso and Intendant Juan Ventura Morales, promulgated between 1770 and 1779, might certainly lead one to this conclusion.[8] But actually these regulations were seldom, if ever, enforced. An American official, arriving in St. Louis in 1804, asserted that the regulations were neither posted nor acknowledged by the district commandants whose "thirst for money" was exceeded only by the "most mercenary despot of Tripoli or Morocco."[9]

---

[6]Clarence W. Alvord (ed.), *Kaskaskia Records, 1778-1790* in Illinois State Historical Library Collections (Springfield, 1909), V, xlix. A local land jobber (who later fell victim to the lure of the west bank) reported that Father Edgar was being high-pressured into embarking for St. Louis by Col. Auguste Chouteau. "His departure will effectually ruin the village," the man deplored. *Ibid.*, p. 554, John Rice Jones to Hamtrack, October 29, 1789. See Beverley Waugh Bond, *Civilization in the Old Northwest* (New York, 1934), Chap. III, "Government in the Wilderness," for an excellent discussion of unrest and discontent in the Kaskaskia settlement.

[7]Whitaker, *The Spanish-American Frontier*, Chap. VII.

[8]Don Alexander O'Reilly, the fiery Irish soldier of fortune who replaced Ulloa as Governor of Louisiana following an uprising of New Orleans merchants in August, 1769, drastically revised the immigration policy to weed out any opportunity for speculation in land. For example, the colonist who received a tract of land bordering a river was obligated to construct and maintain suitable dikes and levees. Every grantee, no matter where his land was located, was obligated to construct all necessary bridges, keep the roads that crossed his property in good repair, clear the whole front of his grant to a depth of two arpents, and enclose the whole front with appropriate fencing material. All this had to be accomplished in the space of three years. Failure to comply with these conditions entailed forfeiture of the grant, but with no compensation for the partially completed improvements. Severe penalties were imposed upon the owners of stray livestock. Most important, under no condition could the grant be sold or transferred during the first three-year period. See *American State Papers* (38 vols., Washington, 1832-1861), *Public Lands* (Gales and Seaton edition), V, 229-30. Regulations of O'Reilly, February 18, 1770. Hereafter cited as *ASP, Lands.*

[9]Clarence Edwin Carter (ed.), *The Territorial Papers of the United States* (20 vols. to date, Washington, 1934-), XIII, 29-31, William C. Carr to John Breckinridge, July 7, 1804. Hereafter cited as *Territorial Papers.*

Spanish officials in the district of Upper Louisiana pursued their own haphazard colonization program. Lieutenant governors and post commandants acquiesced to any and all petitions for land. Seldom were the concessions surveyed and recorded in a plat book because description by metes and bounds was sufficient for all. Typical descriptions ran thus: an island off the mouth of the Meramec River; 324 arpents, more or less, in the lower fields of St. Charles; 10 arpents frontage on the Mississippi River running back to the road leading from St. Louis to Carondelet.[10]

As Spain's grip upon the Mississippi Valley daily became more precarious in the last five years of the 18th century, and as it became obvious after 1800 that the United States was maneuvering toward ultimate annexation of the Louisiana province, the pillage of the public lands on the west side of the river quickened. This was the critical period in the history of the private land claims of Missouri when the powerful junto composed of the French inhabitants and speculators emerged.

THE TRANSITIONAL PERIOD, 1803-1804

Historians generally have neglected to give the private land claims in Missouri proper significance during the transitional period, 1803-1804, when the territory was purchased and formally ceded to the United States. One historian gave brief mention to a land panic that gripped St. Louis when many citizens became convinced that their unconfirmed concessions were worthless and unloaded them "for almost nothing."[11] A second alluded to a "mania for land grants" that seized all classes.[12] A third concluded that the "inhabitants . . . neither rejoiced nor were they even reconciled either at the time when the treaty of cession became known or later when the actual transfer was made."[13] Research convinced a fourth that the "general apathy of the French inhabitants at the time of [cession] leads many to think that the inhabitants were not fit for self-government."[14] Men on the scene in St. Louis reported an extremely negative attitude prevalent among the men of wealth who feared a quick liberation of their slaves "of which they have great num-

---

[10]*ASP, Lands*, II, 678, 683, 684.

[11]Richard Edwards, *Great West* (St. Louis, 1885), p. 284.

[12]W. F. Switzler, *Illustrated History of Missouri* (St. Louis, 1881), p. 160.

[13]Floyd C. Shoemaker, *Missouri's Struggle for Statehood* (Jefferson City, 1916), p. 11.

[14]Houck. *A History of Missouri*. II, 375.

bers."[15] The most pessimistic men of property spoke of selling out and fleeing to New Mexico.[16]

Actually, the prospects of cession acted like a King Midas touch upon land values. The inhabitants, on the whole, had interpreted the treaty of cession as a favor-able attitude on the part of the United States toward all prop-erty rights: "The inhabitants . . . shall be maintained in the full enjoyment of their property."[17] During a time lag of almost a year between the treaty of cession April 30, 1803, and the actual occupation of Upper Louisiana March 10, 1804, the land jobbers were grabbing up every available title to land (complete or incomplete) con-fident that all would be con-firmed by the American govern-ment. Positively amazed, Capt. Amos Stoddard, the first U. S. official to arrive in St. Louis, reported that "200,000 acres . . . have been surveyed to various individuals in the past few weeks." Each order of survey bore the signature of "M. . . .;" continued Stoddard, it had

Courtesy Read Studio

Raising the American Flag at St. Louis, March 10, 1804.

been five years since "M. . . ." had been lieutenant governor of the district.[18]

The land jobbers attended public auctions, solicited widows, commissioned agents to canvass the districts, in fact, did anything to acquire concessions, orders of survey, or permissions to settle that would serve as title to land. The animating pursuit of speculation

[15]*Territorial Papers*, XIII, 7, Thomas Davis to Thomas Jefferson, October 5, 1803.

[16]Thomas Ashe, *Travels in America* (London, 1808), p. 287; Robertson, *Louisiana*, II, 50-51.

[17]*United States Statutes at Large*, VIII, 202, Article III, Treaty of April 30, 1803.

[18]*ASP, Lands*, I, 193, Stoddard to Jefferson, January 10, 1804. One may wonder why Stoddard delayed his official arrival in St. Louis until March 10, 1804, when he had received his instructions to proceed to Louisiana at "the earliest opportunity" in November, 1803. See *Territorial Papers*, XIII, 9, the Secretary of War to Stoddard, November 7, 1803.

tempted John Rice Jones and Rufus Easton to drop their affairs in Kaskaskia, Illinois, and take the fastest ferry across the river. Easton, upon arrival, exclaimed that property values had advanced at least 200 percent.[19] Other men reported that land values had gyrated upward 500 percent.[20]

The transitional period reflected a scramble for land titles, and it was a foregone conclusion that Congress would confirm every one.

Rufus Easton Came to Buy Land

Between January and March, 1804, Rufus Easton acquired four tracts of land in the lower districts.[21] In May, 1803, Jacques St. Vrain began purchasing at a fantastic pace, and by March of the following year he had gathered up twenty-two titles that formed two solid tracts of considerable size, one 6400 arpents, the other 8750 arpents, in the district of St. Charles.[22] Simultaneously, Louis Labeaume bought up twenty claims totaling some 14,200 arpents adjacent to St. Vrain's smaller tract. All in all, Labeaume amassed a solid block of twenty-six claims prior to May, 1804.[23] Charles Gratiot picked up titles to three tracts (including one for 7056 arpents) between November, 1803, and May, 1804.[24] Even Auguste Chouteau, Sr., who held a large portfolio of concessions from lieutenant governors Trudeau and Delassus could not resist the temptation to further enlarge his concessions or unload some of them upon an active market. For instance, his

[19]Houck, *History of Missouri*, III, 34.

[20]Amos Stoddard, *Sketches of Louisiana* (Philadelphia, 1818), p. 266; Henry M. Brackenridge, *Views of Louisiana* (Pittsburgh, 1814), p. 140.

[21]*ASP, Lands*, II, 634, 642. By January, 1808, Easton had obtained fifteen titles embracing more than 14,000 arpents of land.

[22]*Ibid.*, II, 592-94; 617-18.

[23]*Ibid.*, II, 616-17.

[24]*Ibid.*, II, 542, 660, 681.

purchases included four town lots, two in St. Charles and two strategically located on the St. Louis waterfront.[25]

The relentless buying spree did not subside with the actual transfer to the United States on March 10, 1804. Easton, St. Vrain, Labeaume, Auguste and Pierre Chouteau, Jacques Clamorgan, James Mackay, and John Mullanphy continued their purchasing activities until 1808. Mullanphy in particular began purchasing as late as January, 1805, and continued to buy until the latter part of August, 1808. His efforts netted him a total of thirteen titles embracing slightly more than 6600 arpents of land.[26]

What were the strategic factors behind this pursuit of land titles? To the former inhabitants and recently arrived speculators, cession to the United States represented a combination of factors that made investment in lands an irresistible temptation. Land would be the first and foremost demand of a horde of new immigrants pouring into the territory from as far back as the headwaters of the Ohio, but it might be years before the public lands could be surveyed and made ready for actual sale. This was a hypothesis that had been borne out in the territories of Ohio and Indiana where the government surveyors had bogged down in swamp lands, had been repulsed by mosquitoes as well as Indians, and had run into complicated private land claims that demanded immediate adjudication.

Hence, confronting the immigrant to upper Louisiana was a belt of land extending from New Madrid to a point roughly 150 miles above St. Louis and ranging inward from the banks of the Mississippi River anywhere from 60 to 120 miles, where settlement was greatly complicated by the blanket of overlapping, unsettled, private land claims, making it necessary for the immigrant to purchase a concession or permission to settle from a former resident or land speculator.[27]

An atmosphere of uneasiness settled over the territory in March, 1804, when Stoddard issued his first official proclamation requesting that all public records pertaining to the private land claims be surrendered immediately to the United States.[28] About a month later the powder keg blew up when the inhabitants were informed of

---

[25]*Ibid.*, II, 533, 556, 569, 632, 638, 655, 666.

[26]*Ibid.*, II, 466, 467, 472, 620, 641, 647, 653.

[27]Curiously, Amos Stoddard recommended that new settlement be limited to a fifty or sixty mile belt along the Mississippi because of apparent unrest among the Indians of the interior. See his *Sketches*, pp. 264, 265.

[28]Thomas Maitland Marshall (ed.), *The Life and Papers of Frederick Bates* (St. Louis, 1926), I, 21.

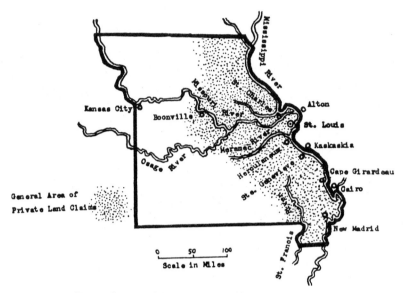

General Area of Private Land Claims in Missouri

the act of March 26, 1804, which primarily partitioned the Louisiana Purchase into two territories, Orleans and Louisiana, with the latter falling under the direct supervision of the Governor of the Territory of Indiana.[29] Attachment to Indiana was immaterial; but the death knell to the schemes of many a land jobber was contained in the section that declared null and void all grants of land issued between the Treaty of St. Ildefonso on October 1, 1800, and actual cession to the United States authorities in New Orleans on December 20, 1803. Were the innumerable concessions parceled out by irresponsible post commandants after October 1, 1800, nullified? Were the assiduous efforts of the French settlers and speculators to obtain any and all titles to land, valid as well as fraudulent, to have been in vain? A great deal was at stake.[30]

---

[29] *United States Statutes at Large*, II, 283. Upon entering the second territorial stage of government in June, 1812, Louisiana was named Missouri. I shall refer to it as Louisiana until that date.

[30] The French landowners of Orleans and Louisiana were determined to secure redress. "It is a fact well known," they exhorted, "to your honorable body [Congress] that after the treaty of St. Ildefonso, the Spanish authorities continued in possession of this territory, exercised their usual acts of sovereignty, and were supposed by her subjects to enjoy their former unlimited right of granting away the soil. Hence proceeded that confidence which allured adventurers to this country, induced them to accept surveys of land, to enter into possession, and faithfully to perform the usual conditions . . . your memorialists hope that some provision will be made, by which claimants under Spanish titles dated since the first day of October, 1800, shall be confirmed in their rights." *Territorial Papers*, IX, 526-32. Memorial to Congress by the Territorial House of Representatives [Orleans], November 14, 1805.

Courtesy Mo. Hist. Soc.

The Chouteau House, Where Landowners Made Plans

During the month of April, 1804, a group of St. Louisans frequently met at the home of Auguste Chouteau, Sr., and during the course of these gatherings a special committee of five men, Charles Gratiot, Peter Provenchere, Louis Labeaume, Bernard Pratte and Auguste Chouteau, Sr., was organized to keep Congress informed of the wishes of the inhabitants. By mid-summer the committee went on record as being deeply opposed to free elections in the territory, but by September it became evident that the committee's chief purpose was to put down all rumors afloat that tended to characterize the inhabitants of St. Louis as "a set of covetous, rapacious land jobbers, who by false, antedated, counterfeted deeds, had monopolized" all the vacant lands of the territory.[31] "Not an inhabitant of this district," the committee deplored, "was on the spot [meaning the floor of Congress] to destroy those unfounded accusations."[32] In January, 1805, the committee dispatched Elgius Fromentin and Auguste Chouteau, Sr., to Washington to lobby for the repeal of the hated act of March 26, 1804.[33] The fortunes of the land claimants hung in balance as Fromentin and Chouteau set off for Washington.

Meanwhile, in the American settlements of the Ste. Genevieve district another committee had been formed and from its meetings emerged resolutions condemning the St. Louis committee as an "apparent design . . . to form and carry into effect a plan, whereby the opinions and wishes of a few might be palmed upon the public;

[31]*Territorial Papers*, XIII, 33-37, Committee of the Inhabitants of St. Louis to Citizens of Upper Louisiana, July 28, 1804.
[32]*Ibid.*, XIII, 43-46, Minutes of a Meeting at St. Louis, September 14, 1804.
[33]*ASP, Misc.*, I, 400-405.

upon the Constitutional authorities of the Country and upon Congress, as the sentiments of the majority of the people of Upper Louisiana." The American committee vowed to appoint its own representatives to consult with Congress and Governor William Henry Harrison.[34] This was the final step in setting the stage for the bitter struggle over the land claims.

Louisiana's attachment to the Territory of Indiana proved to be temporary, and on July 4, 1805, the notorious General James Wilkinson arrived in St. Louis to assume the responsibilities of Territorial Governor of Louisiana.[35] The inhabitants of St. Louis were especially elated at his arrival. Auguste Chouteau, Charles Gratiot, and Antoine Soulard proclaimed: ". . . the political wishes of the citizens of St. Louis are accomplished. The many vicissitudes of Government . . . have . . . been brought to a close. Apprehensions for our future destiny, the clouds of uncertainly, of inquietude . . . are dissipated, by the dawn of political liberty, which now begins to expand and brighten the Western Hemisphere."[36] Wilkinson's arrival produced a happy effect everywhere except in the Ste. Genevieve district.[37]

Courtesy Filson Club

General James Wilkinson, Territorial Governor of Louisiana.

Certain men in key territorial administrative positions had been careful to make preparations for General Wilkinson's arrival. Amos Stoddard wrote long letters to Wilkinson which were full of vital information about the land claims issue.[38] Governor Harrison, an obliging friend of Auguste Chouteau, Sr., and Julien Dubuque, contacted Wilkinson and suggested that he form an alliance with

[34]*Territorial Papers*, XIII, 41-43, Resolutions of a Committee of Ste. Genevieve and New Bourbon, September 2, 1804.

[35]*Ibid.*, XIII, 155, Proclamation by Governor Wilkinson, July 4, 1805; Marshall, *Bates Papers*, I, 23.

[36]*Territorial Papers*, XIII, 149-50, Citizens of St. Louis to Governor Wilkinson, July 3, 1805.

[37]*Ibid.*, XIII, 164-72, Governor Wilkinson to the Secretary of War, July 27, 1805.

[38]*Ibid.*, XIII, 8-9, (footnote 14). References to the Stoddard Manuscript Collection in the Missouri Historical Society.

the French inhabitants as soon as he arrived in St. Louis.[39] Not long after Wilkinson arrived, it was reported that he had been warmly received by the French.[40]

Upon the arrival of Wilkinson, open warfare broke out among the rival land claimants. "There is probably no part of the United States so much torn to pieces as Louisiana," one observer deplored. By Christmas, 1805, the factional strife had stripped the territory of any semblance of unity.[41] Meanwhile, certain inhabitants, apparently oblivious to the chaos about them, assured President Jefferson that they were perfectly satisfied with the administration of Governor Wilkinson, and despite the barrage of petitions to the contrary, they wished to express their utmost confidence in him.[42]

The initial step in adjudication of the land claims was the appointment of a surveyor general for the territory with instructions to collect all evidence pertaining to all claims to land arising from the French and Spanish dominion, survey them at private expense, and record all results (along with all pertinent documents) in a suitable book for presentation to the Board of Land Commissioners. Recommendations for the appointment had been presented to the Treasury as early as December, 1803. However, it was deemed good policy to retain Antoine Soulard, who had served as Surveyor General for Upper Louisiana under Trudeau and Delassus, "not only because he is as well or better qualified to discharge [the duties] than any other person who can be found there, but because he is a foreigner; and his appointment will strongly endear his friends to the government." The French, in other words, would be on their good behavior in hopes that they, too, might receive appointments.[43]

Of course, there was no end of mellifluous praise for Soulard. He was perfectly honest, an excellent draftsman, and a man of "honor and probity."[44] But, unfortunately, there was a degree of subterfuge woven into this fabric of political expediency and professional excellence.

---

[39]*Ibid.*, XIII, 134. The Governor of Indiana Territory to James Wilkinson, June 7, 1805.

[40]*Ibid.*, XIII, 269-70, Judge Lucas to the Secretary of the Treasury, November 12, 1805.

[41]*Ibid.*, XIII, 270-73. William C. Carr to the Attorney General, November 13, 1805; *Ibid.*, pp. 319-24, Carr to the Attorney General, December 24, 1805.

[42]*Ibid.*, XIII, 329-49, Memorial to the President by the Citizens of the Territory, December 27, 1805. Just seven of the petitioners. Auguste Chouteau, Sr., Charles Gratiot, Jacques Clamorgan, Manuel Lisa, Antoine Soulard, Bernard Pratte, and James Richardson, later submitted collectively for confirmation by the Board of Commissioners more than seventy claims that embraced roughly one million arpents of land. See *ASP, Lands*, II, 463-688.

[43]*Territorial Papers*, XIII, 11-12, George Muter and Benjamin Sebastian to John Breckinridge, December 12, 1803.

[44]*Ibid.*, XIII, 26. John B. C. Lucas to the Secretary of the Treasury, June 25, 1804.

In November, 1804, Soulard launched his work with great enthusiasm and promised to follow carefully the instructions mapped out for him by Governor Harrison.[45] When James Wilkinson assumed the responsibilities of the territorial governorship of Louisiana in July, 1805, he not only extended Soulard's commission but also streamlined the latter's duties to such a degree that their performance was mere routine.[46]

Antoine Soulard, Surveyor General of the Territory.

Heretofore, the surveys of all public lands had fallen under the direct supervision of the surveyor general of the United States. Why was an exception made for the Territory of Louisiana? Ironically, it was to prevent untold "confusion, frauds and pillage," which were likely to spring up as a result of District Judge Rufus Easton's decision to allow any individual claimant to survey his own claim and present the plats to the recorder of land titles. For that reason Governor Wilkinson retained Soulard as surveyor general of the territory under a clause in the act of March 2, 1805, which, in his opinion, gave him unlimited powers to "avert impending mischief."[47] Easton's decision, tailored for the benefit of the small land claimant, in the lower districts especially, had been checkmated by Governor Wilkinson who acted in behalf of the St. Louis land junto.

Circumstances gave Soulard a free hand on the surveys. All survey plat books pertaining to Louisiana on deposit in the Spanish

[45]*Ibid.*, XIII, 81-82, Advertisement Relative to Surveys, January 2, 1805.

[46]*Ibid.*, XIII, 435-36, Governor Wilkinson to the Secretary of State, November 12, 1805. Fast action was implied in Wilkinson's new set of instructions. Soulard could commission as many deputies as he felt the situation demanded. In the case of overcrowding or overlapping, only Soulard's verbal consent would be required to remove the concession elsewhere. The surveying fees were on a regressive scale: two cents per acre for the first 1000 acres; one and one-half cents for the next 500 acres; one cent for tracts between 1500 and 3000 acres; and one-half cent for all tracts in excess of 3000 acres. *Ibid.*, XIII, 437-38, Regulations for Surveying by Governor Wilkinson, November 2, 1805.

[47]*Ibid.*, XIII, 435-37, Governor Wilkinson to the Secretary of State, November 12, 1805.

archives in New Orleans had either been burned in 1788 or 1794, or had been packed off to Pensacola by the Intendant Don Juan Ventura Morales before United States authorities could lay their hands on them, and now Soulard was searching the territory for the remaining ones.[48] How could his work be challenged when all the original evidence had been either burned or lost or was now in his hands? It was a foregone conclusion that no amount of persuasion could induce him to surrender the valid surveys. However, despite the unreliability and much publicized notoriety of Soulard's surveys, the land claimants were requested to present these very surveys before the Board of Land Commissioners in order to substantiate the validity of their claims.

The only solution was to eclipse the authority of Soulard and place the surveys under the direction of the Surveyor General of the United States.[49] Accordingly, an act of February 28, 1806, extended the powers of the surveyor general to the Territory of Louisiana, and Soulard's official activities came to an abrupt halt.[50] However, Governors Wilkinson and Harrison immediately used their influence on the Treasury, urging the retention of Soulard and his assistants.[51] To Surveyor General Jared Mansfield, stationed in Cincinnati, this was a preposterous request; fortunately, he succeeded in having his good friend Silas Bent appointed Principal Deputy Surveyor to Louisiana.[52]

To resume Soulard's work proved no easy task for Silas Bent, who arrived in St. Louis in mid-September. First, the pursuit of Soulard and the stolen records proved to be no small task. Eventually he found them, "blush of accuracy," full of "erasures and apparent alterations, in the possession of the clerk to the Board of Land Commissioners."[53] In the course of his field work Bent's suspicions of alteration and fraud were substantiated more convincingly than he had expected. Trees, certified as blazed in 1799, had scarcely more than three grains of bark grown over their outer

---

[48]*Ibid.*, IX, 526-32, Memorial to Congress by the Territorial House of Representatives [Orleans], November 14, 1805.

[49]*Ibid.*, XIII, 432-35, The Secretary of the Treasury to Thomas Worthington, February 8, 1806.

[50]*United States Statutes at Large*, II, 352. The purpose of the act, remarked Secretary of the Treasury Albert Gallatin, "was to secure the survey and other records here-to-fore in the possession of Mr. Soulard." See *Territorial Papers*, XIII, 536, The Secretary of the Treasury to Jared Mansfield, July 3, 1806.

[51]*Territorial Papers*, XIII, 491, Governor Wilkinson to Jared Mansfield, April 19, 1806; *Ibid.*, p. 492, The Governor of Indiana Territory to Jared Mansfield, April 19, 1806.

[52]*Ibid.*, XIII, 519-20, Jared Mansfield to the Secretary of the Treasury, June 14, 1806; *Ibid.*, p. 536, The Secretary of the Treasury to Jared Mansfield, July 3, 1806.

[53]*Ibid.*, XIV, 8-9, Silas Bent to Jared Mansfield, September 22, 1806.

edges seven years later. "The Records," Bent concluded, "have evidently undergone revolution . . . leaves cut out, plats and surveys pasted in . . . names rewritten;" the frauds were easily detected by the "striking contrasts in the colors of ink used."[54]

The actual field surveys had been "executed in a most careless manner." Field notes were never taken, and the sources were laid down at variance up to seven degrees. In fact, the surveys of Soulard were so chaotic that an attempt to iron out all the inconsistencies to the satisfaction of every land claimant, Bent estimated, would cost more than a survey of the whole territory.[55] The concessions were so faded, torn, and plastered with "indecipherable markings," giving no clue to their relative position, that Bent was compelled to go out and look for the tracts in question himself. The majority of Bent's deputies quit in disgust, complaining that they would not travel without allowances.[56]

Meanwhile, Soulard frequented the board meetings to vindicate his past actions and argue that his honor and integrity were impervious to criticism because, of all the former Spanish officials, he had laid claim to the least amount of land—some 3130 arpents of which title to 1042 was complete.[57] Months later he asserted with amazing glibness that the obvious and careless manner in which he had altered the records could be regarded "as a proof of sincerity and good faith." The same intention performed for a good friend, he concluded, "could have been better effected by loosening the strings of both ends of the quire [a quire is a medieval expression for a collection of loosely bound manuscripts] and substituting in the room of the old sheet a new whole one containing the Same Plots with the designed alterations."[58] That he should be held above suspicion seemed obvious to Soulard, but he had helped compound the already difficult and tangled problem of the ownership of land in the new Territory of Louisiana.

This is the first of three articles on private land claims in Missouri. "Part II: The Board of Land Commissioners" will appear in the April issue.

---

[54]*Ibid.*, XIV, 13-14, Silas Bent to Jared Mansfield, October 5, 1806.

[55]*Ibid.*, XIV, 51-52, Silas Bent to Jared Mansfield, December 21, 1806. Orders to survey concessions bordering the road between Carondelet and St. Louis could not possibly be carried out with accuracy, because now many new roads connected the towns.

[56]*Ibid.*, XIV, 408-409, 432, 509-12, 590, letters from Silas Bent to Jared Mansfield, 1810-1812.

[57]*Ibid.*, XIII, 533-35, Antoine Soulard to the Land Commissioners, May 2, July 24, 1806. His figures show a marked disparity to the first report of the Board of Land Commissioners which revealed that he submitted claims to land embracing 5100 arpents. See *ASP, Lands*, II, 534.

[58]*Ibid.*, XIV, 29-33, Antoine Soulard to the Land Commissioners, November 5, 1806.

PRIVATE LAND CLAIMS IN MISSOURI

BY LEMONT K. RICHARDSON*

PART II: THE BOARD OF LAND COMMISSIONERS

We have examined briefly in the first article the storm of protest that greeted the act of March 26, 1804, the first Congressional attempt to adjudicate the private land claims in the Louisiana Territory. Only a temporary expedient, the hated act was repealed March 2, 1805, by a new act which provided for a Board of Land Commissioners to ascertain the validity of the claims.[1] However, the limits of eligibility defined by the act were extremely rigorous: any person residing within the territory who had, prior to October 1, 1800, obtained from either the Spanish or French government any duly registered warrant and on that date had begun actual habitation and cultivation of said tract would have his claim confirmed. Claims based on permissions to settle in accordance with the laws, usages, and customs of the Spanish government and granted prior to December 20, 1803, would be confirmed providing actual habitation and cultivation had been in effect on that date. The date October 1, 1800, referred to the Treaty of San Ildefonso when Spain relinquished her claims in the Mississippi Valley to France; the later date, December 20, 1803, marked the official transfer of Louisiana to the United States. Claims of all minors were disallowed, and the size of all confirmations was limited to one square mile. Finally, failure upon the part of the claimant to deliver the proper documents and plats in writing to the recorder of land titles by March of the following year resulted in forfeiture of the claim.

The act was designed for the benefit of the honest landholder, the bona fide settler upon a small tract of land. Temporarily, the hopes of men such as Auguste Chouteau, Sr., Jacques Clamorgan, Bernard Pratte, Charles Gratiot, and Antoine Soulard had evaporated.

These were men who, some in the span of a lifetime, others in the space of a few months, had amassed claims ranging from 1,000 to

*Lemont K. Richardson was born in Wisconsin, attended Reed College, received his A.B. degree from the University of Wisconsin, his M.A. from Cornell University, and returned to the University of Wisconsin to complete his Ph.D. The research for this series of articles was done at Cornell under the direction of Professor Paul Gates.
[1]*United States Statutes at Large*, II, 331-32.

100,000 arpents of land, few of which had been conceded prior to October 1, 1800, and still fewer of which had been developed according to Spanish law, custom, and usage.

The attitude and action of the early inhabitants were not unique. Basically, their attitude toward government supervision of the public lands and adjudication of the private land claims was no different from that expressed by cattlemen and homesteaders who crossed the 98th principal meridian some eighty years later. A land system with an open end supply and rapid and easy transfer of title was desired by small homesteader and cattle baron alike. The General Land Office took no cognizance of the local attitude toward the public lands in 1885, and neither did the Jefferson administration lend a sympathetic ear to the complaints of the old settlers of Louisiana. The Jefferson administration held unswervingly to two principles: protection of the bona fide settler on a small tract of land and cash sales as a valuable source of revenue. The latter was characteristic of the federal government's attitude toward the public lands during the first half of the nineteenth century. This attitude explains the persistence of the cash sales system and the reluctance of Congress to adopt either free homesteading or pre-emption, which would permit purchase at the minimum price of $1.25 per acre.

Appointing boards of land commissioners to the various territories carved out of the Louisiana Purchase provided an excellent opportunity for the Jefferson administration to fulfill necessary patronage appointments. By the middle of May, 1805, James Lowry Donaldson, Clement Biddle Penrose, and John B. C. Lucas had packed their bags and were bound for St. Louis to serve on the Board of Land Commissioners for the Territory of Louisiana. Donaldson, an Irish-born lawyer, had been engaged in Maryland politics. Penrose was descended from a prominent Philadelphia family, the Biddles, and Lucas had been active in Pennsylvania politics, having succeeded Albert Gallatin as representative to Congress from the Allegheny district when the latter was appointed Secretary of the Treasury in 1802. Of the three only Lucas, who also had been appointed territorial judge, had any real legal ability, and none was able to read or speak Spanish.[2]

---

[2]Clarence Edwin Carter (ed.), *The Territorial Papers of the United States* (20 vols. to date. Washington, 1934-   ), XIII, 112-14; biographical material from Thomas Maitland Marshall (ed.), *The Life and Papers of Frederick Bates* (2 vols., St. Louis, 1926), II, 97; Frederic L. Billon. *Annals of St. Louis in Its Territorial Days, 1804-1821* (St. Louis, 1888), pp. 213-18.

Within a matter of days after the first hearings opened in St. Louis, the board had succumbed to hostility from without and temptation from within. In short, it became two separate and distinct boards: Penrose and Donaldson on the one hand, and Lucas on the other, each avowing to do justice to the land claimants. At the beginning of 1806, after six months of board hearings, Lucas submitted a wrathful report to his old Pennsylvania politician friend, Secretary of the Treasury Albert Gallatin: "It is impossible for me to give a precise account of the operations of the Board since about the beginning of June last," he began, "for reasons that will appear to you very extraordinary . . . the intimacy of [Penrose and Donaldson] which had been very

Courtesy Mo. Hist. Soc.

J. B. C. Lucas

great from the beginning . . . appeared to become greater . . . their [sympathies], the similarity of their opinions created the Most Perfect understanding between them, and being a majority, they were able to form a board when they pleased; and to accomplish whatever they thought proper to do."[3]

In June, Lucas resumed, Penrose and Donaldson proposed to remove the board to New Madrid and commence working up through the lower districts and eventually terminate the hearings in St. Louis. As the claims in the New Madrid district were relatively unimportant and his presence at the current session of the district court was imperative, Lucas agreed wholeheartedly with the decision and proposed to join the board at Cape Girardeau or at least before Ste. Genevieve where the "claims of Lead Mines and other claims to a large amount were to be decided." Two days later, Penrose and Donaldson decided to go first to Ste. Genevieve and then proceed to the lower districts. Completely caught off guard, Lucas was unable to accompany them. Later he learned from United States

---

[3]Judge J. B. C. Lucas to Secretary of the Treasury Albert Gallatin, January 4, 1806, in Carter, *Territorial Papers*, XIII, 372-83.

Commissioner William C. Carr that in Ste. Genevieve Penrose and Donaldson had "hurryed business so much that they decided all the claims of that district in one week." Carr deplored that he scarcely had sufficient time to investigate the most important claims—many of which seemed to him fraudulent.

Having returned to St. Louis, Penrose and Donaldson removed their families to the cantonment located fourteen miles outside St. Louis and began to hold hearings at "irregular hours and without previous adjournment." Whenever a hearing was scheduled for the town chambers, Lucas would spend hours waiting, become disgusted and leave, only to learn the next day that Penrose and Donaldson had come a few moments after his departure. On one rare occasion when Lucas and Penrose held hearings, Lucas departed to dine with his family leaving the latter alone; but upon returning, he discovered that Donaldson had arrived in his absence and the board was in full swing. Due to culpable neglect on the part of the board clerk, the board had remained "seated" and had confirmed a dubious warrant for 1600 arpents belonging to Auguste Chouteau, Sr.

Donaldson's behavior as Recorder of Land Titles outlined by Lucas in his reports to the Secretary of the Treasury Gallatin indicates that there was an understanding between him and certain members of the land junto. Donaldson categorically refused to record any claim not accompanied by a survey laid down or certified by Antoine Soulard.[4] Consequently, only the claims of the early inhabitants of the St. Louis district were eligible for recording. Claimants, primarily Americans, from the lower district where Soulard had never bothered to extend his surveys, might as well have forgotten about appearing before the board. Lucas' protests and insistence that all claims be recorded regardless of whether Soulard had a hand in the surveys, Donaldson managed to dodge by simply stamping the word "Refused" upon the packets in question, and the clerk generally neglected to return the unopened packets to the respective claimants.

The cumulative effect of these tactics, plus the arduous trips into town and long hours of patient waiting for scheduled hearings that did not materialize, convinced many a small claimant that the costs of confirmation far outweighed the real value of the claim itself. Many gave up in disgust and transferred their concession or order of

---

[4]The reader will recall the anxiety of Governor Wilkinson and others to have Soulard appointed Surveyor General for the Territory of Louisiana and later retained as Principal Deputy Surveyor under the act of February 26, 1806.

survey to a more patient land jobber for a mere pittance.[5] This may explain why the transfer or sale of concessions and permissions to settle continued at an accelerated pace until as late as 1808.

By the summer of 1806, the vehemence of Lucas' letters to Secretary Gallatin show that Lucas was perfectly cognizant of the grave dangers that were piling up around him. Penrose and Donaldson had been absenting themselves from the board to secure "subscriptions" to a petition urging the retention of James Wilkinson as territorial governor. Men who balked at signing the petitions were cajoled into reconsidering by the threatened application of rifle butts and clubs. Violence had broken out openly and parties were aroused to the "highest pitch of animosities." Lucas deplored that he was not quite sure whether he would be "mobbed or assassinated." Friends urged him to waste little time in repairing to Pittsburgh, but Lucas decided to stay on with the pronouncement: "My [honor] and independence is more precious to me than my safety."[6]

Meanwhile, events had transpired in Washington necessitating the removal of Wilkinson from the territorial governorship.[7] By the first week of July, 1806, it was evident that things were not going well for the land junto: ". . . the worst is apprehended and the anxiety of [Wilkinson's] friends is extreme," deplored James Donaldson. The opposition had assumed new confidence, and "there is no villainy private or public" that this "Knot of unprincipled Scoundrels" was ready to undertake.[8] Anything to retain Wilkinson in Louisiana was in order. Penrose and Donaldson circulated petitions in behalf of Wilkinson but, at the same time, denied that he exercised any influence upon the decisions of the Board of Land Commissioners. Next, they hastened to add that in many instances his opinions on important claims had materially differed from theirs.[9] Finally, Donaldson most solemnly labeled all the injurious insinua-

---

[5]Lucas to Clement B. Penrose, November 25, 1806, in Carter, *Territorial Papers*, XIV, 40-43.

[6]Lucas to Gallatin, February 13, 1806, in *ibid.*, XIII, 444-47; Lucas to Gallatin, August 5, 1806, in *ibid.*, 559-60.

[7]Jefferson suffered considerable abuse, especially at the hands of John Randolph, for appointing Wilkinson, a general of the army, to a civil post. Jefferson rationalized his action by insisting that Louisiana was "not a civil government, but merely a military station" when he made the appointment. However, as expediency proved to be the better policy, Wilkinson was hurried off to New Orleans to quell "hostile encroachments" of the Spanish. See Jefferson to Samuel Smith, May 4, 1806, in *ibid.*, pp. 504-505; Secretary of War Henry Dearborn to Wilkinson, May 6, 1806, in *ibid.*, pp. 505-507.

[8]James L. Donaldson to William Stewart, July 5, 1806, in *ibid.*, pp. 537-39.

[9]"Statement of Clement B. Penrose and James L. Donaldson," April 26, 1806, in *ibid.*, p. 502.

tions heaped upon Wilkinson as "part of the system of inveterate underhand persecution which has been unceasingly carried on here, against every person who has endeavored to support the lawful authority of the Governor."[10]

For the land junto the appointment of a new governor meant uncertainty and, perhaps, a new alignment of forces with themselves in the minority. Long in advance they had begun to brace themselves for any such rupture. Governors Harrison and Wilkinson had deluged Surveyor General Jared Mansfield with recommendations

for the appointment of a principal deputy surveyor for Louisiana. They put Antoine Soulard forward as a man of exceptional ability and unequaled qualifications. It was Soulard or no one at all; that is, no one from west of the Mississippi.

Auguste Chouteau, Sr., posted a "petition of the inhabitants of the Territory" to President Jefferson recommending that Joseph Browne, then secretary of the territory, be appointed governor. At the very top of the petition were the signatures of John Mullanphy, Pierre Chouteau, Antoine Soulard, Charles Gratiot, Manuel Lisa, Bernard Pratte, and James Lowery Don-

Auguste Chouteau, Sr.

aldson.[11] Meanwhile, the other petition, dominated by Americans of the Ste. Genevieve district, circulated about the territory expressing the fullest confidence in Colonel R. J. Meigs and Colonel Samuel Hammond. Either of these men, if appointed to the governorship, "by their mildness, and Republicanism" would, the petitioners asserted, "restore harmony to the Territory." Americans of the Ste. Genevieve district appeared at the head of the list.[12]

Wilkinson, hearing of this petition, dispatched an admonishing

[10]Donaldson to [Gallatin], April 26, 1806, in *ibid.*, 493-98.

[11]Auguste Chouteau to Jefferson, July 15, 1806, in *ibid.*, 550-55.

[12]Memorial to the President by Citizens of the Territory [no date, 1806] in *ibid.*, 468-86.

note to Senator Samuel Smith of Maryland: "For God's sake caution the President against Hammond — He is an unsound Man engaged in every species of speculation [&] the Creature of Lucas & his pack."[13] Obligingly, Smith informed the President that "Hammond has been and continues to be a snake in the Grass."[14]

By November, 1806, the land junto had successfully made the transition. To their satisfaction, Joseph Browne had been appointed acting territorial governor. The Board of Land Commissioners was hopelessly split; Recorder Donaldson had made off with the records, for the second time, and was on the way to his Maryland home via the Mississippi River to New Orleans and the Atlantic Ocean. Board action could not be resumed until the papers were returned, but this, Lucas realized, was too much to expect.[15] In the field, the attempts of surveyor Silas Bent to solve the riddle of mutilations and forgeries left by Antoine Soulard were actually being challenged at gun-point. By this time Bent was so desperate for fees to sustain his family, which he had optimistically brought over from Cincinnati, that Surveyor General Mansfield was compelled to ask the President for immediate relief for his favored deputy.[16] In short, no further surveys were being projected in Louisiana. It was evident that the settlement of the private land claims in the Territory of Louisiana had come to a standstill.[17]

In less than eighteen months, the Congressional attempts to adjudicate the private land claims, despite the partiality displayed by the majority of the Board of Land Commissioners, had sown seeds of discontent throughout all Louisiana. Clarification of the act of March 2, 1805, was demanded by all parties. Were all claims now limited to 800 arpents? What about the status of claims to town lots and common field strips? Were all concessions awarded in recognition of valuable services to His Majesty the King of Spain to be automatically rejected because the grantee had failed to begin actual cultivation and habitation prior to October 1, 1800? Large and small land claimants considered the act extremely harsh and not at all

[13]Wilkinson to Samuel Smith, March 29, 1806, in *ibid.*, 466-67.

[14]Smith to Jefferson, April 28, 1806, in *ibid.*, 502-503. Smith, apparently, was serving as the Congressional agent for the Louisiana land claimants. He talked the Presid·nt into appointing Donaldson to the Board of Land Commissioners, cautioned him against the removal of Wilkinson, and tried valiantly to block Hammond's nomination. See the letters of Smith to the President in *ibid.*, pp. 111, 113, 115-16.

[15]Lucas to Gallatin, November 4, 1806, in *ibid.*, XIV, 27-28.

[16]Jared Mansfield to Jefferson, October 31, 1805, in *ibid.*, pp. 23-25.

[17]William C. Carr to Gallatin, November 20, 22, 1806, in *ibid.*, pp. 36-39.

compatible with the articles of the treaty that ceded Louisiana to the United States.[18]

Characteristic of federal statutes of the nineteenth century pertaining to the public lands, the interpretations arising out of the acts were more significant than the acts themselves. In Louisiana the conflict of interpretation over the act of March 2, 1805, saw Penrose and Donaldson favoring leniency and clemency on every count as opposed to an uncompromising adherence to the letter of the law advocated by Judge Lucas. For example, on the question of extinguishment of Indian title, Penrose and Donaldson considered extinguishment as implicit in the concession, whereas Lucas required positive proof in each case. Next, Penrose and Donaldson hit upon a so-called settlement right. To them the settlement right could be construed as a "free and generous largess" upon the part of Congress which permitted the Board of Commissioners to confirm any claim based on a permission to settle. This permission to settle, Penrose and Donaldson argued, in view of the extreme liberality of the Spanish colonial land system, was never refused. Unquestionably, the local officer's reply to an application for land was: "Why do you apply to me, go and settle, the axe and the plow are your best title." If the presumption of permission was always in the settler's favor, why require positive proof?[19]

Next, the most controversial clause limiting the size of each settlement right to 800 arpents was thoroughly overhauled. If the Board adhered strictly to Spanish law, usage, and custom, Penrose and Donaldson argued, one settler with no children would be entitled to as much land as one with twelve. The question arose of whether a man with twenty slaves would be considered an ordinary settler. On six points bordering on the "liberal intention of Congress to grant land to the settler in proportion to the number of his family," that is, in proportion to the particular needs of the settler, Penrose and Donaldson decided that the quantity of land granted to one claimant, or settler, might exceed 800 arpents.[20]

By this time the President's cabinet had taken an interest in the situation. Voicing disapproval of what they considered the board's intention to carve unlimited tracts from the public domain, cabinet

[18]Carr to Attorney General John Breckinridge, October 14, 1805, in *ibid.*, XIII, 237-38.

[19]Donaldson to Gallatin, April 26, 1806, in *ibid.*, pp. 493-502.

[20]An opinion of the Land Commissioners, enclosed in a letter from Donaldson to Gallatin, April 26, 1806, in *ibid.*, pp. 499-501.

members urged President Jefferson to remove the commissioners
without delay.[21]

Meanwhile, the land claimants heaped upon Congress petition
after petition, memorial after memorial, to register their objections
to the manner in which the land claims were being settled. Invariably these petitions stated that the arbitrary nullification of all
concessions granted between 1800 and 1804 was extremely unfair,
because Spain had maintained "uninterrupted possession" of
Louisiana during that period. Secondly, attention was directed to
the innumerable tracts of land granted for the "use & support of
works, such as mines, salines, mills, distilleries, quarries, & objects of
general utility." Hence, "occupancy & cultivation have not always
been the Condition on which lands [were] granted, but on the

A Settler's House

Sketch by C. A. LeSueur

Contrary . . . most ancient titles of the Coutry [*sic*] have been
Conceded without Condition." The Indian menace had reduced
farming on an isolated plantation to a flirt with death and had
prompted many inhabitants to abandon their farms and congregate
in fortified settlements. Consequently, habitation of one's concession was impossible or incidental to Spanish law, usage, and custom.[22]

---

[21]Gallatin to Jefferson, March 16, 1806, Jefferson to the Cabinet, March 16, 1806, Secretary of
State James Madison to Jefferson, March 16, 1806, Dearborn to Jefferson, March 17, 1806, in
ibid., pp. 454-55.

[22]Petition to Congress by Inhabitants of the Territory, February 1, 1806, in *ibid.,* pp. 425-30;
Annals of Congress: Debates and Proceedings in the Congress of the United States (42 vols., Washington, 1834-1856), 8 Cong., 2 Sess. (1804-1805), pp. 1597-1620; *American State Papers* (38 vols., Washington, 1832-1861), *Public Lands* (Gales and Seaton edition), II, 671, hereafter cited as *ASP, Lands;*
Private Acts of the Third General Assembly of the State of Missouri, 1824 (St. Louis, 1824), p. 52.

This combination of forces was bound to endanger the Jefferson administration's adherence to a rigid settlement of all land claims. Some of the Creole inhabitants of the territory, the Chouteaus, Gratiot, Pratte, and Clamorgan, for example, had amassed extensive land holdings of what they undoubtedly considered to be valid concessions. On the other hand, there were the avowed speculators who had drifted into the territory shortly after cession to the United States to buy up any available titles to land. Here one may cite Rufus Easton and John Rice Jones who had become adept at speculation in private land claims in the Kaskaskia district across the river.[23]

Early settler and speculator alike realized that claims to land stemming from concessions did not stand well with the federal authorities who had been cautioned against their fraudulent nature.[24] The brazen attempts of Antoine Soulard to alter the surveys and record book tended to augment federal suspicion against all concessions. A better approach to confirmation, bona fide claimant and speculator eventually decided, was to exercise the settlement right to the maximum. It became easy for one claimant to testify before the board to another's habitation and cultivation of a parcel of land on or before a specified date; it was simply a matter-of-fact policy pursued by the early settlers who were merely attempting to get what they thought rightfully belonged to them.

Still the stipulation that written permission be attached to the permission to settle barred the path to confirmation. Penrose and Donaldson had already tried to circumvent this stipulation by arguing that the permission was implied, but it was possible that their construction was tailored for the benefit of the Creole inhabitant or the speculator who was naturally intrigued by the animating pursuit of speculation in land titles.

The demands of the claimants were partially satisfied by a supplemental act passed on April 21, 1806, which recognized actual settlement as sufficient evidence that permission to settle had been given by the proper Spanish official, although the claimant could not produce permission in writing. Confirmation was extended to all

---

[23]Easton obtained confirmation of six claims totalling 1200 arpents. Jones held fifty-one claims, including claims for land improvements, donations to heads of families, donations to militiamen, and claims to common fields. By January, 1811, he had obtained confirmation of claims embracing 1700 arpents. See Report of the Land Claims in the District of Kaskaskia, January 2, 1811, in *ASP, Lands*, II, 123-241.

[24]Captain Amos Stoddard to Jefferson, January 10, 1804, in *ibid.*, I, 193-94; Gallatin to Carr July 9, 1805, in Carter, *Territorial Papers*, XIII, 157-60.

claims not in excess of 640 acres (764.67 arpents) which had actually been inhabited and cultivated by the claimant for a period of ten consecutive years prior to December 20, 1803.[25] With the requirement of written permission abandoned, this Congressional action pointed the way toward a policy of increasing liberality in the confirmation of private land claims during the following years.

Beginning with the liberal interpretations of the act of 1806, one can see the change from a determination to thwart all inroads upon the public domain to a blanket endorsement of claims.[26] Remaining untold, however, is the bitter struggle between the claimants and the Board of Land Commissioners and among the claimants themselves as the territory matured and eventually entered the union in 1821.

The era of increasing liberality was launched with the passage of the act of March 3, 1807. The maximum size of any claim allowed on the basis of ten years' possession was raised from 800 to 2,000 arpents. The deadline for delivering evidence to the recorder of land titles to substantiate a claim was extended for one year. Actual survey of the confirmed tracts began under the direction of the surveyor general, and the Board of Commissioners was allowed "full powers to decide according to the laws and established usages and customs of the French and Spanish governments, upon all claims in excess of one square league (7,056 arpents) within their respective districts." All board decisions in favor of the claimants were final.[27]

However, Secretary of the Treasury Albert Gallatin had tried to remove the clause which extended wholesale confirmatory powers to the board. He argued that what were called the laws, usages, and customs of the French and Spanish governments consisted primarily of deviations from the very land ordinances the board was supposed to obey.[28] After this, any brochure of instructions on the adjudication of the land claims submitted by either the Secretary of the Treasury or the Attorney General to the Board of Commissioners was disregarded.

[25]*United States Statutes at Large*, II, pp. 391-95.

[26]Professors Eugene M. Violette and Louis Pelzer stress this point in their chronological examinations of the settlement of the land claims. See Violette, "Spanish Land Claims in Missouri," *Washington University Studies*, VIII, *Humanistic Series*, No. 2 (St. Louis, 1921), pp. 167-200; Pelzer, "The Spanish Land Grants," *Iowa Journal of History and Politics*, XI (January, 1913), 3-37.

[27]*United States Statutes at Large*, II, 440-42. The act pertained to the adjudication of private land claims in all territories carved from the Louisiana Purchase.

[28]Gallatin to John Boyle, January 20, 1807, in Carter, *Territorial Papers*, XIV, 79-81.

The Board of Commissioners, however, had become aware of the fact that things were not well in Washington. President Jefferson displayed discontent over the "perversions" of duty and "frittering" of responsibility.[29] Accordingly, the board tried to assume a new moral tone. Penrose denounced his former colleague, James Donaldson. Frederick Bates, former deputy-postmaster of Detroit, land commissioner of the Michigan Territory, and ardent Jeffersonian who arrived in St. Louis in April, 1807, to take over the responsibilities of territorial secretary and recorder of land titles, was appointed to replace Donaldson on the Board of Land Commissioners. Bates enjoyed the confidence of the authorities at Washington, and he approved the conduct of Lucas as commissioner, reporting that Lucas was a man of "superior parliamentary information [and] more independent in principle and conduct" than most men in the territory.[30]

The arrival of Frederick Bates marked the beginning of a period when the board functioned smoothly. From 1807 to 1810, the commissioners made an annual circuit of the territory to receive and weigh evidence on new as well as on old claims. By February 1, 1810, the board had recorded 3,056 claims and taken testimony on 2,699. It began action on the claims on December 8, 1808, and by February 1, 1810, it had acted on 638, confirming 323 based on permission to settle or ten years' possession and 167 based on concessions or orders of survey, while 139 were rejected. Throughout this period, the board had been extremely lenient toward tardy claimants, three times extending the deadline for submitting new evidence.[31]

Following somewhat loosely the instructions of Secretary of the Treasury Gallatin, the board had arranged the claims into forty-nine groups which could be further reduced to five general categories: first, claims derived from French and Spanish grants dated prior to October 1, 1800, that exceeded 800 arpents but were smaller than one square league, based on either habitation or cultivation prior to December 20, 1803, or construction and completion of projects of general utility such as grist mills and sawmills; second, claims not exceeding 800 arpents which were derived from French or Spanish grants for construction of mills and distilleries where all

[29]Jefferson to Gallatin, January 4, 1807, in *ibid.*, pp. 57-58.
[30]Marshall, *Bates Papers*, I, 14-27; Bates to August B. Woodward, June 18, 1807, in *ibid.*, p. 146; Carter, *Territorial Papers*, XIV, 117n.
[31]The land commissioners to Gallatin, February 1, 1810, in *ibid.*, pp. 366-68.

the terms had been fulfilled; third, claims derived as in the first two groups, not exceeding 800 arpents, where the claimant had had no other tract granted or confirmed to him; fourth, all claims based on habitation and cultivation prior to December 20, 1803, with or without written permission to settle; fifth, all village claims, town lots, commons, common fields, and adjacent field strips given to the village inhabitants for cultivation prior to December 20, 1803.[32]

The board's policy, however, was not liberal enough to satisfy the land claimants, and deep-seated discontent pervaded the whole territory. Lucas, the most conservative member of the board, was the principal target of criticism. He felt that he was being "assailed by a powerfull host" whose attacks were directed exclusively against him.[33]

Repaying an obligation, Moses Austin cautioned Recorder Bates in August, 1809, to be on the alert for a recently organized committee which opposed certain board members and threatened to mutilate the record books. "You know what I should suffer was it known that I made a communication to . . . you," Austin closed.[34] He was referring to the "Land Claimants' Convention" held in Ste. Genevieve during the month of April. The delegates dispatched the colorful John Smith T (T standing for Tennessee) to Congress to petition for the second grade of government and the removal of Judge Lucas from the Board of Commissioners.[35] This was the beginning of a new controversy in which the opposition to the board's action was mingled with the new issue of admission to higher territorial status.

Quickly, "A Land Claimant" appeared on the scene to caution everyone about signing the petitions for the removal of Lucas. "Look before you leap, and think twice before you sign once. . . . John Smith T [is] the GREAT instrument to tear down the standing of Judge Lucas . . . to bring about a general confirmation of *all kinds*

---

[32]*ASP, Lands,* II, 377-79, 388-603.

[33]Lucas to Gallatin, October 19, 1809, in Carter, *Territorial Papers,* XIV, 334-35.

[34]Moses Austin to Frederick Bates, August 27, 1809, in Marshall, *Bates Papers,* II, 77. Bates had been backing Austin's speculative and mining ventures in the Ste. Genevieve District. To the Secretary of the Treasury he gave the highest recommendation to Austin's proposed road project from Mine à Breton to the mouth of Joachim Creek. Eventually, the road was constructed to the mouth of the creek, and there the village of Herculaneum sprang up to be the principal lead exporter of the territory. In 1815, Austin and Hammond brought their lands into sale: 100 town lots, ea h 120' x 150'. (*Missouri Gazette,* September 23, 1815, June 19, 1818.)

[35]*Missouri Gazette,* October 12, 1809. The *Gazette* was initially published by Joseph Charless on July 12, 1808, and was called the *Missouri Gazette* until November 23, 1809. From then until shortly after Missouri's admission to the second territorial stage of government (June 14, 1812), it was called the *Louisiana Gazette,* and thereafter it became the *Missouri Gazette* once more.

of claims to land in this territory." "Land Claimant" did not entertain the slightest doubt that "John Smith T., and the other gentle-
man who claim the right of representing you, would be willing to mix
their large or elastic 10,000 or 20,000 acre claims with your *Bona fide*
claims of moderate size . . . the very name and nature of col. Smith's
own claims will render all he could do for you suspicious."[36]

The select committee of the Ste. Genevieve convention retaliated
with an assertion to the small claimants: "An injury to your claim
would be an injury to theirs [meaning the large claimants]. . . . The
property of the Territory is as much their interest as yours . . . 'Land
Claimant's' patron [Lucas] has already inflicted more wounds on
this infant country than she will speedily outgrow." Not until the
"Ethiopean changes his skin, and the Leopard his spot," concluded
the committee, "will this 'Land Claimant' and his worthy associates cease to calumniate the virtuous and the respectable, and to
injure a country whose only blemish is, giving protection to her
enemies."[37] About four months later "Land Claimant" was assured
great bodily harm would befall him if he persisted in his defense
of Judge Lucas.[38]

The land claimants felt that the liberal benefits afforded in the
act of March 3, 1807, were not being extended to them. They
assailed the commissioners in the *Gazette*, accusing them of employing Spanish laws, usages, and customs, heretofore unknown to the
claimants, to refute bona fide "contracts made in good faith" under
the Spanish government.[39] The vitriolic comments of one land
claimant who entitled himself "A Louisianan" were representative:
"People of Louisiana! Nothing can save you but unanimity and
courage . . . you will be saddled for life, or as long as there is a land
claim in Louisiana to be decided, with those whom you are so justly
anxious to remove, and if continued in office, will be sure to assail
with redoubled fury your property and reputation, and bring ruin
on you and your posterity."[40]

This opposition to the Board of Commissioners had produced
some curious alliances. Wealthy St. Louisans united with small
claimants to castigate the decisions of the board and challenge the

---

[36]*Ibid.,* October 19, 1809.

[37]*Ibid.,* October 26, 1809.

[38]*Louisiana Gazette,* March 8, 1810.

[39]*Ibid.,* January 1, 1810.

[40]*Ibid.,* February 1, 1810.

surveys in the field. There were few indeed who would not subscribe to a petition for the removal of Lucas. Moses Austin, Rufus Easton, and John Smith T together clamored for confirmation of the mineral claims and adoption of a more liberal leasing policy on the government controlled mineral lands.

The opposition forces disagreed among themselves, however. Members of the select committee of the Ste. Genevieve convention were labeled "strangers to truth and propagators of falsehoods." William Russell, mail contractor, deputy surveyor, and spokesman for the claimants, was considered a tool of Auguste Chouteau, Sr., and James Mackay. His application for the transcripts of the board's proceedings was branded a "wedge whereby the books [might be] thrown open to all erasures."[41] It was "proven" that a "Mr. Louisianan," James Mackay, Jacques St. Vrain, and fellow Creoles had broken into the record books to alter water courses and double the size of confirmed claims."[42]

"Slander, Detraction and Violence" stalked the Ste. Genevieve district. Conditions had reached such a state of alarm that Recorder Bates seriously considered calling in the federal troops. Whenever a rich mine was discovered, he related, "the owner of a floating concession locates it immediately, and strengthens the establishment with a gang of ruffians who defy removal."[43] Land claimants were at one another's throats. Men were pursued into their own homes, attacked and butchered on the spot. On one occasion John Smith T received a ball in the thigh, but his "antagonist was dreadfully Mangled and expired on the spot." A $500 reward was offered to any person who "would discover and prosecute the villian who fired cannon balls" into Moses Austin's parlor.[44] But the violence halted abruptly when it became apparent to the citizens of the territory that the question of entering the second territorial stage of government had to be settled. After a brief lull the tempest broke out with renewed vigor.

By January, 1812, the Board had finished its work and adjourned. It reported that of more than 3,000 claims submitted for

[41]William Russell to the land commissioners and William C. Carr, March 14, 1810, in Carter, *Territorial Papers*, XIV, 379-82; Russell to Silas Bent, January 25, 1812, in *ibid.*, 508-13; *Louisiana Gazette*, August 9, 1810. As an agent for the land claimants, Russell in 1812 submitted to the board a docket of 312 claims, of which twenty-three, embracing 14,740 arpents, were confirmed. (*ASP*, *Lands*, III, 365, 370.)

[42]*Louisiana Gazette*, August 9, 1810.

[43]Bates to Gallatin, May 30, 1807, in Marshall, *Bates Papers*, I, 134-35; Bates to Richard Bates, May 31, 1807, in *ibid.*, p. 135.

[44]*Louisiana Gazette*, February 7, 21, 28, 1811.

review, it had confirmed 1,342, approximately one third of the total.[45] The controversy was then carried back to the floor of Congress, where a more liberal policy of confirmation was gradually evolved. The question of the presentation of the claims, however, was closely tied to the issue of entry into the second stage of government, when the Territory of Missouri would be entitled to a delegate to Congress. Heated debate continued to rage over that subject during the months that followed the adjournment of the Board of Land Commissioners.

This is the second of three articles on private land claims in Missouri. "Part III: The Era of Increasing Liberality" will appear in the July issue.

[45]*ASP, Lands*, II, 689-729.

extending inland from the banks of the Missouri River to a small parallel creek.[53]

The incoming waves of immigrants found that this blanket of private land claims west of the Mississippi formed an obstacle to quick location and settlement. Some, perhaps, became discouraged and moved elsewhere, while others squatted and prepared to fight for the lands they wanted.

The United States had acquired, as a result of its purchase of Louisiana, a tangled problem of land ownership which remained a major issue throughout the territorial period. The land grants by the French and Spanish governments had offered a rich field for speculation, and the resulting confusion and controversy over their confirmation by the United States government caused strife and violence in the territory and greatly delayed the sale of public lands in Missouri.

This is the last of three articles on "Private Land Claims in Missouri." The first two appeared in the January and April, 1956, issues.

---

[53]*Ibid.* See map opposite.

PRIVATE LAND CLAIMS IN THE SOUTH

Paul W. Gates

Private Land Claims in the South

By PAUL WALLACE GATES

THE FIRST TASK OF THE UNITED STATES GOVERNMENT IN the management of the public domain it acquired by the Treaty of Paris of 1783, the Louisiana Purchase, and later territorial acquisitions was the adjudication of a mass of confused, ill-defined, overlapping, and inadequately documented claims to land, the legacy of predecessor governments. On the Southern frontier, where colonial authority had been tenuously maintained, and in Missouri, the French, Spanish, and the British had lavishly distributed land grants and bounties to attract loyal immigrants, reward military officers, soldiers, and governing officials, satisfy settlers, pacify pirates, and gain political favor and "the affection of [the] inhabitants." Grants had also been made to induce construction of sawmills, tanneries, distilleries, and roads, for stocking cattle ranges, and as compensation for losses sustained at the hands of marauding Indians and enemy whites.[1] Since there had been no intention of using the public lands as a source of revenue, they were generously given to heads of families, their wives, and children,[2] thereby enabling persons with numerous children to gain control over considerable areas. Few of the grants contained prescribed boundaries or acreages. Some were little more than

---

[1] The principal published source on the private land claims is the Gales and Seaton edition of *American State Papers, Public Lands* (8 vols., Washington, 1832-1861), hereafter cited as *Public Lands*. For some odd reason the Supreme Court references are to the Duff Green edition. Joseph M. White prepared a detailed study of Spanish land grants which appeared in Vol. VI of the Gales and Seaton edition, pp. 631-774. White later revised his study and brought it out as *A New Collection of Laws, Charters and Local Ordinances of the Governments of Great Britain, France and Spain, Relating to the Concessions of Land in Their Respective Colonies* (2 vols., Philadelphia, 1839). Charles L. Mowat has a brief account of "The Land Policy in British East Florida," in *Agricultural History* (Chicago, 1927-   ), XIV (April 1940), 75-77. See also Charles L. Mowat, *East Florida as a British Province, 1763-1784* (Berkeley and Los Angeles, 1943), and Clinton N. Howard, *The British Development of West Florida, 1763-1769* (Berkeley and Los Angeles, 1947).

[2] W. H. Sparks, *The Memories of Fifty Years . . . Spent in the Southwest* (Philadelphia, 1882), 246.

warrants to locate, and practically none other than urban lots had been surveyed and the proper papers completed that conveyed full title.

Many grants, particularly in the French Acadian portion of Louisiana and at Detroit, Vincennes, and Kaskaskia, were laid out in long, ribbon-like strips fronting on the rivers and bayous for a few hundred feet and extending back forty arpents, or nearly one and a half miles. Waterways provided the only means of communication in the early period; hence, desirable locations were right on them. Both sides of the Mississippi were lined with grants from well below New Orleans to Natchez. Similarly, grants extended for a distance of ninety miles along Bayou Lafourche and elsewhere on the Red River near Natchitoches, on the Ouachita, and on the Atchafalaya in Louisiana, and on the Alabama and Tombigbee rivers in Alabama and the St. Johns in Florida.[3] Poorly drained and subject to frequent overflow, these disease-infested lands took a heavy toll of their inhabitants. But their alluvial soil was richly productive and admirably adapted to the growth of indigo, rice, sugar cane, and cotton.

Congress not only assured confirmation of all land claims for which there existed any actual proof of ownership, residence, and improvement but declared that every person, a head of a family, twenty-one years of age, in Louisiana, Florida, Mississippi, Alabama, Arkansas, and Michigan who was not pressing any other claim and who at the time of transfer to American possession was in actual possession of and occupying land which he had improved, though he had no title, should have confirmed to him a maximum of 640 acres.[4] Heads of families who were residing on land in Indiana and Illinois at the time it became American territory were allowed 400 acres if they were still living in one of the two territories or returned to it between 1791 and 1796 to take up the land.[5] In Missouri up to 800 arpents (680 acres) were allowed settlers or their representatives who were

[3] Township maps in the Bureau of Land Management, United States Department of the Interior, show the location of these grants. Also useful are "Norman's Chart of the Mississippi River from Natchez to New Orleans" (1858) and William Darby, The Emigrant's Guide to the Western and Southwestern States and Territories (New York, 1818), 7.

[4] Acts of March 3, December 20, 1803, March 3, 1807, May 26, 1824, 2 U. S. Stat. 229, 326, 438, 4 U. S. Stat. 47.

[5] Act of March 3, 1791, 1 U. S. Stat. 221.

cultivating and living upon their land claims in 1803 and 1804.[6]

Private land claims ranged in size from city lots in Mobile, Natchez, Pensacola, New Orleans, Detroit, and St. Louis to the great 1,275,000-acre tracts of Elisha, Gabriel, and William Winter in Arkansas, the 1,427,000-acre claim of John Forbes and Company in Florida, successor to Panton, Leslie and Company,[7] and the 881,563-acre Bastrop grant in Arkansas. Far more common were the grants and settlement rights of 400 to 800 acres, except in the Acadian parishes where with few exceptions the claims were small, many being for less than 100 acres.[8]

With transfer of the area containing these claims to the United States there ensued a scramble to acquire ownership that now appeared likely to appreciate substantially in value. John W. Monette described this scramble in a somewhat jaundiced vein:

> Claims and evidences of title were to be raked up from old records, musty documents, antiquated titles, concessions, settlement-rights, transfers, entails, and every species of oral and written evidence of title, real and factitious.
>
> Claims of this character were eagerly sought by the land speculator, and as freely produced by the needy creole, and the avaricious fabricator. An active commerce sprung up between the artful land-jobbers and the docile, unlettered settler; titles, complete and incomplete, were multiplied in endless variety.[9]

Territorial officials, like Winthrop Sargent, Nathaniel A. Ware, and Harry Toulmin, respectively governor, secretary, and judge of Mississippi Territory, and a host of other officials, like Generals Ferdinand L. Claiborne and Edmund P. Gaines, joined in this scramble. Other eminent Americans who dealt largely in private land claims were Edward Livingston, Aaron Burr, Stephen Girard, Wade Hampton, Daniel Clark, John McDonogh, and John Slidell. The story of their intrigues and political pressures to secure confirmation of claims provides the key to much of the early history of the newly developing South and West. As some of the claims overlapped others, long and tedious conflicts fol-

---

[6] Act of June 13, 1812, 2 *U. S. Stat.* 750.

[7] Robert S. Cotterill, "A Chapter of Panton, Leslie and Company," in *Journal of Southern History* (Baton Rouge, 1935-   ), X (August 1944), 275 ff.

[8] In the heart of the Acadian country in Assumption Parish, township 13 south, 14 east, 57 of 178 claims were for less than 100 acres. The average size of the claims was 110 acres. There were a number of claims for 500 acres and more; seven claims for 1,912 acres were confirmed to Thomas de Villaneuva.

[9] *De Bow's Review* (New Orleans, 1846-1880), VIII (May 1850), 409.

lowed between interested parties. Distress sales resulting from debt, taxes, or other liens cut off rights of original owners who misunderstood American land law. When it was found that sheriffs were buying property at such sales a Louisiana governor had to issue an admonishing order against the practice.[10]

The Creoles, already unhappy at the transfer of territory to the United States, were not made easy in mind by the machinery of the new government to validate and confirm land titles. Persons whose rights to their land through original concessions, settlement rights, or the right of occupancy which had been previously unchallenged now found it necessary to go through an involved procedure of assembling witnesses and searching government archives for evidence that would aid in proving their ownership. To occupants claiming title by ancient custom or concession the very necessity of proving ownership was deeply resented.[11] New immigrants who were seeking concessions or claims promptly presented their proof, but the older residents, especially the smaller owners in the more remote areas, were slow to take action and even slower to present proof of ownership that was acceptable to the commissioners.

Boards of land commissioners were appointed to sift through evidence presented in support of land claims and to recommend for confirmation those which satisfied the provisions of the law; others they were to reject. Early instructions to the commissioners were more legalistic than those of later times, for Congress gradually relaxed its standards in its efforts to assure justice to all deserving claimants, even if their proof of title was not legally complete, and to appease influential groups. Governing officials knew it was expedient to cultivate the Creoles and to allay fears about titles in so far as lenient administration of the law was possible. But as standards of confirmation of titles were relaxed dubious claims were more vigorously pressed. Since there was no regularity or system in the layout of the claims, each one had to be individually surveyed before confirmation, which was

<hr/>

[10] Charles Gayarré, *History of Louisiana: The American Domination* (New York, 1866), 146.

[11] George W. Cable, *The Grandissimes: A Story of Creole Life* (New York, 1880) brings out the tension in New Orleans in 1804 over American occupation and the fear that Spanish titles would be rejected. Memorials of the territorial legislatures of Mississippi of November 25, 1803, and of Louisiana of November 14, 1805, contain an eloquent appeal for more liberal treatment in the confirmation of claims than the existing legislation sanctioned. *Public Lands,* I, 161, 250-51.

no small task in view of the vague character of the early concessions. Local officials who were overburdened with their tasks,
a Washington officialdom which was never adequately staffed
in the nineteenth century by a people inherently suspicious of
bureaucracy, and a group of claimants many of whom were illiterate and ignorant of American land law, all combined to cause
delay in the process. A harassed official offered other reasons for
the long delay in determining titles:

. . . the refusal by the Spanish officers to deliver the plats and books
relating to foreign grants; the refusal of the late deputy surveyor south
of Tennessee to deliver to his successor his field-notes, plats, etc.; the
meagerness and inaccuracy of the description of titles and boundaries
given to the old boards of commissioners by claimants; bad translations
of the old titles, which were sometimes very bad French, Spanish, or
English, or a mixture of the three; and last, but not least, the refusal
or neglect of parties to point to true locations, or to give any assistance
to the deputies while employed in the field, together with misdirections
by others, with a view to obtain a tract of land free of interference
with other claims, or through ignorance of their rights.[12]

Lands contained in private land claims which had neither been
confirmed nor rejected, or which, after rejection, were appealed
to higher authority, were neither open to settlement and purchase
nor were they surveyed under the rectangular system of townships and ranges. Squatters inevitably moved upon them if they
were not being used, as was the case with the backlands in the
Houmas claims, the Dauterive claims, or the large claims in the
disputed territory east of the Mississippi. Being unable to obtain
a good title the squatters made few permanent improvements,
stole the timber, and depreciated the value of the lands; at the
same time the claim owners, whether developing their holdings
or not, were angered at their failure to gain a clear title.[13] Some
disputed land was surveyed, opened to settlement, and pre-
emption entries accepted, only to be rejected when claims were
later revived. Still other lands, like those in the Florida parishes
of Louisiana, which were permitted to be sold were later con-

[12] M. Birchard, January 9, 1840, in *House Docs.*, 26 Cong., 1 Sess., No. 155
Ser. No. 366), 17.
[13] The Little Rock *Arkansas Gazette*, December 23, 1820, comments on the unfortunate effect "the large and numerous" Spanish land claims, many of which had
not been confirmed, had upon the development of the territory.

firmed to early claimants who were, however, given in lieu thereof scrip subject to entry on an equivalent amount of land elsewhere.

The problem of the confirmation or rejection of the land claims became, in Louisiana and Missouri, a major political issue, with Thomas Hart Benton taking up the side of the large claimants in Missouri and a succession of governors of Louisiana calling for speedy action to end the litigation, uncertainty of title, and neglect and abuse of land. With two million acres in Louisiana— roughly 7 per cent of its area—in this category of no man's land because it was claimed and unconfirmed, pre-empted but the filings rejected, sold and patents issued but the original claims revived by subsequent law, it is easy to understand the significance of the problem. Beginning with Governor T. B. Robertson in 1820, each successive chief executive of Louisiana through 1843 flayed the federal government for its failure to adjudicate these issues and end the long period of neglect.[14] The state legislature directed a stream of angry memorials to Washington urging that legislation be adopted to permit trying the large unconfirmed claims in the courts so that final decisions concerning ownership could be reached.[15]

The House Committee on Private Land Claims reflected this highly critical attitude in its report of 1836:

The State of Louisiana . . . has been crippled in her energies, paralized [sic] in her wealth and resources, and greatly restrained in her population and political power; and, furthermore, she has been arrested in her progress, and thrown far behind many of her sister States in the construction of those valuable works of internal improvement which would benefit that country so peculiarly. All this has been produced by the circumstance, that a considerable portion of . . . the State is covered by . . . unsettled titles, so that purchasers or emigrants could not know of whom to buy or take title from.[16]

---

[14] Gayarré, *History of Louisiana: The American Domination*, 638, 643-45, 647 48, 652, 655, 656, 663-64. That Gayarré used "domination" in the subtitle of each of the three volumes of this history is significant.

[15] Between 1831 and 1844 eleven memorials relating to land claims in Feliciana Parish, to back concessions, to the Bastrop and Maison Rouge claims, and to claims generally, were forwarded by the Louisiana legislature to Washington. See especially resolutions of March 15, 1839, and February 24, 1842, in *Laws of Louisiana* (1839), 230-34, and *ibid.* (1841-1842), 156.

[16] *House Repts.*, 24 Cong., 1 Sess., No. 554 (Ser. No. 295), 2. See also *De Bow's Review*, III (March 1847), 227.

Again, John Slidell, speaking for the House Committee on Public Lands in 1844, condemned the "vicious legislation" which prevented the confirmation of titles to a number of large holdings and produced "sufferings, privations, and, in many cases, the absolute ruin" of individuals.[17]

The slow grinding of the legal mills seems justified despite the hardship it produced, for it prevented the confirmation of large claims that had little or no basis in law or equity. The inflated Vinter claims, for example, were twice recommended for confirmation, and twice favorable reports were issued recommending that the heirs be permitted to try their case in the courts. Not until 1832 was it brought out that the claims rested on false certificates and inconsistent translations, that no authority had existed for making such large grants, and that no record of an original grant had been produced.[18] The handling of the Bowie claims in Arkansas came in for severe castigation by a later investigator who found no basis for any, though 117 grants for 60,000 acres had been approved and were, presumably, on the way to patent, even were still on the docket, and 188 had been dropped for failure of claimants to give security.[19] It was of these claims that John W. Monette acidly commented on the "men of deep thought and great legal attainments" of Natchez and other parts of Mississippi who were suspected of being jointly interested.[20] Notwithstanding Monette's comments there is less evidence in the South of the "incredible forgeries, subornation and perjuries," and nepotism which Francis Philbrick found in the record of Illinois and Missouri claims.[21]

The principal issues in determining confirmation were the nature of the concession, whether the grantee had met its requirements, the dates of settlement, improvements and continued

---

[17] Report of January 9, 1844, in *House Repts.*, 28 Cong., 1 Sess., No. 4 (Ser. No. 45), 5.

[18] *Public Lands.* III, 170, 289, 429; *ibid.*, VI, 423, 941.

[19] *Ibid.*, VI. 5.

[20] *Ibid.*, VI. 4-8. John W. Monette. "Public Lands Acquired by Treaty, etc.," *De Bow's Review*, V (February 1848), 116 ff. Claims of Elijah L. Clark and Lewis Clark for 733 and 640 acres were reported with thirty-three other claims as a base attempt to defraud the Government" in 1823. *Public Lands*, III, 599-609. Four years later the House Committee on Private Land Claims was induced to recommend confirmation and in 1830 Congress so acted. *House Repts.*, 19 Cong., Sess., No. 28 (Ser. No. 159); Act of February 27, 1830, 6 U. S. *Stat.* 406.

[21] Francis S. Philbrick (ed.), *The Laws of Indiana Territory (Collections of the Illinois State Historical Library*, XXI, Law Series, II [Springfield, 1930]), lxxxvii.

occupancy, and a continuous title sanctioned by succeeding governments.

Lawyers enjoyed a prolonged field day in arguing for confirmation before the boards of commissioners and registers and receivers of the local land offices, and in carrying appeals to the commissioner of the General Land Office, to department heads, to presidents, to federal courts, and to Congress. The stakes were large and fees were in proportion. Few lawyers of eminence were not employed on land claims at one time or another. Among the most distinguished lawyers who appeared frequently in behalf of claimants were Seargent S. Prentiss, Edward Livingston, Reverdy Johnson, Caleb Cushing, Daniel Webster, John A. Campbell, Francis Scott Key, Pierre Soulé, Hugh Lawson White, John McP. Berrien, Richard K. Call, Thomas Hart Benton, William Wirt, William Cost Johnson, and Judah P. Benjamin. Congressmen, even before they became "lame ducks," took on such cases to augment their income.

It was the practice of Congress to confirm recommendations of the special commissioners who were appointed to investigate the private land claims. A series of more than a score of such statutes, beginning in 1807 and running to 1858, followed the recommendations of the commissioners with a few exceptions which were specifically noted.[22] Many other claims the commissioners had rejected, or for which Congress had originally refused to follow the recommendations of the commissioners, were confirmed by numerous private acts.[23] Beginning with the first individual act, of February 10, 1814, which confirmed a claim of 1,000 arpents in Missouri to Daniel Boone, 134 such measures were enacted by 1861.[24] Additional private laws gave claimants

[22] Claims in excess of a square league (4,428 acres) were denied confirmation in the acts of April 29, 1816, and February 5, 1825, even though they had been approved by the commissioners. 3 U. S. Stat. 328; 4 U. S. Stat. 81.

[23] Representative of those claims which the original commissioners rejected in 1816 on grounds of fraud were those presented by Hyacinthe Bernard, amounting to 3,706 arpents. Fourteen years later, after additional testimony had been offered, a favorably inclined House committee approved and Congress confirmed 2,640 arpents. Public Lands, III, 123; 6 U. S. Stat. 408. Another instance of Congress reversing an early judgment of the land commissioners is that of Bernard Marigny, a prominent Creole planter of New Orleans. In 1832 claims for 4,794 arpents were thus confirmed. 6 U. S. Stat. 480.

[24] 6 U. S. Stat., passim. The act of June 25, 1832, confirmed ninety-five small claims on Terre aux Boeufs, two of which, containing thirty-eight arpents, were owned by Laurent Millaudon. 6 U. S. Stat. 499.

whose land had been otherwise disposed of the right to enter an equivalent amount of land elsewhere.

Claims of 1,000 arpents or less were confirmed without much difficulty if actual residence and improvements could be proved, but the larger claims in excess of 1,000 and 2,000 arpents, especially those greater than a square league, were more rigidly scrutinized. A number of these larger grants, notably the Bastrop and the Maison Rouge grants in Louisiana, had been conditioned upon extensive development and the settlement of a considerable number of immigrants upon them. The grantees' failure to fulfill conditions or even to try did not prevent them from maintaining that a right had been granted which could not be revoked, and they or their assignees made every effort to secure confirmation. Attorneys refused to accept one or two rejections and continued to press for confirmation, arguing that new evidence had been found, that new witnesses were ready to swear to early cultivation and settlement, that earlier requirements were being relaxed, and that justice and equity required confirmation. When all other efforts failed, they appealed to Congress, where large claim owners had strong friends and some members had substantial interest in such claims.

Claims were persistently urged upon Senate and House committees for sixty and more years, absorbing an appalling amount of time in their consideration. Said a House committee in 1836:

Congress has been perpetually harassed, for upwards of twenty years, by the claimants, praying for the adoption of some mode . . . for the final determination of . . . and the settlement of those titles. Every succeeding year brings forth new and additional applicants, produced by the circumstances of speculators and companies, in various States of the Union, becoming interested by purchase in those grants, as well as by the multiplication of heirs of some of the original grantees. By these and other causes, the claimants are becoming more imposing from their wealth, numbers, and influence, yearly.

Speaking of the Bastrop, Maison Rouge, and Winter claims, the committee observed that "many persons of high standing, influential stations, and character, have become deeply interested in those claims." They had retained the "most distinguished lawyers in Louisiana and other places" to argue their rights. The committee rightly prophesied that the longer the determination of ownership was postponed, the more formidable their supporters would become "and the more incessant will be their applications to Congress." It failed, however, to devise a way by which a final no could be said to claimants.[25] Naturally those claims with much at stake—as large acreage, like Clamorgan (448,000 arpents), Dubuque (75,000 to 150,000 arpents), Houmas, Bastrop, and Maison Rouge, or extremely valuable location, like the Batture claim in New Orleans—were revived for reconsideration over and over again, and the small claims that were early rejected were not likely to be heard from again.

Fifty-five years after present Louisiana was acquired from France the government could list 1,472 claims for an aggregate area of 1,230,400 acres which were "wholly or partially unsatisfied" in that state.[26] Twenty-two years later, in 1880, the surveyor general for Louisiana drew up twenty-five detailed pages of located but unconfirmed private land claims ranging from city lots to 4,514 acres and embracing some 80,000 acres.[27] In addition, ownership of the Houmas claims, among the largest presented for confirmation, still remained for further adjudication.

Whig members, it was reported, were more inclined to favor confirmation of big claims than Democrats, though notable Democrats like Edward Livingston, John Slidell, and Thomas Hart Benton fought hard for approval of claims in which they were directly interested or whose owners were influential in their states. Rice Garland, Whig representative from Louisiana, and Judah P. Benjamin, Whig senator from Louisiana, followed Livingston in arguing for confirmation of large claims in the Florida parishes of Louisiana in which they were interested either as attorneys for claimants or because of direct ownership.[28]

Two groups of claims were before the commissioners, Washington officials, and the courts for half a century before definite rejection was given one and a qualified confirmation was given the other. The first of these related to grants made by the British in West Florida between 1763 and 1783; the second group consisted of grants or sales of land by the Spanish in the Florida parishes between 1803, when the American claim to the territory

[25] *House Repts.*, 24 Cong., 1 Sess., No. 554 (Ser. No. 295), 2 ff.
[26] *Sen. Ex. Docs.*, 49 Cong., 2 Sess., No. 67 (Ser. No. 2448), 2.
[27] *Ibid.*, 46 Cong., 2 Sess., No. 111 (Ser. No. 1885), 7–32.
[28] Natchez *Mississippi Free Trader*, June 8, 1842.

was established, and 1810, when it came under American control. There was some overlapping of the claims.

During their occupation of West Florida the British made forty-five grants for 350,000 acres, conditioned upon their being settled and developed within ten years. Grants of 10,000 and 20,000 acres were made to aristocratic friends of the government who never resided in the colony. No more than half of the grants in West Florida were presented for confirmation, and on the others few or no improvements were made nor was any effort exerted to maintain ownership during the period of Spanish control.[29] The Spanish, in consequence, regranted the land, and by 1803 the area contained in the original British grants, much of it near Natchez, was well developed. British claims to the amount of 16,375 acres came into the possession of Elihu Hall Bay of South Carolina, who urged Congress year after year that they be confirmed. Between 1823 and 1844 Bay submitted eight petitions for confirmation. Nine bills were considered in the Senate and eight reports were issued on his claims by the House or Senate committees on private land claims. Early reports were somewhat favorable, but no action was taken; finally, in 1844 the Senate committee declared that the claimants had "no legal or equitable" right to any lands and thus put a quietus on their importunities.[30]

The Spanish claims in the Florida parishes of Louisiana were larger, more numerous, and had much stronger support among influential Louisianians and in Congress. Most of these grants or claims, contrary to past policy, had been sold by Spanish officials between 1803 and 1807 when West Florida belonged to the United States under the treaty with Napoleon for the purchase of Louisiana. Though the United States maintained the right to the land, it did not attempt to occupy it for years, and Spanish

---

[29] Cecil Johnson, *British West Florida, 1763-1783* (New Haven, 1943), has a chapter on "The Distribution of Land," 115 ff.

[30] *Public Lands*, II, 892-93; *ibid.*, III, 165-68; *ibid.*, IV, 877; *ibid.*, VI, 573-75; *Sen. Docs.*, 26 Cong., 2 Sess., No. 236 (Ser. No. 379), 38-39; *ibid.*, 28 Cong., 1 Sess., No. 48 (Ser. No. 432), 1. The early reports are brought together in "Reports of the Committees on Private Land Claims of the Senate and House of Representatives," in *Sen. Misc. Docs.*, 45 Cong., 3 Sess., No. 51, Pts. 1-3 (Ser. No. 1836). Philip Livingston of the New York Livingstons picked up many British claims in the Florida parishes of Louisiana amounting to 22,717 acres. These claims, with others amounting altogether to 38,859 acres, were acquired by Daniel Boardman and presented for confirmation, but without success. Johnson, *British West Florida*, 130; *Public Lands*, III, 469-70.

officials continued to administer and to manage the lands. The Spaniards and French previously had not sold lands for revenue, but with the rise in real estate that accompanied the transfer of Louisiana territory to American possession, officials in the disputed territory still held by the Spanish opened wide the door to speculation. Wealthy Louisiana planters like Daniel Clark, John McDonogh, and Bernard Marigny bought great tracts ranging from 10,000 to 120,000 arpents at three to twenty-five cents an arpent.[31]

For fifty years holders of these claims in the Florida parishes of Louisiana failed in their efforts to secure confirmation since administrative officers, Congress, and the Supreme Court held that the territory was American at the time the grants were made and the Spanish officials, though they occupied it, had no right to sell the land.[32] The size of the grants and influence of their owners, including Caleb Cushing and Judah P. Benjamin, among the sharpest and shrewdest claim lawyers in the United States, virtually assured that relief would be forthcoming. On the eve of the Civil War Benjamin introduced a bill to confirm these grants, which promptly drew the fire of senators opposed to large scrip donations and the confirmation of questionable claims, and the measure was passed over.[33]

Apparently the opposition thought the West Florida claims were now dead, or at least quiescent, for it did not watch another bill which Benjamin phrased in such a vague and indefinite way as to make it appear to be intended for the benefit of small claimants, but which was to make possible confirmation of the great speculative claims. Benjamin's second measure also was designed to confirm the vastly inflated Houmas claims, but the section providing for this was defeated before the final passage

31 James Wilkinson to Secretary of War, January 3, 1804, in Clarence E. Carter (comp. and ed.), *The Territorial Papers of the United States* (21 vols. to date, Washington, 1934-), IX, 151; *Public Lands*, III, 58-59; *ibid.*, VI, 501; Lewis E. Atherton. "John McDonogh–New Orleans Mercantile Capitalist," in *Journal of Southern History*, VII (November 1941), 479.

32 Edward Livingston, Secretary of State, did make a report on the diplomatic background of the disputed territory which favored confirmation of the claims in which he was interested, and John Marshall, speaking for the Supreme Court, conceded that the owners had an equitable though not a legal claim. *Public Lands*, VI, 495-505; 2 *Peters* 253.

33 Benjamin's report in support of the West Florida claims is in *Sen. Repts.*, 35 Cong., 1 Sess., No. 279 (Ser. No. 939), 1-24; *Cong. Globe*, 35 Cong., 1 Sess., 2692.

of the bill.[34] As later and, one may say, mistakenly determined by the Supreme Court, this second bill was "intended to validate grants to *bona fide* grantees of land" in the disputed territory of the Florida parishes.[35] Reading of the discussions in Congress at the time on the contrary indicates feeling against the confirmation of large grants and the desire to limit the application of the measure to apply to small holders. Since the land included in the claims in the Florida parishes had long since been surveyed and in large measure conveyed to others, the claimants, if successful, were to be granted scrip locatable on other public lands in lieu of that portion of their claims that did not come into their hands.

In the next twenty years major bounties were handed out to the heirs or assignees who had long fought for these claims. Large beneficiaries and their bounties were the heirs of Bernard Marigny, scrip for 50,000 acres; Caleb Cushing, scrip for 64,101 acres; the heirs of Joseph Reynes, scrip for 34,000 acres; and the cities of Baltimore and New Orleans as heirs of John McDonogh, scrip for 104,146 acres. The heirs of Thomas Power had 68,000 acres confirmed and received 57,184 acres in scrip. The heirs of Bernard Dauterive, including the powerful Bouligny clan, also were successful in securing confirmation under this act of an ancient claim of 212,255 acres and were allowed 135,757 acres in scrip. Twenty-four individuals and groups had confirmed to them 624,743 acres in scrip. Altogether, under this act and a somewhat similar one of 1858, scrip to the amount of 812,000 acres was issued in lieu of claims in Louisiana. Some 283,000 acres in scrip were awarded Missourians under the act of 1858.[36]

The second great Dauterive claim—500,000 arpents—dated back to 1717 when the grant was made by the French Mississippi Company. A century later Edward Livingston attempted to secure confirmation, without success because of the size, failure to develop, and the fact that the area granted had meantime been

[34] *Cong. Globe,* 36 Cong., 1 Sess., 2674.

[35] Act of June 22, 1860, 12 *U. S. Stat.* 85; *United States v. Lynde,* 11 *Wallace* 646.

[36] Act of June 2, 1858, 11 *U. S. Stat.* 294; Thomas Donaldson, *The Public Domain* (Washington, 1884), 289-90; compilation from records in the National Archives. The radical land commissioner William A. J. Sparks held in 1886 that the act of 1858 "has largely served the purpose of speculators, who procured the opening of the succession, purchased unlocated claims at 'succession sales' for a nominal sum (simply the costs of court), and procured the scrip." *Sen. Ex. Docs.,* 49 Cong., 2 Sess., No. 67 (Ser. No. 2448), 2.

given to others. In 1839 the claim was revived, to the consternation of many in Iberville Parish who feared that if it was confirmed they might lose land they had long held and of which
possession had been approved.[37] In 1864 a favorable report was
obtained from the House Committee on Private Land Claims,
and in 1867 Congress enacted that one-sixth part of the claim
which was held in the Civil War by a "loyal citizen"—John E.
Bouligny, a former member of Congress—should be confirmed
and scrip given in lieu of the land.[38] The statute provided that
the other five sixths were not confirmed since "the loyalty of the
other claimants is not known."[39] The owners of a claim of 299,000
acres in the Neutral Ground of western Louisiana were also rewarded for their patience and loyalty in 1862 when Congress
authorized the issuance of scrip to the amount of 17,477 acres.[40]

Missouri heirs to the Jacques Clamorgan claim of 488,000 arpents, near the junction of the Missouri and Mississippi rivers,
despite numerous rebuffs, continued to seek redress as late as
1880, though without success. They did, however, win confirmation of two other large claims for 196,000 acres, for which they
received scrip for 44,800 acres.[41]

The Bastrop and Maison Rouge claims, because of their size
and their attractiveness to settlers and speculators, excited the
most clamor. They were rights that had to be earned by the
settlement of numerous immigrants, a requirement to a good
and valid title which the Supreme Court was to hold had not
been met. Shares of large tracts of each were hawked around
among Americans who bought mostly on credit. The Maison

[37] *Grand Gulf (Miss.) Advertiser*, October 31, 1839.

[38] Bouligny is said to have been the only representative from the seceding states
who did not withdraw from Congress upon secession. *A Biographical Congressional Directory, 1774 to 1903* (Washington, 1903), 403.

[39] *House Repts.*, 36 Cong., 1 Sess., No. 343 (Ser. No. 1069), 1-6; *ibid.*, 37
Cong., 3 Sess., No. 30 (Ser. No. 1173); *ibid.*, 38 Cong., 1 Sess., No. 63 (Ser. No.
1269); Act of March 2, 1867, 14 *U. S. Stat.* 635.

[40] *Public Lands*, IV, 124-216; J. Villasana Haggard, "The Neutral Ground between Louisiana and Texas, 1806-1821," in *Louisiana Historical Quarterly* (Baton
Rouge, 1917-), XXVIII (October 1945), 1006; 15 *Howard* 1; Act of March 17,
1862, 12 *U. S. Stat.* 371.

[41] The legislative story of the Clamorgan claims is told and the pertinent docu-
mentary materials are listed in Lemont K. Richardson, "Private Land Claims in
Missouri" (M.A. thesis, Cornell University, 1955), 175-88. The substance of this
thesis is appearing in "Private Land Claims in Missouri," in *Missouri Historical
Review* (Columbia, 1905-), L (January 1956), 132-44, and in later numbers.
Sen. Misc., Docs., 45 Cong., 3 Sess., No. 81, Pt. 2 (Ser. No. 1836), 810; 11 *U. S.
Stat.* 294.

Rouge grant of thirty square leagues, or approximately 211,680 acres, fell into the grasping hands of Daniel Clark of New Orleans and his Philadelphia partner, Daniel W. Coxe, who over the succeeding years retailed it to large and small purchasers. Titles were for long years in dispute, until in 1844 the claim was pronounced invalid.[42]

More complicated is the story of the Bastrop claim, parts of which were acquired by Aaron Burr (400,000 acres), Edward Livingston, Stephen Girard, and other less well-known figures. Burr planned to colonize his purchase with restless Americans who were roving over the frontier in their search for opportunity and land.[43] After numerous sales and resales, Stephen Girard, the outstanding commercial figure in Philadelphia, acquired much of the Bastrop claim and on his death willed it to the cities of Philadelphia and New Orleans, as John McDonogh left most of his vast estate to Baltimore and New Orleans, for educational purposes. With Pierre Soulé as principal attorney for the two cities in their defense of their title to the Bastrop lands, the best possible case was presented but to no avail.[44]

Settlers had meantime taken up land within these tracts, either as purchasers or grantees of the original claimants and their successors or as squatters. Congress, importuned to grant relief to occupants who had already bought their tracts once, enacted a series of measures that attempted partially to compensate for the forfeiture of rights the settlers thought they had gained in the past. Forty-eight claims acquired within the Bastrop grant by purchase from Bastrop's grantees, and on which permanent improvements and sustained settlement had been made, were confirmed either *in situs* or, if the land had passed to other persons, in floating rights or scrip for an equivalent acreage.[45]

[42] *Public Lands*, III. 463-65; Jennie O'Kelly Mitchell and Robert Dabney Calhoun, "The Marquis De Maison Rouge, the Baron De Bastrop, and Colonel Abraham Morhouse. Three Ouachita Valley Soldiers of Fortune. The Maison Rouge and Bastrop Spanish Land Grants," in *Louisiana Historical Quarterly*, XX (April 1937), 352, and *passim*; 3 *Howard* 773.

[43] Nathan Schachner, *Aaron Burr* (New York, 1937), 325 ff. For a more critical estimate see John W. Monette, "Early Spirit of the West," Pt. 2, in *De Bow's Review*, VIII (May 1850), 107 ff.

[44] 11 *Howard* 610; Mitchell and Calhoun, "The Marquis De Maison Rouge . . . ," 369 ff.

[45] These claims were recommended for confirmation by the local land officers and were confirmed by Congress on June 29, 1854. *Sen. Ex. Docs.*, 32 Cong., 2 Sess., No. 4 (Ser. No. 661), 2 ff.; 10 *U. S. Stat.* 299; also Act of July 29, 1854, 10 *U. S. Stat.* 802.

One may wonder whether John Monette did not have Edward Livingston in mind when he wrote of the "artful land-jobbers" who eagerly sought Creole claims. Livingston arrived in New Orleans in 1804 just after control had passed to the Americans. In a short time he acquired part ownership of the Batture claim to a valuable piece of land in the city of New Orleans which promised to add greatly to his fortune.[46] Two plantations and a block of the Bastrop claim also came into his possession. Although Livingston had to fight long years to secure the confirmation of his Batture claim, when some lots included in that claim were released to him he was able to induce the government to accept them in satisfaction of the claim it had against him for an earlier defalcation.[47]

Whether or not the Hevin-Toulmin claims in Mississippi and Alabama, amounting to an estimated 300,000 to 400,000 acres, were fabricated as charged, there was no basis for the extensive acreage. Judge Harry B. Toulmin entered into an agreement with the alleged owners whereby he was to press for confirmation and, if successful, was to have two thirds of all land that was conceded. When the nature of the claim and Toulmin's agreement was revealed, the judge unctuously denied knowledge of the former and denounced as political enemies those who brought out the information.[48]

Litigation over the Houmas claim (or claims) involved notable Louisianians such as Oliver Pollock, Wade Hampton, also of South Carolina, Daniel Clark, John Slidell, Judah P. Benjamin, and John S. Preston. As granted in 1774 and 1777, frontage on the Mississippi River for a distance of 96 arpents, or three and one half miles, "with the common depth of 40 arpents" was conceded and with the right to "back lands" which were ill defined. Because of the curve of the Mississippi, the side lines fanned out to include great breadth, thus making the grant large even though only one or two usual depths of forty arpents were included.

[46] Agreement between Abraham Morhouse and Edward Livingston, in *Sen. Ex. Docs.*, 32 Cong., 2 Sess., No. 4 (Ser. No. 661), 382-83.

[47] For Livingston's land and claim business in Louisiana see Charles H. Hunt, *Life of Edward Livingston* (New York, 1864), 110, 115, 244, 310. The Batture claim receives detailed analysis in William B. Hatcher, *Edward Livingston* (University, La., 1940), 138 ff.

[48] *Public Lands*, III, 20-33; Carter, *Territorial Papers*, VI, 431-39. Toulmin and General Edmund P. Gaines secured confirmation of other claims.

When Louisiana was transferred to the United States the Houmas claims were acquired by Daniel Clark and John McDonogh, who enlarged their scope by maintaining they fanned out from the points of origin on the Mississippi and ran back to Lake Maurepas on one side and to a bend of the Mississippi on the other, a distance of nineteen and fifteen miles respectively. This enabled them to claim well in excess of 200,000 acres on the left bank of the Mississippi, comprising a considerable part of the sugar lands of Louisiana.[49] This "exorbitant and unreasonable" extension of the claims cut across and included ninety-five Spanish grants containing 27,556 acres, was a late interpretation, and ran counter to clear decisions of the Supreme Court.[50] There seemed so little justification for the enlarged limits of the claims that the local land office opened the backlands to settlement and permitted some 269 pre-emption entries to be made, many of which passed into the hands of Laurent Millaudon, a leading land dealer.

In 1811, in one of the biggest real-estate transactions of the time, Clark sold to General Wade Hampton, for $300,000, of which one third was paid in cash, his Sligo plantation and an undivided one half of his Clarksville plantation in Wilkinson County, Mississippi, the latter consisting of 3,023 arpents and having twenty-eight slaves, an undivided half of the Houmas Point plantation with its fifty-four arpents of frontage on the right bank of the Mississippi and eighty-five slaves, and the great Houmas plantation on the left bank of the Mississippi with its 37,282 arpents and 200 slaves.[51] Other parts of the Houmas claims were acquired by businessmen and politicians, chief of whom was John Slidell who thereafter became, with Judah P. Benjamin, an advocate of confirmation.

Meantime, the Houmas plantations became large sugar producers under Hampton and his two sons-in-law, J. S. Preston and J. L. Manning, though they still lacked clear title to the backlands, or, for that matter, to frontage on the Mississippi. There could be no doubt, however, that the frontage without the backlands constituted a valid claim which when separated from them would be confirmed. With John McDonogh, the two sons-in-law

---

[49] See maps in *Sen. Docs.*, 28 Cong., 2 Sess., No. 45 (Ser. No. 450), especially that opposite p. 132; *ibid.*, 25 Cong., 2 Sess., No. 144 (Ser. No. 316).
[50] *Sen. Repts.*, 36 Cong., 1 Sess., No. 150 (Ser. No. 1039), 41, and *passim*.
[51] *House Ex. Docs.*, 27 Cong., 3 Sess., No. 21 (Ser. No. 419), 121 ff.

of Wade Hampton, and John Slidell and Judah P. Benjamin arguing for confirmation of the entire claims, and Laurent Millaudon joining with the 269 settlers who had entered pre-emption claims and ninety-five owners of small private claims that had been confirmed opposing confirmation, the stage was set for a major legal and political battle.[52] Two parts of the Houmas claims, containing 64,699 acres, were actually confirmed and the patents issued by the General Land Office, but were subsequently declared void by the Attorney General of the United States in 1847.[53] Two years earlier the Supreme Court refused to confirm the controversial backlands.[54] Thereafter, efforts in behalf of confirmation were concentrated upon political action.

Slidell, the political boss of Louisiana and the power behind the throne in the Buchanan administration,[55] came near accomplishing his objective in 1858 with the aid of his colleague Benjamin. They added an amendment to a bill to confirm certain private land claims in Missouri that would make the measure applicable to Louisiana. Seemingly innocuous, when carefully analyzed it appeared that this amendment would give validity to the inflated Houmas claims.[56]

Slidell's act "excited a great commotion" among Houmas occupants who condemned the action of Congress in validating a doubtful claim of such size.[57] Much was made of the five hundred squatters on the tract. In defense, Slidell urged that his investment had been unprofitable, that even with confirmation he could not recover costs, that he was not motivated by personal interest, and he denied that he had used improper influence to have the amendment adopted. The pleas of Slidell and Benjamin were unconvincing, and a bill to repeal the amendment was rushed through with large majorities. To make absolutely certain that title to the enlarged Houmas claims might not be approved, Congress in 1860 specifically refused confirmation, though only after another effort had been made to have it validated.[58]

[52] House Repts., 28 Cong., 1 Sess., No. 81 (Ser. No. 445), 1-6.
[53] Sen. Repts., 36 Cong., 1 Sess., No. 150 (Ser. No. 1039), 35.
[54] 3 Howard 693.
[55] Allen Johnson, Dumas Malone, and Harris E. Starr (eds.), Dictionary of American Biography (21 vols. and index, New York, 1928-1944), XVII, 211; Allan Nevins, The Emergence of Lincoln (2 vols., New York, 1950), II, 42.
[56] Cong. Globe, 35 Cong., 1 Sess., Appendix, 561.   [57] 111 U. S. Reports 435.
[58] Cong. Globe, 36 Cong., 1 Sess., 2674, 3178, 3252; acts of March 3, 1859, and June 21, 1860, 11 U. S. Stat. 442, 12 U. S. Stat. 866.

During Federal occupation of New Orleans condemnation proceedings were brought against Slidell's property and it was confiscated. Despite this action and long-continued failure to gain confirmation of the enlarged Houmas claims, his heirs were pressing as late as 1883 for the full acreage Slidell had claimed, only to be rebuffed by the Supreme Court, which held that ownership extended only eighty arpents deep.[59]

John F. H. Claiborne, that jaundiced and thoroughly prejudiced historian, described, undoubtedly with some truth, how Daniel Clark, one of the most flamboyant and roistering figures of the new Southwest, accumulated his extensive holdings. Clark, in association with Daniel Coxe, "embarked largely in land speculation in Louisiana, purchasing lots and lands at low prices, hunting up defective titles, intimidating ignorant holders, thus getting possession of a vast real estate." Clark, Claiborne wrote, "was a man of talent and energy: his wealth gave him much influence, and in 1806 the Territorial Legislature elected him delegate to Congress. He repaired to the seat of government with the prestige of a Croesus, and adopted a style corresponding with his reputation. His equipage was princely; his expenditure profuse; his charities ostentatious; his gallantries notorious."[60] Claims to the amount of 19,000 acres were confirmed to Clark and his partners. In addition, claims for 148,000 acres were rejected, and the buyers of his Houmas claims waited long to obtain confirmation.[61]

William Dunbar, explorer, scientist, member of the American Philosophical Society, and friend of Jefferson, was one of the

[59] 111 *U. S. Reports* 412. In 1880 the United States surveyor general for the district of Louisiana could not decide whether the Houmas claims "are confirmed or unconfirmed" and did not include them in a long list of located but unconfirmed private land claims in Louisiana. *Sen. Ex. Docs.*, 46 Cong., 2 Sess., No. 111 (Ser. No. 1885), 1.

[60] J. F. H. Claiborne, *Mississippi, as a Province, Territory and State* (Jackson, 1880), 247. Cf. Arthur P. Whitaker, *The Mississippi Question, 1795-1803* (New York, 1934), 92, which pictures Clark as "a molelike individual." Claiborne himself seems to have had no personal aversion to land speculation, for he possessed 10,000 acres of sugar land below Donaldsonville in Louisiana which he offered for sale in 1846. *Natchez Mississippi Free Trader*, January 3, 1846. Furthermore, his father, Ferdinand L. Claiborne, while civil commandant in Concordia, had acquired twelve claims, part of which were later confirmed.

[61] Other prominent Louisianians having large claims were Dr. John Sibley, 23,410 acres; William Miller and Alexander Fulton, 61,410 acres; the heirs of C. J. B. Fleuriot, 121,029 acres; the de la Houssaye family, 27,146 arpents, of which 20,074 were confirmed.

most persistent land grabbers in Mississippi, having some 14,000 or 15,000 acres confirmed to himself, his wife, and his sons and daughters.

In Missouri, a group of St. Louis capitalists associated with the fur trade gobbled up many claims. Auguste Chouteau, Sr., had thirty-five claims for 23,500 acres and twelve town lots confirmed; Pierre Chouteau had claims to 22,700 acres confirmed; Marie Le Duc gained confirmation of 12,900 acres; and Antoine Soulard had 10,500 acres confirmed.[62] These were in addition to a number of claims whose owners received scrip ranging from 10,000 to 44,000 acres.

Through the admirable work of the Historical Records Survey, the Spanish land grants in Florida have come in for study and the publication of their principal documents.[63] The Spanish were lavish in their grants in East Florida which, when confirmed by the American officials, revealed a concentration of ownership greater than existed elsewhere in the eastern United States. Largest of the confirmed claims was that of John Forbes and Company, successor to the fur trading company of Panton, Leslie and Company, amounting to 1,427,289 acres.[64] With the approval of the Spanish and American governments the land was conceded by Creek and Seminole Indians for claims the trading company had against them. Other individuals or families having large claims confirmed to them in East Florida were the Arredondo family, 346,321 acres, George J. F. Clarke, 51,450 acres, Joseph Delespine, 54,400 acres, and Moses E. Levy, 83,975 acres. Thirty confirmed grants in Florida included 2,038,145 acres.[65] Fifty-two town-lot claims, twenty-one claims having no known acreage, and 371 claims containing roughly 2,856,000 acres were rejected.

Altogether in the six public land states with which we have been primarily concerned, 15,769 private land claims containing 9,324,011 acres were confirmed, the average size being 591 acres. This average size is not particularly meaningful since many town lots and grants running up to a maximum of 1,427,289 acres are

---

[62] Richardson, "Private Land Claims in Missouri," 105-106.

[63] Historical Records Survey, *Spanish Land Grants in Florida* (5 vols., Tallahassee, 1940). There is some duplication in the figures given in this work.

[64] In 1836 1,200,000 acres of the Forbes claim, said to contain the finest cotton and sugar lands, were offered for sale. Cincinnati *Daily Gazette*, February 10, 1836.

[65] These thirty grants were confirmed by the United States Supreme Court under legislation allowing owners to carry appeals from the land commissioners to the high court. The cases are found in 6-16 *Peters*.

included in the calculation. Also, it should be remembered that some people acquired five, ten, twenty, and even thirty-five separate claims.

CONFIRMED PRIVATE LAND CLAIMS[66]

	Number of claims	Acreage	Average size
Alabama	448	251,602	561
Arkansas	248	110,090	443
Florida	869	2,711,290	3,121
Louisiana[67]	9,302	4,347,891	467
Mississippi	1,154	773,087	669
Missouri	3,748	1,130,051	301
	15,769	9,324,011	591

Since we know the number of town-lot claims in Missouri and Alabama, we have the following table for these two states:

AVERAGE SIZE OF CLAIMS EXCLUDING LOTS

	Number of claims including town lots	Number of town lots	Excluding town lots	Including lots Acres	Excluding lots Acres
Alabama	448	100	348	561	721
Missouri	3,748	1,500	2,248	301	502

Federal policy in dealing with land claims, particularly the large claims for which there were grounds for withholding confirmation, was worked out slowly, to the extreme dissatisfaction of the claimants. While hardships resulted from this slowness, it is notable that when machinery for final adjudication was completed delay continued, as much the responsibility of claimants as of the government. The most extreme and least justified of the claims had been denied confirmation, but claims difficult to decide were generally given the benefit of the doubt. Congress and administrative officers had shown remarkable patience in

[66] From the Florida total should perhaps be deducted the two grants of a township of land each to the Marquis de Lafayette, in reward for military services, and to Dr. Henry Perrine, for the introduction of tropical plants. "Report of the Public Lands Commission," in Sen. Docs., 58 Cong., 3 Sess., No. 189 (Ser. No. 4766), 140.

[67] This last available tabulation of private land claims in Louisiana as of June 30, 1904, is exclusive of "458 confirmed claims which had not been surveyed or otherwise satisfied, their aggregate area approximating 180,000 acres." Ibid.

reconsidering time after time claims with new evidence. It might be argued that more firmness in rejection would have saved much expense and time, but the American way provided that every possible opportunity to appeal from the commissioners to the General Land Office, the Secretary of the Treasury, the President, state and federal courts, and Congress should be available to all. The process was cumbersome, the delay in adjudication long, but the results were, we may conclude, generally fair. Notwithstanding the voices of dissent that were heard in the early years of American occupancy, the government policy toward these claims contributed to the easy assimilation of the various elements making up the population.

Private land claims delayed the survey of the public lands and their opening to settlement because of the confusion over titles and boundaries. As a result the first public sales in Louisiana were held seventeen years after the purchase of the territory; the first public sales in Missouri were not held until 1818, and in Florida not until 1825. Before the public offering immigrants had no legal right to take up public land. With much of the best land included in the grants and a considerable part unavailable for development because of confusion over title and litigation, and the long-continued and heavy expense of this litigation over boundaries and titles, the public-land states felt the blighting effect of their heritage in land claims from the French and Spanish periods. Residents of these states found it easy to place responsibility for their plight upon the federal government, though with less than justice.

A pattern of landownership was established by the early French, British, and Spanish grants that varied widely from the small, narrow-strip farms in the Acadian parishes of Louisiana to the large plantations of the lower Mississippi, lower Missouri, Tombigbee, and St. Johns rivers, and the huge speculative tracts of Forbes and Arredondo in Florida. On the numerous plantation holdings of Daniel Clark, Bernard Marigny, Wade Hampton, William Dunbar, the Surget family, and John McDonogh along the lower Mississippi, there developed perhaps the most intensive form of large-scale commercial agriculture in America.

THE GOVERNMENT LAND SURVEYOR
AS A PIONEER

Dwight L. Agnew

THE GOVERNMENT LAND SURVEYOR AS A PIONEER

By Dwight L. Agnew

The system of public land surveys of the United States extends over our country in a great network of imaginary lines. This intricate web was woven by the efforts of thousands of deputy surveyors who followed the pointing of the compass back and forth across the land and blazed their trails through the forest, or erected on the open prairie mounds of sod to mark their lines. There were streams and swamps to cross, dense woods to penetrate, mosquitoes to combat, Indians to be dealt with, and inclement weather to endure. But the result of the hard and hazardous work was a system of records by which every settler who bought land from the government might claim and accurately identify his plot of ground, no matter how large or how small it might be.

The presence of an abundance of cheap land in the West has been recognized as one of the great determining factors in our history. The control and administration of that land was of obvious importance. The men who performed the necessary task of subdividing the public domain formed only one division of that great army of individuals connected with the General Land Office. Yet their service was unique in that it often involved personal danger and subjection to the living conditions of the frontier. With the fur traders, the miners, and the early settlers, they formed the vanguard of a civilization.

Immediately after the passage of the Land Ordinance of 1785, surveys were begun in the wilderness of Ohio by Israel Ludlow, a deputy surveyor, and were continued by him, "subject to many interruptions from Indian troubles, state of the weather, etc." [1] From the first, the surveys were made according to the rectangular system, an orderly arrangement provided for in the Ordi-

---

[1] T. C. Mendenhall and A. A. Graham, "Boundary Line Between Ohio and Indiana, and Between Ohio and Michigan," Ohio Archaeological and Historical Society, *Publications* (Columbus), IV, 1895, p. 131.

nance of 1785, which stated that the public lands should be divided into "townships of six miles square, by lines running due north and south, and others crossing these at right angles."[2] The township thus became the unit of land division, divided so as to contain thirty-six sections, each one mile square. The superiority of this system over that of private and heterogeneous surveys is obvious, and is demonstrable in the endless litigation necessary to establish claims where the system has not been used, as in the case of the original states and of Kentucky and Tennessee.

In the beginning the surveyors were appointed by Congress and performed their duties under the supervision of a Geographer,[3] but in 1812 a General Land Office was established in the Department of the Treasury and placed under the supervision of a commissioner.[4] Within the General Land Office a principal clerk of surveys supervised surveyors general who in turn engaged deputy surveyors for the actual field work.

A young man who had sufficient technical knowledge and the requisite ambition applied for a commission which stated that the surveyor general reposed "special trust and confidence in the integrity, ability, and discretion" of the deputy.[5] The surveyor was then required to acknowledge in writing the receipt and acceptance of the commission, and to transmit his official oath duly signed and sworn to. The deputy was required to give bond, the amount of which was double the pay he was to receive from his first contract.[6] This bond was surety that the proper instructions would be followed and that true field notes of the surveys would be submitted within the period named in the contract or contracts. The contract, drawn up and signed by the surveyor general, the deputy, and their witnesses, contained a legal description of the land to be surveyed, agreements about the method to be followed, instructions concerning the making out of plats and notes, and a guarantee of the rate of pay.[7] Upon

---

[2] *Journals of the Continental Congress, 1774-1789* (Washington, 1904-1937), XXVIII, 375.

[3] *Ibid.*

[4] In 1849 the General Land Office was shifted to the Department of the Interior.

[5] Thomas Donaldson, *The Public Domain* (Washington, 1884), 583.

[6] *Ibid.*, 586; *Revised Statutes* (Washington, 1878, 2nd ed.), Sec. 2230, p. 391.

[7] Report of William Rector, Surveyor General at St. Louis, to William H. Craw-

accepting a contract, the deputy took oath that he would faithfully discharge his duties.[8] Even all this legal procedure seemed to be insufficient to prevent fraud, for a law of 1846 provided that upon completion of the surveys, the United States deputy surveyor should take a final oath to the effect that he had done his work according to the stipulations of the contract.[9]

The task of the deputy surveyor involved more than the running of lines. The field of operations might be hundreds of miles from the office of the surveyor general. Assistants must be hired, and they, together with needed equipment and provisions adequate for several months' stay, must be transported to the scene of action. Compensation was made to the deputy for the "whole expense of surveying, making the plats, descriptions, and calculations."[10] Out of the amount of the contract came the pay of the assistants and the money necessary for the purchase of supplies and equipment for the entire party. Flour and pork were bought by the barrel, beans and dried apples by the bushel, and sugar, rice, oatmeal, pepper, and salt by the pound. Seventy pounds of coffee and ten pounds of saleratus[11] would supply a party of six men for a period of four months.[12] Supplies were often hard to procure. Israel Ludlow, then in the Ohio region, wrote in June 1797 to his surveyor general: "I have hopes of seeing you at Tuscarawas & being able to procure flour from you but fearing some disappointment, I shall drive two or three small cattle to furnish ourselves with provision. . . ."[13] J. A. Rousseau, another deputy, wrote in 1837 from Saginaw Bay to his surveyor general in Cincinnati:

> It is greatly to our disadvantage, too, to buy here; we have to give for flour $15 per barrel, and for pork, and that of an inferior quality, $33 per barrel, and other things in proportion. . . . Do not fail to

ford, Secretary of the Treasury, August 1, 1823, *American State Papers, Public Lands* (Washington, 1832-61), IV, 24-25.

[8] James C. Zabriskie, *Public Land Laws of the United States* (San Francisco, 1877), 531.

[9] *Statutes at Large*, IX, 79.

[10] Report of William Rector, *loc. cit.*, 24-25.

[11] A form of potassium bicarbonate. Baking powder has now taken its place.

[12] William A. Burt, *A Key to the Solar Compass and Surveyor's Companion* (New York, 1888), 79.

[13] Clarence E. Carter, ed., *The Territorial Papers of the United States* (Washington, 1934-), II, 609-610.

supply us immediately with money, for we are not, by any means, in an enviable position; in a strange land, among strangers, 1,000 miles from home, without money, and out of provisions.[14]

Occasionally wild game might supplement the diet. In speaking of an Iowa survey in 1849, a deputy wrote: "On this trip I remember one of the boys shot a deer, and once we found a 'bee-tree' containing several gallons of honey; and once, with the aid of a big dog, a jack staff and a convenient snow bank, we captured a two hundred and fifty pound wild hog."[15]

The typical expedition took only the minimum of equipment. One large tent for the surveying party and a small one for the packmen were needed. Bedding consisted of six mackinaw blankets and three "common" blankets to spread on the ground. Two dozen boxes of matches (the best kind) were taken. Four tin pails made to fit into each other and two "half round" cans which would fit inside the pails, together with fourteen tin basins, three light frying pans, two tin pepper boxes, one meat knife, and, for making bread, two mixing cloths of heavy cotton drilling, one yard square each, made up the culinary equipment. Each member of the crew had a knife and fork, a spoon, and a "soldier's drinking cup." Miscellaneous items included needles, awls, thread, twine and small cord, and papers of three ounce tacks for nailing boots. McDonald, an early Ohio deputy, said that in his day "the surveyor not accepted [sic], carried his rifle, his blanket and other articles that he might stand in need of."[16] Among the instruments and tools required were one solar compass, one standard chain, eleven tally pins, two marking tools and two pocket compasses. Field books, mapping and writing paper, ink, pens, pencils, India rubber, and "mouth glue" were necessary for note taking.[17]

The means of transporting the party and its equipment varied according to circumstances. Wagons were used on the prairies and plains but not always to advantage. Ira Cook, an Iowa sur-

[14] Letter from J. A. Rousseau, Deputy Surveyor, to R. T. Lytle, Surveyor General, September 1, 1837, *Executive Documents*, 25 Cong., 2 Sess., VII, no. 197, pp. 8-9.

[15] Ira Cook, "Government Surveying in Early Iowa," *Annals of Iowa* (Des Moines), Series 3, II, 1897, p. 606.

[16] W. H. Hunter, "The Pathfinders of Jefferson County," Ohio Archaeological and Historical Society, *Publications*, VI, 1900, p. 170.

[17] Burt, *Solar Compass*, 80.

veyor, related that the men of his party were often confronted by "a broad, deep river, some of the numerous branches of the Grand or Missouri Platte, no bridge, no ford, and but very limited means at our command to overcome the obstacle. All the same the job was there and we must cross, with horses, wagon and camp equippage, provisions, etc." Sometimes two cotton-wood trees opposite each other along the banks were cut so they would meet and form a footbridge. In this manner the small articles of equipment were transported across the stream. The horses were made to swim to the opposite bank. Then, said Cook, the next step was to "so fasten the axles and wheels of our wagon to the box that they would float; then when that was floated to the other shore hitch the horses to the end of the wagon tongue and, with the aid of the strong arms of the men, land the same on the bank, load up and go on our way rejoicing." [18]

Pack horses or pack mules performed excellent service. These were provided with bells, spancels, and saddlebags. More frequently than not, supplies and articles of equipment were carried by the men themselves, where swampy or rough ground made the use of wagons or even pack mules and horses impossible. The "portage strap" was used by the packmen. It was ten or twelve feet long, made of leather, and consisted of three sections. The middle part, two feet long and three inches across at the center, was tapered toward the ends. At each end of the middle section was fastened a thong of leather, and these pieces were tied around the pack. With the broad part of the portage strap resting on his forehead or chest, the packman was able to transport large quantities of supplies great distances. His usual load weighed from seventy-five to one hundred and twenty-five pounds.[19]

When the surveyor reached the neighborhood described in his contract, his first task was to find a corner of some previous survey from which to start his own. Notes of former surveys would help him. Settlers in the vicinity could give him the needed information, but quite often there were no settlers. A day or two was usually spent in tracing lines to the beginning point of the new survey. The old survey might be defective and some-

[18] Cook, "Surveying in Early Iowa," *loc. cit.*, 605.
[19] Burt, *Solar Compass*, 82.

times the marks were obliterated so that entirely new points had to be made. One deputy who was new at the job became discouraged at the very outset. After several hours of fruitless search he cried out, "I will give any man $50 that will show me my starting point." [20]

The living quarters of the surveyor usually consisted of a tent. Grass was gathered or small boughs of fir were picked to make a padding for beds. One group of surveyors working in the swamps of Michigan was frequently obliged to lay poles on the ground and cover them with hemlock boughs to keep out the water; and on one occasion they built a campfire "on the earth-covered roots of an overthrown hemlock." [21] In the prairie country, camps were made in the timber along the streams and much time was frequently lost in tramping to and from work.

The surveying party usually ate breakfast before dawn. The morning meal consisted of strong tea or coffee, fried or cold boiled pork and "shortcake yellow with saleratus and rich with pork drippings." [22] The men were ready to work before sunrise, although the "line" might be three or four miles from camp. The surveyor led the way, carrying his Jacob's staff [23] in his right hand, and with his compass swung on his left shoulder. On his right hip the surveyor carried a buckskin pouch suspended by a shoulder strap. It was the receptacle for his instructions, field notes, and papers, and it contained "an ink-horn, opened at the smaller end, containing 'home-made' ink brewed from forest bark; another horn, opened at the larger end, containing dry sand, which he used in his tent, as a blotter is used now; a dozen or more wild goose feathers, from which to make quill pens, etc." [24] Clothing for each of the party was practical. A common wool hat was considered best for all seasons. Trousers were made large and of strong cloth. The light coat or frock was supplied with waterproof pockets as a protection for books and

[20] Quoted in Hervey Parke, "Reminiscences," Pioneer Society of the State of Michigan, *Collections* (Lansing), III, 1881, p. 582.

[21] *Ibid.*, 587.

[22] *Ibid.*, 590.

[23] A support for a surveyor's compass, consisting of a single leg instead of the tripod ordinarily used.

[24] George R. Wilson, "Early Indiana Trails and Surveys," Indiana Historical Society, *Publications* (Indianapolis), VI, 1919, pp. 418-419.

papers. A large silk handkerchief was tied around the ears and neck if flies and mosquitoes were bothersome. Boots were larger than for ordinary use. A single sole projecting a quarter of an inch from under the upper leather protected the boot from bushes and grass. Tacks nailed in the bottom of the sole kept the boot from slipping.[25]

The flagman, wearing a red flannel shirt that he might be more easily distinguished, carried his rods and flags, the chainmen their tapes, chains and tally pins, and the axemen or moundmen their marking tools. Each man carried his own lunch. In areas where horses could not be used the camp moved with the work. In that case each man would carry a share of the blankets, clothing, provisions, and equipment on his back.

The deputy, with the use of his compass and the aid of the flagman, determined the course of the line. The Ordinance of 1785 provided that lines were to be run according to the true meridian.[26] This regulation caused the surveyor some embarrassment, for in order to run his lines according to the true meridian, observations of the stars were necessary. One of the deputies in Ohio was unable to take an observation for six weeks because of fogs and clouds. A surveyor general was able to obtain but two observations in the course of a month.[27] The magnetic compass proved worthless when used in the presence of minerals. In the mineral region of Wisconsin the "agency of the 'needle' " was "entirely lost" because of the presence of tap rock which caused violent fluctuations.[28] In the Lake Superior region the variation of the needle was particularly noticeable. Surveyor William Burt found that his solar compass was especially valuable there. This compass, invented in 1835, made daylight observations possible and was not influenced by magnetic attraction. "What could be done here without my compass?" he would say to his assistants. So great was the force of the local attraction that at one time the north end of the

25 Burt, *Solar Compass*, 83.

26 *Journals of the Continental Congress*, XXVIII, 376-377.

27 Letter of Rufus Putnam, Surveyor General, Marietta, Ohio, to Congress, March 10, 1798, *American State Papers, Public Lands*, I, 83.

28 Report of George W. Jones, Surveyor General at Dubuque, Iowa, to the Commissioner of the General Land Office, October 18, 1848, *Senate Executive Documents*, 30 Cong., 2 Sess., II, no. 2, p. 107.

magnetic compass needle pointed a few degrees south of west.[29] Even the solar compass did not remove all difficulties for it could not be used unless the sun was shining. Burt's own party was once held up by rain and cloudy weather until provisions were exhausted,[30] and another spent as much as three weeks at a time in waiting for a ray of sunshine.[31]

The task of the chainmen was to measure distances along the line and inform the compassmen when forty chains or a quarter of a mile had been traversed, then eighty chains or a half mile, and so on. Posts on which the township and section numbers had been scratched with a marking iron were set up by the axemen at section and quarter section corners. "Bearing trees" in the neighborhood were blazed and marked so that the corner could be easily found. The procedure had to be somewhat varied in open prairie country. There, corners were made by raising mounds of earth two and one-half feet high. A stake or post marked with a description of the township, the range and the section was driven into the top of the mound. Field notes were kept from which plats of the survey could be made.

After the morning's work, wrote a veteran surveyor, "a small fire is built, each one sharpens a crotched stick, and on it hangs a slice of his pork and broils it over the fire, letting what fat he can fall on his bread as a lubricant."[32] The bread was made at camp by the cook, or if no regular cook was attached to the party, each man took his turn. The "mixing cloths" were used in bread making. A blanket was laid on the ground and the cloth spread over it. The next step was to "pour enough flour upon it for a mixing, and make a hollow in it; then pour in some lard from the can and add saleratus and salt dissolved in warm water, stirring the flour with a spoon to a proper consistency for kneading with the hand, taking care not to reach the bottom of the flour so as

[29] Peter White, "The Iron Region of Lake Superior," Michigan Pioneer and Historical Society, Collections (Lansing), VIII, 1886, p. 147.

[30] E. C. Martin, "Leaves from an Old Time Journal," Michigan Pioneer and Historical Society, Collections, XXX, 1906, p. 409.

[31] Letter of Henry A. Wiltse, Deputy Surveyor, to the Surveyor General at Dubuque, Iowa, August 20, 1847, Sen. Exec. Doc., 30 Cong., 1 Sess., II, no. 2, p. 96.

[32] C. S. Woodard, "The Public Domain, Its Surveys and Surveyors," Michigan Pioneer and Historical Society, Collections, XXVII, 1897, p. 322.

to wet the cloth."[33] Loaves were baked in frying pans before the fire.

This practice of using a cloth for a kneading trough brought disaster to one Michigan party. The cook had used an old secondhand tarpaulin, discarded as useless for sea service but used by the men for a tent as well as by the cook for his bread. At a trading post to which the surveyors came for supplies, the tarpaulin was discovered by a number of hungry swine which had been "attracted by the adhering dough." The tent was nearly devoured, and the men were reduced to blankets for shelter.[34]

Difficulties of one kind or another might be expected at some time during the day. Particularly during the early days of government land surveying in Ohio, the Indian menace was a major problem for those engaged in the service. The red men resented the intrusion of the American white men on their hunting grounds. They sensed that the man with the compass was the forerunner of the man with the rifle and the man with the plow. One deputy stated that the Indian hated the surveyor even worse than he did a settler or even a soldier. "The figures and letters on the posts and surrounding trees, the chisseling on the stone, the hasty notes and scrawling diagrams made by the surveyor and then stuffed into his field wallet form a combination which the imagination of the Indian magnifies into some misterious [sic] 'bad medicine' whose ills he must not dare to invoke."[35] Encouraged at the outset by the British of the Great Lakes forts, they stubbornly resisted the attempts of the Americans to plant permanent marks of civilization beyond the Ohio River.

In the year following the passage of the Ordinance of 1785, Fort Steuben was erected in eastern Ohio for the protection of the surveyors of the Seven Ranges. Each party had, in addition to the protection of the fort, an armed guard of soldiers. One such party which set out in September, 1786, numbered fifty men, thirty-six of whom were soldiers. The work had not progressed far when an express rider informed them that the "Shawanese" were on the warpath and were making prepara-

33 Burt, *Solar Compass*, 80-81.

34 Parke, "Reminiscences," *loc. cit.*, 576.

35 J. L. Ingalsbe, "Northwestern Iowa in 1855," *Iowa Journal of History and Politics* (Iowa City), XVIII, 1920, p. 276.

tions to scalp the surveyors and all the other white people in the Ohio country. This news caused a hasty retreat.[36] Cases of robbery by the Indians of a part or all of the surveyor's equipment were frequent as more and more lands to the west were opened for settlement.

The white man as well as the red man often objected, even forcibly, to the operations of the surveyor. Offenses against deputies must have been rather frequent, for the protection of the surveyors of public lands was the subject of a special message to Congress from President Jackson in 1830. There appeared to be no law, he said, for the "punishment of persons guilty of interrupting the public surveyors when engaged in the performance of the trusts confided to them."[37] The result of the President's message was the passage of an act providing punishment for stopping or threatening to stop the public surveys. The act further authorized the President to order a guard, if one were needed, for the protection of the surveyor.[38]

The objection of the settler is understandable in view of the confusion arising where claims were staked out before the arrival of the surveyor. A pioneer of Wisconsin recalled that squatters came to the site of Waukesha in 1836 before the government lines had been run. Three settlers staked claims on land near a mill site, and when the survey was made it was revealed that the farms of the three men were all on one quarter section. Each was anxious to claim the waterpower, and the matter was for some time, so the pioneer said, "a bone of contention."[39]

Generally, however, the squatter looked forward eagerly to the establishment of permanent government records. When the compass preceded the plow, and the land was immediately opened for sale, the purchaser could secure an indisputable title to the tract which he chose to occupy. Then, too, the prospective settler could be guided in his choice by consulting the surveyors' field books which were kept on file at the office of the surveyor general. The intention of the General Land Office was to make

[36] Hunter, "Pathfinders," loc. cit., 196-199.

[37] Message of President Andrew Jackson to the House of Representatives, May 13, 1830, American State Papers, Public Lands, VI, 180.

[38] Statutes at Large, IV, 417.

[39] Alexander F. Pratt, "Reminiscences of Wisconsin," State Historical Society of Wisconsin, Collections (Madison), I, reprinted 1903, p. 135.

these records very complete. Instructions concerning data to be recorded in the field books were extremely detailed. Not only was a general description of the country to be included but also notations of all types of natural resources. In the surveys of the Upper Peninsula of Michigan, deputies were required to note outcroppings of mineral and obtain a small specimen which was quilted into a piece of cotton cloth, numbered, and referred to in the field books so that the location could be easily traced.[40] Some instructions recommended that surveyors should plant seeds of fruit and shade trees for the benefit of settlers. The deputy sometimes carried the title of "Land-looker." The original surveyor of the territory around Milwaukee claimed that he sent American settlers south and the Irish north and west, while the hilly country to the east was reserved for the Germans. The latter, he felt, could, by their customary hard work, best adapt themselves to the less desirable locality.[41]

Just how often the surveyor found the settler waiting for him is hard to determine. The migration into Iowa, then a part of Michigan Territory, began three years before any surveys were made. The council of the territory presented in 1836 a petition for the survey and sale of the lands in the counties of Dubuque and Desmoines where there were, according to "those best acquainted with their numbers," ten thousand inhabitants.[42] Late that year the first work of subdivision was begun. In December a deputy and his party found shelter in the squatters' cabins while their equipment was being transported across the Mississippi River.[43] The plats of the first surveys in Nebraska Territory were not delivered to the land offices until 1856. Yet by September 30, 1855, seven hundred and eighty-six preëmption claims had been filed.[44] The surveyor general of Nebraska Territory strongly urged in his report of 1859 that surveys be made at the foot of the Rocky Mountains (now a part of Colorado) where, he said, "a busy population are turning their attention

[40] Woodard, "Public Domain," loc. cit., 319.
[41] William F. Whyte, "The Settlement of the Town of Lebanon, Dodge County," State Historical Society of Wisconsin, Proceedings (Madison), LXIII, 1915, p. 105.
[42] American State Papers, Public Lands, VIII, 514-515.
[43] Parke, "Reminiscences," loc. cit., 588.
[44] Addison E. Sheldon, Land Systems and Land Policies in Nebraska, Nebraska State Historical Society, Publications (Lincoln), XXII, 1936, p. 35.

to the various mechanical and agricultural pursuits."[45] In his report of the following year, he recommended even more emphatically that the land in the neighborhood of Denver and Boulder be subdivided immediately. The population of that section, he thought, was about sixty thousand.[46] At the same time the surveyor general of Washington Territory reported that subdivision in the valleys of the Walla-Walla and Klickitat was imperative. There were six hundred preëmptors there at that time, he said, and soon there would be a thousand or more on unsurveyed land.[47]

On the other hand the surveyor often found few marks of civilization in his whole district. The first house in Shelby Township, Macomb County, Michigan, was erected during the winter (1816) in which the first lines were run.[48] The supply depot of a Michigan party was at Woodworth's Grove, where two families formed the westernmost settlement in 1823.[49] A member of one surveying crew recalled that in the southeastern part of Wisconsin there were in 1835 one or two families at Kenosha and a dozen at Racine, but that there was not a single farmer or farmhouse away from the lake shore.[50] A Michigan deputy complained in a letter dated June 27, 1837, that he was placed nearly one hundred miles from a post office or place of business.[51] When the fifth principal meridian was run through Missouri in 1815, the line did not touch a single settlement from the southern border of the state to the Missouri River. The surveyors were compelled to rely on wild game for food.[52]

Like others of the frontier, the surveyor took hardship as a

45 Report of Ward B. Burnett, October 1, 1859, *Sen. Exec. Doc.*, 36 Cong., 1 Sess., I, no. 2, p. 304.

46 Report of Ward B. Burnett, October 1, 1860, *Sen. Exec. Doc.*, 36 Cong., 2 Sess., I, no. 1, p. 179.

47 Report of James Tilton, September 20, 1860, *Sen. Exec. Doc.*, 36 Cong., 2 Sess., I, no. 1, pp. 225-226.

48 George H. Cannon, ''History of the Township of Shelby, Macomb County,'' Michigan Pioneer and Historical Society, *Collections*, XVII, 1892, p. 425.

49 Parke, ''Reminiscences,'' *loc. cit.*, 580.

50 Franklin Hatheway, ''Surveying in Wisconsin, in 1837,'' State Historical Society of Wisconsin, *Collections*, XV, 1900, pp. 390-391.

51 Letter from John Brink, Deputy Surveyor, to R. T. Lytle, *Exec. Doc.*, 25 Cong., 2 Sess., VII, no. 197, p. 6.

52 John L. Thomas, ''Some Historic Lines in Missouri,'' *Missouri Historical Review* (Columbia), III, 1909, p. 228.

part of the day's experience. There was this difference: the deputy was required to leave the beaten path and was often compelled to do his work at seasons of the year when others considered work impossible. A day's exposure to rain might soak everything except pocket compass and matches, but the surveyor's feet never became wet, a deputy testified, for a hole in the toe of each boot let the water out as fast as it came in at the top.[53] "During four consecutive weeks there was not a dry garment in the party, day or night," reported a Wisconsin deputy. The line of march led through country shunned as impassible by the Indians.[54] A deputy who had worked in a district west of Burlington, Iowa, recalled that during one winter night the prairie winds blew out all the fires. His assistants found sleep impossible and ran to the nearest settler's cabin. They made the journey in their stocking feet for there was no fire to thaw out their frozen boots. The deputy surveyor remained until sunrise, but the entire supply of blankets was insufficient protection, and he, too, sought the warmth of a squatter's kitchen.[55]

A letter written in a surveyor's camp of eastern Michigan bore the heading: "Musquito Headquarters." "In addition to the swamps," the deputy wrote, "there is another annoyance for the present, even less tolerable. I allude to the musquitoes and gnats. They are more numerous and more voracious than I have ever met with elsewhere." He believed there were sufficient mosquitoes on every quarter acre of land to consume "the last drop of blood" in his entire company. "They swarm about us a cloud, not to guide us through the wilderness, but to devour."[56]

"We worked early and late," wrote an Iowa deputy, "in sunshine and storm; amid rain, sleet and snow we toiled on, but we had glorious appetites and our rations of bread, beans, salt pork and coffee never went begging, but were eaten with a hearty relish. . . ." And although sleeping in a tent at sub-zero weather might seem disagreeable, they slept, and slept well, he said.[57]

[53] Dorr Skeels, "The Surveyor the Advance Guard of Civilization," Michigan Engineering Society, *Proceedings* (Lansing), 1897, vii.

[54] Letter of Henry A. Wiltse, *Sen. Exec. Doc.*, 30 Cong., 1 Sess., II, no. 2, pp. 94-97.

[55] Parke, "Reminiscences," *loc. cit.*, 588.

[56] Letter from Lewis Clason, Deputy Surveyor, to R. T. Lytle, August 13, 1837, *Exec. Doc.*, 25 Cong., 2 Sess., VII, no. 197, pp. 6-7.

[57] Cook, "Surveying in Early Iowa," *loc. cit.*, 610.

Hot bean soup with bread and tea served around the campfire at night was welcomed by all. Bedtime would follow close behind supper at the end of a surveyor's day, but a smoke and the exchange of a few yarns would be a necessary prelude to slumber.

Few monuments, if any, have been erected to the memory of government land surveyors. Their work was not spectacular. All that they did was accomplished in the rôle of paid workers, so they are not often thought of as pioneers. Yet those who did their work honestly succeeded in doing what all pioneers do — they helped to open up new country for those who came to stay. They blazed trails through uncharted forests. They recorded the existence of natural resources important to the settler. They answered accurately the questions of distance and location. Most important of all, their work gave the settler a feeling of security in the possession of his land. Perhaps no monuments need be erected to the pioneer land surveyors. They left their own marks, records which will remain so long as the Federal Government stands.

PRIVATE LAND CLAIMS IN MISSOURI

BY LEMONT K. RICHARDSON*

PART III: THE ERA OF INCREASING LIBERALITY

It has been supposed that citizens of every territory carved out of the public domain were united in one purpose—to progress as rapidly as possible through the stages of advancement prescribed under the Northwest Ordinance and enter the Union on an equal footing with all other states. Having entered the second territorial stage, a territory could ostensibly lay her requests or grievances upon the floor of Congress through her territorial delegate. In the case of Missouri, appropriations to improve navigation on the Missouri and Mississippi rivers were urgently demanded. Also, a territorial delegate could press Congress into an accelerated and liberal confirmation of the private land claims. Missouri, however, lagged behind as her enthusiasm for entering the second territorial stage was suppressed by the large land claimants, a vested interest that, to all outward purposes, had everything to gain by the presence of a territorial delegate on the floor of Congress.

The conflict of opinion cropped out early in the *Louisiana Gazette* when a salvo of editorials reprimanded an overzealous citizen, referred to as "Subscriber," who desired immediate entry into the second territorial stage.[1] "Subscriber" struck back, accusing the editor of keeping the "people in ignorance" by neglecting to print his petitions for the second grade of government.[2] Prepared to exchange blow for blow, editor Joseph Charless dismissed the petition as being full of "sophistical inferences and argument." The ultimate goal of state government, he elaborated, could be achieved only through the medium of population. To do anything humanly possible to increase the influx of settlers from surrounding states and territories was, therefore, the correct policy. Any decision tending to double or triple the tax burden of the territory would discourage this influx of settlers. "None can deny that this would be the consequence of entering into the second grade of territorial govern-

---

*Lemont K. Richardson was born in Wisconsin, attended Reed College, received his A.B. degree from the University of Wisconsin, his M.A. from Cornell University, and returned to the University of Wisconsin to complete his Ph.D. The research for this series of articles was done at Cornell under the direction of Professor Paul Gates.

[1]*Missouri Gazette*, January 25, March 1, 1809.

[2]*Ibid.*, February 3, 1809. The petition referred to by "Subscriber" appeared in the February 3 issue of the *Gazette*, but this was a full month after it had been circulated.

ment," he ventured. The inhabitants ran the risk of having to bear additional tax burdens if they progressed at that time into the second stage.

An additional sum of $4,500, editor Charless estimated, would have to be raised to defray the expenses of the second grade. Doubling the already burdensome taxes upon houses, town lots, cultivated lands, Negroes, horses, and cattle would produce no more than $2,500, leaving a deficit of $2,000 to be levied upon new objects. And as the public lands and disputed private land claims were non-taxable, the whole deficiency would come to rest upon the present land holders. "If we then compare the quantity of lands which have been confirmed to individuals with the amount of tax to be levied on them," editor Charless boded, "we shall find that the tax on these lands will be àt least four times as great as the land tax paid in any state or territory of the U. States." His reflections, he concluded, were submitted for the consideration of the land holders.[3]

The call to arms had been issued. By the summer of 1811, concentrated efforts were underway to suppress the enthusiasm for the second territorial stage of government.[4] Making no effort to disguise his partiality, "An Old Farmer" cautioned the "Ancient Inhabitants," or pre-Purchase residents, many of whom had been circulating petitions favoring the second stage, to wait until the federal government was more favorably inclined toward all land claims: "Taxes without property to support [us] would soon bring us to ruin and beggary."[5]

On the other hand, enthusiastic arguments were offered to soothe the fears concerning increased tax burdens. "Baptiste," who identified himself as the little man who could "with some confidence," if his claims were settled, improve his small cabin and bring a few more acres under cultivation, predicted that popular resentment would block all attempts to tax the unconfirmed lands.[6] Altering his statistics slightly, "Alknomack" demonstrated that the annual expenses incurred by entering the second stage would be no more than ten cents per capita, or $2,750 divided among 27,500 people.[7]

[3]*Ibid.*, March 1, 1809.
[4]*Louisiana Gazette*, July 1, 1811.
[5]*Ibid.*, November 16, 1811.
[6]*Ibid.*, December 14, 1811.
[7]*Ibid.*, November 23, 1811. Census figures for 1810 list the population of Missouri as 20,845, of which slightly more than 17,000 were white. (*Aggregate Amount of . . . Persons Within the United States . . . in the Year 1810* [Washington, 1811], p. 84.)

The large land claimants, chiefly the Creoles of St. Louis and the Americans of the Ste. Genevieve district, were determined to preserve the existing form of government. Forty-five inhabitants of St. Louis petitioned Congress: "Let us by a few years of Patient industry acquire property the Surplus of which weill defray the expenses of government . . . that the present order of things, may not be changed until time and Circumstances have prepared us to receive that change as a blessing rather than a curse."[8] Many of the signers, Manuel Lisa, Pierre Chouteau, Auguste Chouteau, Sr., Charles Gratiot, James Mackay, Antoine Soulard, Bernard Pratte, and Marie P. LeDuc, had amassed title to comparatively large blocks of land through confirmation of their claims; furthermore, they held large portfolios of unconfirmed claims. Pierre Chouteau had acquired roughly 9,000 acres through confirmation; Soulard, 6,600; Mackay and Gratiot, each 1,200 acres.[9]

Courtesy Mo. Hist. Soc.

Manuel Lisa

Much was at stake. The speculators intended to reserve from sale these enlarged tracts accumulated through confirmation of their claims until the price had been bid up by incoming settlers. Now these idle tracts were threatened with tax liens, and eventually, confiscation and sheriff's auction. Moreover, as the editor of the *Gazette* had remonstrated, increased tax burdens might deter settlement and thereby depress the market price of land. Finally, the territorial government in its quest for additional revenues could assess the great unconfirmed

---

[8]Petition to Congress by inhabitants of St. Louis, November 9, 1811, in Clarence Edwin Carter (ed.), *The Territorial Papers of the United States* (21 vols. to date, Washington, 1934-   ), XIV, 486-87.

[9]*American State Papers* (38 vols., Washington, 1832-1861), *Public Lands* (Gales and Seaton edition), II, 689-729.

tracts of land—a move which, in the space of a few years, might render ultimate confirmation worthless.

During this controversy the Board of Land Commissioners was preparing to adjourn. It had acted on all claims filed and closed its work on January 24, 1812.[10] Out of more than 3,000 claims reviewed, certificates of confirmation were issued on 1,342, or roughly one-third.[11] There was still hope for those whose claims had been turned down, however, because the negative decisions of the board could be reversed by act of Congress.

For the large land claimants, the tax burdens implied in the second stage of government outweighed the advantages to be gained through having a territorial delegate on the floor of Congress. The land claimants already enjoyed access to Congress through private agents who, for a slight fee, worked zealously to secure confirmation. In 1806, James L. Donaldson, through still a member of the Board of Commissioners, had advertised himself as the "proper person" to lay the claims before Congress. He charged two dollars per claim. Four years later, Thomas F. Riddick, clerk of the board, advertised that he would go to Washington as soon as the board had completed its business. Those who entrusted their claims to him could calculate with some certainty that "proper attention would be given."[12]

It was a discouraging matter for the small claimants when the Board of Commissioners closed its books. One of them complained: "Individual claimants are either obliged to abandon their claims to what constitutes the best support of their families, or expend money, hard to earn, and difficult to obtain, in paying an agent, and that agent vested with no power, authority, or privilege to speak, except when the 'committee' shall deign to permit him."[13] To them, a delegate in Congress appeared advantageous.

Seemingly, the large land claimants suffered a defeat when the territory entered the second stage on June 14, 1812,[14] but they controlled the territorial legislature and nominated eighteen of their

---

[10]Eugene M. Violette, "Spanish Land Claims in Missouri," *Washington University Studies*, VIII, *Humanistic Series*, No. 2 (St. Louis, 1921), p. 184.

[11]*ASP, Lands*, II, 689-729.

[12]Settler Jesse Cain had entrusted his claim to Donaldson, and unfortunately that was the last he ever heard of it. Deposition of Cain, October 30, 1806, in Carter, *Territorial Papers*, XIV, 22-23; *Louisiana Gazette*, October 4, 1810.

[13]*Ibid.*, July 1, 1811. The well-known select committee of the Ste. Genevieve Convention of 1809 was implied.

[14]*United States Statutes at Large*, II, 743-47. The territory was renamed Missouri.

own men to the territorial council. The President of the United States, in turn, selected nine from the eighteen nominees in June, 1813. Among the nine were Auguste Chouteau, Sr., and Samuel Hammond of St. Louis, and John Scott and James Maxwell of Ste. Genevieve.[15] These selections must have been gratifying to the larger land claimants.

Courtesy Mo. Hist. Soc.

Edward Hempstead

In the territory's first delegate to Congress, Edward Hempstead, they also had a firm friend. Hempstead, an aggressive lawyer who had arrived in St. Louis from Vincennes in 1805, was appointed attorney general for the territory in 1809.[16] He soon allied himself with the land junto, serving first on the St. Louis committee of 1809 with Bernard Pratte, Alexander McNair, and Auguste Chouteau, Sr., and later with John Smith T and George C. C. Harbison on the select committee of Ste. Genevieve.[17] His legal services were much in demand, and, unquestionably, the various resolutions and memorials to Congress bore evidence of the penetrating pen of the lawyer. His activities in land claims, begun after his arrival in St. Louis, indicated a drive to accumulate as many titles to land in as many ways as possible. He attended auctions, enlisted the aid of agents, and made direct purchases himself, obtaining eleven unconfirmed titles to land totaling 4,660 arpents.[18]

Hempstead's opponents, Rufus Easton, Samuel Hammond, and Matthew Lyon, were land claimants themselves and promised liberal action toward all land claims.[19] Rufus Easton, Hempstead's

[15]Frederic L. Billon, *Annals of St. Louis in Its Territorial Days, 1804-1821* (St. Louis, 1881), pp. 43-46.

[16]*Ibid.*, p. 206.

[17]*Ibid.*, pp. 44-45; *Missouri Gazette*, December 19, 28, 1812.

[18]*ASP, Lands, II*, 469, 532, 535, 545, 547, 625, 638, 642, 650, 652, 659.

[19]*Missouri Gazette*, October 24, 31, 1812.

primary adversary, was closely allied with Moses Austin and his fellow Americans of the Ste. Genevieve area, and at that time the eligible American-born voters far outnumbered the eligible French inhabitants.[20] However, Hempstead was backed by powerful interests, the Creole inhabitants of St. Louis, the wealthiest and most influential men of the territory, and the *Missouri Gazette*, the only newspaper in the territory.[21]

Hempstead took his seat in Congress January 4, 1813,[22] and his record shows a desire to accelerate and liberalize confirmation of the private land claims. He repeatedly lampooned the irregularities of the Board of Commissioners. In New Orleans the board had been extemely generous in adjudicating the claims, but the St. Louis board was more parsimonious. Hempstead advocated similar treatment for all land claimants under the various Congressional acts and the abolition of the board, transferring its functions to the recorder of land titles. He proposed to inquire into the expediency of a speedy and final confirmation of all grants of land in the Territory of Missouri, extend confirmation to all claims not in excess of 640 acres which were inhabited and cultivated prior to December 20, 1803, and allow the claimants to test the validity of their rejected claims in the federal courts.[23]

Legislative steps were finally taken. Congressional confirmation was extended to all village or commons claims of the inhabitants of Portage des Sioux, St. Charles, St. Ferdinand, St. Louis, Village à Robert, Carondelet, Ste. Genevieve, New Madrid, New Bourbon, and Little Prairie.[24] Section four of the act of March 3, 1813, confirmed 640 acres to practically everyone who had previously held 640 acres or more but had been granted less by the board. Two hundred and thirty-five certificates, most of them for 640 acres, were issued.[25] Under an act of April 12, 1814, passed for the "final adjustment of land titles in the State of Louisiana and the Territory of Missouri," the powers and duties of the boards were transfrered

---

[20]Hattie M. Anderson, "Missouri, 1804-1828: Peopling a Frontier State," *Missouri Historical Review*, XXXI (January, 1937), 156-63.

[21]*Missouri Gazette*, October 24, 31, November 7, 14, 1812.

[22]*Annals of Congress: Debates and Proceedings in the Congress of the United States* (42 vols., Washington, 1834-1856), 12 Cong., 2 Sess. (1812-1813), p. 510.

[23]*Ibid.*, pp. 846-47; *Annals of Congress*, 13 Cong., 1 Sess. (1813-1814), p. 787.

[24]*United States Statutes at Large*, II, 748-52. Confirmation was also extended to 1342 certificates of confirmation issued by the Board of Land Commissioners between December, 1808, and January, 1812. (*ASP, Lands*, II, 689-729.)

[25]*United States Statutes at Large*, II, 812-15; *ASP, Lands*, III, 327-31.

to the recorder of land titles in each district, and all land titles in Missouri that fell into two classes were confirmed.[26]

First, grants made by a French or Spanish concession, warrant, or order to survey issued prior to March 10, 1804, were confirmed if the claimant was an actual resident of the territory at the time of the concession. This mollified the land claimants on one of the most urgent issues, as all previous acts had nullified all Spanish concessions dated after October 1, 1800, when Spain secretly ceded Louisiana to France. Second, grants previously denied for lack of evidence of habitation prior to December 20, 1803, were now confirmed. Eventually, confirmation was extended to 392 claims falling under these categories.[27]

Frederick Bates

According to the four reports of Recorder Frederick Bates, 2,318 claims, slightly more than seventy-five percent of the 3,056 claims submitted, were confirmed or enlarged. Still unconfirmed and in dispute were the claims of John Smith T, Moses Austin, Julien Dubuque, and Jacques Clamorgan. These claims ranged from 10,000 to 500,000 arpents, each one a story in itself.

To the large landholder and claimant, Hempstead's efforts were especially gratifying. Many doubled and tripled their holdings. As Missouri's public lands were nowhere ready for cash sale or pre-emption entries, this proved to be most profitable.[28] Auguste Chouteau, Sr., who prior to January, 1813, held twenty-four confirmatory certificates entitling him to 9,000 acres and seven town lots in St. Charles and St. Louis, acquired title to five more town lots and six field tracts to bring his total holdings to

---

[26] *United States Statutes at Large,* III, 121-23.

[27] *ASP, Lands,* III, 332-44.

[28] The first Presidential proclamation ordering land sales to begin at the land offices in St. Louis and Franklin was issued April 30, 1818. See *Territorial Papers,* XV, 385.

23,500 acres. Marie P. LeDuc expanded his holdings from one town lot in the village of New Madrid to almost 13,000 acres. Pierre Chouteau now commanded five tracts totaling more than 22,700 acres; his estates, collectively, had amounted to little more than 500 acres before. Antoine Soulard, already assignee to more than 6,600 acres of confirmed land, acquired four more tracts totaling 3,900 acres. One included a tract of 3,250 arpents strategically located on the north bank of the Missouri River near its junction with the Mississippi. Jacques St. Vrain, meanwhile, received confirmation to an identical adjacent tract, so that the two men controlled more than 5,600 acres at the mouth of the Missouri. John Mullanphy, whose confirmed land holdings prior to January, 1813, comprised seven scattered tracts of less than 750 acres, added three outlots (two near St. Louis and one near St. Ferdinand) and three plantations, totaling 2,900 acres, to his holdings. Even territorial delegate Edward Hempstead benefited by securing confirmation of a town lot in St. Louis and two field strips north of the town.[29]

Generous plantations and field strips ranging anywhere from 800 to 3,000 arpents, generally situated in the districts of St. Charles and St. Louis, were confirmed to a small group of men. Similarly, valuable river frontages in St. Charles, St. Ferdinand, and St. Louis, which in time would become wharf landings, railroad sidings, or warehouse sites, as well as strategically situated outlots, were confirmed to these same men. If the village desired to develop its waterfront or to expand, it was compelled to purchase its so-called "Lebensraum" at a high price. To assess the impact of the confirmation of these village and outlot claims upon the early communities of the Missouri Territory is a project rich in historical speculation.

In a general evaluation of the effects of the private land claims upon Missouri's development, it is necessary to try to determine their influence upon the sales of public lands. Preparations for surveys and sales were initiated with the passage of the act of March 3, 1811,[30] but the first land office did not open in St. Louis until 1815,[31] and actual sales did not begin until 1818. We see, therefore, that the land sales were unquestionably postponed.

With the arrival of the surveyors, anticipation of cash sales of the public lands swept the territory, and the claimants intensified their

[29]The above tabulations have been compiled from the listings of confirmatory certificates issued by Recorder of Land Titles Frederick Bates under the acts of 1812, 1813, and 1814, in *ASP, Lands*, II, 689-729; *ibid.*, III, 314-44.
[30]*United States Statutes at Large*, II, 662-66.
[31]Carter, *Territorial Papers*, XIII, 126n.

efforts to have their respective claims properly located before the sales began. Their sanctuary was the famous section ten of the act of March 3, 1811, which reserved all duly registered unconfirmed claims from cash sales. To reserve these claims proved to be no easy task. Time and time again, sales had to be postponed because the claims were not properly registered. In early July, 1817, William Rector reported that his surveys were practically completed and that by the first Monday of the following November the lands would be ready for sale.[32] The people, he remarked, "were generally anxious for the public sales." Most of the land would sell immediately and "some of it at a high price."[33] "Nowhere had the sales been more anxiously awaited," Alexander McNair, the territorial marshall, wrote.[34] However, the necessary Presidential proclamation was not issued, and the following spring Rector was still trying to get the General Land Office to bring the lands into immediate sale. Five and seven-tenths million acres were ready at that time.[35] Finally, the Presidential proclamation was issued on April 30, 1818, ordering land sales to begin at the land offices in St. Louis and Franklin no later than the first Monday of September, 1818.[36]

On the eve of the sales, territorial delegate John Scott, who had once promised to work for the opening of additional land offices and acceleration of the land sales,[37] submitted a frantic plea for postponement.[38] Scott's initial plea touched off a concerted drive to postpone the actual sales. In June, Recorder of Land Titles Frederick Bates, feeling much "anxiety on the subject," announced that he was unable to decide judiciously which lands were exempt from sale under section ten of the act of March 3, 1811.[39] Simultaneously, William Rector divulged that Bates had refused to make a list of properly reserved claims, because he did not feel authorized to make such a list.[40] Samuel Hammond, recently appointed receiver of the public monies at the land office in St. Louis, reported that he was considerably embarrassed in his attempts to administer section ten and that, as a result, there were many unconfirmed tracts in a

---

[32]William Rector to Josiah Meigs, July 7, 1817, in *ibid.*, XV, 288-90.

[33]Rector to Meigs, September 15, 1817, in *ibid.*, 306-308.

[34]Alexander McNair to Meigs, June 16, 1817, in *ibid.*, 282-84.

[35]Rector to Meigs, March 28, 1818, in *ibid.*, 367-68.

[36]Proclamation of Land Sales at St. Louis and Franklin, April 30, 1818, in *ibid.*, 385-86.

[37]*Missouri Gazette*, November 8, 1817.

[38]Delegate John Scott to Secretary of the Treasury William H. Crawford, May 5, 1818, in Carter, *Territorial Papers*, XV, 388-90.

[39]Bates to Meigs, June 21, 1818, in *ibid.*, 401.

[40]Rector to Meigs, June 24, 1818, in *ibid.*, 402-403.

"precarious" situation which could not possibly be adjusted prior to the approaching sales.[41]

Finally, Commissioner Meigs, unable to bring the Missouri public lands into sale, acquiesced to the demands made by Scott and seconded by Recorder Bates and Samuel Hammond; he instructed Rector to withdraw all claims from sale without additional survey.[42] With the claims safely withdrawn, it seemed that the sales could begin.

Then from the Franklin land office came a request that all public sales be further postponed. Because of the confused status of all pre-emption claims, the registrar and the receiver believed that the two week period prior to the commencement of the sales for registering pre-emption claims was insufficient, and requested at least two months.[43] When it was announced that the sales at Franklin would be postponed until January 1, 1819, an anonymous letter appeared in the *Missouri Gazette* charging the Franklin agents with full responsibility because of their refusal to do anything to adjudicate the status of pre-emption, New Madrid relief, and Spanish claims.[44]

Delaying the land sales only intensified the problem of adjudication. In the meantime, the number and variety of claims increased. Pre-emptioners and New Madrid relief claimants moved in, military bounty warrants were located, and the old private claims were confirmed.

Meanwhile, an influx of settlers created pressure on the demand side. Between 1814 and 1820, Missouri's population was increasing at an annual rate of 6,800.[45] Many had been attracted by the promise of abundant lands. "Every ferry on the river," reported the *Missouri Gazette*, "is daily occupied in passing families, carriages, wagons, negroes, wagons, carts . . . respectable people . . . Come one, Come all, we have millions of acres to occupy, and provisions are cheap and in abundance."[46]

The gazetteers did not hesitate to praise Missouri's attractions. Missouri soil was described as the "richest kind," consisting of a black alluvium of "unknown depth." It was a vegetable soil, suggested another, having a uniform "depth of forty feet, and earth thrown up from the bottom of wells is as fertile as that on the

[41] Samuel Hammond to Meigs, June 25, 1818, in *ibid.*, 403-405.
[42] Meigs to Rector, August 1, 1818, in *ibid.*, 422.
[43] Henry Carroll to Meigs, August 22, 1818, in *ibid.*, 425-26.
[44] *Missouri Gazette*, August 28, 1818.
[45] Anderson, "Peopling a Frontier State," p. 151.
[46] *Missouri Gazette*, October 26, 1816.

surface." The Ste. Genevieve district was reported to be "rich in Mineral [treasures]" which, according to all testimony, were inexhaustible. There was no "country in the world where cattle and hogs can be raised with so little trouble . . . no country better adapted to the raising and keeping of large flocks of sheep." Missouri was reputed to have the most extensive and continuous "tract of productive soil in the United States," and the Missouri River afforded a navigable channel to the very heart of this rich agricultural country. There was unlimited water power, and pine forests crowded both banks of most steams. Missouri's prairies were not extensive in the least but stretched into "picturesque hills, infinitely varigated in altitude, and form and beauty."

No stagnant waters, no repositories of mud and slime, no "pestilential airs from decaying vegetables and drying ponds" were found in Missouri. Winds from the west swept in, drying all fens and pools of stagnant water. "Fever and ague is a very rare thing." "Epidemics are unknown." And the settler was categorically guaranteed immunity from "miasmata."

No western country held out greater advantages to the new settler than Missouri, according to these accounts. Few towns west of the Alleghenies held better prospects for "future eminence" than St. Charles, St. Louis, and Ste. Genevieve. Of course, there were abundant lands for all. A safe estimate was twenty million acres. Opportunities for purchase abounded at modest terms. Land titles were unquestionably secure, as they had been confirmed by Congress. And finally, it was advised, the best terms could be obtained from the earlier settlers.[47]

The gazetteers mentioned but occasionally the actual status of the unconfirmed land claims and the public lands. As far as can be determined, only one guide book specifically informed the immigrant that the only lands for sale in Missouri, as late as August, 1818, were the confirmed private land claims.[48] Therefore, since the right of pre-emption had been extended only to those settlers who were

---

[47]The above accounts have been randomly drawn from the following sources: Henry R. Schoolcraft, *A View of the Lead Mines in Missouri* (New York, 1819), pp. 34-35, 227; Schoolcraft, *Travels in the Central Portion of the Mississippi Valley* (New York, 1825), p. 234; [Samuel Augustus Mitchell], *An Accompaniment to Mitchell's Reference and Distance Map of the United States* (Philadelphia, 1835), p. 317; John Mason Peck, *A Guide for Emigrants* (Boston, 1831), pp. 95, 97; John Melish, *The Traveller's Directory through the United States* (Philadelphia, 1822), p. 40; Alphonso Wetmore, *A Gazetteer of the State of Missouri* (St. Louis, 1827), pp. 26-28; William Darby, *Universal Gazetteer* (Baltimore, 1827), p. 489; Darby, *A New Gazetteer of the United States of America* (Hartford, 1833), pp. 313-14.

[48]William Darby, *The Emigrant's Guide* (New York, 1818), p. 146.

actually inhabiting or cultivating a tract of land in Missouri on or before April 12, 1814,[49] all immigrants who arrived in Missouri after 1814, expecting lands to be had for the asking, were obliged to purchase a confirmed title to a plantation or town lot from one of the earlier inhabitants, to purchase a New Madrid relief certificate, or to band together with others who had been similarly lured by the promise of abundant lands and await the public sales.

Unfortunately, the federal officials had no idea who should be removed from the public lands or what lands had been properly reserved from cash sales and private entry. Pre-emption claims under the act of April 12, 1814, could not be filed at the district land office until two weeks before the land sales commenced, and only a sprinkling of private land claims had been surveyed and officially recorded at the land office. For example, on thirty-five township plats submitted to Commissioner Meigs by Missouri land office authorities prior to the commencement of sales in 1818, not one private land claim had appeared. Meigs then presumed that there were no private land claims.[50] Local authorities concluded from the same evidence that the claims did exist and that the claimants had not been allowed sufficient time to file them.

Was the settler who was cutting timber and harvesting fruit on Antoine Soulard's planation[51] really violating the law? Perhaps he was a lawful pre-emptioner, but no one could tell until all surveys had been completed and the lands brought into sale.

Cutting across the classic township, section, and quarter-section pattern of land ownership which characterized the public land states, an irregular pattern of land ownership had been laid down in Missouri. The river bottoms in a tier of counties about fifty miles deep, bordering the Mississippi River and extending up the Missouri River as far as Franklin in Howard County, were covered with a jumble of surveyed holdings that ran from the various stream courses in all directions.[52] There were no uniform extensions back to the foothills, and depths were jagged and irregular. The common field strips belonging to the villages were preserved intact as late as 1880. Adjacent to the village of St. Ferdinand, north and west of St. Louis, lay a cluster of narrow field strips, uniform in breadth,

[49]*United States Statutes at Large*, III, 121-23.
[50]Josiah Meigs to William Rector, October 19, 1820, in Carter, *Territorial Papers*, XV, 658.
[51]*Missouri Gazette*, September 4, 1818.
[52]*Plat Book of St. Louis County, Missouri* (Des Moines, 1909), Map No. 7.

THE FORFEITURE OF RAILROAD LAND GRANTS, 1867-1894

David Maldwyn Ellis

THE FORFEITURE OF RAILROAD LAND GRANTS, 1867-1894

By DAVID MALDWYN ELLIS *

The policy of granting land to aid in the construction of railroads in the western and southern states bequeathed to the United States a legacy of thorny problems. Stephen A. Douglas who maneuvered through Congress the first railroad land grant in 1850 could hardly have foreseen that within the next two decades Congress was to set aside for railroad construction approximately 174,000,000 acres.[1] Still less could he have anticipated the controversial history of the land grants from the Civil War to the present day: the revulsion of public sentiment which by 1871 forced Congress to refuse additional grants; the groundswell of public opinion which throughout the 1880's demanded the recovery of grants to companies failing to observe the requirements of the law; the endless litigation which surrounded almost every clause in the grants; the vexatious delays which marred the administration by the General Land Office; the interminable debates in Congress which accompanied every effort to recover unearned grants; the curious legal issues involved in the government's action to cancel the Oregon and California land grant during the 1910's; the contemporary struggle to repeal the provisions which required land grant railroads to transport mail, troops, and government property at reduced rates.

* It is a pleasure to acknowledge the aid of the Social Science Research Council in collecting some of the material used in this paper. I am also indebted to Professor Richard C. Overton of Northwestern University and Professor Paul Wallace Gates of Cornell University for helpful suggestions and criticism.

[1] The railroads actually received by 1943 a total of 131,350,534 acres. U. S. General Land Office, *Annual Report of the Commissioner*, June 30, 1943, table 76. This paper will list the main grants making up the 35,000,000 acres of forfeited land. The railroads released to the government in 1941 approximately 8,000,000 acres of unpatented land still in the process of adjustment in order to take advantage of a clause in the Transportation Act of 1940. For a discussion of this act and of the recent struggle to repeal railroad land grant rates, see David Maldwyn Ellis, "Railroad Land Grant Rates, 1850-1945," *The Journal of Land & Public Utility Economics*, XXI (August, 1945), 207-222.

28   THE MISSISSIPPI VALLEY HISTORICAL REVIEW

These problems and a host of other questions scarcely less important deserve careful study before any evaluation of our land grant policy can be made.

Within recent years government departments, railroad associations, and independent scholars have begun to penetrate the haze which all too often has surrounded the history of land grants. The first two groups have been primarily concerned with the current argument whether the total amount of rate reductions on United States military traffic — these concessions in 1944 totalled more than $200,000,000 — have offset the value of the original grants. But the historian is less interested in whether the government drove a sharp bargain than he is in the fate of the 174,000,000 acres of Federal land and the approximately 49,000,000 acres of state lands which were offered to the railroads.[2] Several questions loom large. What effect did the land grants have upon the construction of railroads, the colonization of the West, the pattern of land ownership, and the establishment of large timber holdings? What caused western opinion to demand the end of land grants and the forfeiture of unearned grants? What part did the forfeiture movement play in the upsurge of anti-railroad sentiment so noticeable during the last quarter of the nineteenth century? The recent studies describing the activities of the land grant railroads in colonizing the prairies illustrate and underscore the need of further research.[3] This paper will attempt to analyze the movement demanding the forfeiture of unearned grants and the partial success achieved by its advocates in Congress.

Between 1850 and 1871 Congress provided land grants for some seventy-odd railroad companies. Prior to 1862 the grants were made to the various state governments which thereupon conveyed the land to private companies. The agitation for a grant to help build a transcontinental railroad across the west-

2 U. S. Federal Coordinator of Transportation, *Public Aids to Transportation* (4 vols., Washington, 1938-1940), II, 32.

3 Paul Wallace Gates, *The Illinois Central Railroad and Its Colonization Work* (Cambridge, 1934); James Blaine Hedges, "The Colonization Work of the Northern Pacific Railroad," MISSISSIPPI VALLEY HISTORICAL REVIEW, XIII (December, 1926), 311-42; James Blaine Hedges, *Building the Canadian West: The Land and Colonization Work of the Canadian Pacific Railway* (New York, 1939); Richard C. Overton, *Burlington West* (Cambridge, 1941). These writers have made significant contributions in this field.

ern territories culminated in the act of 1862 which transferred land earned by construction directly to the Union Pacific and Central Pacific companies. Almost all subsequent grants were made directly to the corporations, notably the Northern Pacific, the Atlantic and Pacific, and the Texas Pacific.[4]

Each grant included not only the right-of-way but also alternate sections along the right-of-way within a certain distance of the road. The government retained the intervening section within the primary limits but raised the minimum price of such lands to $2.50 an acre. Mineral rights except coal and iron remained the property of the government. The railroad received compensation for these sections and for land already disposed of to settlers or reserved for public purposes by being given the right to secure an equivalent (if available) amount of land within a secondary zone paralleling the primary zone. In the case of the Illinois Central grant which served as the model for subsequent acts, the railroad secured the even-numbered sections for six miles on each side of the right-of-way and the right to select lieu lands among the even sections in the zone lying between six and fifteen miles from the road.

I

Nonfulfilment of many land grant provisions, inept administration by the General Land Office, self-seeking tactics of many railroad companies, and the intensification of ''homestead'' sentiment made inevitable the movement to forfeit the unearned land grants. Most crucial of all provisions was the time limit which appeared in almost every grant. If the railroad did not

[4] Note that land grants were made to predecessors often two or more times removed from present owning or operating companies. Seven present systems or predecessor companies ''received 83 per cent of the net federal acreage conveyed. . . .'' *Public Aids to Transportation*, I, 12. The Northern Pacific received 39,843,053 acres; the Santa Fe has acquired 14,886,795 acres; the Southern Pacific received 21,648,681 acres including the 2,966,384 forfeited acres for which the Oregon and California, a subsidiary, was paid $2.50 an acre by the Federal government; the Union Pacific acquired 18,979,659 acres. These four systems, which swallowed up many smaller companies, account for 73 per cent of the total Federal lands conveyed to railroads. U. S. Board of Investigation and Research, ''Land Grants to Railroads and Related Rates,'' *A Report submitted to the House Committee on Interstate and Foreign Commerce with Reference to H. R. 4184* (Washington, March 1944), 8-9. An old but standard treatment of Federal land grants is John Bell Sanborn, *Congressional Grants of Land in Aid of Railways* (Madison, 1899).

complete its line within a certain number of years (usually ten), the land was to revert to the government. The intent is obvious. In fact, the whole justification for land grants rested on this provision. The government expected that the land grant would enable the railroads to push construction ahead of settlement. Private capitalists either did not dare to risk, or more usually did not command, financial resources sufficient to build new lines into the undeveloped sections of the country.

Unfortunately a large number of railroads failed to meet the time requirement. Repeatedly Congress extended or renewed grants which had expired. In the meantime the land along the projected route was withheld from settlement until adjustments had been made and titles ascertained. The fact that forty out of some seventy-odd subsidized railroads were not completed within the time limits including extensions reveals the importance of such withdrawals.[5]

At first the opinion prevailed among railroad lawyers as well as government officials that the General Land Office had the power to restore to entry the lands of a railroad which had failed to complete its road on time.[6] Delinquent companies were careful to secure renewed authorization from Congress. But in 1874 the Supreme Court handed down a decision which clarified the legal issues but complicated the process of forfeiture. Schulenberg v. Harriman deserves careful analysis as the most important case dealing with land grants.[7]

The judges declared that the grants were in *praesenti*, "immediately transferring title, although subsequent proceedings might be necessary to give precision to that title" and "attach it to specific tracts." The decision went on to hold:

In what manner the reserved right of the grantor for breach of the condition must be asserted so as to restore the estate, depends upon

[5] U. S. Department of Commerce and Labor, Bureau of Corporations, *The Lumber Industry: Part I — Standing Timber* (Washington, 1913), 248. Note that the total number of grants varies according to the method used in computing the number. For example, the first grant to the Illinois Central also was made to the Mobile and Ohio Railroad Company. This writer considers this grant as actually one grant. The Coordinator's report estimates that approximately 70 railroads received grants. *Public Aids to Transportation*, II, 13.

[6] U. S. General Land Office, *Annual Report of the Commissioner, 1875*, pp. 106-107. Hereafter these reports will be cited as G. L. O. *Report.*

[7] 21 *Wallace* 44.

the character of the grant. If the grant be a public one, it must be asserted by judicial proceedings authorized by law . . . or there must be some legislative assertion of ownership of the property for breach of condition.

No one therefore could take advantage of a condition subsequent except the grantor which was the government. If the government did not see fit to assert its right, the title "remained unimpaired in the grantee." The effect of this decision was to make forfeiture a matter for Congressional action. In effect, it threw the burden of initiative upon the land reformers and anti-railroad bloc, while the railroads were content to delay the drive for forfeiture. In the meantime the railroads could continue construction and receive the patents for the land as fast as they earned them. They could feel confident that once they received the patents Congress would not take away their lands. Railroads were thus able to acquire millions of acres earned after the time limit. One report in 1885 estimated that almost 100,-000,000 acres lay opposite those sections of the railroad which had not yet been built or had not been built within the original time limits.[8]

The absence of a constructive and consistent land policy and the inept administration of the General Land Office made still more difficult the smooth working out of the railroad land grants.[9] The contempt for inconvenient laws so characteristic of frontier groups from the humble squatter to the cattle baron made a mockery of our land laws. Indeed the preëmption law and the commutation clause of the Homestead Act became the tools of speculators who continued to engross large tracts after 1862.

[8] G. L. O. *Report, 1885*, p. 44. This repeats the estimate of the House Committee on Public Lands in 1878. *House Reports*, 45 Cong., 2 Sess., No. 911. Perhaps 79,000,-000 acres would be more accurate. The General Land Office estimated in 1888 that the land opposite all portions of the roads (4,598 miles) not completed within the time limits amounted to 54,000,000 acres. *House Reports*, 50 Cong., 1 Sess., No. 2476. To this figure must be added about 29,000,000 acres already forfeited by 1888.

[9] Elihu B. Washburne was perhaps indulging in hyperbole when he stated in 1886 that the General Land Office had been the "most corrupt Department that ever existed in any government on the face of the earth." *Cong. Record*, Appendix, 49 Cong., 1 Sess., 259. For a typical attack, see George W. Julian, "Railway Influence in the Land Office," *North American Review*, CXXXVI (March, 1883), 237-56. A recent study indicates that the land office was guilty more of inefficiency than of fraud. John B. Rae, "Commissioner Sparks and Railroad Land Grants," MISSISSIPPI VALLEY HISTORICAL REVIEW, XXV (September, 1938), 211-30.

Illegal fencing of range land, dummy entrymen, and raids on Indian reservations were contemporary expressions of the widespread belief that the public domain was inexhaustible and that everyone had the right to seize whatever he could. The special Congressional committee of 1883 succinctly described the situation: "The present system of laws seems to invite fraud." [10] It is not strange, therefore, that unscrupulous speculators and over-sanguine promoters often diverted Federal aid into their own pockets as well as robbing the equities of private investors.

Perhaps the withdrawal of indemnity lands provides the most glaring example of poor administration by the officials of the land office. The General Land Office withdrew from public appropriation not only the primary limits as required by law but also the lands within the indemnity limits. This action was taken after the line had been projected and the map of definite location filed in the land office. After the companies had made their indemnity selections, the remaining lands were restored to market.[11] If the adjustment had been made properly, i.e. if the titles to the land within the primary zone had been ascertained and the amount of indemnity land speedily awarded, this practice would have caused only a temporary inconvenience. But several factors interfered with the orderly administration of the indemnity lands. The government sometimes neglected to survey the lands thus preventing early selection by the railroads. The railroads often failed to patent lands which they had selected because they hoped to avoid local real estate taxes. The status of all indemnity lands remained in jeopardy as long as it was not known how many sections the railroads would need to compensate them for land lost to them in the primary limits. The General Land Office was notoriously slow in adjusting the grants. Thus the indemnity lands of nearly all the railroads were withdrawn for over thirty years.[12]

Secretary Lucius Lamar graphically described the confusion into which land grants had thrown titles in large sections of the country.

Maps of "probable," "general," "designated," and "definite"

[10] Thomas Donaldson, *The Public Domain* (Washington, 1884), 536.
[11] G. L. O. *Report, 1857*, pp. 88-9.
[12] Sanborn, *Congressional Grants of Land in Aid of Railways*, 339.

routes of the roads were filed with rapidity in the Department, and withdrawals thereunder asked and almost invariably granted until the public land States and Territories were gridironed over with railroad granted and indemnity limits; and in many instances the limits of one road overlapping and conflicting with other roads in the most bewildering manner, so that the settler seeking a home could scarcely find a desirable location that was not claimed by some one, or perhaps two or three, of the many roads to which grants of land had been made by Congress.[13]

This discussion of withdrawn lands illustrates the confusion into which our land grant policy and the bungling tactics of the land office had thrown titles in large sections of the western states and territories. The frontiersman's habit of squatting on vacant lands also added confusion. For decades disputes between homesteaders and land grant railroads bedeviled government officials, required judicial determination, and attracted the attention of Congress.[14] It is difficult to apportion blame. The settler often did not observe all the legal technicalities in proving his title. Like a true gambler he hoped "something would turn up" to safeguard his claim. Quite frequently Congress would pass special acts for the relief of certain classes of homesteaders, who had inadvertently or, more often than publicly admitted, deliberately selected lands belonging to the railroad. The corporations, however, treated many settlers badly and used their influence in the land office and the courts to browbeat recalcitrant homesteaders.[15] The General Land Office, laboring under the handicaps of insufficient funds and inadequate staff, failed to attack the problems resolutely.[16] Endless disputes arose. Did railroad rights attach at the time of definite location or at the time of withdrawal of lands by the land office (and which office)? Were the companies entitled to indemnity for lands disposed of prior to the date of the grant as well as for those disposed of between that date and the definite location of the line? Could

[13] U. S. Dept. of the Interior, *Annual Report of the Secretary, 1887*, p. 8.

[14] The most extensive treatment is found in Roy M. Robbins, *Our Landed Heritage* (Princeton, 1942), 255-67.

[15] Julian, "Railway Influence in the Land Office."

[16] Rae, "Commissioner Sparks and Railroad Land Grants," 211-30. A contemporary defense of the land office is found in Henry Beard, "Railways and the United States Land Office," *Agricultural Review and Industrial Monthly* (New York), I (April, 1883), 1-16.

deficiencies along one portion of the road be made up in indemnity selections farther west?

It is small wonder that many officials and settlers looked upon forfeiture as a simple solution to the difficulties presented by the land grant policy. If the land was recaptured by the government, it could be thrown open to public entry under the homestead and preëmption laws.

The forfeiture movement drew much strength from the fear of land monopoly and the distrust of railroad practices. Land reformers had found that monopolization of western lands continued despite their hard-earned victories in securing the Homestead Act and in bringing an end to land grants. The "speculators were generally able to secure the most desirable lands, that is, those easily brought under cultivation, fertile and close to timber, water, markets, and lines of communication."[17] The census of 1880, revealing for the first time the large number of tenants, spurred land reformers to redoubled activity. The news that one in every four farmers was a tenant (and this proportion was still higher in the prairie states) came as a shock to Americans who had always denounced tenancy as a hated Old World institution incapable of taking root in democratic America. Congressmen, editors, and leaders of farm states began to echo the charges of monopoly which the reformers had been advancing. "Land for the landless" became the "demogogue's yelp."[18] Land-hungry farmers, their numbers reinforced by the heavy immigration of the 1880's, clamored for the opening of Oklahoma, the adjustment of indemnity lands, the destruction of vast landed estates which many cattle syndicates had seized by fraudulent methods, and last but not least, the forfeiture of railroad land grants.

The unearned land grants were particularly vulnerable to at-

[17] Paul Wallace Gates, "The Homestead Law in an Incongruous Land System," *American Historical Review*, XLI (July, 1936), 662.

[18] *Nation*, XLI (August 6, 1885), 114. Alarm at the scarcity of land is seen in a House report of 1886. It stated that "less than five millions of acres of arable, agricultural land . . . remain for the settler. . . ." *House Reports*, 49 Cong., 1 Sess., No. 3455. Recent studies by Paul Wallace Gates have admirably documented the activities of frontier speculators. See his "The Role of the Land Speculator in Western Development," *Pennsylvania Magazine of History and Biography*, LXVI (July, 1942), 314-33, and *Frontier Landlords and pioneer Tenants* (Ithaca, 1945).

tack. At least 80,000,000 acres were at stake inviting forfeiture. In addition, there were the indemnity lands which had been withdrawn from public entry. Homesteaders naturally joined the chorus demanding forfeiture.

Anti-railroad sentiment gave aid and comfort to the advocates of forfeiture. Distrust of the railroads which the Granger movement had first crystallized was nourished by new abuses in addition to the old and continuing evils of high rates, free passes, discrimination, and poor service. With fear and alarm the farmers watched the consolidation of competitive lines into huge systems and the organization of pools. Far from remaining the servant of the people, the railroad was threatening to become the master, a fear which the haughty attitude and political chicanery of many railroads did little to dispel. The public at large and the farmers in particular suspected that the financial legerdemain of the Goulds and the Sages would have to be paid for in higher rates.

The land grant railroads were particularly exposed. The charges of land monopoly and tax evasion were added to the general indictment of abuses which all the railroads shared.[19] The companies shielded themselves behind the Supreme Court decision which held that technically the title did not rest in the railroads until formally certified and patented. Consequently the lands remained government property and therefore tax-exempt. Admittedly, the General Land Office was partly responsible in that it delayed public survey, postponed adjustment of grants, and often failed to settle disputes between railroads and between railroads and homesteaders. Sparsely settled townships found it exceedingly difficult to support schools and good roads. They were incensed at those railroads which delayed patenting their lands. In almost every Congress determined efforts were made to remedy this evil. Finally on July 10, 1886, Congress passed a statute requiring railroad corporations to pay taxes even though their land had not yet been patented.[20] This law, however, applied only to lands opposite completed portions of the road. It also did not apply to unsurveyed land.

[19] Contemporary pamphlets charged the railroads with assigning land to speculative rings. Charles W. Hassler, *Railroad Rings and Their Relation to the Railroad Question in this Country* (New York, 1876).

[20] 24 *Statutes at Large*, 143.

This rapid survey of the background of the forfeiture movement demonstrates the obvious need for reform of the land
grant system. To be sure, the forfeiture question was never a
major political issue in the country at large, although it did become for a short time the most absorbing issue for several western states and territories. The demand for forfeiture was an
integral part of the agrarian and industrial unrest which characterized the decades following the Civil War. The long, grinding deflation in farm prices and the emergence of huge monopolies in transportation and industry led to a series of agrarian
revolts which threatened the political and economic supremacy
of the business class. The forfeiture movement must be seen
therefore in this context of discontent. It stirred up the same
controversy — although less intense — as those created by the
drive to regulate the railroads and the trusts, the attempt to
lower the tariff rates, and the bitter fight to force through free
coinage of silver. But the conservative forces, acting for the
most part through their favorite agency, the Republican party,
were able to wage as successful a rearguard action on the forfeiture front as on the currency, tariff, and trust battle fronts.
The advocates of forfeiture, however, did succeed in eliminating the egregious shortcomings of the land-grant policy and provided valuable aid to the movement calling for a general overhauling of our land laws.

II

The movement to forfeit railroad land grants ran its course
in the period between 1867 and 1894. It reached its high point
during the middle years of the 1880's. Three chronological divisions appear:

1. 1867-1877. This period witnessed the end of land grants
and the first efforts to forfeit unearned grants. The main arguments for forfeiture became well-defined. Failure to construct,
fear of land monopoly, and distrust of railroads transformed
enthusiasm for railroads into active opposition. The general
feeling that nothing should be done to jeopardize the building
of railroads stifled the isolated outcries for forfeiture. Moreover
many grants did not expire until after 1877.

2. 1877-1887. The movement gained momentum as the evils

of land grants became more apparent. Congress heeded the demand by recovering over 28,000,000 acres from notorious defaulters. The Secretary of the Interior restored the indemnity lands to settlement. The Northern Pacific and other roads building their lines after the time limit successfully warded off forfeiture.

3. 1887-1894. Land reformers concentrated on a general forfeiture act. The Senate Republicans made good their insistence that only those lands adjoining uncompleted portions of the railroad should be recaptured. Democratic efforts to forfeit all lands not earned within the time limit won House approval but met Senate opposition. The act of 1890 was a mild measure recovering the grants from railroads which had failed to construct their lines.

The forfeiture movement was an outgrowth of the increasing opposition to the policy of granting land for railroad construction.[21] Popular resentment toward this policy, which the enthusiasm for railroads had never completely silenced, first found vigorous expression in Congress after the Civil War. In 1867 there was an abortive move to forfeit grants to railroads in the southern states. Whether the motive behind the move was primarily revenge or reform is hard to say. It is significant, however, that several Republican "railroad statesmen" such as James Blaine, William Allison, and Grenville Dodge deserted their party to join the Democrats in opposition. Perhaps more significant was the determined effort by the land reform bloc to attach a "homestead clause" to all grants awarded after 1866. This clause provided that the railroads must sell their holdings in lots not over 160 acres in size and for not more than $2.50 an acre to "actual settlers only."[22] This clause was callously disregarded. In 1916 Congress did recover almost 3,000,000 acres from the Oregon and California Railroad which had failed to observe this requirement. The debates over the southern land grants and the "homestead clause" publicized the more glaring evils of the land grant system. They also served as a sounding board for representatives from the Granger states. Extor-

[21] David Maldwyn Ellis, "The Forfeiture of Railroad Land Grants" (Unpublished M. A. thesis, Cornell University, 1939), 10-19.
[22] *Cong. Globe*, 40 Cong., 2 Sess., 4438.

tionate rates, discriminations between long and short hauls, bribery, reckless financing, and corrupt construction operations had so aroused the farmers of the Old Northwest that they favored any move designed to punish the railroads.

Perhaps the most determined foe of land grants in 1870 and the most vigorous advocate of forfeiture for the following two decades was Representative William S. Holman of Indiana. In 1870 Holman introduced a resolution which declared that the public lands should be held for the "exclusive purpose of securing homesteads to actual settlers under the homestead and preëmption laws. . . ."[23] Ironically enough, the same House, which endorsed the Holman resolution, granted an additional 20,000,000 acres within the next year.

By 1871 popular opinion forced Congress to discontinue the land grant policy. Farm groups, labor organizations, land reformers, and politicians were bringing pressure on Congress.[24] In 1872 the platform of the Republican party included a plank against additional grants which the Liberal Republicans and the Democrats had already adopted. The more radical elements of labor and agriculture had been attacking the policy of land grants ever since the Civil War.

The opponents of land grants found it necessary throughout the decade of the seventies to prevent further raids on the public domain and the Treasury by the railroads. The panic of 1873, by drying up the flow of speculative capital in Europe and in the eastern financial centers, brought almost all railroad construction to a halt. Desperate promoters besieged Congress and begged for subsidies. Swarms of lobbyists among whom Collis P. Huntington and Tom Scott were the most conspicuous thronged the corridors and drawing rooms of the capitol. But the aroused anti-railroad bloc did not relax its vigilance. In 1875 they won a notable albeit fruitless victory by defeating the proposal extending the time limit for construction of the Northern Pacific Railroad.[25]

Prior to 1877 Congress recovered about 650,000 acres from

23 *Ibid.*, 41 Cong., 2 Sess., 2095.
24 See New York *Times* of August 4, 1869 and January 29, 1871 for attacks on the land grant policy.
25 James Blaine Hedges, *Henry Villard and the Railways of the Northwest* (New Haven, 1930), 48-9.

five minor grants. In 1870 the New Orleans, Opelousas, and Great Western Railroad lost its grant.[26] In 1874 Congress answered the request of the California legislature by forfeiting the two small grants to the Placerville and Sacramento Valley and the Stockton and Copperopolis railroads.[27] The complaints of land-hungry settlers in Kansas caused Congress to forfeit the grants to the Leavenworth, Lawrence, and Galveston and the Kansas and Neosho Valley railroads.[28] These forfeitures did not arouse much debate and were regarded as local bills since they were endorsed by representatives from the affected localities.

The forfeiture movement rapidly gathered momentum after 1877 and reached full speed by 1884. In that year both major parties, trailing as usual the minor agrarian and labor parties, yielded to the popular demand and incorporated forfeiture planks in their platforms. Without and within the halls of Congress land reformers found more and more people willing to listen to their charges of land monopoly, nefarious practices, and failure to construct. The friends of the railroads fought back skillfully and for the most part successfully. Every stratagem of delay and obstruction was employed to prevent the "agrarian madness" from getting out of control. But labor and farm groups along with the General Land Office and a few politicians gave the forfeiture movement strong support.

The small group of land reformers led by William Holman and George Washington Julian enlisted the support of labor and farm organizations. American labor had a long tradition of agrarianism, using that expression in a broad sense. George Henry Evans and the coterie of labor leaders associated with the National Reform movement took a keen interest in the land question. Their slogan, "Vote yourself a farm," and their demand that the public domain be reserved to "actual settlers only" had attracted wide attention before the Civil War. The National Labor Union took up the cry against land grants directly following the Civil War. Terence Powderly, Master Workman of the idealistic Knights of Labor, declared in 1883 that the land ques-

[26] 16 *Statutes at Large*, 277.
[27] 18 *Statutes at Large*, 29, 72.
[28] For more details, see Ellis, "The Forfeiture of Railroad Land Grants," 27-8.

tion was the " 'one great question of the hour.' " [29] In his opinion land reform was as important to the worker as the securing of higher wages and shorter hours. The various labor parties of the 1880's made the forfeiture of railroad grants one of their major demands.

Farmers, especially those living in the Old Northwest, furnished the strongest mass support. A casual reading of the debates reveals quite clearly a growing impatience with railroad practices and a deep-rooted fear of land monopoly. Naturally the agrarian parties, which have so checkered the political history of the Middle Western states during the post-Civil War period, joined in the drive. Thus the Greenback National Party in 1880 and 1884 wanted to reclaim the unearned grants for the people.[30] Gradually the various agrarian parties merged into the powerful Populist party of 1892. The section in its platform dealing with land reform called for the recovery of all land "held by railroads and corporations in excess of their actual needs, and all lands now owned by aliens."

The much maligned General Land Office urged Congress in 1877 either to extend the time for completion or forfeit the expired grants.[31] Year after year it kept urging Congress to take remedial action. But it was not until the appointment of William Andrew Jackson Sparks in 1885 to head the land office that this agency took decisive steps. Sparks openly advocated forfeiture as the only effective method of solving the evils of the land grant system.[32] His crusading zeal infused new life into the moribund land office. Sparks not only furnished useful information to the forfeiture advocates, but he also tried to attack the problem through a vigorous and bold administration.

In 1884 and again in 1888 the politicians framing the platform in both the Republican and Democratic conventions took cognizance of the public demand for forfeiture. The Republicans, unlike the forthright Democrats, hedged their plank with the provision that forfeiture should be accomplished in all cases "where

29 T. V. Powderly, *Thirty Years of Labor, 1859-1889* . . . (Columbus, Ohio, 1890), 341.

30 Kirk H. Porter, *National Party Platforms* (New York, 1924), 102, 126. For other party platforms, see *ibid.*

31 G. L. O. *Report, 1877*, p. 13.

32 G. L. O. *Report, 1885*, p. 44.

there has been no attempt in good faith to perform the condition of such grants.'' Obviously such a qualification minimized the threat to the railroads. It reflected the attitude of the conservative classes, who were unwilling to permit the forfeiture of any grant except those where no effort to construct had been made.[33]

The major battleground was the floor of Congress, for the Supreme Court had put the question of forfeiture squarely up to the legislators. To be sure, pressure groups could and did agitate, pass resolutions, and elect forfeiture champions; but Congress alone could act. In 1878 anti-railroad sentiment flared up in Congress. The Thurman bill, which forced the Union and Central Pacific companies to create sinking funds for their debts to the government, engendered a bitter debate. The House Committee on Public Lands in a scathing report denounced the land grant railroads for failure to construct and for monopolizing land.[34] But except for an occasional report, the opponents of forfeiture were able to sidetrack the demand for forfeiture until 1884. As the pressure increased, the partisans of the railroads disclosed that their strategy was one of delay. For example, the Senate Committee on the Judiciary in 1883 suggested that judicial proceedings and not congressional action were necessary to accomplish forfeiture.[35] Obviously long-drawn-out suits in courts, where the judges were notoriously friendly to corporations, would practically guarantee the delinquent roads ample time to earn their grants. The advocates of forfeiture were able to defeat crippling amendments requiring judicial proceedings.

The forty-eighth Congress (1883-1884) saw a barrage of reports on the various forfeiture bills. No longer were forfeiture bills conveniently buried in committee as Holman charged as late as 1883. The flood tide of public opinion was sweeping before it every obstacle. Especially was this true of the House of Representatives, where on January 21, 1884 this branch of Congress passed Holman's resolution by the vote of 251 to 17. The

[33] Note that in 1892 the Democrats urged the recovery of all lands unlawfully held by corporations, whereas the Republicans dodged the issue. Porter, *National Party Platforms*, 162.
[34] *House Reports*, 45 Cong., 2 Sess., No. 911.
[35] *Senate Reports*, 47 Cong., 2 Sess.; No. 906.

resolution recommended the recovery of all unearned grants. To make effective this recommendation, the resolution gave to forfeiture bills a privileged place on the calendar.[36] The period between 1884 and 1887 was the heyday of the forfeiture movement. Declaring that they were carrying out the mandate of the people as expressed in 1884 through the platforms of the two great parties, the forfeiture advocates redoubled their attacks on individual grants and intensified their demands for a sweeping act forfeiting all unearned land. The railroad statesmen, however, were able to prevent the movement from getting out of hand. In the case of the Northern Pacific grant, the greatest prize of all, they successfully stalemated the agrarian "madmen." Nevertheless, they could not prevent the forfeiture of several grants embracing more than 28,000,000 acres. Moreover, decisive action by the General Land Office speeded the process of adjusting grants and released millions of acres of withdrawn lands to settlement.

The following table lists the important grants which were recovered.[37]

Railroad	Location	Acres	Statute
1. Iron Mountain	Pilot Knob, Mo. to Helena, Kansas	601,000	June 28, 1884 (23 *Stat.* 61)
2. Oregon Central	Oregon	810,880	Jan. 31, 1885 (23 *Stat.* 296)
3. Texas Pacific	New Mexico Arizona	15,692,800	Feb. 28, 1885 (23 *Stat.* 337)
4. Atlantic and Pacific	California and New Mexico	10,795,480	July 6, 1886 (24 *Stat.* 123)
5. New Orleans, Baton Rouge and Vicksburg	Louisiana	352,587	Feb. 8, 1887 (24 *Stat.* 391)
		28,252,747	

The obstructionist attitude of the Senate and the bold leader-

36 *Cong. Record*, 48 Cong., 1 Sess., 547-51.
37 G. L. O. *Report, 1888*, p. 100. This list does not include minor grants forfeited in the southern states. 24 *Statutes at Large*, 140.

ship of the General Land Office deserve further attention before the struggles over individual grants are examined. Resigning themselves to a lukewarm opposition in the House, the railroads concentrated their pressure on the Senate. Bills were killed in committee, placed far down on the calendar, or burdened with stultifying amendments. For example in February, 1885 the Texas Pacific bill temporarily lost its place at the head of special orders.[38] This move, however, failed to check the drive to forfeit this land grant. Tactics of this nature earned for the upper chamber the unenviable title of ''The Land Grabbers' Senate.''[39]

The Cleveland administration made notable efforts to revitalize the Land Office and to check the more flagrant abuses of our land laws. Cleveland confessed to ''special gratification'' that his administration was able to restore to public entry some 81,000,000 acres of land.[40] No doubt his most significant act was the appointment of William Andrew Jackson Sparks as Commissioner of the General Land Office.

Mention of Spark's activities has already been made in the discussion of indemnity lands. His annual reports unsparingly denounced the ''looters'' of the public domain, while his vigorous orders suspending entries on public lands and revoking land withdrawals stirred up much opposition as well as public interest. His order, recapturing the land grant to the Atlantic and Pacific from Ventura to San Francisco, received the approval of his superior, Secretary Lucius Lamar. Encouraged by this success, Sparks examined other grants in search of violation of conditions. Unfortunately Secretary Lamar dampened his enthusiasm by refusing to sustain Spark's order which forfeited the lands adjoining the Northern Pacific line from near Portland to Tacoma.[41]

The need for a drastic overhauling of our land grant policy was gradually forcing itself upon public attention, when the

[38] New York *Times*, February 9, 14, 1885.
[39] Editorial in Albany *Argus*, June 17, 1886.
[40] Allan Nevins, *Grover Cleveland* (New York, 1932), 361.
[41] Rae, ''Commissioner Sparks and Railroad Land Grants,'' 219; U. S. Dept. of the Interior, *Annual Report of the Secretary, 1887*, p. 8. The Seattle *Weekly Post-Intelligencer* of February 4, 1886 praised this action and defended Sparks from the attacks of the railroad press.

Guilford Miller case suddenly dramatized the issue. Miller had homesteaded a quarter section in Washington Territory in 1878, but he had failed to file a claim until 1884. In passing, it should be noted that Miller, like a true son of the frontier, was at the same time trying to acquire a quarter section under the preëmption law. But swearing to two separate places of residence was not an unusual practice for land-hungry settlers. In the meantime the Northern Pacific company claimed and selected his holding as part of its indemnity grant. Subsequently the Attorney General confirmed the selection on the ground that the withdrawal was legal and that during the withdrawal Miller could acquire no right or title. Popular outcry spurred Cleveland to overrule his Attorney General and to order the Secretary of the Interior to administer land grants in such a way as to protect settlers from injury. Cleveland deplored the withdrawal of millions of acres to which the railroads had no fixed or definite interest.[42]

Shortly thereafter, Congress directed the Secretary of the Interior to adjust land grants as speedily as possible. Lamar asked the railroads for whose benefit the withdrawals had been made to show cause why such withdrawals should not be revoked. He studied their objections and decided that since the original withdrawals had been ordered by executive authority, he had the power to revoke the withdrawals. Thereupon Lamar restored approximately 21,323,600 acres of indemnity lands to public entry.[43]

III

The movement to forfeit railroad land grants before 1887 was largely a succession of struggles over individual grants. Thereafter the advocates of forfeiture stressed the need of a general forfeiture bill. The arguments for and against the forfeiture of each grant were quite similar, although the circumstances surrounding each case differed widely. Most important, most interesting, and most controversial were the debates over the Northern Pacific grant. The fight to forfeit this grant illustrates clearly the fundamental issues at stake; it brings out the cross-

[42] Fred. Perry Powers, ''The Guilford Miller Case and the Railroad Indemnity Lands,'' Political Science Quarterly, IV (September, 1889), 452-79.

[43] U. S. Dept. of the Interior, Annual Report of the Secretary, 1887, pp. 10-12.

current of forces, both local and national, which buffeted land grants for twenty years and more.

In 1864 Congress granted an imperial domain, larger than all New England, to the Northern Pacific Railroad Company. This great enterprise, long the dream child of America's first transcontinental enthusiast, Asa Whitney, was to run from Lake Superior to Puget Sound "with a branch line via the valley of the Columbia to a point at or near Portland in the State of Oregon." The history of this railroad is a story replete with drama. The "boom" cities of the Northwest — Portland, Tacoma, and Seattle — compete desperately for terminal rights. Jay Cooke and later Henry Villard perform amazing feats of finance to promote its construction. Anti-monopolists direct their most barbed shafts against this company that earned most of its land grant after the time limit had expired. Even homesteaders find their "cause célèbre" in the martyrdom of Guilford Miller.

The original grant was of odd sections within a limit of twenty miles of either side of the road in the states and of forty miles in the territories. The grant amended in 1866 and 1870 likewise provided an indemnity limit ten miles wide on each side of the primary grant within the states. Within the territories the indemnity limits extended ten miles (sometimes twenty miles) beyond the place limits. Needless to say, the task of adjusting this huge grant presented baffling problems to the General Land Office and the Federal courts. The final settlement of the Northern Pacific grant in 1941 reveals that the railroad received 39,843,053 acres. Of course, the amount originally offered was more. Thus failure to build the Portland-Wallula section cost the Northern Pacific about 2,900,000 acres. In 1941 the railroad directors surrendered claims to about 4,500,000 acres in order to take advantage of the benefits of the Transportation Act of 1940.[44]

The financial vicissitudes of the early years need not detain us. Sufficient to say that in 1873 the house of Jay Cooke crashed, bringing down with its collapse the infant undertaking. Con-

---

[44] Federal Judge Lewis B. Schwellenbach handed down a decree on August 28, 1941 bringing to a conclusion the twenty-year suit between the Northern Pacific and the United States as to the final amount of land to which the railroad was entitled. *Railway Age*, CXI (September 6, 1941), 385.

struction halted and was not resumed on any important scale until 1879. Citizens of the Pacific Northwest immediately raised the cry of forfeiture as soon as they saw their hopes for a transcontinental railroad shattered. Calling for forfeiture seemed good strategy. Perhaps the threat of forfeiture would spur the railroad promoters to redouble their efforts. Perhaps citizens could secure part of the 20,000,000 acres of land which had been withdrawn in Washington Territory pending the selection of a route.[45] The mania for land speculation as often collided as coincided with the desire to acquire a transcontinental railroad.

Forfeiture became a weapon in the rivalry between western cities for commercial supremacy and between railroads for strategic advantage.[46] The Puget Sound cities, notably Seattle and Tacoma, and their common rival, Portland, begged the directors of the Northern Pacific to make their city the terminal. To Seattle's chagrin and wrath, the directors of the railroad selected Tacoma where they hoped to secure handsome profits from the operations of the Tacoma Land Company. At once Seattle groups demanded forfeiture of the land grant along the route from Wallula to Puget Sound. They wished to transfer the grant to the Seattle and Walla Walla Railroad Company, a local enterprise organized to cross the Cascade Mountains by way of Snoqualmie Pass. Orange Jacob was sent as Territorial Delegate to Congress to press for this transfer. They also sent John McGulbra to Washington to demand forfeiture of the Cascade Division branch of the Northern Pacific.[47]

Portland likewise, as the leading commercial city of the Northwest, pressed its suit most ardently upon the Northern Pacific. Its citizens feared that the construction of a direct line across the Cascades to the Sound would divert from Portland not only the through traffic but also deprive it of the trade of eastern Oregon and Washington. Portland citizens were painfully conscious (and Seattle papers would not let them forget the uncomfortable fact) that Portland lacked good harbor facilities. Partly to coerce the Northern Pacific and partly to outdistance

[45] Roy M. Robbins, ''The Federal Land System in an Embryo State,'' *Pacific Historical Review*, IV (December, 1935), 366.
[46] James Blaine Hedges has written an excellent account of railroad strategy in the Pacific Northwest. See his *Henry Villard and the Railways of the Northwest*.
[47] New York *Tribune*, December 21, 1877.

its rivals in railroad connections, Portland's leaders initiated negotiations with the Central Pacific. Collis P. Huntington, who bestrode the western railroad world like a colossus, visited Oregon in 1875. Somewhat arrogantly he demanded perpetual tax exemption and a guarantee that the state would not regulate any line he would build. The Portland Board of Trade rejected these terms.[48]

A group of Portland promoters led by W. W. Chapman proposed to construct a railroad from Portland to Salt Lake City and eventually make connection with the Union Pacific. Of course, capital was needed, but Chapman devised an ingenious plan to raise funds. Realizing that the temper of the country would not permit further land grants, Chapman proposed that Congress forfeit part of the Northern Pacific grant and transfer the land to the new railroad. In 1877 Senator Mitchell supported a bill whereby the Northern Pacific would receive an extension of its time limit in exchange for which it would give up its land grant down the Columbia valley. Hedges aptly describes the measure:

> The measure was so designed . . . it would accomplish the purpose of the Portland promoters in either of two ways. The forfeiture of the Northern Pacific land grant would insure the miscarriage of that company's plan to build its road to the sound, and leave Portland free to develop control of the Northwest trade. But if this forfeiture did not materialize, Portland would still be assured of a road of her own, whose interest it would be to build up that city. . . .[49]

The friends of the Northern Pacific were able to defeat the bill in the House Committee on Public Lands.

In the meantime Henry Villard had embarked upon his remarkable career as a railroad promoter. His Oregon Railway and Navigation Company held a tight monopoly of transportation in Oregon. The Northern Pacific was a direct threat. If the Northern Pacific were to build its own outlet to the Sound, it would injure the trade of Villard's company and divert business from Portland. Consequently Villard used every device including agitation for forfeiture of the Northern Pacific land grant to hamper his rival. In 1880 his agent attempted to persuade

---

[48] Hedges, *Henry Villard and the Railways of the Northwest*, 40-47.
[49] *Ibid.*, 52.

President Hayes, who was visiting the Northwest, that the United States should recover that portion of the Northern Pacific grant lying between Wallula and Portland. At the same time Villard kept pressing Senator Mitchell to introduce bills providing for forfeiture of the Northern Pacific grant.[50]

Suddenly in 1881 Villard startled the country by secretly buying control of his rival. Overnight Villard and Portland reversed their attitude. The overjoyed business men of Portland were confident that Villard would protect his Oregon properties by refusing to build the line from Wallula across the Cascades to Puget Sound. But Villard took a more statesmanlike view. He reassured the citizens of Tacoma and Seattle that his company would not discriminate against their interests. He likewise sprang to the defense of the Northern Pacific land grant, which was under heavy fire from the land reformers in Congress. His dangerous rival, the Central Pacific, was probably behind the Cassidy bill of 1882 calling for a restoration of the Northern Pacific land grant.[51]

In 1882, 1884, and again in 1886, strenuous efforts were made in Congress to forfeit the unearned grant. The report of the House Judiciary Committee in June, 1882 checked for a time the forfeiture drive.[52] This report stressed the rapid rate of construction and the danger of destroying the credit of the Northern Pacific. The minority outlined the discrepancies between construction costs and the value of the grant. The inaction of Congress stirred up a storm of protest especially in the Washington Territory.

In 1884 both House and Senate reports recommended forfeiture.[53] These reports, however, revealed a fundamental difference as to the extent of forfeiture. This cleavage emerged again and again. The House committee called for the forfeiture of all lands opposite the 1,739 miles of road uncompleted on July 1, 1879 when the time limit expired. On the other hand, the Senate committee asked for the forfeiture of only those lands adjoining

---

50 *Ibid.*, 69-70.

51 *Ibid.*, 105-106.

52 *House Reports*, 47 Cong., 1 Sess., No. 1283. The *Prairie Farmer*, July 29, 1882, bitterly denounced lack of action by the House.

53 *House Reports*, 48 Cong., 1 Sess., No. 1256; *Senate Reports*, 48 Cong., 1 Sess., No. 804.

the portions of the road which were uncompleted in 1884. The latter proposal was much less drastic since the Northern Pacific had constructed most of its line between 1879 and 1884.

In 1884 and to a slightly lesser extent in 1886 the fight to forfeit the Northern Pacific grant dwarfed all other issues in Washington Territory. Passions ran high.[54] The Northern Pacific had earned the hatred of many Seattle citizens by its selection of Tacoma as its western terminus. Alarm turned to rage in 1884 when the railroad selected a new route across the Cascades instead of using the Stampede Pass. The abandonment of the latter route injured Seattle's hopes for terminal rights. Moreover, the Northern Pacific was trying to secure the coal and timber lands adjoining the twenty-five miles of the Payallup coal road which Seattle citizens had helped to finance and whose trade they intended to develop.

In the backcountry forfeiture sentiment found a receptive audience. The farmers and land speculators echoed the familiar complaints of land monopoly, exorbitant prices, tax evasion, and political corruption. Certain policies of the land department of the Northern Pacific caused much hard feeling. On November 19, 1879 the directors had agreed to sell lands west of the Missouri River to actual settlers at $2.60 an acre. But in May of 1883 Henry Villard announced that settlers after that date would have to pay the appraised value of the lands. Settlers who had already gone on railroad land in good faith and improved it for a home could buy their land at the old rate for cash or four dollars an acre on time.[55]

Space permits only the barest outline of the bitter fight over forfeiture in Washington Territory.[56] Seattle citizens held mass meetings and collected a fund to send a lobbyist to Washington. His duty was to press for the forfeiture of the Cascade Division land grant. The Seattle *Post-Intelligencer* assumed the leader-

[54] Thus the editor of the Port Townsend *Argus*, a foe of forfeiture, attacked the Seattle *Post-Intelligencer* as the "Guiteau of the West; the howling idiot of the Sound; conceived in forfeiture, born in the lap of 'sorehead' Democracy, and nursed at the breast of a declining constituency." Seattle *Post-Intelligencer*, October 30, 1884.

[55] *Ibid.*, February 21, March 27, 1884.

[56] The details of this fight can be traced in the Seattle *Post-Intelligencer*, 1884-1887.

ship of the forfeiture drive. It printed daily editorials attacking the Northern Pacific and the latter's "journalistic lackeys." It published the famous "Black Cloud" pamphlet and map which showed the railroad land claims covering two thirds of Washington Territory. This map attracted much attention at the national convention of the Republican party. The *Post-Intelligencer*, which prided itself on its staunch Republicanism, bolted the party choice for territorial delegate. Denouncing the Republican convention of September 4, 1884 as a rubber stamp for Northern Pacific lobbyists, the paper threw its support to Charles S. Voorhees, the Democratic candidate. Voorhees won a sweeping victory which he repeated two years later. There seems little doubt that a good majority of the citizens of Washington Territory were eager to forfeit the Northern Pacific land grant after 1883. The construction of the Cascade Division in 1887 ended most of the agitation. No opposition and little interest were evidenced in 1890 when Congress finally recovered the land adjoining the route from Wallula to Portland.[57]

The Congressional struggle to forfeit the Northern Pacific reached its climax in 1886. In January Commissioner Sparks began the assault by reinterpreting the joint resolution of 1870 in such a way as to deprive the railroad of its land grant from Portland to Tacoma. Approximately 2,500,000 acres were involved, but Secretary Lamar overruled this act as unjustifiable.[58] In Congress each side girded its strength. At stake was the fate of the seventy-five miles of land adjoining that portion of the Cascade Division still uncompleted. Apparently the railroad statesmen, led by Senators Dolph and Mitchell of Oregon and Edmunds of Vermont, had reconciled themselves to the loss of the Wallula-Portland sector along which another railroad (a Northern Pacific ally) had already built its line. Rumors circulated widely that the Northern Pacific was spending hundreds of thousands of dollars to stop any drastic forfeiture bill.[59]

When Senator Van Wyck from Nebraska, a Republican with strong populist leanings, proposed an amendment to forfeit the lands along the Cascade Division, Dolph and his allies swung

[57] *Ibid.*, September 11, 1890.
[58] Rae, "Commissioner Sparks and Railroad Land Grants," 219.
[59] New York *Times*, March 29, 1886.

into opposition. A motion to table the amendment lost by the narrow margin of 23 yeas to 28 nays.[60] Not one of the affirmative votes was cast by a Democrat whereas four Republicans were recorded among the negative voters. Dolph and Edmunds immediately "organized a campaign of delay." But Van Wyck skillfully pushed through his amendment which mustered 24 votes to the opposition's 18.[61] A drastic measure calling for the forfeiture of all lands not earned by July 1879 attracted only 12 votes in the Senate.

But in the House popular pressure forced the passage of this drastic forfeiture. The vote was overwhelming — 184 to 52.[62] Almost unanimously the Democrats lined up for the measure. Only half of the Republicans approved. Significantly, the Republicans supplied 50 of the 52 nays. Most of these Congressmen came from districts in the northeastern states where the bulk of railroad securities were held.

The two branches of the legislature had taken widely diverging positions. Conferences proved fruitless in this session and in the subsequent session. Neither side would yield its position. In the meantime the Northern Pacific rushed through completion of the Cascade Division by 1887.

The long struggle to forfeit this grant came to an inglorious close in 1890. In that year Congress passed a general forfeiture act which included the forfeiture of all land adjoining the Wallula-Portland section of the route. The advocates of forfeiture could take no comfort in this act. As Congressman Holman charged on the floor, the act was a Northern Pacific measure deliberately designed to forestall a more drastic forfeiture.[63] The railroad already had acquired a road down one bank of the Columbia. It was quite willing to yield its rights on the other side of the river.

For over a decade the land reformers and anti-railroad bloc had concentrated their fire on this grant not only because it comprised the most valuable tract but also because victory would open the way to wholesale forfeiture of other grants. The

[60] *Senate Journal*, 49 Cong., 1 Sess., 826.
[61] *Ibid.*, 909. Dolph insinuated that the Union Pacific was backing Van Wyck. Chicago *Daily Inter-Ocean*, May 29, 1886.
[62] *House Journal*, 49 Cong., 1 Sess., 2360-61.
[63] *Cong. Record*, 51 Cong., 1 Sess., 10423.

friends of the Northern Pacific adopted a strategy of delay. The longer they could postpone Congressional action, the more lands the railroad could earn by construction. Their efforts were crowned with success. The act of 1890 was virtually an official confirmation of the millions of acres ''earned'' by the Northern Pacific after July 1879.

IV

Previous to 1888 the forfeiture movement had concentrated its attack on specific railroad land grants.[64] True, some attempts had been made to pass a general forfeiture act. As early as 1878 the Joyce bill was introduced in the House and throughout the 1880's Holman had introduced a series of general forfeiture bills. In fact, the Holman resolution of 1884 was a clear call for the recovery of all expired land grants. The pressing need for a general settlement of the land grant problem — the adjustment of grants, the opening of indemnity lands, the recovery of expired grants — forced the Cleveland administration to act.

General forfeiture of unearned land grants would have come in 1888 had it not been for a triangular fight over the extent of land to be recovered. Three alternatives faced Congress. The majority of the House Committee on Public Lands upheld the traditional viewpoint that some 54,000,000 acres adjoining all portions of the road not completed within the official time limit must be forfeited. A minority of three endorsed the Senate stand which would forfeit only the 5,600,000 acres opposite portions of the road uncompleted regardless of time limits. A minority of two advanced the radical proposal of forfeiting the entire land grant in all cases where the time condition had not been strictly observed. This last proposal would have forfeited 78,500,000 acres.[65]

The grand old man of the forfeiture movement, Representative William S. Holman of Indiana, cautioned the extreme radicals not to jeopardize the cause of forfeiture. He pointed out

[64] For accounts of the struggle to forfeit other land grants, see Ellis, ''The Forfeiture of Railroad Land Grants,'' 87-127. The grants discussed include the Oregon Central, the Oregon and California, Texas Pacific, Atlantic and Pacific, the New Orleans branch of the Texas Pacific, Iron Mountain, Ontonagon and Brule.

[65] *House Reports*, 50 Cong., 1 Sess., No. 2476. See also estimates of the General Land Office cited by Holman, *Cong. Record*, 50 Cong., 1 Sess., 5913.

that patents had already been issued in many cases and that titles had been vested in the state or corporations. To recover these lands would lead to endless litigation. It would visit extreme hardship on persons who had purchased land from the railroads in good faith. It would never win judicial approval. Nevertheless, the radical faction composed almost exclusively of Democrats persisted in their demand. An amendment incorporating their proposal mustered surprising strength in July 1888. The radicals rallied 60 votes as compared with 106 for the opposition.[66]

The mild Senate version likewise failed to win a majority of the members of the House. Shortly thereafter, the Democratic majority in the House reaffirmed its conviction that all lands not earned within the time limits should be recovered. The vote was practically unanimous — 179 to 8.[67] But the Senate turned down the House bill and the matter was postponed to the next Congress. In 1889 a similar stalemate occurred, but the opponents of forfeiture displayed much more strength in the House.

The conservatives rested their case partly on legal points and partly on grounds of equity. They argued that all grants were *in praesenti* thereby vesting an immediate estate in the grantee. The failure of Congress to forfeit at the time of expiration was in effect a waiver of its right to forfeit the land earned after that date. The Supreme Court had held in Van Wyck *v.* Knevals that "so far as that portion of the road which was completed and accepted, is concerned, the contract of the Company was executed, and as to the lands patented, the transaction on the part of the government was closed and the title of the Company perfected." [68] As the years passed, the practical difficulties of forfeiture increased. Forfeiture would unsettle thousands of land titles bought in good faith by innocent purchasers. It would jeopardize the investments of "widows and orphans." The railroads had frequently sold their bonds on the strength of the land grant. Drastic forfeiture would strike a body blow at railroad credit. It would also discourage many companies from completing their lines.

[66] *House Journal*, 50 Cong., 1 Sess., 2275-6.
[67] *Ibid.*, 2284-5.
[68] 106 *U. S. Reports*, 360.

New England furnished the staunchest opposition, followed by the Middle Atlantic states. Contrarywise, the states of the Old Northwest produced most of the leaders of the movement, notably George Washington Julian and William S. Holman. With the growing industrialization of this area and the corresponding increase in conservative as contrasted with agrarian strength, the number of Congressional opponents of forfeiture tended to rise. The Democrats invariably took a more advanced position than the Republicans, although party lines were often ignored by members of both parties.

In 1890 it was the conservatives, alarmed at the spread of Populist ideas, who pushed through the general forfeiture act.[69] More positive in its program than the earlier Greenback, Granger, and Anti-Monopolist movements, the Populist party called for government ownership of railroads and telegraphs, government regulation of natural resources, the end of the protective system, and the adoption of free silver and banking reforms. These measures were designed to orient government policy to aid agriculture. Land reform and the forfeiture of land grants were minor objectives of the Populists.

The act of 1890 must be viewed in the setting of this social ferment. A bill providing for the forfeiture of grants opposite uncompleted railroads received Senate approval. The opposition came from staunch advocates of forfeiture such as Holman, who condemned the measure as one sponsored by the Northern Pacific Railroad. Nevertheless, the House swung over to the Senate position. Many members undoubtedly felt that any bill was better than nothing.

The act forfeited the following grants:

1. Gulf and Ship Island	652,800	acres
2. Coosa and Tennessee	140,160	
3. Coosa and Chattanooga	144,000	
4. Mobile and Girard	536,064	
5. Selma, Rome and Dalton	89,932	
6. Atlantic, Gulf and West India Transit	76,800	
7. Marquette, Houghton and Ontonagon	294,400	
8. Ontonagon and Brule River	211,200	
9. Wisconsin Central	406,880	

[69] 26 *Statutes at Large*, 496.

10. Northern Pacific	2,000,000
11. Southern Pacific	1,075,200

5,627,436 acres[70]

In 1890 the House had surrendered to the Senate. Forfeiture sentiment fanned by the growing agrarian unrest did not die. It reasserted itself in the House in 1892 when a bill calling for the recovery of all lands not earned within the time limit received an overwhelming majority.[71] No doubt a considerable number of congressmen voted for the measure for purely political reasons. They knew full well that the Senate would reject any drastic measure. The Senate was obdurate; it refused to reconsider its former stand.

Two years later the advocates of forfeiture made a last effort to recover the land grants completed after the time limit. The bill provoked much opposition. The conservatives, composed mainly of Republicans, tried to amend the bill so as to guarantee title in all cases where the land had been sold to bona fide purchasers. The Democrats had already included a provision that the government would not contest the title to those purchasers who held less than 320 acres. The opponents of forfeiture failed to prevent passage of the House bill.[72]

The Senate gave short shrift to the forfeiture bill. Senator Dolph voiced the opinion of most Senators when he warned that "vast interests, large farms, vast tracts of lands, the interests of the purchasers of the railroad companies . . . would be destroyed." The bill was accordingly tabled.

The movement to forfeit railroad land grants came to an end in 1894. To be sure, sporadic attacks on the land grants broke out from time to time. For example, in 1907 Congress authorized the attorney general to compel the Oregon and California railroad to observe the terms of its charter. This action set in train a complicated series of court decrees and forced Congress to act on several occasions to protect the interests of innocent purchasers, the state of Oregon and its local government units, and the rights of the railroad. Finally in 1916 the government actually

70 Compiled from the table in *House Reports*, 52 Cong., 1 Sess., No. 1426.
71 The vote was 143 yeas to 12 nays. *Cong. Record*, 52 Cong., 1 Sess., 5125.
72 For details, see Ellis, "Forfeiture of Railroad Land Grants," 139-41.

did recover almost 3,000,000 acres of land, although the railroad managed to salvage the equivalent of $2.50 an acre for its original grant.[73] The Northern Pacific grant became embroiled in an equally complicated mass of litigation. But these controversies grew out of a substantially different set of circumstances and require separate treatment. By 1894 the fight to recapture land grants on the ground that the companies had not completed their railroads within the time limit was over. The conservative Republicans of the Senate had succeeded in delaying the movement until most railroads had "earned" their grants by construction. The advocates of forfeiture, however, could take some solace in the fact that their efforts had recovered approximately 35,000,000 acres and had forced the government to speed the adjustment of all grants.

V

A critical reappraisal of our land grant policy is long overdue. What the land grant railroads did with their grants — over 11 per cent of the area of continental United States — is an important chapter in American expansion. Fortunately recent studies have brought to light the role of these railroads in colonizing the prairies and plains. More recently Colonel Robert S. Henry has highlighted the danger of an uncritical use of the traditional land grant map and has urged textbook writers to give adequate attention to the impressive amount of rate reductions granted to the government.[74] Much more work, however, needs to be done before anything more than a tentative evaluation of our policy may be hazarded.

The forfeiture movement reflected the attitude of many Americans belonging to the generation (1870-1890) most directly affected by the operations of the grants. Their attitude deserves careful consideration. Contemporary opinion as voiced by labor and farm groups, outlined in political platforms, and expressed in Congressional debates considered that the evils outweighed the benefits. Failure to construct, the withdrawal of indemnity lands, the delays in adjusting grants, tax evasions, and other

[73] 39 *Statutes at Large*, 218.

[74] Robert S. Henry, "The Railroad Land Grant Legend in American History Texts," MISSISSIPPI VALLEY HISTORICAL REVIEW, XXXII (September, 1945), 171-94.

annoyances aroused public indignation against land grants and their administration by both the government and the carriers. The mantle of time has tended to cover these shortcomings. Of course, champions of forfeiture took only a partial and myopic view. They ignored the crucial problem of raising credit, especially after the depression of 1873 dried up the springs of finance. They failed to take account of the prodigious difficulties of constructing railroads into undeveloped territory. They singled out abuses of the land grant system at a time when virtually all land laws were being outrageously violated and when the general level of public service and business ethics had reached ebb tide. They passed over unnoticed the very real contributions which the land grant railroads made in opening the West and in promoting colonization.

The dangers of making sweeping generalizations about the wisdom, effectiveness, and consequences of our land grant policy should be obvious. Certain observations would appear to be pertinent. The majority of the people, particularly those in the western states, were determined to secure railroads no matter what the cost. Between 1850 and 1871 they favored or at least acquiesced in the policy of granting lands to aid railroad construction. Furthermore, there seems little question that the right to mortgage the grants bolstered the precarious credit of many companies. The land was a tangible asset even though somewhat difficult to liquidate. Land grants did spur certain speculative enterprises to life. For example, the Northern Pacific failed to show much vigor until Congress passed the joint resolution of 1870 permitting it to place a mortgage on its land. Land grants gave substantial help to other railroads. The Burlington used revenues from its land sales to help construct its line across Nebraska ahead of settlement.

But a grant of land by no means assured construction. How else explain the long list of forfeited grants? How else account for the roster of companies which failed to earn their land within the time limit? Contrarywise, unaided lines sometimes maintained a faster rate of construction than aided companies. The Great Northern under Jim Hill's driving leadership crossed the Plains and Rockies without Federal aid. The Southern Pacific constructed its line eastward from California without a Federal land grant despite the fact that its rival, the Texas Pacific, had received a large grant from both the Federal government and the state of Texas. The latter failed to earn any of its Federal grant. Similarly the Atlantic and Pacific was a miserable failure and failed to earn its grant. In short, each enterprise must be studied individually before it can be determined whether a land grant was necessary, helpful, ineffectual, or harmful.

The remarkable colonization work of the Illinois Central, the Chicago, Burlington, and Quincy, and still later the Canadian Pacific has perhaps conveyed the impression that all land grant railroads were equally vigorous in promoting settlement. These companies were not typical. Neither were the score of companies which failed to construct any part of their line and consequently failed to earn any land. Again each enterprise must be studied separately. The above railroads, which possessed good land and boasted vigorous leadership, accomplished great results in bringing in immigrants. On the other hand, companies such as the Texas Pacific and the Atlantic and Pacific would have found it difficult to colonize their holdings since most of their land lay in the semi-arid regions of the West. In some cases land grants actually retarded settlement or dispersed it unnecessarily. Land within the primary and indemnity zones was withdrawn for decades, preventing anyone but squatters from improving the land. Controversies between railroads over overlapping grants and between railroads and homesteaders likewise cast a blight upon large sections of the countryside.

Possession of a land grant was not necessary to interest far-sighted railroad leaders in promoting colonization. Jim Hill, than whom there was no greater exponent of colonization work, attracted thousands of homesteaders to the Great Plains despite the fact the Great Northern had practically no land to sell.

Perhaps it is captious to suggest that the very success of some railroads in promoting settlement of the plains and mountain country was not an unmixed blessing. For example, many of the farmers whom Jim Hill had persuaded to settle in eastern Montana later found it impossible to make a living on the parched and wind-swept plains. The construction of railroads ahead of the frontier line tended to disperse the population. Withdrawal of land by the government and withholding by railroads likewise prevented compact settlement. The scattered population was less able to support such social services as schools, churches, and roads. The practice of granting alternate sections worked badly in both the semi-arid and timbered areas. Well-suited to the humid and fertile Mississippi Valley states, the alternate section scheme was a complete failure west of the 100th meridian. A unit of 160 acres was much too small for efficient ranching. Of course Congress was mainly at fault for failing to adapt the land laws to the peculiar needs of the Great Plains. But the patchwork of railroad land grants complicated the problem of readjusting our land policy for decades to come.[75] Needless to say, no railroad could expend the large sums necessary for reclamation and irrigation even if it had owned solid tracts of land.

Another unforeseen result of our land grant policy was the establishment of large timber holdings by the Northern Pacific in the Pacific Northwest and the engrossing of valuable oil lands by the Southern Pacific in California. Moreover, the alternate-section pattern has created administrative difficulties for the United States Forest Service in those regions where the railroad grant overlaps a national forest.

Clearly, final judgment concerning our land grant policy must await further study. The experience of each land grant railroad in earning its grant and disposing of its land is as individual a story as the founding and settlement of the thirteen colonies. The Oregon and California railroad found that its grant was largely valuable for the timber on it. The directors callously and perhaps realistically disregarded the provision requiring the company to sell its holdings to actual settlers in lots of not more than 160 acres and for no more than $2.50 an acre. The Illinois Central rapidly sold its tract most of which was fertile agricultural land. The Texas and Pacific failed to earn its grant and was therefore spared the problem of administering millions of acres of desert lands. The Northern Pacific held land of every description — agricultural, forest, and mineral; prairie, plain, and mountain; humid and semi-arid. Practically nothing is known about the history of land grant railroads in the southern states except that few companies earned their grants.

[75] A pioneer study in tnis field is Sanford A. Mosk, *Land Tenure Problems in the Santa Fe Railroad Grant Area* (Berkeley, Calif., 1944).

The movement to forfeit Federal land grants was the inevitable outcome of our lavish and poorly-administered land grant policy. This drive shows that the era of the open frontier was drawing to a close and that the country was seeking to recover some of its landed heritage. It is no coincidence that the general forfeiture act of 1890 corresponded with the announcement of the census report that the frontier no longer existed as a definite region for settlement.[76] Both events reflect a new America of the closed frontier, an America which was slowly recognizing the principle that the public lands must be conserved for the benefit of future generations.

[76] This did not mean that there was no more land available for homesteading. See Fred A. Shannon, "The Homestead Act and the Labor Surplus," *American Historical Review*, XLI (July, 1936), 637-51. The Forest Reserve Act of 1891 is perhaps another sign of the trend toward conservation.

THE OREGON AND CALIFORNIA RAILROAD LAND GRANT, 1866-1945

David Maldwyn Ellis

The Oregon and California Railroad Land Grant, 1866-1945

*David Maldwyn Ellis**

THE LAND GRANT RECEIVED by the Oregon and California Railroad Company has probably stirred up more controversy over a longer period of time than any other land grant—always excepting the gigantic grant to the Northern Pacific Railway. Three distinct disputes stand out. Failure to construct its line within the time limit led to a demand for the forfeiture of the grant during the 1880's. Secondly, the federal government attempted between 1907 and 1916 to recapture the grant, on the ground that the company had failed to sell the land according to the terms of the original award. Success in this endeavor forced Congress to make provision for the proper administration of the land and the disposition of the revenues therefrom. Thirdly, in more recent years the Department of the Interior challenged the jurisdiction exercised by its old rival, the Department of Agriculture, over approximately 470,000 acres of land lying within the "indemnity limits" of the original grant but also within the borders of the national forests. All three quarrels have stirred up the citizenry of Oregon, forced Congressional action, and required judicial determination.

At the outset it should be noted that the officials of the Oregon and California Railroad Company shared the usual problems facing practically all promoters of land-grant railroads, namely, earning the grant by construction, using the grant for credit purposes, organizing and operating a land department, and defending the grant from such dangers as forfeiture bills, taxes, homesteaders, and timber pirates. To all these ills (and more) the Oregon and California company fell heir.

More unusual, in fact, unique, were the troubles stemming from a provision in the grant popularly known as the "homestead clause." It stipulated that the lands should "be sold to actual settlers only, in quantities not greater than one quarter section to one purchaser, and for a price not exceeding $2.50 per acre."[1] To be sure, Congress attached similar provisions to many railroad grants made after 1866.[2]

* It is a pleasure to acknowledge the aid of the Social Science Research Council and the Committee for Research in Economic History in collecting the material used in this paper.

[1] The Act of April 10, 1869 (16 *Stat.* 47) added this clause to the original act of July 25, 1866 (14 *Stat.* 239).

[2] The House passed a resolution on July 24, 1868, declaring all future grants should be sold to actual settlers in lots of 160 acres, and for not more than $2.50 an acre. 40th Congress, 2nd Session, *Congressional Globe*, 4428.

Nevertheless, only the Oregon and California company was to lose any land because of failure to observe the terms of this provision.

During the Civil War the Oregon Steam Navigation Company acquired a monopoly of river transportation within the state of Oregon. Its directors, however, showed little interest in railroad promotion until a group of aggressive California businessmen began to lay plans for a railroad from the Sacramento Valley to Portland. Thereupon Oregon enthusiasts organized in 1866 the Oregon Central Railroad Company, to build a line southward to the California border along the west side of the Willamette River.

In that same year Congress granted to the states of Oregon and California portions of the public domain for the purpose of helping build a railroad from California to the Columbia River. This was an important link in the network of railroads which received Congressional aid in the form of land grants between 1850 and 1871. The Oregon legislature promptly turned over the federal land grant to the backers of the Oregon Central. The company was to receive the odd-numbered sections (640 acres), nonmineral in character, in a place strip extending twenty miles on each side of the railroad right-of-way. Theoretically the railroad would receive a maximum of 4,220,000 acres. Actually, however, homesteaders had already preëmpted alluvial lands along the Willamette since the 1840's. Moreover, speculators had rushed to buy land along the route of the projected railroad. Only after the railroad had filed its map of definite location in the land office did the General Land Office withdraw the land along the route from public entry. To compensate the railroad for lost acreage of this nature, Congress followed its usual practice of permitting the railroad to select odd-numbered sections within an additional strip extending ten miles on each side of the place or primary zone. It later developed that even this concession did not make up for all the acreage lost within the primary limits. Consequently this railroad, like many others, never did receive its theoretical maximum of land. The final court adjudication held that the Oregon and California Railroad Company (the heir of the Oregon Central) was legally entitled to about 3,728,000 acres within the primary and the indemnity zones.[3]

This railroad land grant, in common with those made to a number of other railroads, had several strings attached to it. By these clauses Congress hoped to safeguard the public interest. Most crucial of all was the time limit. If the company did not complete the first twenty miles within two years, the land would revert to the government. If the railroad did not reach the California border by July 1, 1875, the grant would be subject to forfeiture. The purpose of this clause is obvious. In fact, the whole justification for land grants rested on this provision. The government expected that the land grant would enable the railroad to push construction ahead of settlement. Private capital-

---

[3] A convenient source for statistics is the accounting suit of 1925: 8 *Fed.* (2nd) 645.

ists did not dare to risk, and often did not command, financial resources sufficient to build lines into an undeveloped region such as that between Portland and Sacramento.

A minor provision which caused some embarrassment to the Oregon and California railroad in the 1920's was the clause requiring the railroad to carry all government traffic and troops at no charge. Practically all land-grant railroads had to make reductions to the government, but only a few charters specified free service.

The early history of the railroad is fairly well known, even though the tangled skein of events is difficult to unravel. Participants such as Joseph Gaston and Henry Villard have left their recollections, and historians have often described the *opéra bouffe* antics of such colorful figures as Ben Holladay and Henry Villard.[4] The California promoters, temporarily outsmarted by their rivals in Portland, organized another company which bore the same name, the Oregon Central Railroad Company. It was locally known as the "East Side" road, since it planned to run its line up the east bank of the Willamette.

The two companies fought each other bitterly. Ben Holladay, who got control of the East Side company in 1868, conducted a brilliant publicity campaign. Indeed, his high-powered lobby pressured the Oregon legislature in 1868 to strip his rival of the land grant and to transfer it to his own company. He sent agents to Washington to persuade Congress to make an extension of the grant,[5] and the Oregon delegation helped get Congressional approval for an extension to July 1, 1880. In addition, Congress extended until December 24, 1869, the period in which the first twenty miles were to be completed. Another amending act in 1869 fell under the scrutiny of land reformers in Congress. George W. Julian and William Holman were vigilant to amend every land grant after 1866 with the homestead clause. They were genuinely concerned with the danger of creating huge land monopolies in the West. In almost every instance the homestead clause met callous neglect. Nevertheless, it did provide a legal peg whereby the United States government was eventually to hang its case for recovery of the Oregon and California land grant.

In 1870 the leaders of the West Side company capitulated to Holladay. The promoter, in the meantime, had organized a new company called the Oregon and California Railroad Company to replace the Oregon Central of Salem (East Side). The new company acquired control of the original Oregon Central (West Side) and of several steamships as well. The enterprising Holladay was also able to secure from Congress in 1870 a land grant for the Oregon Central, the

4 This account of the early history of the Oregon railroads relies largely upon the following studies: John Tilson Ganoe, "The History of the Oregon and California Railroad," *Oregon Historical Society Quarterly*, XXV (September, 1924), 236-83, 330-52; James Blaine Hedges, *Henry Villard and the Railways of the Northwest* (New Haven, 1930); Henry Villard, *The Early History of Transportation in Oregon*, ed. Oswald G. Villard (Eugene, 1944).
5 15 *Stat.* 80.

newly acquired subsidiary. This railroad was to receive alternate sections within ten miles of each side of the right-of-way which ran from Portland to Astoria, in addition to a branch line from Forest Grove to the Yamhill River near McMinnville.[6]

Holladay managed to build his first twenty miles within the deadline. By 1872 he had constructed about 200 miles of track to Roseburg. Approximately 160 miles of rough territory lay between that town and the state line. Holladay likewise pushed the construction of the subsidiary, the Oregon Central, which by 1872 had reached McMinnville west of the Willamette River.

Holladay was a master of financial and political legerdemain. He approached Milton S. Latham, president of the London and San Francisco Bank, who had excellent contacts in Europe. Latham placed millions of bonds through banking houses in Germany. The land grant and other assets were pledged as security. Ostensibly the trustees for the bondholders planned to use the proceeds of the land grant as a sinking fund for the redemption of the bonds. Probably the real object of the separate trust for the land grant was to convey the land to a land company at a nominal figure.[7] The trustees actually did convey the grant to the European and Oregon Land Company, which was committed to pay the trustees only $1.25 an acre before April 1, 1889. Such practices were quite common among railroad promoters of that era. Thus promoters used the Credit Mobilier to strip the Union Pacific of many of its assets, and the Big Four—Stanford, Huntington, Crocker, Hopkins—transferred the land grant and other assets of the Central Pacific to their construction company. Holladay was an apt student in the rough-and-ready school of railroad promotion.

The German bondholders sent out an investigator in 1873 to inspect their properties. He pointed out several weaknesses: failure to complete the road south of Roseburg, scarcity of population, and the failure to sell much land to settlers. When the Oregon and California Railroad Company defaulted on its bonds later in the same year, the German investors delegated Henry Villard to visit Oregon and to protect them from further loss. Villard was an excellent choice. He had spent several years in America as a journalist, and he had considerable experience in railroad finance. Villard made a careful examination of the properties. After long negotiations he persuaded Holladay to enter into an agreement whereby the receipts of the railroad would be turned over to a financial agent appointed by the bondholders. The trustees also agreed in 1874 to give the land grant back to the railroad. Holladay proved faithless in the agreements, but Villard finally forced him by 1876 to transfer his stock in the Oregon and California Railroad Company to his creditors and to drop out of the transportation business in Oregon.

---

[6] 16 *Stat.* 94.
[7] Hedges, *op. cit.*, 9; Villard, *op. cit.*, 27.

The officers of the Oregon and California paid much more attention to land selling and colonization between 1874 and 1881 than to new construction. The land department sent agents to the Eastern states and to Europe to induce immigrants to settle in Oregon.[8] The company priced its lands attractively, some as low as $1.25 an acre. It offered liberal credit terms, even granting a ten-year period in which to pay off the mortgage. Lack of capital, however, forced the directors to postpone the completion of the railroad to the California line. The panic of 1873 had dried up the sources of speculative capital both here and abroad. Moreover, the mountainous terrain south of Roseburg presented serious problems for the engineer. Upon the expiration date, July 1, 1880, there still remained a gap of nearly three hundred miles between the Oregon and California line, and its sister road, the California and Oregon, was likewise uncompleted.

In 1880 the Oregon and California, Oregon Central, and Western Oregon were merged into one corporation, which continued to bear the name Oregon and California. The company, under Villard's leadership, was able to raise $6,000,000 from first mortgage bonds, and the infusion of new capital revived the construction program of the railroad. Villard was determined to keep control of all the gateways to Portland. In 1881 he astonished the financial world by secretly buying control of the Northern Pacific which was threatening to invade the Columbia Valley from the east and thus break up his tight monopoly of transportation in Oregon.

By January, 1883, funds to build the Oregon and California had almost run out, and the railroad was still short of making a connection with the Central Pacific. Ever ingenious, Villard turned to his Oregon and Transcontinental Company which held a controlling interest in most of the steamship and railroad lines of the Pacific Northwest. Two contracts were signed, one providing that the Oregon and Transcontinental Company lease the Oregon and California Railroad Company, the other authorizing the Oregon and Transcontinental Company to complete the road to the state line.[9] By 1884 the construction crews had reached Ashland, situated some twenty miles from the Oregon boundary.

Many citizens of Oregon chafed under the railroad monopoly of Henry Villard. Not only had the Oregon and California Railroad Company failed to complete its road, but its satellite, the Oregon Central, which had been acquired in 1881, had failed to build its line from Forest Grove to Astoria. Both the Astoria Chamber of Commerce and the Board of Trade felt that Villard was ignoring their city. In 1882 they petitioned Congress to open the grant to settlement. Villard in 1883 enraged Astoria business circles still further by frankly stating that he was abandoning the project.[10] Immediately the Cham-

---

[8] Hedges, *op. cit.*, 113, 121 f.
[9] *Ibid.*, 102.
[10] 48th Congress, 1st Session, *House Reports*, No. 383, p. 4.

ber of Commerce, some two thousand settlers, and even the former president of the Oregon Central memorialized Congress to forfeit the grant. The question became a lively issue in Oregon, where the state legislature hastened to join the forfeiture movement.[11]

Villard vigorously opposed the forfeiture movement, which by 1884 was sweeping against his land grants. His address to the Astoria Chamber of Commerce condemned forfeiture as unwise and unfair.[12] Would not cautious investors, already smarting from heavy losses after the panic of 1873, refuse to invest in pioneer railroads? Furthermore, he insisted that interest in lands yet to be acquired was mortgaged as well as the lands already conveyed to the company. Meanwhile, he instructed Senator John H. Mitchell to spur the Secretary of the Interior to approve a map of definite location extending the Oregon and California railroad to thirty-eight miles north of the California line and withdrawing the lands along the route.[13] Mitchell likewise secured the appointment of a board of commissioners to report for approval forty-five miles of completed road. Such steps would help cement the company's claim against the threat of forfeiture.

A determined movement got under way that same year, 1884, to forfeit the grant to the Oregon and California railroad, its subsidiary, the Oregon Central, and its sister road in California.[14] Many merchants blamed the management of all three roads for their half-hearted efforts to complete the road. Settlers were angry about the long delay in construction and the uncertainty of land titles in the indemnity zone because of the policy of not patenting the land to which it was entitled, a policy which threw the burden of local taxation on the inhabitants, since the lands could not be taxed until title passed from the government. High rates, discrimination between persons, localities, and goods, poor service, unsavory political influence—the long catalogue of abuses which the Granger movement had attacked in the 1870's—stirred up considerable anti-railroad feeling in Oregon. Fearfully the shippers, especially the farmers, watched the railroad barons consolidate lines into huge systems. Villard's clever maneuvers won admiration, but his monopoly of transportation facilities created distrust. To be sure, his financial difficulties in 1883 temporarily broke the monopoly of the Oregon and Transcontinental Company, permitting the Oregon and California railroad to slip from its grasp in 1884. But within a year another railroad baron, Collis P. Huntington of the Central Pacific, swallowed up the Oregon and California into his own

[11] 48th Congress, 1st Session, *Congressional Record*, 4792.
[12] Portland *Sunday Oregonian*, April 29, 1883.
[13] John H. Mitchell to Henry Villard, April 3, 1883, Villard Papers, Houghton Library, Harvard University.
[14] 48th Congress, 1st Session, *House Reports*, No. 2025. For a report concerning the forfeiture of the California and Oregon Railroad Company, see 48th Congress, 1st Session, *House Reports*, No. 793. For a more detailed story of the forfeiture movement, see the following article: David Maldwyn Ellis, "The Forfeiture of Railroad Land Grants," *Mississippi Valley Historical Review*, XXX (June, 1946), 27-60.

great system. No railroad man in America, with the exception of Jay Gould, was more feared and more hated than the powerful survivor of the Big Four. His entrance into the Oregon railroad scene intensified public resentment. Agitation for forfeiture of the land grant was, therefore, just another expression of the public fear of monopoly.

The House Committee on Public Lands in 1884 urged the forfeiture of all land opposite the sections of the Oregon and California and the Oregon Central not completed within the time limits.[15] The House debated at length the bill to forfeit the land grant to the Oregon Central. Should the entire grant be forfeited or only the portion opposite uncompleted sections of the road? The majority insisted on complete revocation and succeeded in beating down amendments which would have limited the amount of land to be recovered.[16] The Senate Committee on Public Lands refused to accept the House position and urged forfeiture of only those lands not earned by construction.[17] Senator John T. Morgan of Alabama attempted to attach an amendment calling for judicial review of the forfeiture procedure, but it was badly beaten, 15 to 28.[18] The Republicans furnished all the affirmative votes, but seven Republicans joined with the Democrats to defeat the amendment.

In 1885 the House yielded to the Senate viewpoint. As a result only those lands adjoining the uncompleted portions of the Oregon Central were forfeited.[19] This action recovered approximately 810,880 acres. It likewise permitted the General Land Office to throw open to settlement the withdrawn government lands along the proposed route from Forest Grove to Astoria.

The Oregon and California company was more successful in keeping its own grant than it was in keeping that of its subsidiary. True, the House Committee on Public Lands advised forfeiture of all lands opposite portions of the road not completed in 1880. The minority, however, advanced the argument which the Senate usually used in refusing to forfeit lands which had been earned by construction even after the time limit expired.[20] It held that the failure of Congress to exercise its right to forfeit in 1880 was in effect a waiver of its right to forfeit the land earned after that date.

In the meantime Huntington was pushing construction of both the Oregon and California and the California and Oregon. The gap narrowed rapidly, and in 1887 the two roads met at the state line. Apparently the chance to push the forfeiture of either land grant had slipped by. The United States Senate stood guard against any attempt to forfeit lands "earned by construction," and the federal courts could be expected to take a similar view.

---

[15] 48th Congress, 1st Session, *House Reports*, No. 2025.
[16] 48th Congress, 1st Session, *Congressional Record*, 4792.
[17] 48th Congress, 1st Session, *Senate Reports*, No. 358 *passim*.
[18] 48th Congress, 2nd Session, *Congressional Record*, 481.
[19] 23 *Stat.* 296.
[20] Ellis, *loc. cit.*, 52-56.

The land department of the Oregon and California Railroad Company paid little if any attention to the homestead clause.[21] In 1908 a government report estimated that the company had sold approximately 813,000 acres, broken down as follows:

127,000—not more than $2.50 an acre, and not more than 160 acres to any one settler.
170,000—more than $2.50 an acre, but not more than 160 acres to the purchaser.
515,000—more than $2.50 an acre, and more than 160 acres to the purchaser.[22]

More than half of this acreage passed in units of more than 2,000 acres in size. The total area of approximately 813,000 acres brought in over $4,000,000, or an average of about $5.00 an acre, just twice the figure set by Congress.

The company made little effort to patent more than 323,184 acres before 1890.[23] Technically the title did not pass until the government formally certified and patented the land. David Loring, who worked in the Oregon and California land office, carefully explained the reasons to a court in 1916:

and it was the policy of the company to avoid selecting as long as possible, in order to keep them off the tax rolls. . . . But indemnity selections were made as rapidly as surveys would permit, because a great deal of land was being lost. The place limit lands were not selected until required in a general way, first, to avoid the fees, and *second, to avoid taxes.*[24]

The General Land Office was partly responsible for slowness in patenting. It delayed public surveys, thus preventing early selection by the railroad. Until it was known how many sections the railroad would need to compensate it for land lost in the primary limits, the indemnity lands remained in doubtful status.

The framers of the original act of 1866 and its amendment in 1869 were badly misinformed as to the agricultural potentialities of the region through which the railroad was to run. After thirty years of effort the land department of the Oregon and California could boast of selling only some 300,000 acres.[25] The value of the land grant lay not in the soil but in the thick stands of Douglas fir. Prior to 1895 the railroad sold small parcels to actual settlers at prices ranging from $1.25 to $7.00 an acre. Virtually all buyers were farmers who wanted

[21] See testimony of Charles W. Eberlein, Acting Land Agent, in the United States Supreme Court, *Transcript of Record, October Term, 1916, No. 492, Oregon and California Railroad et al., Petitioner vs. United States,* 18 vols. (Washington, 1917), XIII, 7115. This transcript contains a vast amount of historical information. Hereafter it will be cited *Transcript of Record (1916).*

[22] 60th Congress, 1st Session, *House Reports,* No. 1301. The figures for the acreages have been rounded off to the nearest thousand acres.

[23] Ganoe, *loc. cit.,* 339.

[24] *Transcript of Record (1916),* XI, 5509-15.

[25] *Ibid.,* XIII, 7115.

land along the right-of-way and in the river bottoms. The steep rock-strewn slopes were naturally avoided by settlers.

The lumber industry of the Lake States was beginning to cut its last good stands of white pine by 1890. Already farsighted lumbermen like Frederick Weyerhaeuser had acquired millions of acres of timber lands in the Southern states. In the early 1890's they turned their eyes to the Pacific Northwest, where grew the magnificent Douglas fir. Jim Hill, who had completed the Great Northern to Seattle in 1893, was anxious to build up eastbound traffic for his railroad. He set rates low enough to permit Western mills to compete in the markets of the Middle West. Hill also got control of the Northern Pacific Railway with its huge land grant. He sold 900,000 acres of land in Oregon and Washington to Weyerhaeuser at $6.00 an acre.

The Puget Sound region was the first area in the Northwest to attract the lumbermen, since the timber could be easily brought to deep water. Before long the reports of timber cruisers sent out by the Southern Pacific to examine the land grant of the Oregon and California excited the interest of lumbermen. The railroad hastened to patent its land, which after 1895 was sold rapidly. The Land Department, which had been reorganized by the Southern Pacific, found its task greatly simplified. It could sell large tracts at rising prices to men of capital. No longer did it have to send agents to the East and to Europe to attract farmers who, when they arrived, frequently needed liberal credit terms. Prices ranged from $5.00 to $40 an acre. One purchaser bought 45,000 acres at $10 an acre. Approximately 363,000 acres passed into the hands of thirty-eight large buyers.[26] In short, the railroad ignored every phrase of the homestead clause.

In January, 1903, the Oregon and California Railroad Company suddenly brought its sales to a halt. Actually, of course, the decision came from Edward H. Harriman, president of the Southern Pacific Railroad, which had earlier swallowed the Central Pacific. Apparently his aim was to keep for his company any rise in stumpage values. Harriman was reported to have stated on September 2, 1907:

> The agricultural land we will sell, but the timber-land we will retain, because we must have ties and bridge timbers, and we must retain our timber for future supply. . . . Yes, we will sell to settlers, but speculators will get none.[27]

At first the company withdrew all lands from sale indefinitely. Later, under the lash of public opinion, Harriman made a gesture of selling agricultural lands. In 1904 the company appointed a special acting land agent to reorganize the land office and to clear the tax titles. Unfortunately for the company, not to mention the historian, the San Francisco fire of April 18, 1906, burned the records of the

---

[26] 60th Congress, 1st Session, *House Reports*, No. 1301; 60th Congress, 1st Session, *Congressional Record*, 5091; 8 *Fed.* (2nd) 645.
[27] *Transcript of Record (1916)*, VIII, 4265.

land office. This disaster hampered the work of the land office, although the company was later able to replace many records by utilizing duplicate records held in Portland, examining the records of the United States Land Office, and consulting the recorder's office in many counties in Washington and Oregon.[28]

The refusal of the railroad to sell its land stirred up much ill feeling against it. Throughout the course of American history settlers and businessmen in pioneer communities have heartily denounced those landholders who have failed to develop their lands as rapidly as possible. Indeed, certain groups have attacked not only individuals and corporations but even the government. At various times from 1907 to 1948 the national forest reserves have been under attack by certain economic groups. Many citizens of Oregon, already alarmed at the more rapid pace of development in Washington, were accusing Harriman of locking up the resources of the state. Admittedly, out-of-state speculators were equally active in buying timber lands. Nevertheless, the average Oregon citizen had a stake in the growth of business of which lumbering was a very important part.

Harriman's action stirred up a hornet's nest. It came at a time when the public in Oregon, as well as the nation at large, was demanding curbs on such railroad abuses as high rates and discrimination. The people of the Pacific Northwest were particularly sensitive to the sins committed by the railroads. In 1903 the titanic struggle between Hill and Harriman for control of the Northern Pacific Railway spotlighted the issue of monopoly. When the Northern Securities Company was formed to control the Great Northern, Northern Pacific, and the Burlington railroads, their fears of monopoly were intensified. Rumors that the Hill combination of northern transcontinentals and the Harriman system had reached an agreement to divide traffic and territory were confirmed early in 1907.[29] Farmers and businessmen saw their last hope for competitive rates fading.

Harriman's withdrawal order must, then, be considered against this background of anti-railroad feeling. Many Oregonians would support any measure which would harass and harry the railroads. A. C. Dixon made the unsupported statement to the House Committee in 1912 that the land issue was first brought into a meeting which was originally called to protest freight rates.[30] To many citizens of a booming frontier state the refusal to sell the huge railroad land grant seemed the most unkindest cut of all—a deliberate attempt to retard the development of the state.

Early in 1904 the vigilant eye of George Andrews, Acting Land Agent for the Oregon and California, spied an alarming notice in the Portland *Oregonian*. An antiquarian-minded citizen had unearthed

---

[28] *Transcript of Record (1916)*, V, 2240 ff.
[29] Portland *Sunday Oregonian*, January 6, 1907.
[30] "Oregon and California Land Grant," *Hearings before the House Committee on Public Lands* (Washington, 1912), 62.

the "homestead clause" in the charter to the Coos Bay Wagon Road Company. Congress in 1869 had made a small grant to help construct a military wagon-road from Coos Bay to the town of Roseburg. The land area involved was about one hundred thousand acres in the heart of the timber region. Nevertheless, Congress had attached the clause requiring the company to sell its lands for not more than $2.50 an acre and in units of not more than 160 acres. Obviously a successful attack on the Coos Bay company would jeopardize the grant to the Oregon and California. The local officials of the railroad were so alarmed that they wrote to the chief counsel of the Southern Pacific Railroad asking for guidance. More specifically, they wanted to know whether they should keep silent or help defend the Coos Bay grant. They were advised to adopt a policy of watchful waiting.[31]

It did not take long for enemies of the Oregon and California to seize upon the homestead clause as a weapon to bludgeon the railroad to disgorge its withdrawn holdings. An officer of the railroad later accused A. C. Dixon of the Booth-Kelley Lumber Company of Detroit of spearheading the drive.[32] This company had already acquired 70,000 acres, but it needed additional stumpage. If the government should force the railroad to sell the land at $2.50 an acre (far below current values), the large lumber companies would secure sizable tracts by bypassing the 160-acre maximum in some manner or other. The Eastern capitalist, as well as the Western settler, had had long experience in ignoring the spirit and twisting the letter of our land laws. But big timber speculators alone could not secure mass support for their selfish aims. Small speculators likewise joined the hue and cry. Businessmen in the cities along the route of the railroad naturally favored any move which would unfreeze the timber holdings of the railroad. Those who disliked railroad management in general joined the chorus. Politicians recognized a popular issue.[33] Governor George E. Chamberlain, who later as Senator was to pilot the settlement of 1916 through the upper house of Congress, toured the state addressing public gatherings and spurring the local chambers of commerce to demand the reopening of the land grant to sale under the terms of the homestead clause. His castigation of the railroad management before the National Irrigation Congress, which met in Sacramento in 1907, disturbed Edward Harriman so greatly that the railroad magnate rushed to the convention to defend his policies.[34] The public outcry prompted the Oregon legislature to adopt and dispatch to Congress a memorial which was presented on February 14, 1907, urging Con-

---

[31] *Transcript of Record (1916)*, XI, 5495.
[32] *Ibid.*, V, 2240 ff.
[33] Portland *Sunday Oregonian*, January 13, 1907; 60th Congress, 1st Session, *House Reports*, No. 1301; 64th Congress, 1st Session, *Congressional Record*, 8939-40. Oregon opinion likewise called for the forfeiture of the Coos Bay Wagon Road Grant which had also failed to observe the homestead clause. Portland *Morning Oregonian*, February 6, 1907.
[34] 64th Congress, 1st Session, *Congressional Record*, 8944.

gress to grant relief from the continued violation of the homestead clause.

Oddly enough, the Oregon people found their champion in a picturesque figure from the deep South. Senator "Pitchfork Ben" Tillman of South Carolina introduced a resolution asking Theodore Roosevelt (with whom he quarreled bitterly) for information concerning the land grant. Attorney-General Charles Bonaparte made an investigation and submitted a report confirming the violations.[35] Mr. Bonaparte, however, felt reluctant to commence action for forfeiture without express Congressional authorization. Such reluctance is understandable, considering the disquieting effect drastic and arbitrary legal steps would have on land titles along the railroad. Tillman, in February, 1908, introduced a joint resolution directing the Attorney-General to enforce compliance and to recover the land for the government.[36] In brief, the resolution called for forfeiture of the grant because the railroad had failed to observe the homestead clause.

A few conservative members of the Senate and the House attempted to block the resolution. Representative Joseph W. Fordney of Michigan complained that forfeiture would challenge the title of many lumber companies which had bought their holdings in good faith. His effort to attach an amendment guaranteeing the holdings of bona fide purchasers failed to muster more than a few votes.[37] Most of the support came from Congressmen representing Wisconsin and Michigan districts where most of the large purchasers resided. Friends of the resolution suspected, and with good reason, that the amendment contained a "joker" and would embarrass the Department of Justice in its suit to recover the land.

The passage of the resolution was the signal for professional speculators to lay claim to a share of the spoils and to inveigle gullible investors to advance money for fees and claims. Already, in the fall of 1907, Abraham Lafferty, a shrewd lawyer who later became representative from Oregon, advised sixty-five settlers to squat on the land. They had earlier tendered to the Oregon and California Railroad Company an offer of $2.50 an acre, or $400 for each quarter-section, but the company had refused to accept it. It seems clear that these so-called settlers were speculators or dummies for speculators who hoped to make good their title to valuable timber lands at a nominal sum. Other speculators sent out circulars to many individuals offering to "locate" land within the disputed territory for a fee. Tillman denied he was in collusion with land sharpers. He branded the activities of the St. Paul and Pacific Timber Syndicate of Portland, Oregon, as fraudulent.[38]

[35] 60th Congress, 1st Session, *House Reports*, No. 1301.
[36] 35 *Stat.* 571; Portland *Morning Oregonian*, April 24, 1908.
[37] Fordney openly defended the interests of the Booth-Kelley Lumber Company which had bought 67,000 acres and whose bonds were held by the Detroit Trust Company. 60th Congress, 1st Session, *Congressional Record*, 5135-39.
[38] *Ibid.*, 2216. For examples of locator's advertisements, see *Transcript of Record (1916)*, IV, 1964-68.

George Wickersham, who succeeded Bonaparte as Attorney-General under William H. Taft, began the long, tortuous, legal proceedings which have filled so many volumes of court records and proved a bonanza to scores of lawyers. Progress was slow, so slow, in fact, that the Senate passed a resolution on January 24, 1910, directing Wickersham to report on the steps he had taken to bring suit against the alleged violations of the terms of the land grant. Wickersham replied that the large number of interventions and demurrers had complicated and delayed the suit.[39] His office had begun suit against the Oregon and California Railroad Company on September 24, 1908. Some forty-five more suits were instituted in January and February, 1909, against parties who purchased lands from the railroad in quantities of more than 1,000 acres.

The Attorney-General caused a bill of equity to be filed in the United States district court for the district of Oregon to have it judicially determined whether the railroad company had not forfeited its unsold land. Counsel for the government rested its case on the contention that the homestead clause was in the nature of a condition subsequent. Failure to fulfill the terms therefore operated to forfeit the grant. Counsel suggested two alternatives: the appointment of a receiver to sell the lands, or an injunction ordering the company to sell the land according to the original terms. Either course pleased interested citizens of Oregon, since either would lead to the rapid sale of the timber. Outright forfeiture, however, might give the government the opportunity to establish additional forest reserves, the particular *bête noir* of Western "boomers."

The Oregon and California demurred to the bill of complaint.[40] It held that the homestead clause was merely a simple covenant and not a condition subsequent. The clause was so vaguely phrased as to be impossible of performance; it was repugnant to the purpose of the grant which was primarily to complete the railroad and not to regulate land settlement. Moreover, the government had waived its right to protest by its apparent acquiescence in recognizing deeds of record, accepting the use of the railroad, and issuing patents to the company from 1871 to 1906. Quite properly the company lawyers pointed out that speculators were instituting intervening suits. Judge Charles E. Wolverton overruled the demurrer in 1911. Two years later he declared the grant forfeited.[41]

---

[39] 61st Congress, 2nd Session, *Senate Documents*, No. 426.

[40] William D. Fenton, *Oral Argument of Mr. William D. Fenton for Oregon and California Railroad Company, Southern Pacific Company and S. T. Gage, Trustee . . . in U.S. Circ't Court, District of Oregon* (n. p., 1910). For the argument of one of the large lumber concerns which had purchased land from the railroad, see Mark Norris, *Brief, Amicus curia and of counsel for Booth-Kelley Lumber Company, Defendant . . . In the Circuit Court of the United States for the District of Oregon, United States v. Oregon and California Railroad Company et al.* (n.-p., 1910).

[41] 186 *Fed. Rep.* 861. The decision can also be found in 62nd Congress, 1st Session, *Senate Documents*, No. 27.

to actual settlers. Indeed, such a step would tend to facilitate the sale of the land itself to actual settlers by relieving them of the task of clearing away the trees.[45] This devious but ingenious reasoning did not prevent the Southern Pacific from offering to sell its rights, title, and interest to the government for $10,000,000 cash. In addition, the government was to assume the payment of unpaid taxes and to repeal the right of the government to transport goods without charge over the line of the Oregon and California. Mr. Blair made no mention of the $4,000,000 which the railroad had already received from land sales. When the final settlement was made, this amount was charged up against the total award to the railroad.

Land speculators hastened to batten on the spoils of the land grant. Franklin K. Lane, Secretary of the Interior, estimated in 1916 that 14,000 to 15,000 applications to buy land had been filed with the railroad company.[46] Practically all of these applications were speculative in character. It would be wrong, not to say uncharitable, to condemn these individuals as dishonest. Every Westerner, indeed every American, was a speculator in the sense that he hoped to "grow up" with the country. George Washington's lands in the Ohio Valley, Andrew Jackson's speculations in Tennessee lands, Theodore Roosevelt's flyer in a South Dakota ranch, William Jennings Bryan's ventures in Florida real estate in the 1920's—all illustrate the American (should we not write human?) penchant for land speculation. Mark Twain's famed Colonel Sellers with his elusive Tennessee lands and Sinclair Lewis' immortal George F. Babbitt are fictional tributes to this type of promoter. Of course, Oregon citizens were particularly eager to claim some of the spoils. If the railroad were to be forced to sell its land at the bargain rate of $2.50 an acre, they wanted to get possession of at least one quarter-section.

Inevitably professional "locators," whose ranks included some unsavory gentry, flocked to the scene. They sent circulars throughout the United States and Canada urging people to apply for a quarter-section. They offered to select the most valuable parcels and to make proper applications in exchange for a fee of $50 to $250. So fraudulent did their claims become that the Department of Justice brought several indictments and convicted at least nine of them for misrepresentation and fraud.[47]

Perhaps the most notorious—certainly the most articulate—of these professional gentlemen was Stephen A. Douglas Puter. Puter has left us a curious confession of his earlier activities in the book, *Looters of the Public Domain*, which is his apologia for the famous

[45] *Hearings before the House Committee on Public Lands* (Washington, 1916), 120-23. Hereafter this reference will be cited as *House Hearings (1916)*.
[46] 64th Congress, 1st Session, *Senate Reports*, No. 494.
[47] One unsubstantiated claim estimated that Puter and other locators collected about $2,000,000 from the public. 64th Congress, 1st Session, *Congressional Record*, 8584.

land-fraud cases of 1905.[48] In 1916 Puter willingly disclosed his activities to members of the House Committee on Public Lands. In fact,
Puter volunteered to appear before the committee on behalf of the
1,300 clients whom he claimed to represent.[49]

Puter first became interested in the disputed lands shortly after the
act of 1912. He immediately obtained from the abstract companies a
description of the sections not yet sold or applied for. He then located
the parcels. By circulars and by personal contact he persuaded about
one hundred persons to make agreements with him. By exchanging
names with other locators, Puter collected a mailing list of 4,000 to
5,000 people. His plan was simplicity itself. He tendered to the acting
land agent of the Oregon and California Railroad Company the sum of
$400 in full payment for a quarter-section of land. Of course, this
action was only a formality, since the railroad could not legally sell
any land after 1908. Nevertheless, Puter charged $100 for this service.
Furthermore, the would-be purchaser agreed to transfer an undivided
one-half interest in any land thus acquired. Puter in turn was to
furnish the purchaser a certificate from reputable abstracters that the
application was the first and only one on file for the quarter-section.
Scott Ferris of Oklahoma, chairman of the committee, forced Puter
to admit that he did not submit a complete abstract to potential
buyers of the claims, and furthermore, that he failed to inform them
that the Oregon and California had raised money secured by a
mortgage on the land grant. He also conveniently forgot to inform the
purchasers that it would be necessary for them to reside on any claim
if they wished to make good their title.

These speculators had their champions in Congress. Chairman
Ferris elicited the admission that Puter's attorney had drawn up the
bill which Representative William W. Wilson of Illinois had introduced in the House. This bill (H.R. 9814—January 22, 1916) was
designed to protect the rights of persons who had applied to the
Oregon and California for a quarter-section. Irwin Rittenhouse, who
had worked for twelve years in the General Land Office and who
managed a lobbying agency with the impressive title of National
Information Service, served as Puter's agent in the capital. He also
framed a bill introduced by Representative Albert Johnson of Washington which provided that a claimant should receive a patent from
the United States upon the payment of $2.50 an acre, if he had actu-
ally filed an application with the railroad company and had tendered
its representative $2.50 an acre. This disclosure brought Representa-
tive Johnson before the committee to defend his action.[50] Johnson
claimed that hundreds of people in his district were vitally interested

---

[48] The government convicted Senator John Mitchell, a Congressman, two
former United States district attorneys, and several members of the Washington
legislature for fraud in regard to land laws.
[49] This account of Puter's activities is taken from the *House Hearings (1916)*,
322 ff.
[50] *Ibid.*, 391 ff.

in the passage of the bill. These constituents had made application in good faith. Disclaiming any knowledge of speculators, Johnson declared that he had asked the Department of Justice to prosecute locators who were using the mails to defraud. He defended his bill as a necessary step to attract additional settlers to an underpopulated state.

Several government departments were on the watch to protect the public against Puter and his associates. The Department of the Interior set an agent on his trail to warn people against him. The Post Office likewise watched his activities, but Puter was careful to avoid written commitments. He was brought under indictment but escaped conviction. While still under indictment Puter ran full-page advertisements in the Washington newspapers demanding consideration for his clients.[51]

The fate of the Oregon and California land grant aroused great excitement in Oregon. Speculators, both amateur and professional, lumbermen, and homesteaders hoped to gain portions of the valuable timber lands. State and local officials, as well as businessmen, were eager to prevent the lands from going off the tax rolls. Governor James Withycombe called a conference to discuss the situation. Over 300 delegates descended on Salem September 15, 16, and 17, 1915, to make known their views.[52] The convention called on Congress to define the status of "actual settlers" and to provide for the immediate sale of the land in 160-acre lots for not more than $2.50 an acre. The convention likewise stated that it was "unalterably opposed" to any increase in forest reserves in the state of Oregon.

There seems little doubt that articulate opinion in Oregon wanted the timber resources along the route of the railroad to be exploited rapidly. Equally desirable in the minds of many Oregonians was the diversion of a high percentage of the proceeds from the grant into the coffers of local governmental units. Businessmen, editors, and politicians tended to oppose the establishment of additional forest reserves.[53] To be sure, the advantages of the tourist trade and the orderly exploitation of our forests through such techniques as sustained-yield plans were not yet apparent. These men indulged in visions of a new empire in the Pacific Northwest based on the rapid development of the agricultural, timber, and mineral resources of the

[51] 64th Congress, 1st Session, *Congressional Record*, 8584.
[52] Portland *Morning Oregonian*, September 13, 16, 17, 1915; Portland *Sunday Oregonian*, September 12, 19, 1915. This convention was not representative according to Mr. Williams, attorney for the Department of Justice. 64th Congress, 1st Session, *Congressional Record*, 8942.
[53] Mr. Williams visited every county in the land-grant region. Without exception he found the citizens opposed to the establishment of more forest reserves. *Ibid.*, 8939-44; *House Hearings (1916)*, 8 ff. The Portland *Sunday Oregonian*, September 12, 1915, carried a picture of a large map showing 62 per cent of the land of eleven Western states tied up for settlement. It condemned forest reserves as retarding the growth of Oregon. For a more detailed treatment of the Western attitude toward conservation, see Roy Robbins, *Our Landed Heritage* (Princeton, 1942), 343-63.

state. Representative Willis C: Hawley of Oregon was only echoing the sentiments of many of his constituents when he uttered the following banality in the House: "While I do not think the bounties of nature should be wasted, I am for men, women, and children. (*Applause*)."[54]

Tax exemption was another question closely tied to the conservation issue. County officials had assessed the patented railroad lands at a rate well above $2.50 an acre. They relied on the tax revenue for the support of schools and roads. When the federal district court in 1913 had decreed forfeiture, the railroad had promptly refused to pay taxes. Between 1913 and 1916 tax arrears accumulated to a sum exceeding $1,000,000.[55] County and town officials were up in arms against the permanent removal of the lands from the tax rolls through the creation of national forests.

The apparent unanimity of opinion against the creation of a national forest from the forfeited land grant did not extend to the problem of its proper disposition. Representative Hawley introduced a bill calling for the immediate sale of the land in tracts of not more than 160 acres and for not more than $2.50 an acre. Senator George E. Chamberlain of Oregon, backed by Representative Clifton N. McArthur, also of Oregon, opposed the sale of quarter-sections of land containing from $5,000 to $20,000 worth of valuable timber for a paltry $400. Chamberlain urged that the land be disposed of in such a way that the bulk of the proceeds go into the school-and-road fund of Oregon. Ultimately the latter ideas prevailed.

Amid the welter of clashing interests a voice was heard which approached the problem realistically and objectively.[56] David F. Houston, the Secretary of Agriculture, evinced a keen interest in the fate of the land grant. He noted that the heavy capital investment would force most individuals to liquidate their timber holdings because they would not be able to carry the heavy charges of interest and taxes and provide adequate fire protection. The annual burden, estimated at 7 per cent, was becoming more onerous, especially since stumpage prices had failed to rise since 1908. Moreover, the Secretary did not see any immediate prospect of the Oregon timber coming upon the market. Certainly the lumber industry would first clear off the more accessible stands in Washington and California. Nevertheless, hard-pressed purchasers of lands on the Oregon and California railroad land grant would have to throw their lumber on the market. Such action would demoralize still further the industry which the outbreak of World War I found seriously disorganized. Houston advanced the sound proposal that the government withhold the raw timber until the time came when the country needed it. For this reason he favored granting discretionary power to the Department of the

[54] 64th Congress, 1st Session, *Congressional Record*, 8593.
[55] *Ibid.*, 8941.
[56] *House Hearings (1916)*, 200-08.

Interior to sell the timber on the most convenient terms. Furthermore, he urged that the revested lands (later estimated at about 470,000 acres) lying within the indemnity limits and the national forests be placed under the National Forest Service of the Department of Agriculture.

The act of 1916 represented a compromise among the rival interests. The House vote of 186 ayes to only 6 nays reflects widespread agreement.[57] First of all, the act returned the unsold grant lands approximating 2,891,000 acres to federal ownership. The Department of the Interior was given jurisdiction over the revested acreage. The act directed the Secretary of the Interior to classify the lands into power-site, timber, and agricultural land. It defined the timber lands as those containing 300,000 or more board feet per forty acres. The Secretary of the Interior was authorized to sell for cash the timber from the land as rapidly as reasonable prices could be obtained in a normal market. After the timber had been cut, these lands, as well as those originally classified as agricultural lands, were to be opened to homestead entry at the price of $2.50 an acre.

The act established the Oregon and California Land Grant Fund, which was to receive the income from both timber sales and homestead fees. The first charge upon this Fund was the payment to the Southern Pacific Railroad of an amount sufficient to bring its receipts up to the $2.50 an acre specified in the Supreme Court ruling. The railroad was to receive only $4,102,215.28, which represented the difference between the total value of the grant, sold and unsold, at $2.50 an acre and what the railroad had already received from the 837,000 acres it had sold, including due allowance for interest and back taxes. The second charge upon the Fund was the reimbursement of the United States Treasury, which had advanced to the land-grant counties $1,571,044.05 for back taxes in 1913, 1914, and 1915.

The issue which stirred up the most wrangling in Congress was the distribution of the revenues from the Fund after these two fixed charges had been paid. The representatives from Oregon naturally demanded for their state all the revenues. They argued with more vehemence than plausibility that Oregon had already suffered incalculable damage through the failure of the railroad to develop the southwestern part of the state. To divert the revenues into the federal Treasury, they insisted, would deprive the people of Oregon of the benefit of increased land values. Senators from the other Western states sympathized with this attitude, except that they wished to divert part of the revenues into the Reclamation Fund available for projects throughout the West. The final agreement awarded 50 per cent of the revenues to Oregon to be divided equally between the state school fund and the counties in lieu of taxes. The Reclamation Fund was to receive 40 per cent and the federal Treasury a scant 10 per cent.

---

[57] 64th Congress, 1st Session, *Congressional Record*, 8649.

The act of 1916 was more a triumph of expediency than a statesmanlike solution. The interests of conservation were poorly served, both in the failure to place some of the land in forest reserves and in the inadequate provision for reforestation. For example, the clause opening cut-over timber lands to homestead entry betrayed poor judgment. Probably the share given to Oregon was too high. At any rate it was much higher than that given by the National Forests which generally remit 75 per cent of their revenues to the federal Treasury. Nevertheless, the act did approximate a certain measure of rough justice. The railroad received the value of the land at the figure intended by Congress and without the speculative increment. The counties got income from their resources without running through the cycle of hasty cutting and blight.

Lawyers for the Southern Pacific made a final attempt to salvage additional benefits. They secured a Supreme Court verdict upon their contention that the homestead clause applied only to the land itself, and that the railroad still held good title to the timber. The Supreme Court made short shrift with this specious reasoning and dismissed the claims.

It took several years before the government and the railroad reached any agreement as to the total acreage due the railroad under the grants, the total gross proceeds of sales previously made by it, and the net amount due the railroad by the government. The accounting suit explored many complicated details before final figures were reached.[58] For example, both the government and the railroad agreed that 1,692,092 acres had been "lost" in the primary limits. But the government held that there were only 946,637 acres available in the indemnity limits for the railroad, since the rest had already been disposed of. The railroad disagreed with the latter figure, claiming more lands in the indemnity limits. The details of the accounting suit need not detain us. It should be noted, however, that the court held that the railroad should receive credit for about 470,000 acres lying within the indemnity limits and included within the forest reserves. The federal court charged the government with negligence for not being aware of the deficiency in the land grant. It held that the government could not take acreage within the indemnity limits necessary to make up this deficiency and place it in the forest reserves. In the late 1930's these lands were to become a bone of contention between the Department of the Interior and the Department of Agriculture.

A minor issue arising from the land grant of 1866 was the clause requiring the railroad to carry government freight and military personnel at no charge. Commissioner Joseph Eastman, the secretaries of War, Navy, and the Interior, as well as the Postmaster-General, testified in favor of extending to that portion of the Southern Pacific between Portland and Roseville, California, the right to charge the

---

[58] 8 *Fed.* (2nd) 645; *Railway Age,* vol. 79 (September 19, 1925), p. 537.

standard 50 per cent rate for government traffic.[59] Such a step would simplify the problem of estimating charges, and it placed this portion of the railroad upon an equal footing with the rest of the land-grant railroads. In 1928 Congress acceded to this request. In 1947 Congress abolished all railroad land-grant reductions. This no-charge clause of the land grant of 1866 is, therefore, no longer in force.

In passing, we may note that several towns along the Siskiyou route of the Southern Pacific cited the land grant of 1866, when the railroad discontinued passenger services along the route during World War II. The management was routing most of its trains over the Cascade line which had been opened in 1926 from Eugene into California. The Southern Pacific pointed out the savings in units of equipment but promised to restore the services which the cities of Roseburg, Medford, and Ashland claimed under the act of 1866.[60]

The fate of the Coos Bay Wagon Road land grant, whose history so closely parallels that of the Oregon and California Railroad Company, deserves a passing glance. Its land grant of 1869 contained the homestead clause, without any mention, however, that the land must be sold to "actual settlers." The Attorney-General in 1908 received Congressional authority to bring proceedings to forfeit 96,000 acres sold in violation of the terms. The United States Circuit Court of Appeals upheld the government's position, advancing the same reasons used in the Oregon and California decision. In 1919 some 93,000 acres of unsold land were reconveyed to the federal government. The government paid the Southern Oregon Company, which controlled the Coos Bay Wagon Road land grant, a sum equivalent to the total acreage multiplied by $2.50 an acre, less, of course, the unpaid taxes and earlier income from sales of land and lumber. The government did not disturb the purchasers of land from the Southern Oregon Company. It did agree to give $547,224 in back taxes to Douglas and Coos counties in which the land grant was located.[61]

The framers of the 1916 act looked for a rapid transfer of all revested lands to private ownership and consequently to the local tax rolls. Actually, very little of the "agricultural" land was ever homesteaded. Indeed, some which had earlier been homesteaded returned to county ownership for non-payment of taxes. The Department of the Interior sold timber from the timber lands in the following manner. Blocks of timber lands were opened up to cash bids. The successful bidder had ten years in which to cut and remove the timber. Thereafter the Department reclassified the land as open to homesteading, but very few of these cut-over lands were ever occupied.

The slow shift to private ownership alarmed the counties, and their failure to receive any money from the Oregon and California Land Grant Fund created serious problems. The revenue that did come in

[59] 70th Congress, 1st Session, *House Reports*, No. 1538.
[60] *Business Week*, No. 773 (June 24, 1944), p. 46.
[61] 40 *Stat.* 1197; 241 *Fed. Rep.* 16.

to the Fund went first to the Southern Pacific Railroad and second to the United States Treasury as reimbursement for its advance payment to the counties for unpaid taxes (1913-1915). Some of the eighteen land-grant counties found it very difficult to maintain essential services, since between 1916 and 1926 they received no payments in lieu of current taxes.[62]

By 1926 the outcry from Oregon officials became so shrill that Congress investigated their grievances. Testimony brought out the dire financial straits of many counties. Congress agreed to a new arrangement whereby the government granted to the counties amounts equal to the taxes that would have accrued against said lands for the years 1916-1926, if the lands had remained privately owned. Proper safeguards were included as to the rate of assessment and the rate of taxes. The Stanfield Act of 1926 appropriated $7,135,-283.36 to the land-grant counties for the eleven-year period.[63] This money was to be reimbursed to the government from anticipated revenues from land and timber sales.

The Stanfield Act of 1926 did not work out well for the hard-pressed county officials. The Attorney-General interpreted the act in such a way as to prevent the payment of funds equivalent to the taxes which the railroad had paid. Perhaps the following table will illustrate the discouraging story of the O. & C. Fund before 1937:

Paid to the Southern Pacific $4,102,215.28
Paid as taxes from U. S. Treasury 1913-15 inc. . 1,571,044.05
Paid in lieu of taxes 1916-26 inc. 7,135,283.36
Paid in lieu of taxes from O. & C. Fund
1927-33 inc. 3,866,646.01
Owed in lieu of taxes 1934-37 inc. 2,067,423.77

Total paid or owed $18,742,612.47
Receipts from sales of O. & C. land and timber . $8,269,719.09

Obligations payable from future receipts . . . $10,472,893.38[64]

In brief, the policy of land and timber disposal to private ownership was a failure. By 1937 the Oregon and California Fund had run a deficit of $10,472,893.38.

In 1937 Congress again tackled the problem of the proper handling of the Oregon and California revested lands.[65] The financial arrangements were altered. Fifty per cent of the income from the lands was to go to the counties. An additional 25 per cent was applied to the unpaid tax claims. Once these claims were paid, this 25 per cent was to be devoted to payment of the deficit in the Oregon and California

[62] *Forever Timber* (Portland, n. d.), 10; see also "Oregon and California Land Grant Lands," *Hearings before the Senate Committee on Public Lands and Survey* (Washington, 1926).
[63] 44 *Stat.* 915.
[64] This table is compiled from *Forever Timber*, 11.
[65] 50 *Stat.* 874.

Land Grant Fund, and after this latter deficit had been paid, the 25 per cent would go to the interested counties. In other words 75 per cent of the total revenues would eventually return to the counties. But the provision of the act which authorized sustained-yield operation of the timber land was of far greater significance. It envisioned coöperative action between the government and private owners in combining private and public forest lands in management units for sustained-yield timber production. It laid down the policy of sustained yield; i.e., the annual cut was to be about the same as the annual timber-growing capacity. The Secretary of the Interior appointed an advisory committee of Oregon citizens to represent the interests of the state, the Forest Service, the timber operators, the counties, and other groups. In 1938 Secretary Harold Ickes established the Oregon and California Revested Land Administration, whose management of the timber land has won wide acclaim. The agency has made an inventory of the lands in order to determine how much timber can be cut annually. Forestry units, each capable of supporting on a permanent basis one average western Oregon sawmill, have been established. These local sustained-yield operating units have been grouped into twelve master units.[66] Financially the Revested Land Administration has enjoyed great success. The wartime demand at high prices naturally gave it a fine start. During the first eight years of operation it has paid over $4,000,000 to the counties in lieu of current taxes, over $1,000,000 more to satisfy back taxes to the counties, and paid in $1,567,066.91 to the Treasury toward the original deficit in the O. & C. Treasury Fund. No doubt this success is largely due to the especially valuable Douglas fir on the land. The framers of our land-grant policy could hardly have foreseen this curious but significant by-product of their grant of 1866 to help build a railroad in Oregon. This paper has only sketched the story of the sustained-yield forest units, since our chief concern is with the acquisition, division, and eventual disposition of the acreage involved.

Perhaps the most curious development arising from the Oregon and California land grant was the quarrel between the Department of Agriculture and the Department of the Interior over jurisdiction of a portion of the revested land grant. Both departments hoped to make good their claims to approximately 470,000 acres of timber land valued at upwards of $10,000,000. This row—merely another incident in the prolonged feud between these rival departments—soon spread to Oregon. The people in the eighteen counties in which the land grant had been located scented the possibilities of securing more federal money to supplement local taxes. Local officials rushed to the support of the Department of the Interior, because more money would reach their treasuries if that department extended its jurisdiction over the acreage in dispute. Lumber interests likewise backed the Interior

---

[66] *Forever Timber,* 14-32; New York *Times,* November 30, 1947.

Department which has usually shown more willingness than the National Forest Service in the Department of Agriculture in opening timber lands to logging operations.[67] Which lands were those in dispute? To answer that question, one must reëxamine the principal statutes and relevant court decisions. Under the original granting acts of 1866 and 1870 the railroad received every odd-numbered section of public land not mineral to the amount of twenty alternate sections per mile (ten on each side of the route). The law following the usual pattern of land grants provided that, if any of the alternate sections had already been granted, sold, reserved, occupied by homestead settlers, preëmpted, or otherwise disposed of, the company might select odd-numbered sections within a secondary zone extending for ten additional miles on both sides of the primary zones or place limits. But the company delayed patenting much of its land partly because it hoped to keep it off the tax rolls.

The Supreme Court decision of 1915 enjoined the Oregon and California Railroad Company from disposing of any land until Congress could act. The Revestment Act of 1916 specifically forfeited the unpatented claims as well as those sections already acquired by the company, except those already sold. No one contested the authority of the Interior Department over the odd-numbered sections within the primary limits of the grant including the approximately 300,000 acres lying within the exterior boundaries of the national forests. Furthermore, the Interior Department administered without challenge those sections within the indemnity limits which the railroad had selected or patented prior to the establishment of the national forests. But the Department of Agriculture vigorously asserted its claims to the unpatented lands within the indemnity limits lying within the borders of the national forests. Both departments eyed covetously some 470,000 acres valued at more than $10,000,000.

The quarrel developed out of the accounting suit of 1925. The circuit court sided with the attorneys of the Oregon and California railroad by declaring that these unpatented indemnity lands were included in the acreage for which the company was entitled to a credit of $2.50 an acre. Government lawyers, spearheaded by counsel for the Department of the Interior, had long maintained that lands within the indemnity limits were in the nature of a floating grant until selected. Consequently the company had no right to the land until selection had been actually made and approved. These lawyers argued that executive proclamation had reserved these lands which had long since become a part of the national forests. Between 1892 and 1907 several proclamations had set aside national forests in western

---

[67] Since the days of Gifford Pinchot, the National Forest Service has prided itself on its conservation attitude. The Department of the Interior, especially under Secretary Ickes, has tried to recapture this agency from the Department of Agriculture.

Oregon. Therefore, the unpatented indemnity lands had never gone into the hands of the company. The circuit court refused to accept this reasoning. It maintained:

All these reserves and additions were set apart by the President long subsequent to the time, as shown by the evidence, that a deficiency was found to exist within the indemnity limits to meet the losses sustained to the place limits, and it was therefore inadmissible for the Government to reserve or appropriate to its own use any of such lands.

This decision followed the precedent established in 1921 in the case of United States v. Northern Pacific Railway Company.[68] The Supreme Court considered the propriety of setting aside for forest purposes lands within the indemnity limits of a railroad grant. The justices held that after the date of the granting act to the railroad the government could not appropriate to its own use lands within the indemnity limits which were known at the time to be needed to supply losses in the place limits of the grants. This decision naturally caused some alarm in the ranks of conservationists. Ironically enough, the Department of the Interior has adopted this position which it formerly denied to the railroad. Since it fell heir to the lands of the railroad, it has naturally wanted to acquire as much acreage as possible, even though it means taking it away from the national forests.

The lawyers of the Department of Agriculture proved resourceful in combating the legal position of their rival department.[69] They argued that Congress passed the Revestment Act of 1916 five years before the Northern Pacific decision. Consequently Congress was legislating on the well-established assumption that the railroad company acquired no interest whatever in indemnity lands until it had selected them for the purpose of covering losses in the place limits. Moreover, they asserted that the President enjoyed independent authorization to issue the proclamations creating the forest reserves. They explained away the Oregon and California decision of 1925 as purely an accounting suit. The fact that payment was made to the railroad for these lands did not mean that the railroad was entitled to receive a patent for them. It merely meant that the government was to compensate the railroad for the "full value" of the grant. The railroad lost its right to select the lands even though it received payment for them.

To skirt around the barrier of the Northern Pacific decision required great ingenuity. The Department of Agriculture had to recognize the rule; but its lawyers were adept in restricting its implications. Thus counsel argued that this decision did not determine

---

[68] 256 U.S. 51.
[69] "Oregon and California Railroad Land Grants," *Hearings before the Senate Public Lands Commitee* (Washington, 1943), 4-10, 151 ff. Hereafter this reference will be cited as *Senate Hearings (1943)*.

whether a selection was necessary by the railroad company in order for the company to be entitled to a patent. All it determined was that a selection by the railroad company after a deficiency is ascertained is unnecessary to terminate the power of the United States to reserve the land for public purposes. The Department of Agriculture vigorously denied that, as soon as it was clear that the sections within the indemnity limits would not make up the losses in the primary limits, equitable title to the land in indemnity limits was automatically vested in the railroad company. It pointed out that land in the indemnity limits was available to actual settlers until a selection had been made by the railroad company. This rule would lead to the anomalous situation where equitable title would vest in the company but settlers could also enter this land. Therefore, there was no actual title in the railroad company until a selection had been made. The case of Wisconsin Railroad Company *v.* Price County was cited to show that the lands in the place limits were subject to state taxation even though no patent had been issued.[70] The act of location vested equitable title in the railroad company. But lands in indemnity limits, even though a deficiency was known to exist and a selection had been made but not yet approved, still remained in the public domain, since title had not yet passed. The promise of the government to give indemnity lands created no legal interests and no title. Such were the legal points advanced by the Department of Agriculture.

These legal distinctions are much less convincing than the indisputable fact that the Department of Agriculture had exercised continuous jurisdiction over the lands in question for over thirty-five years. Equally persuasive is the fact that the Department of the Interior acquiesced in this jurisdiction during the same period. For example, in 1908 the Department of the Interior had rejected application by the Oregon and California Railroad Company to make indemnity selections in a certain township on the ground that the lands had been withdrawn for forest reserves.[71] Perhaps the most conspicuous example of its former position was the opinion of Assistant Secretary of the Interior E. C. Finney, made on August 9, 1923:

> At that time [1916] the general understanding of the law was, as consistently held by this Department, that the company had no right to invade a forest reservation in making selection within the indemnity limits of its grants. Therefore . . . Congress could not have had in contemplation the lands which were then, and had been long prior thereto, reserved for forest use.[72]

Let it be reiterated that the Forest Service for decades considered these lands as part of the national forests. It made timber sales, pro-

---

[70] 133 *U.S.* 496.

[71] *Decisions of the Department of the Interior*, XXXVI, 349-51.

[72] Quoted by Martin White, Solicitor of the Department of Agriculture, *Senate Hearings (1943)*, 133. Secretary Ickes discounted the Finney statement in a letter of December 18, 1940, to the Attorney-General. He stressed the fact that Finney was writing two years prior to the O. & C. decision of 1925. *Ibid.*, 139.

tected the growth from fire, issued grazing permits, controlled all private occupancy, and constructed many improvements. The Forest Service had included receipts from these lands as part of the national forest receipts in making payments to Oregon.

The interdepartmental dispute did not break open until 1938. The forestry personnel of the Department of the Interior discovered that employees of the National Forest Service were selling timber off these lands. A formal protest followed. Harold Ickes refused to accept the position of the Department of Agriculture that the lands were part of the national forests. His department advertised for bids on timber located on some of the sections. The dispute was referred to Washington where the Solicitor-General held that the National Forest Service held jurisdiction.[73]

In 1940 Ickes asked the Attorney-General for an opinion on the legislative intent of the acts of June 9, 1916, and August 28, 1937. The latter declared that the Department of Agriculture should continue to exercise control, since its jurisdiction had gone unchallenged for decades. But the self-styled "Curmudgeon" refused to yield. He asked reconsideration, claiming that the Attorney-General had acted upon insufficient evidence. Furthermore, he insisted that the people of Oregon had substantial interests at stake. Attorney-General Homer Cummings agreed to reopen the case. He called a conference of the interested parties at which it was arranged that the two departments would submit to him an agreed statement of facts. Subsequently the two departments drew up statements which they exchanged. The two positions, however, were so widely divergent that no agreement was possible. On February 20, 1943, the Department of Agriculture advised the Attorney-General that it could not reach any agreement with the Interior Department. Secretary Ickes requested Attorney-General Francis Biddle to withdraw the original opinion and to leave the matter to Congress.[74]

In the meantime Oregon interests joined forces with the Department of the Interior to get control of the controverted lands. The hearings of 1916, 1926, 1937, and 1943-1944 saw representatives of Oregon counties and lumber firms testifying for measures which would divert more money to their state. The local officials angrily blamed the Revestment Act of 1916 for depriving them of tax revenues. Their importunities had been largely responsible for the changes in the financial arrangements made in the acts of 1926 and 1937. No inconsiderable revenue was at stake. Thus for the tax years 1917-1943, inclusive, the payments to the eighteen counties totaled $14,859,-367.62. Three counties—Douglas, Lane, and Jackson—received over half of this money.

---

[73] For somewhat different accounts, see *ibid.*, 6 ff., and *Hearings before the House Committee on Public Lands (1944)*, 227. This reference will be cited hereafter as *House Hearings (1944)*.

[74] *Senate Hearings (1943)*, 135-40.

Officials of the land-grant counties backed the Interior Department for two major reasons. First, the Oregon and California Revested Lands Administration turned over 50 per cent of its revenues to the counties. After the deficit in the Oregon and California Fund has been paid, the local governments will receive 75 per cent of the revenues. In contrast to this generous treatment the Forest Service pays only 25 per cent to the counties. In short, 25 per cent and eventually 50 per cent of the revenues from almost 500,000 acres of valuable timber land were at stake. Less important, but still persuasive, was the general belief that the Department of the Interior would be more sympathetic to the local lumber industry than would the Department of Agriculture. Rightly or wrongly, the Forest Service has been accused by certain Western interests of refusing to recognize the legitimate ambitions of timbermen and grazers.

The Department of Agriculture denied the assertion that the land-grant counties had fared badly. In fact, few counties in the country had received such a high percentage of their revenues from federal forest lands. Moreover, the lands in question had never been selected by the railroads, had never been on the tax rolls, and had never paid the counties any money.

But its most convincing argument was the fact that the National Forest Service had administered these lands for decades, as has been pointed out above. To turn the lands back to the Interior Department would aggravate the problem of efficient management. The odd-numbered sections would be administered by the Interior Department; the even-numbered sections, by the Department of Agriculture. Such a checkerboard pattern would gravely complicate the most effective utilization of the forests. Divided responsibility would prevent the orderly development of logging operations, timber-cutting practices, timber-sale-contract clauses, grazing permits, and sustained-yield arrangements. Inevitably confusion would result, and the two government agencies would quarrel. People using the lands would have to deal with two federal agencies, each with different policies.

The Forest Service, smarting somewhat from figures submitted by the Oregon and California Revested Lands Administration which showed handsome profits for the latter agency as contrasted to some of their activities, insisted that national forest lands were generally more inaccessible.[75] Most of the revested O. & C. lands were within ten miles of the railroad. These lands were at lower levels and had better stands. Roads, highways, and railroad permitted their rapid development. Moreover, the Forest Service had spent large sums for purposes other than forest management. It had built roads, protected the forests from fires, and provided recreational facilities. It had likewise adopted the more expensive but more accurate method of scaling timber instead of selling it on the basis of cruise.

---

[75] *House Hearings (1944),* 251.

The Department of the Interior failed in 1944 to persuade Congress to pass the bills providing for the transfer of these controverted lands to the Oregon and California Revested Lands Administration. The lands remain parts of the national forests and are currently administered as national-forest lands. There were bills, however, in the last Congress providing for the transfer of the lands to the Department of the Interior.[76]

The controversies over the Oregon and California railroad land grant provide an excellent case study of the wide variety of perplexing problems which sometimes arose from the policy of granting land in aid of railroad construction. Like a majority of land-grant railroads the Oregon and California Railroad Company failed to build its road on time. In the middle 1880's the demand rose for forfeiture. The company did succeed in keeping all the land opposite the completed portions of the road irrespective of the time limit. This grant clearly demonstrated the shortcomings of the alternate-section pattern, especially when applied to forested regions. The battle between railroad and the little speculator once more flared up. Charges that the railroad was retarding the development of the country and avoiding taxes were reiterated. The cry of land monopoly so often raised against many land-grant railroads was used to denounce the Oregon and California.

This land grant experienced a unique fate among the eighty-odd grants to railroads between 1850 and 1871. The United States government recaptured its unsold holdings in 1916 on the ground that the railroad failed to observe the provisions of the homestead clause. Furthermore, Congress established an agency to administer approximately 2,600,000 acres of valuable forest lands recovered from the railroad. The Oregon and California Revested Lands Administration has enjoyed considerable success in operating these lands upon a sustained-yield basis. Oddly enough, the recovery of this land added fuel to the long-standing feud between the Department of Agriculture and the Department of the Interior. After a good deal of bickering the United States Forest Service has managed to retain jurisdiction over the unpatented "indemnity" lands (approximately 470,000 acres) lying within the national forests.

A participant on a quiz program would find it difficult to say whether or not the land grant of 1866 was a success. Strictly speaking, the act was a failure. The railroad did not reach the California line until 1887, more than ten years after the original time limit had expired. Furthermore, the company virtually ignored the homestead clause attached to the grant in 1869.

Nevertheless, the government derived more benefits than might be expected, considering its lack of knowledge of the Oregon countryside and its lavish and poorly administered land-grant policy. First of all, the railroad did get built many years ahead of the time when private capital would have dared assume the risk. The forfeiture of the unsold

---

[76] H.R. 2363; S. 580.

portions of the land grant in 1916 gave the government another chance to work out an equitable arrangement between federal and local interests, innocent purchasers and the railroad, lumbermen and conservationists. The railroad lost the speculative increment but kept the value of the original grant ($2.50 an acre). The bona fide purchasers from the railroad retained their property rights in the act of 1912. The land-grant counties after many delays received payments in lieu of taxes. "Actual settlers" retained their right to secure a quarter-section. Lumbermen found it possible to buy stumpage as they needed it without overinvesting in timber lands. Most important of all, Congress finally set up in 1937 an agency called the Oregon and California Revested Lands Administration which is supervising one of the world's largest experimental laboratories in practical forest management. Sustained-yield operations on the old land grant have proved a courageous and intelligent method of utilizing and conserving the timber resources of the region.

THE NORTHERN PACIFIC RAILROAD
AND MONTANA'S MINERAL LANDS

Thomas A. Clinch

The Northern Pacific Railroad and Montana's Mineral Lands

THOMAS A. CLINCH

Thomas A Clinch is associate professor of history in Carroll College, Helena, Montana.

Transportation was a vital factor in Montana's economic development. The geographic location of the region, lying to the north of such well-traveled routes as the Oregon Trail, dictated the development of wagon roads into the gold fields. These included the Bozeman and Bridger Roads, The Mullan Road, the Minnesota-Montana Road, the Niobrara Road, and the Corinne, Utah-Virginia City Road. Travel on such routes in the placer-mining period was satisfactory, although tedious and expensive, but the advent of quartz mining and the growth of cattle and sheep raising demanded railroad transportation. For some time, the nearest railhead was 1,400 miles distant at Omaha, Nebraska.[1]

The situation was sufficiently difficult for the stockgrowers, but costs were practically prohibitive for the mine owners. The smelting of ore and the determination of its value were their great concerns. Silver smelting at the mine was practical, but copper smelting demanded complex equipment not locally available until William A. Clark built the Colorado and Montana Smelter at Butte in 1879 and Marcus Daly his at Anaconda in 1883. Prior to the construction of such works, mine owners had often shipped cuprous ores as far as Swansea, Wales, Freiberg, Germany, and Baltimore, Maryland.[2] Once local smelting problems had been solved, the problem remained of getting processed copper, silver, and other metals to eastern and European markets.

The author gratefully acknowledges the assistance rendered him by Mr. Donald Garrity, deputy attorney general of Montana, in acquiring source material at the State Law Library in Helena, Montana.

[1] James M. Hamilton, *From Wilderness to Statehood, A History of Montana, 1805–1900* (Portland, 1957), 359; for general data on western transportation, see Robert F. Riegel, *The Story of the Western Railroads* (New York, 1926).

[2] Merrill G. Burlingame and K. Ross Toole, *A History of Montana* (New York, 1957), I, 348.

Transportation difficulties ultimately made Montanans extremely vocal in urging construction or a transcontinental railroad through the region. In 1853 Isaac I. Stevens, territorial governor of Washington, conducted a government survey for such a road. However, the first railroad that actually reached Montana was the Utah and Northern, the brainchild of Salt Lake City businessmen eager to link mineral and agricultural lands to the north with the Union Pacific. At the head of this enterprise was John W. Young, son of Brigham Young, who facilitated construction by securing the technical and financial assistance of the two New York railroad contractors, Joseph and Benjamin Richardson. Despite financial difficulties, the Utah and Northern reached Silver Bow Junction, a few miles from Butte, in December, 1881. In 1883 this line built a spur westward to connect with the Northern Pacific at Garrison.[3] The Utah and Northern was a tremendous boon for the mining industry of southwestern Montana, but it did not serve the entire region nor did its completion lessen the intensity of arguments for a transcontinental road. An additional factor to be considered was the fact that the Utah and Northern was a narrow-gauge railroad until 1888. This was something of a drawback in connecting with other roads.[4] In any event, Montanans fixed their aspirations and attention on the Northern Pacific.

Interest in a northern transcontinental railroad had been persistent for some time. In 1845 the enthusiastic Asa Whitney had presented Congress with a plan for such a road connecting Lake Michigan, the Pacific Coast, and potential Asiatic outlets.[5] Eight years later Isaac I. Stevens conducted his survey over much of the subsequent Northern Pacific right of way.[6] Finally, in 1864, Josiah Perham, Whitney's successor as propagandist for such a route, won a charter for a railroad beginning at a point on Lake Superior and running westward north of the forty-fifth parallel to some point on Puget Sound with a branch running through the Columbia River valley to a point at or near Portland.[7] The charter established the Northern Pacific Railroad, and Perham became its first president. His plans for financing through stock subscriptions in small amounts failed, however, and it was not

[3] *Ibid.*, II, 71–72.

[4] *Ibid.*, 72.

[5] Henry Nash Smith, *Virgin Land, The American West as Symbol and Myth* (New York, 1950), 32.

[6] Joseph Schafer, "Isaac I. Stevens," *Dictionary of American Biography* (New York, 1928–1944), XVII, 612–614.

[7] John F. Dillon, *Pacific Railroad Laws* (New York, 1890), 47 ff.

until Jay Cooke, the famed Civil War financier, put the power of his banking firm behind the enterprise that it assumed serious dimensions. Construction began in 1870, and three years later the road reached Bismarck, North Dakota.[8] At that point, construction stopped with the failure of Cooke's banking firm and the resultant Panic of 1873. Bismarck remained the railhead through the ensuing years of financial difficulty until Frederick Billings reorganized the company in 1879 and resumed westward construction.[9] Meanwhile, Henry Villard entered the picture. In 1879 he purchased the Oregon Steam Navigation Company from Simeon G. Reed, organized the Oregon Railway and Navigation Company, and began construction of a railroad eastward from Portland, Oregon. In this enterprise he clashed with the Northern Pacific and finally decided to buy a controlling interest in it through his famous "blind pool." Under his direction the Northern Pacific reached completion with the driving of the last spike at Gold Creek Montana, in September, 1883.[10]

The Northern Pacific was a land grant railroad, receiving from the government ten alternate sections on either side of the track in the states and twenty in the territories for every mile constructed. The area in which lands might be selected extended fifty miles on either side of the track. In Montana this gave the company a total of 14,000,000 acres of land. Specifically excluded from the grant, however, were mineral lands except those containing iron or coal.[11]

The charter provided that, as each twenty-five miles of track reached completion, the President would appoint three commissioners to examine the work and that if it proved satisfactory the land along it might be patented to the company. It also provided that, once the route was fixed, the President would authorize the survey of lands up to a distance of forty miles on either side of the track.[12]

The charter also provided for beginning and completion dates, originally stipulating that construction was to begin within two years of issuance and that the road was to be finished by July 4, 1876. Congress extended both dates by two years in 1866.[13]

With Jay Cooke's failure in 1873, the most pressing problem be-

---

[8] Ellis P. Oberholtzer, "Jay Cooke," *Dictionary of American Biography*, IV, 383–384.

[9] John D. Hicks, "Frederick Billings," *ibid.*, II, 265–266.

[10] James B. Hedges, "Henry Villard," *ibid.*, XIX, 273–275; James B. Hedges, *Henry Villard and the Northwest Railways* (New Haven, 1930), 97, 109.

[11] Dillon, *Pacific Railroad Laws*, 49–50; K. Ross Toole, *Montana, An Uncommon Land* (Norman, 1959), 92.

[12] Dillon, *Pacific Railroad Laws*, 50–51.

[13] *Ibid.*, 61–62.

326 PACIFIC HISTORICAL REVIEW

came meeting the deadline for completion. The straitened economic circumstances of the corporation indicated that it would not meet the deadline. Congressional friends of the enterprise thus turned their attention to winning an extension. In 1876 Senator Samuel J. R. McMillan of Minnesota introduced Senate Bill 14, providing for an eight-year extension, and it passed the upper house. In the house of representatives the measure received a favorable committee report, but it passed over to the next session. At that time the confusion attending the disputed election of 1876 delayed consideration until the final day. Despite an eloquent defense of the charter and the corporation by Martin Maginnis, territorial delegate from Montana, the measure failed to pass the House.[14]

The failure of subsequent attempts to win a Congressional time extension convinced the company that it need only continue construction and rest on its original charter rights. In 1879 President Hayes's attorney general, Charles Devens, decided that the completion date with a one-year grace period was July 4, 1879.[15] He added that until Congress took steps to declare a forfeiture of the land grant, it would remain in full force. Congress did not so declare, and the company completed the road under these conditions.[16]

However, the technicality that the company had not complied with the letter of the charter and its amendments was to provide ammunition for its opponents in Montana once it attempted to acquire mineral lands within its grant in terms of a tortured interpretation of what the charter meant in originally excluding them.

With the completion of the Northern Pacific in 1883, Montana began to enjoy the advantages gained with a transcontinental avenue of travel and commerce running through the territory. On its part the company began a continued and vigorous campaign to bring settlers into the area of its land grant. However, the enthusiasm marking Montana's interest in the completion of the road and the rejoicing that marked the accomplished fact soon underwent a radical change.[17]

The railroad waited for over a year before beginning the selection of lands lying within its grant. On November 18, 1884, company repre-

---

[14] 44 Cong., 2 sess., *Cong. Record*, 2131. Northern Pacific officials held Maginnis in high regard. In 1883 they gave him and his wife a pass good for the year 1884. T. F. Oakes to Martin Maginnis, Dec. 27, 1883, Maginnis Papers, Montana Historical Society Library, Helena, Montana.

[15] Eugene V. Smalley, *History of the Northern Pacific Railroad* (New York, 1883), 224.

[16] *Ibid.*, 225.

[17] *Proceedings. Helena Convention on the Northern Pacific Land Grant* (Helena, 1888), *passim*. Hereafter referred to as *Proceedings, Northern Pacific Land Grant*.

sentatives filed the first selection at the land office in Helena.[18] Between that date and October 22, 1887, they selected slightly over 2,000,000 acres under the provisions of the charter.[19] In the process the company began to select mineral lands in western Montana as being agricultural in character.

Meanwhile, incoming President Grover Cleveland appointed William Andrew Jackson Sparks as his first commissioner of the General Land Office.[20] Sparks felt that the office had previously been a tool of such interests as the land grant railroads and in his *First Annual Report* in 1885 stated: "I found that the magnificent estate of the nation in its public lands had been to a wide extent wasted under defective and improvident laws, and through a laxity of public administration astonishing in a business sense if not culpable in recklessness of official responsibility." [21]

On April 3, 1885, Sparks issued an order withholding the granting of patents for lands in certain regions, including Montana. This meant that Northern Pacific selections in the area would be tentative despite their being recorded and legal fees paid. The order was also to establish an important principle embodied in the supreme court decision which finally settled the mineral land question in 1894.[22]

Public sentiment was slow in developing opposition in Montana to the company's program until 1888, when the threat became serious. On February 7 and 8, 1888, leading citizens from the mining areas met at Helena to discuss ways and means of dealing with the problem. The threat was not illusory. If the railroad could pick known mineral lands on odd-numbered sections, existing mines therein might become company property, for the Northern Pacific was working on the assumption that mineral lands within its grant would have to be known as such when it received its charter in 1864.[23]

Among the ninety-four delegates present at the convention in Helena were such leading mine owners and political figures as James A. Leggatt of Butte, owner of the Gambetta Mine; Thomas Cruse, Irish immigrant and owner of the fabulously productive Drum Lum-

[18] *Ibid.*, 225.

[19] *Ibid.*, 14–15.

[20] Harold H. Dunham, "William Andrew Jackson Sparks," *Dictionary of American Biography*, XVII, 434–435.

[21] John B. Rae, "Commissioner Sparks and the Railroad Land Grants," *Mississippi Valley Historical Review*, XXV (1938), 211.

[22] Dunham, "William Andrew Jackson Sparks," *Dictionary of American Biography*, XVII, 435.

[23] *Proceedings, Northern Pacific Land Grant*, 3–4.

mon Mine at Marysville; Robert Burns Smith, Democratic district attorney for Montana; and Thomas H. Carter, a Republican lawyer from Helena and future territorial delegate.[24] Eleven western Montana mining counties sent delegates to the convention.[25]

During the course of the meeting, the delegates denounced the Northern Pacific's policy in a series of vigorous resolutions and discussed sending protests to the president, the secretary of the interior, and the territorial delegate, Joseph K. Toole. However, the delegate was fully cognizant of current developments and so also was the executive branch of the federal government. During the proceedings, correspondence between Secretary of the Interior Lucius Q. C. Lamar and a resident of Helena revealed that the government had not issued patents for lands chosen by the railroad.[26] On the basis of this assurance, the delegates wasted no time on protests and proceeded at once to the establishment of a permanent territorial executive committee headed by Thomas G. Merrill of Helena and a finance committee including Leggatt and Cruse as members.[27] Each of the counties represented was to have an executive and financial subcommittee as well.

In addition to organizing executive and finance committees, the convention was important in collecting affidavits from some 700 mining men proving that lands selected by the Northern Pacific were mineral in character.[28]

To sustain interest in the controversy, a second convention met at Helena in November, 1889.[29] In the meantime, however, in June 1888, a small group of "miners" had discovered lodes of ore containing gold, silver, and other precious metals on the western outskirts of Helena on odd-numbered sections claimed by the Northern Pacific. Whether this deliberate test of the legality of the Northern Pacific' selection of lands directly stemmed from the convention of 1888 is not known, but it is very likely that it did. Among the members of the group were Richard P. Barden, city treasurer of Helena; William A. Muth, a Helena mining broker; Harpin Davies, a prominent miner; and an unidentified William Welles.[30] Muth and Davies had

---

[24] *Ibid.*, 12–13.
[25] *Ibid.*, 13.
[26] Lucius Q. C. Lamar to A. J. Davidson, Jan. 7, 1888, *ibid.*, 7–8.
[27] *Ibid.*, 14–15.
[28] Helena *Daily Herald*, Feb. 9, 1888.
[29] *Ibid.*, Nov. 30, 1889.
[30] A. W. Ide, comp., *Helena City Directory for 1888* (Helena, 1888), 95, 118, 181.

served as delegates at the mineral lands convention held in February, and Barden had probably been there also.[31] Between June 20, 1888, and May 9, 1889, they located the Vanderbilt, Four Jacks, New York Central, Hudson River, and Chauncey Depew quartz-lode mining claims.[32]

In October, 1890, the Northern Pacific obtained a complaint praying the ejection of the group from their claims and forfeiture to the company of the value of ores extracted. The defendants, Barden and his associates, demurred to the complaint, and the case came before the federal district court for Montana in Helena. Judge Lorenzo Sawyer of the ninth circuit presided, and District Judge Hiram Knowles of Montana sat with him in the hearing.[33]

Counsel for the railroad argued that the company had accepted the charter in 1864, that in 1872 it had fixed its general route, and in 1882 its definite route through Montana, and that after the establishment of definite location it had filed a plat of the route with the commissioner of the general land office. Following definite location, they held that the disputed lands lay within the forty-mile limits of the land grant on odd-numbered sections and that the Helena townsite survey in 1868 had shown the lands as being agricultural and not mineral. They further emphasized the company's filing of the list of selections, including the lands in question, in the district land office in Helena in November, 1886, and payment of the required legal fees. The heart of the company's argument, however, lay in contending that with definite location in 1882 the lands, not then known as mineral, had automatically become its property.[34]

Counsel for the defendants did not dispute these facts until they reached the contention that the disputed lands had automatically become company property with definite location in 1882. Their position was that the lands in question belonged to their clients in view of the government's failure and refusal to issue patents.[35]

In announcing the decision of the court on June 12, 1891, Circuit Judge Lorenzo Sawyer used a similar case decided in California in December, 1889, *Francoeur* v. *Newhouse*. At issue in that case was the charter issued to the Central Pacific Railroad in 1862 and the company's ejection of gold miners operating on lands lying within its

[31] *Proceedings, Northern Pacific Land Grant,* 13.
[32] *Northern Pacific Railroad Co.* v. *Barden et al.,* 46 Federal Reporter, 593.
[33] *Ibid.,* 592.
[34] *Ibid.,* 594.
[35] *Ibid.*

grant. The court decided that unless the lands in question were known to be mineral-bearing when the Central Pacific had met the charter's conditions, miners could be ejected from lands claimed by it despite the government's failure to issue patents. In this case the court had held that the patent was "only a convenient instrument of evidence that conditions have been performed and title vested." [36]

Using this case as a precedent, Judge Sawyer overruled the demurrer and decided in favor of the Northern Pacific, giving the defendants ten days to file their answer.[37] District Judge Hiram Knowles dissented, but in situations of this sort the opinion of the circuit judge took precedence. Knowles placed great emphasis on the Federal Mining Law of 1872, which declared, "in all cases lands valuable for minerals shall be reserved from sale, except as otherwise expressly directed by law." [38] He held that legislative grants must be construed most strongly against the grantee and must not be enlarged by implication, as he held the charter had been in this case. He further demonstrated that in the previous twenty years the General Land Office had issued patents to miners for mineral lands lying within the Northern Pacific grant and on odd-numbered sections.[39] As far as *Francoeur* v. *Newhouse* was concerned, he took sharp issue with the decision, and concluded by arguing for classification of lands lying within the Northern Pacific's land grant by competent and experienced experts.[40]

Following the delivery of Sawyer's decision, the defendants decided to appeal the case to the United States Supreme Court. In the meantime, the state of Montana had decided to aid Barden and his associates. The second legislature had created a mineral land commission in March, 1891, with former territorial delegate Martin Maginnis as commissioner. His salary for a two-year term was $3,000, and he enjoyed an expense account in the same amount to be used, among other objectives, for the employment of counsel "to protect Montana and her mineral interests." [41]

With the financial resources derived from the mineral lands conventions and the state appropriation provided in the creation of the mineral land commission, the defendants were well able to bear the expense of an appeal to the supreme court. En route, they acquired the

[36] *Ibid.; Francoeur* v. *Newhouse*, 40 Federal Reporter, 618.

[37] 46 Federal Reporter, 608–609.

[38] *Ibid.*, 609–610.

[39] *Ibid.*, 611.

[40] *Ibid.*, 623.

[41] *Laws, Memorials and Resolutions of the State of Montana Passed at the Second Regular Session of the Legislative Assembly* (Helena, 1891), 178–180.

services of a galaxy of extremely able legal minds. Appearing for them
were Edwin W. Toole, brother of Governor Joseph K. Toole; William
Wallace, Jr., Edwin Toole's partner; and William W. Dixon, Montana's congressman from 1891 to 1893.[42] Also appearing on their behalf were members of the offices of United States Attorney General and
Solicitor General. The title of the case, on appeal, was *Richard P.
Barden et al. v. Northern Pacific Railroad Company.*

Counsel for the opposing sides finally appeared before the supreme
court on first argument on January 23, 30, and 31, 1893. Toole and
Wallace bore the burden of the task then. Re-argument occurred on
April 11, 1894, with Solicitor General Lawrence Maxwell, Jr., and
Dixon appearing for the plaintiffs in error, Barden and his associates,
at that time.[43] The arguments presented by opposing counsel were the
same as those offered in the lower court.

On May 26, 1894, Associate Justice Stephen J. Field read the majority opinion of the court in favor of the plaintiffs in error. The court
had split six to three in the decision. Concurring with Justice Field
were Chief Justice Melville W. Fuller and Justices Henry B. Brown,
John Marshall Harlan, Howell E. Jackson and Edward D. White.
Justice Brewer dissented, stressing the rights of the railroad's investors
and accepting the railroad's argument that the disputed lands had
passed into its possession with definite location in 1882, and Justices
George Shiras, Jr., and Horace Gray agreed.[44]

The majority opinion, overruling the lower court's decision and
that in *Francoeur* v. *Newhouse*, stressed three major conclusions: (1)
the Northern Pacific Railroad Company cannot recover under the
grant to it by the act of congress of July 2, 1864, mineral lands, from
persons in possession thereof who have made locations, although the
mineral character of the land was not discovered until the year 1888,
no patent having been issued to the company therefor; (2) it was the
intention of congress to exclude from the grant of lands to the Northern Pacific Railway, of July 2, 1864, actual mineral lands, whether
known or unknown, and not merely such as were at the time known to
be mineral; (3) nothing will pass by a government grant to the grantee
by implication or inference, unless essential to the enjoyment of the
thing granted, and exceptions intended for the benefit of the public
are to be liberally construed.[45]

[42] *Richard P. Barden et al. v. Northern Pacific Railroad Co.,* 154 U.S. 288.
[43] *Ibid.*
[44] *Ibid.,* 332.
[45] *United States Supreme Court Reports* (Rochester, 1894), XXXVIII, 994.

It would be difficult to overemphasize the importance of the decision in the Barden case for the mining industry in Montana and the general rejoicing marking its announcement. However, a concurrent problem had meanwhile become apparent—the need for a thorough classification of the lands in the Northern Pacific grant as being mineral or otherwise.

In February, 1888, Territorial Delegate Joseph K. Toole, realizing the need for a thorough examination of Northern Pacific lands in Montana, introduced a measure to that purpose. The house referred the measure to the committee on public lands, and there it died.[46] A like fate met later measures for the same purpose introduced, after the attainment of statehood, by Representatives Thomas H. Carter and William W. Dixon and Senator Thomas C. Power.[47] These later measures included Northern Pacific lands in Idaho.

The state legislature subsequently interested itself in the need for such legislation. Among the duties of the mineral land commissioner was that of preparing "an act or acts to be introduced into Congress to save both discovered and undiscovered mineral lands."[48] Although no evidence directly links Martin Maginnis, the first commissioner, with subsequent legislation concerning the matter, he doubtless had a hand in its inspiration, since he spent considerable time in Washington, D. C., in the performance of his duties.

Finally, on February 26, 1893, Representative Charles S. Hartman of Montana introduced House Resolution 3476 "to provide for the examination and classification of certain mineral lands in the States of Montana and Idaho." Again the house referred the measure to the committee on public lands.[49] The bill passed over to the second session of the fifty-third congress and received a favorable report on February 27, 1894.[50] On July 24, 1894, the house debated the measure with Hartman eloquently defending it against minor objections raised by Representative Joseph G. Cannon of Illinois concerning per diem compensation for the commissioners provided in the bill. Hartman specifically linked the bill with the Barden case in emphasizing the

---

[46] 50 Cong., 1 sess., *Cong. Record*, 986.

[47] *Ibid.*, 51 Cong., 1 sess., 2513, 8722; 52 Cong., 1 sess., 1728; 52 Cong., 2 sess., 92, 109–110.

[48] *Laws, Memorials and Resolutions of the State of Montana Passed at the Second Regular Session of the Legislative Assembly*, 178–180.

[49] 53 Cong., 1 sess., *Cong. Record*, 1827. Hartman's sponsorship of H.R. 3476 was rather ironic. Prior to his election to Congress in 1892, he had been a Northern Pacific attorney. After receiving the Republican nomination, however, he severed all connections with the railroad. See *Bozeman Weekly Avant Courier*, Sept. 10, 1892.

[50] 53 Cong., 2 sess., *Cong. Record*, 2451.

need for classification to settle all possible disputes that might arise over the character of Northern Pacific lands. H.R. 3476 provided that the secretary of the interior should "as speedily as practicable" examine and classify all of the Northern Pacific land and indemnity grants in Montana and Idaho with regard to their mineral or non-mineral character and disallow all Northern Pacific claims to mineral lands. The actual work was to be done by three commissioners in each of the Bozeman, Helena, and Missoula land districts in Montana and in the Coeur d'Alene land district in Idaho. At least one of the commissioners in each district was to be a practical miner and resident of the area. The bill empowered the commissioners to examine the lands and call witnesses prior to the submission of their reports to the commissioner of the general land office. The measure also provided that all lands previously patented as mineral would retain their classification as well as all other lands which evidenced indications of mineral-bearing characteristics or probable market value because of minerals contained therein.[51]

Where previously surveyed, the land was generally to be classified in sections and in no case in acreage of less than "legal subdivisions." Unsurveyed lands were to be classified in terms of natural or artificial boundaries as the commissioners might designate. In the process of the survey, the commissioners were to make monthly reports of their findings to the register and receiver of the land district in question and to the secretary of the interior. The register and receiver was then to make weekly publication of this data in local newspapers. Any person, corporation, or company could then protest within sixty days and be heard by the local register with the right of appeal to the secretary of the interior, the United States attorney for the judicial district involved representing the government. In all cases, the decision of the secretary of the interior was to be final. Where no protest occurred, the decision of the local commissioners was to constitute the last word. The Northern Pacific was to receive no patents until the survey had been completed, and those previously issued in violation of the act were to be void.[52] No provision of the act was to be construed as recognizing a Northern Pacific claim to lands that it might otherwise forfeit. The bill finally provided an appropriation of $80,000 to pay the survey's expenses.[53]

---

[51] *Ibid.*, 7838–7839.
[52] *Ibid.*, 7839.
[53] *Ibid.*

On July 24, 1894, the bill passed the house. The senate did not take it up until late in the second session of the fifty-third congress, referring it then to the committee on public lands. Senator Thomas C. Power of Montana, a member of the committee, was its manager. On December 17, 1894, the committee returned it to the senate. Power proposed a number of amendments on February 4, 1895, and two days later the bill passed the senate.[54] The amended version differed from that of the house in a number of particulars. It placed a four-year time limit on the duration of the survey, reduced the total appropriation for expenses from $80,000 to $20,000, cut per diem compensation for United States attorneys involved in potential litigation, and lengthened the section containing details on classification.[55]

Following senate passage of its version of the mineral lands bill, the house refused to concur. On February 11, 1895, the senate reconsidered its version, added minor amendments, and passed it a second time.[56] The house conferees finally agreed that it did not differ in spirit from the original measure. On February 25, 1895, President Cleveland signed the bill.[57]

The supreme court decision in the Barden case and passage of H.R. 3476 secured the mineral lands of Montana against wholesale depredations by a land-hungry railroad, although subsequent to the classification of its land grant, the Northern Pacific did acquire timber lands with mine works located on them through obvious corruption of the commissioners authorized by the bill.[58] However, such acquisitions in no way approximated those which might have taken place had there been no Barden case nor congressional legislation in the controversy.

The Montanans' protest against the Northern Pacific was not the typical agrarian complaint of this and earlier periods directed against an inflated rate structure.[59] As late as 1891 and 1892, the *Rocky Mountain Husbandman*, the state's leading agricultural newspaper, thanked the Northern Pacific for a favorable rate on wheat shipped to Minneapolis and congratulated it for bringing new population into the re-

---

[54] *Ibid.*, 3 sess., 1817.
[55] *Ibid.*, 1716, 2404–2405.
[56] *Ibid.*, 2128, 2015, 2520.
[57] *Ibid.*, 2876.
[58] See C. W. Wilber, "The Way of the Land Transgressor. How Montana was 'Done'," *Pacific Monthly* (Jan., 1908), 109–115.
[59] Farmers in some areas seem to have had complaints about freight rates, notably those on farm equipment. See Journal of the Gallatin County Farmers' Alliance, Number Four (unpublished manuscript, Montana State College Library, Bozeman, Montana).

gion.[60] The protest against the Northern Pacific was industrial and not agricultural and arose in western Montana, heartland of the mining industry. Mine owners began the fight at the mineral lands conventions in 1888 and 1889 and sustained it thereafter. Also important in the controversy was the non-partisan character of opposition to the Northern Pacific. Democrats such as Joseph K. Toole, Martin Maginnis, and William W. Dixon and Republicans such as Thomas H. Carter, Thomas C. Power, and Charles S. Hartman forgot partisan differences to bring the problem to solution. Montana's Populists, whose strength lay in trade unions dependent on the mining industry for full employment, also lent their voices to the protest. In 1892 the Populist platform in Montana advocated Northern Pacific forfeiture of its entire land grant for failure to meet the deadline for completion.[61] The Northern Pacific became the bête noire of western Montanans of all walks of life and of all political faiths because it threatened the basis of their principal industry—mining.

---

[60] White Sulphur Springs *Rocky Mountain Husbandman*, April 16, 1891; Jan. 21, 1892.

[61] *Anaconda Standard*, Jan. 21, 1892; Butte *Semi-Weekly Intermountain*, June 19, 1892.

TIMBER EMPIRE FROM THE PUBLIC DOMAIN

Roy. E. Appleman

TIMBER EMPIRE FROM THE PUBLIC DOMAIN

By Roy E. Appleman

During the years spanned by the period of this study, 1897 to 1910, there was intense activity among special interests in securing profit and advantage from what remained of the public domain of the United States. There was stiff competition among those who strove to acquire the choice timber lands, the most valuable mineral lands, and the richest grazing lands. The public land laws and the officials who were supposed to enforce them were only obstacles in the way to fortune to be removed or ignored as the occasion demanded.

In the 1890's, timber kings were turning their steps toward the great forests of the Pacific slope. By this date the timber of the Great Lakes region had been cut over and the rush to the southern pineries was well under way. A few years later the lumber boom had migrated to the Pacific Northwest.[1] The old "saw-log dynasties" of the middle region were taking their methods as well as their fortunes westward. So powerful was the influence of these interests that, years later, a graduate student in one of the state universities in the lake states dared not publish his thesis on the history of the pine lands. Too many state legislators were involved in the disclosures.[2]

The economic basis for the scramble among the powerful for forest wealth is apparent. James Jerome Hill, in a speech in 1905, said that one acre of timber land was worth to a railroad more than forty acres of agricultural land.[3] Within a decade southern pine which had been bought for $1.25 an acre was held

[1] Thomas H. Sherrard, "National Forests and the Lumber Supply," *Yearbook of the United States Department of Agriculture* (Washington, 1907), 1906, pp. 447-452. See also Robert T. Hill, *Public Domain and Democracy, Columbia University Studies in History, Economics, and Public Law* (New York), XXXVIII (1910), and address of Governor James O. Davidson of Wisconsin, *Proceedings of Conference of Governors in the White House, Washington, D. C., May 13-15, 1908* (Washington, 1909), 125.

[2] John Ise, *United States Forest Policy* (New Haven, 1920), 371.

[3] Stephen A. D. Puter in collaboration with Horace Stevens, *Looters of the Public Domain* . . . (Portland, Ore., 1908), 456.

for $60 an acre, and Douglas fir in the Northwest which had been obtained from the government at $2.50 an acre reached a value of $200 an acre.[4] One operator records that fifty quarter sections he sold in 1899 for $4 an acre were resold in 1907 for $87.50 an acre, and the following year were held at $150 an acre.[5] Single trees of fir and cedar varieties often were worth $100 to $150, and it was not uncommon for a square mile of timber land to have an estimated capacity of 100 million board feet of lumber, worth $1,500,000 on the retail market at current prices in the closing decade of the nineteenth century.[6] This timber land the government sold at $1600 a square mile.

An official report in 1905 stated that the land laws, court decisions, and departmental practices had become so complicated that the settler was at a marked disadvantage in trying to get his share of the public lands when pitted against the wealth and superior legal services of corporations.[7] Laws intended to serve homeseekers were used to achieve the goal of financial interests. This is evidenced by such practices as were used in eliminating 400,000 acres from the Olympic National Forest in 1900 and 1901, on the ground that it was valuable chiefly for agriculture. But no sooner had this area been set aside for agricultural purposes than it was entered by dummies as "valuable chiefly for timber, but not fit for cultivation" and was soon in the hands of timber speculators.[8] In 1910 only 570 acres of the 400,000 were

[4] H. H. Schwartz, ''The Timber and Stone Act, and the Commutation Clause of the Homestead Act,'' *Senate Documents*, 60 Cong., 2 Sess., XII, No. 676, *Report of the National Conservation Commission*, III, 401.

[5] Puter, *Looters of the Public Domain*, 75, caption under photograph. Puter tells a most interesting story of how the *Deschutes Echo*, of Bend, Oregon, had its origin in the rush to the pine forests of that region which took place about the turn of the century. An old hand press worth about $50 was brought in, spiked to a leveled pine stump, and timber claim notices were ground out at the rate of $10 each. In six weeks 1,500 land notices had been printed on this pioneer press. *Ibid.*, 83.

[6] Edward A. Bowers, ''Present Condition of the Forests on the Public Lands,'' *Publications of the American Economic Association* (Baltimore), VI, 1891, No. 3, pp. 61-62.

[7] *Report of the Public Lands Commission*, *Senate Documents*, 58 Cong., 3 Sess., No. 189, pp. XXIII-XXIV.

[8] *Lumber Industry* (Washington, 1913-1914), pt. 1 p. 267. This monograph in four parts (3 vols.) published by the Bureau of Corporations in 1913-1914, and bringing its data down to the year 1910, is a most valuable work on the concentration of timber wealth in the United States. It is a scientific work, based on the records of the General Land Office in large part. It contains many maps and charts of importance.

cultivated. In a certain county in Washington on twenty-three homesteads totaling 3,676 acres, only 33 acres were unforested, whether naturally barren or cleared, and were on not more than 3 and may have been entirely on one of the 23 claims.[9] Similar practices were common throughout the public land states.

The outright cutting of timber from the public domain was the object of considerable concern by successive secretaries of the interior. Practically all the annual reports of the Department of the Interior during the last twenty years of the nineteenth century and during the first decade of the twentieth century contain long lists of cases of timber suits. Reservation notices in the national forests were torn down almost as soon as they were posted. In 1894, Commissioner Silas W. Lamoreux of the General Land Office wrote in response to a Senate inquiry, ''The regulations are practically inoperative, and it is beyond the power of this office to effectively control the cutting of public timber. But, aside from this, it seems to me that the time has arrived when the Government can not afford to give away its timber.'' [10]

Irregular dealings in obtaining choice timber lands reached to high places, even to the United States Senate. It was alleged that Senator John H. Mitchell of Oregon agreed to facilitate final proof of thirty-three quarter sections of land in the Pacific Northwest for Minneapolis interests and was to receive $25 for each quarter section patented. Stephen Puter states that he gave Senator Mitchell two one thousand dollar bills in Washington to induce him to use his influence with Binger Hermann, commissioner of the General Land Office, to have patents issued for twelve quarter sections of land. When the patents were issued, the entire acreage, which fell within the terms of the Lieu Land Act, was sold by Puter to Minnesota lumbermen at the rate of $5.25 an acre. This deal netted Puter a nice personal profit after deducting the $2.50 an acre paid to the government and the two thousand dollars given to Senator Mitchell. The entire transaction had been in violation of the land laws.[11]

[9] *Ibid.*, 262-263.

[10] August 4, 1894, *Senate Executive Documents*, 53 Cong., 3 Sess., No. 45, pp. 2-3.

[11] Puter, *Looters of the Public Domain*, 46-66; the Lieu Land Act, a rider to the 1898 appropriations bill, authorized the selection of land in lieu of claims relinquished in national forests. See *U. S. Statutes at Large*, XXX, 36.

When President Cleveland, on February 22, 1897, by executive order established a large number of new national forests a veritable storm of criticism was unleashed by western Senators, congressmen, and state legislators. One man on the floor of Congress spoke of the President's action as the "arbitrary, iniquitous proclamations of February 22."[12] Western Senators and congressmen during this period seldom supported attempts made to enforce the land laws or to promote the cause of conservation.[13] The climate of opinion was such in the western part of the country that the land laws could be enforced only with the greatest difficulty. During this period, nearly everywhere in the West, local interest and influence were exerted against the principle of conservation. Quick exploitation of the natural resources was the dominant economic impulse of the section. This sentiment favored those who hurriedly acquired princely areas and magnificent potential wealth from the public domain.

In 1910 almost one-eighth of all the privately owned timber land in the United States was included in 3, and one-half in 195 holdings.[14] In one study of 7,370,000 acres of forest land in railroad, wagon road, and canal land grants, intended by the government to find its way quickly to small holders, it was shown that only fifteen per cent had actually done so. The remainder, or over 6¼ million acres, was still in the hands of the original grantees or their assignees. Of 82,500,000 acres granted to three western railroads in the 1860's, forty per cent of the land was still held by them in 1910 after a lapse of nearly half a century. Timber holdings showed great concentration of ownership. In southwest Washington, two holders held forty-nine per cent, in west Oregon five held thirty-six per cent, in northeast California six held seventy per cent, in the redwood belt of California ten held over fifty per cent, and in north central Idaho four owners held fifty-nine per cent of the timber resources. All this was held speculatively, far in advance of any actual use.[15]

Far flung principalities dominated by one man or a corporation were not uncommon in the golden West. Sutter's was not the last, and those who followed him were often better able to strengthen their grasp on lordly kingdoms. Henry Miller, a

12 *Congressional Record*, 54 Cong., 2 Sess., XXIX, pt. 3, p. 2973.
13 *Ibid.*, 2548, 2480; 55 Cong., 1 Sess., XXX, pt. 2, p. 1568.
14 *Lumber Industry*, pt. 1, pp. 12-13.
15 *Ibid.*, pt. 2, pp. xvii-xviii, 11-12.

penniless German youth, who had migrated to America in 1905, was said to control over 14½ million acres of land on the West Coast, a holding twice as large as Belgium.[16] John Clay, who saw him in the 1880's, wrote admiringly of his matchless energy in exploiting the San Joaquin Valley.[17] Thomas B. Walker, in 1913 the largest non-corporate holder of timber, was said to own 750,000 acres of superb timber land in northeast California.[18] Half the state of Florida in 1910 was held by 290 owners, the largest single holding amounting to 1,730,000 acres. One owner of timber and iron land in the Upper Peninsula of Michigan held nearly sixty-six townships, and had this vast holding been in a compact square the boundary line would have been 195 miles long. In Texas and Louisiana one company held 700,000 acres of timber and oil land.[19]

The movement for the establishing of national forests gained great headway around the turn of the century, and received a great impetus in 1907, when fifty-seven new national forests were proclaimed by presidential decree, bringing the total of such areas to over 150 million acres.[20] It must not be supposed, however, that all this territory was owned by the government. Much of the land inside a forest reserve actually might be private property. In the five states of California, Oregon, Washington, Idaho, and Montana, with over 96 million acres in national forests, over 14½ million acres, or more than 15 per cent, were privately owned. In California 22.9 per cent of the national forests was privately owned. In Mt. Shasta National Forest 62 per cent of the reserve was in private hands. Nearly always the private holdings in a national forest constituted the most densely forested parts of the reserve. Within the national forests in the five states mentioned the government had only three-sevenths as much timber as was held by private owners, although the acreage owned was more than two and a half times greater.[21]

Among the important concentrations of land and natural re-

---

16 Bailey Millard, ''The West Coast Land Grafters,'' *Everybody's Magazine* (New York), XII. 1905, p. 589.

17 John Clay, *My Life on the Range* (Chicago, 1924), 27.

18 *Lumber Industry*, pt. 2, pp. 90-91.

19 *Ibid.*, pt. 3, pp. 190, 219.

20 *Annual Report of Secretary of Interior, 1907*, I, 10.

21 *Lumber Industry*, pt. 2, pp. 15-16. Private owners held 31,620,000 acres with an estimated timber stand of 1013 billion feet; the government held 82,080,000 acres with an estimated timber stand of 440 billion feet.

sources, those of the transcontinental and western railroads were the greatest. The Southern Pacific system, holding under five grants, in 1910 led in timber resources. Its main line, running from Sacramento, California, to Portland, Oregon, a distance of 682 miles, traversed a heavily wooded region in which the railroad owned alternate sections to a depth of thirty miles on either side of the track. What it did not own the railroad controlled by reason of its transportation monopoly. Owning nearly 4 million acres of timber land, with an estimated stand of 105 billion feet, the railroad stood first among all private owners of timber in the United States. Out of 17 million acres granted by the government from 1862-1871, the railroad still held in 1910 nearly 14 million acres, or eighty per cent of the original grants.[22] But a policy of too willfully flouting the land laws and of ignoring the purpose of the granting act finally led the great corporation into trouble and resulted in the loss of an empire in timber. The great timber holdings of the Southern Pacific were chiefly in Oregon where about 2 million acres of splendid forest, with a stand of 60 million feet of timber, were held through a subsidiary company, the Oregon and California Railroad, under the old Oregon and California Railroad grants of 1869 and 1870. In 1907 it was rumored that Senator Jonathan Bourne of Oregon had taken the matter to President Roosevelt, charging willful violation of the terms of the grant.[23]

The next year the storm broke when the Oregon legislature presented a memorial to Congress alleging the violation of the terms of sale of the land included in the grant. It was charged that the railroad company had failed to dispose of the land according to law. The grant had required that the land be sold to actual settlers in tracts not to exceed 160 acres and at not more than $2.50 an acre. It was alleged that 370,000 acres of the grant had been sold to thirty-eight timber speculators, that settlers were denied the privilege of buying the land, and that the railroad still held over 2 million acres of the grant and, after January 1, 1903, had virtually withdrawn its land from the market.[24] The federal government entered a suit in the federal courts seeking a forfeiture of the grant. This was the first time in the

22 *Ibid.*, pt. 1, p. 233; pt. 2, pp. 46, 53; pt. 4, p. 6.
23 New York *Sun*, October 22, 1907.
24*Lumber Industry*, pt. 1, pp. 250-251.

history of American-land policy that the government had sought to secure the forfeiture of a grant because of violations of the internal conditions of the grant prescribing the manner of its execution. In 1911 the United States district court in Oregon rendered a decision on the case which forfeited the entire remaining acreage of the grant to the government. The case was appealed to the United States Supreme Court, where in 1915 a decision was handed down reversing the lower federal court. The Supreme Court held that the suit was ''one to enforce the covenants and not to annul the patents.'' The railroad, however, was enjoined from disposing of the land in any way until Congress had had a reasonable time to enact legislation looking toward the enforcement of the terms of the grant. If after six months had elapsed and Congress had taken no action, the railroad company then might apply for a modification of the decree. On June 9, 1916 the President approved an act of Congress which returned the lands, about 2,300,000 acres, to the government. In return, the Southern Pacific Railroad was to receive compensation at the rate of $2.50 an acre, the value conferred on the land by the granting act for the railroad's benefit.[25]

Of all the princely grants of land made by Congress, those to the Northern Pacific Railroad, by their sweep and grandeur, most excite the imagination. The two grants to the Northern Pacific, the first in 1864, and the second and supplementary one in 1870, gave a theoretical total of 44 million acres to the promotors of the railroad. The original grant gave a strip of alternate sections 20 miles deep on each side of the track in the state and 40 miles deep in the territories through which it passed. This meant a 40 mile strip through Minnesota and 80 miles the rest of the way to Puget Sound. There was to be an indemnity strip 10 miles wide on each side of the track beyond the borders of the main grant, and by the act of 1870, an additional 10 mile strip on either side of the line was added along the edge of the

25 United States v. Oregon and California Railroad, 186 *Federal Reports*, 861-933, April 24, 1911; Oregon and California Railroad v. United States, 238 *United States*, 408, June 21, 1915. Both the cases cited are very long, and each has a statement of fact which has much information concerning the litigation. Over 2,500 pages of brief were submitted to the Supreme Court. The legislation of 1916 justly has been called admirable. See also *Annual Report of the Commissioner of the General Land Office*, in *Annual Report of Secretary of the Interior, 1916, Administrative Reports*, I, 172 ff.

first indemnity strip, making a total of forty miles for indemnity selections, which, if added to the primary grant, brought the belt of railroad land to the staggering breadth of 120 miles, cutting a great swath from Minnesota to the Pacific. The indemnity lands were designed to permit the railroad to secure the maximum acreage under the terms of the original grant. If settlers had taken up entries within the confines of the railroad grant before the road applied for patent, the grant was automatically reduced by such amount. Because of this, many of the railroads actually realized only a fraction of the acreage theoretically made possible by munificent grants. In Iowa, for instance, railroad grants practically covered the state, but the railroads actually received only about one-eighth of the total land in the state.[26] Because it passed through an unsettled wilderness and the land department of the railroad was zealous in getting land patented, and because its interests were well served by legislators in Washington, the Northern Pacific Railroad actually became possessed of far more land than any other of the land grant beneficiaries. Up to June 30, 1910, the Northern Pacific had patented 32,664,651 acres of land. It was estimated that about 10½ million acres more possibly might be obtained by the terms of the grants.[27] In each of three states, North Dakota, Montana, and Washington, the amount selected and patented by 1910 ranged from nearly 9 million to nearly 11 million acres.[28]

Virgin forests had fallen within the limits of the Northern Pacific grant. Had it not been for an early disposition to alienate much of its best timber land, the Northern Pacific easily would have been the leading private holder of timber resources. Despite the large sales to speculators, the Northern Pacific Railroad in 1910 still had over 3 million acres of forest land with an estimated stand of over thirty-six billion feet of merchantable timber.[29] This placed it third in private holdings, being surpassed only by the Southern Pacific Railroad and the Weyerhaeuser interests. As a result of the Supreme Court decision in 1915 and the subsequent purchase in 1916 by Congress of the Southern Pacific Railroad forest lands in Oregon which reduced

26 *Lumber Industry*, pt. 1, p. 222.

27 *Ibid.*, pt. 1, pp. 234-235.

28 *Ibid.*, pt. 1, p. 235, note.

29 *Ibid.*, pt. 2, p. 7.

that company to 'third place among private holders of timber, the Northern Pacific stepped up to second place in timber wealth, of which about forty-five per cent was on patented land. The remainder, or fifty-five per cent, was on unpatented land claimed by the railroad.

At the close of the period of this study the Northern Pacific had reversed its earlier policy and had practically withdrawn its timber land from the market. Early sales had chiefly benefited the Amalgamated Copper Company, which had bought one million acres in western Montana, and the Weyerhaeuser firm, which had purchased heavily in western Washington. In 1910, nearly five-sixths of the unsurveyed land in the national forests falling within railroad grants belonged to the Northern Pacific Railroad. This corporation was in no hurry to have the land surveyed and selected for patenting, as in the meantime it escaped state taxation of the land, a sum which it was estimated would have reached $300,000 annually.[30]

If ever worked out, the intricate story of the land policy of the Northern Pacific Railroad would unfold a tale of subtle political influences reaching to the nation's capitol. One of the ventures into practical politics undertaken by the Northern Pacific serves as an introduction to the story of Weyerhaeuser in the Pacific Northwest. Mt. Rainier National Forest was one of the reserves set aside by President Cleveland in 1897. As its grant passed directly through the national forest, one million acres, or about half the acreage in the reserve, was owned by the Northern Pacific Railroad. Much of the land owned by the railroad in Mt. Rainier National Forest was barren and rocky. Little of it had commercial timber of any quantity. The Lieu Land Act of June 4, 1897 gave any holder of land within forest reserves the right to exchange it for surveyed land elsewhere in the public land states. Much of the best timber land still in the public domain was unsurveyed. Hence it was not open to selection, for entries could be made only on land which had been surveyed. To eliminate this obstacle a cunning scheme was successfully slipped through the legislative channels in Washington. On March 2, 1899, the Mt. Rainier National Park was created. It was situated within the boundaries of the forest reserve. The important part of the act was a clause that permitted the North-

[30] Annual Report of Secretary of Interior, 1900, Administrative Reports, I, 11.

ern Pacific Railroad to exchange its lands within the park limits for land elsewhere, unsurveyed as well as surveyed, in any state penetrated by its line.[31] There were no settlers within the park boundary. Clearly, the result was special legislation for the Northern Pacific Railroad. The way was now open for it to exchange worthless land for the best timber acreage in the Northwest. To give the railroad still a freer hand in getting the choice spots in the Northwest, it was allowed to cruise the unsurveyed timber land in which it would make its lieu selections.[32] This amounted to a hand picking by specialists of the best timber land in the Pacific Northwest.[33]

It has been charged that this bit of legislation was framed in the land office of the Northern Pacific Railroad in St. Paul, Minnesota.[34] That it was high finance in the best sense of the term to exchange glaciers for timber land worth $200 an acre no one will deny. Within a few months the effect of the law could be seen by anyone who examined the filings in the General Land Office. From 1897 to 1900 only about 71,000 acres had been exchanged under the general Lieu Land Act. In 1900 the total jumped to 523,000 acres. One authority estimated that the Northern Pacific reaped benefits totaling almost $53,000,000 as a result of the Mt. Rainier National Park legislation of 1899.[35] While other railroads were slow to see the usefulness of the general Lieu Land Act,[36] not so the Northern Pacific with its special legislation, and under Ballinger the General Land Office

[31] *United States Statutes at Large*, XXX, 993-995.

[32] Puter, *Looters of the Public Domain*, 368-385; *Annual Report of Secretary of Interior*, 1899.

[33] This objectionable feature regarding the selection of lieu lands was removed by a law effective October, 1900 (31 *Stat.* 614), requiring that all lieu land selections must be on surveyed land.

[34] Charles P. Norcross, "Weyerhaeuser Richer than John D. Rockefeller," *Cosmopolitan Magazine* (New York), XLII, 1907, p. 256; Puter, *Looters of the Public Domain.*

[35] Puter, *Looters of the Public Domain*, 378-379. Puter gives an itemized account of the manner in which the Northern Pacific Railroad profited to this extent. The writer of this paper thinks the sum needs revision in light of other evidence he has seen. The net gain to the railroad was probably less.

[36] The Santa Fe Railroad, owner of the old Atlantic and Pacific land grant, and four purchasers from the Atlantic and Pacific grant effected relinquishments in Arizona and took up forest lands to the amount of 735,000 acres under the Lieu Land Act, all but about 70,000 acres being in the Pacific Northwest. *Lumber Industry*, pt. 1, p. 242.

was kept busy approving the scrip selections of the railroad, or of those to whom it had sold hundreds of thousands of acres in lieu land scrip from Mt. Rainier National Park at a price ranging from $6 to $8 an acre. The chief purchaser of this Northern Pacific lieu land scrip was the Weyerhaeuser Timber Company. With this scrip the Weyerhaeuser firm took up the virgin unsurveyed forests of southwestern Washington, the finest on the continent. The beginning of Weyerhaeuser's career goes back to the middle of the nineteenth century, but his entrance into the lumber regions of the Pacific Northwest coincides almost precisely with the years which begin the period of this study. It was late in the century that the name of Weyerhaeuser became a power on the Pacific Coast. But before that time he had become king of the lumber lords.

Frederick Weyerhaeuser would have made a fit hero for an Alger chronicle. A German youth of eighteen, he had arrived in this country in 1852, bringing with him his mother and sister.[37] The family stopped four years in Erie, Pennsylvania, where Frederick worked in a brewery at four dollars a week. After a fitful effort at farming the boy took his little family to Rock Island, Illinois. Here he obtained work in a lumber mill piling slabs for a dollar a day. In two years he and another German immigrant had bought the small mill of their employer on credit, and the start had been made which was to lead to unrivaled supremacy in American timber. German thrift paid dividends, even though they were small at first. This was a period in which it was not uncommon to lose one-quarter of the logs between the point where the raft was made up and its arrival at the mill. Weyerhaeuser's boast later in life was that he never lost a log.

In 1864, leaving his partner to manage the mill, Weyerhaeuser went north to visit the fabulous Chippewa white pine region of the Lake States. The ruinous waste he saw there shocked him. When he returned from Wisconsin, he had made his first investment in timber lands.[38] In 1870, he had three mills. In 1872, he began to form his great syndicate. This was the famous Mississippi River Boom and Logging Company. Of one hundred partners, none knew the business of the others, except Weyerhaeuser. An observant but silent spectator at a meeting of the big lumbermen of the Middle West at the Briggs House in Chicago in 1870, he had come out as one of three members of the executive committee of the embryo lumber trust.[39] Under the managing genius of Weyerhaeuser this organization wiped out the middleman. Weyerhaeuser became the president of the company in 1872 and held that post for the next forty years, during which time he was virtually dictator of the organization.

By the 1890's Weyerhaeuser was the greatest single figure in the lumber industry of Wisconsin, Minnesota, Illinois, and the Mississippi Valley in general. At the time of his death in 1914, his control extended from Canada to Mexico, from Maine to Puget Sound. His wealth was estimated at various figures, ranging from three hundred million to six hundred million dollars.[40] In 1907 he was said to be richer than John D. Rockefeller, although this, if true, did not remain so in the next decade.[41] It was not until 1906, when his name was brought into the Interstate Commerce Commission's investigations of coal and mineral land grabs by railroads, that the general public learned of his existence.

Frederick Weyerhaeuser worked quietly and steadily from seven o'clock in the morning until ten at night. He shunned society. He was seldom seen at social functions. He used neither drink nor tobacco. He read little and affected no acquaintance with culture.[42] He attended the Dutch Reformed Church as had his forefathers. He confined his operations to lumber, and moved down that groove with a singleness of purpose that was never deflected. His portraits show a strong, shrewd face, similar to that of James J. Hill, his friend and neighbor of St. Paul.

Much of his early operations are shrouded in mystery. That he was not averse to stretching the spirit as well as the letter of the land laws can be inferred from the fact that an impending congressional investigation of his Chippewa timber dealings was averted when Weyerhaeuser went across the Mississippi River to Iowa and enlisted the services of a friendly congressman.

39 *Literary Digest*, XLVIII, April 18. 1914, pp. 949-950; *New York Times*, April 5, 1914.

40 *New York Times*, February 16, 1930; New York *World*, April 5, 1914.

41 Norcross, ''Weyerhaeuser Richer than John D. Rockefeller,'' *Cosmopolitan Magazine*, XLII, 1907, pp. 252-259.

42 *New York Daily Tribune*, April 5, 1914.

The inquiry in Washington was dropped.[43] There can be little
doubt that much of the Weyerhaeuser holdings in the Lake
States, and later in the South and in the West, was obtained
through a circumvention of the land laws. In the years of his
greatest power, however, it is very unlikely that Weyerhaeuser
had any direct connection with such practices. It was not necessary. Smaller men, anxious to make a few hundred or a few
thousand dollars, would do the necessary ground work and run
the risk of falling athwart the arm of the law. They would sell
their lands to the larger operators and speculators after the
patents had issued from the General Land Office.

From 1880 to 1896 Weyerhaeuser's interests increased one
thousand per cent. He and his associates controlled 10 million
acres of timber along the Mississippi, Missouri, and Ohio River
valleys. A triangle whose points were West Virginia, Louisiana,
and Minnesota knew the weight of his word. By the first decade
of the twentieth century he was a factor in the politics of the
Northwest States. William Lorimer of Chicago, expelled from
the Senate because of corrupt practices, was said to have been
his instrument in Washington. Governor Frank Steunenberg of
Idaho, father-in-law of William E. Borah, was charged with
having been the Idaho agent for a Weyerhaeuser company.[44]

In 1891, began Weyerhaeuser's friendship with James J. Hill.
It was in that year that Weyerhaeuser moved to St. Paul. Two
years later he bought a house on Summit Street, between the
million dollar mansion of Hill and the less pretentious home of
Hill's son.[45] In the next year, 1894, Hill sold Weyerhaeuser
990,000 acres of timber land from the old St. Paul and Pacific
grant for two dollars an acre.[46] In the years that followed, a
clearly marked affinity between Hill and Weyerhaeuser interests
can be seen. Hill was willing to let his friend control the timber,
while he controlled its transportation from the Northwest to the
markets in the Mississippi Valley. This close tie between the
two most powerful men in the Northwest was signalized in a
fitting way, even beyond life, when F. E. Weyerhaeuser, a son

[43] Charles E. Russell, "The Mysterious Octopus," *World Today* (Chicago), XXI,
1912, p. 1740.

[44] *Ibid.*; also the issue of March, 1912; New York *World*, April 5, 1914.

[45] *St. Louis Daily Globe Democrat*, August 4, 1907.

[46] Russell, "The Mysterious Octopus," *World Today*, XXI, 1912, p. 1747.

of the elder Weyerhaeuser, in 1916 was elected to fill the vacant directorship on the Northern Pacific Railroad, left by the death of James J. Hill.[47]

It was about 1900 that the Weyerhaeuser Timber Company was formed and became the holder for the vast tracts secured from the Northern Pacific Railroad. Taking advantage of the railroad's need for cash, in 1900 the Weyerhaeuser Timber Company added to its holdings at the expense of the Northern Pacific by buying from that company 900,000 acres of timberland at an average price of six dollars an acre.[48] This land lay in the odd sections of the railroad grant. Shortly thereafter the Weyerhaeuser Timber Company bought about 220,000 acres of lieu land scrip from the same railroad, made available by the Mt. Ranier National Park legislation of 1899 which had so greatly benefited the Northern Pacific Railroad.[49] The prompt sale to the Weyerhaeuser interests of the large block of scrip acreage, which was immediately exchanged in the General Land Office for even sections in the densely forested area of southwestern Washington and joining the odd sections already purchased from the railroad to make an immense solid block of virgin forest, excites the suspicion that the Weyerhaeuser genius might have had a part in formulating the iniquitous Mt. Rainier National Park lieu land legislation. After 1900, the Weyerhaeuser Timber Company was dominant in southwestern Washington. Other purchases by the Weyerhaeuser Company from the Northern Pacific Railroad followed, until a total of 1,525,000 acres of timber land had been bought from that railroad.[50] In southwestern Washington ninety per cent of the Weyerhaeuser holdings, or 1,231,857 acres, had originated in the Northern Pacific land grant.

The Weyerhaeuser purchases from the Northern Pacific Railroad were heaviest in Washington, but they were also considerable in Oregon and Idaho. In 1910 the Weyerhaeuser Timber Company held 1,901,436 acres of timber, with a footage of 95.7 billion feet of lumber in the three states of Washington, Oregon,

---

47 *New York Times*, October 14, 1916.

48 *Lumber Industry*, pt. 2, pp. 6-7; *American Review of Reviews* (New York), XXXVI, 1907, pp. 572-573; Russell, ''The Mysterious Octopus,'' *World Today*, XXI, 1912, p. 1747.

49 *Lumber Industry*, pt. 1, p. 239.

50 *Ibid.*, pt. 2, pp. 6-7; pt. 1, pp. 239-240.

and California. Over three-fourths of this, 1,515,932 acres, was in Washington,˙with Oregon having approximately one-fifth, or nearly all the remainder, the Weyerhaeuser Timber Company owning only about 5,000 acres of timberland in California.[51]

Prior to 1916 the Weyerhaeuser Timber Company had been the second largest private holder of timber in the United States, but in that year it became the largest, due to congressional action in restoring to the United States government over 2,000,000 acres of heavily forested land which had been held by the Southern Pacific Railroad. Eighty per cent of the Weyerhaeuser Timber Company's land originally had been part of the Northern Pacific land grant. Thus, the land grant policy of Congress can be charged with direct responsibility for the two or three greatest private holdings of timber wealth in the country.

It would be a great mistake to measure the Weyerhaeuser power and wealth in timber by considering only the holdings of the Weyerhaeuser Timber Company. This company's holdings all date from 1900 and after and were confined largely to land bought from the Northern Pacific Railroad. If all the Weyerhaeuser interests had been grouped together, and they numbered scores of the largest timber firms in the nation, the total timber resources of the family would have been found to have been at least three times greater than that of the Weyerhaeuser Timber Company alone. While the Weyerhaeuser Timber Company in 1910 was estimated to control about 95,000,000,000 feet of standing timber, the combined Weyerhaeuser interests were said to own 291,900,000,000 feet of standing timber. Of this staggering forest wealth well over two-thirds was in the Pacific Northwest, about one-sixth was in southern pine, and the remainder was scattered throughout the Lake States.[52]

The actual strength of the Weyerhaeuser monoply in timber was increased beyond what its large ownership would presuppose by its strategic control of ingress and egress to other holdings, and by having the power to isolate them from the market. Other large owners held the same advantages. The small owner

[51] *Ibid.*, pt. 2, pp. 6-7, 37.

[52] *Ibid.*, pt. 2, pp. 6-7. The footage of timber in the various areas was divided as follows:

Pacific Northwest	228.5 billion feet.
Southern Pine	48.7 billion feet.
Lake States	14.7 billion feet.

of valuable timber was often compelled to sell to one of the big holders at a sacrifice when an offer was made by the latter. If the small owner persisted in his refusal to sell, his tract might be cut around, leaving the constant threat of fire running through the slashings nearby with resultant destruction of his timber. Or if entirely isolated by being cut around, the cost of bringing in expensive machinery for the heavy timber of the Northwest might be prohibitive for a small tract, no matter how heavy the timber stand.[53] Thus, for years, many of the large holders of timber acreage did not cut from their own holdings, but were able to keep their mills running by purchasing from small owners whose holdings stood in jeopardy. The Weyerhaeuser Timber Company sold very little of its Washington timber. When it did sell it was always to an operator at a top price for immediate consumption. As an example, a few years after its purchase from the Northern Pacific Railroad at $6 an acre, a section of timber land in Thurston County, Washington, was sold by Weyerhaeuser for $76,000, or $120 an acre.[54] In Oregon, where the company was not a dominant holder, its policy was not to sell at all.[55]

While the Weyerhaeuser Timber Company was not the dominant holder of timber in Oregon, it was one of the greatest. At the close of the period of this study it owned 380,599 acres of superb timber land in the state. Furthermore, it was following a policy of buying up small holdings from individuals and was absorbing other companies when given the opportunity. This was especially true in Klamath and Lake counties, the heart of the south central pine region. The Weyerhaeuser and the Hill interests worked together in order to gain control of this important area. In 1910, when the Oregon Trunk Railroad, a Hill enterprise building up towards the region from Deschutes, quietly bought up an old land grant which ran through this section, as yet undeveloped and unexploited, a new empire in timber seemed to be rounding out in central Oregon.[56]

[53] H. H. Schwartz, ''The Timber and Stone Act, and the Commutation Clause of the Homestead Act,'' loc. cit., 389.

[54] Norcross, ''Weyerhaeuser Richer than John D. Rockefeller,'' Cosmopolitan Magazine, XLII, 1907, p. 254.

[55] Lumber Industry, pt. 2, p. 30.

[56] Ibid., pt. 2, pp. 55-56.

THE HOMESTEAD ACT:

Free Land Policy in Operation, 1862-1935

Paul W[allace] Gates

PAUL W. GATES

The Homestead Act: Free Land
Policy in Operation, 1862–1935

TWO GENERATIONS of agitation by land reformers, including
workingmen's advocates, Jeffersonian arcadians, and western
agrarians, finally produced the Homestead Law of 1862 which
offered free a quarter section of public land in the West to
citizens or intended citizens who settled upon and improved it.
These free-land advocates anticipated Henry George in maintaining that wild, undeveloped land on the frontier had no value
until it was improved by the toil of farm makers; the taxes of
residents that provided roads and schools; town and county government; subventions that assisted in opening up canals and railroads; and high transportation rates that helped to pay for the
railroads. Since it was the investment of the farmer's labor and
the public's money that made land valuable, it seemed to the
western citizen double taxation to make him pay for government
land.[1] The Homestead Act was intended to reward him for his
courageous move to the frontier by giving him land, the value
of which he and the community would create.

If classical economists found little but sophistry in this reasoning, the western pioneer and the eastern land reformers cared
not.[2] Free land, they hoped, would make the life of the pioneer
easier, enable him to use his meager capital to purchase farm
machinery and livestock, relieve him of debt to the government or
to loan sharks (who frequented the land offices to lend their
funds at frontier interest rates of 20 to 40 per cent), remove the
specter of crushing mortgages, and thereby assure a larger proportion of success among farm makers.

The Homestead Law was the culmination of a series of
moves intended to end the policy of using the public lands as a
source of revenue for the government. Prior to 1862, the revenue
policy had been frequently modified but prices had been reduced
only moderately. Now, in one simple act, it seemingly had been

28

replaced by what conservatives regarded as a radical policy of giving land freely to anyone willing to undertake the obligations of farm making.

Not all westerners subscribed to the view that land on the outer fringe of settlement had no value. Some could see that as the western population movement expanded, it shortened the period in which, on successive frontiers land values rose swiftly from little or nothing to a number of dollars an acre. Like speculators from the East, they were prepared to gamble that the land would acquire value with the expected immigration and the improvements the people made. Consequently, they looked for every opportunity to accumulate ownership, whether by one or two quarter sections beyond their needs or acres numbered by the hundreds or thousands. The ambivalence of western attitudes is clear, for with free land established, the West interposed every kind of objection to plans to curb the alienation of homesteads or to provide effective administration of land laws that would prevent accumulation.

The Homestead Law was not without opponents in 1862. Some held it was partial and discriminatory in that the donation would go only to persons who went West. Others held it would drain off population from high-priced land and thereby lower land values in eastern communities; that it would deprive older states of their share in the lands and reduce the value of soldiers' land bounties and railroad grants. But these were the cries of conservatives who feared the elevating effect that free land would have on the propertyless poor, the day laborer, the immigrant.

If conservatives viewed with alarm the social results they foresaw from homesteading, the land reformers were disappointed that the thoroughgoing reconstruction of American land policies they had sought was not achieved. Homesteads were to be alienable, and weak and inadequate safeguards were included to prevent abuse of the law and accumulation of homesteads by capitalists. The privilege of buying public land in unlimited quantities to anticipate settlers' needs was not ended. Huge grants of land were made after the adoption of the Homestead Law to railroads, wagon roads, and states and territories which could make their selections before settlers appeared and thereby acquire the better and more desirable tracts. Indian land, when opened to settlement, was commonly to be sold, not given to settlers, and individual Indian allotments were likewise to be sold. Altogether, between 400 and 500 million acres were selected by states and territories, railroads, and investors and were held for future sales. These were not, therefore, subject to homestead.[3] In fact, the area not open to homestead, though undeveloped, was much greater than the total acreage that homesteaders finally won as free grants. Congress even required in 1889 and 1890 that the 23 million acres it granted the six new states that entered the Union during these years should be sold at a minimum of ten dollars an acre.[4]

Free-land policy as embodied in the Homestead Law was then grafted upon a land system to which it was ill-fitted and incongruous. The two systems existed side by side for the next twenty-eight years, indeed longer, during which time the choicer selections of the railroads, states, and speculators were being sold. Hence the amount of homesteading was smaller than otherwise it surely would have been.[5]

That revenue was not abandoned as a basic feature of government land policy is shown by the fact that homesteaders, desiring to expand their holdings beyond the 160 acres they could acquire by right of development, had the choice of buying additional tracts from railroads, states, or territories—or from the federal government if in areas where land had been proclaimed for sale in unlimited amounts. If the land was in unoffered areas, they might secure a preemption, or take a desert-land entry which would cost them $1.25 an acre, or enter a tree claim with its obligation of setting out trees on forty of the 160 acres. Actually, more government land was sold between 1862 and 1891 than was successfully homesteaded and patented between 1862 and 1899. Or, to put it differently, the government derived from the sale of public land in the sixty years following the adoption of the Homestead Act a far greater sum ($223,000,000) than it did in the first sixty years of its land administration ($186,000,000).

The land reformers had not succeeded, when writing the Homestead Act, in providing that all public lands henceforth should be reserved for actual settlers. Nor had they succeeded in restricting the quantity of land that might be purchased in offered areas. But they did prevail on the government not to offer newly surveyed land at unlimited sale except for timbered land in Michigan, Wisconsin, Minnesota, Colorado, Oregon, and Washington.[6] Henceforth, there were two classes of land in official terminology: offered land which was subject to private entry in unlimited amounts and unoffered lands which could only be acquired through settlement laws: homestead, preemption, timber culture, timber and stone, and their variations. Approximately two-thirds of Kansas, a larger fraction of Nebraska, all of Oklahoma and the Dakotas, and all of the public land farther west except for California and small areas in Colorado, New Mexico, and Washington were not offered. In these states, speculators could not use their cheaply acquired military bounty-land warrants, or their agricultural college scrip that cost them as little as fifty or sixty cents an acre, to build up huge holdings such as the 263,000 acres that the Brown-Ives-Goddard group of Providence, Rhode Island, established mostly in Illinois, Iowa, and Nebraska; the half million acres of pine lands in Wisconsin to which Ezra Cornell acquired the patent; or the huge 650,000 acres of land that William S. Chapman came to own in California.

Yet it is true that in the unoffered areas large estates were created, such as the bonanza farms of the Dakotas, and the equally large cattle ranches of Wyoming and elsewhere. Some of these holdings, like the bonanza farms, were bought partly from the railroads which placed few limitations on the size of tracts they would sell, and partly from the states. And partly they were acquired through the use of dummy entrymen who took advantage of the loopholes in the settler laws.[7] Others, including some of the large cattle ranches, were not ownerships but enclosures, illegally erected on the public lands which, when the order went out for the removal of the fences, became thereafter open to settlement. These large holdings, together with even larger acquisitions of the timber companies (elaborately documented in the report on forest ownership of the Bureau of Corporations of 1913),[8] and the discovery that millions of acres of land have passed into private hands by the fraudulent use of the settlement laws, have led historians to misunderstand and underestimate the role of the Homestead Law and related settlement measures. Recent textbook writers have declared that the Homestead Law was "not a satisfactory piece of legislation"; it was "a distressing disappointment"; "farmers only benefited slightly" from it; it ended "in failure and disillusionment"; two-thirds of all "homestead claimants before 1890 failed."[9]

A reason for the frequency of these misconceptions of homestead is the continued reiteration in the annual reports of the Commissioners of the General Land Office, of the widespread and indeed common violation of the spirit and even the letter of the law by land-hungry settlers, land lookers, petty and large speculators and their agents, and cattle and mining companies. Defective legislation, insufficient staff, poorly paid personnel in the Washington office, the low level of people filling the local land offices, and the practical impossibility of scrutinizing critically the entries made under the various land laws, all combined to make the Commissioners' task of administering the laws most frustrating.[10] Their comments on the amount of perjury, subornation, and misuse of the law became increasingly sharp until finally, the Commissioner under Cleveland, harassed by the degree of maladministration and the widespread dishonesty of people trying to take advantage of the government, took the drastic step of suspending many thousands of land entries moving toward patent to allow time for examination and the cancellation of fraudulent entries. This action led to swift political pressures by western politicians, forcing Cleveland to reverse his subordinate, no matter how just his action. So absorbed were the Commissioners in their efforts to make homestead function as it was intended to, that they devoted the space allowed them for recommendations for future action very largely to the frauds and malfunctionings of the system. Historians have reflected this jaundiced view, relying upon these continued reiterations, and not finding much in the reports about the hundreds of thousands of people successfully making farms for themselves.

I must confess that I may have contributed to this misunderstanding some twenty-six years ago when I wrote a paper. "The

Homestead Law in an Incongruous Land System." As the title suggests, the paper was intended to show that the principle of free lands to settlers clashed with the revenue principle on which the federal land system was based. My opening sentence might well do for introduction here, and I quote:

> The Homestead Act of 1862 is one of the most important laws which have been enacted in the history of this country, but its significance has been distorted and grossly misrepresented.[11]

The article was intended as a corrective for some of the ideas then prevalent concerning the measure, as, for example, the notion that most of Iowa passed into private hands through the Homestead Act; that homestead replaced other methods of land disposal; that cash sales in unlimited amounts ended in 1862; or that the revenue basis of the land system was abandoned.[12] Correction was necessary but, as is often the case, the revision was carried too far, until some writers seem ready to discount the Homestead Law as of little more than minor significance. Such judgment is unsound.

In any attempt to appraise the significance of the Homestead Law it should be borne in mind that settlers on unoffered land had more protection for their selections and improvements than they did on offered land. Since speculators could not enter or offer to buy their selections or improvements by falsely swearing at the land office that there were no claims against the land, the settler had less fear, once he had filed his original entry, of being dispossessed.

Having filed his original entry (even though he lacked the means with which to develop his claim), the homesteader had an equity that became increasingly valuable and negotiable as population increased the pressure upon the land supply. In the vanguard of settlement on every frontier were land speculators great and small who spied out choice tracts they wished to hold for the expected rise in value that incoming immigration would bring. The extensive speculator might assemble tracts running to tens of thousands of acres. But of equal importance, possibly, was the small man with no capital for the arduous task of farm making who nevertheless took up a piece of land to which he expected to acquire a preemption right. Frontier custom assured that his claim of one hundred to two hundred acres was his to do with as he wished. With patience and little labor he might improve slightly, sell, and then move to another tract and do the same thing. Government conceded only one preemption right, but that right was almost sacrosanct on the frontier and the same person might make a number of fortunate selections in succession and dispose of them profitably. Some contemporaries were not certain whether the first occupation of pioneers was farm making or land speculation. A settler on his homestead claim in central Kansas in 1878, noting how so many of his neighbors were attempting to engross and acquire title to far more land than they could utilize observed:

> The curse of this country is land-grabbing. Few men are satisfied with one claim; they must have a pre-emption, homestead and timber filing, and between the three they have so much work they don't know which end they stand on.[13]

In addition to the three usual claims it was not unknown for different members of a family to file on adjacent tracts, even though they were violating the spirit if not the letter of the law.

Having established a number of claims which they might be doing little or nothing to develop, settlers had the choice of selling relinquishments to others, borrowing to commute and then skipping the country, attempting to make their improvements with loans until they could get the benefit of rising land values, or holding for long range development. The location, sale, and relinquishment of claims became a major business on the frontier as it proceeded into western Kansas, Nebraska and Dakota.[14] Relinquishments in the middle Eighties sold for $25 to $50 in Kansas, for $50 to $400 in South Dakota and for as little as $5 and a shotgun to $700 in North Dakota.[15] Variations in price partly depended upon the nature of improvements. Undoubtedly, the business of selling relinquishments was carried beyond all justification but it should be emphasized that it permitted persons who lacked the means with which to begin farming to acquire some cash, farm machinery, and stock and

FEDERAL LAND POLICY IN THE SOUTH, 1866-1888

Paul Wallace Gates

after two or three false starts and sale of relinquishments to succeed finally in establishing ownership of a going farm. The process of claim making with the intention of selling was greatly
abused, particularly in the Eighties, but despite that abuse it
provided opportunities for many settlers to reach their goal of
farm ownership.

Land office reports, accounts of the cattle and lumber industry, and other government documents are replete with stories of
the use of dummy entrymen by individuals and companies eager
to get control of large areas of the public lands. The process was
fairly simple. Employees of the cattle, mining, or lumber companies would be induced to file claims under one of the settlement laws, possibly make some slight improvements on their
claims, take title by commuting their claims and swear before
the land officials that their claims were intended for their own
use and that they had entered into no agreement to transfer ownership. Funds for their commutation and a fee for their services
that ranged from $50 to $200 were provided by the company.[16]
As competition for land intensified, compensation to dummy
entrymen reached as high as $1,000 for a quarter section.[17]

A third source of income that the weakly administered public
land system made possible to westerners was the practice of mort-
gaging newly entered land with insurance companies at well
beyond its going value and then skipping out with the proceeds
of the loan and unloading the property on the credit agency. The
West had not always been blessed with abundance of capital but
in the Eighties, attracted by high interest rates, money flowed
into the Great Plains in such quantities that agents of eastern
insurance companies and petty capitalists vied with each other
in pushing their loans on settlers, offering some well beyond the
cash value of the land at the time. So marked was this rivalry
that agents, eager for their fees, paid little attention to the quality
of improvements on the land and only insisted on a mortgageable
title. It was reported from northwestern Nebraska in 1886 that it
was easy to get an $800 loan on any quarter section of wild land
on which a settlement right had been established.[18] In central
North Dakota, in 1903, loans to permit commutation of homesteads were being made as high as $1,500.[19] Settlers who had put

little effort into their claims could commute their timber claim (before 1891) or homestead, at a cost of $200 for 160 acres, pay all fees and still have left from $600 to $1,300 for a second try under one of the other settlement laws, the privilege of which they had not yet used.

Many western settlers had larceny in their hearts when it came to dealing with the government, and it did not stretch their consciences unduly to take advantage of the insurance companies or other absentee sources of capital. As one insurance adjuster later said, "it became really too easy for settlers to cash in on their western venture and 'go back to their wives' folks.' They borrowed more than the land was worth and fled."[20] An agent for a Kansas bank said of the borrowers in western Kansas: "As soon as their loans are completed they abandon the land, if they can sell it to someone for a nominal sum above the mortgage they do so."[21]

Whether the early settler was defrauding the government, cheating the insurance company, or making the later immigrant buy a relinquishment from him, he was accumulating the means with which he could finally establish himself as a stable farm maker. This is not to say that all persons establishing claims on the public lands were ultimately to become farmers; many had no such intention. They were out for a speculation. But a very considerable portion of the misuse of the public land laws resulted, it appears, from the credit needs of actual settlers.

A common error in appraising the Homestead Law has been the assumption that homesteading was only important in the Great Plains and Interior Basin where the unit of farming characteristic of the more humid regions was not suitable. The fact is that 23 per cent (689,000) of all original homestead entries were filed in the states east of the Mississippi and in the first tier west of that river. Twenty-four per cent of the homestead entries that went to final patent were located in this region. During the first ten years of the operation of the Homestead Law, Minnesota outranked all states in number of final entries of homesteads and was exceeded only by Kansas in the number of original entries. Altogether, 82,845 free homesteads were patented in Minnesota.[22] This constitutes 66 per cent of the farms of Minnesota of 100 acres or more as listed in the census of 1920. It probably would not be far from the truth to say that the abstracts of two-thirds of Minnesota farms trace back to the patent of the homesteader. East of the Mississippi, 143,360 homestead entries for 15,990,533 acres were carried to patent, mostly in Alabama, Florida, Wisconsin, Mississippi, and Michigan.

In all the states around the Great Lakes, in the South, and in the first tier west of the Mississippi, a considerably higher proportion of the original filings were carried to final entry than elsewhere and there were fewer commutations.

In substantial portions of the second tier of states beyond the Mississippi (extending from Dakota to Oklahoma), the 160-acre unit of farming was not altogether unsuited for farm practices in the late Nineteenth Century. The line of 20-inch rainfall begins roughly just west of the Red River of the North and extends in a gentle southwestward direction. East of that line is perhaps a fifth of North Dakota, a third of South Dakota, more than half of Nebraska, and two-thirds of Kansas. The line of 24-inch rainfall leaves, to the east, a small corner of South Dakota, a fifth of Nebraska, and half of Kansas. To and somewhat beyond the 24-inch rainfall line, corn flourished and the 160-acre unit of agriculture seemed reasonably well adapted to farming. I have conservatively estimated that 150,000 homestead applications were filed in the more humid portions of the Great Plains. This means that, together with the 689,000 entries previously mentioned, 839,000 homesteads or 28 per cent of the total number of homesteads were commenced in areas generally suitable in the Nineteenth Century for 160-acre farm units.

Furthermore, it is important to note that of these early homesteads established from Kansas north to Dakota territory before 1881, 58 per cent of those in Kansas were successfully carried to final entry, 61 per cent in Nebraska and 52 per cent in Dakota. Sixty-seven per cent of the entries in Dakota made before 1876 were patented by 1880. This is perhaps the best test of the applicability of homestead to these areas. For the country as a whole, slightly less than 50 per cent of the original homesteads were carried to patent.[23]

Doubtless there are other and perhaps smaller areas in the

West where the 160-acre homestead unit seemed to work well at the time. One example is in California where 63 per cent of the original entries made in the years from 1863 to 1875 were carried to completion.

A second error frequently observed in appraisals of the Homestead Act is forgetting that it took five years, later reduced to three (veterans' military service could be counted), for the original entries to mature.[24] Actually, even more than five years was required for many homesteaders who were driven out by drought, grasshoppers, or other misfortunes, and who had to be allowed extensions of time in which to prove up.

In the land selection process many choices were made by settlers and speculators who were misled by the descriptions on the surveyors' plats; by the land lookers who for fees guided settlers to what soon proved to be questionable locations; and by settlers themselves who may have had little knowledge of the quality of land in the vicinity of the 100th meridian. Some settlers, like those who participated in the great rushes into Oklahoma or who desperately tried to get a claim on the Rosebud Reservation in South Dakota, had no time to pick and choose but had perforce to take the first vacant land they could find. Inevitably, mistakes were made. Study of the correspondence of the General Land Office and of western congressmen illustrates the frequency with which errors of location were made from the very outset of the public land system, and the disappointments and frustrations of the land locators who sought the privilege of making exchanges. In the absence of land classification, settlers made many errors that resulted in a high rate of failure on homesteads.

Nebraska well illustrates this tendency to err in the selection of land. When homestead was adopted, or shortly thereafter, the grants to the state for educational purposes, and to railroads for aid to construction had reduced the public domain to less than 37 million acres. Of this amount speculators quickly grabbed up an additional million acres. Yet the records show that settlers filed on nearly 51 million acres either for homesteads or timber-culture claims. Some of these filings led to contests between homesteaders and the railroads or between different homesteaders; other filings proved to be unattractive and were abandoned or relinquished, and perhaps the rights transferred to others. For Nebraska, 51 per cent of the homestead entries and 46 per cent of the combined homestead and timber-culture entries were carried to patent as free land. If commuted entries are included, the percentages reaching patent becomes 58 and 53. Those that did not reach patent were either relinquished for a fee to others or simply abandoned for better selections elsewhere. What is important is that ownership of 74 per cent of the land available for homesteading in Nebraska was actually achieved either through the Homestead Act or the Timber Culture Act, with their privilege of commutation. Or, we may go one step farther and say that at least 80 per cent of the land area of Nebraska available for settler location became owned by homesteaders through settler-oriented laws, though some of this ownership was quite unstable and was not acquired by the first owner for farming.

In Kansas, where little more than 24 million acres were available for homesteading when the act was passed, settlers filed for homesteads and timber-culture claims for more than 35 million acres. The business in relinquishments was large in Kansas as in Nebraska: an estimated 93,000 homestead claims were either relinquished or abandoned. Of the land available for homesteading 50 per cent was carried to patent as free land, 14 per cent was patented as commuted homesteads and 8 per cent was patented to timber-culture claimants.

Since 1607, settlers had been moving westward adapting themselves to different ecological conditions from those to which they were accustomed. The oak openings of Michigan and the rich bluegrass region of Kentucky were as strange to settlers from New York and Virginia as were the prairies of Illinois and Iowa and the Great Plains of Kansas and Nebraska. Adaptation to environment wrought swift changes in methods of farming; those who could not adapt failed. American settlers on whatever frontier were prepared to make these changes and soon did. They did not realize, so general was this process of adaptation, how different their methods—and indeed their whole way of life—had become from those they had followed previously.

Not long after the hungry land seekers crossed the Missouri they came into contact with a region where rainfall was less than they had been accustomed to and the variations greater from year to year; where drought, winter blizzards, and grasshopper plagues were met, and where more extensive farm practices were essential. These conditions made larger farm units necessary. It is interesting to note how the average size of farms in Kansas increased with a certain regularity from east to west as is shown by the census of 1920: 153 acres was the average in Miami County on the eastern Kansas front, 167 in Osage County, 192 in Lyons County, 244 in Morris County, 354 in Ellsworth County, 590 in Ness County, and 900 acres on the western border in Greeley County.[25]

Historians have been troubled that the homestead unit was fixed at 160 acres just when, as they say, settlers were preparing to break into the less humid region of the Great Plains where larger farm units were desirable. Paradoxically, they have also been troubled that the Preemption Law which, with homestead, made possible larger farm units, was kept on the statute books.[26] Following the judgment of the Commissioners of the General Land Office who harped on the amount of fraud involved in preemption, they have given undue emphasis to this aspect and insufficient attention to the fact that preemption was consciously retained by Congress surely because of the greater flexibility it allowed settlers in adapting themselves to farming in the dryer portions of America where land was not offered.[27] There is no mention of repeal of preemption in the discussion leading to the adoption of homestead in 1862 and the Law itself carefully provided for saving all preemption rights that may have been established prior to its adoption. Furthermore, just a few days after the adoption of the Homestead Law, Congress, without a word of opposition in either house, enacted a bill that said all lands to which Indian title had been or should thereafter be extinguished should be subject to preemption. We must conclude that Congress had no intention of establishing an inflexible 160-acre unit for settlers in the unoffered areas.[28]

In 1872 and 1873 the two houses of Congress finally came to agreement on a bill to encourage the planting of trees on the

Great Plains. An additional quarter section was thereby offered to settlers who would plant and care for forty acres of trees (later reduced to ten acres) for a period of ten years. An effort to limit its benefits to settlers who had not taken up a preemption or homestead, failed. Timber culture was designed further to adapt the post-1862 land system to farming in sub-humid America. The law was not carefully drafted and as with all other land legislation it quickly became subject to abuse and was repealed in 1891. But it had in the meantime, notwithstanding its abuse, served its purpose. With preemption and homestead it provided a flexibility that after its repeal was to be assured by the more direct method of enlarging the homestead unit to 320 and then 640 acres.

How significant was the Homestead Law in enabling settlers to acquire land and to establish themselves on going farms? It is clear that it was most successful in the period from 1863 to 1880 when the greater proportion of homesteads were being established in the states bordering on the Mississippi River. It was successful also in parts of Kansas and Nebraska well east of the 98th meridian where there was abundance of rain, and where commutations, relinquishments, and abandonments were fewer than they were to be in other areas later. In these eighteen years, homesteaders filed on 469,000 tracts and by 1885 had made their final entries and were in process of getting title on 55 per cent. Doubtless some would complete their residence requirements in later years.

The misuse of the Homestead Law was becoming common between 1880 and 1900. As shown, misuse was by persons not primarily interested in farm making but concerned to sell relinquishments to immigrants or to transfer rights to cattle, timber, and mining companies. But the most glaring abuses occurred later. Between 1880 and 1900, approximately half of the homestead entries were filed in the six states and territories extending from Oklahoma to North Dakota and including Minnesota. These all were major farm states and the Homestead Law was contributing largely to the development of farm ownership, notwithstanding its abuses.

In these states and territories, free government land, advertised by the America letters which earlier immigrants had sent back to their families in the Old World, by the government immigration bureaus, by even the colonization departments of the railroads and land companies, provided the lodestone, the directing force, that set in motion continued waves of settlers in search of free land. It was the prospect of disposing of their lands to these settlers and transporting their goods that made possible the financing and construction of the railroads through the Plains, into the Interior Basin and to the Pacific Coast. Homestead, above all other factors, made possible the fast growth of the West and all the problems this rapid growth brought with it.

Altogether, 1,413,513 original homestead entries were filed between 1863 and 1900, but even more were to be filed in the twentieth century for a substantially larger acreage. The great day of farm making with the material aid of Uncle Sam was over, however. True, some twentieth century entries were made with the enlarged units for small stock raising farms or ranches or even wheat farms but the evidence seems strong that the great bulk of the entries filed after 1900 were for large ranching, mining, and lumbering companies. The numbers of original and final homestead entries, when compared with the number of farms in the Rocky Mountain States, provides startling evidence that the homesteads were being assimilated into larger aggregations of land. Using round figures, we find that Idaho had 92,000 original homestead entries, 60,000 final entries and in 1910–1930 its highest number of farms was 42,000. Colorado had 205,000 original, 107,000 final entries, and at its most 59,000 farms. Arizona had 38,000 original, 20,000 final entries, and 9,000 farms. Wyoming had 115,000 original, 67,000 final entries, and 15,000 farms. In six mountain states the original entries came to 848,000, final entries 492,000, and the maximum number of farms 217,000. Thus it seemed to take about four original entries and two final homestead entries to produce a farm, and most of these homesteads were of the enlarged variety.

Major John W. Powell's recommendation of 1879 that the public lands be classified for use and that a 2,560-acre pasturage homestead be established for lands fit only for grazing was somewhat premature, but certainly by 1900, land classification and larger homestead units were essential.[29] Yet the evidence is strong that the enlarged units of 1904, 1909, and 1916 were not altogether wise or successful. The old evils of careless drafting of land legislation, weak and inefficient administrations (inadequately staffed), and the anxiety of interests to take advantage of loopholes in the laws, all brought the Homestead Acts into contempt and censure. But their noble purpose and the great part they played in enabling nearly a million and a half people to acquire farm land, much of which developed into farm homes, far outweigh the misuse to which they were put.

NOTES

1. The western point of view concerning the public lands and homestead was perhaps best expressed over and over again in the 1850's by Horace Greeley in the *New York Tribune* when he was vigorously campaigning for the adoption of a homestead law and for drastic curbs on speculative purchasing of public lands. Theodore Roosevelt, no radical as almost everyone would agree, accepted, with his keen understanding of western problems, the traditional western view concerning land values in his *Winning of the West* (4 volumes, New York, 1889–1896), III, 252–253.

2. Reference should be made to the standard works on public land policy for the period to 1860: George M. Stephenson, *Political History of the Public Lands from 1840–1862* (Boston, 1917); Benjamin F. Hibbard, *History of the Public Land Policies* (New York, 1924); Roy M. Robbins, *Our Landed Heritage. The Public Domain, 1776–1936* (Princeton, 1924); Paul W. Gates, *The Farmers' Age* (New York, 1961).

3. The following statistics of acreage of land and numbers of entries are compiled from the *Annual Reports* of the Commissioner of the General Land Office. Compilations that sometimes differ from data continued in these reports are Thomas Donaldson, *The Public Domain. House Miscellaneous Documents*, 47 Cong., 2 Sess., No. 45, Part 4, 1884, and *Report of the Public Land Commission, Senate Documents*, 58 Cong., 3 Sess., No. 189, 1905.

4. Herbert S. Schell, *History of South Dakota* (Lincoln, 1961), p. 222.

5. Paul W. Gates, *Fifty Million Acres: Conflicts Over Kansas Land Policy, 1854–1890* (Ithaca, N.Y., 1954), pp. 237ff. Also the same author's "The Homestead Law in an Incongruous Land System," *American Historical Review*, XLI (July, 1936), 652 ff.

6. Between 1866 and 1876 the public lands of Alabama, Arkansas, Florida, Louisiana, and Mississippi were open only to homesteaders but in the latter year they were restored to unlimited entry and the best of them were quickly

44 THE HISTORICAL BACKGROUND

bought up by lumbermen from the North. Paul W. Gates, "Federal Land Policy in the South, 1866–1888," *Journal of Southern History, VI* (Aug., 1940), 303 ff. Elsewhere, lands that had once been offered for unrestricted sale and later withdrawn to permit railroads to select their alternate sections as granted by the United States were restored to the offered and unrestricted status when the selections had been made.

7. Harold E. Briggs, "Early Bonanza Farming in the Red River Valley of the North," *Agricultural History, VI* (Jan., 1932), 20 ff.

8. Bureau of Corporations, Department of Commerce and Labor, *The Lumber Industry,* 3 Parts, 1913–1914 (Washington, 1913–1914), especially Part 1, Chap. VI, "Public-Land Policy a Primary Cause of the Concentration of Timber Ownership," pp. 218 ff.

9. T. Harry Williams, Richard N. Current and Frank Freidel, *History of the United States* (2 Vols., New York, 1959), II, 142; Thomas D. Clark, *Frontier America* (New York, 1959), p. 727; Ray A. Billington, *Westward Expansion. A History of the American Frontier* (New York, 1949), pp. 696 ff.; Dumas Malone and Basil Rauch, *Empire for Liberty, The Genesis and Growth of the United States of America* (2 Vols., New York, 1960), II, 43. Actually 58 per cent of those who homesteaded through 1890 succeeded in gaining title to their land either through final entry or through commutation. James C. Olson, *History of Nebraska,* (Lincoln, 1955), p. 166, contemplating the slow alienation of public lands in Nebraska by the homestead route before 1900, asks why did the Homestead Act "fall so short of expectations." Much of western Nebraska was still in public ownership and largely unused save for grazing in 1900 but this was nature's fault, not the fault of the act. In 1900 there were 121,525 farms in Nebraska. It may not be unfair to say that 68,862 of these had been partly or wholly acquired through homesteading for that is the number of homesteads that had gone to patent at that time. In addition, 5,004 homesteaders were to reach the final entry stage in the next five years and should be included in the number of homesteads which were probably a part of the farms of the time.

10. Harold H. Dunham discusses the inadequacies and weaknesses of the personnel of the General Land Office in *Government Handout: A Study in the Administration of the Public Lands, 1875–1891* (New York, 1941), pp. 124 ff.

11. *American Historical Review,* XLI (July, 1936), 652.

12. Edgar Harlan, director of the Iowa Historical, Memorial, and Art Department assured the writer in 1936 that most of the land of his state was homesteaded and was greatly surprised when he was shown that only 4 per cent went to patent. Congressman Harvey B. Ferguson stated in 1914: "It was great statesmanship that created the homestead laws under which such a State as Iowa developed." *Grazing Homesteads and the Regulation of Grazing on the Public Lands,* Hearings before the Committee on the Public Lands, House of Representatives, 63 Cong., 2 Sess., 1914, Part 1, p. 358. See also Leifur Magnuson, *Disposition of the Public Lands of the United States With Particular Reference to Wage-Earning Labor* (Washington, 1919), p. 29; Theodore L. Nydahl, *Social and Economic Aspects of Pioneers in Goodhue*

County, Minnesota, Norwegian-American Historical Association, *Studies and Records,* V (Northfield, Minn., 1930), 53.

13. John Ise, ed., *Sod-House Days. Letters from a Kansas Homesteader, 1877–1878* (New York, 1937), p. 212; Francis J. Rowbotham, *A Trip to Prairie-Land* (London, 1885), p. 240.

14. On the basis of careful research in newspapers and in correspondence of the land offices in Kansas, George W. Anderson emphasizes the institutional character of the location of claims by land lookers and the purchase and sale of relinquishments in "The Administration of Federal Land Laws in Western Kansas: A Factor in Adjustment to a New Environment," *Kansas Historical Quarterly,* XX (Nov., 1952), 233 ff. Newspaper proprietors, he found, were deeply involved in this business.

15. Anderson, *ibid,* p. 240; Herbert S. Schell, *History of South Dakota,* p. 173; *North Dakota Historical Collections,* II (1908), 169, 202, 237; and III (1910), 167; *North Dakota History,* XVIII (October, 1951), 242.

16. For the prevalence of the $200 fee see General Land Office, *Report,* 1886, p. 83. Charles Lowell Green has summarized some of the evidence of frauds in the administration of the public land laws in South Dakota in "The Administration of the Public Domain in South Dakota," *South Dakota Historical Collections,* XX (1940), 199 ff.

17. *Report of the Public Lands Commission, Senate Documents,* 58 Cong., 3 Sess., 1904, p. 121. This sum was paid for the services of eight dummy entrymen and women in southern Pierce County, by the Prowly & Church Cattle Co.

18. The Aetna Life Insurance Company, which had an average of $8,677,000 invested in western farm mortgages from Ohio to Texas between 1867 and 1890, was forced to take over 812 properties having a book value of $1,877,000. The number of foreclosures was doubtless greater in Kansas, Nebraska, and Dakota than in the region farther east. The figures were kindly provided by Robert H. Pierce, formerly of the Aetna Company. Allan G. Bogue in his *Money at Interest: The Farm Mortgage on the Middle Border* (Ithaca, N.Y., 1955), p. 193, shows that J. B. Watkins of Lawrence, Kansas, and his mortgage company took over 2,500 farms between 1873 and 1893, or between 10 and 20 per cent of the total number of farms on which they made loans.

19. Beatrice *Gage County Democrat,* June. 25, 1886; *Report of the Public Lands Commission, Senate Documents,* 58 Cong., 3 Sess., 1904, No. 189, p. 122.

20. Seth K. Humphrey, *Following the Prairie Frontier,* p. 95; General Land Office, *Report,* 1885, p. 54. Humphrey was a claim agent who tried to chase down some of the defaulting mortgagors. His disillusionment with absconding debtors led him to write: "By far the greater number of landseekers took up government land with the intention of unloading it on somebody else...." *op. cit.,* p. 132.

21. Quoted in Allan G. Bogue, *op. cit.,* p. 146.

22. Since much of Minnesota land had been offered and was therefore subject to purchase in unlimited amounts there was less resort to the use

of dummy entrymen in this state than in areas farther west. The Mesabi Range, partly, and much of the timber land, was open to cash purchase and well over a million acres of potentially valuable land were acquired through outright purchase in large blocks by capitalists.

23. I have omitted Oklahoma from consideration because its lands came into settlement so much later.

24. Cf. Roy M. Robbins, *Our Landed Heritage, The Public Domain, 1776–1936*, p. 240; Fred A. Shannon, *The Farmers' Last Frontier* (New York, 1945), p. 54.

25. *Fourteenth Census of the United States*, 1920, Vol. VI, *Agriculture*, 732–41.

26. Cf. Hibbard, *History of the Public Land Policies*, p. 409; Robbins, *Our National Heritage*, pp. 238, 285–86.

27. In 1870, Joseph Wilson, Commissioner of the General Land Office, recommended that persons be allowed to enter only one tract of 160 acres under either the preemption or the homestead laws. His successor, Willis Drummond, urged the repeal of the preemption law in 1871–1873. In 1877, Commissioner J. A. Williamson, and in 1882, Commissioner N. C. McFarland, resumed the attack upon the preemption law with recommendations that it be repealed. Thereafter, until 1891 when the act was repealed, the successive commissioners laid down an increasing barrage against its continuation on the ground that it enabled persons having no intention of developing the land to acquire ownership.

28. *Congressional Globe*, 37 Cong., 2 Sess., April 17, 1862, p. 1711; May 29, 1862, pp. 2432, 2439.

29. The recommendation for the 2,560-acre homestead on "pasturage" lands is made in the Preliminary Report of the Public Lands Commission, *House Ex. Doc.*, 46 Cong., 2 Sess., 1880, Vol. 22, p. lxxvi.

THE HOMESTEAD IN PERSPECTIVE

Mari Sandoz

MARI SANDOZ

The Homestead in Perspective

THE HOMESTEAD ACT was the hope of the poor man. Many who had wanted a piece of government land felt that preempting, which required an eventual cash payment of $1.25 or more an acre, was too risky for the penniless. If the preemptor failed to raise the money at the proper time, in addition to building a home in the wilderness and making a living for a family, he lost the land and with it all his improvements, his work, and his home. The Homestead Act offered any bona fide land seeker 160 acres from the public domain with no cash outlay beyond the $14 filing fee and the improvements he would have to make to live on the place the required five years. His house, barn, sheds and corrals, his well, the tilled acreage and the fencing, all counted toward the final patent to the land, and most of these improvements could be made by the homesteader's own hands, his and the family's.

It was this offer of free land that drew my father, Old Jules Sandoz, west to a homestead in the unorganized region that was to become Sheridan County, Nebraska, and he stressed "free land" in all the letters he wrote to the European and American newspapers for the working man, letters that drew the hundreds of settlers he located.

The home seeker, as late as the end of the Kinkaid Homestead days of my childhood, came by every possible means, even afoot. I was born too late to see the Czechoslovakian couple who crossed much of Nebraska pushing a wheelbarrow loaded with all their belongings, including, it was said, the wedding feather tick. But we saw many land seekers walk in, some coming much farther than the seventeen miles from the railroad. There were dusty men, worn and discouraged until they got a good wash-up at the Niobrara River near our house or at our well, followed by one of mother's hearty suppers and a big dose of Old Jules' enthusiasm and faith in the country. Some came by livery rig or the mail wagon, or were picked up by a settler returning home from town. Many of the more serious land seekers left their families back east until they were located. Often these drove in by wagon in the old way although the wire fences of settlers, and, in the free-land regions, the cattlemen, prevented the accustomed movement up along the streams, as Old Jules himself had come, following the Niobrara to Mirage Flats.

We children had the usual curiosity about outsiders but we were even more thoroughly disciplined than most homesteader children, who were taught to keep out of the way and never push into grown-up affairs. But we tried to hear the answer to Old Jules usual western query: "What name you traveling under?"

This question from a rough, bearded man with a strong foreign accent and a gun on his arm was not reassuring to strangers. But perhaps a potential settler should realize from the start that homesteading was not for the timid, and as soon as a man could say "I'm looking for me a piece of government land——" he was among friends. He and any family he had were welcome to eat at our table and sleep in our beds even if we children were moved to the floor. This was naturally all free beyond the twenty-five dollar locating and surveying fee Old Jules charged whenever the settler managed to get the money. Often the family stayed with us until their house was up, the wife perhaps criticizing father's profane and bawdy tongue and complaining contemptuously about mother's bread from unbleached macaroni wheat that we grew and hauled to the water mill on Pine Creek.

For us children the important home seekers were the boomers, the covered wagon families. Evenings we watched them come down into the Niobrara valley, rumble over the plank bridge, and climb the steep sandy pitch to the bench on which our house stood. There, on a flat camping-ground, the panting horses were allowed to stop, and barefoot children spilled out of the wagon, front and back, to run, galloping and bucking like calves let out of a pen. We stared from among the cherry trees, or in the summer, from the asparagus patch where the greenery stood over our heads. We saw the tugs dropped, the harness stripped off and piled against the wagon tongue, while the woman ordered the children to this and that task as the fire began to smoke in the little pile of stones always there for campers.

Finally the man might come to draw a bucket of the clear water from our well, water so cold it hurt the teeth on hot days.

By the time we were old enough to notice, father had no trouble waiting until after supper to talk land to such men.

"Boomers!" he would say, in contempt. "Probably been to Oregon and back, living off the country, picking up anything that's loose. Hey, Mari, go hide all the hammers and bring in my rifle——" meaning the 30-30 that usually hung on the antlers outside the door.

"And shut up the chickens——" mother would add.

Old Jules was usually right about the boomers of the 1906–12 period. The man would come in to talk land but even if he showed any enthusiasm for homesteading, the family might be pulling out at dawn, seldom with anything of consequence that belonged to us. That stack of guns in a corner of our kitchen-living room, and father's evident facility with firearms, discouraged more than petty thefts of, say, a pair of pliers or a slab of bacon from the smokehouse.

"Sneaky thieves!" mother would snort. "If they were so hungry I would have given them more than that, so long as we could spare it."

A few stayed to follow father's buckskin team into the sandhills, to live in the covered wagon until a dugout or a soddy could be prepared on the new homestead. Some of these left when the drouth and hot winds of August struck, along with others who had walked in or came by hired rig. The winters seemed particularly hard to the latter-day boomers, and often the first fall blizzard sent them rolling toward Texas or Arkansas. Some stuck it out. Several of these Kinkaid-day boomers are growing fine blooded stock in Nebraska, the older members spending the winters in Florida or California and damning the government.

We tend to forget that the homesteaders were not a type, not as alike as biscuits cut out with a baking-powder can. They varied as much as their origins and their reasons for coming west. There were Daughters and Sons of the Revolution located next to the communal communities of the Mennonites, say, or the Hutterians. An illiterate from some other frontier might be neighboring with a Greek and Hebrew scholar from a colony of Russian Jews in the Dakotas. A nervous-fingered murderer who fled west under a new name might join fences with a nonviolent River Baptist or a vegetarian who wouldn't kill a rabbit eating up his first sprouts of lettuce, no matter how hungry the settler might be.

Yet there was apparently a certain repetition of characters in the homestead communities. Those who thought that Old Jules Sandoz was incredible or at least unique should go through the many thousands of letters I received from homesteaders and descendants of homesteaders. Apparently, men with some Old Julesian traits lived in every pioneer community—even as far away as Australia and New Zealand—men with the vision of the community builder, the stubbornness to stick against every defeat, the grim ruthlessness required to hold both themselves and their neighbors to the unwelcoming virgin land.

There was considerable difference between the homesteaders who came into western Nebraska in the 1884–90 period and the Kinkaiders of 1906–12, that is, after the cattleman fences were removed from the government land. The homesteaders of the earlier period were generally young, many under the required twenty-one years, but with a family or a flexible conscience. In the height of the Kinkaid Homestead days many were in their forties and some much older—usually office workers or teachers and so on—retired people or those who had lost their jobs in the retrenchment of 1906–08. There were many women among these, not only among the fraudulent entries by the cattlemen (often only names of old-soldier widows) but among the bona fide homesteaders. These women were classified roughly into two groups by the other settlers. Those with genteel ways, graying hair, downy faces and perhaps good books to loan to a settler's reading-hungry daughter, were called Boston school teachers, no matter who or where from. The others, called Chicago widows, weren't young either, or pretty, but their talk, their dress, and their ways were gayer, more colorful, more careless; their books, if any, were paperback novels, with such titles as *Wife in Name Only*, or *Up from the Depths*. Several had a volume of nonfiction called *From Ballroom to Hell*, with every step of the way well illustrated and described. Among the tips offered was a solution for a recurring problem: To fill out your corset cover, roll up two stockings and pin into place, but be sure the stockings are clean, to avoid an offending odor.

It is true that in the largely male population of our homestead regions more of the Chicago widows got married than the Boston school ma'am type.

There was a saying among the settlers that the first spring of a new homesteader told whether the man or the woman was the boss. If the house was put up first, plainly the woman ran things; if a corn patch was broken out before any building, the cowboys told each other that this homesteader would be hard to drive off. But there were other factors to be considered. An April settler was wise to throw up a claim shack of some kind and leave the sod breaking for May, after the grass was started well enough so it would be killed by the plowing. Nor were the women, bossy or not, always easy to drive out. Some clung to the homestead even after their husbands were shot down by ranch hirelings. Nebraska's State Senator Cole grew up in the sandhills because his mother stayed with her two young sons after their father was shot off his mower.

Old Jules' first claim dwelling was half dugout, half sod, but the home of his family was a frame house in which the water froze in the teakettle in January. We envied our neighbors with good sod houses, the deep window seats full of Christmas cactus, century plants, and geraniums blooming all winter, the fine shadowiness of the interior cool and grateful in the summer, while our house was hot as an iron bucket in the sun. Old Jules permitted no cooling blinds or curtains at the windows. He wanted to see anyone coming up. Evenings he always sat back out of line of the lighted windows.

Although I never lived in a sod house I went to school in one and taught school in two others, both pretty decrepit at the time, with mouse holes in the walls; one with a friendly bullsnake living there. Sometimes the snake was fooled by the glowing stove on a chilly fall day and came wandering out and down the aisle during school hours. A snickering among the boys always warned me, and the snake too. Licking out his black forked tongue speculatively, the autumn-logy snake turned slowly around and moved back to his hole in the wall.

The three immediate needs of the new settler were shelter, food, and water. Of the three, only the food that he must grow had a tyrannical season. As locater Old Jules never showed a home seeker a place without a piece of corn land. At a potential site he would push his hat back, estimate the arable acreage, and sink his spade into an average spot. Turning up a long sod, he examined the depth and the darkness of the top soil and shook out the rooting of the grass. If he was satisfied, he looked around at the weeds, not just on spots enriched by some animal carcass long ago, but in general. Where sunflowers grew strong and tall, corn would do well.

But even the best of sod had to be turned and planted at the proper time. With two fairly good draft horses, preferably three or four against the tough rooting, and a sod plow, the settler could break the prairie himself. Or he could hire it done, usually by exchange of work with some of his neighbors. I like to remember the look on the faces of some of these new homesteaders as they tilled the first bit of earth they ever owned. Like any toddler, when I was two, three years old I couldn't be kept from following in the furrow of any plowing done near the house. Later it seemed to me there was something like a spiritual excitement about a man guiding a breaker bottom through virgin earth, with the snap and crackle of the tough roots as they were cut, the sod rolling smooth and flat from the plow, a gull or two following for the worms, and blackbirds chattering around.

Sometimes corn, beans, or potatoes were dropped in the furrow behind the sod plow and covered by the next round but more often the corn was planted later by a man, a woman, or an energetic boy or girl. With an apron or a bag tied on for the seed, and a spade in the hand, the planter started. At every full man's step or two steps for the shorter-legged, the spade was thrust down into the sod, worked sideways to widen the slit, two kernels of corn dropped in, the spade swung out and the foot brought down on the cut to seal it. All day, up and down the sod ribbons, the rhythmic swing of step and thrust was maintained. To be sure, the spade arm was mighty work-sore the next morning, but every homesteader's child learned that the remedy for that was more work.

Millions of acres were planted this way, sometimes with beans and pumpkin seeds mixed with the corn for a stretch. Good breaking grew few weeds except a scattering of big sunflowers, so the sod field was little care. With the luck of an early August rain, turnip and rutabaga seed could be broadcast between a stretch of rows for the winter root pit. Up in South Dakota, some homesteaders tried flax instead of corn, the seed harrowed into the sod just before a rain, and were rewarded by an expanse as blue as fallen sky in blooming time.

The second spring the sod was backset, and ready for small grain, perhaps oats or rye but more often the newer varieties of wheat broadcast on the fresh plowing from a bag slung under one arm, much like the figure of the Sower on the Nebraska capitol. The seed was covered by a harrow or drag. If there was no harrow, a heavily branched tree, a hackberry, perhaps, would be dragged over the ground by the old mares or patient oxen. Mechanical seeders drawn by fast-paced horses or mules helped spread bonanza wheat farming from the Red River down to Oklahoma and deep into Montana and Alberta. But the new homesteader still broadcast his small grain by hand.

The settler too late for the land along the streams was in urgent need of water from the day of his arrival. True, there might be buffalo wallows and other ponds filled by the spring rains for the stock a while, but many settlers hauled at least the household water ten, twelve miles, and farther, until a well could be put down, or had to be, to quiet the womenfolks. Where the water table was not too deep the first well was usually dug— cheap but dangerous for the novice. Every community had its accidents and tragedies. Uncurbed wells caved in on the digger.

People, adults and children, fell into the uncovered holes and were perhaps rescued by a desperate effort of everyone within fifty miles around, or were left buried there, with a flower or a tree planted to mark the grave.

The well in our home yard was the usual dug one, curbed to the bottom, with a windlass and a bucket that had been a black powder can, larger than the usual pail, the fifty-pound powder size, I think, and came painted a water-proof blue outside. All of us were very careful around wells, perhaps because we had a constant example before us. Old Jules was crippled his first summer on his claim on Mirage Flats. He had finished his new well and was being drawn up by his helpers. As he neared the top the two practical jokers yanked the rope to scare him. The rope, frayed by all the strain of lifting the soil from the sixty-five foot hole, broke. The digger was dropped to the bottom and crippled for the rest of his life. Only the extraordinary luck of getting to Dr. Walter Reed, of later yellow-fever fame, at the frontier post, Fort Robinson, kept him alive at all.

Our well on the river had a solid ladder inside the casing, the kind of ladder that could have saved Old Jules all those crippled years if he had nailed one into the curbing of his first well and climbed out instead of standing in the dirt bucket to be drawn up. Whenever a foolish hen jumped up on the water bench of our well and let the wind blow her in, it was Old Jules who clambered ponderously down the deep hole after her. Practically any other emergency, except something like sewing up a badly cut leg, he let his wife or his children handle—ordered them to handle—but he was determined there would not be another well accident in his household.

In the deep-soiled sand hills, most homesteaders put down their wells with a sand bucket—a valve-tipped short piece of pipe on a rope to be jerked up and down inside the larger well piping that had an open sand point at the bottom. Water was poured into the pipe, to turn the soil into mud under the plunging sand bucket and be picked up by the valve in the end. Full, it was drawn out, emptied and the process repeated. Occasionally, the larger pipe was given a twist with a. wrench until its own weight forced it down as fast as the earth below was soaked and lifted out in the sand bucket. When a good water table was reached the end of the sand point was plugged, a cylinder and pumprod put in, and attached to a pump, home-made or bought from a mail order catalogue, and the home-steader had water.

"Nothing's prettier'n a girl pumpin' water in the wind," the cowboys used to say, obviously of homesteader daughters, for no others were out pumping.

As long as there were buffaloes, settlers could go out to the herd ranges for meat and even a few hides to sell for that scarcest of pioneer commodities, cash in the palm. The early settlers learned to preserve a summer buffalo or two in the Indian way, cutting the meat into flakes thin as the edge of a woman's hand to dry quickly in the hot winds, with all the juices preserved. Well-dried, the meat kept for months and was good boiled with a touch of prairie onion or garlic. With vegetables, the dried buffalo or deer or elk made good boiled dinners or meat pies, and was chopped into cornmeal mush by the Pennsylvanians for scrapple until there was pork.

Much could be gleaned for the table before the garden even started. Old Jules brought water cress seed west and scattered it wherever there was a swift current and in the lake regions where the earth-warmed water seeped out all winter, and kept an open spot for cress and mallard ducks. Dandelions start early and as soon as they came up brownish red, we cut them out with a knife for salad, very good with hard boiled eggs, the dressing made with vinegar from wild currants, plums, or grapes and the vinegar-mother we borrowed from a neighbor who had brought it in a bottle by wagon from Kentucky. Later there was lambs-quarter, boiled and creamed and perhaps on baking days spread into a *dunna*, which looked like a green-topped pizza. Meat the homesteaders could provide—antelope and deer, and after these were gone, grouse, quail, and cottontails, with ducks and geese spring and fall. Old Jules was an excellent trapper and hunter as well as gardener and horticulturist, with his wife and the children for the weeding and the harvest. Consequently we seldom lacked anything in food except the two items that cost money—sugar and coffee. Roasted rye made a cheap and poor coffee substitute. Other homesteaders grew cane and cooked the sap into hard and soft sorghum but our sweetening was often nothing but dried fruits eaten from the palm or baked into buns and rolls. Once a whole winter was sweetened by a barrel of extra dark blackstrap molasses father got somehow as a bargain. It made fine pungent cookies.

Mother was a good pig raiser and we usually had wonderful sausage looped over broomsticks in the smoke house with the hams and bacon, the good sweet lard in the cellar in crocks. In our younger days butchering was a trial. It meant father had to be disturbed from his plans, his thinking, to shoot the fat hog. The washboiler was put on the stove, with buckets and the tea-kettle filled for extra scalding water. A barrel had to be set tilted into the ground with an old door laid on low blocks up against the open barrelhead. When everything was ready, the hog up close and everybody out to keep it there, Old Jules had to be called, mother shouting to him, "That one there! Shoot quick!"

But by then the hog might be gone, to be fetched back after a chase through the trees. When father got a shot he put the bullet cleanly between the eyes but he was often experimenting with the amount of powder that would kill without penetrating into the good meat. Sometimes the hog was not even stunned but ran squealing for the brush, and had to be shot again. Sometimes it fell soundlessly and mother thrust the sticking knife into father's hand. With disgust all over his face, he drove the knife in the general direction of the jugular vein and when the dark blood welled out, stepped back while mother ran in to roll the animal to make the blood flow faster. When grandmother was still alive she usually hurried out with a pan for the makings of her blood pudding but none of the rest of the family would even taste it.

Now the hog was dragged up on the old door, ready for the scalding. Everybody ran for the boiling water, the washboiler, the buckets.

"Look out! Look out!" father kept shouting most of the time as he limped around. When the barrel was steaming with the hot water, he and mother shoved the dead pig down into it head first, because that was the hardest to scald well, and worked the carcass back and forth by the hind feet, to get every spot wet, while mother yanked off handsful of the loosening bristles, shaking the heat from her fingers. Then the hog was drawn out upon the door, turned and the hind half thrust into the stinking hot water, and pulled out upon the door again. Now everybody fell to scraping, clutching butcher knives by the back or working with ragged-edge tin cans, the bristles rolling off in wet clumps and windrows.

No butchered animal looks finer than a well-scalded and scraped hog—pink and plump and appetizing. That evening there was fresh liver for supper, and the frothing brain cooked in a frying pan. I liked pork tenderloin with the animal heat and sweetness still in it. I fried this for myself, and never tasted a finer dish. Meat still animal-warm was credited with helping to cure many sufferers from bleeding stomachs sent west to a government claim by their doctors. Whole communities of stomach patients settled on the Plains, and usually died of other complaints, including old age.

Butchering for most homesteaders, particularly the lone ones, was a matter for neighborly help, as were many larger undertakings, particularly threshing. Most of the threshing outfits that finally reached the homesteader were small horse-powered machines with the owner probably feeding the separator himself to keep greenhorns from choking it, tearing it up. Usually three, four hands, including the horse-power driver, came with the outfit. The rest of the sixteen, eighteen man crew was drawn from the settlers, exchanging work. Often neighber women came to help with the cooking. Reputations were made or broken by the meals put out for the threshers, and many a plain daughter owed a good marriage match to the wild plum pie or the chicken and dumplings of her mother at threshing time.

The homesteader got most of his outside items through mail-order catalogues, including, sometimes, his wife, if one could call the matrimonial papers, the heart-and-hand publications, catalogues. They did describe the offerings rather fully but with, perhaps, a little less honesty than Montgomery Ward or Sears

Roebuck. Unmarried women were always scarce in new regions. Many bachelor settlers had a sweetheart back east or in the Old Country, or someone who began to look a little like a sweetheart from the distance of a government claim that got more and more lonesome as the holes in the socks got bigger. Some of these girls never came. Others found themselves in an unexpectedly good bargaining position and began to make all kinds of demands in that period of feminine uprising. They wanted the husband to promise abstinence from profanity, liquor, and tobacco and perhaps even commanded allegiance to the rising cause of woman suffrage. Giving up the cud of tobacco in the cheek was often very difficult. A desperate neighbor of ours chewed grass, bitter willow and cottonwood leaves, coffee grounds, and finally sent away for a tobacco cure. It made him sick, so sick, at least in appearance, that his new wife begged him to take up chewing again. Others backslid on the sly, sneaking a chew of Battle Axe or Horseshoe in the face of certain anger and tears.

But many bachelors had no sweetheart to come out, and some of these started to carry the heart-and-hand papers around until the pictures of the possible brides were worn off the page. In those days the usual purpose really was marriage, not luring the lonely out of their pitiful little savings or even their lives. "We married everything that got off the railroad," old homesteaders, including my father, used to say.

Usually the settler was expected to send the prospective wife a stagecoach or railroad ticket. Perhaps, even though he had mortgaged his team to get the ticket, the woman sold it and never came and there was nothing to be done unless the U.S. mails were involved. Most of the women did arrive and many of these unions, bound by mutual need and dependence, founded excellent families. Of course, there was no way to compel a mail-order wife to stay when she saw the husband's place. Usually she had grown up in a settled region, perhaps with Victorian sheltering, and was shocked by her new home, isolated, at the best a frame or log shack with cracks for the blizzard winds, or only a soddy or dugout into some bank, with a dirt floor and the possibility of wandering stock falling through the roof.

The long distance to the stagecoach or the railroad, with

walking not good, kept many a woman to her bargain. There are, however, stories of desperate measures used to hold the wife— ropes or chains or locked leg hobbles, but the more common and efficacious expedient was early pregnancy. That brought the customary gift for the first child—a sewing machine, and many a man, including my own father, scratched mightily for the money.

The women, particularly the young ones, brought some gaiety to the homestead regions, with visitings, berryings, pie socials, square dances, play parties, literaries at the schools, and shivarees for the newlyweds. The women organized Sunday Schools, and sewing bees. When calamity or sickness struck, the women went to help, and if there was death they bathed and dressed the corpse, coming with dishes of this and that so the bereaved need not trouble to cook and were spared the easing routine. Doctors were usually far away and scarce and expensive. Old Jules, with his partial training in medicine, had a shelf of the usual remedies and for years he was called out to care for the difficult deliveries. Several times middle-aged people have come to me to say that Old Jules brought them into the world, perhaps back in the 1880's or 1890's.

There were problems besides sickness and death, besides the lack of cash and credit that dogs every new community, besides the isolation and drouth and dust storms. Fires swept over the prairies any time during practically ten months a year, although the worst were usually in the fall, with the grass standing high and rich in oily seed. The prairie fires could be set by fall lightning, by the carelessness of greenhorns in the country, by sparks from the railroads and by deliberate malice.

"Burning a man out" could mean destroying his grass, crops, hay, even his house and himself. Once started, the heat of the fire created a high wind that could sweep it over a hundred miles of prairie in an incredibly short time. Settlers soon learned to watch the horizon for the pearling rise of smoke from prairie grass. At the first sign of this, everyone hurried to fight the flames with water barrels, gunny sacks, hoes, and particularly plows to turn furrows for the backfiring. Even more important was the awareness of the danger ahead of time, early enough so fireguards were plowed around the homestead, at least around the buildings. In addition everyone was told the old Indian advice: "Come fire, go for bare ground, sand or gravel or to big water. Make a backfire against small creek or bare spot, to burn only into wind, and stay where ashes are. Best is to go on a place with no grass, and do not run."

Old Jules' Kinkaid in the sandhills bordered on the Osborne valley, which had a prairie-fire story. An earlier settler and his wife and two small boys had lived in the Osborne—a wet hay flat with miles of rushes and dense canebrakes, and a small open lake in the center that dried up in the summers. Early one fall a prairie fire came sweeping in toward the place. The settler and his wife hurried out to help fight the flames, commanding the two boys to stay in the house. It was sod, with a sod roof, and surrounded by a wide fireguard. Here they were safe. But when the smoke thickened and the fire came roaring over the hill toward the house the boys ran in terror to the swamp, clambering through the great piles of dead rushes and canes for the lake bed. The fire caught them.

After that the settler and his wife moved away but the story of the boys remained as a warning to all of us. When my brother James and I were sent down to hold the Kinkaid for a few months alone, we often went to the Osborne swamp to hunt ducks but never without searching the horizon for prairie-fire smoke. There were mushrooms growing where the sod house of the early settler had been, good mushrooms, fine fried with young ducks or prairie chicken.

The most dreaded storm of the upper homestead region was and still is the blizzard. The first one to kill many people was the Buffalo Hunter's Storm of the 1870's, although the School Children's Blizzard of 1888 is sadly remembered, and even the one of 1949. Most of the people who died in blizzards died through some foolishness, some stupidity, and a few years later would have known better. There are always signs before the worst storms: unseasonal warmth, calm, and stillness, as on January 12, 1888, and old timers were ready with warnings of what to do if caught in a blizzard. "If lost in the sand hills, any blow-out will give the directions. The wind cuts the hollows from the northwest and moves the sand out southeastward. If so confused that directions are useless or you are too far from shelter, dig in anywhere to keep dry, with a fire if possible, but dry, even if it's only under a bank somewhere, into the dry sand of a blowout. Don't get yourself wet and *don't* wear yourself out. Practically anyone with a little sense and a little luck can outlast a blizzard."

Not all the danger is in the storm itself. The homestead region had few trees and fewer rocks and a May blizzard left an unbelievable glare of unbroken whiteness in the high spring sun, enough to make cows snowblind, and people, if the eyes were not protected. Of all the dangers of homestead life, our family escaped all but two, Old Jules' well accident and my snowblindness in a May blizzard that cost me all useful sight in one eye.

Much of what I have been saying comes out of my childhood but could have come out of the childhood of practically anyone brought up on a homestead. Those first years on a government claim were a trial, a hardship for the parents, particularly the women, but the men too. Usually only one in four entrymen remained to patent the claim; in the more difficult regions and times only one in ten, or even fifteen. A large percentage of those into any new region had been misfits in their home community, economic, social, or emotional misfits, both the men and the women. Some of these, unsettled by the hardships and the isolation, ended in institutions or suicide if they did not drift on or flee back to relatives or in-laws. Those who stayed might be faced by drouth, grasshoppers, and ten-cent corn, sometimes followed by the banker's top buggy come to attach the mortgaged team or the children's milk cow. The men gathered at the sales and at political meetings, with many women, too, speaking for reforms, for a better shake for the sparsely settled, sparsely represented regions.

None of these things could be kept from the children. They saw the gambles of life and the size of the stakes. They shared in the privation and the hard work. All of us knew children who put in twelve-, fourteen-hour days from March to November. We knew seven-, eight-year-old boys who drove four-horse teams to the harrow, who shocked grain behind the binder all day in heat and dust and rattlesnakes, who cultivated, hoed and weeded corn, and finally husked it out before they could go to school in November. And even then there were the chores morning and evening, the stock to feed, the cows to milk by lantern light. If there had been tests for muscular fitness as compared to European children then, we would have held our own.

Often there was no difference in the work done by the boys and the girls, except that the eldest daughter of a sizable family was often a serious little mother by the time she was six, perhaps baking up a 49 pound sack of flour every week by the time she was ten. Such children learned about life before they had built up any illusions and romanticisms to be clung to later, at the expense of maturity. Almost from their first steps, the home-steader's children had to meet new situations, make decisions, develop a self-discipline if they were to survive. They learned dependence upon one's neighbors, and discovered the interrela-tionships of earth and sky and animal and man. They could see, in their simpler society, how national and international events conditioned every day of their existence. They learned to rescue themselves in adulthood as they had once scrabbled under the fence when the heel flies drove the milk cows crazy. What they didn't have they tried to make for themselves, earned money to buy, or did without. Perhaps somewhere there are individuals from homestead childhoods who grab for fellowships and grants, for scholarships and awards, for special influence and privilege but I don't know of any. The self-reliance, often the fierce inde-pendence, of a homestead upbringing seems to stay with them. They may wander far from their roots, for they are children of the uprooted, but somehow their hearts are still back there with the old government claim.

Federal Land Policy in the South

1866-1888

By PAUL WALLACE GATES

There is a striking difference between Federal land policy in the public domain states of the South after 1865 and that in force elsewhere in the United States at the same time.[1] In fact, the South was a laboratory for experiments in land reform. Prior to the Civil War public lands in the South were open to unrestricted entry, but between 1866 and 1876 they were reserved for homesteaders and large purchases could only be made illegally. In 1876 all limitations were removed and the lands were again opened to unrestricted cash entry, although elsewhere newly surveyed lands were not being opened to large-scale purchasing.[2] Another sharp reversal in policy was made in 1888 when the southern lands were

[1] A Social Science Research Council Fellowship for 1933-1934 and grants-in-aid for 1936 and 1938 made possible the research for this article.

[2] When the Homestead Act was adopted in 1862 there were available for unrestricted purchase 83,916,649 acres of public lands located, for the most part, in the states of the Mississippi Valley, including the five southern public land states. After the Civil War Congress was reluctant to have newly surveyed lands opened to cash entry because the campaign against land monopoly was gaining ground rapidly and it was felt that the cash entry system favored speculators. Nevertheless, more than 25,000,000 acres in the Lake states, Kansas, Colorado, New Mexico, Washington, and Oregon, were opened by executive order to cash purchase. Furthermore, Congress in 1868 provided for the establishment of a new land district in Nebraska and authorized the President to offer the land at public sale. 15 *United States Statutes at Large*, 224. Although public auctions were being announced as late as 1875, most of the lands surveyed subsequent to 1870 were not so offered and were only subject to entry under the Homestead, Pre-emption, Desert Land, Timber Culture, and Timber and Stone acts. These "unoffered" lands, as they were called in contradistinction to the "offered" lands, were located in western Kansas and Nebraska, the Dakotas, Colorado, Wyoming, Montana, Arizona, New Mexico, Nevada, Utah, Idaho, and parts of the Pacific Coast states. See Paul W. Gates, "The Homestead Act in an Incongruous Land System," in *American Historical Review* (New York, 1895-), XLI (1936), 652-81.

once more restricted to entry under the Homestead Act. Reformers thus had an opportunity to compare the results of the two methods of disposing of the public domain and neither gave them much satisfaction. Despite all the efforts of reform and antimonopoly groups, it seemed impossible to devise a system which would protect the lands from near monopolization by a comparatively small group of speculators. Nevertheless, it was the restrictive policy, first tried out in the South between 1866 and 1876, which was, in 1888 and 1889, adopted for all the public land states except Missouri. Southern land policy in these experimental years is important, therefore, for the part it played in the development of the national policy. It is also important because, as a result of the unrestricted cash entry system in operation from 1876 to 1888, large blocks of the most valuable stands of timber in the South passed into the hands of lumbermen and speculators, mostly nonresidents. The process of getting the South into hock, to reverse President Roosevelt's expression, was carried far in this short period.

In 1861 there remained in Federal ownership in the five public land states of the South, Alabama, Arkansas, Florida, Louisiana, and Mississippi, 47,700,000 acres,[3] or somewhat less than one third of their area. Much of this land was swampy, poorly drained, and unsuitable for settlement without large expenditures of capital. Heavy stands of yellow pine and cypress covered these lands. As there was little demand in the South for such timber, the forest cover was looked upon as worthless and as an obstacle to settlement and development. Part of this land had been open to entry for years at $1.25 per acre, and since the adoption of the Graduation Act in 1854 had been subject to sale at prices ranging from 12½ cents to $1.00 per acre, depending upon the length of time it had been on the market.

After the Civil War the administration of these remaining public lands became intricately involved with Reconstruction and the land reform movement. In their vindictive hatred of the ex-Confederates,

[3] The amount of unsold land in the five southern states in 1866 was given by James M. Edmunds as 46,398,544 acres. Quoted in *Congressional Globe*, 39 Cong., 1 Sess., 715 (February 7, 1866), 2736 (May 22, 1866) The Commissioner of the General Land Office, in his *Annual Report*, 1867, p. 367, gave the amount of unsold land as 47,726,851 acres.

northern radicals proposed to restrict public land entries in the South to loyal citizens. They also wished to preserve the public lands for the freedmen who were finding it difficult to acquire their forty acres and a mule. To achieve these ends the radicals proposed to modify the land system in the South drastically by ending cash sales and pre-emption entries, reserving the public lands for homesteaders only and denying the homestead privilege to all ex-Confederates. They also proposed to declare forfeited the land grants which had been given the southern states to aid in the construction of railroads.

George W. Julian, long an abolitionist Indiana Representative and chairman of the House Committee on Public Lands,[4] was partly responsible for these proposals and he supported them with fervor. He regarded them as a two-edged sword wherewith to strike a blow at both the old slaveholding aristocracy and land monopoly. In Julian there were combined the worst qualities of the fanatical abolitionist, now vindictively persecuting the South, with the virtues of the social reformer. Few radicals in Congress were any more bitter in their hatred of the ex-Confederates and none were more ingenious in their efforts to destroy the southern aristocracy than Julian. His animosity to the South was not, however, insincere or self-seeking in its nature, nor was it a cloak to cover hidden economic or political motives. The South had erred, its social system must be destroyed, and the ex-slaves raised to the ranks of farm and homeowners, like the great majority of Julian's constituents. To destroy the Old South it was necessary to disfranchise

---

[4] That Julian considered his fight against slavery the most important part of his political career is evident from his *Political Recollections, 1840 to 1872* (Chicago, 1884), and from the biography prepared by his daughter, Grace Julian Clarke, *George W. Julian* (Indianapolis, 1922). Paul L. Haworth, who wrote the sketch of Julian for the *Dictionary of American Biography*, 20 vols. and index (New York, 1928-1937), X, 245-46, is apparently of the same opinion for he gives no attention to Julian's fight against railroad land grants, the cash sale system, and other features of the Federal land policy which permitted speculators to acquire great tracts of land. It is the opinion of this writer that Julian's place in American history must rest as much on his career as a land reformer as on his fight against slavery. The Julian manuscripts in the Division of Manuscripts, Library of Congress, are disappointing. Julian's diary and some of his letters in the Indiana State Library contain interesting comments on land frauds in the Far West. For Julian's fight to end abuses in the disposal of Indian lands in Kansas, see Gates, "The Homestead Act in an Incongruous Land System," in *loc. cit.*, 677-78.

its leaders, confiscate their property, and prevent them from acquiring new lands from the government. Julian was obsessed with the idea that the old aristocracy was impatiently waiting for the reopening of the Federal land offices in the southern states to swoop down upon them and to select the most valuable tracts for speculation. All these lands were needed, he contended, for homesteads for the freedmen and he wanted to reserve them for this class.[5]

Julian's sympathy for the landless classes comprehended the poor whites and the impoverished immigrants as well as the freedmen. He believed that the remaining public lands of the United States should be reserved for actual settlers and should not be granted to railroads or sold to capitalists and corporations in large tracts.[6] To achieve these aims he endeavored to have the entire land system overhauled but found the railroad lobby and the lumbering and land speculating interests too powerful to overcome at once.[7] Here in the South, however, was a splendid opportunity to combine land reform and punitive reconstruction measures which delighted him. He must have looked with sardonic glee upon the spectacle of those northern radicals who bitterly opposed his general land reform bills, voting to restrict land entries in the South.

In addition to Julian, the chief advocates of the policy of reserving the public lands in the South for homesteaders were James M. Edmunds, Commissioner of the General Land Office, John H. Rice and Abner C. Harding, representatives from Maine and Illinois, respectively, and Senator Samuel C. Pomeroy of Kansas. Edmunds seemed to feel that the welfare of the landless classes in the South demanded the reservation of the public lands in that section for settlement only, but he could not agree with Julian that the same policy might well be applied to all the public domain.[8] Harding deplored speculation in the public

<hr/>

[5] *Cong. Globe*, 39 Cong., 1 Sess., 716 (February 7, 1866).

[6] Of the cash sale system which, in 1868, he was trying to end, Julian said, "Nothing could be more vicious in principle or more ruinous to the public interest than has been this policy." *Ibid.*, 40 Cong., 2 Sess., 1714 (March 6, 1868).

[7] *Ibid.*, 97 (December 9, 1867), 371 (January 7, 1868), 1712-15 (March 6, 1868), 1861 (March 12, 1868), 2380-87 (May 7, 1868).

[8] Communication of Edmunds, *ibid.*, 39 Cong., 1 Sess., 715 (February 7, 1866).

lands because it had proved so detrimental to the development of Illinois and he wished to avoid such errors in the administration of the
southern lands.[9] Rice likewise argued that a restrictive policy would
withhold the lands "from the rapacious talons of the monopolist and
the speculator," and would assure to the landless homesteads which
are "nurseries of independence, citadels of liberty."[10] Pomeroy, who
needs no characterization here, spoke feelingly of the needs of the colored men for whom his heart yearned.[11] It was to assure homesteads for
them that he favored restricting southern lands to homestead entry.
Most of these speeches, except those of Julian, are characteristic of the
demagogues who paid lip service to the squatter democracy of the
pioneer West while frequently voting against its interest.

The Southern Homestead Act, as it was finally adopted,[12] provided
that the public lands in the five southern states should be subject to
entry only by homesteaders and that for a period of two years the unit
of entry should be eighty acres. Until 1867 only citizens whose loyalty
had been unquestioned during the Civil War could make entries. The
measure passed the House on February 8, 1866, the voting being very
nearly on straight party lines. Only two Republicans voted against it,
John F. Driggs, who avowedly represented the lumbermen of Michigan,
and George R. Latham of West Virginia. Offsetting the vote of Driggs
was that of John W. Longyear, himself a large owner of timberland in
Michigan.[13] The discussion in the Senate was brief and no roll call was
taken.[14] On June 21, 1866, the measure was signed by the President.
One may doubt whether it could have been passed had the South been
fully represented in Congress. In the light of the failure which met
Julian's efforts to restrict land entries to homesteaders in other parts of

[9] *Ibid.*, 718 (February 7, 1866). In few states, if any, had there been so much speculation and absentee ownership of lands as in Illinois, a fact of which Harding was doubtless aware.

[10] *Ibid.*, 717 (February 7, 1866).

[11] *Ibid.*, 2735 (May 22, 1866). By 1870 Pomeroy was arguing for the repeal of the
act of 1866. *Ibid.*, 41 Cong., 2 Sess., 2897 (April 22, 1870).

[12] 14 *U. S. Statutes at Large*, 66-67.

[13] *Cong. Globe*, 39 Cong., 1 Sess., 748 (February 8, 1866).

[14] *Ibid.*, 2736 (May 22, 1866).

the country, it is evident that support was given the act, especially in the Senate, more because it would further punish the South and delay its recovery than because it would prevent land monopoly. That Pomeroy was in charge of the measure in the Senate is fair evidence of this since he rarely voted for settlers' interests when they were in conflict with those of land speculators and railroads.

The southern railroad companies, like most of the western railroads which had received Federal land grants, had not completed their lines within the time prescribed by law. The lands had been granted but not patented, and they were not taxable nor were they open to settlement. Residents in the vicinity of these grants were grieved that the land was lying idle and demanded that the grants be declared forfeited and that the land be reopened to settlement.[15] Julian had a particular grievance against some of these southern railroads which, it was believed, were largely southern owned, and he fathered a bill to forfeit the grants which Congress had made in 1856. The amount of land involved was about 5,000,000 acres, much of which was suitable for settlement.[16] In 1868 Julian secured the passage of the measure in the House after one of the grants had been specifically exempted.[17] The vote was close, however, and shows that many northern radicals were not prepared to support this kind of measure, even though it was as bitterly antisouthern as the Southern Homestead Act of 1866. Such staunch representatives of business and railroad interests as James G. Blaine of Maine and William B. Allison of Iowa, despite their radical propensities on reconstruction measures, obviously could not favor a bill the principle of which might well be applied to numerous unearned railroad land grants in the West. The Senate Public Lands Committee under the chairmanship of Pomeroy was careful not to report the House bill and the effort to reopen these lands to homesteaders was a failure.[18]

The Southern Homestead Act of 1866 was such an obviously dis-

[15] David M. Ellis, "The Forfeiture of Railroad Land Grants" (M. A. thesis, Cornell University, 1939), 10-13.

[16] *Cong. Globe*, 40 Cong., 2 Sess., 310 (December 20, 1867).

[17] *Ibid.*, 985 (February 5, 1868). See also, *ibid.*, 1 Sess., 615-16 (July 12, 1867).

[18] *Ibid.*, 3 Sess., 1364 (February 19, 1869).

criminatory measure that it was certain to be challenged by the southern states as soon as they were restored to good standing in the Union. Southern leaders pointed out that the lands remaining in Federal ownership had not been entered under the Graduation Act nor were they being entered under the act of 1866, except to a limited extent. This, they argued, was clear proof that the lands were not suitable for farming and it was, therefore, absurd to continue to withhold them from commercial use.[19] In their opinion the restrictive policy was in effect a "hoarding policy," and was intended to be discriminatory.[20] With the agrarian philosophy implicit in the act of 1866 they were, moreover, totally out of sympathy.[21]

That Southerners actually believed the remaining public land in their section to be unsuitable for settlement is scarcely credible. True, the lands best adapted to cotton cultivation and most easily brought into production were already in private ownership and the remaining public lands would require heavy labor and large investments of capital to make them suitable for farming. But settlers had cleared timbered sections elsewhere and made successful homes for themselves and there was no reason why they could not do the same on these lands. Furthermore, only a part of the southern lands had been available at graduated prices after 1854. Over 14,000,000 acres in Florida and Louisiana were unsurveyed before 1866 and had never been subject to entry.[22] Also some 5,750,000 acres had been withdrawn from entry in the 1850's pending the selection of railroad grants.[23] Nor were the number of homestead entries as inconsiderable as Southerners maintained. On the contrary, between 1867 and 1876 there was more homesteading in that section in proportion to the amount of land available than there was elsewhere in the public land states. In this period 40,000 original entries were made.[24] Doubtless a large number of them were filed by

---

[19] *Congressional Record*, 44 Cong., 1 Sess., 3291 (May 24, 1876).
[20] *Ibid.*, 3289-94 (May 24, 1876).
[21] *Ibid.*, 3290 (May 24, 1876).
[22] Commissioner General Land Office, *Annual Report*, 1866, p. 53.
[23] *Ibid.*, 1886, p. 183.
[24] Computed from *ibid.*, 1867-1876.

dummy entrymen acting for the lumber companies, as the Commission of the General Land Office pointed out,[25] but certainly some of them were made by bona fide settlers. The future was to show that a con siderable part of the southern lands then in public ownership was cap able of producing crops and providing homesteads for settlers.

Economic recovery was long delayed in the South but after home ru was re-established it proceeded more rapidly. Southern timber was com ing into demand as a result of the rapid depletion of northern resource and the increasing use of iron and steel was stimulating the develop ment of mines and mills in new areas. The standing timber and the iron and coal deposits of the public lands were attracting increasing interest in the 1870's and Southerners wished to have all restriction upon them removed so that extensive areas could be acquired by cap talist groups which might utilize their resources. Representative Gold smith W. Hewitt of Alabama charged the North with adopting the a of 1866 because it feared southern economic rivalry and wished "t clog" southern progress. He asserted that the iron interests of the North were unfavorable to the growth of a rival industry in Alabama, that the coal mining industry of Indiana was averse to the exploitation of the "superior" coal lands of Alabama, and that the Michigan lumbermen were opposed to the opening of the timberlands of the South to com mercial use. Hewitt charged that those land reformers who were op posed to the repeal of the act of 1866 because they wanted to prevent monopoly were actualy aiding monopoly by preventing competition from developing in the South.[26]

Southern members of Congress were most concerned at the restrictive effect which the act of 1866 had on the lumber industry in their section They urged that the deplorable economic condition of the South would be relieved and its lumber industry stimulated by throwing the publ lands of the section open to unrestricted purchasing.[27] It seems, how ever, that lumbering had not been altogether retarded by the act of

---

[25] *Ibid.*, 1875, pp. 17-19.

[26] *Cong. Record*, 44 Cong., 1 Sess., 3289-92 (May 24, 1876).

[27] *Ibid.*, 815 ff. (February 2, 1876), 850-51 (February 3, 1876).

1866, for the Commissioner of the General Land Office in 1875 spoke of the "wholesale depredations" being committed on the public domain and the "extensive mills" which were manufacturing the timber thus fraudulently cut.[28] Southern congressmen admitted this and argued that the repeal of the act of 1866 would induce purchasing and bring in revenue to the government.[29] Clearly by 1876 the southern land question had ceased to be confused with reconstruction issues and had become a problem in land economics and business policy.

Opposition to the repeal of the Southern Homestead Act was led by William S. Holman of Indiana. In 1870 the old war horse of the land reformers, Julian, had been retired from Congress[30] but in his place was Holman, who was an equally persistent fighter. Holman wanted to keep the restrictions upon land entries in the South and to extend them to all public land states.[31] He was not deterred by the southern contention that the remaining lands were not suitable for agriculture because he was convinced that they possessed valuable timber resources the ownership of which, if distributed under the homestead policy, would be widely diffused. Such a policy, he held, would check the "growth and centralization of the wealth of the country, which in a republic is a positive evil." Holman predicted that if the act of 1866 were repealed capitalists would monopolize the remaining lands and "coin them into imperial estates." "The robbery of the public lands," he said, "is far more fatal than the robbery of the Treasury. It deprives

---

[28] Commissioner General Land Office, *Annual Report*, 1875, p. 18.

[29] *Cong. Record*, 44 Cong., 1 Sess., 815-16 (February 2, 1876), 850-51 (February 3, 1876).

[30] After his retirement from Congress in 1871 Julian continued his deep interest in the land question, and in the midst of the campaign to repeal the Southern Homestead Act of 1866 he wrote a long letter to the New York *Tribune*, January 29, 1876, in favor of the continuation of the measure. The *Tribune*, in commending the letter, agreed with Julian that the act of 1866 should not be repealed.

[31] Holman argued that the land system, including the cash sales feature, had worked satisfactorily in Indiana in an earlier generation and that "The great body of the lands . . . was purchased by actual settlers." *Cong. Globe*, 44 Cong., 1 Sess., 2605 (April 19, 1876). This was certainly true for Holman's section of southern Indiana but in the prairie counties it would not apply at all. See Paul W. Gates, "Land Policy and Tenancy in the Prairie Counties of Indiana," in *Indiana Magazine of History* (Indianapolis, Bloomington, 1905-), XXXV (1939), 1-26.

the laboring masses of homes and firesides and hope, and the Republic of independent and virtuous citizens." In final condemnation of the move to repeal the restrictions on land sales, Holman said:

No scheme could be devised more injurious and unjust to labor than the un-limited right to purchase the public lands at a nominal price. . . . For when this public domain shall be exhausted, the young man leaving the old home . . . finds no lands within his reach; monopoly dictates the price; he becomes a tenant . . . and the landlord takes the bread he has earned. . . .

Land monopoly . . . means stately palaces, luxury, idleness, and licentiousness on the one hand and on the other squalid and hopeless poverty.[32]

The move to repeal the Southern Homestead Act came to a head in 1876, after a long fight. An aggressive and nearly unanimous South then succeeded in attracting sufficient support from the older states of the North to force through both houses of Congress a repeal measure. Holman could not muster sufficient votes to defeat the bill. Unlike Julian, he lacked the aid of the radical reconstructionists whose votes had carried the act of 1866, and he had not yet succeeded in obtaining a sufficient following of land reformers to carry his program. To be sure, he had the strong support of representatives of the lumbering states of the North and Far West who were opposed to reopening the southern lands to unrestricted entry, although even they were not unanimous. Nathan B. Bradley,[33] owner of a large lumber mill in Bay City, Michigan, opposed repeal as had Omar Conger in the preceding Congress. Conger had then stated that the lumber operators of his dis-trict did not approve of his stand but were actually waiting in Florida, Louisiana, and Arkansas to buy the southern lands as soon as they were open to entry.[34] Two senators from Minnesota and one from Wisconsin

[32] Cong. Record, 44 Cong., 1 Sess., 2604-2605 (April 19, 1876).

[33] Few lumbermen have received sketches in the Dictionary of American Biography and most of those who are included apparently won attention because of their political and philanthropic activities rather than because of the part they played in the development of one of the most important and picturesque industries of the nineteenth century. Not even Frederick Weyerhaeuser is included! Uncritical but detailed sketches of most of the out-standing lumbermen of the nineteenth century may be found in Henry Hall, America's Successful Men of Affairs, 2 vols. (New York, 1895-1896), and in American Lumber-men, 3 series (Chicago, 1905-1906). For Nathan B. Bradley, see Hall, America's Success-ful Men of Affairs, II, 106-107.

[34] Cong. Record, 43 Cong., 1 Sess., 4634 (June 5, 1874).

also seem not to have feared southern competition, and there was other scattered support for repeal in the lumbering states as the following table shows:[35]

VOTES OF THE LUMBERING STATES ON THE BILL TO REPEAL THE ACT OF 1876

| | Senate | | House | |
	For	Against	For	Against
California	1	1	0	2
Maine	0	2	0	2
Michigan	0	1	0	6
Minnesota	2	0	0	2
Oregon	1	0	0	0
Wisconsin	1	1	2	4
Totals	5	5	2	16

In the House, where the vote was 108 to 97 in support of repeal, only 8 southern votes were cast against it. On the other hand, there was strong support in Illinois, Ohio, Pennsylvania, and New York. In the Senate the vote was 41 to 17, with the South favoring repeal, except for a Texas Senator, and the public land states of the North and West generally opposing it. The bill became a law without President Grant's signature.[36]

The act of 1876 repealed all restrictions upon the sale of public lands in the five southern states and directed that the lands be offered at public sale "as soon as practicable."[37] The task of preparing the lands for market was not an easy one and it took the General Land Office four years before they were all made available for entry.

The repeal of restrictions on land entries greatly expedited the process of transferring the public lands to private ownership in large blocks, as Holman had feared. From 1881 to 1888 there flocked to the southern land offices not hordes of settlers seeking land or small farmers who wanted to expand their cultivated areas, but lumbermen and

---

[35] Ibid., 44 Cong., 1 Sess., 1090 (February 15, 1876), 3655 (June 7, 1876).
[36] Ibid., 4469 (July 8, 1876).
[37] 19 U. S. Statutes at Large, 73-74.

capitalists who either anticipated their future needs or those of others by buying huge tracts of land. So much excitement was aroused by the reopening of the southern lands to speculative entry that the Illinois Central Railroad ran a series of special trains from Chicago to Mississippi and Louisiana for the benefit of the numerous "land lookers."[38]

Many fortunes had already been made in Maine, New York, Pennsylvania,[39] and the Lake states in the purchase and sale of timberlands and in the lumber business. When the lumber industry passed its peak in the eastern states its leaders migrated to Michigan, Wisconsin, and Minnesota[40] where they operated on a far larger scale than formerly. Here they learned that the profits of the lumber business were to be obtained more by speculating in timberland than from the actual logging, sawing, and marketing of the timber.[41] In the Lake states the public lands had always been open to unrestricted purchases and there had been nothing to prevent a small group of speculators from monopolizing extensive areas of timberlands.[42] Actual lumber operators were subsequently obliged to buy stumpage or lands from them at high prices. When there were no more easily accessible timberlands to be purchased from the government in the Old Northwest, the land dealers, their

[38] *Northwestern Lumberman* (Chicago, 1873-1898), May 31, 1884, p. 7; June 14, 1884, p. 2.

[39] For the lumber business in the eastern states, see Richard D. Wood, *History of Lumbering in Maine, 1820-1861,* in University of Maine *Studies* (Orono, 1900-), XXXVII, No. 7 (1935); James E. Defebaugh, *History of the Lumber Industry of America,* 2 vols. (Chicago, 1906-1907).

[40] The names of Bradley, Coburn, Hersey, Higgins, Morrison, Staples, Stephenson, Washburn, and Woodman are prominent on the rolls of Maine lumbermen before 1850 and equally prominent on the Michigan, Wisconsin, and Minnesota rolls thereafter.

[41] This was clearly the view of the leading journal of the lumber trade in the Lake states. The *Northwestern Lumberman,* April 11, 1885, p. 1, reported a wealthy Muskegon pine manufacturer as saying that his profits had come entirely from the rise in stumpage values and not from logging. Again on July 19, 1890, p. 3, the *Northwestern Lumberman* said: "Almost every man in Michigan who has made any money out of pine has made it by the rise of stumpage, rather than manufacturing and selling it." See *post,* n. 49.

[42] There is much material on the concentration of timberland ownership in the upper peninsula of Michigan in a report of the Department of Commerce and Labor, Bureau of Corporations, *The Lumber Industry,* 4 pts. (Washington, 1913-1914), Pt. III, *Land Holdings of Large Timber Owners,* 188-216.

pockets overflowing with profits, went elsewhere for investments.[43] They preceded the actual lumbermen to new areas where timberland was now coming into demand. Some went to the Far West to buy the rich fir, spruce, and redwood forests of Washington, Oregon, and California,[44] while others went into Louisiana, Alabama, Mississippi, Florida, and Arkansas where they sought out the yellow pine and cypress stands.[45] Some actual lumbermen accompanied the vanguard of land buyers in these new areas but even they seemed to be more concerned with land speculation than with cutting the timber.

Speculative purchasing of southern timberlands was chiefly concentrated in Louisiana and Mississippi. Such a notable Michigan lumberman as Bradley, who, as a member of Congress in 1876 had voted against reopening the southern lands to unrestricted entry, purchased 111,188 acres of timberland in Louisiana, all of which was subsequently sold to other lumbermen. Similarly, a group of Chicago capitalists including Franklin H. Head, Nathaniel K. Fairbank,[46] and Turlington W. Harvey,[47] bought 195,804 acres which they later sold to the Long

[43] Large entries of timberlands in the upper peninsula of Michigan and in parts of northern Minnesota were made in the 1880's but they were less accessible and consequently more difficult to lumber on than the lands elsewhere in the Lake states. After 1889, when cash sales of public lands were virtually ended, there still remained valuable stands of pine on Indian reservations which were sold in unrestricted amounts. The story of the disposal of the Indian reservations still remains unexplored by historians.

[44] The best stands of timber in the Pacific Coast states passed generally into private hands through land grants to railroads, the Forest Lieu Land Act, and other acts which provided for restricted entries. They were not subject to cash entry, except in certain areas of Oregon and California, and the large lumbermen bought either from the railroads, the states, or employed dummy entrymen to secure titles which were promptly conveyed to the lumbermen. See John Ise, *United States Forest Policy* (New Haven, 1920), *passim.*

[45] The bulk of the southern lands which were sold in the 1880's was purchased for cash at the minimum price of $1.25 per acre. Most of the military land warrants issued under the acts of 1847, 1850, 1852, and 1855 and the Agricultural College Scrip issued under the Morrill Act of 1862 as well as other miscellaneous issues of scrip, except perhaps for the Chippewa issue, had already been used and there was little remaining on the market. The abstracts of cash entries for the land offices in the five southern states are in the General Land Office, Department of the Interior, Washington, D. C. From them has been compiled the data on land entries presented in this article.

[46] Hall, *America's Successful Men of Affairs*, II, 294.

[47] *Ibid.*, 371. Harvey was said to handle "more lumber than any other individual operator on American soil." *Northwestern Lumberman*, July 1, 1882, p. 4.

Bell Lumber Company and other operating companies. Perhaps the largest speculator in southern timberlands was James D. Lacey[48] of Grand Rapids, Michigan. When the southern lands were opened to cash entry he put in an early appearance in Louisiana and Mississippi and bought for himself and partners 107,461 acres. But this was only the beginning. From 1880 to 1905 he and his agents roamed throughout the southern states as well as the Pacific states, British Columbia, and Central America in their search for timberlands. Altogether Lacey is said to have bought more than 5,000,000 acres of timberland, the greater part of which was in the South. This vast acreage was acquired from the state and Federal governments, railroads, and private owners. Lacey held the lands for subsequent resale to firms who bought to log them, and he was frank to admit that the profits of the loggers and sawmill operators were small, where they existed at all, but that the profits of the timberland dealers were large. Although he engaged in lumbering, his principal business was "buying and selling timber lands."[49]

The firm of Edward A. and Edward F. Brackenridge, formerly of Oscoda, Michigan, but later of New Orleans was, like Lacey and his associates, more of a dealer in timberlands than a lumbering company. Its members entered the business of buying, selling, and locating southern lands on a commission basis as soon as the public lands were reopened to large-scale purchasing. They personally inspected a large part of the pine and cypress lands of Louisiana and Mississippi, selected

[48] American Lumbermen, Ser. I, 235-38.

[49] Lacey made some highly illuminating remarks before the House Ways and Means Committee, at its hearing on the tariff in 1908, concerning the relative profits in lumbering and speculating in timberlands. He said: "But while there has been a moderate profit on the lumber manufactured, in the same locality there has been an increase of several hundred per cent in the value of the stumpage itself, and the whole question to-day, in the increased cost of lumber, resolves itself down to the increased value of stumpage and the increased value of labor.' Tariff Hearings before the Committee on Ways and Means of the House of Representatives, 9 vols. (Washington, 1909), III, House Document, No. 1505, 60 Cong., 2 Sess., 3019-20. Again, "Well so far as the manufacturer of lumber is concerned, I do not think there is a lumberman in this room that can show that he has ever made much profit on the strict manufacture of lumber; he has made his money in buying low-priced stumpage and holding until changed conditions of some kind advance it to a manufacturing profit." Ibid., 3024.

those tracts they deemed the most valuable, and offered their lists to northern lumbermen looking for choice tracts. In some three years they were said to have selected and located nearly 700,000 acres of pine land for others, including many of the northern purchasers whose names appear in the tables below.[50]

Other timber agents offered their services to the northern lumbermen in their quest for choice locations in the South. L. N. Dantzler of Moss Point, Mississippi, offered to survey, locate, and buy government pine lands in his vicinity for Northerners at a commission of 30 per cent or for a third interest in the investments.[51] A Wisconsin lumberman, James L. Gates, who claimed to own 300,000 acres of southern pine lands, offered to guarantee 10 per cent and a generous profit to capitalists who would aid him in marketing his holdings.[52]

There were, it is true, northern lumbermen who bought lands in the South with the intention of cutting their timber and among them were some of the most successful operators in Michigan and Wisconsin. Delos A. Blodgett[53] of Grand Rapids, when his Michigan lands approached exhaustion, acquired 126,238 acres of yellow pine land in Mississippi. The Wright-Blodgett Lumber Company, of which he was the principal stockholder, later bought well over half a million acres of additional land in Louisiana. William C. Yawkey[54] of Bay City, Michigan, whose family name has been more recently connected with baseball history, ranged far in his search for timber. From the Saginaw Valley he pushed into Wisconsin and Minnesota and acquired large tracts there. Then in the 1880's he bought of the Federal government 47,176 acres in Alabama, Florida, and Louisiana. He also purchased lands on the Pacific Coast. Charles H. Hackley[55] of Muskegon, Mich-

[50] In the years from 1882 to 1888 the *Northwestern Lumberman* gave a great deal of publicity to the Brackenridges who advertised in the journal. *Northwestern Lumberman,* December 23, 1882, p. 7; January 27, 1883, p. 19; November 3, 1888, p. 6; and elsewhere.

[51] *Ibid.,* February 18, 1888, p. 24.

[52] *Ibid.*

[53] Hall, *America's Successful Men of Affairs,* II, 95-96; *American Lumbermen,* Ser. II, 209-12.

[54] Hall, *America's Successful Men of Affairs,* II, 900-901; *American Lumbermen,* Ser. I, 151-53.

[55] Hall, *America's Successful Men of Affairs,* II, 362; *American Lumbermen,* Ser. I, 223-26.

igan, bought 89,743 acres in the Calcasieu Basin of Louisiana from which he intended to cut the timber. Isaac Stephenson of Wisconsin, whose wealth was to send him to the United States Senate, purchased with associates 70,274 acres in Louisiana after his Michigan and Wisconsin lands approached exhaustion. In 1899, eleven years after Stephenson and his associates had acquired their Louisiana land, the *Lumber Trade Journal* reported that they planned to shut down their plant at Menominee, Michigan, and re-establish it at Alexandria, Louisiana.[56]

Some of the northern lumbermen who bought extensively in the South transferred their business and residence there. Most notable of these expatriated Northerners were Henry J. Lutcher and G. Bedell Moore of Williamsport, Pennsylvania. Following the Civil War these men, who jointly owned a lumber mill in Williamsport, moved to Orange, Texas, where they opened a large sawmill. They purchased 500,000 acres of pine and cypress in Louisiana and Texas, 108,000 acres of which in the former state were bought from the Federal government in the 1880's.[57] So rapidly did their business expand that they were called the "lumber kings of the world" and "giants of the south." By 1890 it was stated that no lumberman in the South and few in the North were cutting as much timber as Lutcher and Moore.[58]

The movement of northern timber land speculators and lumbermen into the South can be seen by statistics of individual purchases which, however, are only for Federal lands. The total acreage would be greatly increased if the records for state and railroad lands were included. In Louisiana forty-one groups and individuals from the North bought 1,370,332 acres and nine from the South purchased 261,932 acres. In Mississippi thirty-two from the North acquired 889,359 acres and eleven from the South secured 134,270 acres.

[56] *Lumber Trade Journal* (New Orleans, 1881-), March 1, 1899, p. 34. In addition to large holdings in Michigan, Wisconsin, and Louisiana, Stephenson owned a substantial acreage of redwood forest in California. Isaac Stephenson, *Recollections of a Long Life, 1829-1915* (Chicago, 1915), contains interesting information on Stephenson's career as a lumberman and politician.

[57] For a sketch of Lutcher, see Hall, *America's Successful Men of Affairs*, II, 520.

[58] *Northwestern Lumberman*, August 2, 1890, p. 5.

PURCHASES OF 5,000 ACRES AND MORE IN LOUISIANA, 1880-1888

BY NORTHERNERS

Name	Residence	Acres
Avery, G. E.	Detroit, Mich.	6,520
Barnard, E. T.	Greenville, Mich.	7,882
Barker, S. B.	Chicago, Ill.	28,380
Birkett & McPherson	Livingston Co., Mich.	19,178
Brackenridge & Wasey	Wayne Co., Mich.	49,325
Bradley, N. B.	Bay City, Mich.	111,188
Brown, A. C.	Marinette, Wis.	42,842
Chesbrough, A. M.	Lucas Co., O.	11,785
Comstock, C. C.	Grand Rapids, Mich.	33,139
Culver, L. S.	Bay City, Mich.	9,526
Cummer, J. & W.	Wexford Co., Mich.	14,897
Eddy, J. F.	Bay City, Mich.	17,613
Fairbanks & Harvey	Chicago, Ill.	86,159
Gay, G. W.	Grand Rapids, Mich.	13,097
Gould, J.	New York, N. Y.	27,464
Hackley, C. H.	Muskegon, Mich.	89,743
Hake & Coach	Grand Rapids, Mich.	6,768
Hamlin, B. D.	Smithport, Pa.	26,907
Hamlin, H.	Smithport, Pa.	18,002
Head, F. H.	Chicago, Ill.	109,645
King, H. W.	Chicago, Ill.	5,640
Lamport, Alway, et al.	Ontario, Canada	23,554
Leatham & Smith	Door Co., Wis.	6,343
Morley, W. B.	St. Clair Co., Mich.	41,014
Nason, R. H.	Saginaw Co., Mich.	19,276
Penoyer, W. C. & W. V.	Iosco Co., Mich.	13,574
Prentice, S. R.	Oakland, Cal.	18,525
Reinhart, H.	Sac Co., Iowa	5,660
Rice, W. M.	Somerset Co., N. J.	48,608
Robinson, Lacey, et al.	Grand Rapids, Mich.	60,025
Silliman, J. R.	New York, N. Y.	23,843
Smith, M. J.	Wayne Co., Mich.	10,080
Van Schaick & Carpenter	Chicago, Ill.	70,274
Wasey & Winchester	Detroit, Mich.	18,581
Watkins, J. B.	Douglas Co., Kan.	145,335
Wetmore, L. D.	Warren Co., Pa.	8,460
Wetmore & Jefferson	Warren Co., Pa.	6,660
Winchester, C.	Ashburnham, Mass.	15,100
Woods, J. L.	Cleveland, O.	84,279
Woods & Pack	Cleveland, O.	9,650
Tawkey, W. C.	Bay City, Mich.	5,790
TOTAL		1,370,332

BY SOUTHERNERS

Name	Residence	Acres
Bradford, J. L.	New Orleans, La.	17,338
Beer, H. & B.	New Orleans, La.	17,807
English & Drew	Calcasieu Parish, La.	13,475
Forest Land Co.	Little Rock, Ark.	14,832
Lutcher & Moore	Orange Co., Texas	108,051
Perkins & Moore	Calcasieu Parish, La.	6,097
Poitevant & Favre	Hancock, Miss.	39,771
Thomson & Knapp	Calcasieu Parish, La.	24,681
Violett, A.	New Orleans, La.	19,880
TOTAL		261,932

PURCHASES OF 5,000 ACRES AND MORE IN MISSISSIPPI, 1880-1888

BY NORTHERNERS

Name	Residence	Acres
Bewick & Comstock	Detroit, Mich.	65,486
Blodgett, D. A.	Grand Rapids, Mich.	136,238
Birkett, McPherson, et al.	Howell, Mich.	18,746
Cartier & Dempsey	Manistee, Mich.	9,563
Chesbrough, A. M.	Toledo, O.	13,180
Conkling, O. F.	Grand Rapids, Mich.	9,120
Doud & Bonner	Winona, Minn.	6,202
Hamlin, H.	Smithport, Pa.	12,195
Heald & Nufer	Montague, Mich.	15,377
Henry, F.	Warren Co., Pa.	9,600
Hills, C. T.	Muskegon, Mich.	69,828
Kent, G.	Delhi, Ontario	6,169
McKeown, J.	Parker City, Pa.	24,646
Moores & McPherson	Lansing, Mich.	11,425
Plock, O.	New York, N. Y.	42,588
Ransdell, D. M.	Indianapolis, Ind.	69,843
Rich, S. B.	Wayne Co., Mich.	18,052
Robinson & Avery	Detroit, Mich.	22,485
Robinson, Lacey, et al.	Grand Rapids, Mich.	6,360
Sage, H. W.	Ithaca, N. Y.	34,559
Schlesinger, B.	Boston, Mass.	7,475
Southwell, H. E.	Milwaukee, Wis.	5,420
Squier, D. W., A. T., & F. W.	Ashland, Mich.	39,648
Tippin, G.	Defiance, O.	9,672
Tomlinson, S. J.	Lapeer Co., Mich.	5,960
Tuttle, B. B.	Naugatuck Co., Conn.	10,015
Vaughan & Johnson	Lapeer Co., Mich.	8,509
Wagar & Wells	Ionia, Mich.	17,680
Ware & Blanchard	Grand Rapids, Mich.	10,090
Watson, A. B.	Grand Rapids, Mich.	82,885
Weston, I. M.	Grand Rapids, Mich.	33,716
Wilson, R. T.	New York, N. Y.	49,717
TOTAL		889,359

BY SOUTHERNERS

Name	Residence	Acres
Butterfield, J. S.	Brookhaven, Miss.	20,599
Brackenridge, E. A.	Orleans Parish, La.	7,520
Colley & Warner	Marion Co., Miss.	8,580
W. F. Evans & Co.	Lauderdale, Miss.	6,323
Griffin & Perkins	Perry Co., Miss.	10,406
Kamper, J.	Laurel, Miss.	14,600
Leinhard, H.	Harrison Co., Miss.	7,524
Orrell, J. C., et al.	Jackson Co., Miss.	17,068
Persons, J. W.	Lincoln, Miss.	5,580
Richardson, W. P.	Hinds Co., Miss.	21,210
Waddell, S.	Union City, Tenn.	14,860
TOTAL		134,270

The sales abstracts of Alabama, Arkansas, and Florida[59] do not reveal such a concentration of purchasing by a few groups nor as many northern buyers as do the records of Louisiana and Mississippi, but Northerners are by no means absent. Seven Northerners bought 121,983 acres in Alabama; in Arkansas seven Northerners bought 114,334 acres; and in Florida six Northerners bought 64,243 acres. The largest purchaser in these states was Daniel F. Sullivan, a native of England, who acquired in Alabama and Florida 250,000 acres of which 150,000 were bought directly of the government.[60] Sullivan, who was characterized as the "timber and lumber king of Florida," a "sort of Gulf Coast Jay Gould in the timber business,"[61] was reported in virtual control of Pensacola through ownership of railroads, piers, and lumberyards, and was reaching out for similar control of Mobile.[62] His death in 1885 revealed ownership of bonds and cash to the amount of $1,000,000 in addition to his vast land and lumber business.[63] The following tables show the large purchases in Alabama, Arkansas, and Florida.

[59] Florida received title to 20,224,022 acres of swamplands which it disposed of largely to railroad and drainage companies in the post Civil War period. The extent of concentration of timberland ownership in Florida in 1911 which resulted from the land policies of the state is revealed in the report of the Bureau of Corporations, *The Lumber Industry*, Pt. II, *Concentration of Timber Ownership in Important Selected Regions*, 217-36.

[60] *Northwestern Lumberman*, May 2, 1885, p. 2.

[61] *Ibid.*, June 28, 1884, p. 7; May 3, 1884, p. 3.

[62] *Ibid.*, May 24, 1884, p. 10.

[63] *Ibid.*, May 2, 1885, p. 2.

PURCHASES OF 5,000 ACRES AND MORE IN ALABAMA, 1880-1888

BY NORTHERNERS

Name	Residence	Acres
Davis, H. L.	Philadelphia, Pa.	39,996
Hall, J. M. W.	Suffolk Co., Mass.	7,647
Peters, R. G.	Manistee, Mich.	5,673
Sage, H. W.	Ithaca, N. Y.	39,031
Wentworth, J. & G. K.	Bay City, Mich.	5,580
Wright & Burrows	Dunkirk, N. Y.	6,410
Yawkey, W. C.	Detroit, Mich.	17,646
TOTAL		121,983

BY SOUTHERNERS

Name	Residence	Acres
Ashe, C. B.	Colbert Co., Ala.	14,320
Boddie, Handley & Lyons	Jefferson Co., Ala.	26,820
Bradfield, L. T.	Montgomery, Ala.	19,880
Carney, J. A.	Baldwin Co., Ala.	8,658
Creary, J. E.	Santa Rosa Co., Fla.	8,390
Durr, J. W.	Montgomery, Ala.	10,660
Ernst, M. L.	Uniontown, Ala.	19,106
Foster & Satterfield	Selma, Ala.	6,240
Fowlkes & Satterfield	Selma, Ala.	5,920
Frazier, S. T.	Union Springs, Ala.	5,740
Friedman, Loveman, et al.	Tuscaloosa, Ala.	23,56C
Gaines, W. H., et al.	Geneva Co., Ala.	8,840
Henderson, Lossing, et al.	Wilcox Co., Ala.	10,66C
Hill, N., Trustee	Jackson Co., Ala.	9,600
Howison, A. P.	Randolph, Ala.	5,16C
Hunter, J.	Mobile, Ala.	18,01C
Jackson, E. E. & W. H.	Salisbury, Md.	43,41S
Millner, J. T.	Jefferson Co., Ala.	7,55S
Muscogee Lumber Co.	Escambia Co., Fla.	13,94I
Robinson, G. W.	Escambia Co., Fla.	14,37:
Roman, S.	Montgomery, Ala.	11,52C
Scott, D. W.	Selma, Ala.	11,55C
Sullivan, D. F.	Escambia Co., Fla.	146,94:
Tyler, W. F.	Shelby Co., Ala.	5,77S
Woodstock Iron Co.		6,59I
TOTAL		463,24

PURCHASES OF 5,000 ACRES AND MORE IN ARKANSAS, 1880-1888

BY NORTHERNERS

Name	Residence	Acres
Ainsworth, C. R. & J. R.	Moline, Ill.	21,22
Cremer, B.	Peoria, Ill.	14,12
Eyke, W.	Muskegon, Mich.	5,25
Goodlander, C. W.	Bourbon Co., Kan.	5,65
Lindsay, J. E.	Scott Co., Iowa	15,60
Lindsay Land & Lumber Co.	Scott Co., Iowa	42,61
Nettleton, G. H.	Jackson Co., Mo.	9,86
TOTAL		114,33

BY SOUTHERNERS

Name	Residence	Acres
Blackburn, J. A. C.	Benton Co., Ark.	9,000
Doyle, T. F.	Pulaski, Ark.	8,598
Forest Land Co.	Ark.	18,913
Hillman, E. H.	Grant Co., Ark.	5,865
Gibson, T. M.	Little Rock, Ark.	42,898
Hall, L. C.	Dardanelle, Ark.	6,100
Jacoway, W. D.	Dardanelle, Ark.	,51,080
McDaniel, H. F.	Washington Co., Ark.	14,436
Smith, J. A.	Smithson, Ark.	7,449
Warren, A. J.	Little Rock, Ark.	19,607

TOTAL 183,946

PURCHASES OF 5,000 ACRES AND MORE IN FLORIDA, 1880-1888

BY NORTHERNERS

Name	Residence	Acres
Foster, G. E.	Venango Co., Pa.	6,366
Hower, J. G.	Cleveland, O.	5,486
Louderback, W. S.	New York, N. Y.	7,981
Morse, C. H., Trustee	Chicago, Ill.	9,983
Seipt, A. H.	Shippack, Pa.	10,687
Yawkey, W. C.	Detroit, Mich.	23,740

TOTAL 64,243

BY SOUTHERNERS

Name	Residence	Acres
Adams & Hall, Trustees	Santa Rosa Co., Fla.	13,202
Bridges, R. R. & P. L.	Wilmington, N. C.	37,503
Byrne, McDavid, et al.	Escambia Co., Fla.	7,837
Doyle, Mann, et al.	Hernando Co., Fla.	8,340
Ingraham, J. E.	Orange Co., Fla.	5,200
Inman, S. M.	Atlanta, Ga.	5,994
Jackson, E. E. & W. H.	Salisbury, Md.	12,640
McMillan, McDavid & Co.	Escambia Co., Fla.	6,240
Muscogee Lumber Co.	Escambia Co., Fla.	6,708
Trafford, E. R.	Orange Co., Fla.	5,800
Wright, Anderson, et al.	Santa Rosa Co., Fla.	5,809
Wright, Milligan, et al.	Escambia Co., Fla.	9,899

TOTAL 125,172

That many of these large purchases were made for speculation is clear from the journals of the lumber trade which record sales made by the original purchasers to actual operators. Corroborative evidence is to be found in a report of the United States Bureau of Corporations for 1913 which analyzes sales of Louisiana timberlands during the 1880's totaling a million acres. Here one finds that the Long Bell Lumber Company[64] whose total landholdings today run to more than 1,000,000 acres, acquired 203,000 acres in the Calcasieu Valley of Louisiana, all of which was bought from nineteen individuals or groups who had entered the lands between 1880 and 1888. Lutcher and Moore enlarged their holdings by acquiring 12,000 acres from second parties, the Central Coal and Coke Company[65] bought 76,300 acres from second parties, and numerous other groups acquired large tracts by buying from speculators at second hand. The following table lists some of these other lumber companies with their purchases in Louisiana and the number of groups from whom they acquired their lands:[66]

Company or Group	Acres Bought	Number of Groups From Whom Acquired
Industrial Lumber Company	58,320	14
Chicago Lumber and Coal Company[67]	54,960	6
W. R. Pickering Lumber Company	47,880	8
Calcasieu Pine Company and Southern Lumber Company	46,760	3
Edgewood Land and Logging Company and Lock, Moore and Company	53,200	14

One is also impressed with the advertisements in journals of the lumber trade offering for sale large blocks of land in the five southern states. For example, the New York Timber Land Company in 1882 advertised for sale 640,000 acres in Mississippi, 65,000 acres in Florida, and 44,000 acres in Arkansas, in addition to large tracts elsewhere in

[64] Bureau of Corporations, *The Lumber Industry*, Pt. II, *Concentration of Timber Ownership in Important Selected Regions*, opposite 148. The Long Bell Lumber Company was incorporated in Missouri in 1884. Its landholdings in Louisiana and Texas in 1913 totaled 393,000 acres, most of which was in long- and shortleaf pine. See *Moody's Manual of Railroad and Corporation Securities*, Fourteenth Annual Number, 2 vols. (New York, 1913), II, 4915-16. The *Annual Reports* of the Long Bell Lumber Corporation (successor to the Long Bell Lumber Company) for recent years give data as to the amount of standing timber which the corporation owns but do not give the acreage.

[65] For the Central Coal and Coke Company, see *Moody's Manual*, Eighth Annual Number (New York, 1907), 1964.

[66] Taken from the Bureau of Corporations, *The Lumber Industry*, Pt. II, *Concentration of Timber Ownership in Important Selected Regions*, opposite 148.

[67] For the Chicago Lumber and Coal Company, see *Moody's Manual*, Fourteenth Annual Number, II, 4184-85.

the South.[68] In 1890 the *Northwestern Lumberman*[69] carried the following advertisements: W. A. Webber and Company of Chicago offered 10,000,000 acres of yellow pine, oak, and cypress lands for sale; S. T. Randle of Yazoo City, Mississippi, advertised 250,000 acres of virgin oak, ash, and cypress; Chamberlin and Amendt of Chicago had 300,000 acres of timberland in Florida for sale; and George W. Clark of New York announced 800,000 acres of yellow pine land in Florida and 300,000 acres of oak and ash land for sale in Arkansas.

Between 1877 and 1888 a total of 5,692,259 acres of Federal lands were sold in the southern states, as shown by the following table:[70]

TABLE OF FEDERAL LANDS SOLD IN THE FIVE SOUTHERN STATES, 1877-1888

Year	Acres	Year	Acres	State	Acres
1877	2,095	1883	1,103,407	Alabama	878,413
1878	14,262	1884	891,836	Arkansas	628,744
1879	16,036	1885	212,863	Florida	1,021,112
1880	86,873	1886	210,100	Mississippi	1,296,775
1881	212,488	1887	882,817	Louisiana	1,867,215
1882	835,710	1888	1,223,772		

These large sales by the Federal government were duplicated by the states which disposed of their swamp, education, and internal improvement grants with equal rapidity. Of course state lands were not subject to the same restrictions as were the Federal lands before 1876, and one finds northern purchasers taking up large tracts as early as 1874. In that year the *Lumberman's Gazette* reported the following purchases in Mississippi: C. H. Shepherd of Lansing, Michigan, bought 40,000 acres in Hancock and Pearl counties; J. D. Norton and T. A. Flowers of Pontiac, Michigan, bought 40,000 acres in Lawrence, Copiah, and Marion counties; T. Hall of Ann Arbor, Michigan, bought 30,000 acres on the Pearl and Pascagoula rivers; and S. M. Wilcox, likewise of Michigan, bought 12,000 acres in Marion county.[71] Perhaps the largest sale

---

68 *Northwestern Lumberman,* May 27, 1882, p. 14; September 16, 1882, p. 18.
69 *Ibid.,* July 12, 1890, p. 21; October 18, 1890, p. 22.
70 This table was compiled from the *Annual Reports* of the Commissioner of the General Land Office by Douglas Schepmoes, formerly of the Resettlement Administration and now of the United States Department of Agriculture.
71 These lands had been granted to the Pearl River Navigation and Improvement Company which sold them to Vose and Baldwin of Jackson, Mississippi, and were sold by

of state land was that made by Florida to a syndicate headed by Hamilton Disston in 1881. Four million acres were thus purchased, a part of which later passed into the hands of the Florida Land and Improvement Company in which British and Dutch capitalists had an interest.[72] Another large purchase was made by R. L. Henry of Chicago who, in 1888, acquired 122,000 acres from the state of Florida.[73] For a part of this land Henry paid as low as twenty-five cents an acre. Southern opposition to the sale of Federal lands in large quantities, as noted below, did not seem to affect state land policies for Florida, Louisiana, and Mississippi continued long after 1888 to sell large tracts to Northerners as well as Southerners.[74]

Southern railroads were also disposing of their holdings in large

them to the above-mentioned parties. Vicksburg *Herald*, quoted in *Lumberman's Gazette* (Bay City, Mich., 1871-1896), August 8, 1874. Vose and Baldwin, in 1874, advertised for sale 400,000 acres in Mississippi, 110,000 in Florida, and 100,000 in Georgia. *Lumberman's Gazette*, May 23, 1874, p. 4.

[72] *Northwestern Lumberman*, July 2, 1881, p. 6; January 21, 1882, p. 5.

[73] *Ibid.*, May 12, 1888, p. 11. Mississippi advertised 250,000 acres of swamplands for sale in 1885 for $1.00 per acre. New Orleans *Times-Democrat*, quoted in the *Northwestern Lumberman*, June 13, 1885, p. 1.

[74] The land policies of the railroads and the state and local governments in the South except for those in Texas, have not been studied. The following sales or advertisements of land by local governmental agencies in 1899 and 1900 were taken from the *Lumber Trade Journal*, published at New Orleans. The General Land Commissioner of Florida sold 325,000 acres of timberlands in Lafayette, Jefferson, Taylor, Madison, and Wakulla counties to the East Coast Lumber Company of Wisconsin *(Lumber Trade Journal,* October 15, 1899, p. 21); 80,000 acres were sold by the Fifth District Levee Board of Louisiana *(ibid.,* September 15, 1899, p. 26); Tyre, Clark, and Brown of Indianapolis purchased 21,000 acres in East Carroll Parish from the Fifth District Levee Board of Louisiana *(ibid.,* October 1, 1900, p. 23); the Tensas Delta Land and Improvement Company purchased a tract of heavily timbered levee land from the city of Monroe, Louisiana, for $155,000 *(ibid.,* January 15, 1899, p. 24); Lutcher and Moore bought the timber on sixteen sections of school land in Newton and Sabine counties from the state of Texas for $32,347 *(ibid.,* July 1, 1900, p. 19); John H. Kirby of Houston bought the timber on 7,000 acres of school land in Jasper County, Texas, for $30,187 *(ibid.,* June 1, 1900, p. 21); over 20,000 acres of land in Jackson and Houston counties, Mississippi, belonging to the University of Mississippi, were offered for sale by the Chancellor *(ibid.,* January 1, 1900, p. 28); the Alcorn Agricultural and Mechanical College of Rodney, Mississippi, sold 23,040 acres for $95,000 to Hemphill Brothers and Company of Hattiesburg, Mississippi, J. J. Newman Lumber Company, Hattiesburg, Knapp, Stout, and Company, Menominee, Wisconsin, D. A. Blodgett, Grand Rapids, Michigan, and Sage Land Improvement Company, Albany, New York *(ibid.,* January 1, 1900, p. 25).

racts. In 1882 the Mobile and Montgomery Railroad sold 35,560 acres of Alabama pine lands to an Appleton, Wisconsin, syndicate for $60,000;[75] the New Orleans Pacific Railroad sold in 1886, 60,000 acres to General Grenville M. Dodge and 20,000 to a General Swain, both of New York;[76] and in 1900 the Illinois Central Railroad and the Yazoo and Mississippi Valley Railroad companies sold 156,750 acres in Mississippi for a price in excess of $1,000,000. This tract was called "the largest virgin forest still standing in the South."[77]

The era of the public domain was coming to an early end, not only in the South but elsewhere in the United States, and the threatening disappearance of free or cheap land gave an impetus to the demands for reform in land policies. Holman, who had long battled to reserve the public lands for actual settlers, now found assistance among those who feared the growing monopoly and trust movement and who looked upon the rapid engrossment of the public lands by speculators, lumber, mining, and cattle companies as a grave danger to American democracy. He also enjoyed the support of the conservationists who were stimulated to action by the threatened exhaustion of the lumber resources. The combination of land reformers, antimonopolists, and conservationists swept the country with their demand for restrictive legislation to safeguard the remaining arable lands for settlers and the timbered lands for future controlled use.[78]

Southerners had good reason to reconsider their attitude on land policy. They realized that the reopening of the southern lands to large-scale purchasing had not brought the economic expansion they had expected; instead it had resulted in the purchase of large tracts of valuable lands by speculators, generally nonresidents, who withheld them from development while they waited for their profits. Some northern capitalists doubtless bought lands to keep them out of competition with their northern lands and mills. Others were later to cut the timber, prepare

[75] *Northwestern Lumberman*, August 5, 1882, p. 9; October 21, 1882, p. 10.
[76] *Ibid.*, July 24, 1886, p. 7.
[77] *Lumber Trade Journal*, June 15, 1900, p. 13.
[78] Gates, "The Homestead Law in an Incongruous Land System," in *loc. cit.*, 679-81.

328 THE JOURNAL OF SOUTHERN HISTORY

the rough lumber, and ship it to their northern mills for finishing, thereby depriving the South of the industrial expansion it anticipated. Nor had the act of 1876 ended timber stealing. In 1888 the Commissioner of the General Land Office reported that organized trespassing and plundering upon the public lands existed in all the southern states.[79] Furthermore, it was becoming apparent that the earlier view concerning the soil qualities of these public lands was erroneous.

Homesteading, which in the period from 1866 to 1876 had been regarded as largely the work of dummy entrymen acting for the lumber companies, had continued after 1876 on a more extensive scale. Whereas before 1876 there had been an incentive for the lumbermen to use dummy entrymen to acquire land, there was no such need thereafter. Small operators doubtless continued to take advantage of the preemption and homestead laws to acquire lands illegally, but the larger operators could buy in unlimited amounts at a small price and they had no further use of dummy entrymen. Still the number of homestead entries increased, as did also the area under cultivation in the southern states. No doubt some of this land was taken up by people who intended to sell it to lumbermen. But many of these homestead entries were made by settlers who established farms in the timbered sections. Calcasieu Parish, in which a large part of the remaining public land in Louisiana was located, doubled the number of its farms in the 1880's, quadrupled its acreage in farms, and increased the value of its farms eightfold.[80] Other timbered sections of the five states also enjoyed substantial farm increases. The realization that many thousands of new farms might be established if the remaining lands were withdrawn from speculative purchasing[81] produced a revulsion of sentiment in that section against the wide-open land system and the act of 1876 which had placed it in operation.

The South was alarmed and angry at the rapid disappearance of pub

[79] Commissioner General Land Office, *Annual Report*, 1889, pp. 50, 53-54, 57-58.
[80] *Tenth Census of the United States*, 1880, *Agriculture*, 118; *Eleventh Census of the United States*, 1890, *Agriculture*, 211.
[81] That the South was coming to realize that timberlands were suitable for farming seen in a dispatch in the *Northwestern Lumberman*, October 8, 1877, p. 1.

lic lands[82] and its representatives co-operated with the land reformers of other sections in bringing about a complete reorganization of the land system. But the land question was a complicated one and called for long debate. Furthermore, at the very moment when changes in the system were being discussed in Congress, there was a concerted dash by timbermen, speculators, and others to secure the remaining lands before the wide-open policy was reversed. Cash sales and homestead entries boomed in 1887 and 1888. Despairing of quick congressional action upon the land reform question, the Southerners determined to rush through Congress a measure to suspend all large-scale purchasing in Alabama, Arkansas, and Mississippi until the end of the session. On April 17, 1888, such a bill was introduced into the Senate. It passed the upper house on the twenty-third and on May 3 it passed the lower house, each time without debate, and became a law on May 14.[83] Within a month representatives of Louisiana and Florida were urging Congress to extend the suspension to their states where, it was pointed out, those who were formerly buying in the closed states were now threatening to enter all the remaining lands. A second resolution was rushed through Congress to suspend all cash entries in the South until the end of the Fiftieth Congress by which time it was anticipated a general reform law would be adopted.[84] The next three years witnessed the

[82] As early as 1884 it was apparent the South was becoming disillusioned about the economic effects of the act of 1876. When a group of Michigan lumbermen sought to secure from the Mississippi legislature an act to incorporate the Pascagoula Improvement, Log Running, and Booming Company, they were defeated because of fear that the group would acquire a monopoly of the lumber business in the southeastern part of the state. *Northwestern Lumberman*, April 5, 1884, p. 1. Three years later the New Orleans *Times-Democrat* regretted the large sales of public lands to Northerners and opposition generally was being expressed to continued sales. Quoted in *ibid.*, March 12, 1887, p. 1; May 28, 1887, p. 1.

[83] *Cong. Record*, 50 Cong., 1 Sess., 3032 (April 17, 1888), 3221 (April 23, 1888), 3707 (May 3, 1888), 3771 (May 7, 1888); 25 *U. S. Statutes at Large*, 622. The *Northwestern Lumberman*, May 5, 1888, p. 2, said that this measure would operate to the disadvantage of many who wished to speculate in southern timberlands but that it came "at a rather late day, the larger part of the more desirable lands having already been secured."

[84] *Cong. Record*, 50 Cong., 1 Sess., 5479 (June 21, 1888), 5828 (July 2, 1888), 5859 (July 3, 1888); 25 *U. S. Statutes at Large*, 626. On March 2, 1889, all public lands except those in Missouri were closed to private or cash entry. *Ibid.*, 854.

termination of cash sales[85] and the long-awaited reorganization of the land system combined with the beginning of a new policy of forest conservation.

There yet remained a substantial fragment of the public domain in the five southern states, amounting to 14,398,148 acres.[86] Although the best of the timber, the mineral, and the arable lands were gone, home steading went on for another generation, during which time 134,000 original entries were made. The story of that homesteading is worthy of study but space does not permit an analysis here. Meantime, absentee ownership of great tracts of timberland had been established in the South as was also northern control of most of the resources of that section. This absentee ownership was to evoke in the present decade a notable "Report on the Economic Conditions of the South,"[87] and an equally challenging polemic by a professor at a southern university entitled *Divided We Stand*.[88] The South had invited the investment of northern capital by the repeal of the act of 1866 but instead had gotten mere speculation and retarded development. When it awoke to its error it reverted to the policy of 1866 but the change came too late. Northern ers controlled the best stands of yellow pine and cypress lands and were to reap the benefit by taking the cream of the profits from the rising lumber industry.

[85] In 1889 Congress ended cash sales of public lands in all states but Missouri. The following year it was provided that no person should acquire more than 320 acres of the Federal government. 25 U. S. *Statutes at Large*, 845-55; 26 *ibid.*, 391. In effect this left none but fragments of sections generally and isolated tracts in Missouri which still could be purchased. Certain Indian lands were subsequently to be sold, however.

[86] Commissioner General Land Office, *Annual Report*, 1890, p. 12.

[87] Prepared by the National Emergency Council and submitted to the President of the United States on July 25, 1938.

[88] Walter P. Webb, *Divided We Stand. The Crisis of a Frontierless Democracy* (New York, 1937).

THE ADMINISTRATION OF FEDERAL LAND LAWS
IN WESTERN KANSAS, 1880-1890

George L. Anderson

THE KANSAS
HISTORICAL QUARTERLY

Volume XX   *November, 1952*   Number 4

The Administration of Federal Land Laws in Western Kansas, 1880-1890: A Factor in Adjustment to a New Environment[1]

GEORGE L. ANDERSON

THE careful interpretive studies of James C. Malin,[2] some of which have appeared in earlier issues of this *Quarterly*,[3] have demonstrated that adaptation to the physical characteristics of the grassland region was the greatest single problem confronting the settlers in the western half of Kansas. Malin has shown that the successful types of adaptation were the results of folk-processes; and that the most fruitful technique for the historian is to study a community in its entirety, with the emphasis upon the role of individuals as portrayed in local newspaper and manuscript sources.

This study involves only certain selected phases of the question. It is based upon the assumption that the administration of the federal land laws was an important component of the problem of adjustment. It is intended to illustrate the use that can be made of certain types of archival materials and to provide a background for further studies. It does not represent a commitment to the point of view that fraud and speculative activities constitute the most important aspects of the problem.

It should be clear that the history of the administration of the land laws cannot be reduced to some capsule-like generalization

DR. GEORGE LAVERNE ANDERSON is chairman of the history department at the University of Kansas, Lawrence.
1. An earlier version of this paper was presented at the 1944 meeting of the Mississippi Valley Historical Association.
2. "The Adaptation of the Agricultural System to Sub-humid Environment," *Agricultural History*, Baltimore, v. 10 (1936), July, pp. 118-141; *Winter Wheat in the Golden Belt of Kansas: A Study in Adaptation to Subhumid Geographical Environment* (Lawrence, 1944); *The Grassland of North America: Prolegomena to Its History* (Lawrence, 1947); "Grassland, 'Treeless,' and 'Subhumid': A Discussion of Some Problems of the Terminology of Geography," *The Geographical Review*, New York, v. 37 (1947), April, pp. 241-250.
3. "The Turnover of Farm Population in Kansas," v. 4 (1935), November, pp. 339-372; "The Kinsley Boom in the Late Eighties," v. 4 (1935), February, May, pp. 23-49 and 164-187; "J. A. Walker's Early History of Edwards County," v. 9 (1940), August, "Introduction," pp. 259-270; "An Introduction to the History of the Bluestem-Pasture Region of Kansas: A Study in Adaptation to Geographic Environment," v. 11 (1942), February, pp. 3-28.

that will faithfully portray developments in even a part of one state, much less accurately reflect developments in all the states and territories west of the Missouri river. For too long a time a summary of the laws padded with quotable portions of congressional debates, and seasoned with the more dramatic generalizations of officials in Washington, has passed for a history of the subject. Even this formula is so diluted or distorted in some instances as to leave the impression that the operation of the federal land laws was relatively unimportant. In pursuing the study of a subject in an entirely different field Joseph Schafer remarked:

> The author's chief reason for calling sharp attention to the futility of the speculative method hitherto commonly used by historians in dealing with subjects of this kind is to protest against an outworn methodology. The "guessing game" is no longer permissible to those who claim the right to be called historians, in the American field at least. Like Hamlet, we demand "proofs more relative" than those supplied by ghosts.[4]

Much of the historical literature in the field of public land studies is vulnerable to this criticism. Also, it cannot escape the judgment Malin makes concerning population studies that are based exclusively upon printed federal materials: "As in outline surveys or general histories, it is writing from the top down and partakes too much of the fitting of generalizations to particular cases rather than arriving at the generalization from the study of the underlying detail."[5]

Another characteristic of many of the historical accounts of the public lands which this study seeks to avoid is the almost universal preoccupation of the writer with the large speculator, the "bonanza farmer," the cattleman or the corporation. Thus Paul W. Gates excludes from a study of the homestead law the "many farmers who speculated in a small way."[6] The histories of the range cattle industry tend to limit land frauds to fencing the public domain and the use of hired or dummy entrymen.[7] The authors of a widely used general history accept this point of view so completely that they are able to say, "Land frauds in the cattle kingdom were so universal

4. "Who Elected Lincoln?" *The American Historical Review*, New York, v. 47 (1941), October, p. 63.
5. "Local Historical Studies and Population Problems," in Caroline F. Ware (ed.), *The Cultural Approach to History* (New York, 1940), p. 300.
6. "The Homestead Law in an Incongruous Land System," *The American Historical Review*, New York, v. 41 (1936), July, p. 652.
7. Ernest S. Osgood, *The Day of the Cattleman* (Minneapolis, 1929), pp. 190-215; Ora B. Peake, *The Colorado Range Cattle Industry* (Glendale, Cal., 1937), pp. 69-84. Louis Pelzer, *The Cattlemen's Frontier* (Glendale, Cal., 1936), pp. 173-191. The reports of the registers and receivers of the local land offices and those of special agents that were sent to the General Land Office during October and November, 1884, are devoted almost exclusively to these forms of fraudulent practice. "Report of the Commissioner of the General Land Office," 1885, in *Report of the Secretary of the Interior, House Ex. Doc. No. 1* (serial no. 2,378), 49 Cong., 1 Sess. (1885-1886), v. 1, pp. 202-216.

as to make impertinent the suggestion of mere individual wrong-doing." [8]   This relegation to the realm of the "impertinent" leaves the individual settler a shadowy figure, always present, but rarely made the specific object of attention. How he came to be in a particular community; how he obtained his land; whether he was a permanent settler, transient drifter or would-be speculator; how the operation of the land laws affected his adjustment to his environment if he stayed; these and many other questions have been answered only in a fragmentary way if at all.

The nature of the problem of research in this field, if printed federal materials are used exclusively, can best be emphasized by quoting conflicting statements of two commissioners of the General Land Office. Each had access to the same type of material and each had come to the office from the Middle West after long periods of public service and political experience. William Andrew Jackson Sparks was a member of the Democratic party and an anti-monopoly crusader; [9] his successor, William M. Stone, was one of the organizers of the Republican party.[10]   Said Commissioner Sparks in 1885, after six months in office:

> I found that the magnificent estate of the nation in its public lands had been to a wide extent wasted under defective and improvident laws and through a laxity of public administration astonishing in a business sense if not culpable in recklessness of official responsibility. . . . I am satisfied that thousands of claims without foundation in law or equity, involving millions of acres of public land, have been annually passed to patent upon the single proposition that nobody but the government had any *adverse* interest.
>
> The vast machinery of the land department appears to have been devoted to the chief result of conveying the title of the United States to public lands upon fraudulent entries under strained constructions of imperfect public land laws and upon illegal claims under public and private grants.[11]

Following these introductory remarks there are estimates of fraud under the several land laws ranging from 40% in the case of the homestead law to 100% under the commutation clause of that law.[12]

Thus Commissioner Sparks, using materials accumulated by the preceding administrations, drew a blanket indictment that was

8. Samuel Eliot Morison and Henry Steele Commager, *The Growth of the American Republic* (New York, 1942), v. 2, p. 94.

9. There is a brief biography by Harold H. Dunham, in the *Dictionary of American Biography* (New York, 1946), v. 17, pp. 434, 435.

10. Benjamin F. Gue, *History of Iowa* (New York, 1903), v. 4, p. 253.

11. "Report of the Commissioner of the General Land Office," 1885, *loc. cit.*, pp. 155, 156.

12. *Ibid.*, p. 223. In this report reference is made, pp. 201, 202, by Commissioner Sparks to his order of April 3, 1885, suspending the further entry of land in a group of Western states and territories including western Kansas. This order remained in effect until April 6, 1886, when it was revoked upon direct orders of Secretary of the Interior L. Q. C. Lamar.

tantamount to saying that the settlement and development of the Western plains prior to 1885 was largely based upon fraud. The quotation given above is reasonably characteristic of those that have gained entrance into the general histories, but in fairness, Commissioner W. M. Stone should be heard in rebuttal. Making direct reference to the Sparks report of 1885 and quoting several paragraphs from it, he said:

> This wholesale arraignment of claimants on the public domain should not have been made without the most conclusive evidence to sustain it. It contains in express terms, without discrimination and without exception, a charge of the gravest character against these hardy and courageous pioneers of our advancing civilization well calculated to challenge the credulity of the lowest order of American intellect.
>
> This astounding condition of things . . . may or may not have existed during his administration, but it affords me infinite pleasure to inform you that during my more than four months of intimate connection with the duties of this office I have found no evidence of general misconduct on the part of our western settlers, and have failed to discover any general system of fraud prevailing upon the government in reference to the public domain. Instances of attempted fraud are to be expected, but justice requires me to say that they are exceedingly rare and notably exceptional. I speak now of the individual settler.[13]

It is elementary to point out that both of the honorable commissioners could not be right and that the truth must lie somewhere between the two extremes. It is more important to note certain factors, other than political, that may serve to explain their disagreement. The General Land Office, although charged with the responsibility of administering a landed heritage of imperial proportions, was handicapped by an undermanned staff, an antiquated building, a pint-sized budget and an overwhelming flood of business.[14] The information that came to Washington from the cutting edge of settlement was from special agents with too little time to

13. "Report of the Commissioner of the General Land Office," 1889, in *Report of the Secretary of the Interior, House Ex. Doc. No. 1* (serial no. 2,724), 51 Cong., 1 Sess. (1889-1890), v. 1, p. 9. Commissioner Stone was much too optimistic. Statements that he thought would challenge "the credulity of the lowest order of American intellect" have come to be accepted almost without question as accurate descriptions of the administration of the federal land laws. There is no question concerning the existence of practices that the commissioners described as fraudulent. The question is whether they were well nigh universal and characteristic. N. C. McFarland, the predecessor of Sparks, wrote on August 5, 1881, to J. R. Hallowell, United States district attorney for Kansas, "This fraudulent entry business has become too common as I have reason already to know."—Correspondence of the United States District Attorney's Office, Kansas State Historical Society manuscript collections. Unless otherwise indicated all correspondence used in this paper is contained in this collection.

14. Harold Hathway Dunham, *Government Handout: A Study in the Administration of the Public Lands, 1875-1891* (New York, 1941), pp. 124-144. The chapter cited is entitled "The Inadequate Land Office." This study, which is a product of the seminar of Allan Nevins at Columbia University, illustrates a statement made earlier in this paper. The opening sentence of the paragraph in the preface, p. v., which describes the bibliography that was used is as follows, "Emphasis on the administration of the public lands did not call for an exhaustive analysis of the literature of the West."

do an enormous piece of work; from partisans in the local land offices; from cranks and malcontents; as well as from honest settlers with legitimate complaints and views. The alternate advance and recession of settlement produced by alternate periods of drought and rainfall brought a complex mixture of humanity to an unfamiliar environment and piled entry upon entry, relinquishment upon relinquishment and contest upon contest until even the plat books were hopelessly out-of-date and the basement and corridors of the land office were piled high with unclaimed patents, unsettled contests and unstudied correspondence.[15] "Going back to the wife's folks" may be just a convenient euphemism to the historian, but it more than doubled the work of the General Land Office. The sequence of entry, abandonment without record, relinquishment or sale may have added up to fraud in the humid regions farther to the east and south; but in western Kansas it may have meant that optimistic settlers, becoming discouraged by death, drought, dust and grasshoppers, were giving up the fight and were only trying to salvage enough from their battles with and on Uncle Sam's land to get out of the country.[16]   For this reason, among others, the emphasis in this study is shifted from Washington to the local scene, from federal officials to individual entrymen, from the public domain of several millions of acres to the individual quarter section of 160 acres.   Obviously broader questions must be considered, but the center of attention is the individual entryman on a particular quarter section of land.[17] This paper is, in a sense, a preliminary move in the direction of studying the history of the operation of the federal land laws in the western half of Kansas from the ground up.[18]

15. Any researcher with a specific project in hand who has used even a small portion of the mass of material in the General Land Office section of the National Archives, Washington, D. C., with the assistance and guidance of skilled personnel and modern technical aids, will appreciate the difficulties that confronted the staff of the General Land Office when the public lands were being entered at the rate of several millions of acres annually.

16. See article entitled "Governmental Evictions in Kansas" in the Kirwin *Independent*, July 7, 1887, for a suggestion that the homesteader was really just betting his $14 against Uncle Sam's 160 acres that he could live on the land for five years.

17. A study somewhat comparable in objective was made in 1887 at the request of Commissioner Sparks.   He directed that a thorough study be made of representative townships by special agents and inspectors to discover how the several land laws operated in particular instances.   After giving specific directions for carrying out the study, Sparks stated its purpose as follows: "The purpose of these examinations is to ascertain what becomes of public land taken up under the public land laws, and the general character of the different classes of entries on different classes of land, and to what extent they are made to sell or mortgage, or for the benefit of land and loan agents, speculators, syndicates, and corporations."—"Report of the Commissioner of the General Land Office," 1887, in *Report of the Secretary of the Interior, House Ex. Doc., No. 1* (serial no. 2,541), 50 Cong., 1 Sess. (1887-1888), v. 1, p. 144.

18. Almost without exception the examples selected involve entries west of the 98° meridian.   The principal local land offices for the area were located at Wichita, Salina, Concordia, Cawker City, Kirwin, Larned, Garden City, Hays, Wakeeney, Colby and Oberlin.

Reduced to its simplest term, the process of alienating land from the public domain to private ownership under the pre-emption and homestead laws consisted of three steps: settlement, residence and improvement. The timber culture act required a sequence of breaking, planting and cultivating. The performance of these various activities had to be verified before the local land officers by the entryman through the filing of sworn affidavits and the sworn testimony of two witnesses. Indeed, there was so much swearing in the process that it is reminiscent of the medieval practice of compurgation or oath helping.[19] It was this same abundance of swearing that made perjury the most frequent offense under the land laws. Forgery was quite prevalent, but it was the swearing to the truth of the forged statement that made it actionable. If, in the judgment of the officers of the local land office, the final proof was satisfactory a final certificate was issued, and if no contest had been filed the entry would be reported to the General Land Office for the issuance of the patent. If the entry was contested the case was heard in the first instance at the local land office with the right of appeal to the commissioner of the General Land Office and ultimately to the Secretary of the Interior.[20] Under some circumstances entries that had been suspended because of the failure of the entryman to comply with the law could be referred to the Board of Equitable Adjudication for final determination.[21] The almost limitless variation of this process of entry, proof, contest, appeal and patent; the numerous technical features of the laws; the frequent contradictions in the interpretations of the laws and the administrative procedures used in enforcing them imposed heavy burdens upon the individual entryman. In nearly two-thirds of the suspended entries referred from the area under consideration

19. The following contemporary comments suggest that the act of swearing to the truth of statements contained in land entry papers had become so commonplace that it had lost its value as an inhabitant to fraud: "The fact is land law is almost disregarded. The people make affidavits much as they eat pie without any regard for their moral digestion."—Frank Thanhouser, Garden City, to W. C. Perry, May 1, 1886. "It is a positive fact that a class of land lawyers in this country tell their clients that there is no danger of getting into any trouble by swearing what they please and a certain class are acting accordingly to the annoyance of honest settlers. . . ."—Charles Morrison, Hillside, to W. C. Perry, June 25, 1887. "There has been so much looseness in these land claims and many persons think they are perfectly safe to swear to anything in a land claim or entry that in those cases false swearing is no crime this idea which is quite prevalent should be corrected and those persons who are disposed to swear falsely should be taught that it is perjury. . . ." —L. V. Hollyfield of Cherryvale, to J. R. Hallowell, March 23, 1880. "Our atty's here claim there is no law against perjury and that there never was a party sentenced to the Pen. for this kind of false swearing in the state of Kansas. They argue this way: that a man is compelled to swear falsely in order to start a contest and whenever a party is compelled to swear in order to start a suit it is not considered a crime. . . . This president of affairs has existed in this county until perjury is considered witty and cute."—C. H. Barlow, Goodland, to W. C. Perry, April 12, 1888.

20. The contest division was established in 1887 upon the recommendation of Commissioner W. A. J. Sparks. It was designated Division H.—"Report of the General Land Office," 1887, loc. cit., pp. 435-438.

21. There is no readily available source of information concerning this agency.

to the Board of Equitable Adjudication, "ignorance of the law" was the reason given for failure to make proof within the required period of time.[22]

The position of the individual entryman was further weakened by the fact that the federal land laws did not make adequate provision for the punishment of criminal fraud. So weak was the position of the government that W. C. Perry, United States district attorney, wrote warningly to a United States court commissioner: "I write this letter not for public use, as it is better not to let every one know the weakness of the federal statutes with reference to the punishment of frauds against the public domain." [23]   Even the avenue of prosecution for perjury was so restricted as to permit all but the most glaring cases to go unpunished.   In discussing a land case Perry defined perjury as "wilful and corrupt swearing to some material matter, which was known at the time by the party so swearing to be untrue." [24]   It had to be "positive, unequivocal, malicious and knowingly false." [25]   There had to be proof that the alleged acts were intended to and did actually defraud the United States and not merely a private individual.[26]   Moreover it should be noted that the statute of limitations barred prosecution after three years had elapsed [27] and that in all cases where the land involved had been passed to patent the district attorney was helpless and could prosecute only upon orders from the Attorney General, who in turn could act only if requested to do so by the Secretary

22. H. Booth, former receiver of the Larned land office, expressed the opinion that not one settler in a thousand could fill out the entry and proof papers correctly without assistance from an attorney.—Larned *Chronoscope*, July 10, 1885.   The editor of the paper agreed with Booth.   The comments were inspired by the order issued on June 24, 1885, by Commissioner Sparks which curtailed the activities of land attorneys.   Every suspended entry referred to the Board of Equitable Adjudication was of course open to contest.   The fact that such a large number of vulnerable entries escaped contests has caused this writer to study the operations of the board in some detail.

23. W. C. Perry to J. M. Tinney, U. S. commissioner at Kirwin, April 28, 1886. The letter was written from Topeka and concerned the D. N. Whipple case.   On October 10, 1885, Perry had written to A. H. Garland, Attorney General of the United States, requesting more assistance because ". . . a large portion of the State is, or, rather, formerly was public domain and many cases have, and are arising out of frauds and perjuries perpetrated in the entries of public lands under the homestead, pre-emption and timber culture statutes and more will and should arise under these laws, as the violating thereof are notoriously and shamefully frequent."

24. W. C. Perry to R. A. Crossman, Vilas, Colo., November 29, 1887. In another case Perry emphasized wilful and false testimony to "material matter."—Letter to Charles Fickeissen, Buffalo Park, May 6, 1886.   In an undated letter to J. M. Tinney, Kirwin, Perry included "a dishonest or corrupt motive" as part of his definition of perjury. In letters to R. G. Cook, U. S. commissioner at Dodge City, April 23, 1886, and to Thomas J. Richardson, special agent of the General Land Office at Wichita, November 9, 1888, Perry commented upon the difficulty of securing convictions in perjury cases.

25. W. C. Perry to C. W. Reynolds, Chalk Mound, July 9, 1886.   Perry to A. D. Duncan, special agent of the General Land Office at Kirwin, October 20, 1886.

26. W. C. Perry to C. H. Carswell, Coronado, December 7, 1887.   Same to J. G. Allard, special agent of the General Land Office, Oberlin, June 12, 1888.

27. The evidence in a case involving Charles Miller and Gust Mauer of Hays, seemed to indicate that fraud had been used by the former in 1881, but it was not discovered until 1885 thus taking "it out of the Statutes."—A. D. Gilkerson to Perry, November 10, 1885; Perry referred to the statute of limitations in letters to Louden and Freeman of Ness City, February 4, 1887; and to Doctor H. Tant, Medicine Lodge, June 29, 1888.

of the Interior.[28]   Thus a fraud could be committed under the preemption act, the land be patented and sold to an innocent third party and the whole process go unnoticed and unpunished.[29]   The same legal and technical complications that laid heavy handicaps upon the entrymen provided the foundation for the profitable activities of land attorneys, land agents, professional locators and chronic claim jumpers.   It seems clear that these men contributed in considerable measure to the confusion and instability that were characteristic of communities during their early years.   They made a practice of buying and selling relinquishments;[30] of hiring men to make entries in order to prevent legal entrymen from initiating claims to choice tracts;[31] of loaning money to prove up,[32] and in some cases of preventing by violence the entering of bona fide settlers.[33]   Instances are on record of one of these agents securing 12 quarter-sections on two separate occasions;[34] of another paying individuals $5 for the use of their names in making homestead entries and retaining the claims until they could be sold to bona fide entrymen for $25 to $50,[35] and of a third getting control of a local

28. W. C. Perry, to J. E. Anderson, Salina, February 25, 1889. Note in Perry's handwriting on letter of June 13, 1887, received by him at Fort Scott from Lovitt and Sturman of Salina.

29. In a letter to Thomas J. Richardson, special agent of the General Land Office at Wichita, May 26, 1888, W. C. Perry emphasized the difficulty of canceling an entry that had reached the final receipt stage and the land in question had passed in good faith to an innocent third party. Other references to the "innocent purchaser" doctrine are contained in letters from Perry to Clark S. Rowe, special agent of the General Land Office at Larned, March 20, 1888; to W. F. Galvin, Stockton, December 4, 1888, and to Rowe, March 16, 1888.

30. A rapid examination of almost any newspaper published during the period under consideration in the western part of Kansas will confirm this statement.

31. Randolph Burt, Gettysburg, to W. C. Perry, May 3, May 12, and June 2, 1886. Henry Kern, Palco, to Perry, April 2, 1889. The material relating to the activities of such large scale operators as J. L. Gandy, J. G. Hiatt and A. M. Brenaman is relevant, but is much too voluminous to be cited here.

32. Land agents on frequent occasions mentioned "loans to make final proof" as a specialty. The Lane County Herald, Dighton, April 22, 1886, contained two examples.

33. Allegations to this effect are so numerous in the incoming correspondence of the United States district attorney as to make listing impracticable. There is some reason to believe that "Homesteaders' Unions" and "Old Settlers' Protective Associations" were devices to protect illegal entrymen. W. C. Perry to E. E. Thomas, special agent of the General Land Office at Salina, July 31, 1886, relative to organized intimidation in Scott county; Perry to G. M. McElroy of Oberlin, August 27, 1886, concerning a similar organization in Cheyenne county; E. R. Cutler, Meade Center, to W. C. Perry, December 20, 1886, asking for help against mob violence in Meade county; J. Word Carson, Wakeeney, to Perry, November 22, 1887, calling attention to the situation in Greeley county; Charles P. Dunaway, Stockton, January 2, 1888, to Perry asking him to investigate the activities of the Homesteader's Union in Rooks county. The Hoover case in western Ness county and the Widow Edsall case in Sherman county produced a voluminous correspondence with the district attorney's office during the spring and early summer of 1888.

34. The Eye, Oberlin, September 18, and November 20, 1884, referring to the activities of A. J. Cortell. The Cortell-Zimmermann contest case attracted a great deal of attention in 1887-1888.

35. The Lincoln (Neb.) Journal quoted in the Oberlin Eye, January 28, 1886, describing the activities of the firm of Wilson, Tacha and Parker. S. F. McKinney wrote to W. C. Perry from Salina on April 7, 1887, "I . . . am a poor man & have a family to support & look after and I have got very poor health also & I have been swindled out of my land & home just by such law pettifoggers & western swindle schemers as this Robert W. Carter & J. W. Brooks & many others in Ellsworth that stand ready to gobble up a poor mans hard earned property & lie him out of it." W. Jones to Perry from Conway Springs, April 30, 1888.

landoffice by placing beds and cots in front of the door for his "rustlers" to sleep on so that they could anticipate even the early rising settlers in making and shifting relinquishments, entries and contests.[36] In many cases they were the publishers or editors of the local newspapers and in some they were intimately familiar with local land office procedures either through previous experience or current connections.[37] The notion that a settler reached the frontier and "gazing upon almost endless stretches of rich agricultural land" made his selection does not fit the facts. More often than not he located his claim under the watchful eye of a land locator who may have located some other person on the same tract at an earlier date.[38]

The activities of land agents and attorneys received special attention from Commissioner W. A. J. Sparks in several of his annual reports [39] and in the day-to-day correspondence of his office. His determination to eliminate those who were engaging in dishonest practices is indicated in a number of letters written to law firms in Kansas towns. In November, 1885, W. A. Frush, of Garden City, was debarred from practice before any bureau of the Department of the Interior for failing to give a satisfactory explanation of a charge that he had forged the signature of an entryman in connection with the relinquishment of a timber culture entry.[40] During the same month Sparks was extremely critical of a circular issued by Milton Brown, also of Garden City, advising union veterans of

36. "Report of the Commissioner of the General Land Office," 1886, in *Report of the Secretary of the Interior, House Ex. Doc. No. 1* (serial no. 2,468), 49 Cong., 2 Sess. (1886-1887), v. 2, p. 86.
37. C. J. Lamb, editor of the Kirwin *Independent*, advertised real estate for sale in the issue for February 3, 1887; R. H. Ballinger, editor of the Larned *Chronoscope* and Henry Booth, receiver of the land office in Larned were partners in a real estate firm; Ed Martin, a loan agent in Oberlin had served as a clerk in the land office at Kirwin according to the Kirwin *Independent*, March 31, 1887. William Don Carlos of Kirwin began his career as chief clerk in the Kickapoo land office; his son, the junior partner in the firm, had been a clerk in the General Land Office in Washington, D. C.—*Ibid.*, March 10, 1887. H. A. Yonge who became register of the land office at Kirwin in March, 1887, had been editor of the Beloit *Democrat* and a member of the firm of Yonge and Scott; Tully Scott had been appointed register of the Oberlin office at an earlier date.—*Ibid.*, March 31, 1887. W. J. A. Montgomery, editor of the Stockton *Democrat* on March 26, 1886, ran the following advertisement: "Say—If you want a good claim that you can put a pre-emption, homestead or timber entry on, call at this office. If you want to make your home here, buy a claim and lay your homestead or timber entry on it and save from 7 to 13 years' taxes." The following land office officials were accused of having had illegal if not corrupt dealings with land firms: Tully Scott, Oberlin, Oberlin *Eye*, March 8, 1888; C. A. Morris, Larned, Larned *Weekly Chronoscope*, November 25, 1887; B. J. F. Hanna, and W. C. L. Beard, Wakeeney, *Lane County Herald*, August 25, and September 1, 1887.
38. The firm of Borton and Spidle of Ness City advertised in the *Lane County Herald*, July 17, 1885, "Will locate you. Win a contest for you. Make out your final proof. Make out filing papers for you. Sell you horses and cattle. Furnish you money to pay out on your claims. Make a soldier's filing for you, if you cannot come in person, and win law-suits for you." One partner was a lawyer, the other a locator.
39. The "Report for 1887" is typical. It is contained in *Report of the Secretary of the Interior, House Ex. Doc., No. 1* (serial no. 2,541) 50 Cong., 1 Sess. (1887-1888), v. 1, pp. 134-136.
40. Sparks to Frush, August 18, September 3, and November 21, 1885—"General Land Office Correspondence," A, Miscellaneous, pp. 233, 234, 272 and 449, in the National Archives.

the Civil War that they were entitled to 160 acres of government land which they could obtain *"without residence on the land"* and informing them that the filing and locating could be accomplished *"without their leaving their eastern homes."* In his first letter to Brown, Commissioner Sparks asserted that "these statements are false and misleading and . . . can be regarded only as attempts to defraud either the soldier or the government or both." In his second letter Sparks declared that the "statements in said circulars are unwarranted by any provision of the laws and are calculated to encourage and induce frauds upon the government in the procurement and promotion of illegal entries and claims.[41] In a letter to a third Garden City firm Sparks commented that their circular was a palpable invitation to fraud and that its apparent purpose was "to deceive soldiers, impose upon their widows and orphaned children and promote frauds on the government." Critical reference was made to their requirement of the soldier's discharge papers, a power of attorney and a fee of ten dollars.[42] In other letters Sparks asked one firm to explain charges that it had accepted a fee for filing a contest and then had dismissed the case without notice to its client;[43] and another one to explain why it had filed a contest, dismissed it without notice to its client, and then filed a fictitious contest against the client's entry.[44]

It should be apparent that the entryman's problem of adjustment to his new environment began with his first encounter with the local land officers and with those residents of the community who sought to exploit his ignorance for their own profit. It should be added that some entrymen had the benefit of honest and capable legal advisers when they became entangled in administrative regulations. The firm of William Don Carlos and Son, of Kirwin, was held in high esteem. The editor of *The Independent,* Kirwin, a critic of almost every other aspect of land office administration, stated that this firm was composed of "competent, energetic men, always wide awake and attentive to the interests of their clients. . . . In the twelve or thirteen years that this firm has been doing business here

41. Sparks to Brown, November 4, and December 12, 1885.—*Ibid.*, pp. 411, 412 and 486.

42. Sparks to Bennett and Smith of Garden City, December 23, 1885.—*Ibid.*, pp. 12, 13.

43. Sparks to Kimball and Reeves, Garden City, August 10, 1886.—*Ibid.*, 499, 500.

44. Sparks to Morris and Morris, Larned, November 17, 1885.—*Ibid.*, p. 435. A summary of the practices of the Garden City firms is contained in the "Report of the Commissioner of the General Land Office," 1886, *loc. cit.*, pp. 85, 86. Larned *Weekly Chronoscope*, November 25, 1887. An earlier instance is described in a letter of Secretary of the Interior Henry Teller to Commissioner N. C. McFarland, September 26, 1883, in *Decisions of the Department of the Interior Relating to the Public Lands*, v. 2, pp. 58-62.

we have never heard them charged with unfair practice, or wrongful action toward their clients." [45]

One phase of the operation of the land laws that was particularly productive of friction, insecurity and uncertainty was the invitation extended to all comers to contest the entry of any settler upon the public domain.[46] Entries were subject to contest at any time; and, if they escaped contest prior to the time that the entryman was required to make his final proof, the published notices, six of which were required in pre-emption and commuted homestead entries, were almost sure to produce a contest. There is some reason to believe that timber culture entries were particularly vulnerable to contest.[47] The possibility of encountering a contest must have operated as frequently to discourage improvement and cultivation as it did to encourage complete compliance.[48] In effect every transient in a community and every person who had not exhausted his rights under the land laws was asked to keep his eye on the entryman and advertise alleged noncompliance by filing a contest. In a sense the right to contest placed a premium upon snooping and exalted the role of the talebearer. When witnesses in the proof-taking process were asked questions concerning smoke from the chimney, chickens around the shack, lights in the windows and the exact diameter of trees, it seems clear that the land officials expected that neighbors in a community would see each other as actual or at least potential defrauders and therefore scrutinize even routine activities with the vigilance and zeal of a secret police agent. As commissioner of the General Land Office, W. A. J. Sparks introduced elaborate and detailed forms for the presentation of proof. The new procedures received some support in the newspapers of western Kansas,[49] but the preponderance of comment was in opposi-

45. March 10, 1887.
46. The Ness City *Times* reported a statement of the county attorney that three-fourths of the contestable claims in the county were already under contest and that in a few more weeks timber claims would be obtainable only by purchase. Reprinted in the *Lane County Herald*, May 1, 1885, together with an invitation to entrymen to come to Lane county for homesteads and timber claims. About six months later, October 29, 1885, the *Herald* reported that timber claims were becoming scarce in Lane county. The *Rooks County Record*, Stockton, April 29, 1887, in condemning the frequency of contests said, "There are few of the farmers in Rooks county whose titles are not open to attack on some petty technicality."
47. O. F. Searl, receiver of the land office in Salina, in discussing the contest case of Russell C. Harris vs. Anderson Stoops with W. C. Perry on June 21, 1887, stated the usual grounds for contesting timber claims as failure to plant and cultivate trees and the entering of land not naturally devoid of timber. Nearly three out of the eight pages of the *Lane County Herald*, October 15, 1885, were devoted to land notices which were for the most part announcements of contests against timber culture entries.
48. The uncertainty involved in obtaining a final patent under the homestead, pre-emption and timber culture acts was emphasized in a letter written by George Cotton of La Crosse to W. C. Perry, July 29, 1887.
49. *Rooks County Democrat*, Stockton, January 13, 1887.

tion to them.   The following critical comment appeared in the columns of the *Rooks County Record*:

A government is in a big business when it tries to find out what kind of a crib the baby sleeps in, whether the farmer and his wife recline on wire-woven springs or ante-diluvian bed cords, or whether the woman of the house bakes her beans in a stone jar or brass kettle.   Sparks is a thousand times more particular about a homesteader's exact compliance with each infinitessimal iota of the law than he is with a railroad grant or the stock ranch of an English syndicate.   Yet that is the general style of this great business administration, which constantly strains at gnats and swallows dromedaries by the caravan.   After 1888 there will be a new deal and a more just equation of the peoples' rights.[50]

The editor of the Kirwin *Independent* expressed his views in an editorial entitled "Tom Foolery."   It was a mixture of general criticism of the Sparks policies and specific objection to the high costs of making proof that resulted:

Commissioner Sparks of the General Land office is a beautiful beast, a red tape dude, a go-off-half-cocked sort of a man.   When he assumed the duties of his office he also assumed that the people of the west were perjurers, swindlers and fugitives from justice at large in a Garden of Eden. . . .

It wouldn't be quite so bad if all of this tomfoolery didn't have to be paid for out of the homesteaders pocket, but this arrant nonsense costs men who, as a class are poor, several extra dollars, in counties where, as a rule, dollars are scarce.   Take this in connection with the swindle requiring claimants to advertise their lands, an act passed to benefit newspaper men, and the homesteader who has to shell out here and there to obstructionists along the road to a final proof, is not apt to entertain a very high opinion of the simplicity of a democratic form of government.

As to Sparks we believe that he is honest, but he is the biggest old nuisance that ever a pioneer community had to depend upon for titles to well earned land. [51]

Just as contemporary reaction to Commissioner Sparks ranged from one extreme to the other so the contemporary evaluations of the contest process varied a great deal.   Commissioner Sparks and those who supported his policies seemed to assume that a contested entry involved deliberate fraud either on the part of the contestee or the contestant, whereas his critics tended to look upon the right of contest as an almost automatic inhibitant to fraud.   At no point does the doctrine of simple causation or broad generalization with

50. November 26, 1886.
51. January 6, 1887.   The editor elaborated one aspect of his views in the issue for January 20, when he remarked: "Since Sparks became commissioner of the general land office he has so ruled and managed the business of the office as to make all the land fraudulently proved up on, cost honest settlers not less than $25 per acre.   He suspicions dishonesty and so plans that those who are honest shall pay fifteen to twenty-five dollars costs in making a proof that ought to cost not over five or six dollars."   It should be noted in passing that the editor has suggested the answer to those who insist that homestead land was "free" land, a subsidy from the federal government to the agricultural interests of the nation.

respect to the administration of the land laws break down so completely. Contests were initiated for almost every conceivable reason. Some were the results of poor advice given by land agents and professional locators; [52] others were encouraged by local land office men because the fees in such cases constituted a large portion of their remuneration; [53] and still others were deliberate attempts to secure desirable tracts of land.[54] There were friendly contests to conceal a fraudulent entry until the relinquishment could be sold to an innocent third party.[55] There were collusive contests initiated by friends or relatives to bar a legitimate contest or to "smuggle" a tract of land, that is, keep it from being legally entered until a son reached his majority or a friend could enter it.[56] The most vicious contests were outright cases of blackmail and were accompanied by violence or threats of violence.[57] They were commenced by professional claim jumpers to force a legal·entryman to fight a contest or pay the contestant to withdraw his suit.[58] Fre-

52. W. J. Calvin to the editor of the Larned *Chronoscope*, February 19, 1886; Thomas J. Richardson, special agent of the General Land Office, Wichita, to W. C. Perry, January 4, 1887; E. Sample, Medicine Lodge, to Perry, October 16, 1887; B. W. Dysart, Ansonia, Ohio, to Perry, October 15, 1888.

53. "Report of the Commissioner of the General Land Office," 1885, *loc. cit.*, p. 42.

54. Mrs. M. E. Warner, Oxford, wrote several letters to J. R. Hallowell urging him to continue the legal sifting of claims in Pratt county and the canceling of fraudulent entries so that she might be able to secure one of the canceled entries. Her letter of July 8, 1885, is particularly relevant. C. O. Erwin, Harper, wrote to W. C. Perry on April 11, 1886, accusing several men of making fraudulent proof, asking to be informed of the best method of procedure in securing one of the claims, and offering Perry a $100 fee for securing one of the claims for him; M. B. Bailey, Wichita, to Perry, January 12, 1889; Larned *Weekly Chronoscope*, September 30, 1887.

55. "Report of the Commissioner of the General Land Office," 1886, *loc. cit.*, pp. 85, 86; *ibid.*, for 1887, pp. 149, 150; D. H. Henkel, U. S. circuit court commissioner at Wakeeney, to W. C. Perry, January 25, 1888.

56. There are several cases described in the *Decisions of the Department of the Interior Relating to the Public Lands*. Some examples are: R. W. Satterlee vs. C. F. Dibble, v. 2, pp. 307, 308, in which the original Dibble entry was contested by three different relatives; A. Moses vs. J. B. Brown, v. 2, pp. 259, 260, wherein the right to contest was denied to S. H. Brown, a relative of the plaintiff; and Caroline E. Critchfield vs. W. M. Pierson, v. 1, pp. 421, 422, which involved a divorce on the grounds of adultery in order to qualify Mrs. Critchfield as a contestee. Charles Fickheisen, Buffalo Park, to W. C. Perry, April 29, and May 16, 1886; M. B. Bailey, Wichita, to Perry, January 12, 1889.

57. E. C. Cole, U. S. commissioner at Larned, to W. C. Perry, April 15, 1887; *Rooks County Record*, May 20, 1887. *The Eye*, Oberlin, January 19, 1888, reprinted the following comment from the Atchison *Champion*: "For a number of years past persons in the western third of Kansas who have in good faith, entered land as timber claims, have been annoyed and harassed by a class of irresponsible and mischievous vagabonds who have made it a business to go prowling around to find a few bushes and saplings on timber claim entries as a basis of contest, making these few scattering trees an excuse for annoying and expensive litigation, instituted solely for the purpose of blackmail." On April 9, 1889, W. C. Perry wrote to J. M. Barrett, register of deeds at Canton, concerning an unsigned letter accusing B. A. Dupree and Joe Smalley of instituting contests and then offering to drop them for $250. An unsigned letter to Perry dated April 11, 1889, quoted the following from a telegram from F. G. White of McPherson, "R. A. Deupree and Jack Smalley are in the business of Swearing out contest papers for the purpose of *Black Male* [sic] and then compel parties to By [sic] them off. . . ."

58. W. J. Crumpton in a letter to the Larned *Chronoscope*, February 19, 1886, emphasized the blackmail aspect of many contest cases, but more importantly called attention to the fact that the effect of the contest procedure was to compel the entryman to pay far more than the market value for a tract which the law intended him to have in return for cultivation and improvement. Crumpton stated explicitly what most later historians have not understood, namely that land was not free for the taking; administrative procedures among other factors nullified the law and defeated the avowed intent of those

quently the process was repeated by a whole series of contestants until either the settler had to pay out more money in fighting contests than the land was worth or give up his entry.[59]   The quest for personal revenge was a fruitful source of contests.[60]   A community quarrel, a jilting by a boy friend,[61] a real or imagined loss in a business deal, a political controversy, all of these and many more excuses of similar character were involved in the initiation of contest cases.[62]   The persistent habits of some pioneers of telling tales, informing on neighbors, writing letters, venting prejudices and going

who drafted it. J. A. Nelson of Buffalo Park, on May 20, 1886, wrote Perry a detailed description of his experiences with the professional claim jumper. In his case the original price for being left alone was $250; this was reduced to $200 and later to $87. He refused all offers to compromise and made a successful defense. Wm. Don Carlos, of Kirwin, in writing to Perry on May 28, 1887, concerning a perjury case that had developed out of a contest affidavit, asserted that it was founded upon spite and was brought for the purpose of scaring some money out of the defendants. He continued, "This class of cases, is becoming frequent, and in my mind are generally brought, or instigated, for the purpose of making money out of a compromise, by certain Attys, and witness fees, and mileage by other impecunious parties." James P. Burns of Oberlin, wrote to Perry on February 3, 1888, "Now there is lots of this contesting going on for the mere purpose of extracting money out of parties holding claims, or for the mere purpose of annoyance." Frequent reference is made to the professional claim jumpers in the contemporary discussion of homesteaders' protective associations. In this connection The Eye, Oberlin, on December 29, 1887, reprinted the following from the Atchison Champion: "Next to prairie dogs, jack rabbits and coyotes, one of the worst pests of a new country . . . is the 'claim jumper,' the party who prowls around like a wolf to hunt up opportunities to dispossess some honest and well meaning settler. . . ."

59. In a letter to J. R. Hallowell on October 6, 1884, M. B. Jones of Corwin, estimated the cost of prosecuting a contest against an entry at $200. In a letter on December 26, 1885, to W. C. Perry, Y. R. Archer estimated the cost of defending against a contest at $100 to $1,000. The Rooks County Record, May 20, 1887, placed the cost of defending at $50 to $200. M. F. Dean, Sappaton, told Perry on January 16, 1888, that one of his neighbors had been forced to defend his claim against four contests.

60. L. D. Seward, St. Louis, to J. R. Hallowell, September 5, 1881; J. P. Campbell, Harper, to Hallowell, March 20, 1882. The Zickefoose-Shuler contest case in the Wakeeney land office seems to have originated in a desire by Zickefoose for revenge. W. H. Pilkenton, receiver of the Wakeeney office to W. C. Perry, April 7, 1885. Wm. Lescher, Lawrence, wrote Perry on February 12, 1886, alleging "malicious meanness" as the cause of the sequence of contests against his entry in the Oberlin land district. W. T. S. May, Kirwin, to Perry, June 5, 1886. Ira T. Hodson, Burr Oak, to Perry, June 9, 1886. W. C. Perry, to John McDonald, Dun Station, November 11, 1886. George Cotton, La Crosse, to Perry, July 29, 1887. W. C. Perry to Clark S. Rowe, special agent of the General Land Office at Larned, December 14, 1887. J. P. Burns, Oberlin, to Perry, February 3, 1888. Frank Thanhouser, Garden City, to Perry, August 10, 1888. R. M. Wright, Dodge City, to Perry, September 22, 1888. W. C. Perry to E. E. Thomas, special agent of the General Land Office, Salina, November 28, 1888.

61. Such an instance is described in a letter by W. C. Perry to J. G. Allard, special agent of the General Land Office at Oberlin, September 20, 1888. Perry's remarks, based on an affidavit made by Dolly Hayes, contained the following: "In the first place Dolly having kept with the young man for three years and that beautiful and heavenly relation now having ceased, is undoubtedly angry with Alvin, and if he is keeping company with some other young lady, is also undoubtedly suffering from a severe attack of the green-eyed monster."

62. W. M. Skinner, Gaylord, in letters to J. R. Hallowell, July 14 and 15, 1882, recited a particularly long tale of woe concerning contests growing out of personal quarrels and political differences. Hallowell had received letters from H. C. Sunderland, Gaylord, on February 13, 1880, and from G. W. Hodson, Gaylord, of March 22, 1880, relative to the Skinner case and had written to the commissioner of the General Land Office on February 24, 1880, describing the case as a neighborhood quarrel. Tully Scott, receiver, Oberlin land office, to W. C. Perry, October 27, 1885, describing the Wheelock-Cass contest as a "neighborhood fight." C. H. Barlow, Kansas Banking Company, Goodland, in a letter to Perry on April 12, 1888, said that the man who had contested his claim "is owing this Bank of which I am a member and he came around and hinted as though he would release the contest if I would cancel his note and informed me that we did not treat him right last fall in some of our deal is why he contested it." J. G. Lowe, Washington, to Perry, October 10, 1886.

to law probably confused the federal land officials as completely as they do the historians of today.[63] Probably there was as much informality with respect to the residence requirements as toward any other feature of the operation of the federal land laws. Again, as far as the evolving community was concerned, the immediate effect of such informality was to contribute to instability and impermanence. It was regular practice for the business and professional men in the towns to enter a tract of land, go through the motions of compliance by eating a meal— sometimes cooked in a hotel and carried to the claim—or by sleeping on the land at infrequent intervals, and then make final proof before the local land office.[64] Sen. Preston B. Plumb stated in the senate that these practices were considered normal and legal in the parts of Kansas with which he was familiar. While defending the settlers in Kansas against charges of fraud he described the contemporary attitudes and practices in the following words:

A man goes out from the East; he is a tinner, a shoemaker, a blacksmith, a wagon-maker, or a tradesman of some kind. He goes West for the purpose of getting a home, and in the mean time he must live. He goes into the nearest town, follows his calling, and takes a quarter-section of land outside, lives upon it between times, so to speak, having his domicile part of the time perhaps in the town and part of the time on his claim, and at the end of six months he proves up on it. Perhaps the intent and the act do not fully combine, and yet the intent is as good as that of any man ever was to make that place his home, and to all intents and purposes it is his home. . . . It may be called in law a fraudulent entry, and yet so far as the essential elements of fraud are concerned they are entirely lacking." [65]

At almost exactly the time that Senator Plumb was placing a

63. The letters of J. B. Tillinghast, Myrtle, to W. C. Perry, illustrate this point. See the one written on April 16, 1888; A. C. Mende, another resident of the same community, wrote an extraordinarily gossipy letter to Perry on July 15, 1888. Letters written by Mrs. M. E. Warner, Oxford, to J. R. Hallowell on January 19, February 13, and March 26, 1885, are in the same category. In many respects the brochure-length letter written by I. V. Knotts of Schoharie on July 5, 1886, to W. C. Perry, is the most fantastic of them all.

64. *Decisions of the Department of the Interior Relating to the Public Lands,* v. 1, pp. 77, 78. The document referred to is a letter of Secretary of the Interior Henry Teller to the commissioner of the General Land Office, N. C. McFarland, dated October 2, 1882, and concerned with the contest case of W. P. Peters *vs.* George Spaulding. Report of William Y. Drew, special agent of the land office at Wichita, dated November 26, 1884, and contained in the "Report of the Commissioner of the General Land Office," 1885, *loc. cit.,* pp. 206, 207. Report of Walter W. Cleary, special agent of the land office at Garden City included in "Report of the Commissioner of the General Land Office," 1887, *loc. cit.,* pp. 149, 150. Larned *Chronoscope,* March 11, 1887.

65. *Congressional Record,* 49 Cong., 1 Sess. (1885-1886), pt. 6, p. 6,073. In the course of the debate Plumb implied that the zeal with which Commissioner W. A. J. Sparks was enforcing the land laws in the West and Northwest was rooted in partisan considerations. "Is it not a little singular that the individual whose duty it is to scan the horizon should be afflicted with such a political, geographical, isothermal strabismus that he has never allowed his eagle eye to cover anything south of Mason and Dixon's line, but has kept it as steady as the needle to the pole on the West and Northwest?"—*Ibid.,* p. 6,075. A week earlier Plumb had described his own experience at pre-empting a quarter section of land, remarking in one place, "I have no doubt that I committed a fraud upon the law; . . . the claim was my home though I was printing a newspaper in a hamlet a mile away."—*Ibid.,* Appendix, p. 426.

"loose" construction upon the residence requirement in pre-emption entries, Commissioner Sparks was defining his views in response to a series of questions directed to him by a resident of Kansas. In answer to the question, "Can a married man pre-empt or homestead a claim and prove up without his family?", Sparks replied, "The home contemplated is the home of the family. It is inconceivable that a homestead entry is made in good faith when the permanent home of the family is elsewhere. The pre-emptor is also expected to make his home on the land." In reply to the question, "What constitutes six months residence?", the commissioner replied briefly but specifically, "The actual living on the land for the period of six months." [66] The local newspapers took the practices described by Senator Plumb for granted and reported individual instances as news: railroad employees were visiting their claims; school teachers, merchants, and artisans were spending short visits on their homestead or pre-emption entries; entrymen were returning to their claims after a prolonged absence during the winter months.[67] One entryman who was a member of a banking firm that operated banking houses in Goodland, and Burlington, Colo., complained bitterly to the federal district attorney when his claim was contested.[68] Another banker in Sherman county in discussing compliance with residence requirements and in response to a question concerning what he raised on his claim remarked, "Last year I raised 'hell and watermelons.' This year it is too dry to raise anything; I shall try to raise the mortgage next year and skip." [69] Another entryman wrote to Sen. John J. Ingalls protesting against the cancellation of his entry simply because he left his claim to work in a near-by town from Monday morning to Saturday night of each week in order to provide food for his family.[70] Still another tried to retain his claim in the face of a contest, even though he spent the winter months near Boul-

66. W. A. J. Sparks to C. T. Connelly, Terry, June 10, 1886, "General Land Office Correspondence," A, Miscellaneous, pp. 363, 364.

67. *Kansas Herald.* Hiawatha, March 12, 1880; Garnet *Chronoscope.* January 28, 1881; *Lane County Herald*, June 3, July 24, September 11, and September 25, 1885; June 3, September 9, September 16, November 11, and December 16, 1886; February 24, and December 8, 1887; and June 7, 1888. *The Eye*, Oberlin, December 11, 1884; September 10, and November 26, 1885; March 25, and April 1, 1886. *Scott County News*. Scott City, March 19, April 12, May 12, and May 14, 1886. The Oberlin *Eye*, January 27, 1887, in commenting on the shooting of a claim jumper said, "a number of persons whose claims were contested are working on the railroad for a livelihood and were vexed with having contests put on their claims."

68. Charles H. Barlow, Goodland, to W. C. Perry, March 19, April 12, and August 7, 1888.

69. E. E. Blackman, "Sherman county and the H. U. A.," *Kansas Historical Collections*, v. 8 (1903-1904), p. 53.

70. Bishop W. Perkins, representative in congress from Kansas, quoted from the speech by Senator Ingalls during the course of a debate in the house of representatives.— *Congressional Record*, 49 Cong., 1 Sess. (1885-1886), pt. 6, p. 6,289.

der, Colo., working in a mine.[71] Even a United States court commissioner on one occasion closed his office while he undertook to
fulfill the residence requirement by living on his claim.[72] A dili-
gent shoemaker left his family on his claim while he maintained his
shop and residence in Dighton during the entire period that he was
supposed to be in residence on his claim.[73] After the Fort Dodge
military reservation was opened to settlement 75 filings were made
on land within its limits. Of these, 18 were made by gamblers,
saloon-keepers, bartenders and sporting women engaged in business
or plying their trade in Dodge City; four were made by widows
living in town; six were made by railroad employees and five were
unknown. Only eight or ten were made by actual settlers.[74] One
entryman on trial for perjury in connection with his attempt to prove
up replied to the question concerning continuous residence in the
language of a college freshmen, "Yes, except when temporarily
absent." [75] Another one of Teutonic ancestry, extremely anxious
to secure some choice land adjacent to his own claims and unable
to comply with the residence requirement, left the following note
on the back of a township plat:

> Dere Misses——: Know your name as you hat Bad Lugg in your man and
> lost him I tell you I am for sale I am a widderwor and after Land and
> woman and home I have som land Now how would this sude you, you gitt
> a devores and a home state & timber clame and I have some land now and
> I gitt a home state and timber clame and we can have lots of land Com and
> see me in Rume No 1 or rite.[76]

Beyond the physical facts of unimproved land and undeveloped
claims the effects upon community spirit of such activities as have
been described, together with the accompanying absentee ownership and control, must have been important. Certainly it was discouraging to newcomers to discover that the land near town, although apparently unoccupied was in the hands of nonresident

71. James Baird writing from Langford, Colo., to W. C. Perry, January 15, 1888.
72. W. T. S. May, Kirwin, to W. C. Perry, November 25, 1886.
73. *Lane County Herald*, December 8, 1887. Actually the news item revealed the
fact that the entryman was proving up on his second claim. The *Herald* for June 3, 1886,
reported that a carpenter who was working in Dighton was surprised while paying a visit
to his claim to discover that he had become the father of twins, the first set to be born
in Lane county.
74. "Report of the Commissioner of the General Land Office," 1886, *loc. cit.*, p. 96.
75. Letter from the commissioner of the General Land Office to J. R. Hallowell, March
3, 1880.
76. Oberlin *Eye*, August 12, 1886. It should be suggested that the plan would have
been perfectly legal. On August 11, 1879, the commissioner of the General Land Office
wrote to Hughes and Corse of Larned that if a man and woman having adjacent homestead entries should marry they could fulfill the residence requirement by living in a house
on the dividing line between the two claims. "Report of the Commissioner of the General
Land Office," 1880, in *Report of the Secretary of the Interior, House Ex. Doc. No. 1*
(serial no. 1,959), 46 Cong., 3 Sess. (1880-1881), p. 484.

18—4168

entrymen.[77]   One homesteader who had to walk a good many
miles to a small town remarked in a letter that the only thing wrong
with the town was that everyone in it had land for sale.[78]
The problems arising out of contests and the evasion of residence
requirements led to the formation of various types of protective
associations.   In many respects they were the direct descendants
of the claim associations of an earlier period.   There were all kinds
of protective associations.   Some were organized by entrymen who
were residing on their claims for the purpose of protecting themselves against chronic contestants and professional claim jumpers.[79]
Others, although masquerading under such names as "Old Settlers'
Association" or "Homesteaders' Union," were composed of residents
of towns and villages who had never settled on their claims and did
not propose to do so.[80]   Their objective was to maintain their entries
by intimidation if need be until final proof could be made or a
relinquishment sold.[81]   Whatever might have been their purpose
or form of organization, these protective associations introduced a
disruptive influence into the early development of some communities.[82]   The incoming correspondence of the federal district attorney's office was burdened with letters describing incidents of intimidation and violence to which entrymen had been subjected.[83]   It

77. The complaint of T. B. Hatcher, Grenola, addressed to W. C. Perry on September
25, 1886, with reference to the activities of J. G. Hiatt is reasonably typical: "The masses
here want to see the land grabbers punished for we know to what extent it is practiced
and detrimental to the settling of the country.   West and north of us the people have no
direct roads to town but have to go 5 & 10 miles around and have no schools on account
of the large tracts that are fenced."
78. John Ise, editor, Sod-House Days: Letters From a Kansas Homesteader, 1877-1878
(New York, 1937), p. 153.   These letters written by Howard Ruede of Osborne county
contain a great deal of information on matters pertaining to entering claims, proving up,
residence requirements and the like.
79. The Larned Chronoscope alleged that this was the motive behind the formation
of an Old Settlers' League near Larned.   See the issues for March 12, March 19, May 14,
and May 21, 1886.   W. J. Calvin in a letter to the Chronoscope which appeared in the
issue for February 19, 1886, suggested a protective league as the answer to the epidemic
of contests that had broken out.   He attributed the frequency of contesting to the Sparks'
policies.   The Chronoscope echoed this point of view in the issue for May 14, 1886.
80. The character of the Rooks County Homesteader's Union was argued in the columns
of the Rooks County Record and the Rooks County Democrat during the spring and summer
of 1887.   The issues of the Record for April 29, May 6, 20, and 27, September 2, 9, 16,
and 23, and of the Democrat for May 17 and August 23, contain particularly relevant
information.   The varied activities of one organization are described in Blackman, loc. cit.,
pp. 50-62.
81. E. R. Cutler, Meade Center, in a letter written to the United States district attorney
for the Garden City land office on December 20, 1886, and forwarded to W. C. Perry, described a typical instance.   In a letter to Walter W. Cleary, special agent for the General
Land Office at Garden City, on February 23, 1887, Perry described the type of evidence
that would be necessary for the successful prosecution of the individuals accused by Cutler.
82. The Stockton Democrat on May 21, 1886, used the phrase "guerilla warfare" to
describe the friction between rival settlers in northwest Kansas.   It was stated that five
persons had been killed, that the sheriff had refused to act, and that an appeal for
assistance had been sent to the governor.
83. Charles L. Chittenden, Nickerson, to W. C. Perry, January 28, 1886; John W.
McDonald, Dun Station, to Perry, November 7, 1886; J. W. Carson, Wakeeney, to Perry,
November 22, 1887; Charles P. Dunaway, Stockton, to Perry, January 2, 1888; Blanche
Hoover, Beelerville, to Perry, November 21, 1887; C. B. Dakin, Colby, to Perry, May 2,
1888, describing the Edsall case and commenting upon the character of the Sherman
County H. U. A.

should be noted in this connection that the federal laws did not afford any protection against the threats or acts of an individual. It was only when two or more persons conspired to deprive an entryman of his rights under the federal land law that a prosecution by federal officials could be undertaken.[84] It should be clear that it was in precisely such instances that the entryman was outnumbered by the parties whom he was accusing. As a result the federal district attorneys were never optimistic concerning the likelihood of securing convictions. Vigilante activities, with all of the disturbing features that usually accompany them, seem to have been a characteristic feature of the instances of overt or threatened violence that plagued entrymen in some new communities.[85]

It has been pointed out by many writers that the federal land laws were not well adapted to the Great Plains environment. It has also been pointed out in connection with the homestead act that it "would have worked badly on any frontier" because of the incompatibility of the five-year residence requirement with the frontier tendency toward mobility.[86] It may be suggested that it was not only the land laws that were unadapted to the Great Plains, but the rules and regulations with which they were surrounded—the administrative procedures as well as the laws. It may be remarked further that the tendency toward rapid turnover among early settlers was stimulated rather than checked or restrained by the operation of the federal land laws. The technical and involved rules of procedure, the invitation to contest, and the absence of any effective method of dealing with violations of the laws contributed to the atmosphere of uncertainty and insecurity that surrounded western Kansas communities during their early and formative years.

84. W. C. Perry to G. E. Rees, Scott City, January 14, 1888; Perry to C. B. Dakin, Colby, May 7, 1888; Perry to Thomas J. Richardson, Wichita, May 26, 1888. In the last letter Perry quoted section 5508 of the federal statutes, "if two or more persons conspire to injure, oppress, threaten or intimidate any citizen in the free exercise or enjoyment of any right or privilege secured to him by the constitution or laws of the United States, or because of his having exercised the same, he shall be punished. . . ."

85. G. E. Rees, Scott City, to W. C. Perry, January 6, 1888, alleging that a vigilante committee was trying to intimidate legal entrymen in Scott county is a case in point.

86. James C. Malin, "Mobility and History: Reflections on the Agricultural Policies of the United States in Relation to a Mechanized World," *Agricultural History,* v. 17 (1943), October, p. 181.

LAND DISPOSAL IN NEBRASKA, 1854-1906

Homer Socolofsky

LAND DISPOSAL IN NEBRASKA, 1854-1906;
THE HOMESTEAD STORY

BY HOMER SOCOLOFSKY

THE magnetism of land ownership has long been a primary attraction or lure in drawing settlers to remote and distant frontiers. The time from the official opening of the territory of Nebraska in 1854 until 1906, when the first results of the Kinkaid Act were coming in, was probably the most active period in the disposal of the nation's vast public domain. This era saw changes of revolutionary proportions, not only in land disposal everywhere, but in most activities related to the use of land.

In 1967, as Nebraska celebrates her centennial of statehood, it is appropriate to re-examine the accounts of public land disposal in that state, with particular emphasis on the homestead story. Although few regions in the United States have had as extensive and prolonged research into the matter of land transfers from public to private ownership, the subject is far from exhausted. These past studies are open to revision. In addition, inquiry into the topic of subsequent transfers of land ownership opens

Dr. Socolofsky, a professor of history at Kansas State University, delivered this paper at the Organization of American Historians meeting in Chicago on April 27, 1967.

a new dimension in the history of that period, which is virtually untapped.

Even before Nebraska was organized as a territory, the region attracted boomers who encouraged settlement illegally.[1] As many as 250 illegal claims were located in each of the Missouri River counties before the passage of the organic act of the territory.[2] Many of these sooners, and the legal settlers who came after them, followed the pattern of their Iowa neighbors in organizing claim associations to furnish protection for their land.[3] In some areas these extra-legal organizations were soon replaced by local governmental institutions and the first registered deed record came less than a year after approval of the Kansas-Nebraska Act.[4]

Territorial Nebraska history emphasized the activity of the land speculator and town boomer. Contemporary newspaper comment, such as that from the *Nebraska Advertiser* of Brownville, in southeastern Nebraska's Nemaha County, shows the expected strong support for actual settlers as opposed to absentees. Editor Robert W. Furnas rejected suggestions for the use of the public domain of Nebraska

> . . . other than making such arrangements that the actual settlers can pre-empt, and pay for their land at $1.25, per acre, . . . at such times as they are able. We are satisfied that great injury would result from bringing the Public Lands to sale, short of two years hence, at least. Give set-

---

[1] James C. Malin, "Thomas Jefferson Sutherland, Nebraska Boomer," *Nebraska History,* Vol. XXXIV, pp. 181-214; James C. Malin, *The Nebraska Question, 1852-1854,* (1953), pp. 77-85, 128-137.

[2] A. T. Andreas, *History of the State of Nebraska,* (1882), pp. 473, 679-682, 1200, 1246, 1301.

[3] "Burt County Claim Association Record, 1857," bound manuscript, Nebraska State Historical Society; Donald F. Danker, "The Nebraska Winter Quarters Company and Florence," *Nebraska History,* March 1956, pp. 28-34; Earl G. Curtis, "John Milton Thayer," *ibid.,* October-December 1947, p. 228; Everett N. Dick, "Free Homes For the Millions," *ibid.,* December 1962, p. 215.

[4] Nemaha County Deed Records. Nebraska's number one recorded deed, drawn up April 12, 1855, was filed May 24, 1855, much sooner than any federal land office existed in the territory.

tlers time to open up their farms, get things comfortable
around them, and *then* pay for their land.[5]

Topics involving land issues, surveying, approval of
land offices, and settlement, were found in almost every
issue. Naturally, settlement was promoted and encouraged. Proudly the editor announced that:

> STILL THEY COME.—Since our last issue over 50
> families have taken claims and settled in this county. All
> who come and see this country with the intention of . . .
> [acquiring] homes, are sure to settle here—the country only
> wants to be seen to be admired and taken possession of.
>
> If the half starved farmers East, in the States—where
> it requires 15 years to get 10 acres of land in a proper and
> easy state of cultivation—could but see the 'fairest portion
> of God's creation' out here, waiting only the plow and fence,
> to make it surpass the boasted 'Bottom Lands,' the entire
> Territory would fill up in a few years. Well, they are be-
> ginning to find it out. [6]

Of vital concern to a pioneer anywhere was local protection for his right to land. A challenge to a just claim
was viewed with alarm and was reported widely. Thus
one settler wrote that:

> On arriving at Omaha we ascertained that difficulties
> existed somewhere in the neighborhood in reference to the
> claim of a young man who had recently died in town, and
> had been jumped up [by] some unprincipled man on the day
> of the burial. The citizens took it in hand and on further
> investigation it was ascertained that the miscre[an]t was a
> Dutch pettifog[g]er who resides here in town. He appeared
> determined to hold it right or wrong, and did not yield his
> claim to it until the people met in mass, and passed resolu-
> tions condemnitory of his course, and resolved to put him
> across the river if he did not comply. Thieves only submit,
> when overtaken in their evil deeds, and are compelled to
> surrender. 'Claim jumpers' have poor encouragement in
> this country, as very few are successful, and always get
> off with lasting disgrace. [7]

Loyal to his local area, the *Nebraska Advertiser's* editor wrote in glowing terms of new arrivals, of peace and

---

[5] *Nebraska Advertiser*, (Brownville, N. T.,) June 21, 1856;
"Nuckolls manuscripts," Nebraska State Historical Library. These
records show extraordinary activity on town lot sales during the
territorial period.
[6] *Nebraska Advertiser*, July 5, 1856.
[7] Letter to the editor in *ibid.*, Nov. 29, 1856.

tranquility and of universal recognition of law and order
in Nemaha County. He treated as gross exaggeration the
story of the rival *Nebraskian* that the

> . . . larger portion of the land within twenty miles of the
> Missouri River, are covered by *pretended claims*. That men
> living in the towns have control of 'claims'—some of them
> many claims—who never saw them; that these claims are
> daily bought and sold, with as much facility as a horse
> or an ox is sold. [8]

Nemaha County also was described in pleasant contrast with violence found elsewhere, particularly in the
twin territory of Kansas to the south.[9] Statements that
no one had asserted his right to more than 160 acres and
that no claim had been jumped were shattered in mid-1857
with a story of the death of a recent arrival to the area.

> The cause leading to this unfortunate difficulty was
> 'claim jumping.' . . . We have boasted of our peace and
> harmony in claim matters, and attributed it very properly
> to our *observance of the laws*. Let us not sully our fair
> reputation at home and abroad, by following the example
> of some other points in this Territory and Kansas in regard
> to settling claim difficulties. [10]

The panic of 1857 had depressing effects on the national economy which were not felt in frontier Nebraska
for several years. Much of the frenzied rush to engross
valuable properties in the territory came to naught by the
end of the fifties as a consequence of that depression. No
doubt, President James Buchanan's order to auction land
in the area in the midst of hard times, an action that found
almost no supporters in Nebraska, produced political align-
ments still apparent more than a century later.

By 1860, with a population grown to 28,841, there
were many pioneers out in advance of government surveys
and much Nebraska land was claimed. Although early
observers declared that little effort was being made to develop farms and many remained unimproved for another

---

8 *Ibid.*, Feb. 12, 1857, reporting a story from the *Nebraskian* of
Feb. 4, [1857].
9 *Ibid.*, April 30, May 17, 1857.
10 *Ibid.*, June 18, 1857.

dozen years, there were more than 2,500 farms averaging two hundred acres in the territory. This represented about 20 acres per capita, with about one-fifth of this area improved. The cost of purchasing land was considerably reduced through the extensive use of military bounty land warrants. By 1860 six out of every seven acres acquired from the federal government in Nebraska Territory were paid for with land warrants rather than cash.[11] In spite of low cost and the lack of improvements, Nebraska farm land had an average value of $8.26 per acre.

A discussion of contemporary farm-making costs suggests that improvement of a quarter-section of raw Nebraska land came to $531.37.[12] Naturally, expenses of this nature eliminated many potential home-seekers. Nevertheless the availability of such opportunity was portrayed in idyllic splendor as follows:

> The bold and determined settler of an early day, enjoyed the palatable venison, joyously chased the elk over the hills and plains, while the buffalo has been killed beyond consum[p]tion. He now reaps the luxuriant harvest from one-hundred and fifty-five acres out of 160, while his children enjoy the fruit and sports under the trees which he planted.
>
> A [quarter-section] farm containing one hundred and sixty acres, with forty acres broke, and fenced, with a little

---

[11] Addison E. Sheldon, *Land Systems and Land Policies in Nebraska*, (1936), pp. 59-60. Sheldon reported that land warrants in 1858 were selling at prices ranging from 75c to $1.00 an acre in New York and as much as $1.75 on a credit plan in Nebraska. Basic statistics are drawn from the United States Census Reports as well as the annual reports of the Nebraska State Board of Agriculture. The 1860 federal census reported 2,473 farms in Nebraska Territory, whereas a revised figure in the 1900 census was 2,789. Averages given were 203 and 226 acres respectively.

[12] *Nebraska Farmer*, June 1861. An enumeration of these expenses was:

A house	$250.
Breaking 40 acres	120.
500 walnut fence posts	25.
500 holes for posts	5.
Lumber for fence	125.
Nails	6.37
	$531.37

house upon it, constitutes a farm. A man can attend that
number of acres and rest more than one third of the year.
Its products will support a family, pay their expenses, and
allow them four hundred dollars in cash to lay up every
year. 13

Soon after the outbreak of the Civil War, the U.S.
Surveyor General for Kansas and Nebraska, Mark W.
Delahay, wrote Salmon P. Chase, Lincoln's Secretary of
the Treasury, of the urgent necessity of further surveys
to prepare for an expected rush to the public domain in
his area. He told of loyal southerners who had moved north
and had made "settlement far West of the present Survey's," and that "a large number of Volunteers now bearing Arms under their Country's Call, will after the Rebellion is put down, require homes in Kansas and Nebraska." Because of this necessity Delahay asked Chase's
support. Expecting that military bounty warrants would
again be used following the war he wrote:

> In consideration of the foregoing suggestions, will not
> Congress feel it to be a Patriotic duty, intimately connected
> with the earliest Legislation, to make the necessary Ap-
> propriations in order to prosecute the Public Surveys in this
> District, so the lands will be in Condition, whereon the War-
> rants granted to the Soldiers in the present War may be
> located. 14

Little was done immediately to boost Delahay's request
for needed surveys. However, the wind was blowing strongly for free homesteads and the Homestead Act of 1862 was
passed with the backing of a sizable majority of Westerners and especially the citizens of the territory of Nebraska.
Territorial Governor Alvin Saunders, in his best political
manner, extolled the beneficence of the federal government
in a message to the territorial council when he said:

> What a blessing this wise and humane legislation will
> bring to many a poor, but honest and industrious family.
> Its benefits can never be estimated in dollars and cents. The
> very thought, to such people, that they can now have a tract

---

13 *Ibid.*
14 Letter from Mark W. Delahay to Salomon [sic] P. Chase,
Secretary of the Treasury, June 20, 1861, National Archives. Delahay had similar correspondence with Commissioner J. M. Edmunds,
of the General Land Office, see *Land Office Reports,* 1861, pp. 591-2.

of land that they can call their own, has a soul-inspiring effect upon them, and makes them feel thankful that their lots have been cast under a Government that is so liberal to its people. [15]

An "anti-Homestead" leader in Nebraska was J. Sterling Morton, who long voiced his criticism of free grants of land for any purpose.[16] After ten years of operation he still described the Homestead Act as "a questionable piece of legislation." Sometimes he served as spokesman for the settler but at other times he lumped homesteaders and land-grant railroads together as beneficiaries of an unfair preferred status on the matter of local taxation.[17]

Another Nebraska critic of the Homestead Act was Benton Aldrich, a perceptive farmer-philosopher from southeastern Nebraska, who ignored the Homestead Act to pay cash for forty acres of public domain in Nemaha County in 1865. Born in New Hampshire in 1831, Aldrich moved west and married at age twenty in Wisconsin. After three years he pushed on to Minnesota where he remained until 1864 when he sought land in the west that was suitable for planting an orchard. With only enough money to pay the $50 cash price he nevertheless placed much of his initial effort on his land in planting trees and an orchard that succeeded beyond his hopes. The attitudes of neighbors caused him to "become thoroughly dissatisfied," and after six years he "tried to sell [his] farm and failed." Gradually conditions improved, he became the local postmaster, and he started a circulating library, which brought about more desirable neighborly relations, and he stayed

15 *Homestead Act Centennial*, hearing before the Subcommittee on Federal Charters, Holidays, and Celebrations . . . on S. J. Res. 98, July 26, 1961. Statement of Tom V. Wilder, p.11.

16 *Nebraska Advertiser*, October 4, 1860.

17 Leslie E. Decker, *Railroads, Lands, and Politics*, (1964), pp. 27-8, from a Morton letter to the Omaha *Weekly Herald*, August 27, 1873. The letter was dated August 17; James C. Olson, *J. Sterling Morton*, (1942), pp. 178 ff; James C. Olson, *History of Nebraska*, (1955), pp. 172-3.

on his farm, which was eventually enlarged to 490 acres.[18] In his old age, when he had forgotten some of his earlier indecision, Aldrich wrote strong indictments against the Homestead Act and other "free land" schemes. Families possessing sufficient foresight to obtain and to keep land even when it was high priced were credited with high moral character by Aldrich.[19]

On the other hand the usual response from Nebraskans was strong endorsement of the Homestead Act. Without doubt, the best known "success story" is that of homesteader Daniel Freeman, whose land became the site of the National Homestead Monument.[20] In Nebraska, state history, as well as local accounts, personal memoirs, letters, and reminiscences, and even newspaper stories, view the Homestead Act as a positive benefit to the state. The opportunity made available by the law provided initial economic development in many parts of the area. Many of the homesteaders were young and idealistic, and their immediate problems, associated with pioneering, were frequently overlooked in their optimistic view of the future. Jules Haumont, who settled in Custer County in 1880, at the age of 23 years, recalled in 1932 that:

> We came here to this beautiful country, in those early days, young, strong, healthy, filled with hope, energy and ambition. . . . I do not know how large a bank account, some of the old settlers may have today, I do not care, they will never be as rich as I felt, when I first settled on my homestead. I remember the time I did not have the money to buy a postage stamp. I remember the hard winter, the drought of 1894. The many obstacles to overcome. We

---

18 Benton Aldrich collection, Nebraska State Historical Society Archives; Nemaha County Deed Records; Andreas, *op cit.*, pp. 1133-4; *A Biographical and Genealogical History of Southeastern Nebraska*, (1904), Vol I, pp.353-8.

19 Benton Aldrich collection, manuscript written January 1915.

20 Andreas, *op cit.*, pp. 896, 908; Ray H. Mattison, "Homestead National Monument: Its Establishment and Administration," *Nebraska History*, March 1962, pp. 1-28. Typical of pro-Homestead comment were the editorials and stories in the *Nebraska Advertiser*, May 29, July 3, 1862, and Jan. 3, 1863. At the same time this newspaper did not avoid the more cautious approach when they used an *American Agriculturist* story on July 9, 1862 which counseled that a "farm for ten dollars is not particularly cheap."

came to win the battle, and we did. . . . We were empire builders. [21]

Another Nebraska settler, in writing to relatives a few years earlier, said, "You at home have no idea of the rush to the West." His success in securing a desired homestead at the Beatrice land office was rated as, "The only streak of luck I ever had in my life."[22] While most homesteaders did not leave written records of this phase of their activity, a few echoed similar sentiments. One young farmer from Missouri repeatedly heard "disturbing rumors that the good homestead land would soon all be taken," so he located his claim in central Nebraska in 1884.[23] Only a year later, this young homesteader, now married, expressed his vigorous land hunger again when he wrote that:

> We are thinking of proving up on the homestead and renting it out and going further west and using my other two wrights [sic]. They say that timber claim and pre-emption is going to play out this summer. If so I want to use my wrights [sic] before it is to [sic] late. [24]

Two illustrations serve to introduce other situations found in claiming a Nebraska homestead. John R. Maltby was one "claim jumper" who successfully challenged the homestead right of a Civil War veteran, and he lived in the community long enough to become one of the honored pioneers in his county.[25] Maltby arrived in Nebraska from New England in 1867 almost penniless after more than a dozen years of travel and work all over the world. In 1869 he filed on a pre-emption claim for 80 acres in Polk County but failed to prove up on his land. After following various non-farming occupations Maltby and a partner, William

---

[21] Jules Haumont, "Pioneer Years in Custer County," *Nebraska History*, October-December 1932, p.236. Haumont emigrated from Belgium to Iowa in 1875 and settled in Custer County in 1880.

[22] Esther Bienhoff, "Homesteading in Nebraska," *Nebraska History*, October-December 1929, pp. 381-4.

[23] Charles J. Wilkerson, "The Letters of Ed Donnell, Nebraska Pioneer," *Nebraska History*, June 1960, pp. 123-140.

[24] *Ibid.*

[25] Homer E. Socolofsky, "Why Settle in Nebraska—The Case of John Rogers Maltby," *Nebraska History*, June 1963, pp. 123-132.

A. Way, contested the Clay County homestead claim of James C. Vroman in a land office hearing on June 15, 1871, where the officials recommended that "the complaint be dismissed."[26]

Included in the record of the proceedings forwarded to the General Land Office was a petition from Maltby and a copy of Vroman's official receipt showing that he had abandoned the homestead. With this evidence Commissioner Willis Drummond reversed the local land office and ordered cancellation of Vroman's claim.[27] Maltby and Way settled on adjoining eighty acre tracts of the homestead and were improving their holdings when Vroman appealed for a new hearing and eventually lost the contest. In the meantime the Burlington and Missouri River Railroad built across Clay County. Maltby became the first Probate Judge of the new county, and his homestead which he commuted to cash purchase became part of the county seat town of Sutton. Litigation over the homestead was now replaced by several years of trouble with the railroad company for Sutton was not an "approved" town site. Eventually conditions stabilized and Maltby lived out his days in Clay County as one of the leading pioneers.[28]

A second illustration is Niels Chris Nielsen, Danish immigrant, who arrived in Nebraska in 1879 from several years' residence in Illinois, and homesteaded a quarter section in Dawson County by obtaining a relinquishment from the original homesteader. Expenses for paying off the first settler and for filing his homestead and timber cul-

---

26 "Hearing Papers, Maltby vs. Vroman," National Archives.
27 "Petition of J. R. Maltby to Hon. Willis Drummond," "Copy of Vroman's Receiver's Receipt #6380, with endorsement," and "Letter from Drummond to R & R, Lincoln, Nebraska, Aug. 25, 1871," National Archives.
28 Andreas, op cit., 547-8, 559, 563; Burr, Buck, and Stough, History of Hamilton and Clay Counties, Nebraska, Vol. I, 673; John Rogers Maltby papers, Nebraska State Historical Society.

ture claims totaled $100.00.[29] During his first year in Ne-
braska he harvested 1,600 bushels of corn on a farm he
operated in neighboring Buffalo County so he got off to
a good start as a pioneer in a new land. However, crop
production was down for Nielsen during the next four
years while he was proving up on his homestead. He sold
some livestock, he worked for hire as much as 130 days
in a year, and his income averaged about two hundred
dollars annually, or about half the amount predicted for
a smaller acreage twenty years earlier. The final proof
for his homestead was acquired in 1884 and he had another
good crop. With land ownership assured he could now
borrow more capital and he set about improving his property.[30]

During Nielsen's first years on the land the improvements consisted of a sod stable costing $35.00 and a sod
house which was built for $50.00. Gradually land was
broken, fences and other outbuildings were put up, and
trees were planted. Not until the homestead was his did
he have a well dug and he added a granary and a cattle
shed the same year. By 1887, the year he obtained proof
on his adjacent timber claim, Nielsen had paid for the
breaking of 124 acres of prairie sod at two dollars an acre.
Two years later a $250 dwelling replaced the sod house
and the growing Nielsen family could easily recognize the
bounty which their hands had helped to produce. Beginning
in the 1880's Nielsen rented out all or part of his land, and

---

[29] Niels Chris Nielsen and T. C. Jensen, "Farm Record Book
1879-1961, Dawson County, Nebraska," microfilm, Nebraska State
Historical Society; Land Office Records, Tract Book 83, Nebraska
State Historical Society. Nielsen's homestead, the NE¼ of 20-11-
22W, was entered July 12, 1879, and the final certificate and patent
came five years later. His timber culture claim was the NW¼ of
the same section with the date of entry on April 28, 1879, the final
certificate on May 21, 1887, and the patent issued on April 18, 1890.

[30] Ibid. His borrowing for the years 1879 through 1882 had
caused an interest and repayment of $15, $10, $15, and $35, and no
doubt his personal property had provided security for this loan.
Between 1885 and 1898 Nielsen had a total outlay of $1,832 for
interest, commissions, and repayment of his loan. He had some
money collecting interest during the same period.

with the sale of 79 acres in 1891 for $1,010 his holdings dropped to 240 acres. During the next twenty years Nielsen farmed no more than two-thirds of his land, preferring to rent out the remainder. Hardship, poverty, illness, poor crops, heavy debts, and even death, was visited on this family during the pioneering years. Their eventual release from the monotony and the exhausting labor of the years of early settlement was in keeping with the dream of virtually all homesteaders.[31]

Willa Cather aptly stated that before 1860 "civilization did no more than nibble at the eastern edge" of Nebraska, and that even "as late as 1886 the central part of the state, and everything to the westward, was, in the main, raw prairie."[32] Population in Nebraska by 1870 showed an increase of 425 percent for the decade. By 1880 there were 452,402 residents, a figure which more than doubled by the time of the 1890 census. Population growth was almost stationary in the nineties, when the gain for the decade was about one-third of one percent. In the next ten years the total reached 1,192,214. The acquisition of land in Nebraska shows a close correlation to this population data. The use of cumulative figures for lands in the process of being alienated, as well as those officially transferred, emphasizes a condition of increasing scarcity of land which was highly visible to the incoming settler, who was attracted by the idea of acquiring a Nebraska homestead. [See Chart A] The ratio between appropriated or reserved land and population from 1880 to 1910 was remarkably consistent, ranging from a low of 35 acres per capita in 1890 to a high of 40 in 1880.[33]

---

[31] *Ibid.* In 1903 a house, with furniture and a new well, was built for Nielsen at a cost of more than a thousand dollars. After retiring from the farm he lived in Cozad.

[32] Willa Cather, "Nebraska: The End of the First Cycle," in Virginia Faulkner, *Roundup: A Nebraska Reader,* (1957), pp. 2, 4.

[33] The ratio of acres per capita was for 1880—40.5; 1890—35.5; 1900—36.8; and 1910—39.6.

CHART A

A CUMULATIVE TOTAL FOR THE DISPOSITION
OF NEBRASKA'S 49,031,680[a] ACRES OF LAND SURFACE

Years	Total acres encumbered—all classes of entries[b]	Total acres vacant and not appropriated	Improved Real Estate (acres)	Unimproved Real Estate (acres)	Original Homestead Entries (acres)	Final Homestead Entries (acres)	Original Timber Culture entries (acres)	Final Timber Culture entries (acres)
1870	5,342,237	39,766,857	647,031	1,426,750	1,921,516	104,357	—	—
1880	13,632,604	30,678,899	5,504,702	4,440,124	7,295,607	3,085,854	1,799,329	—
1890	35,103,185	11,226,584	15,247,705	6,345,739	16,587,534	6,578,763	8,681,428	363,712
1900	39,765,561	9,798,688	18,432,595	11,479,184	19,820,601	9,560,399	8,879,809	2,364,913
1910	56,511,282	1,879,486	24,382,777	14,239,454	34,614,710	11,862,568	8,876,351	2,546,698

[a] Territorial Nebraska had an estimated size of 219,160,320 acres.

[b] Railroad land grants from the United States to corporations in Nebraska totaled 7,641,755.78 acres and from the State (using internal improvement lands) 531,103 acres for a total of 8,172,859 acres. Grants to the State for common schools, public buildings, saline lands, land grant college and state university totaled 3,025,779 acres. The figures in the total acres encumbered column reflect railroad and state selections, generally in the decade in which this land was patented, or transferred to the State, and they show the repeated entries, under preemption, homestead and timber-culture laws on the same land. Federal reserved land was a small amount at this time.

Useful in compiling the figures on this chart were the *Annual Reports of the General Land Office*, the published U.S. Census returns and the land figures compiled by Addison E. Sheldon, James C. Olson, and Leslie E. Decker and used by them in their books.

The homestead story has been described most frequently with repeated recital of deficiencies found in provisions
of the law. Further shortcomings were found in its en-
ticement of settlers into situations offering little chance
for success, with a resulting high rate of homestead abandonment. Other criticisms suggest that the law was mis-
interpreted and that it failed to play the important role in
settlement that was expected. Some criticisms are softened
be recognizing that about three-fourths of Nebraska was
available for homesteading and that almost three-fourths
of that area was eventually acquired by the individual
settler through the use of either the Homestead Act or the
Timber Culture Act.[34]

When all provisions of the Homestead Act are considered there were 167,797 homesteads filed on by 1905
with final certificates issued to 95,998 settlers or 57
percent of the total by 1910 when those filing five years
earlier were eligible for completion of their claim.[35] Timber
Culture final certificates for Nebraska were only 30 percent of all entries under that law. Together, these settler-
oriented laws gave land to 48 percent of the Nebraska
settlers who entered a claim under either law.

Benton Aldrich, long a critic of free land provisions,
was sure that acquisition and eventual loss of land obtained
under the Homestead Act was associated with moral decay.
He offered no other way to account for the families who
willingly sold their fertile eastern Nebraska land as soon
as it reached $5.00 per acre in order to relocate on the
western Nebraska frontier or in the Dakotas where the
price was no more than $1.25 per acre. Other critics do
not usually express their views in the moral tones of
Aldrich. Instead, they consider the economic impact to

---

[34] Benjamin H. Hibbard, *A History of the Public Land Policies*,
(1924, 1965), p. 408; Paul W. Gates, "The Homestead Act: Free Land
Policy in Operation, 1862-1935," in *Land Use Policy and Problems in
the United States*, Howard W. Ottoson, ed., (1963), pp.32-43; Gilbert
C. Fite, *The Farmer's Frontier, 1865-1900*, (1966), pp. 16-23.

[35] This data includes two years of intense activity under the
Kinkaid Act, with its 640-acre homestead.

Land seekers, Broken Bow, 1904.

Settlers moving into Custer County, 1886.

Chrisman sisters' homestead, Custer County, 1886.

J. Cramer sod house, Custer County, 1880's.

the newly settled area and some present the idea that sale of land at comparatively high prices assured a far more successful completion of the pioneer stage of farm making than those who used the Homestead Act.[36]

In Nebraska, the sales contracts for disposal of land grants of the Burlington, the land-grant college, and the Union Pacific show a successful completion rate of about 70 percent, 80 percent, and 90 percent, respectively.[37] When compared to these figures the Nebraska homesteaders with a rate of success of 57 percent do not present as discouraging a picture as when measured against the ideal figure of 100 percent. To properly compare the rate of success of those involved in land grant sales and in homesteading, purchasers who paid immediately for their land should be excluded and those who bought land on an extended sales contract should be considered. The remaining total would further reduce the success rate of sales contracts to a figure more closely approximating the successful completion of Nebraska homesteads. In any case these figures show that pioneering was hazardous, not only to the homesteader, but also to the purchaser of raw land from a railroad corporation or from the state.

---

[36] Benton Aldrich papers, Nebraska State Historical Society; Thomas Le Duc, "History and Appraisal of U. S. Land Policy to 1862," in *Land Use Policy and Problems in the United States,* pp. 26-7.

[37] Richard C. Overton, *Burlington West: A Colonization History of the Burlington Railroad,* (1941), pp.383, 416, 421, 425, 431, 439, 450-1; Agnes Horton, "Nebraska's Agricultural-College Land Grant," *Nebraska History,* March 1949, p. 62; Decker *op cit.,* p. 112. A Kansas township study showed successful government land entries patented at a rate of 66 percent whereas Santa Fe sales contracts for lands in the same area were completed 53 percent of the time. An Illinois study shows completion of half of the sales contracts involving 42 percent of the land. See Allan G. Bogue, "Farmer Debtors in Pioneer Kinsley," *Kansas Historical Quarterly,* May 1952, p. 88, and Homer E. Socolofsky, "William Scully: His Early Years in Illinois, 1850-1865," *Journal of the West,* January 1965, pp. 47-8. Carl J. Ernst reported that most of the Burlington forfeitures of 1874 were made by settlers "scared out by the [grass]hoppers." See his papers, Nebraska State Historical Society.

The time lag between entering a claim for a homestead and getting the final certificate five years later must
have been a time of severe trial to many homesteading
families. The *Decisions of the Department of Interior Relating to Public Lands* and the dockets of the Board of
Equitable Adjudication provide ample examples of problems encountered at the "grass-roots" level. Death of the
homesteader necessitated Board action so that the widow
or other heirs could obtain a patent. In some years Indian
hostilities or overflowed land might handicap legal entry.
A sample of the annual dockets shows a substantial number of female homesteaders who had failed to comply with
the regulations found in the law. Some were not of lawful
age when entry was made, others failed to make settlement
or proper cultivation, they might have been absent for
longer than six months or they might have been an abandoned or deserted wife seeking patent in her own name.
One widow was further delayed by the Land Office bureaucracy because she signed her name "Matteson" but
the papers had been drawn up originally for a "Madison".[38]

But even official bureaucracy could maintain a sense
of humor, as seen in a letter to a Nebraska correspondent
in 1879.

> The fact that the legal wife of the homestead party to
> whom you refer resides in the East, and the party upon
> receipt of patent conveys the land to a concubine who has
> resided with him, is a question that does not come within
> the jurisdiction of this department. [39]

Two aged Nebraska women were among those who required Board affirmation to gain their patents when they
failed to file their final proof in time. One was an 81-year-
old homesteader who had not applied for her final proof
within the required seven years because she "thought she

---

[38] *Land Office Reports, 1880,* pp. 238-258; "Abstract of Cases
Submitted to the Board of Equitable Adjudication," National
Archives.
[39] "Letter press book, General Land Office, December 6, 1879
to January 24, 1880," Book 26, p. 225, letter to M. O'Sullivan, River-
ton, Nebraska, December 30, 1879, National Archives.

had another year. [She had] not had sufficient money of late to pay the expenses of making the proof." The other, a 65-year-old widow, had lived on her homestead ten years, the first few years it was entered under the Timber Culture Act, then relinquished to a homestead. Her failure to prove up as required was due to sickness. [40]

These cases, decided by the Board of Equitable Adjudication, show some of the trials of the homesteader but they are not necessarily typical of what happened in Nebraska. Most of these tracts were patented to the claimant, whereas some 43 percent of the homestead entries in Nebraska were lost by the entryman. Many relinquishments made by Nebraska homesteaders were voluntary— they were paid by another settler for the right to enter their land. Such an action might have been motivated by hardship, laziness, or the realization that they could not succeed. Others were merely abandoned and no formal notice was made at the Land Office. The action of relinquishment, cancellation and new entry could delay patenting for many years. One example, not too unusual, was a quarter section in Box Butte County which was entered as a timber claim in 1884, canceled four years later and filed on as a timber claim in each of the next three years. In 1901 the fourth timber claim on that quarter was canceled and it was restored to entry. Five years later it was homesteaded only to be abandoned and a new homestead was filed in 1910, which went through to patent in 1914, or thirty years after the original entry on the land. An adjacent quarter section had been patented for 24 years by that time.[41]

Settlers who lost their homestead rights were defeated because of poverty, or poor crops, or illness, or death, or lack of educational or religious opportunities, or because of improper decisions, laziness or unwillingness to stick it out. They might have been burned out by prairie fire, eaten out by grasshoppers, or frozen out by bitter winter

[40] "Abstract of Cases . . ."
[41] NE¼ of Section 19-27-48W, in Box Butte County.

weather. Some incorrectly located their claim and improved property that was not their own. Discouragement and frustration helped them to give up their idea of getting free land from Uncle Sam. On occasion homesteaders who had failed in their first try for land might have gained enough equity from their claim to succeed when they made use of another of the federal land laws. The ones who did not succeed in their undertaking, as well as the entrymen who failed, helped to identify Nebraska as a "Homestead State."[42]

The study of Nebraska land values in the years after settlement has generally been confined to averages based on the decennial census figures or on average assessed values from various state annual reports. Federal census reports show the spectacular increase in the relative value of all farm property in Nebraska so that by 1910 only three other states exceeded Nebraska's farm property totals. The figures through the decades are shown in chart B.

[42] Third Annual Report of the State Board of Agriculture, . . . State of Nebraska, 1871, pp. 14-15.
[43] All farm property equals land, buildings, implements, machinery, and domestic animals. The figures are drawn from state reports and the Twelfth Census of the United States, 1900, Vol. V, and the Thirteenth Census of the United States, 1910, Vol. VII. In 1890 the average improved farm value nationally was $3,523, almost identical to the Nebraska figure. The increasing divergence begins with 1900, when the national average was $3,563, and continues at an accelerated rate through the first decade of the twentieth century so that the 1910 national average was $6,444 or 40 percent of the average Nebraska farm.

CHART B
VALUE OF ALL FARM PROPERTY IN NEBRASKA[43]

Years	Number of farms	Average per acre	Average per farm	Value of Farm Property as a Percent of the U. S. Total
1860	2,789	$ 6.14	$ 1,391	.07
1870	12,301	11.67	1,967	.34
1880	63,387	10.65	1,671	1.27
1890	113,608	18.63	3,542	3.18
1900	121,525	19.31	4,753	3.66
1910	129,678	41.80	16,038	5.07

In a detailed study of a rural Nebraska community, Robert Diller has shown that land values reflect those (shown in the table above) of Nebraska as a whole, except that a smaller area reveals a much more rapid increase in land values.[44] The modifying effect of new western lands, shown in a state-wide average, holds down the state figures. Land is not a commodity to be sold in the same way as industrial and agricultural products, it cannot be easily divided and each piece of property has individual characteristics which enhance or detract from its value. The fact that every area has a finite quantity of land should cause an increase in land value as settlers fill the area. Moreover, subsequent sales of a particular farm would show real value only at infrequent and irregular intervals, and some valuable farm real estate in Nebraska does not enter into available figures on sales values because such land has never been sold.

Preliminary figures drawn from a small sample study of fifteen of Nebraska's 93 counties show the following

---

[44] Robert Diller, *Farm Ownership, Tenancy, and Land Use in a Nebraska Community*, (1941), p. 30. Another area in eastern Nebraska was dealt with by Evan E. Evans, in his "An Analytical Study of Land Transfer to Private Ownership in Johnson County, Nebraska," Master's thesis, University of Nebraska, 1950.

characteristics for farm real estates.[45] In areas where land patents were obtained by 1890 or earlier, land values generally rose to an average of $10 or more per acre during the first decade, with regular increases in value in later years. In counties where patents were obtained after 1890 a mixed situation existed with some land sales indicating a per acre value of $10 within a decade but more generally values rose to $6 to $8 per acre with declines likely in later years. The available figures reveal no differences in the values of subsequent real estate transactions in a single county which can be related to the fact that the land in question was originally homesteaded, or pre-empted, or owned by a railroad corporation. Slight differences in value seem to exist where land was acquired under the Timber Culture Act, but the acreage involved was small. Perhaps a timber claim possessed a smaller value because it could be acquired without establishing a residence on the land. In almost all cases, the major advance in land prices came after 1900.

In east-central Nebraska the government tracts within railroad land grants were pre-empted or homesteaded and their patents received from ten to fifteen years earlier than the adjacent railroad land was patented. In all of these cases the land was occupied for a number of years before receiving a patent. Subsequent sales of the adjoining tracts of railroad land grants and other lands show a comparable per acre value. Where marked differences existed, the extra value of improvements presumably accounted for the variation. At times the higher priced land was former railroad land-grant and at other times it was originally homesteaded, but more generally there was no discernible difference in value of side-by-side tracts which could be based on the manner in which the land was origi-

---

45 Samples were taken from the following Nebraska counties: Box Butte, Dawson, Dodge, Douglas, Grant, Hall, Harlan, Keith, Nemaha, Nuckolls, Perkins, Pierce, Valley, Washington, and York. Each sample covered nine sections which were uniformly located within each county.

nally taken from the public domain. Much evidence exists showing differences in value of land in various parts of Nebraska, but within a small area there seems to be considerable uniformity in the price for which land sold in a given year.

In central and western Nebraska the sale of railroad land grants came at about the same time that patents were received on adjoining tracts which were acquired under other land laws. In the central part of the state the value of railroad land grants and adjoining tracts was relatively equal. In the west the railroad land was sometimes sold below the minimum government price of $1.25 per acre and subsequent sales prices, based on the limited area of the sample, were below that of nearby land which was homesteaded or obtained through other land laws. Much study of subsequent land sales in Nebraska is needed in order to evaluate properly the changes that occurred and the meaning of these changes.

Within a half century after the organization of the Territory of Nebraska more than a million people had become citizens of the area. Many of them were born there and their loyalty to the region was based on the accident of birth, but why had their parents and the other pioneers of Nebraska settled in the west? What motivated movement to Nebraska and why did these settlers feel that it was necessary to depart from their earlier home? Perhaps Benton Aldrich was thinking of himself when he wrote that many people went west because they were "too poor or too mean to live at home." He further held that:

> . . . nearly all that have come west in these years . . . have come from overpopulated farms, towns, States and countries. There was a lack of land for the family of each. . . . Hence the west has been settled by those who have a deficiency of the home-spirit.—And after having sold out the home, the family lacked the means to buy a suitable farm near by, that is, it was too poor to stay—and preferred to come west.
>
> By a parrallel [sic] course of reasoning I think I could show that these persons and families were of little more than average courage, had better than average health, were more daring—perhaps *reckless* would be a better word.

It is something that an individual or a single family dared
to go among strangers for life! [46]

In Aldrich's case, the land opportunities in Nebraska
served as a powerful attraction to the area. Conversely he
believed that opportunity was lacking in his native New
Hampshire, in Wisconsin, Minnesota, and Iowa, so he settled with his limited resources in Nebraska. John R. Maltby
shows a similar motivation for removal to Nebraska, so
that he could find employment available in the new land,
with an eventual goal of speculation in farm lands and
town property. In Maltby's case, the crisis which caused
him to depart from his home and business in Massachusetts in 1867 was his wife's refusal to live with him. When
reconciliation seemed impossible, Maltby headed west and
it was almost five years later, when he was well-located,
that Mrs. Maltby finally followed him.[47] Because he was
less articulate than either Aldrich or Maltby, Nielsen's
motivation for settling in Nebraska was less clear. The lack
of opportunity in Denmark and in Illinois caused him to
seek a location where his meager capital could best be employed and Nebraska in 1879 was most attractive to him.[48]

In general the primary attraction bringing a settler
to Nebraska was the economic opportunities to be found
in the new land. In comparison with their own residence
and their own opportunities for the future, those found in
the exploitation of Nebraska's resources were enough to
bring them into unsettled country. Whether they were
making use of the Homestead Act, or buying land from a
railroad, settlers were also influenced by the political,
social, and religious institutions of the area of their homeland. Some fled to Nebraska to escape oppression of these
institutions, while others hoped to quickly build a civilization in the new area. Benton Aldrich observed that, "It may

---

[46] Benton Aldrich papers.
[47] "Cash Book, John Rogers Maltby," entries for November 29,
1867, September 24, 1872, and January, 1873. Nebraska State Historical Society.
[48] Nielsen and Jensen, "Farm Record Book 1879-1961."

be painful to us who saw and felt the early conduct and influences of a settlement on new land, to reflect that it was a degrading process. Old ties and restraints were left, and new ones were not promptly formed."[49] According to another pioneer most of the settlers, after getting through the first few years, were "less interested in going 'back east' than . . . in having eastern comforts in Nebraska."[50]

Most settlers in early Nebraska came to the new land individually or with their immediate family, rather than immigrating with an organized colonizing party. Publicity and advertisements, enumerating the advantages of settling in the state, were widely distributed by railroad corporations, land companies, and even by the state itself. Through a combination of circumstances land promotion in Nebraska found a ready reception in the booming 1880's. Addison E. Sheldon, after personal experience in this land rush, wrote that:

> Suddenly, as if by unanimous agreement, about one hundred thousand of us started out to settle that region. For seven years all the westward trains were crowded with passengers, household furniture and livestock. All the dim trails stretching to no-man's land were thronged with white-topped wagons. Every settler in the northwest Nebraska region could secure 480 acres of land in his own right under the pre-emption, homestead and tree-claim acts. [51]

The 1880's alone saw the appropriation of almost one-half of the total area of Nebraska. After 1890 the opportunities to be found in cheap, fertile, well-watered Nebraska land were gone. Many who had participated in the boom days described by Sheldon were retreating from the hazards they had experienced from settling on marginal land which was cursed by a highly variable climate. Land disposal activities in the nineties were virtually nil in Nebraska and the federal land offices no longer were an im-

---

[49] Benton Aldrich papers.
[50] H. Clyde Filley, "Elijah Filley," manuscript, Nebraska State Historical Society.
[51] Addison E. Sheldon, "The Deficiency Judgment: A Story of the Nebraska Nineties, The Farmers' Alliance and the Supreme Court," *Nebraska History*, October-December 1932, p. 289.

mense asset to the economy of a frontier Nebraska community. The combination of hard times and sandhill pastureland offered little inducement to the incoming settler. Occupation of Nebraska's vast public domain had averaged about 10 miles per year and agriculture was growing rapidly. But in the first decade of the twentieth century the disposal of public land in Nebraska again boomed, especially with the passage of the Kinkaid Act of 1904 and its 640-acre homestead, which was limited to about nine million acres in the northwestern part of the state.[52] After a brief flurry of excitement prompted by new settlers coming in to occupy the last remaining public domain in the state, Nebraskans turned their attention to their own agricultural pursuits, the development of their business, and the advancement of their transportation lines. The "empire builders" of the homesteading generation had been replaced by a new generation which was to build on the solid foundations laid down by the earlier settlers. Certainly by the early twentieth century in Nebraska an old era was gone and a new pattern of life was to emerge.

---

[52] Howard W. Ottoson and others, *Land and People in the Northern Plains Transition Area*, (1966), p. 58; Hibbard, *op cit.*, p. 392-3, says that 7,000,000 acres were available under the Kinkaid Act.

THE DESERT LAND ACT IN OPERATION, 1877-1891

John T. Ganoe

THE DESERT LAND ACT IN OPERATION, 1877–1891

With the passage of the Desert Land Act in 1877, serious misgivings at once arose as to its advisability. In his report for the same year, the Commissioner of Public Lands recommended its repeal and the substitution of a law which would give the arid lands to individuals or corporations for reclamation on the same principle as that applied to other lands.[1] The Secretary of the Interior protested against entry on land before its character was determined and suggested that a commission be formed to study the situation.[2] In response, Congress provided on March 3, 1879 for a commission of three persons in addition to the Commissioner of the General Land Office and the Director of the Geological Survey to codify all laws relating to the disposition of the public domain and to classify the land by types. The commission was also expected to present a system for land surveys and to make recommendations as to the best method of distributing western land to actual settlers.[3] The commission's report in 1881 was probably the most extensive survey of the public lands made up to that time.[4]

Although the report revealed little concerning the operation of the Desert Land Act as a national policy, it soon became evident to the Commissioner of Public Lands and to the Secretary of the Interior that the law was being used primarily to gain control of water. The entries were for long narrow tracts along the banks of streams,[5] and if 640 acres could be located in this manner the entrant had a great advantage in irrigating his land.

[1] U. S. General Land Office, *Annual Report of the Commissioner*, 1877:34. Hereafter cited as *G. L. O. R.*

[2] U. S. Department of the Interior, *Annual Report*, 1877:xxii.

[3] *Ibid.* (1879–80), 1:31.

[4] T. C. Donaldson, *The Public Domain* (Washington, 1881). This report was issued as U. S. 47th Congress, 2 sess., *House Miscellaneous Document* 45, part 4 [serial no. 2158].

[5] *G. L. O. R.*, 1880:85–89.

The Commissioner of the General Land Office, J. A. Williamson, considered this procedure a violation of the provision of the act which stated that the land was to be taken in compact form. This, he interpreted as meaning not merely contiguous but a surveyed section or its legal subdivisions and, for unsurveyed land, a form as near that of the legal units as the situation of the land permitted.[6]

Moreover, the Commissioner of Public Lands soon came to the conclusion that the entire national land system was being undermined by fraud. In response to his request, Congress provided for an investigation of fraudulent entries under the various land acts.[7] This authorization was approved on March 3, 1883, and by April 1, the investigators were in the field gathering evidence.[8] The General Land Office had opposed the Desert Land Act from its inauguration and now urged more strongly than ever that the theory on which the law was based was fallacious.[9] The investigators revealed that final proof, supposed to be submitted within three years, never occurred in a large proportion of the entries. Furthermore, no attempt was being made to irrigate the land as it was being taken for stock raising and as a means of controlling the ranges.[10]

The reports of the investigators were startling. W. H. Goucher, the special agent working in California, estimated that only 5 percent of the entries were made in good faith and that 90 percent of those in his district had been made between 1883 and 1885.[11] The land office at Tucson, Arizona, reported that the stockmen were monopolizing the land and stated that "One of the methods whereby large cattle owners acquire title to land enough to control all the water in a large district is the placing of their employés here and there at the different waters and

---

[6] *Ibid.*, 88.
[7] U. S. Laws, Statutes, etc., *The Statutes at Large of the United States of America* . . . (1883) 22:623.
[8] *G. L. O. R.*, 1883:206.
[9] *Ibid.*, 8.
[10] *Ibid.*, 1884:8.
[11] *Ibid.*, 1885:59. The report was dated Nov. 17, 1884.

acquiring title through them."[12]   Charges against the cattlemen were made with monotonous frequency.

The Secretary of the Interior begged Congress to act.   The
land was being patented by the livestock interests in such a
way as to gain control of thousands of acres.   Odd sections were
purchased either from the Government or the railroads and
fenced in a manner that enclosed the intervening land although
it was not owned by the cattlemen.[13]

The governors of the territories did not agree with the complaints of the Commissioner of Public Lands and the Secretary
of the Interior.   The Governor of Idaho Territory asserted:[14]

In a few years an acreage greater than the whole State of Rhode Island will be
reclaimed in the Snake River Valley alone, and changed from an arid, parched,
and unsightly desert into rich and blooming agricultural lands, safe from drought
or floods of rain.   This happy condition is entirely attributable to the desert-
land act, which should not be, and I beg to express a hope, will not be, changed.

The Governor of Montana Territory estimated that not over
5 percent of the entries were fraudulent and complained bitterly
against the suspension of entries pending investigation, claiming
that it was working "untold hardship" on the settlers.[15]

Until 1885, nearly all of the charges made by the Public Land
Commissioner and the Secretary of the Interior were directed
against the cattlemen.   In attempting to formulate a reclamation policy for the arid lands, Congress had not considered their
use for grazing purposes.   The representatives from the Eastern
States who dominated Congress expected the lands to be trans-
muted into a rich agricultural region like that of the Ohio and
Mississippi valleys.   Westerners were fully aware of what was
taking place, and moreover, if the cattlemen seized the lands,
it was not entirely without invitation.   The Governor of Wyoming Territory gloried in the growth of the cattle industry and
frankly advertised the ways to obtain large quantities of land
under the various acts.   In his annual report, he stated:[16]

    [12] *Ibid.*
    [13] Department of the Interior, *Annual Report* (1887) 1:15, 19.
    [14] Idaho (Ter.) Governor, *Report* . . ., 1884:8, 9.
    [15] "Report of the Governor of Montana," in Department of the Interior,
Annual Report (1886) 2:834.
    [16] Wyoming (Ter.) Governor, *Report*, 1883:27-28.

The greatest source of encouragement to men of moderate means desiring to engage in cattle-raising in Wyoming arises from that feature of the policy of the United States Government by which it encourages its citizens to acquire title to the public lands. In Wyoming, by fulfilling the requirements of the land laws, a male citizen may take up the following number of acres:

	Acres
Under the homestead act	160
Under the pre-emption act	160
Under the timber-culture act	160
Under the desert-land act	640
Total	1,120

By the first three acts land may be taken up in 40-acre tracts, and under the desert-land act a tract a mile and a quarter long and three-quarters of a mile wide may be filed upon.

A married couple, the wife being able to enter 640 acres under the desert land act, can get possession of 1,760 acres, sufficient to support several hundred of cattle. If, say, three men having means sufficient to make the payments at the land office necessary when filing upon lands under the four acts referred to, join their entries along a stream of water, they will have grazing land enough for at least a thousand head of cattle. They will be put to the expense of erecting fences around their lands and sheds to protect their herd against violent storms, but that done, their business will, it is thought, be put upon as safe a basis as is cattle-raising in Iowa.

To this governor, the activities of the stockmen were justified. In his opinion, the land of the Government was not worth $1.25 an acre, and since the stockmen had the water rights they might as well run their fences back to the divides as no other settlers would want the land along the watersheds.[17] He also believed that the land laws did not allow enough leeway for action and claimed that the investigations by the Interior Department worked gross unfairness against the honest man who told what he had actually done and exempted the perjurer who claimed fictitious improvements.[18]

The Governor of Utah did not deny that there was fraud but held that the entire national land system, except for the homestead and preemption acts, was an invitation to fraudulence.[19]

[17] Ibid., 48-52.
[18] "Report of the Governor of Wyoming," in Department of the Interior, Annual Report (1885), 2:1202–1207.
[19] "Report of the Governor of Utah," in Department of the Interior, Annual Report (1885) 2:1029

He blamed the Department of the Interior for the troubles, as-
serting that because[20]

the Department [was] holding so strictly to the requirements under the desert-
land act stockmen, in their own interests, have entered lands about the springs
and streams for the purpose of watering stock. The waters are so scarce in the
Territory that a company of four or five men engaged in stock business can enter
the same number of springs and streams, paying the Government for not more
than a section or two of land, and virtually get the use of thousands of acres that
cannot be settled or entered under any of the present land laws.

The only dissenting voice from the territorial governors was
that of Governor Edmund G. Ross of New Mexico. He believed
that land was being taken by fraud and possibly with the con-
nivance of officials, and he saw no reason for changing the laws
to aid the grazing interests because, as he put it, people rather
than "dumb brutes" should inhabit the land.[21] To him the
problem was a conflict between two civilizations, the nomad and
semi-barbarian against the granger, and he insisted that the cattle industry should be curtailed in the interest of the latter.[22]

The statistics show a marked decrease in the number of entries
under the Desert Land Act by 1887, and the Secretary of the
Interior virtuously declared that the reduction was due to new
methods used by the General Land Office.[23] Probably the explanation is that the cattle industry had reached its maximum
development by the middle eighties. Great losses had resulted
from overstocking the ranges and the severe winters, and the
profits of the industry showed a marked decrease beginning in
1885.[24] This situation naturally affected the number of desert-
land entries.

A new epoch in the operation of the Desert Land Act began
with the decline of the cattle industry. In 1882, there were no
irrigation works built on sound engineering principles, but

---

[20] Ibid.
[21] "Report of the Governor of New Mexico," in ibid., 1008–1010.
[22] Ibid. (1887) 1:874–875.
[23] See G. L. O. R., and Department of the Interior, Annual Report (1887) 1:6.
[24] "The Range Cattle Traffic," House Executive Document 267, U. S. Congress, 48th, 2 sess., serial no. 304; U. S. Congress, 51st., 1st sess., Senate Report
829, serial no. 2705.

by 1888, investors were turning from ranching to the rapidly developing irrigation companies.[25] In Wyoming, companies were being incorporated at the rate of one or two per year, usually, however, with a capital of less than $100,000. In 1882, eleven were incorporated; in 1883, nine, including one which was capitalized at $300,000 and another at $1,000,000; in 1884, nineteen; and in 1885, thirty-six.[26]

In 1887 Arizona had at least 400 miles of irrigation canals that cost over a million dollars, and had reclaimed over 200,000 acres. This work had been done by stock companies, controlled by landowners who had obtained land under the Desert Land Act.[27] In California the growth of irrigation and the number of desert-land entries were equally rapid.

The development of irrigation in the intermontane region was no less meteoric. In Idaho, even by 1884, the Governor pointed with pride to the achievements in reclamation.[28]

Near Blackfoot a canal is nearly finished that will reclaim between 40,000 and 50,000 acres. In Cassia County—along the south side of the Snake River—Raft River, Goose Creek, and many smaller streams are owned entirely by the Mormons and used by them for irrigation purposes.

At Shoshone, in Alturas County, 25 miles north of Snake River, Little Wood River has been turned on the desert and a thriving town with its outlying farms has grown and is growing, where but two short years ago was a sage-brush covered, desert plain.

In the Bruneau Valley some 60,000 acres are already under cultivation and a canal has been started to cover from 25,000 to 30,000 acres more. In Wood River Valley a canal has been constructed and irrigates over 20,000 acres, while below these now fruitful acres lie 50,000 acres which will shortly be covered with water and cultivated.

The Idaho Mining and Irrigation Company of New York is constructing a canal with a capacity of 4,000 cubic feet of water per second, which takes the waters of the Boise about 75 miles above its confluence with the Snake River. This canal will irrigate and reclaim about 600,000 acres of land lying on the north side of the Snake River and south of Boise City.

---

[25] U. S. Geological Survey, *Annual Report* (1891–92) 13 (3):115 (Washington, 1893). Hereafter cited as *G. S. A. R.*
[26] "Annual Report of the Governor of Wyoming," in Department of the Interior, *Annual Report* (1885) 2:1191–1193.
[27] "Report of the Governor of Arizona," in *ibid* (1887) 1:754–756.
[28] Idaho (Ter.) Governor, *Report*, 1884:8–9.

On the Payette River two canals are nearly completed that will cover about 50,000 acres, while a third is contemplated that will reclaim 30,000 acres more.

On the Weiser there are about 75,000 acres being brought under irrigating ditches, there being three or four different canals now building. In addition to the above a plan is maturing to take the waters of the Snake River and reclaim nearly 2,000,000 of acres of valley land. This, if carried into effect, will give Idaho land enough to supply the entire Pacific slope with cereals, fruits, and vegetables, and make her the richest of the Territories.

In 1890, the Governor reported that almost all irrigation was being carried on by corporate development and that most of the land was being taken under the minimum provision of the Desert Land Act.[29] The Governor of Utah stated in 1885 that the increase in the number of desert and timber-culture entries was due to the building of canals for reclamation purposes.[30] In New Mexico some owners were beginning to cultivate grasses, and the progress in irrigation by private enterprise and the incorporation of over thirty companies for that purpose was reported.[31]

The development of irrigation was so rapid that the Director of the Geological Survey expressed fear concerning its future possibilities, since, in order to utilize the water supply to the fullest extent, it would be necessary to buy out vested interests amounting to several hundred million dollars. When asked by the Congressional committee on irrigation for an explanation of the rapid growth, he replied that it was obviously because of the lucrative increment. Scarcely a week passed, he declared, without domestic and foreign companies asking for information and offering capital for investment.[32]

To the Public Land Commissioner this trend became the new crux of the land problem. Whereas the reports of the investigators had once complained against the cattle companies, they now turned to the speculators and the land and ditch companies. In Wyoming, seventy-eight desert-land entries comprising some 48,000 acres were transferred immediately after proof to a land

[29] "Report of the Governor of Idaho," in Department of the Interior, *Annual Report* (1890) 3:564-568.

[30] "Report of the Governor of Utah," in *ibid.* (1885) 2:1029.

[31] "Report of the Governor of New Mexico," in *ibid.* (1888) 3:843-844; (1890) 3:458-459.

[32] *G. S. A. R.* (1889-90) 11 (2):233-234 (Washington, 1891).

and ditch company, previously organized for the expressed purpose of acquiring these lands. Most of the entrymen lived in eastern States and had never seen the land. Even the purchase money was supplied by the company.[33] The reports from other districts tended to confirm the inference. The Surveyor General of Arizona reported that "Speculators of all degrees have now turned their attention to the facilities offered by the desert-land law, and 'the woods are full of them'. "[34] In the same Territory, non-residents entered 113,178 of the 199,026 acres between July 1, 1885 and June 1, 1887.[35]

The Census of 1890 indicates in a measure the growth of irrigation during the latter part of the eighties. There were then 3,631,381 acres under irrigation by 54,136 irrigators, but this development cannot be attributed entirely to the Desert Land Act. Colorado, which was not included in the original act, had more than one-sixth of the total number of irrigators and nearly one-fourth of the improved acreage. In terms of States, it stood third in the number of irrigators and first in the proportion of total area irrigated.[36] Moreover, there had been considerable irrigation in California and Utah prior to the passage of the act, and it is reasonable to suppose that it would have continued to increase there. In addition, the homestead entries of the eighties were greater than the number of desert-land entries in the regions covered by the Desert Land Act. Only in Montana and Wyoming, and in some years in Arizona, Nevada, and Idaho, did the desert-land entries exceed those for homesteads.

Reclamation, however, involved the utilization of water as well as land, and analysis of the operation of the Desert Land Act in relation to the various methods of irrigation indicates its influence on water rights. If a farmer made a bona-fide entry for irrigation rather than cattle raising, he had four possible ways of

---

[33] *G. L. O. R.*, 1888:49.

[34] *Ibid.*, 1887:522.

[35] *Ibid.*, 523.

[36] U. S. Census Office, 11th Census, 1890, *Report on Agriculture by Irrigation in the Western Part of the United States at the Eleventh Census: 1890*, by F. H. Newell, special agent, 1-2 (Washington, 1894).

reclaiming the land: build ditches and appropriate water and manage the project by individual effort; affiliate with others to form a cooperative enterprise in which the stock was held by the landowners themselves; join a large group to form an irrigation district which, with the permission of the State, assumed quasi-governmental powers and issued bonds for the construction of projects based on the tax levy of the district; or, finally, purchase water from an irrigation canal company at a fixed rate.

Reclamation by individual effort was most unsatisfactory from the standpoint of conservation. The Desert Land Act was designed to dispose of arid lands to actual settlers, and it looked primarily to the utilization of perennial streams which could be easily diverted. Under the act as it remained until 1891, this was about all that could be done. In most of the arid regions the water supply was quite limited, and since the act recognized the doctrine of appropriation two important problems arose.[37] The appropriator took the land along streams where water could be diverted most easily and cheaply. As a result the water was invariably used first on the land at the lowest level. With the streams thus utilized it was impossible to irrigate the uplands without buying out the vested interests which had accrued below. Thus, the efficient utilization of water from the standpoint of its maximum beneficial use was thwarted.[38]

The other result was the curtailment of future development due to the early appropriation of easy-access streams. Although the doctrine of appropriation was applied to the public domain, title to water did not go with the land. When the land was owned by private individuals, the water rights came from the States. The resulting diversity of laws relating to water generated problems of equity that baffled the courts. The separate control of land and water tended to create water monopolies with the landowners dependent on the owners of the streams.[39]

---

[37] " . . . the right to the use of water by the person so conducting the same, on or to any tract of desert land of six hundred and forty acres shall depend upon bona fide prior appropriation."—Desert Land Act, sect. 1.

[38] G. S. A. R. (1889-90) 11 (2):233-236.

[39] Elwood Mead, *Irrigation Institutions*, 22, 23 (New York, 1903).

President Harrison, in his third annual message, urged Congress to adopt protective measures on the basis of its control over water rights in the Territories.[40] The percentage of irrigation projects carried out as partnership and cooperative enterprises is not known. Almost all of the canals in Utah were built by cooperative effort. The farmers usually formed clubs to furnish both the money and labor and then divided the stock accordingly.[41] In California irrigation was begun by individual enterprise, chiefly by the holders of large estates. The Crocker-Huffman and Galloway canals cost more than a million dollars each.[42] Later, when the canal companies became involved in extensive litigation, reclamation was undertaken through irrigation districts in accordance with the district irrigation law of 1887. Idaho followed Utah closely in its method of development, whereas Wyoming depended largely on individual effort and land and irrigation companies. This diversity makes it impossible to tell with certainty the amount of irrigation promoted by the various methods of reclamation.

Strictly speaking, the Desert Land Act made no provision for relcamation except by individual effort, and it was on the basis of this assumption that Congress had designated 640-acre units. This amount was assumed to be sufficient, but irrigation farming needed more than land and water; it required capital,—often more than the individual settler could command. Since the act merely required that the land be irrigated in order to prove title and did not specify the amount, the farmer could adopt any method so long as his land was under irrigation at the end of the three-year period. Under the Desert Land Act entrymen could join together to build projects and irrigate their land and receive title from the Government. The persons forming this type of company, however, were of limited means. Capital, except in the form of labor, was extremely limited and consequently

[40] U. S. President, *Compilation of the Messages and Papers of the Presidents, 1789-1897* . . . by James D. Richardson, 9:205 (Washington, 1898).
[41] Mead, *Irrigation Institutions*, 233-237.
[42] *Ibid.*, 186.

these small partnership and cooperative concerns followed the practice of individual irrigators and built comparatively small ditches and irrigated only the low lands. The Mormons in Utah found the cooperative system well adapted to their needs, but as related to the efficient utilization of land and conservation of water, it proved little better than individual action.

The relationship between the Desert Land Act and the district plan of irrigation involved the organization of a community to issue bonds with which to build ditches. The security of the bonds would be the tax issues on the district, but back of the tax was a lien on the land. As title to the land resided in the Government until final proof and it could not be made until water was actually delivered, no lien could be placed until after irrigation. Consequently this method of raising money to build projects was eliminated.

In spite of the hardships involved in promoting irrigation, many believed that it, like the railroads, would create vast fortunes. The boom was based on this hope, and it was only through bitter experience that irrigation companies learned that the land law, passed by the Government to aid the development of irrigation, did not operate in their favor. Concerning its actions, Elwood Mead, who was perhaps more familiar with the irrigation problem of the West than any other man, stated:[43]

When the Bear River Canal was begun in Utah, the land it was to water was an unoccupied sage-brush desert. Before its survey was completed, and in less than thirty days after it was begun, every acre of land had been filed upon. Three years later not one acre in fifty was being irrigated by the original entry men. Before the survey of the canal of the Wyoming Development Company was completed, six sections of the best land below it had been filed on by speculators. To protect itself, the company had to organize a syndicate to file on the land under the Desert Act.

It was evident, then, by about 1890, that remedial legislation was necessary, but it was difficult to know what action should be taken. The attempt to reclaim by means of a land law which gave no consideration to the water problem had worked havoc.

[43] *Ibid.*, 20.

In the meantime a movement to repeal the entire desert-land policy had developed. Beginning with the criticism of the Commissioner of Public Lands in 1877, the Desert Land Act was the object of intermittent attacks from numerous sources. Colorado was not included under the act until 1891, although, as has been noted, it was one of the major States in the development of irrigation. The Colorado representatives tried continually to have the act modified. In the first session of the Forty-seventh Congress, they brought forward a bill to settle the question of arid lands in Colorado by leasing them in 5,000-acre tracts for ten-year periods at four cents an acre.[44] The majority of the Committee on Public Lands reported favorably as it was believed that the bill was designed to allow capital to utilize the land and would at the same time guard proprietary rights. The majority also held that the existing laws of other States and Territories would be unsuitable for this land.[45] The minority felt that leasing the land in this manner would, in essence, make the Government a landlord similar to Old World sovereigns and that the bill was a step backward toward feudalism. It recommended that the Government sell in larger plots but not lease.[46] Because of this divergence of opinion the bill failed to pass.

The second source of agitation against the act came from the arid region itself and consisted mainly of attempts to relieve settlers under the Desert Land Act. Several bills were brought forward, one to amend the fees on the ground that the minimum paid for other lands in the United States was too much for desert lands;[47] and another, which is interesting in the light of the investigations made by the Interior Department, to authorize the assignee to make final proof of the reclamation of his land.[48] A number of bills sought to amend the act by extending the

[44] *Congressional Record*, 13:417, 840, 989 (Jan. 16, Feb. 2, 8, 1882). H. R. 2829, providing for the leasing of land in Colorado, was introduced, but the Committee on Public Lands reported H.R. 3857 as a substitute.
[45] U. S. Congress, 47th, 1st sess., *House Report 197* (Washington, 1882).
[46] *Ibid.*
[47] *Congressional Record*, 10:3707 (May 24, 1880).
[48] *Ibid.*, 1774 (Mar. 22, 1880).

time for making proof and payment, and others provided for incorporation of irrigation companies.[49]

A memorial, drawn by the Nevada Legislature in February 1883 and presented to Congress the following December, asked that desert entries, if not proved after the three-year period as provided by the act, be cancelled. The Legislature believed that the land would be entered under other land acts if this were done.[50] In the Forty-ninth Congress, bills were again brought forward to repeal the act as the investigations of land fraud were well under way. Nevertheless, the resulting Senate report held that the law should not be repealed but modified to prevent the existing abuses. Congress, however, merely postponed action,[51] and during the next few years bills for repeal were immediately laid on the table.

Meanwhile, the Commissioner of Public Lands and the Secretary of the Interior continued to plead for repeal. On February 13, 1888, a Senate Resolution asked the Secretary of the Interior whether he considered it advisable to have the Geological Survey segregate the land and lay out sites for reservoirs. Soon thereafter an act was passed providing for the survey of arid lands and investigation of reservoir sites.[52]

This act, apparently innocent enough in its intent, created a great furor. The plans of a Utah corporation to utilize the waters of Bear Lake and Bear River affected Idaho, and when the Idaho convention met to draw up a constitution, resolutions of protest were passed and the Utah company was forced to appeal to the Secretary of the Interior for protection. The

[49] These bills particularly emanated from the California representatives in 1882 during the first session of the Forty-seventh Congress. See *Congressional Record*, 11:1307 (Feb. 7, 1881); 13:275, 417, 1304, 3925 (Jan. 9, 16, Feb. 20, May 15, 1882); 15:154, 1177 (Dec. 18, 1883, Feb. 18, 1884).

[50] *Ibid.*, 15:199 (Dec. 20, 1883).

[51] These modifications provided: 1, Restriction of the amount purchased to 320 acres; 2, Sale only to citizens of the U. S.; 3, The requirement of a five-year residence period; 4, A provision against alienation of land; 5, At least one-half of the land to be reclaimed in five years. U. S. Congress, 49th, 1st sess., *Senate Report 69* (Washington, 1886); *Congressional Record*, 17:6266 (June 29, 1886).

[52] Texts of the various resolutions, letters, etc. relating to this act are conveniently found in *G.S.A.R.* (1888-89) 10 (2):1-17 (Washington, 1890).

Secretary replied that speculators could not take the land by the terms of the act and the Commissioner of Public Lands was instructed on August 5, 1889, to " 'immediately cancel all filings made since October 2, 1888, on such sites for reservoirs, ditches, or canals for irrigating purposes ... and ... hereafter receive no filings upon any such lands'. "[53] When the question was referred to the Attorney General, he ruled that the act reserved the land from settlement. "Entries," he said, "should not be permitted, therefore, upon any part of the arid regions which might possibly come within the operation of this act."[54]

For all intents and purposes, this interpretation meant that the arid lands could not be reclaimed. Coming just at the time when the irrigation boom was at its peak, it caused a protest to the Congressional Committee on Irrigation and Reclamation of Arid Lands.[55] Obviously the law as interpreted was working against the welfare of the country. Since the good land was withdrawn, the settlers were forced to take inferior lands which meant the utilization of water that could not thereafter be put to its best use. As a result the committee recommended the amendment that was approved August 30, 1890, in which that part of the act withdrawing lands from settlement was repealed.[56] Thus, the attempt of the Secretary of the Interior to gain his point by urging the maintenance of the literal provisions of the act had not met with Congressional approval. In the meantime, Congress was still besieged with requests

[53] *G. L. O. R.*, 1890:61.

[54] *Ibid.* The provisions of the act upon which this opinion was based were: "all the lands which may hereafter be designated or selected by such United States surveys for sites for reservoirs, ditches or canals for irrigation purposes and all the lands made susceptible of irrigation by such reservoirs, ditches or canals are from this time henceforth hereby reserved from sale as the property of the United States, and shall not be subject after the passage of this act, to entry, settlement or occupation until further provided by law: *Provided,* That the President may at any time in his discretion by proclamation open any portion or all of the lands reserved by this provision to settlement under the homestead laws."—*Statutes at Large* (1888) 25:527 (Washington, 1889).

[55] For the activities of this committee, see U. S. Congress, 51st, 1st sess., *Senate Report 928* (Washington, 1890).

[56] *Statutes at Large* (1890) 26:391 (Washington, 1891).

to take some action on arid lands. In the first session of the Fifty-first Congress more than fifty bills and resolutions pertaining to this problem were introduced and Congress accordingly passed an amendatory act, approved on March 3, 1891, which was designed to remedy the abuses.[57] In the first place it provided that the party making the entry would have to file a map indicating how he intended to irrigate the land and prove that his water supply was adequate for the purpose. This would eliminate taking land where there was no water, or merely to assign it to others for cattle raising.

In the second place, the act recognized the principle that irrigation could not be done satisfactorily by a single individual working entirely through his own efforts and provided that entrymen could associate together and file a joint map showing their irrigation plans. The importance of this partnership and cooperation plan is shown by the Census of 1910 which estimated that this method was used on nearly half of the acreage irrigated.[58]

The third feature of the act aimed to define reclamation in terms of the money expended on irrigation. When the Desert Land Act was first contemplated the question of what constituted reclamation and of how much water would have to be applied to meet the terms of the act was considered. The only answer made was that there should be enough "to make it an object for people to occupy the land."[59] From that time on, the problem had vexed the Secretary of the Interior. The amendatory act attempted to settle it by providing that at least $3.00 per acre must be expended and proof shown at the end of each year that $1.00 per acre had been spent to secure water. If in any year before the final entry was made, the entryman failed to show such proof, the land was to revert to the United States.

In the fourth place, the amendment limited the act to indi-

[57] *Ibid.* (1891) 26:1096 1097; 6 *Federal Statutes Annotated*, 395.
[58] U. S. Bureau of the Census, Thirteenth Census of the United States, 1910, *Bulletin, Irrigation* . . . 846 [Washington, 1911 12].
[59] *Congressional Record*, 5·1969 (Feb. 27, 1877).

viduals. Hitherto, the cattle companies, many of them controlled by English and Scotch bankers, had been able to acquire large areas of land by manipulating the entries. The amendment provided that the entrymen should be citizens of the United States, and, what was more important, that "no persons or association of persons shall hold by assignment or otherwise prior to the issue of patent, more than three hundred and twenty acres of such arid or desert lands, . . ." This provision was an attempt to limit the acreage by prohibiting corporations from taking more than 320 acres in addition to entries of the individual entrymen. The final section extended the operation of the act to Colorado.

The movement to repeal the Desert Land Act was unsuccessful, and beginning in 1891 irrigation entered upon a new era. The problems of operation had not been solved, and it remained for the future to see what could be done.

JOHN T. GANOE

University of Oregon
Eugene, Oregon

LAND CONTEST IN EARLY UTAH

Gustave O. Larson

ist's conception of the Eagle Gate, en-
nce to Brigham Young's estate, which
trolled access to City Creek Canyon. The
islature made exclusive grants to lead-
Mormons with a view to centralizing
ponsibility and minimizing controversy
the use of timber and water resources.

LAND CONTEST IN EARLY UTAH

By Gustive O. Larson*

The problem of land ownership in America began when Europeans
first set foot on soil occupied by another people. After a century of confusion the Constitution of 1789 provided authority for the new government to treat with the natives in relation to common boundaries. Accordingly, within a decade the results of several treaties were unified by
Congress into a continuous line from Lake Erie to Florida. When the
white population through expansion breached the line, further treaties
moved it westward. The Louisiana Purchase in 1803 provided ample
room for "Indian Country" west of the Mississippi, and three decades
later a "removal policy" placed the red men west of a line determined
solely by the American government. Nevertheless, native rights to the
soil continued to be recognized beyond the Mississippi, and when the
white settlers pushed into the middle-west they relied on their government to negotiate new treaties extinguishing Indian land titles according to the latest advance.

But in the Great Basin circumstances differed. Here the Mormon
colonial projection had overshot the margin of easy acquisition of land
titles into a political vacuum where peculiar circumstances found the
federal government indifferent to repeated calls for help. No govern-

* Mr. Larson is professor of church history at the Brigham Young University,
Provo, Utah.

ment stood ready to push the natives one step further by a treaty involving extinction of land titles. Hence native rights, which were still acknowledged by the United States government, were violated by Mormon colonization. For more than two decades the red men saw every tribal homeland occupied by the invader and the game driven from their hunting grounds. Conflicting claims developed, to be resolved between three groups, each viewing the situation through different eyes. There were the United States government extending sovereignty over its recent territorial conquest, the native defending his heritage, and the Mormon moving in to establish squatters' rights through utilitarian occupation.

Manifest Destiny which dictated conquest of the Southwest may have shunted the Latter-day Saints into a region "abandoned to the Mormons for its worthlessness."[1] But the religious exiles, on the contrary, viewed it as expressed by Brigham Young: "We have been driven from the habitations of man and hurled . . . as a stone from a sling, and we have lodged here in this goodly place . . . just where the Lord wants His people to gather."[2] With this conviction of divine sanction of their location and uncoupled from the processes of the federal government, the Mormons made their own laws. A committee was appointed "to draft and report to the convention a constitution under which the inhabitants of said territory might govern themselves until the Congress of the United States should otherwise provide by law."[3]

Among the laws developed were those governing land surveys and disposition of property. The first governing principles were announced upon President Young's arrival in Salt Lake Valley. "No man should buy or sell land. Every man should have his land measured off to him for city and farming purposes, what he could till. He might till it as he pleased but he should be industrious and take care of it."[4]

The first survey of Salt Lake City was begun by Orson Pratt and Henry S. Sherwood on August 2, 1847. Subsequently the city was divided into ten-acre blocks, each containing eight 1¼-acre lots. Extending away from the city proper were larger areas of five, ten, twenty and

---

[1] Senator Sneddon, quoted by H. H. Bancroft, *History of Utah, 1540–1886* (San Francisco, 1889), 453.

[2] Journal History of the Church of Jesus Christ of Latter-day Saints, August 7, 1847, in Church Historian's Office, Salt Lake City, Utah.

[3] Manuscript History of Brigham Young, 1849, p. 26, in Church Historian's Office.

[4] Diary of Wilford Woodruff, July 25, 1847, MS, in Church Historian's Office.

forty acres measured off for farms and pastures. At first the tens and twenties were enclosed as one big field by co-operative fencing. Both the city homesites and the outlying fields were distributed free to the settlers through drawing lots. Within a year of arrival in the valley eight hundred and sixty-three applicants had drawn property totaling 11,005 acres.

Salt Lake City became the pattern for the far-flung communities of Mormondom. Land surveys surrounding the town and cities were deliberately extensive in anticipation of rapid population growth as "the Gathering" would pour its thousands into "Zion." Responsibility

Orson Pratt and Henry S. Sherwood fixed the Great Salt Lake Base and Meridian of the valley of the Great Salt Lake in 1847. In 1855, David H. Burr, the first surveyor general for Utah, also located here the initial point of public land surveys for Utah and set the stone monument still preserved.

LAND CERTIFICATE.

This is to certify that _____

_____

_____

_____

Salt Lake City, _____ *186__*

Facsimile of a land certificate issued just a few months prior to the formal opening of the federal Land Office in Salt Lake City, March, 1869.

for classification and distribution of lands among the newcomers rested upon the local bishops.

The State of Deseret, organized in March, 1849, could make no provision for disposal of public lands. However, it did undertake to provide rights of occupancy in anticipation of subsequent confirmation of its action by the federal government. By legislative action on March 2, 1850,[5] it created the office of Surveyor General and County Surveyor whose duties were to supervise and certify to all surveys. Certificates approved by them were to constitute titles of land possession when properly registered with the county recorder. The land itself came free to the applicant but a charge of one dollar and fifty cents was made to cover survey and recording costs. An ordinance of February 12, 1851, required the owner to enclose his land with a fence four and one-half feet high to protect against animal trespass.

When the Organic Act of the Territory of Utah, in September, 1850, also failed to provide for acquisition of land titles, further provisional measures became necessary. An act of 1852 placed the public lands under jurisdiction of the county courts. These were empowered to grant permits of occupancy to residents and users of described pieces

[5] "The State of Deseret," *Utah Historical Quarterly*, VIII, nos. 2, 3, 4 (Salt Lake City, 1940), 184.

of property. Transfer of ownership was provided for through quit-claim deeds supported by survey certificates. Also, as protection against trespass and to encourage small land holdings in order to make room for additional settlers, each owner was required, by an act in 1853, to enclose his property with a pole fence within one year. Fencing was considered of such importance that breaching it to "jump a claim" was made a criminal offense. In 1855 the processes of transfer were extended to unsurveyed as well as surveyed lands, and in 1861 a law was enacted establishing land ownership through enclosure.

Water and timber, being equally vital to survival, were also declared communally owned and placed under jurisdiction of the county courts. The objective in their use was equitable distribution to the greatest number. With reference to water the "doctrine of appropriation" developed in Utah in contrast to the law of riparian rights in less arid states. Timber for fuel and construction purposes existed only in the canyons, and building of access roads into wooded areas became community enterprises under direction of the bishops. Upon completion of a road, timber became available to all upon payment of a small maintenance fee. A strict policy of conservation permitted use only of dead wood for fuel. Frequently the legislature made exclusive grants to leading Mormons with a view to centralizing responsibility and minimizing controversy in the use of resources. A typical grant was made to Ezra T. Benson on January 9, 1851:

An ordinance in relation to the timber in the Kanyons and mountains . . . passed December 3, 1850.
Section 1. Be it ordained by the General Assembly of the State of Deseret, that the exclusive control of the timber in the kanyons and mountains leading into Tooele Valley . . . is hereby granted to Ezra T. Benson, who is hereby authorized to control said kanyons, to work roads into them, and to direct when, where, and by whom timber may be taken out therefrom.
Section 5. Nothing in the above ordinance shall be so construed as to prevent, or hinder the citizens of said counties from getting timber, wood, or poles in any of said kanyons for their own use by observing the above regulations.[6]

While in no sense intended as monopolistic, these grants excited early non-Mormon opposition.

Salt Lake Valley stretched as an indefinite borderline between Shoshoni and Ute Indians. A "digger" band from each camped near the newly arrived Mormons on July 31, 1847. The record states,

[6] Ibid., 207.

"The Shoshones appeared to be displeased because the brethren had traded with the Utes. The Shoshones claimed that they were the owners of the land and that the Utes had come over the line to interfere with their rights. They signified to the brethren by signs that they wanted to sell them the land for powder and lead." [7] The next day the pioneers gathered for church service under a hastily prepared bowery. Heber C. Kimball, who spoke for Brigham Young,

discouraged the idea of paying the Indians for the lands, for if the Shoshones should be thus considered, the Utes and other tribes would claim pay also. "The Land," said the speaker, "belongs to our Father in heaven, and we calculate to plow and plant it; and no man will have power to sell his inheritance, for he cannot remove it; it belongs to the Lord. We will all have farms and cultivate them and plant vineyards. And if we are faithful, five years will not pass away before we are better off than we ever were in Nauvoo." [8]

Within a week fifty-three acres had been plowed and planted with some patches of corn and potatoes already greening the gray landscape.

Although the offer of the natives to sell their land was not taken seriously, its implications of ownership continued to haunt the Mormons in varied forms for two decades as they occupied every Indian homeland in the shadows of the Wasatch. "We come as brothers," they said in effect, to the dispossessed, "to teach you to make your lands produce and if we drive the game from your hunting grounds we will help you stock them with cattle." The Ute Chief Walkara voiced a typical Indian response when he said, on the shores of Utah Lake, "The water (and the land) are mine. But tell Brigham that the Mormons may use them. We want to trade." [9] So, without treaty or legal process, the choice lands passed into Mormon control while the natives contented themselves with the expedient of trade.

The Mormon "Kingdom" was exclusive by circumstance and by intent. The "Gentile" who came among them as prospector, merchant, or territorial appointee, was an intruder; and when he multiplied in Zion he became the cause for much concern. It was doubly so as the outsider represented the federal government to which accounting would have to be made in the appropriating of its territory. So a defensive movement developed against the Gentile in the form of re-

[7] Journal History, July 31, 1847.
[8] *Ibid.* The only land purchase made by the Mormons in their initial settlement was the Miles Goodyear ranch in Weber Valley for $1,950.00.
[9] Paraphrased from Journal History, June 2, 1849.

activation of the "law of consecration." This program, tried with in-conclusive results in Missouri, involved the transfer of individual prop-erty to the church to be received back "consecrated" to the service of the Kingdom. More than a third of the membership of the church entered the movement in 1855–56 by signing over their individual prop-erty to Brigham Young as Trustee-in-Trust on especially prepared forms. The president himself turned in property in the amount of $199,000.00. As the plan progressed it became one more ground for a general complaint against the Mormons in Washington, which caused President Buchanan to send an army to put down a so-called rebellion in Utah. Before the economic experiment was abandoned in face of the military invasion, the defensive movement developed into a full-blown "reformation" in 1856[10] in which the local Gentile found little favor.

FEDERAL LAND SURVEYS

It was into this situation that the United States Surveyor General was introduced when he arrived in Salt Lake City on July 27, 1855. The legislative assembly had petitioned Congress for a land survey on March 6, 1852, and President Pierce the following year recommended that the public land system be extended over Utah "with such modifica-tions as the peculiarities of the territory require." Congress responded favorably and David H. Burr was accordingly appointed in 1855 to commence operations in Utah. After establishing the initial point for the survey at the southeast corner of the Temple Block where Brigham Young had previously directed the Mormon survey to commence, he proceeded by contract to determine the principle base and meridian lines from which the survey was extended throughout the valley. Other contracts carried the operations into surrounding areas until over two million acres had been surveyed at the cost of ninety thousand dollars when the "Utah War" brought the survey to a close in 1857.

Unfortunately, both surveyor general and much of his survey met official disapproval. The Mormons charged Burr with fraud and delin-quency in his operations. Brigham Young wrote to Delegate John H. Bernhisel:

The surveying is a great humbug. They have got their own party and sur-veyors imported for the purpose and I am told the surveyors have no trouble in making about one thousand dollars per month and that all they do is of no earthly benefit; they stick down little stakes that the wind could almost

---

[10] See Gustive O. Larson, "The Mormon Reformation," *Utah Historical Quarterly,* XXVI (January, 1958), 45–63.

blow over, neither plant charcoal, nor raise mounds. Not a vestige of all they do will be left to mark where they have been in five years.

The Indians also watched the proceedings with disapproval. Wrote Burr on December 31, 1855: "Some danger has been apprehended from the Indians. They exhibit some uneasiness about the survey of their lands as they call it, and have made some threats. . . . Their chief (Shoshone) recently sent a delegation to the Indian Agent at this place to know why we were surveying the country before purchasing it of them." Soon his letters carried reports that Mormons were prejudicing Indians against the surveyors who were represented as government agents preparing to wrest the land from both Indians and Mormons."[11] Before the end of a year in Utah, Burr made a triple charge against the Mormons: (1) The territorial legislature was granting exclusive canyon rights of government property to certain of its members; (2) Salt Lake City exceeded, in its claims, the area allowed for a townsite described by the Congressional Act of May 23, 1844; and (3) The Saints were conveying their holdings by deed to Brigham Young as Trustee-in-Trust for the church. These were causes, he suggested, for government intervention in Utah.

A committee of rugged Mormons soon waited upon the surveyor general, who was confronted with the charges made and warned against repetition of such messages.[12] A surveying contractor was mauled on the streets of Salt Lake City, and as threats of further violence spread through the community, Burr abandoned his post in July, 1857, without leave and fled to Washington. After making serious charges against the Mormons in his report to the U.S. Land Commissioner, he asked permission to return to his post by overtaking the Utah-bound military expedition. He was, however, dismissed from office and charged with fraud and disregard of regulations in the performance of his duties as surveyor general in Utah. These charges were later confirmed after careful field investigations in 1860 by his successor, S. C. Stambaugh.

Brigham Young, as Superintendent of Indian Affairs, and the territorial legislature repeatedly requested congressional action toward extinguishment of Indian land titles in Utah as the first step towards ownership by the settlers. A memorial on March 6, 1852, asked Con-

---

[11] The Burr letters are on file under Letters Received, in the Land Division of the National Archives, Washington, D.C.

[12] In his letters to the commissioner of the General Land Office, Burr reports considerable hostility to his operations and expresses fear of both Indians and Mormons.

gress to authorize the Indian Superintendent to make treaties with and purchase the lands of the local tribes. In December, 1853, Governor Young pointed out the desirability of locating the natives on a reservation apart from the white settlements, and in 1859 the legislature, in anticipation of the establishment of a land office, made provision for delivery of title to certain claimants. That same year a memorial to Congress urged legislative recognition of the peculiar circumstances surrounding Mormon desert colonization. The Pre-emption Law of 1841, granting one hundred and sixty acres upon condition of fourteen months' residence on the land was not applicable to the Mormon farm-village system. Residence was in the village, and few of the surrounding farms included more than twenty acres with most of them averaging ten.

By this means (read the memorial), from fifty to one hundred farmers cultivate the same section, which is watered by a canal owned by each agriculturist, in proportion to the area of his farm, meadow or garden, . . . Your memorialists would therefore respectfully pray your honorable body to pass a law enabling the occupants of such portions of lands to appoint one of their number an agent who shall be authorized to pre-empt and enter said lands in a body, and distribute the same by giving title to proper claimants.[13]

Congressional response to all such petitions was delayed by reports from federal agents in Utah relative to "Mormon land monopoly," "opposition to public surveys," and "interference with Indian affairs." Surveyor General Stambaugh upon completion of his Burr investigation recommended against further surveys until establishment of a land office would make possible the sale of lands already surveyed. "And," he added significantly, "until a different policy may be devised by Congress to induce other than Mormon emigration to the Territory." [14]

When Samuel R. Fox succeeded Stambaugh as surveyor general in September, 1861, he was reminded by Commissioner Edmunds of the General Land Office that while two million acres of land had already been surveyed in Utah, not one had been sold to offset surveying costs. Ignoring Utah's numerous petitions, he said that there had been no demand for land purchases and further stated that "it is not contemplated to make any additional surveys in your district until provision is made by Congress for the sale of the public lands already sur-

---

[13] *Acts, Resolutions, and Memorials Passed at the Several Annual Sessions of the Legislative Assembly of the Territory of Utah from 1851–1870* (Salt Lake City, 1870).
[14] Stambaugh's reports on file in Land Office Division of the National Archives.

veyed."[15] In 1862, the Utah surveying district was consolidated with that of Colorado Territory and all of its archives removed to Denver. The federal door, which had been opening to land acquisition in Utah was closed for another six years.

EVENTS DURING SUSPENSION

In the meantime events were shaping to effect not only reopening of the survey district but the establishment of a long-delayed land district. To the benefits of the Pre-emption Law enjoyed by citizens of the surrounding territories and anticipated by Utah citizens, was added the Homestead Law of 1862. These two laws, however inapplicable to the Utah situation, became the gateways through which most of her people would ultimately enter into land ownership. Also the townsite laws of 1864–65 were liberalized by a Congressional Act of March 2, 1867, dropping the minimum lot cost from ten dollars to one dollar and twenty-five cents. President Lincoln set aside the Uinta Basin as an Indian Reservation in 1861, which act was confirmed by Congress on May 5, 1864. Then, on February 23 of the year following, that body passed "An Act to extinguish the Indian Title to lands of the Territory of Utah suitable for agriculture and mineral purposes." Accordingly, government officials and Indian chiefs, representing the principal tribes in Utah, met and signed a treaty at Spanish Fork on June 8, 1865. By this instrument the Indians relinquished claim to all lands in the territory except those reserved in Uinta Valley to which it was expected most of the natives would be gathered. Here they were to receive certain benefits to be paid over a period of years.

Unfortunately, the treaty after four years delay was rejected March 15, 1869.[16] Meanwhile, treaty-making with the Indians came into political disfavor which crystalized into congressional action on March 3, 1871, providing "that no Indian nation or tribe within the territory of the United States should thereafter be recognized as an independent power with whom the government might contract by treaty. . . ."[17]

Consistent with the intent of the Spanish Fork Agreement, the earlier Indian farms in Utah, which had already been abandoned, were surveyed and their combined acreage (92,637) made ready for sale. Also Congress acted in harmony with the intent of the treaty by re-

---

[15] Letters on file in Land Office Division, National Archives.

[16] *Executive Journal, U.S. Senate, 1869–71,* Vol. XVII, p. 7.

[17] *U.S. Statutes at Large,* Vol. XVI, 566, 41 Cong., 3 sess. See also, L. B. Priest, *Uncle Sam's Stepchildren* (Rutgers, New York, 1942), 96.

opening the Utah land survey in 1868 in preparation for disposal of public lands. It took for granted the extinguishment of Indian land titles without assuming responsibility for its reciprocal obligation to the native.

Substantial decreases in the territorial boundaries were effected during the period of Utah's suspended surveys. A slice of her eastern border was added to Colorado and her northeastern corner transferred to Nebraska in 1861. Also, that same year 73,574 square miles lying west of the thirty-ninth meridian were formed into Nevada Territory, which, with additional slices from Utah, achieved statehood before the original pioneer community was given a federal land district. The Mormons, who were the first to colonize between the Rockies and the Sierra, became the last to enjoy the privileges of land ownership.

While the Indians, as a result of the failure of the 1865 treaty, continued to assert their inherent rights to the public domain, the Gentiles in growing numbers began challenging Mormon squatters' claims on the ground that, until the national government released its proprietary rights to the soil, local titles were valueless. Their interest in Utah lands had been growing in proportion to coal and other mineral discoveries and the advance of the transcontinental railroad. These were indeed "inducing other than Mormon migration to the Territory" and creating a Gentile as well as a Mormon demand for renewal of the public lands survey and establishment of a land office in Utah. Increasingly they challenged Mormon land monopoly through "jumping" unoccupied pieces of property to which value had accrued through pioneer industry. Such tempting areas included the race course and militia parade ground west of Jordan River, some private claims on the opposite bank, property in the Warm Springs area and on Arsenal Hill, and an open field near the Twentieth Ward. Delegate W. H. Hooper relayed pertinent information on this subject to the General Land Office:

I beg leave to call your attention to the following extract of a letter . . . "several land claims in the vicinity of the city (Salt Lake) have been jumped recently, three or four of them by gentlemen connected with the Land Office in this city, viz. Mr. Clement, brother of the Surveyor General . . . W. H. Hoffman, who is attending to Maxwell's business during his absence in Washington (Mr. Maxwell, register of the Land Office). Last week Mr. Hoffman took possession and claimed a city block. Some of these claims were enclosed and improved by water ditches years ago." [18]

---

[18] Delegate Hooper. Letters Received, General Land Office, March 8, 1871.

The Mormons, jealous of the fruits of their labors, were in no mood to regard land jumping lightly. Brigham Young thundered from the pulpit on August 12, 1866:

If you undertake to drive a stake in my garden with an intention to jump my claim there will be a fight before you get it; if you come within an enclosure of mine with any such intent, I will send you home, God being my helper. . . . We have spent hundreds of thousands of dollars in taking out the water of our mountain streams, fencing in farms and improving the country, and we cannot tamely suffer strangers, who have not spent one days labor to make these improvements to wrest our homesteads out of our hands.

Again, on December 23 he threatened, "If they jump my claims here I shall be very apt to give them a pre-emption right that will last them to the last resurrection. . . . The Latter-day Saints will never again pull up stakes and give their possessions to their enemies." [19]

It was inevitable that the contest, which rose to a high pitch in the sixties, should become violent with life and death involved. The murder of John King Robinson on October 22, 1866, was linked with his having filed upon Warm Springs property inside Salt Lake City's extended boundaries. A shack erected near the Jordan, together with its occupant, was dumped into the river, and threats of similar treatment persuaded others to leave the territory. The prospect of gentile acquisition "caused the 'city fathers' to survey the land lying east of the 20th ward and the 11th ward and give it out gratuitously to the brethren by drawing lots." [20]

Federal officials in Utah, anticipating establishment of a land district in the territory, were as eager to control the processes of distribution as were the Mormons to hold on to their properties. A petition to the President, dated August 29, 1866, was accompanied by a letter of transmittal from acting Governor Amos Reed, which revealed gentile ambitions in relation to control of the program.

Hon. Joseph S. Wilson . . . You will find accompanying this a paper signed by myself and other Federal officers asking the President to establish a land office in this city and the appointment of proper officers to conduct it . . . we now recommend the appointment of William M. Johns, late Lieut. Col. 3rd Vet. Battalion, California Inf., and lately . . . in command of the U.S. military forces near this city, as Register, and Stephen E. Jocelyn, late Captain in the same organization, as Receiver of this Land Office. These gentlemen have served for the greater part of the rebellion in this Territory. They have been most efficient, energetic and patriotic officers . . . . They are now

---

[19] *Journal of Discourses* (26 vols., Liverpool, 1854–86), II, 281.

[20] Manuscript History of Brigham Young. 1866. p. 752.

out of service and settled here. . . . Now, Brother Joseph, (as the Mormons would say,) we are in earnest in this matter. Every interest public and private require this to be done. . . .[21]

Commissioner Wilson concurred with the above. In his report to Secretary of Interior on October 2, 1866, he wrote:

The Surveyor General reports the discovery of rich veins of argentiferous galena and silver which are attracting many miners to Utah, who are building towns in sections of the country heretofore imperfectly known and hence the establishment of a land office is imperatively demanded, with such additional surveys as settlers may require in developing the resources of the Territory.

He recommended that the lands already surveyed in Utah be offered for sale. "This policy it is believed would bring to the Territory loyal settlers and afford them opportunity to acquire title."

Governor Charles Durkee, who, in appreciation of Mormon colonization, had urged federal action a year earlier, repeated his message to the territorial assembly, December 10, 1866:

It is of highest importance to our settlers that they be enabled speedily to avail themselves of the beneficent provisions of the Homestead Act. The occupied lands of the Territory have been reclaimed from their desert state by a marvel of persevering industry, and the title of the occupants who have in truth created for the lands their only value should be placed beyond legal question. I would be pleased to unite with you in a memorial to Congress soliciting an appropriation for completing the public surveys, the appointment of a Surveyor General for the Territory and the opening of an office at this city for the sale and entry of public lands. Under the present laws title to the city and town sites can be perfected, and I urge in these cases the desirableness of immediate action.

Acting on the last suggestion, a number of communities made application through the Land Office in Denver for entry of townsites, only to be reminded from Land Commissioner Wilson in Washington on February 7, 1868: "There being no organized land district in Utah Territory, entries of townsites therein, cannot be allowed at present. The applications however are placed on file for future consideration."

The accumulation of townsite applications waiting the creation of a land district in Utah emphasized the peculiar nature of the Mormon communities. The territorial legislature, in the process of incorporating cities and towns, allowed liberal boundaries in order to include the surrounding fields as well as the residential areas. It was a defensive

---

[21] General Land Office Records in National Archives.

movement on the part of the Mormons to preserve as much land as possible for the original settlers in Utah. The Gentiles protested vigorously on grounds typically expressed by George R. Maxwell, former register, that "the corporate limits of some city or town extends over all the available arable lands of Utah . . . the reason of which is obvious, viz. in plain terms it is to prevent the Gentiles from acquiring title to the public lands. . . ." [22]

In the main, the protests availed little. When the very broad Congressional Townsite Law of March 2, 1867, failed to cover the area embraced in Salt Lake City, a memorial to Congress won as an amendment, "An Act for the Relief of the inhabitants of Salt Lake City in the Territory of Utah." It read in part:

> That the words "not exceeding five thousand in all" contained in an act entitled "An Act for the Relief of the Inhabitants of Cities and Towns upon the Public Lands" . . . shall not apply to Salt Lake City in the Territory of Utah; but said act shall be so amended and construed in its application to said city that lands may be entered as provided in said act for the full number of inhabitants contained in said city not exceeding fifteen thousand.

On October 3, 1867, Mayor Daniel H. Wells submitted a declaratory statement, with accompanying plat, of his intention to enter Salt Lake City under the Congressional Act of March 2, 1867. After five years, during which conflicting claims were eliminated, certificate of title was granted on June 1, 1872.

LAND OFFICE OPENED

Congress responded favorably on July 16, 1868, to a memorial introduced by Delegate Hooper from Utah's territorial assembly, by passing an act "to create the office of Surveyor General in the Territory of Utah and to establish a land office in said Territory and extend the homestead and pre-emption laws over the same. . . ." In his letter of September 26, appointing John A. Clark as Utah's surveyor general, Commissioner Wilson instructed:

> You will select as the sphere of surveying operations such localities as the public interest shall require including actual settlements and where mining operations are carried on under the provisions of an Act of Congress approved July 26, 1866. As the Union Pacific Railroad is rapidly progressing westward and will likely reach Utah Territory the next fiscal year, you will take the requirements of that road into due consideration and direct field operations in the region through which it will pass so that selections of lands

---

[22] Maxwell letter dated February 22, 1877.

granted to that Railroad may be made as fast as the building thereof progresses. . . .

At long last the citizens of Utah were to receive the benefits of land ownership — not because of two decades of heroic desert conquest, but because a government, unresponsive to their earlier petitions, finally decided that "other interests" justified the action. Clark arrived in Salt Lake City in the fall of 1868 as surveyor general, followed soon after by C. C. Clements as register and Lewis S. Hill as receiver of the public moneys. This combination was changed within a year when George R. Maxwell succeeded Clements and the latter assumed the responsibilities of surveyor general. Commissioner Wilson, reporting to the Secretary of Interior on November 5, reviewed progress toward land ownership in Utah over the past fifteen years:

Surveying operations were inaugurated in Utah in the year 1855 and continued to 1857. During that time, 2,425,339 acres were surveyed. In the fiscal year ending June 30, 1867, an area of 92,637 acres were surveyed . . . such area being vacated Indian reservations, increasing the surveyed lands in the territory to 2,517,912 acres. . . . No lands have been disposed of yet in Utah.

Much of the early surveying had been wasteful and contrary to regulations. To suggestions for resurveys Commissioner Wilson replied on January 29, 1869: "In reference to the suggested resurveys . . . I have to say that no such service can be undertaken as there is no positive evidence that former surveys are unavailable and for the reason that moneys appropriated for public surveys cannot be applied to resurveys."

The Land Office opened on March 9, 1869, and from the beginning found itself swamped with business. After two decades of insecurity in face of unquieted Indian titles and gentile challenge of their squatters' rights, the Mormon settlers found relief in legal ownership of their lands. Gentiles, having drifted into the Mormon Kingdom from the westward migration, or through commerce, political appointment, military assignment or mineral prospecting, were no less eager to possess a slice of the once rejected corner of the public domain.

During the first six months of 1869, 148,403 acres were acquired by the citizens of Utah. Of these 51,638 acres sold for cash at one dollar and twenty-five cents per acre, and 96,765 were taken under the Homestead Law. The commissioner's report as of October 27, 1870, showed that a total of 208,073.93 acres had been taken up. At that time 3,211,508 acres had been surveyed.

Notwithstanding congressional failure to provide for it, acquisition of individual land titles was expedited through joint action. A group of land owners, banding together, appointed one of their number as entryman, who, for a small fee, filed on one hundred and sixty acres in his name and then transferred the various tracts to individual owners. Townsites were acquired similarly through the mayor, or probate judge, filing as trustee for the community. Despite gentile complaints against this procedure, Mormon communities lost no time in taking advantage of the opportunity to acquire title to their homes. According to Commissioner Wilson's report of November 1, 1869: "The town site law has given new impetus to building cities and towns on the public domain. . . . During the past year applications have been made to file declaratory statements, under the Acts aforesaid, for a number of towns and cities upon the public land, sixteen of them being in the Territory of Utah."

Looking back upon the long struggle for land ownership in Utah, the historian ponders the question of federal discrimination against her early settlers. Through failure to extinguish Indian land titles and to establish a local land office, the national government withheld the blessing of home ownership in the Mormon territory far beyond its readiness to receive it. The first colonizers in the intermountain region were compelled to watch their neighbors avail themselves of the benefits of the Pre-emption and Homestead laws and even win statehood while they still labored under provisional government which could neither clear Indian titles nor guarantee squatters' rights. The response of a generally liberal government in the distribution of its frontier lands was grudging indeed in relation to appeals from Utah. The explanation lies in a conflict of interest which developed in Utah resulting primarily from certain peculiarities of her colonizers and their methods of colonization.

When the public survey was first extended to Utah in the early 1850's already sufficient deviation from the frontier norm had appeared to prompt President Pierce to advise a survey "with such modification as the peculiarities of the Territory require." In 1861 Surveyor General Stambaugh recommended postponement of the survey until "other than Mormon emigration" could be induced to the territory. Commissioner Wilson in 1866 interpreted delays in Utah land surveys as due to an "anomalous condition of affairs" and urged adoption of a policy to bring "loyal settlers to the territory."

The first surveyor general, David H. Burr, showed little tolerance for these "peculiarities" of the Mormons when they reported his surveys to Washington as fraudulent. He struck back with accusations of illegal timber land appropriations, land monopoly, deeding of private property to the church and interference with the Indians. This unfortunate beginning in land surveys added fuel to earlier fires of prejudice already kindled in the nation's capital by disappointed "runaway officials" in 1851. More fuel was added by charges of federal agents preceding the Utah War of 1857–58, and by a continued stream of correspondence between federal agents in Utah and their department heads in Washington.

Whether soundly based or not, hostility born of misunderstanding and mistrust between Utah Mormons and Gentiles resulted in negation of normal progress towards public surveys and land sales. Not until the rivalry of the opposing parties came to focus in a common desire for land acquisition did Congress respond to their petitions for renewal of suspended surveys. When gentile mining interests and the transcontinental railroad made common cause with Mormon agriculture in demanding land titles, victory was not far away. It would undoubtedly have come sooner if carpetbag government with its divisive influences could have yielded to statehood for Utah in the 1850's when she was prepared for it.

LAND TENURE PROBLEMS
IN THE SANTA FE RAILROAD GRANT AREA

Sanford O. Mosk

Land Tenure Problems in the
Santa Fe Railroad Grant Area

Publications of the
Bureau of Business and Economic Research
University of California

LAND TENURE PROBLEMS IN THE SANTA FE RAILROAD GRANT AREA

By

SANFORD A. MOSK

UNIVERSITY OF CALIFORNIA PRESS

BERKELEY AND LOS ANGELES

1944

UNIVERSITY OF CALIFORNIA PRESS
BERKELEY AND LOS ANGELES
CALIFORNIA

CAMBRIDGE UNIVERSITY PRESS
LONDON, ENGLAND

PRINTED IN THE UNITED STATES OF AMERICA
BY THE UNIVERSITY OF CALIFORNIA PRESS

FOREWORD

THE FOLLOWING STUDY *by Sanford A. Mosk,*
Assistant Professor of Economics in the Uni-
versity of California, is one in a series of re-
search studies conducted under the auspices of the
Bureau of Business and Economic Research of the
University. The Bureau is under the general direc-
tion of a presidential committee consisting at present
of the following members of the Department of Eco-
nomics: Professors J. B. Condliffe (chairman), I. B.
Cross, Stuart Daggett, E. T. Grether (acting chair-
man), and Paul S. Taylor.

The opinions expressed in this study are those of
the author. The functions of the Bureau of Business
and Economic Research are confined to facilitating
the prosecution of independent scholarly research by
members of the faculty.

HOWARD S. ELLIS,
Acting Director

PREFACE

INVESTIGATION ON THE topic of this paper was begun in 1934 when, under the auspices of the University of California Committee on Regional Economy of the Far West, the writer was in New Mexico and Arizona. Discussion of "land-planning" questions with federal and state officials and other informed persons brought out the importance of land-tenure problems in the Santa Fe Railroad grant area and suggested a study to find out how those problems arose. Circumstances made it impossible to bring the study to completion until the Bureau of Business and Economic Research of the University of California provided funds (in 1941) for additional research and field work in the Southwest. Interviews with the persons who actually had to deal with these land problems, as in the earlier field work, provided the writer with the insights and standards of selection that make the documentary record meaningful. Without these interviews the study could not have been made.

It would require a long list to give the names of all those to whom the author is indebted for aid in his investigation. A few, however, must be given special mention. Among these are Mark W. Radcliffe, former field agent for the Office of Indian Affairs; T. W. Cabeen, Vice-president of the New Mexico & Arizona Land Company; the late H. J. Hagerman; Vance Rogers of the Soil Conservation Service; and Professor Carl O. Sauer of the University of California.

SANFORD A. MOSK

Berkeley, July, 1942

CONTENTS

Chapter I

INTRODUCTION

IN THE DEPRESSION YEARS of the 1930's widespread public recognition was given, for the first time, to many latent problems of the American economic and social structure. The broad issue of the period, of course, was to achieve more effective utilization of the nation's resources and manpower for socially desirable ends. But once attention was brought sharply to a focus on this, a multitude of special problems presented themselves. The fact that so many of these problems were attacked at the same time is an impressive feature of recent American experience. Equally impressive is the fact that the nation as a whole became aware of many questions which for years had troubled only specialists working in their particular fields. Among these were a number of problems concerned with the use and conservation of our land resources.

It would be beyond the scope of this paper to examine the various "land-planning" programs that have been instituted since 1933 or even to indicate the principal features of the investigations and studies that have been made in connection with these programs. Much of this research, however, points clearly to the conclusion that our public land policies have failed to promote wholesome, permanent settlement or effective use of our natural resources. The defects of national land policies, and their consequences, are nowhere more apparent than in the grazing areas of the western states.

The western range is one of the great natural resources of the nation. Large in area, important in livestock production, it covers approximately 728 million acres and lies west of an irregular line at or about the 100th meridian; this is about three-fourths of the entire land area between this line and the Pacific Coast, or nearly 40 per cent of the total land surface of the United States. This territory, according to the Forest Service report, *The Western Range* (1936),[1] "produces about 75 per cent of the national output of wool

[1] 74th Cong., 2d sess., Sen. Doc. 199, p. iii.

and mohair, and in pounds about 55 per cent of the sheep and lambs, and nearly one-third of the cattle and calves." The rapidity with which this range has been occupied and depleted of its forage cover is one of the striking features of American economic history, and probably has few parallels elsewhere in the world. Here, indeed, we have an outstanding example of the "destructive exploitation" of natural resources which has developed with the commercialization of economic life in modern times.

Little effort was devoted to livestock production in the range country until the 1880's, when a great boom in cattle raising took place. At that time the range was essentially in its virgin state, its vegetation little influenced by man. Human occupation, however, began to collect a toll from the land. This was a gradual development at first, but it became more intense as the present century advanced. In 1936, about fifty years after stock raising got its initial impulse in this part of the country, the Forest Service took an inventory of the western range and found that more than one-half of its forage resources had been exhausted.

The existing range area has been depleted no less than 52 per cent from its virgin condition, using depletion in the sense of reduction in grazing capacity for domestic livestock. Practically this means that a range once capable of supporting 22.5 million animal units can now carry only 10.8 million.[2]

Lands in all classes of ownership or control have suffered from destruction of forage cover, as the following estimates from *The Western Range*[3] show.

Ownership or control	Depletion (per cent)
Federal	
National forests	30
Public domain	67
Indian lands	51
Other	63
State and county	49
Private	51
Average	52

[2] 74th Cong., 2d sess., Sen. Doc. 199, p. 3.   [3] *Ibid.*, p. 7.

In the conservation record the public domain has suffered the most; the national forests the least. The high figure for private lands, 51 per cent, suggests that private ownership has not been a strong incentive for range preservation under the prevailing conditions. What is the explanation for this sorry record? One is strongly tempted to explore this question fully, for it has meaning in the larger picture of economic development in the United States and reveals important characteristics of American institutions; but only a summary statement can be given here.[4]

The American habit of thinking about natural resources has been excessively optimistic—the outcome of pioneering experience in a huge continent richly endowed with minerals, timber, fertile soils, natural pasturage, etc. That the gifts of nature were unlimited and inexhaustible, that new supplies would always be discovered, and that the advance of technology would offset rapid exploitation of known supplies was a common faith evolved in this country. These attitudes, moreover, were encouraged by great material progress in the nineteenth century—a buoyant, vigorous economic development which insured complete confidence in the future. In this physical and institutional environment, there was little incentive to use resources sparingly and little general interest in the problems of conservation. It is only in the last ten years or so that a significant shift in public attitude on this question has been taking place, although special conservation achievements can be traced back to about 1900.

The spirit of optimism in use of resources is strikingly evident in the history of the western range. Enormous in area, much of it could be used without payment. Moreover, at one time grazing was regarded as a transitional stage to more intensive agricultural development which magnified current operations at the expense of the future. For many years, therefore, the prevailing psychology discouraged the exercise of care and restraint in the use of grazing lands.

The rainfall regime of the western range, generally speaking, is not favorable to continuous renewal of forage resources. Extreme variations in annual precipitation are apt to occur in any part of the

[4] In large part based on material in *The Western Range*.

range country, but in the Southwest it is not uncommon to have a series of drought years. Severe reductions in forage take place under such conditions. Varying the numbers of livestock in rough proportion to forage produced would seem to be reasonable practice, but it has not been typical. "The records show steadily increasing numbers of livestock on the range over entire states during periods of declining precipitation, and hence decreasing forage stand, until the severity of the drought and the scarcity of the feed compelled drastic reductions in numbers by forced sales or by high starvation losses."[5]

Other causes of range depletion, according to the Forest Service, are "rule-of-thumb management" and financial handicaps. So far as the first of these is concerned, it must be remembered that range livestock production is a relatively new feature in the agricultural development of the Anglo-American frontier. Stockmen, in contrast to earlier pioneer farmers in the East and Middle West, did not have an accumulated body of knowledge to rely upon, and they had to learn range management by the slow process of trial and error. This was too slow, we may say, in the face of expansive economic conditions and an optimistic outlook. Furthermore, even when experience and scientific study by federal and state agencies suggested better range practice, other forces often impelled the stockman to carry on in his customary way. Among these forces were what the Forest Service report calls "financial handicaps"; by this they seem to mean chiefly the uncertainties of competitive conditions, although some financial questions, in the narrow sense, are shown to have a bearing on the problem of range use. The tendency to overstock the range has been strengthened, from time to time, by low prices—the operator has tried to maintain aggregate income at the expense of his (and the public's) capital resource.

National land policy, too, must be held responsible for the depletion of the western range. Everyone would substantially agree that the underlying objectives of our public land policy—to insure wide distribution in land ownership and to promote settlement of the country—were highly desirable. As we view in retrospect the mass of land

---

[5] *The Western Range*, p. 16.

laws and as we study their operation, however, we are forced to the conclusion that these objectives have not been attained. In many places, especially in the western range country, effective permanent settlement was impeded by our land policy. In other places land was engrossed within the framework of federal land laws. The two basic objectives sometimes worked at cross-purposes, where holdings were too small for successful settlement. Specific laws have been inconsistent in principle or application, and land policy has been slow to adjust itself to differences in economic and geographic conditions. For a brief critique of American public land policy, one cannot improve on the following statement of Paul W. Gates, an authority whose judgment is fortified by a number of excellent studies on land-tenure questions:

The evolution of our national land system has consisted of a series of slow and bungling changes to which may be ascribed the large-scale speculation in lands, the early development of tenancy, uneconomic farm units, misuse of the lands, reduction in carrying capacity of the range, wasteful treatment of the timberlands, misguided settlement, and misery for thousands of farm families.[6]

Since it is not essential, for our purposes, to trace in detail the many complex ways in which our federal land policy has fostered range depletion, we may summarize them as follows:

(1) Land legislation has favored the small farmer over the stockman, even in the western areas that are suitable mainly for grazing. Public support for this policy was strengthened by the contest for the range between homesteaders and stockmen, which induced the stockmen to pursue tactics and urge policies that laid them open to the charge of land monopolists and gave them unfavorable publicity. Livestock production was forced to concentrate on a smaller area, much of it poorer in quality than the lands homesteaded by farmers, and to use it more intensively. The net effect of these circumstances upon our national economy would have been less detrimental if dry farming had resulted in permanent agricultural settlement, but, as a general rule, it has not. Thousands of dry farms have been aban-

---

[6] National Resources Board, *Report on Land Planning*, pt. 7, p. 85. The section from which this quotation is taken (pp. 60–85) gives a good summary and appraisal of our public land policy, especially for the recent period.

doned, but the attempts to operate them have resulted in spoiling the range land for many years to come, since rehabilitation of a good forage cover is a very slow process.

(2) Our system of public land disposal has, in considerable measure, fostered noneconomic units in stock raising. The land legislation of 1889–1891 especially placed severe restrictions on the amount of land which a person could get from the public domain.[7] Even the 640-acre grant available under the Grazing Homestead Act of 1916 was not adequate to support a family in the semiarid western range country. The fact that about 40 per cent of the acreage included in such homesteads had been abandoned by 1935[8] shows that there was a fundamental weakness in the operation of this law. To criticize our land policy from this standpoint does not imply that we should have tried to establish units of the most economically efficient size. The objective was social rather than economic—to provide land for family units. But the amount of land should have been adequate to enable the family to establish itself on a sound economic base. To overcome the handicap of insufficient land, homesteaders were tempted to graze more stock than their holdings could support and, at the same time, maintain the forage cover at a suitable, permanent level.

(3) The federal government, until very recently, made no attempt to regulate grazing on the public domain—i.e., the lands which had neither passed into private ownership nor had been reserved for special purposes. "First come, first served," was the dominant principle of grazing on public lands. It is true that stockmen made informal range-use agreements among themselves, but these had no legal status and, moreover, were usually short-lived. Temptation to violate these agreements was strong, especially where sheepmen and cattlemen were contesting for the range, and the contribution of the agreements to sound range use was negligible. Appraising this situation in 1905, the Public Lands Commission reported:

At present the public lands are theoretically open commons, free to all citizens; but as a matter of fact a large proportion has been parceled out by

---

[7] National Resources Board, *Report on Land Planning*, pt. 7, p. 69.
[8] *The Western Range*, p. 223.

more or less definite compacts or agreements among the various interests. These tacit agreements are continually being violated. The sheepmen and cattlemen are in frequent collision because of incursions upon each other's domain. . . . There are localities where the people are utilizing to their own satisfaction the open range, and their demand is to be let alone, so that they may parcel out among themselves the use of the lands; but an agreement made to-day may be broken to-morrow by changing conditions or shifting interests.[9]

Uncontrolled use of the public domain inevitably led to overgrazing in the institutional setting of the western livestock industry. This, as we have seen, included an optimistic attitude on the future of resources, generally expanding markets, and a shrinkage in range through the extension of crop raising. Under these pressures the stockman had an incentive to get the most he could from the public domain as quickly as possible. If he exercised restraint, another would not. By 1905 the result was clear to the members of the Public Lands Commission.

The general lack of control in the use of public grazing lands has resulted, naturally and inevitably, in over-grazing and the ruin of millions of acres of otherwise valuable grazing territory. Lands useful for grazing are losing their only capacity for productiveness, as, of course, they must when no legal control is exercised.[10]

From the time of this report to the organization of grazing districts under the Taylor Act, virtually nothing was done to regulate the use of public range lands, and they deteriorated further in forage capacity. The Forest Service estimates of 1936, as we have already seen, show greater depletion on public domain than on lands in other classes of ownership.

(4) Land ownership patterns in the range country are largely the result of federal policies, modified by certain reservations for special purposes, to dispose of the public domain. The methods of disposal included sales; homesteading; land grants to states, railroads, and sponsors of other internal improvements; Indian allotments; and special grants to encourage the development or rehabilitation of resources. The principal reservations are the national forests, Indian

---

[9] 58th Cong., 3d sess., Sen. Doc. 189, *Report of the Public Lands Commission*, p. xxi.
[10] *Ibid.*, p. xxi.

reservations, mineral lands, and, since the passage of the Taylor Act (1934), public domain grazing lands. Before the Taylor Act became effective the public domain was a grazing commons for all who could get their stock on it.

In some parts of the western range these policies have resulted in a complicated tenure condition of broken holdings,[11] making it exceedingly difficult to use the range effectively. This has arisen, in part, from the manner in which grants were made, such as scattered sections to states and alternate sections to railroads; in part from the policy of favoring farmers and small holdings; and in part from the multiplicity of uncoördinated laws and administrative agencies. Moreover, these complex ownership patterns have crystallized and thereby aggravated the problems of regulating grazing on the scattered bodies of public domain and of using associated federal, state, and private holdings so as to meet the requirements of good range management.

Thousands of tracts owned by individuals residing all over the United States; thousands of small farm units interspersed among grazing areas and other ownerships; a large portion of the remaining public domain occurring in isolated, disconnected tracts; state holdings scattered, usually including the sixteenth and thirty-sixth sections of each township; thousands of acres of county land, taken through continued tax delinquency, and occurring haphazardly in small units; railroad lands making a checkerboard effect in some areas, being much more scattered in others; insurance company lands scattered thinly here and there; investment and mortgage company holdings strung out in a disorderly fashion, representing parcels out of larger blocks not yet sold; lands foreclosed by land banks and commercial banks occurring at random here and there ... such is the pattern of ownership established under a policy of "laissez faire," free individualism, and planless settlement. With such a pattern economic instability, overgrazing, and general misuse of the land occurs.[12]

Probably the most awkward tenure patterns in the western grazing country are to be found in the railroad grant areas, where alternate sections were allocated to the railroads, the intervening lands being

[11] The phrase "crazy quilt," used in *The Western Range*, is a good descriptive term for this situation.

[12] From an unpublished manuscript by R. R. Renne of the Montana Agricultural Experiment Station, quoted in *The Western Range*, p. 240. The description pertains to Montana, but it may be applied to range country as a whole.

held by private groups or public agencies. These are called the "checkerboard" areas, from the nature of their basic tenure pattern, and, from the standpoint of effective utilization and preservation of forage resources, they have long been sore spots. But they also present the knottiest problems for the Grazing Service and other agencies which are trying to work out a satisfactory program for the western range. "I think probably the most difficult thing we have in the State of Nevada," said R. H. Rutledge, Director of the Grazing Service, in a recent statement, "is the final working out of the checkerboard land situation."[13] But the Nevada problem is simple when compared to conditions in some parts of the Santa Fe Railroad grant territory in northwestern New Mexico and northern Arizona. In 1919, E. O. Wooton of the Department of Agriculture found the tenure pattern of the latter railroad district to be as complex as any in the stock raising country,[14] and the following years brought complications which have not yet been smoothed out, so that it is still one of the major "problem areas" of the West.

This "problem area," the land-grant territory of the Santa Fe Railroad, is the subject of our inquiry. The writer believes that land-tenure questions more than any other factors are responsible for economic and social dislocations there. The first section of this paper shows how different classes of land ownership and control came to prevail in the region. Next, the unfavorable consequences of these tenure developments are examined in regard to land utilization, ranch organization, conservation, and other questions. Finally, we shall survey and appraise the attempts which have been made in recent years to simplify the tenure pattern, and thereby lay the basis for more effective long-run economic exploitation of the resources of the area.

[13] Testimony given at Elko, Nevada, June 27, 1941, in Subcommittee of Senate Committee on Public Lands and Surveys, 77th Cong., 1st sess., *Administration and Use of Public Lands*, pt. 1, p. 177. Some of the special problems in this "checkerboard" area are brought out in pt. 1, pp. 210 ff.

[14] E. O. Wooton, *The Relation of Land Tenure to the Use of the Arid Grazing Lands of the Southwestern States*, United States Department of Agriculture, *Bulletin* No. 1001.

Chapter II
DEVELOPMENT OF THE TENURE PATTERN

RAILROAD LANDS

T HE BASIC tenure pattern of the area was given by the land grant awarded to the Atlantic & Pacific Railroad shortly after the Civil War. This was one of the four grants to railroad companies, starting with the Union Pacific–Central Pacific railroads in 1862, which proposed to build lines to the Pacific Coast; the others were the Northern Pacific and Southern Pacific companies. All of these grants were large, for Congress acted on the assumption that generous grants were necessary because of the nature of the country through which the lines were to be built. Opposition to all railroad land grants gained headway after these awards were made, on the ground that they restricted unduly the area open to settlement by homesteaders. As a result of this, Congress abandoned the practice in 1871.[1]

The Atlantic & Pacific Railroad Company was chartered by Congress, July 27, 1866, to construct a line from Springfield, Missouri, to the Pacific Coast. The company was granted every alternate section of 640 acres each of public land, designated by odd numbers, for forty miles on either side of the line in territories and twenty miles in states. Mineral lands, as well as lands sold, granted, or appropriated before the construction of the line were not to be acquired by the railroad company, but indemnity lands could be selected from the alternate, odd-numbered sections lying within a belt ten miles wide on either side of the primary grant limits. Most of the grant was forfeited in 1886 (24 Stat. 123), but it remained valid in the area from Albuquerque, New Mexico, to the California boundary, where more than 11,500,000 acres were patented under the terms of the original act.

[1] B. H. Hibbard, *A History of the Public Land Policies*, p. 249.

In 1876 the Atlantic & Pacific Company was taken over by the St. Louis & San Francisco Railroad Company, and four years later a half-interest in the enterprise was bought by the Atchison, Topeka & Santa Fe. In 1884 a million acres of the grant land, mostly in the territory of Arizona, were sold to the Aztec Land & Cattle Company

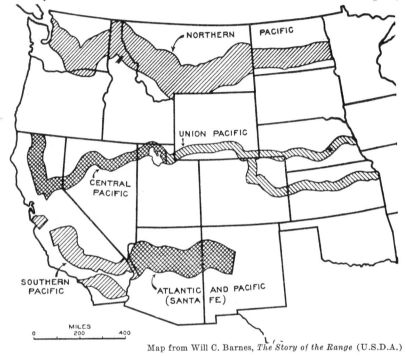

Map from Will C. Barnes, *The Story of the Range* (U.S.D.A.)

Fig. 1. The four principal railroad land grants in the western states. These grants are composed of alternate, odd-numbered sections (640 acres each). The Atlantic & Pacific Railroad Company (Santa Fe Pacific Railroad Company, New Mexico & Arizona Land Company, and Aztec Land & Cattle Company) area is 80 miles wide with additions in ten-mile-wide strips on either side.

for $500,000.[2] The Atlantic & Pacific Company was liquidated in 1894, and the remaining part of the land grant was divided between the two railroad companies. The lands retained by the Atchison, Topeka & Santa Fe were turned over to an affiliate known as the Santa

[2] *Annual Report of the Board of Directors of the Atchison, Topeka & Santa Fe Railroad Company, for the Year Ending December 31, 1884*, pp. 33–34. The A. T. & S. F. invested $150,000 in the capital stock of the Aztec Land & Cattle Company.

Fe Pacific Railroad Company, and the St. Louis & San Francisco transferred its holdings to a subsidiary organization, the New Mexico & Arizona Land Company.

The Atlantic & Pacific grant lands are still held mainly by the three large owners—the Santa Fe Pacific-Railroad Company, the Aztec Land & Cattle Company, and the New Mexico & Arizona Land Company. For a number of years the two latter companies have been operated as a unit, and their lands are administered through a single agency in Albuquerque. The Santa Fe land subsidiary operates in harmony with the broader policies of the parent railroad, and not solely as a land company. The principal business of all three organizations is to lease lands for grazing; they are not engaged in livestock production. Some lands have been sold to stockmen, especially in Coconino County in north-central Arizona, where great numbers of railroad sections have been taken over by a few large livestock outfits. The amount of railroad land disposed of by sale, however, is small in relation to the aggregate holdings of the three land companies.

Leasing railroad sections has been the primary factor in building up ranch units in this area. Stockmen who rent these alternate sections have been in a strong position to control the intermingled public domain, although they have not always been able to keep others from intruding. Railroad land leases usually are subject to renewal—an attractive feature to the stockman as it insures him continuity of use. Annual rental fees for railroad sections vary with the quality of the land, ranging generally from two to five cents per acre.

NAVAJO LANDS

The present Navajo Reservation, which occupies about 15,000,000 acres of land in northwestern New Mexico, northeastern Arizona, and southeastern Utah, has had a complex history. For many years the problem of getting enough land for the rapidly increasing Navajos has been a source of friction and irritation in the Southwest, involving the Indians, the Office of Indian Affairs, other federal agencies, white stockmen, the holders of railroad grant lands, and politicians. The issue is by no means a dead one today, as the following statement by John Collier, Commissioner of Indian Affairs, shows:

... Under the present pattern of ownership, several thousand Navajo families must exist without livestock unless the range available to the tribe is greatly increased. Efforts to enlarge the reservation by purchase of privately owned lands have been consistently opposed by white owners and State officials. Apparently, therefore, the sole possibility of providing the means of self-support for the expanding Navajo Tribe is through the enlargement of the scattered areas of irrigated farm land. That opportunity is limited by the scarcity of water available for irrigation and the high cost of water development. Yet this problem must be faced. More range and more irrigation facilities must be provided if a large part of this virile group of first Americans is not to be placed permanently on a Federal dole.[3]

The Navajo Reservation originally consisted of about 3,500,000 acres, divided almost equally between Arizona and New Mexico. This reservation was created by treaty with the Navajos in 1868, when they were allowed to return from Fort Sumner, New Mexico, where they had been held prisoners for about five years.[4] At the time of their return they were given sheep and goats as a nucleus for larger flocks which, it was hoped, would enable them to support themselves. The number of Navajos at the time the reservation was established is estimated at 8000 to 10,000. One of the fastest growing Indian tribes in the United States, they now have almost 49,000[5] on the enlarged reservation. Additions to the reservation have been made by means of a long series of executive orders and acts of Congress[6] starting with an executive order in 1878 and culminating in the act of June 14, 1934 (48 Stat. 960). Some of these extensions have been very large; the executive order of 1884, for example, added over

---

[3] *Annual Report of the Secretary of the Interior for the Fiscal Year Ending June 30, 1940*, p. 371.

[4] The story of this captivity is told by Frank D. Reeve, "The Federal Indian Policy in New Mexico, 1858–1880," in *New Mexico Historical Review*, XII, No. 3 (July, 1937), pp. 218–269, and XIII, No. 1 (Jan., 1938), pp. 14–62.

[5] *Statistical Supplement to the Annual Report of the Commissioner of Indian Affairs for the Fiscal Year Ended June 30, 1940*, p. 5.

[6] Details are given in H. J. Hagerman, *Navajo Indian Reservation*, 72d Cong., Sen. Doc. 64 (1932). This publication is an official report submitted to the Commissioner of Indian Affairs by Mr. Hagerman, who for several years had served as special commissioner to negotiate with the Navajos on land and other tribal matters.

2,300,000 acres to the Navajos' lands. As white settlement in the area increased, the problems of making extensions became more difficult, and objections to further additions were multiplied. Moreover, some of the additions were handled badly. The reservation boundaries were at times not clearly defined and controversies arose over land titles, while Indians and whites were forced to battle for grazing privileges.

Uncertainty about land titles resulted from two temporary withdrawals, in 1900 and 1901, designed to segregate lands from which additional territory might be granted to the Navajos. The first of these withdrew from sale and settlement "until further ordered" an area of about 425,000 acres of public land in the vicinity of Leupp, Arizona. The second withdrew from sale and settlement the public domain in an area of approximately 1,500,000 acres west of the reservation in Arizona "until such time as the Indians residing thereon shall have been settled permanently under the provisions of the homestead laws or the general allotment act approved February 8, 1887." These withdrawals were intended to be temporary, but the Indian Office chose to regard them as making permanent additions to the reservation. The Santa Fe Pacific Railroad Company held alternate sections in a part of the territory involved, and in 1912 the Federal government completed an exchange for these sections, whereby the railroad selected 327,000 acres of public domain scattered throughout the state of Arizona.[7] The Arizona State Land Commission, however, objected to the transaction on the ground that the base lands had not been definitely incorporated in the reservation. Consequently the commission held that the exchanges could not be legally made.[8] This objection was upheld by the Attorney General of the United States, but the lands were not deeded back to the railroad company. Apparently the Indian Office was trying to make the proposed additions in some other way. Nothing was achieved until

[7] A clause in the Indian appropriation act of 1904 made this transaction possible; this clause provides that private lands over which an Indian reservation has been extended by executive order may be exchanged, at the discretion of the Secretary of the Interior, for vacant, nonmineral, and nontimbered public lands in the same state or territory.

[8] The question is discussed fully in *Report of the State Land Commission of Arizona, June 6, 1912, to December 1, 1914*, pp. 151–157.

1928, when an agreement was reached by the Indian Office and the railroad company whereby the 327,000 acres were to be purchased by the federal government for $1 per acre. Only about 76,000 acres were actually bought,[9] however, the tenure status of the balance remaining undecided until the Navajo Reservation Act of 1934 provided a new means of settlement.

The main Navajo land controversy in New Mexico rose out of a 1907 executive order which added more than 1,000,000 acres in McKinley and San Juan counties to the eastern wing of the reservation. When the Navajos returned from Fort Sumner in 1868 they did not confine themselves to the reservation designated in the treaty but spread over a large district to the east where they had previously lived.[10] Apparently they observed the treaty boundary only on the north, where the Utes were situated. The impulse to use nonreservation lands was strengthened by a clause in the treaty which gave the Navajos the right to hunt on unoccupied land adjacent to the reservation, a provision designed to help them become self-supporting.[11] White settlement in the area was sparse at that time, and no one seemed to object to the Indians grazing their stock on nonreservation lands. The federal government encouraged them to increase their flocks of sheep, and the Navajo economy came to depend almost entirely on sheep raising. As heavier grazing on the arid reservation took its toll of forage, the Indians were drawn increasingly beyond their eastern boundary. Absence of opposition, added to the fact that their tribal range had included these lands before 1863, gave the Navajos a "vested interest" in them. Part of this area was incorporated in the reservation proper in the 1830's and the 1890's. It is significant that objections by local residents were brought before the territorial legislature when southern and eastern extensions were made in 1880.[12] Although local opposition was not strong enough to be effective at that time, it did mark the beginning of a new attitude

---

[9] Hagerman, *op. cit.*, p. 14.

[10] According to John Collier, Commissioner of Indian Affairs, there is no doubt that this had been Navajo country before 1863. See Subcommittee of Senate Committee on Indian Affairs, 75th Cong., 1st sess., *Survey of Conditions of the Indians in the United States,* pt. 34, p. 17534.

[11] Reeve, *op. cit.*, XIII, p. 37.   [12] *Ibid.*, XIII, p. 48.

by white settlers on the question of expanding Navajo lands. This attitude was strengthened as more non-Indians settled in the region. In about 1900 the Navajos strongly began to urge another addition to the reservation. This was to include almost all the remaining lands east of the reservation which they had been using, but which were also being used by growing numbers of white stockmen. Nothing was done, however, until the Santa Fe Pacific Railroad Company leased to whites its alternate-section holdings in several townships of this area, including lakes and springs which the Indians had improved.[18] The Navajos, barred from some of their customary watering places and lands, vigorously renewed their petition to the Indian Bureau to have this district put into the reservation. In 1907 Commissioner Leupp visited the Navajos to study the matter. He recommended the addition, and in the same year it was made by executive order. Over 1,000,000 acres in New Mexico were involved, as well as 1,200,000 acres in Arizona. Now it was the turn of the whites to protest; indignation meetings were held, petitions to have the order rescinded were circulated in western New Mexico, letters and telegrams were sent to territorial and federal officials. It was contended that leases from the railroad company gave the local white stockmen a preference right to graze the area, and that Spanish-Americans from New Mexico had a "vested interest" in the district since they had long used it as a winter range. The protest was effective, and in two steps, in December, 1908, and in January, 1911, the New Mexico extension of 1907 was withdrawn.

This precipitated a bitter conflict between whites and Indians, each group trying to dominate grazing in the area, and generated problems which are by no means solved today. The Navajos, encouraged by the Indian Bureau and other advisers, sought to control the territory through allotments. White stockmen took leases on railroad lands and state sections, and entered homesteads, in order to gain the upper hand.

Navajo allotments were made under the general Indian allotment

---

[18] Rev. Anselm Weber, "The Navajo Indians: A Statement of Facts" (July, 1914), reprinted in Subcommittee of Senate Committee on Indian Affairs, 75th Cong., 1st sess., *Survey of Conditions of the Indians in the United States*, pt. 34, pp. 17560–17575.

LAND TENURE PROBLEMS

act of 1887 and its amendments, which provides for grants to the heads of qualified Indian families. Grazing land up to a maximum of 160 acres could be selected by a Navajo for this purpose from unappropriated public domain. A handful of such allotments was made in this territory before 1907,[14] but most of them were made after that date. Almost 1000 were granted in 1911 alone, bringing the total for the period 1908–1911 to 1900. From 1912 to 1920

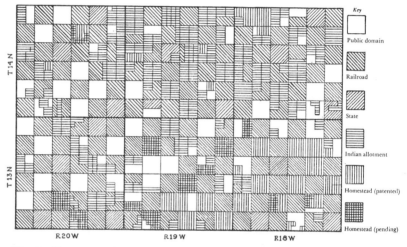

Fig. 2a. The tenure situation in six townships near Gallup, western New Mexico, in 1934. Note especially the scattering of Indian allotments. Homesteads were also common in this area; some were recent entries not yet patented.

allotments averaged about 100 per year. From 1921 to 1933, when the last allotment was made, the average was much lower, although there were two active years—1922 and 1930, when 168 and 417, respectively, were made.

From 1907 to 1933, therefore, about 3800 Navajo allotments were made in the disputed territory, some of them being as far as sixty miles from the reservation boundary. These allotments covered approximately 608,000 acres of land, but they were intended to give the Indians control over a much larger grazing area. It was clear from the beginning that 160 acres in this region were not adequate

---

[14] Some of these were situated on odd-numbered sections before the railroad company applied for patent. The railroad ordinarily made lieu selections elsewhere for these lands.

to support a family even on a low standard of living. Moreover, to assist the Navajos in their fight to dominate the whole area, allotments, wherever possible, were entered on lands containing water, since the water resources were very limited and frequently gave control over a large body of grazing lands. The allotments were not made in large blocks, but were "checkerboarded" in groups of four or less, even in areas where the public domain was extensive; rarely were

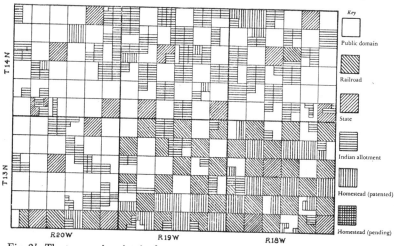

Fig. 2b. The tenure situation in the same six townships shown in figure 2a in 1941. The railroad had by this time relinquished many of its holdings in exchange for other lands. The enlarged public domain was under Grazing Service administration. Comparison with figure 2a shows that some of the homesteads upon which patents were pending in 1934 had been canceled before 1941.

more than four established contiguously. In the railroad grant district of McKinley County, New Mexico, many were spotted on the even-numbered sections. (See fig. 2a.)

A frank statement of the Indian Bureau's Navajo allotment policy was given in a letter written in 1915 by Cato Sells, then Commissioner of Indian Affairs, to the Indian Agent at Leupp. The frankness of this statement merits a rather lengthy quotation.

Sometime prior to the year 1908 the controversy between white and Indian users of the range on the public domain in the vicinity of the Navajo Reservation became so acute that allotting agents were detailed to this locality for the purpose of assisting the Indians to file applications for allotments on the public domain under the fourth section of the general allotment act as amended. Presumably this action was had on the assumption that these Indians having lived on the public domain for a number of years, necessarily at some point they must have made settlement and established homes. Owing to the scarcity of water for domestic and stock-watering purposes, it was also assumed that the allotment of lands to the Indians, containing practically all of the springs or water holes in this locality, would give them an effectual and undisputed control of the entire range, as unless the owners of white stock could get to the water they would not be in a position to use the adjoining pasture lands. In other words, the control of the water resources would practically control the entire range.[15]

This allotment policy, it is now realized, was ill-advised, for the result was to aggravate the tenure situation, to increase greatly the difficulties of securing a compromise settlement, and, as well, to create bitterness between whites and Navajos. It was started as a "second-best scheme," justified, according to Commissioner Collier,[16] as a defensive measure to keep a foothold for the Indians in the region. The tracts were frequently selected "with no reference to whether an Indian was genuinely resident on the spot."[17] This opportunistic attitude continued to hold sway, and it was in fact furthered by the very conflict with white stockmen. The Indian Office made no attempt until about 1930 to formulate a program that would clearly indicate what they thought the Navajos should have and which might resolve the struggle with non-Indian stockmen.[18] Strong protests of the New Mexico Sheep and Wool Growers' Association against continuation of the allotment policy, however, induced the Indian Bureau to make a thorough study of the situation, including field surveys in the disputed area. Allotments were stopped entirely in 1933, and a proposal to extend the reservation boundaries was advanced; this will be examined later.

THE HUALAPAI RESERVATION

The Hualapai Reservation in northwestern Arizona lies entirely within the limits of the Atlantic & Pacific land grant. The railroad

---

[15] Quoted in Hagerman *op. cit.*, p. 67.
[16] See his testimony in Subcommittee of Senate Committee on Indian Affairs, 75th Cong., 1st sess., *Survey of Conditions of the Indians in the United States*, pt. 34, p. 17675.
[17] *Ibid.*, pt. 34, p. 17675.
[18] See testimony of James M. Stewart in *ibid.*, pt. 34, p. 17659.

company's right to the odd-numbered sections in this area was established in March, 1872—several years before the reservation was
created. When the latter was set aside by executive order in January,
1883, no provision was made to exchange the railroad lands for
others outside the Indian grant, and the reservation remained divided
in ownership; the Santa Fe Pacific Railroad Company held the
odd-numbered sections and the federal government held the even-
numbered ones for the use of the Hualapais. This situation, although
unsatisfactory, continued for a number of years without giving rise
to a serious dispute.

Surveys of the reservation lands were conducted in 1919, and at
this time the Indian Office objected to recognition of the railroad
company's title to the alternate sections, claiming the whole area for
the Indians. Prior occupancy by the Hualapais, it was contended,
excluded these lands from the railroad grant of 1866 in spite of the
fact that the reservation was not actually authorized until later. The
raising of this issue made an investigation by the legal staff of the
Department of the Interior necessary, and all available evidence was
examined carefully. This evidence, although meager, seemed to point
to the conclusion that there had been no special Indian occupancy
of the area incorporated in the reservation, but that the Hualapais
simply used it as a part of a vast area of public domain over which
they roamed. These lands, it was held, could not be classed as Indian
in status before the railroad grant, and therefore the odd-numbered
sections in the reservation belonged to the railroad company. On the
basis of this decision, the railroad company was required to pay its
share of the cost of survey,[19] and the "checkerboard" ownership pattern continued.

This tenure situation was certainly awkward, but, because the
Hualapais had enough land for grazing purposes, it was not acute.
As a matter of fact, they used the railroad sections very freely for a
number of years, for the railroad company made no attempt to lease
all its lands inside the reservation. Since there was a surplus of land
for the Indians, the Hualapai Agency for several years leased lands

---

[19] *Decisions of the Department of the Interior,* LIII, p. 484.

in the eastern part of the district to white stockmen, in harmony with Indian Office policy for such instances. These leases included the alternate sections claimed by the railroad. In 1931 about 200,000 acres were rented to one outfit which was permitted to run 2000 head of cattle for an annual fee of $10,000.

One proposed solution for the ownership problem in the Hualapai Reservation was to consolidate Indian and railroad holdings through exchange. The Indian Office accepted this proposal in 1925, and Congress enacted legislation in that year to permit it. An appraisal of all land in the reservation was made jointly by the Indian Office and the railroad company, and an agreement drawn up whereby the central and western parts would be allocated to the Hualapais, with the eastern section remaining in the hands of the Santa Fe Pacific Railroad Company. This division would have given the Indians 462,213 acres valued at $245,221, and the railroad lands would have aggregated 335,736 acres with an appraised value of $212,517. Furthermore, the Indians were to receive 80 per cent of the merchantable timber in the eastern part of the territory, and the railroad promised to supply them with all the water necessary for domestic and livestock purposes in the vicinity of Peach Springs at cost.[20]

Before the agreement could be signed, however, the Indian Office shifted its attitude and insisted on reopening the question of the validity of the railroad company's title to lands in the Hualapai Reservation on the ground that new evidence was available. This occurred in 1931, apparently at the instigation of the Indian Rights Association, and the Solicitor of the Department of the Interior was asked to review the action taken in 1919. He did so, and gave an opinion upholding the railroad company's claim; this opinion was supported by the United States Attorney General.[21] Still reluctant to accept the judgment, the Indian Office refused to sign the agreement and decided to take the issue to the courts for final settlement. The case was carried to the United States Supreme Court which rendered a decision on December 8, 1941, that substantially upheld the Indian Office

---

[20] Subcommittee of Senate Committee on Indian Affairs, 71st Cong., 3d sess., *Survey of Conditions of the Indians in the United States*, pt. 17, pp. 8818–8819.

[21] *Ibid.*, pt. 17, pp. 8836–8843.

position for lands inside the Hualapai Reservation but gave the Indians no rights to lands outside which they had similarly occupied before white settlement.[22] Some months before the decision was given, however, the railroad company had relinquished its claim to Hualapai lands under the Transportation Act of 1940. Section 32 of this law allows a railroad to release claims to granted lands in return for the right to charge the federal government full commercial rates except for that traffic of a military nature. In this way the Hualapai land controversy has finally been settled.

STATE LANDS

New Mexico and Arizona have received large grants from the federal government, starting with awards for the support of the common schools. Four sections in each township have been allocated for this purpose. Sections 16 and 36 were reserved by the organic act which established the territory including the present states of New Mexico and Arizona, although the lands were not actually granted at that time.[23] Additional grants to convey sections 2 and 32 were made upon admission to statehood.[24] In all instances indemnity lands were allowed for designated sections that had been appropriated before the grants were made. Moreover, both states received generous land grants for institutional and educational support such as universities, penal institutions, agricultural and mechanical colleges, public buildings, etc. Lands for each specific institutional grant could be selected from vacant public lands anywhere in the state, and the proceeds derived from leasing or selling them were to be allocated to a special fund to finance the institution for which the grant was made.

The total amount of land granted to Arizona, in round figures, was 10,500,000 acres, consisting of 8,100,000 acres for the common schools and 2,400,000 acres for institutional aid. The total grant to

---

[22] 62 *Supreme Court Reporter*, pp. 248–258.

[23] "Organic Act Establishing the Territory of New Mexico," September 30, 1850, Sec. 15. This applied to both New Mexico and Arizona, as they were not separated until 1863. In 1898 New Mexico was granted sections 16 and 36, as well as other lands. Arizona did not receive an actual grant of school sections until statehood, but was given the right in 1896 to lease such lands under regulations prescribed by the territorial legislature.

[24] "Enabling Act for New Mexico and Arizona," June 20, 1910, Secs. 6 and 24.

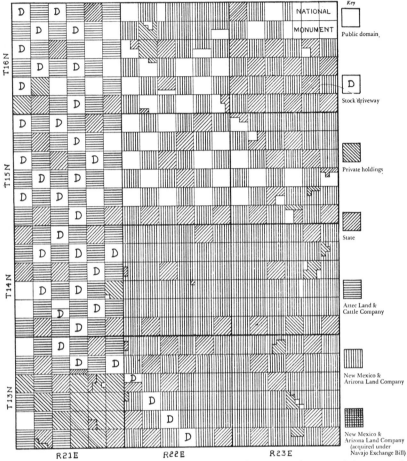

Fig. 3a. The 1934 tenure situation in twelve townships in northeastern Arizona, south of Holbrook. Following are the tenure features illustrated: railroad holdings in alternate-section pattern, owned by the New Mexico & Arizona Land Company and the Aztec Land & Cattle Company, T. 15 N., R. 21 and 22 E.; consolidation through lieu selections, T. 14 N., R. 22 and 23 E.; state school sections, T. 14 N., R. 23 E.; other state holdings, T. 16 N., R. 23 E.; small private holdings, mostly homesteaded, T. 13 N., R. 23 E.; and isolated public domain tracts, T. 16 N., R. 22 E.

New Mexico was 12,700,000 acres, of which 8,800,000 acres were for the common schools and 3,900,000 acres for the various institutions.

One principle has dominated the policy of both states in selecting institutional grant and indemnity school lands: to help livestock

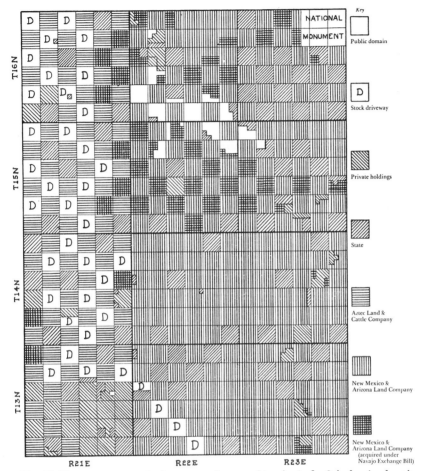

Fig. 3b. The tenure pattern in the same twelve townships (as in fig. 3a) showing how it was modified by 1941. Exchange selections from the public domain, under the Navajo Exchange Bill, enabled the New Mexico & Arizona Land Company to consolidate holdings, especially in T. 15 N., R. 22 E.

operators solve their range problems.[25] Specifically, then, this usually meant that the selection of lands was made so that the livestock operators were enabled to gain control of public range lands or so that they could solidify their holdings through purchase or lease.[26] For

[25] An explicit statement of this policy is given in *Eighteenth Annual Report of the Commissioner of Public Lands of New Mexico* (1917), p. 39.
[26] This is discussed fully by the writer in an article on "Land Policy and Stock Raising in the Western United States," in *Agricultural History*, XVII (Jan., 1943), pp. 14–30.

example, tracts containing actual or potential water resources have been commonly picked by the states, and stockmen who lease or buy them are able to control adjacent range. Several years ago, when the state of New Mexico still had a great deal of land to select, it was customary to hold about 100,000 acres in abeyance, to be chosen at the instance of prospective purchasers or lessees of large tracts.[27]

Numerous selections have been made in the railroad grant territory by both states. In some districts they have chosen all the available even-numbered sections, which are then rented, along with the school lands, to the owners or lessees of the railroad sections. Several consolidated ranch units have been built up in this way. For an illustration of such tenure conditions, see figure 3a.

State holdings in the "checkerboard" country of Arizona and New Mexico are large, and this alone makes them important to the stockmen who operate there. Their importance, however, goes beyond this, for state land policies are usually adjusted to meet the apparent needs of livestock producers even if state revenues have to be sacrificed in the process. In New Mexico, state lands are almost always rented for three cents an acre, the minimum stipulated by state law, regardless of their grazing quality. Leases may not run for more than five years, but a lessee in good standing has a preference right to apply for renewal. In Arizona the minimum fee for a grazing lease on state land is also three cents per acre, but this was cut in half in the recent depression period. The usual term in Arizona is five years, although leases may be executed for twenty years with fee readjustments at the end of each five-year period. It is rare, however, for the state to collect more than the legal minimum.

Comparatively little state land has been sold to stockmen because the minimum prices are too high to make it an attractive investment. These minimum prices were set in the enabling act for the two states, and it has not been possible to reduce them, although suggestions to do so have been made from time to time. The New Mexico minimum figure is $5 per acre for land in, roughly, the eastern third of the state, and $3 elsewhere; any land subject to irrigation under

---

[27] *Sixteenth and Seventeenth Annual Reports of the Commissioner of Public Lands of New Mexico* (1916), p. 27.

a federal reclamation project, however, may not be sold for less than $25 an acre. The state has tried to offset high prices with easy credit terms. Only 5 per cent must be paid in cash, while the balance may be spread over thirty years. The situation in Arizona is very similar. Three dollars per acre is the minimum price in any part of the state, with the same exception for federal reclamation projects. Cash payments must be at least 5 per cent of the purchase price, with the balance covered in thirty-eight annual installments. In the railroad grant area stockmen have confined their purchases of state lands largely to tracts which have strategic value to them, because of water resources or location. Only a few large outfits have bought much state land, and this was selected to fit in with alternate-section railroad lands which they held.

NATIONAL FORESTS

Large national forest reserves have been created within the boundaries of the Atlantic & Pacific grant area, such as the Cibola in New Mexico, and the Sitgreaves, Coconino, Tusayan, and Prescott in Arizona. Some of the railroad sections in these forests were returned to the federal government by the railroad company or a successor to its title, in exchange for other lands. This was done under an act of 1897 which allowed private holdings in forest reserves to be exchanged for an equal acreage selected from vacant public domain anywhere in the country. Flagrant abuse of this privilege forced Congress to repeal the law of 1897 in March, 1905,[28] when fairly heavy private holdings still existed in parts of the forest of this region. In the Cibola Forest the McKinley Land & Lumber Company of Albuquerque was able to acquire large blocks of land by purchasing odd-numbered sections from the railroad and even-numbered sections from the state, which previously had selected them under the university land grant. These state lands were bought by the McKinley Company in 1918. More than 25 per cent of the Cibola Forest is in private ownership, a top figure for the national forests in New Mexico and Arizona. Railroad lands are not the only source of

---

[28] See 73d Cong., 1st sess., Sen. Doc. 12, *A National Plan for American Forestry*, II, pp. 1162–1163.

private holdings in the forest reserves. Many were acquired through homestead entries, either before the reserves were established or under the Forest Homestead Act of 1906. The resulting mixed ownership situation has undoubtedly complicated forest management.[29]

The national forests in this area are, of course, used for grazing, and the Forest Service has built up over many years an elaborate code of regulations for this purpose. In issuing grazing permits for the forests, preference is given to stockmen who own property within or adjacent to the forests. A stockman who owns land situated inside a forest may allow it to be used in common with the public lands or he may fence it for exclusive individual use. If an owner of private land does not have livestock to run, he may permit the Forest Service, in exchange for a share of the net return from grazing fees, to administer and lease the land to stockmen. The Santa Fe Pacific Railroad Company has made such arrangements for most of its lands in the national forests of New Mexico and Arizona. The Aztec Land & Cattle Company, on the other hand, has fenced a number of its alternate sections, individually, in the Sitgreaves Forest of Arizona, and leases them to small farmers in the neighborhood who use them to graze a few head of stock in connection with their farming operations; most of these farmers also work part-time in the sawmills of the vicinity.

The states of New Mexico and Arizona, too, have rights in the national forests. Title to school sections in the forest reserves did not vest in the states, but they are entitled to receive a proportionate share of the forest revenues from the Forest Service which administers them. As an alternative, they have the option of selecting lieu lands. Arizona has allowed most of such school sections to remain under Forest Service administration, whereas New Mexico has made indemnity selections elsewhere in the state. New Mexico has gone even further in drawing out of the forests in recent years by relinquishing some of its institutional grant sections in exchange for lands outside.[30]

---

[29] See 73d Cong., 1st sess., Sen. Doc. 12, *A National Plan for American Forestry*, I, p. 571.

[30] By special act of Congress in June, 1926, such exchanges are allowed in New Mexico on an equal-value basis.

HOMESTEADS

Homesteading has been common in the Atlantic & Pacific grant area, as it has in most parts of the Southwest outside of Texas. In some odd-numbered sections, homesteads were entered before the railroad company's rights attached, making indemnity selections necessary. Large numbers of homesteaders came to the area when the railroad was completed, and the limited amount of land suitable for farming was snapped up quickly. Many homesteads were filed by early stockmen, especially on lands with springs or water holes. The Stock Raising Homestead Act of 1916 gave a strong impulse to homesteading in this area, as it did generally in the western states. Entries under this act have persisted, although experience in this region soon proved that the 640-acre tract was insufficient to support a family.

After the Great War veterans and others crowded into the high plateau area of New Mexico, homesteaded upon the winter range where previously cattle had grazed, and thus seriously affected the interests of those who had large commitments in cattle. It was soon apparent that these homesteaders could not make a subsistence upon the lands, and their situation has been precarious ever since.[31]

Stockmen resident in the area have used the homestead as a means of consolidating ranch units, in part at least, where they already controlled the alternate railroad sections. Many of these homesteads were filed by ranch employees, or other persons, for the livestock operator. Sometimes such homesteads have been taken out to protect the stockman against an entry by an "outsider" who might locate on a strategically placed section and compel the stockman to buy him out at a high price.[32]

In the early 1930's many homesteaders were encouraged to migrate to the region by "colonizing agents" who, for suitable fees, would locate for them public lands open to entry and then assist them

---

[31] National Resources Board, *Report on Land Planning*, pt. 7, p. 74.

[32] Byron O. Beall, Chairman of the New Mexico State Tax Commission, testified before a Senate committee in 1932 that most homesteads currently patented in New Mexico were being sold to livestock operators. See Senate Committee on Public Lands and Surveys, 72d Cong., 1st sess., *Granting Remaining Unreserved Public Lands to States*, p. 134.

to file homesteads. This was purely a promotion game, as most of the homesteaders discovered after trying to make a living on their lands.[33] Many of them relinquished their entries only to have others file on the same sections.[34] Only a few have been able to get patents for their homesteads, since the majority have not had enough cash income to pay even the modest fees necessary to complete their entries. Those who continue to live on the homesteads are, therefore, mostly "squatters," with an exceedingly low standard of living.

In the first months of 1934 many homesteads were filed in anticipation of the passage of the Taylor Bill to regulate grazing on the public domain. It was generally believed that landholders would be given preference for permits to use public lands in whatever grazing districts would be established. The act, as finally passed in the same year, did provide for this preference. Since it also stipulated, however, that no owner, occupant, or settler whose rights were acquired in the calendar year 1934 was to receive preferential treatment until July 1, 1935, the late entries were awarded only a secondary position.

An executive order in November, 1934, withdrew all public lands in the western states from homestead entry to allow the Department of the Interior to establish grazing districts under the Taylor Act. Since that date no new homesteading has occurred in Arizona and New Mexico.

In some parts of the railroad grant area virtually all the even-numbered sections, except those belonging to the state, have been taken up by homesteaders. An illustration of such tenure conditions may be found in T. 13 N., R. 18 W., which is shown in figure 2a.

MEXICAN LAND GRANTS

Several extensive Mexican land grants are found within the borders of the Atlantic & Pacific grant, lying in or adjacent to the Rio Grande Valley in New Mexico. Among the larger ones are the An-

[33] See testimony of S. F. Stacher, Superintendent of the Eastern Navajo Agency in Subcommittee of Senate Committee on Indian Affairs, 71st Cong., 3d sess., *Survey of Conditions of the Indians in the United States*, pt. 18, p. 9593; also, testimony of Clyde S. Ely, newspaper correspondent in Gallup, in *ibid.*, pt. 18, p. 9236.

[34] The tractbooks in the District Land Office at Santa Fe, examined by the writer in October, 1934, showed many recent filings on sections where two or three former entries had been abandoned.

tonio Sedillo, Bernabe Montano, Ignacio Chaves, and Cebolleta. Titles for these lands were not confirmed by the courts for many years, and even when the Mexican titles were upheld, litigation did not end, because several claimants appeared for each grant. It was not until about 1915 that stockmen could safely buy or lease these grants,[35] which offered the advantage of consolidated range lands.

PUBLIC DOMAIN

Public domain in the United States is a residual product which comprises the unappropriated and unreserved lands that belong to the federal government; it does not include lands owned by states or other political subdivisions. The aggregate acreage of public domain in the Atlantic & Pacific grant district is very large, and it has had peculiar importance because of the way in which it is distributed: in the form of isolated tracts. It is rare to find two or more adjacent sections of public domain, since alternate sections were normally railroad property. There were exceptions to this, however. One exception is in lands which were reserved for mineral classification before the railroad applied for patent, and for which the railroad made indemnity selections; subsequently, if the public lands proved to be nonmineral, they were restored to public domain. Most stockmen in the region have used the "checkerboarded" public domain sections in connection with adjacent lands which they owned or leased. This was done informally and without regulation by the federal government. For many years Congress was urged by reliable authorities to control grazing on the public domain, but nothing was done until 1934, when the Taylor Act was passed. This law is bringing about important changes in the use of public lands in all the western states, but we shall examine its effect on the railroad grant area later. For the period before 1934, the absence of public domain grazing regulations accounts for some of the main problems in the use of the resources of the region. These problems were complicated by the selection of public lands for Indian allotments and homesteads.

---

[35] Wooton, *Factors Affecting Range Management in New Mexico*, United States Department of Agriculture, *Bulletin* No. 211 (1915), p. 19.

Chapter III

TENURE PROBLEMS

THE "CHECKERBOARD" land pattern, even in the simple form of alternate railroad and public domain sections, presented serious problems for stockmen in the region as soon as settlement became moderately dense. The lessee or owner of railroad sections had an advantage over others in using the intermingled public lands, and it was natural for him to consider them as a normal part of his range. This attitude was fortified by continuous usage for a period of years. But the existence of public domain sections made it legally possible for other stockmen to enter such a range and physically possible to graze and water their stock on the privately controlled railroad sections as well as on the public lands. Whenever this was done, and it was a frequent occurrence in the "checkerboard" area, the advantages of land ownership or lease were essentially lost. The operators of "tramp sheep herds" who had no definite range of their own found it especially easy to drift across the territory without paying attention to ownership rights, but stockmen resident in the locality were not averse to doing the same thing from time to time. Disputes broke out between owners and interlopers. Obviously the question was a complicated one, both legally and morally, for each side had grounds to support it. The difficulty was inherent in the very ownership pattern. For the lessee or owner of railroad sections it was almost impossible to secure legal redress against invaders, even when he had clear-cut evidence of trespass.[1]

A striking illustration of this tenure problem in the railroad grant area was presented to the Senate Committee on Public Lands and Surveys when it held hearings in Albuquerque in 1925. The following is a quotation from the testimony of Laurence F. Lee, who represented the New Mexico Sheep and Wool Growers' Association:

Now, I know one owner who ranges from 20 to 30 herds of sheep, some 30,000 or more, for four and five months of each year by driving them in

[1] See Will C. Barnes, *The Story of the Range*, p. 50.

the style of many years ago—just start out on a march down through these checkerboarded lands and back on the claim of the right to graze on the Government land, an equal privilege with anybody else. And in order to keep him off that—Senator Jones is familiar with the New Mexico statute—it is necessary that you mark the boundaries of each privately owned section with a proper notice to keep off, which is an absolutely impractical and impossible proposition. The result is that there is one owner—there are others, but this one owner ranges some 30,000 sheep for five months of the year without paying a nickel of taxes on the land or for the grass that they are eating. That makes a situation that is intolerable.[2]

Effective economic utilization of a region is obviously impossible under these conditions. At the Albuquerque hearings just referred to, one stockman testified that he had been forced to abandon part of his winter range in McKinley County, where he actually owned a number of alternate railroad sections, because when he was ready to run his stock on it in the late winter he found that it had already been grazed by others.[3]

Extralegal means have sometimes been used by operators of the larger ranches in the "checkerboard" district to protect what they regarded as their rightful ranges. For example, owners or lessees of railroad sections have fenced their ranges in which are included public domain sections. The enclosing wire was usually called a "drift fence," and it may have performed a function in preventing cattle from "drifting" farther than was desirable, but, at the same time, it kept others from using a stockman's range on the pretext of getting to the intermingled public lands. Such fences were made illegal by act of Congress even before the main settlement of this area took place. This act, passed in 1885, was enacted because of the widespread protest against fencing on the Great Plains, where thousands of square miles of public domain had been enclosed.[4] Exact acreages involved cannot be obtained, but an appreciation of their magnitude may be gained from examples cited by Hibbard.[5]

Two companies in Colorado enclosed a million acres each. Other companies in Colorado, New Mexico, Nebraska and Kansas had around a quarter

---

[2] Subcommittee of Senate Committee on Public Lands and Surveys, 69th Cong., 1st sess., *National Forests and the Public Domain*, pt. 13, pp. 3540–3541.
[3] Testimony of J. F. Branson, in *ibid.*, pt. 13, p. 3656.
[4] Ernest S. Osgood, *The Day of the Cattleman*, pp. 190–193.
[5] Hibbard, *op. cit.*, p. 477.

of a million acres each. In two counties in New Mexico three million acres were enclosed. Thirty-two cases reported to the General Land Office embraced 4,431,900 acres, while in 1888 about seven and a quarter million acres were under investigation. . . . Instances of enclosures of twenty to fifty thousand acres were innumerable.

Many ranchers were required to take down illegal fences in the years immediately following 1885, but, after the first period of enforcement, the Department of the Interior did not attempt seriously to secure general compliance in the Southwest. This lax policy was adopted on the ground that removal of "drift fences" in this region would bring economic disaster to the cattle raisers. During World War I the federal government gave special permission to stockmen in Arizona and New Mexico to erect fences enclosing public domain, and these barriers were not removed after the war.[6] Ample evidence concerning the existence of public domain fences in these two states was presented to the Senate Committee on Public Lands and Surveys in 1925, when it was contended by many stockmen that they were vitally necessary to the conduct of their business.[7] There is little doubt that most of these fences were still standing when the Taylor Bill went into effect in 1934.

Established ranges in the "checkerboard" district were broken up, from time to time, by homesteaders who filed on intermingled public lands. Some of these entries, as we have seen, were not made in good faith, in that they were intended to compel ranchers to buy them out; as time went on, however, it became more difficult to make unfriendly entries, for stockmen, anticipating them, filed homesteads through employees, relatives, and friends. Many homesteaders, of course, were wholly sincere in their entries, intending to set up dry-land farms or small stock ranches. Generally speaking, the physical qualities of the region have not favored success in either type of enterprise, especially the former; as we have already observed, the objective of the homestead laws—to achieve permanent settlement

---

[6] Harold L. Ickes, "The National Domain and the New Deal," in *The Saturday Evening Post*, CCVI (Dec. 23, 1933), p. 11.

[7] Subcommittee of Senate Committee on Public Lands and Surveys, 69th Cong., 1st sess., *National Forests and the Public Domain*, pt. 4, pp. 909, 1016–1017, 1035–1036, 1052; pt. 13, pp. 3563, 3565, 3584.

for family units with normal standards of living—has scarcely been attained here. On the contrary, in breaking up established ranges, in complicating the tenure pattern, in fostering overgrazing, and in tempting people to risk their time, energy, and capital where the chances of success were so slender, homesteading actually was a handicap to effective economic utilization of the physical and human resources of the area.

In the vicinity of the Navajo Reservation, Indian allotments have been a greater impediment to economic development than homesteads. The struggle to dominate grazing in this area, as we have seen, induced the Indian Bureau to "spot" allotments among the railroad sections. Out of this tenure arrangement there developed a condition in which neither Indians nor white stockmen could use the range satisfactorily, and which caused persistent friction between the two groups.

The contest for range between Indian allottees and white stockmen ordinarily boiled down to one of "getting there first." Indian allotments were not fenced, and it was difficult for the rancher to keep his stock off the allotments scattered through his customary range, even if he were inclined to do so. The Indians, on the other hand, made no attempt to confine their flocks solely to their allotments but used the railroad sections as well. In some instances the stockmen dominated; in others the Indians gained the upper hand. But in either situation uncertainty in operations resulted, and the area as a whole suffered an economic loss.

The two sides of the argument have been set forth on numerous occasions, of which the two following quotations are samples:

The white man has a protected range. This is a checkerboard country. They lease the railroad sections, the odd sections, and the Navajos have most of the even sections and the white man has his protected range some place else. When the green feed starts in the checkerboard country he grazes off the grass and leaves the Navajo nothing but the wind.[8]

Through our railroad, school leases, and other holdings we have 65 per cent of this range and all of the permanent waters. The Indians have less than

---

[8] Testimony of J. W. Ashcroft, Stockman for the Crownpoint Indian Agency, in Subcommittee of Senate Committee on Indian Affairs, 71st Cong., 3d sess., *Survey of Conditions of the Indians in the United States*, pt. 18, p. 9572.

15 per cent of the land allotted to them. The other per cent is Government land, which, as tax-paying citizens, we should be entitled to use as much as Government wards who pay no taxes. In spite of the fact that we have more than four times as much range as the Indians, they have run more sheep and goats on the range than we have all of the time we have been out there, besides large numbers of valueless Indian ponies and some cattle. These horses and cattle depend almost entirely upon our waters and it has been impossible to put up a fence around our waters strong enough to keep them out.[9]

These conditions were the basis of range warfare. Mutual distrust between Navajos and whites flared up from time to time in open hostilities and violence, especially in the neighborhood of Crownpoint, New Mexico, where the conflict was most persistent. Both sides were guilty of lawless acts. Cattle belonging to white stockmen were stolen by the Indians and Indian stock were driven off by whites.[10] Some of the larger ranch owners included Navajo allotments within their fenced ranges, thus preventing the Indians from using lands that had been assigned to them.[11] Many of the smaller operators, however, found it so difficult to carry on that they were willing to sell their holdings and move out.

All this country adjacent to the Zuñi Mountains was for many years considered to be Indian country, and when the railroad built through here a good many white homesteaders came in, and there are a good many homesteads still mingled with the Indian allotments throughout this strip. Numbers of homesteaders in the vicinity of Smith's Lake, Mariano Lake, and other parts of the district have found it practically impossible to continue their operations there and would be glad to dispose of their properties.[12]

Organization and management of stock ranches in the "checkerboard" area were affected adversely by the tenure condition. We have already observed how competition occurred among stockmen for the use of public domain sections, and how conflicts were generated between Indians and whites for control of some ranges. These circumstances aggravated the precarious features of stock raising, and can be held responsible for forcing some of the smaller operators

---

[9] Letter from Charles Chadwick & Company to First National Bank of Albuquerque, January 21, 1923, published in Hagerman, *op. cit.*, pp. 77–78.

[10] *Ibid.*, p. 84.

[11] See letter of W. A. Marchalk, Chief of the Land Division, Office of Indian Affairs, to the Commissioner of Indian Affairs, October 23, 1923, published in *ibid.*, p. 94.

[12] *Ibid.*, p. 29; see, also, letter of Charles Chadwick & Company referred to above.

to abandon their enterprises. But because of the alternate-section pattern, even leases of comparatively large amounts of railroad grant lands failed to bring security of tenure. To some extent this disadvantage was overcome by fencing, but these fences were illegal because they enclosed public domain and there was always a threat that strict enforcement of existing laws would compel their removal.

Where ranges were not fenced the typical disadvantages of grazing public lands in common appeared: diminishing total production, lowering of standards of business organization because stockmen were unable to plan operations for several years in advance, continuously diminishing productivity in forage cover, and increasing precariousness in business operations.[13] These were not adequately realized at the time the region was being settled, for the "open range" tradition of earlier Anglo-American frontiers was still strong. Unregulated use of "open range" as a grazing common was suited, at least from the short-run entrepreneurial viewpoint, to primitive pioneering conditions in the livestock industry when the range was not crowded. Cattle raising in Arizona and New Mexico, however, developed with whirlwind rapidity as transcontinental railroad lines were completed through the Southwest in the 1880's. Stockmen from crowded and overgrazed ranges, especially in Texas, rushed into the area, and some eastern and European capital was invested in herds that were shipped to the newly opened ranges. In 1870 there were only about 25,000 range cattle in New Mexico and Arizona; the census of 1880 recorded 172,000, whereas by 1890 the number had risen to 817,000.[14] So quickly did this development take place that by 1890 the southwestern ranges in general were overstocked,[15] and stockmen began to realize the advantages of exclusively controlled pastures. Over a period of years it became apparent to disinterested observers, as well as stockmen, that both public and private welfare would be best served by regulating, in some way, the use of public domain so that it could no longer be used freely by all as a common

[13] Wooton, *Relation of Land Tenure...*, United States Department of Agriculture, *Bulletin* No. 1001, p. 20.
[14] *Eleventh Census, 1890*, Compendium, pt. 3, p. 622.
[15] J. J. Thornber, *Grazing Ranges of Arizona*, pp. 335 ff.

range. Congress, however, remained unconvinced until 1934, when the Taylor Act, regulating grazing on the public domain, was passed. Uncertainty regarding tenure often placed the stockman at a disadvantage in negotiating loans for his business operations. Banks in the whole western range country were cautious about extending loans to stockmen who did not have well-defined control over range land, and such operators were usually required to pay comparatively high interest rates on their loans.[16]

To attain tenure security, some stockmen of the region "blocked" their ranges by purchasing the alternate railroad sections, lieu railroad sections, state lands, and homesteads. This was done on a large scale in parts of Coconino County, Arizona. As elsewhere in the West, land purchases did not always prove economical, for, in spite of the exclusive range control they provided, they added considerably to fixed charges. These additional overhead costs were not only unbearably heavy for some operators in times of low prices or drought,[17] but they also impelled the stockman to increase the number of animals on his ranch and, in this way, fostered overgrazing on privately owned lands.

. . . increase in owned acreage did not increase the area or productiveness of the range unit which he [the stockman] had previously used free of charge as public lands. To meet taxes and interest payments on the enlarged ownership, the stockman usually found it necessary to increase the size of his flock or herd. The result, almost inevitably, has been overgrazing and range depletion.[18]

The tenure pattern of the Atlantic & Pacific grant area, with its resulting problems, has undoubtedly tended to minimize rather than to increase the aggregate of taxable values. On *a priori* grounds one might suppose that the control over public lands implied in alternate-

---

[16] See, for example, the testimony of Vernon Metcalf, Secretary of the Nevada Land and Livestock Association, in Senate Committee on Public Lands and Surveys, 69th Cong., 1st sess., *Grazing Facilities on Public Lands*, pp. 515–516.

[17] Smaller operators in many parts of the West were often forced out of business by the unprofitable purchase of a few homesteaded sections. "Thus," says Gates, "the adoption of the Stock Raising Homestead Act, instead of carrying out its avowed purpose of establishing independent, self-supporting farmers or stockmen has, in fact, forced to the wall many already engaged in the cattle business." National Resources Board, *Report on Land Planning*, pt. 7, p. 75.

[18] *The Western Range*, p. 246.

section railroad holdings would be reflected in higher assessment values for the latter. In some parts of the range country, counties have assessed public lands on the basis of their control over public domain rather than on their forage value,[19] even where control was not exclusively in the hands of one operator. Stockmen in Nevada, for example, assert that the use value of the public domain has been fully capitalized in the value of associated privately owned lands.[20] In New Mexico and Arizona, however, tax assessments have not taken account of this control factor, although it may have been given weight by persons selling or leasing private lands.

In the "checkerboard" district of Arizona and New Mexico, railroad grant lands have actually borne lower assessments than other grazing lands. This has been observed by a number of persons familiar with the situation,[21] and was verified by a survey of tax records made by the writer in 1934. At that time the State Tax Commission of Arizona preferred to have county assessors present on their abstracts of assessment rolls separate figures for "grazing land" and "railroad grant land." On this basis the tax abstracts of the four northern counties of the state showed the following average valuations per acre for the two classes:

County	Grazing land	Railroad grant land
Apache	$0.69	$0.65
Coconino	.51	
Mohave	.85	.40
Navajo	.70	.60

In each of the three counties for which both figures are given, the average valuation of "railroad grant lands" is less than that of "grazing land," with the greatest differential occurring in Mohave County. The Coconino County abstract did not distinguish between the two classes; the writer's survey of the actual tax rolls of this

---

[19] Marion Clawson, "The Administration of Federal Range Lands," in *Quarterly Journal of Economics*, LIII (May, 1939), p. 447.

[20] E. O. Wooton, *The Public Domain of Nevada and Factors Affecting Its Use*, United States Department of Agriculture, *Technical Bulletin* No. 301, p. 47.

[21] See testimony of Laurence F. Lee in Subcommittee of Senate Committee on Public Lands and Surveys, 69th Cong., 1st sess., *National Forests and the Public Domain*, pt. 13, p. 3540; also, Hagerman, *op. cit.*, p. 96.

county, however, showed that more than 90 per cent of the railroad company's holdings were assessed at 40 cents per acre, whereas the average assessment, as shown in the above tabulation, was 51 cents. Since the 51-cent figure is an average that includes a large body of railroad lands at 40 cents, the average for nonrailroad grazing lands must have been appreciably higher.

The tax situation was similar in McKinley County, New Mexico, in 1934. Grazing lands in New Mexico were supposed to be assessed on the basis of their carrying capacity, and the State Tax Commission annually issued schedules of acreage values corresponding to various estimated carrying capacities. In practice, however, county assessors usually carried range land at a constant assessment for a period of years, and, when a modification was made, it took the form of a uniform percentage change on all grazing land. An examination of the McKinley County assessment rolls for 1934 indicated that about 90 per cent of the railroad company's holdings were assessed at 75 cents per acre, though the average assessed valuation of grazing land in the county was 80 cents.

The broken and complicated ownership pattern of the area, because it impedes effective use, is partly responsible for the lower assessments on railroad grant lands, as well as for reduced taxable values of livestock. This was especially true in the areas where. Navajo allottees and white stockmen fought for control of the range, with the result that Indian allotments were spread over a large area far from the reservation limits. No taxes were collected on the acreage allotted, whereas, under other circumstances, some of it would have passed into the hands of stockmen and would have been subjected to assessment by the local taxing authorities. This loss was additional to the reduction of taxable livestock in the disputed territory.[22]

There are other factors, it must be acknowledged, which help to explain the lower assessments on railroad grant lands. The difficulty of appraising separately each tract in alternate-section holdings induced county officials to assess all railroad holdings at a flat rate

---

[22] Hagerman, *op. cit.*, p. 96.

instead of trying to take account of differences in quality. In making this practical solution assessors typically placed the rate below that of other grazing lands on the ground that the railroad lands were not "selected" as were other grazing ranges and that as a consequence they were, on the average, of inferior quality.[23] The fact that the railroad company is a large taxpayer must also be taken into account. In this connection it is interesting to observe that six townships of consolidated railroad lands in McKinley County, New Mexico, were in 1934 assessed at the same rate as the other railroad holdings in the county, most of which were in alternate-section form; this rate, as we have seen, was lower than the average for other grazing property.

Tenure conditions in the Atlantic & Pacific grant area have undoubtedly promoted overgrazing and depletion of forage resources. Competition for the range, in spite of private ownership, goes a long way to account for this. Furthermore, the Santa Fe Pacific Railroad Company, like our other land-grant railroads, has not attempted to manage its lands from the conservation standpoint even where it was feasible to do so. "Not much can be said in favor of the range practice required on most of the railroad lands. It consists simply in leasing the lands without restrictions as to numbers of stock to be grazed or the season during which the land may be so used."[24] Paul W. Gates is authority for the statement that "some of the most destructive erosion" has taken place on the alternate-section holdings of our western railroads.[25]

For years the uncertainty about the Navajo Reservation retarded the development of conservation plans on the reservation proper as well as on surrounding areas, although it was generally acknowledged that the territory was badly overgrazed. This was clearly indicated in Hagerman's report in 1932.

If we all could be assured that the country within the lines above described [reservation boundaries] and with the additional areas recommended for

---

[23] The same reason is offered to explain lower assessments on railroad lands in Nevada. See Subcommittee of Senate Committee on Public Lands and Surveys, 77th Cong., 1st sess., *Administration and Use of Public Lands*, pt. 1, p. 213.

[24] *The Western Range*, p. 229.

[25] Paul W. Gates, "American Land Policy and the Taylor Grazing Act," *Land Policy Circular*, October, 1935 (mimeo.). See also National Resources Board, *Report on Land Planning*, pt. 7, p. 64.

permanent withdrawals were actually in the same clean-cut, exclusive, continuous ownership as the treaty area, then the [Indian] office would be in a far better shape to plan positive programs of water development, rodent control, and real conservation, and to definitely tell the Indians both what they should and must do.[26]

The corollary of overgrazing is excessive erosion, and the "checkerboard" area has made its contribution to the sediment carried by the Colorado River. Writing of that part of the Colorado River basin of which the "checkerboard" area is a segment, an official of the United States Geological Survey in 1932 referred to the region as "an outstanding example of heavy uncontrollable erosion,"[27] and most of the Arizona part of the district was reported in 1936 to have "range in poor condition, erosion heavy."[28]

[26] Hagerman, op. cit., p. 52.

[27] Herman Stabler, "Rise and Fall of the Public Domain," in Civil Engineering, II (Sept., 1932), p. 542.

[28] Reports, Arizona State Planning Board, II, p. 61.

Chapter IV

ATTEMPTS TO IMPROVE TENURE CONDITIONS

THE ATTEMPTS to modify tenure patterns in the Atlantic & Pacific Railroad grant area, thereby making more effective utilization possible, can best be examined separately for two periods; the first of these runs to 1934 when the Taylor Act was passed, and the second covers the period in which this law has been operative.

Before 1934 the principal device for overcoming the disadvantages of "checkerboard" tenure was actual consolidation of holdings through purchase, exchange, and lease. Consolidation through purchase usually was accomplished by buying lieu land scrip as well as odd-numbered sections from the railroad company; the lieu land scrip, which had been issued to the railroad as indemnity for other lands, was then applied on even-numbered sections in the same locality. State school sections within a range built up in this way were ordinarily not purchased because of the high minimum price established by law, but were leased. In some instances the stockman attained exclusive use of the even-numbered sections by asking the state to select them as institutional grant or indemnity lands, after which they would be rented to him. In much less measure, homesteads either were filed or purchased in even-numbered sections in order to consolidate holdings.

The opportunity to consolidate ranges through exchange, before 1934, arose mainly from the extension of the Navajo Reservation and the definition of its boundaries. Such exchanges have had a rather long and complicated history running back to a law of 1904; this act, however, was very limited in scope and application. In March, 1913, Congress enacted legislation allowing railroads in the states of New Mexico, Arizona, and California to exchange some lands which had been occupied by Indian allottees; such exchanges,

[45]

however, were limited to 3000 acres in Arizona and 16,000 acres in New Mexico, and they had to be completed within three years. In 1916 the act was made operative for two years more, and the maximum amounts were raised to 10,000 acres in Arizona and 25,000 acres in New Mexico. Subsequent extensions made the act applicable to March, 1931, the acreage limits remaining unchanged.

A broader exchange measure was provided by the Indian Appropriation Act of March 3, 1921, for the territory east and south of the Navajo Reservation in San Juan, McKinley, and Valencia counties, New Mexico. Exchanges outside the reservation limits in these counties were to be allowed for the purpose of aggregating Indian holdings into large "blocks" and at the same time achieving some consolidation of private lands. In 1922 the General Land Office issued regulations under which such exchanges could take place,[1] but they proved to be so complicated that it was practically impossible to make the actual transactions.

Several conferences on Navajo land problems were held in Santa Fe in the fall of 1923. These meetings, called by Mr. Hagerman, who was then Special Commissioner to the Navajo tribe, were attended by representatives of the Indian Office, the Navajo tribe, the state, the railroad company, and other large landowners and stockmen of western New Mexico. All interested groups seem to have been included, and general agreement was reached on the critical questions involved. The reservation, it was agreed, should be extended to cover substantially all the territory in New Mexico that had been added temporarily in 1907; so far as possible this was to be done by exchanges under the existing laws, with the rest being accomplished by purchase. A detailed program was worked out for the whole area, but when a bill to make it operative was submitted to Congress it failed to pass. Responsibility for this, according to Hagerman, rested with "certain sources antagonistic to the consensus of opinion as expressed at the ... Santa Fe conference."[2] This opposition, presumably, came from stockmen who were not directly involved in the

---

[1] General Land Office, *Circular No. 850*, September 19, 1922.
[2] Hagerman, *op. cit.*, p. 35.

negotiations but who objected strongly to further extensions of the Navajo Reservation in New Mexico.

New opportunities to make exchanges were created in 1930, when the General Land Office modified the regulations which implemented the act of March 3, 1921. It will be recalled that about this time the Indian Office decided to formulate a program for a permanent solution of the Navajo land program. The Santa Fe Pacific Railroad Company filed a first-exchange list under the new setup in April, 1930, and the transaction was completed by January of the following year; this, it might be added, was unusually rapid for such a deal. About 23,000 acres were involved in the actual exchange, but it enabled the railroad company to "block" almost three complete townships in the vicinity of Crownpoint; only some state lands and a few sections belonging to other private owners remained in this area, but these presented no management problem. Exchanges subsequently completed consolidated railroad holdings in the same general region, and by 1934 the railroad company had achieved virtually complete ownership of fifteen townships. About 230,000 acres were traded in the process.

In January, 1932, Mr. Hagerman submitted to the Indian Office his comprehensive report on the Navajo land situation, containing a summary of the complex problems that had arisen in connection with reservation extensions and allotments as well as a review of the various attempts to remedy the obviously unsatisfactory tenure condition. Responsibility for the failure of measures designed to round out the reservation through purchase, exchange, and consolidation was divided, according to Hagerman, between powerful interests in New Mexico and Arizona, on the one hand, and Indian Office policies, on the other. As a permanent solution of the Navajo land problem, Hagerman recommended a number of additions to the reservation. In New Mexico these could be made under the law of March 3, 1921, and the passage of a similar law was suggested for Arizona. Allotments, he believed, should be stopped at once, for they complicated the problems of making exchanges and would not be necessary when the reservation was enlarged.

Field surveys and other investigations necessary to implement such a program were undertaken in Arizona by the Indian Office even before the Hagerman report was submitted; in 1932 similar studies were made in New Mexico. County officials and local stockmen were consulted, many local meetings were held, and the Indian Office was finally able to outline proposed additions to the reservation which seemed to meet with the approval of most of the persons involved in both states.[3] The Arizona situation was much the easier to handle in every respect.

In 1932 a bill to enlarge the Navajo Reservation in Arizona and New Mexico, according to the outlines worked out by the Indian Office, was submitted to Congress, but did not pass. In the following year another measure was tried but it also failed to get Congressional approval. In both these bills the New Mexico situation seemed to be the stumbling block.

In the 1934 session of Congress two separate bills to solve the Navajo land problem were offered, one for.Arizona and one for New Mexico. The Arizona bill was passed and approved in June, 1934. The New Mexico bill received approval in the Senate and was reported favorably in the House but failed to come up for vote. When a similar bill was introduced in 1935, it met strong opposition from the New Mexico senators who voiced objections that had been raised by various groups in the state.[4] The result was that no action was taken. This, and the hearings of 1936, will be considered more fully below.

The actual exchanges consumated prior to 1934 seem pitifully small in relation to the size of the area involved—especially so in view of the critical need, if the region was to be rationally used for stock raising. It is instructive to examine the factors and interests which have retarded exchanges in the Navajo country, for they are typical of the problems that face land planning throughout the western states, and they must be reconciled before anything can be accomplished with such programs.

---

[3] Testimony of James M. Stewart in Subcommittee of Senate Committee on Indian Affairs, 75th Cong., 1st sess., *Survey of Conditions of the Indians in the United States*, pt. 34, p. 17661.

[4] *Congressional Record*, LXXX, pt. 9, pp. 9205–9214.

In the first place, considerable weight must be given to the very struggle for control of the range between white stockmen on the one hand, and Navajos and the Indian Office on the other. Steps which were easy to take in the course of conflict were difficult to eradicate, for "vested interests" were created which had to be taken into account in the tenure adjustment. This, for example, occurred with allotments which were "spotted" on the public domain sections intermingled with railroad lands. The Navajos secured legal rights at the expense of some of the white stockmen, but the latter were so antagonized that they strongly opposed the proposals to extend the reservation and insisted that allotments be suspended, at least before additions were made. The Indian Office, on the other hand, consistently objected to legislation which would prevent allotments in the Navajo area before additions which they regarded as wholly adequate could be made,[5] although they clearly realized that allotments multiplied the problems of consolidation.[6] The situation in Arizona was much less tense and aggravated than in New Mexico, and the tenure pattern was consequently less complicated. Here we have the probable explanation for the passage of the Arizona extension bill in 1934 and for the failure of the New Mexico bill to pass.

Many owners of land in the "checkerboard" area have preferred to sell rather than exchange their lands. This, too, has tended to retard consolidation of holdings. The Indian Office has naturally favored exchanges, because land purchases are extremely costly. Some lands have been bought where exchanges were not feasible, or where they made it possible fully to "block" areas which had been consolidated mainly through exchanges. Only limited funds have been available for purchases, for Congress has made few appropriations for this purpose. The money has come almost entirely from Navajo tribal income, of which more than half was in some years allocated for land acquisition. Lower prices for oil in the early 1930's diminished considerably the Navajo land fund, and, in any event, it was not sufficient for large purchases of the type necessary to solve their land problems.

---

[5] See, for example, Hagerman, *op. cit.*, p. 23. [6] *Ibid.*, p. 140.

Purchases were restricted, furthermore, by the inclination of some owners and the banks, which financed them, to hold out for high prices. This has forced the Indian Office to be extremely cautious about negotiations. A letter written by Hagerman to the Commissioner of Indian Affairs in 1923 tells of negotiations to buy several livestock outfits near Crownpoint, New Mexico, on which mortgages were held by three banks. The following statement from Hagerman's letter is significant:

These banks are undoubtedly impressed with the fact that the present situation offers them the best opportunity they ever have had and probably ever will have of realizing on the indebtedness of these various landholders within this district. I have endeavored to impress upon them this fact and also that if they were unreasonable in their proposals that it would very likely upset the whole plan. . . . I have insisted that the banks and the stockmen themselves cannot presume upon the situation to demand unreasonable considerations.[7]

The potential opportunity to sell land to the federal government explains some of the homesteading which took place several years ago in the vicinity of the Navajo Reservation. There is little doubt that many homesteads were filed merely for the purpose of getting title to land which could subsequently be sold back to the federal government for use by the Navajos. As early as November, 1923, Hagerman suggested that the whole area be temporarily withdrawn from homestead entry in order to prevent filings "for the purpose of holding up the Government."[8] Nothing, however, was done at the time. But a vigorous outburst of this type of homesteading in the latter part of 1930 and the early months of 1931 induced the Department of the Interior to institute a temporary withdrawal in July, 1931, thus putting a stop to the practice.

A third factor which hampered exchange proceedings was the question of mineral rights, for much of the land adjacent to the Navajo Reservation in New Mexico is classified as coal land. The regulations established under the exchange act of March 3, 1921, made it almost impossible to do anything with these lands, although their location required them to be included if satisfactory consolidations were to be worked out. It was not until 1930 that this defect was

[7] Hagerman, *op. cit.*, p. 108.   [8] *Ibid.*, p. 104.

corrected. Since that time it has been possible to exchange public lands which are mineral in character for privately owned or state lands which have mineral resources of approximately equal value.[9] This modification removed an important obstacle to some exchanges.

Navajo land exchanges have run against another stumbling block in the tax question. Exchanges cannot be criticized, as purchases of private land have been, on the ground that they remove property from the tax rolls. On the contrary, by making more effective use of the area possible they should ultimately have the effect of raising taxable values. A problem, however, is still presented by county boundaries. County officials and other local people have insisted that exchanges be completed so as to maintain the aggregate assessed valuation of each county, and it has been necessary to follow this principle in order to get local support for exchange programs. For example, the 1934 act extending the Navajo Reservation in Apache, Navajo, and Coconino counties, Arizona, required a private owner to make his exchange selections in the same county where his original lands were situated. Since the most feasible exchanges do not always fit the pattern of county, or even state, boundaries, such requirements have complicated greatly the problems of consolidation and re-stricted the application of exchange laws.[10]

Another factor in the situation before 1934 was the plan to turn the remaining public domain over to the states. This scheme, which was widely approved and supported in the range states, undoubtedly had the effect of restraining land exchanges in the "checkerboard" district. Both in New Mexico and Arizona state land administration policies have been so strongly shaped by the livestock interests that if the public lands in the vicinity of the Navajo Reservation had been turned over to the states it is almost certain that the Indians would not have been able to hold their own in the contest for extra-reserva-

---

[9] General Land Office, *Circular No. 1208*, March 6, 1930. The Geological Survey must make certification of the approximate equality of mineral values.

[10] This suggests that it is desirable to formulate land-planning programs in regional terms. Regional programs, however, encounter a great obstacle in local political units. This will have to be overcome, probably by wholesale integration of counties and reduction of local autonomy, if public policy adopts the regional criterion in achieving more effective long-run use of our land resources.

tion lands.[11] In 1931 a special commission appointed by the President to study the question of conservation on the public domain recommended that the remaining public lands, which were valuable chiefly for their forage resources, be granted to the states.[12] The bill introduced in Congress that year to achieve this objective, like similar measures in other sessions, was very generally supported in New Mexico and Arizona. This occurred just at the time when the Indian Office was trying to establish better relations with stockmen and to work out a comprehensive exchange program which would involve minimum sacrifices for all parties concerned. Coöperation between the Indian Office and stockmen was therefore handicapped so long as there were bright prospects for the enactment of such a law. But these prospects were dimmed in a few years by growing Congressional support for the alternative policy of keeping the public domain in federal hands and establishing a system of federal regulation for its use. The latter policy dominated when the Taylor Act was passed in 1934. There can be little doubt that this facilitated coöperation between the Indian Office and landowners in Arizona, where other resistances to exchanges were not so great as in New Mexico and where the technical problems were less difficult to handle. The bill for extending the Navajo Reservation in Arizona and the Taylor Bill were both passed in the second session of the seventy-third Congress and approved in the same month. The bearing of the Taylor Act on Navajo exchanges in New Mexico will be considered below.

The Taylor Act of 1934, an important milestone in federal land and range policy, is designed "to stop injury to the public grazing lands by preventing overgrazing and soil deterioration, to provide for their orderly use, improvement, and development, [and] to stabilize the livestock industry dependent upon the public range." This law has already brought about significant changes in the western range industry, and even more far-reaching modifications can be achieved under its provisions, especially in forage conservation. The Secretary of the Interior was authorized by this measure, as

---

[11] See Hagerman, *op. cit.*, pp. 49–50.

[12] President's Committee, *Report on the Conservation and Administration of the Public Domain*, p. 2.

amended in 1936, to create grazing districts from any part of the public domain which is valuable chiefly for grazing; such districts may include, in the aggregate, as much as 142,000,000 acres of public lands. Exchanges of federal domain for state and private lands may be negotiated in order to consolidate holdings and facilitate the administration of grazing districts. The original act permitted the Department of the Interior to lease isolated tracts of public domain to owners of contiguous property, but gave the department no power to rent land from private holders. This defect was remedied in 1938 by the Pierce Act, under which the department may take out a lease on state, county, or private land inside grazing districts for periods ranging up to ten years, at rentals not exceeding the grazing fees which can be collected for the use of such lands.

In January, 1935, a Division of Grazing was established in the Department of the Interior to put into execution the terms of the Taylor Act, and this agency had organized 57 grazing districts in the western states by the end of the fiscal year 1941. These districts comprised a gross area of 266,000,000 acres, of which about 136,000,000 were public domain; in addition, over 8,500,000 acres of other public domain were administered by the Grazing Service under coöperative agreements with various government agencies. The balance of the land in these districts was owned by private parties or state and county units.

Since its organization the Grazing Service has been building up a comprehensive file of records on the public and private lands included in grazing districts, information which is essential for good administration and for planning sound policies. The task is a large one, involving field surveys, research, and mapping to accumulate and maintain systematic records on forage resources and land quality, range facilities, ownership status, etc. Work has necessarily proceeded slowly because of the size of the districts and the limitations of whatever data were available when the Grazing Service started. The ownership records, in which we are especially interested, were about forty per cent complete in the spring of 1941.[13]

---

[13] *The Grazing Bulletin*, April, 1941, p. 8.

Three grazing districts cover parts of the Atlantic & Pacific Railroad grant area, one in the western part of Arizona and two in New Mexico. The two in New Mexico were formerly a single unit, but in 1939 District 7 was split off from the other in an attempt to improve utilization of the range in the "battleground" east and south of the Navajo Reservation. The fact that it was necessary to take this step shows that nothing very significant had been accomplished up to that time in overcoming the defects of the 1934 situation.

When the Navajo Reservation extension bill for New Mexico failed to pass in 1934, the Indian Office did not cease to work for such a measure, but the effectiveness of the opposition was growing at the same time. In 1936 another bill was proposed and extensive hearings were held in Washington as well as in New Mexico,[14] but without success. By this time it was clear that the white stockmen in this area believed that they could gain the upper hand over the Navajo allottees through the Taylor Act grazing district setup, and many who had been willing earlier to exchange lands now refused to support the Indian Office program. Their reasons for holding this opinion were without doubt accurately estimated by Hugh G. Calkins, Regional Director for the Soil Conservation Service in the Southwest, in a statement submitted to the Senate subcommittee in 1936 from which the following pertinent comments are taken:[15]

... The [Taylor] act and the Secretary's regulations pursuant thereto contain certain provisions that would appear to have a somewhat adverse effect upon the welfare of Indian livestock owners occupying the area east of the present Navajo Indian Reservation in New Mexico. ...

The Indians in the eastern Navajo country would in many cases ... be under a disadvantage in attempting to secure [grazing] permits as preference applicants. Frequently it might be found that property qualification was inadequate. This is particularly true because stock water, often stipulated as a necessary qualification, has in the majority of cases been developed by the Government and is, therefore, not the property of the individual range users. In other cases it would doubtless be found that the property owned or controlled by the Indian did not provide "proper protection" as defined by the regulations. ...

---

[14] Subcommittee of Senate Committee on Indian Affairs, *Survey of Conditions of the Indians in the United States*, pt. 34.

[15] *Ibid.*, pt. 34, pp. 17619–17620.

A further disadvantage is that the Navajos would have difficulty in securing adequate representation on the advisory board, which is largely responsible for administration of grazing under the regulations of the Secretary. . . . Many Navajos are unable to write and would, therefore, be ineligible to vote. The Indian living within a reservation is under the protection and guidance of a Government agency organized for this purpose. The Indian living within a grazing district is forced to compete with white men who frequently have greater advantages in education and property resources. It does not seem fair to subject the Indian to such competition if it can be avoided by fair and equitable means.

The distribution of land ownership in the area which the Indian Office proposed to add to the reservation in 1936 is given in the following tabulation:[16]

Ownership	Acreage	Percentage
New Mexico & Arizona Land Co..	55,680	3
White homesteads	92,240	4
State	154,120	7
Railroad	352,700	16
Federal (other than Indian)....	445,330	21
Indian	1,054,480	49
Total	2,154,550	100

In large part, as we have seen, ownership consisted of noncontiguous holdings which enormously complicated the problems of administration by the Grazing Service. One district established in northwestern New Mexico in 1936 is a unique problem area. The amount of non-Indian federal land in the area was only 445,330 acres, of which 393,950 acres were nonreserved public domain; the latter comprised only 18 per cent of the total acreage, and this limited amount was a further handicap to grazing administration. Little improvement occurred in the general situation until the region was made a special grazing district in 1939.

All grazing districts under the Taylor Act have advisory boards, composed largely of local stockmen, but this one has an additional advisory board, made up of representatives of the various government agencies that have an interest in the region—the Indian Office,

---

[16] *Ibid.*, pt. 34, p. 17545.

Soil Conservation Service, and Forest Service. Actual administration, however, is in the hands of the Grazing Service, including the Indian allotments as well as some lands which the Resettlement Administration had purchased and turned over to the Indian Office for use by the Navajos. Another peculiar feature of the district is that it is intended to support many of the smaller white stockmen and Indians on a subsistence, rather than a commercial, basis. A few statements from the rough-hewn testimony of R. H. Rutledge, Director of Grazing, to a Senate Committee in 1940, may be quoted on these features.[17]

I have tried to see where an emergency existed. . . . We put on a special set of regulations, and I will admit that they were designed to take care of the little fellow . . . as I remember the situation, the little fellow who has lived there can only get enough for his subsistence.

Now, speaking for myself, for the grazing service, I would say that our only interest in going in there was to try to see if we could not administer the land as a grazing district rather than as an Indian reservation, which, as you know, some people want. I think it is a try-out to see whether we can handle the Indians, the Spanish-Americans, the small whites, and the big whites on the same area, where there is not quite enough room for everybody.

I am in there just to try to help this thing out, and if anybody can do it better, they are perfectly welcome to go in and do it. It has caused me a lot of headaches.

In this manner, the Grazing Service is at present working toward better use of the land resources of the region. Progress has been slow because the situation is awkward, but there can be little question that improvements have been made since 1939. Informed persons in New Mexico whom the writer interviewed in December, 1941, were agreed on this and believed that the trend would continue. The situation probably gives a minimum of satisfaction to the Navajos, but their problem may in large measure be solved by irrigation development and a shift in their economy, together with some land concessions from local stockmen. The Navajos have many local supporters, particularly in the town of Gallup, which has built up a thriving tourist trade largely through the Indians. It is impossible to appraise

[17] Senate Committee on Public Lands and Surveys, *Amending the Taylor Grazing Act,* p. 25.

this trade statistically, but one may suggest with confidence that the Navajo tourist business will become more important than stock raising as a source of prosperity in the region. So far as consolidation of holdings is concerned, little has been achieved to date under the Taylor Act, although the Grazing Service maintains that it is the most desirable long-run policy for solving the tenure problem of this area. The practical difficulties of making exchanges, however, have been so great that only a handful of transactions has been completed.

The less complex Navajo land situation in Arizona has been met satisfactorily under the 1934 bill to extend the reservation in that state. This act defined the exterior boundaries of the reservation to include a considerable body of new territory, and authorized exchanges with private owners and with the state of Arizona for the purpose of consolidating Indian holdings within the new limits. These exchanges were to be made on an equal-value basis. Navajo allotments were no longer permitted in Arizona, except on the reservation itself. Where it was impossible through exchanges to eliminate private holdings from the reservation, the Indian Office was authorized, to the extent of about $482,000, to buy lands with Navajo tribal funds. The purchase program was actively carried on after the passage of the law, and more than 334,000 acres were added to the reservation by the end of the fiscal year 1938,[18] when the sum was substantially exhausted. As one would expect, exchanges took place at a much slower pace, although negotiations were begun in 1934 with the two principal parties involved, the Santa Fe Pacific Railroad Company and the New Mexico & Arizona Land Company. The large exchanges were completed in 1939, when approximately 321,000 acres were transferred. This not only solidified reservation lands but also enabled the two companies to "block" large areas in the "checkerboard" region and thus overcome the disadvantages of broken tenure patterns. (See fig. 3b.) The act under which this was achieved is certainly a milestone in land policy for the railroad grant territory. Further friction between Navajos and whites has

---

[18] *Annual Report of the Secretary of the Interior for the Fiscal Year Ended June 30, 1938*, p. 212.

been averted, the land can be more effectively used from the short-run entrepreneurial point of view, and long-run conservation measures can be more easily adopted.

The Taylor Act, it will be recalled, authorized the Department of the Interior to negotiate land exchanges with private owners and states, and the Grazing Service hopes to accomplish large consolidations of public land in grazing districts by this method. The principle has been stressed many times in official reports and bulletins, of which the following is a representative sample:

> The exchange program must be pushed. Especially is this true in the matter of State land, to promote better administrative control, to stimulate the production of revenue to the States, and to enable certain isolated tracts of public land outside of grazing districts to become absorbed in the tax-paying structures of the States and counties. Wherever it is in the public interest, applications for exchange within grazing districts should receive early action. There are many examples in which proper blocking of owner-ship immediately would remove existing administrative problems. For the present, exchanges will be encouraged when such exchange will promote better utilization and economical management of the lands involved.[19]

So far, however, very few exchanges have actually been completed in New Mexico and Arizona, or, it might be observed, anywhere else in the West. Data supplied to the writer in December, 1941, by the regional office of the Grazing Service in Albuquerque showed that only about 11,000 acres of private land and 2400 acres of state land had been exchanged in New Mexico, whereas applications were pending on almost 179,000 acres of the former and about 25,000 acres of the latter. These aggregate but a tiny fraction of the potential exchanges in the state. The writer examined the records of the District Land Offices in Santa Fe and Phoenix for sample parts of the "checkerboard" region and found that only a few exchanges had been completed by the end of 1941 in either the Arizona or New Mexico segments. Officials of the Grazing Service and others whom the writer interviewed are convinced that exchanges will be made slowly and that it will take many years to formulate and execute a comprehensive consolidation program in this territory. The task

[19] *The Grazing Bulletin*, March, 1940, p. 9.

of appraising public and private lands is an enormous one, because it involves detailed field surveys over large areas; this seems to be the principal difficulty at present. The Taylor Act requires that federal and private lands be exchanged on an equal-value basis, which makes appraisal necessary. To trade lands with the states is simpler in this respect, for such transactions may be made either on equal-acreage or equal-value terms. The acreage basis does not require appraisal, and state exchanges can be facilitated by taking advantage of this provision of the law. But the states must face another problem; the revenues from specific lands have been allocated to designated state institutions, and it is obviously a difficult task to make wholesale exchanges without upsetting the distribution of these funds.

Exchanges under the Taylor Act have been handicapped, too, by the amount of bureaucratic machinery which has to operate on them. The General Land Office and the Grazing Service must pass on all applications; in some instances other government agencies, such as the Forest Service, the Indian Office, and the Soil Conservation Service, must also give approval. The General Land Office typically moves slowly, and its records are sometimes awkward to work with as well as unclear. The ownership status of some lands in the Atlantic & Pacific Railroad grant area is still in doubt. One gets the impression, too, that coöperation between the General Land Office and the Grazing Service is far from perfect.

Some qualified observers whom the writer consulted in the Southwest question the desirability of eradicating completely the alternate-section pattern of federal holdings. To do so, they argue, would weaken rather than strengthen the conservation program which is being developed for critical watershed districts. The intermingling of private and public ownership, it is held, requires private owners to coöperate with the federal range and soil conservation plans, whereas large consolidated holdings would enable the private owners to dissociate themselves from these programs. On grounds of expediency there is merit to this position. The writer believes, however, that it will be better in the long run to implement the exchange program and to insure conservation by other methods. Highly strategic lands can be kept in public ownership. Those which are consolidated in private hands through exchange can be subjected to a more rigorous and effective conservation policy than is possible under present laws, where the public interest is held to transcend the rights of individual property owners. It must be admitted that this implies a comprehensive land-planning program for the whole region and a much greater degree of coördination among the various federal agencies, as well as between federal and state departments, than prevails at the present time. Indeed, the current multiplicity of government agencies with some authority on land questions is a bureaucratic stumbling block to the development of integrated land-use policies.

Exchange of ownership, as we have seen, proceeds slowly. Meanwhile, more orderly use of lands in "checkerboard" districts can be achieved by exchange-of-use and similar agreements, or by leases. Contracts have been made with the Southern Pacific Land Company since 1937, under which the Grazing Service administers over 200,000 acres of railroad land in Utah and about 2,000,000 acres in Nevada. Late in 1941 negotiations were under way with the Santa Fe Pacific Railroad Company whereby the Grazing Service could lease railroad lands through the Pierce Act. Such agreements cannot constitute a permanent solution of the land-use problem in these areas, for the railroad companies may sell lands at the end of the contract period and in this way break up the established land-use arrangements; but they can be temporarily very valuable and at the same time pave the way for ownership consolidation.

The Taylor Act undoubtedly provides a mechanism for improving tenure and use conditions in the "checkerboard" area, as in other parts of the western range country, and the law can be fitted into a broader program of land planning to be worked out by the National Resources Committee or a similar government agency. There is need for such a program, or rather a set of regional programs,[20] for the

[20] The regions can probably be best defined in terms of drainage basins because land and water are the most important resources exploited in most of the western states. For example, the manner of exploiting the Colorado River plateaus intimately affects the agricultural districts and power development potentialities of the lower Colorado River

western states if their natural resources are to be preserved for permanent use. The writer believes that these plans should be worked out as quickly as possible, before new institutional arrangements become thoroughly crystallized under the Taylor Act. Stockmen have a strong voice in the determination of Grazing Service policies; for example, the grazing district advisory boards, composed of local stockmen, have great weight in the present setup. This is not to be condemned *per se*. Indeed, it may have been necessary at the outset to get the coöperation of the livestock operators, but it must be recognized as a potential threat to the public interest in conservation. It seems fair to say that the Grazing Service has adopted more of the short-run viewpoint of the commercial stock raiser than seems wholesome for long-run conservation policies. Perhaps this viewpoint will shift, but unless it does so before new groups of "vested interests" have been established, the opportunities of attaining desirable land-use adjustments will be seriously restricted.

---

basin. On the importance of applying the regional concept to land planning, see Carl O. Sauer, "Land Resource and Land Use in Relation to Public Policy," in *Report of the Science Advisory Board, July 3, 1933 to September 1, 1934*, pp. 173–260.

LIST OF WORKS CITED

ARIZONA STATE LAND COMMISSION. *Report, June 6, 1912, to December 1, 1914* (Phoenix, 1914).

ARIZONA STATE PLANNING BOARD. *Reports,* II (n.p., 1936).

ATCHISON, TOPEKA & SANTA FE RAILROAD COMPANY. *Annual Report of the Board of Directors for the Year Ending December 31, 1884* (Boston, 1885).

BARNES, WILL C. *The Story of the Range* (Washington, 1926).

CLAWSON, MARION. "The Administration of Federal Range Lands," in *Quarterly Journal of Economics,* LIII, pp. 435–453.

COMMISSIONER OF INDIAN AFFAIRS. *Statistical Supplement to the Annual Report for the Fiscal Year Ended June 30, 1940* (n.p., n.d.).

GATES, PAUL W. "American Land Policy and the Taylor Grazing Act," *Land Policy Circular,* October, 1935 (mimeo.).

HAGERMAN, H. J. *Navajo Indian Reservation,* 72d Cong., Sen. Doc. 64 (Washington, 1932).

HIBBARD, BENJAMIN H. *A History of the Public Land Policies* (New York, 1924).

ICKES, HAROLD L. "The National Domain and the New Deal," in *The Saturday Evening Post,* CCVI, December 23, 1933, pp. 10 ff.

MOSK, SANFORD A. "Land Policy and Stock Raising in the Western United States," in *Agricultural History,* XVII, pp. 14–30.

NATIONAL RESOURCES BOARD. *Report on Land Planning,* pt. 7, "Certain Aspects of Land Problems and Government Land Policies" (Washington, 1935).

NEW MEXICO STATE COMMISSIONER OF PUBLIC LANDS. *Sixteenth and Seventeenth Annual Reports for the two years ending November 30, 1916* (Albuquerque, 1916).

NEW MEXICO STATE COMMISSIONER OF PUBLIC LANDS. *Eighteenth Annual Report for the Fifth Fiscal Year, ended November 30, 1917* (Santa Fe, 1917).

OSGOOD, ERNEST S. *The Day of the Cattleman* (Minneapolis, 1929).

PRESIDENT'S COMMITTEE. *Report on the Conservation and Administration of the Public Domain,* January, 1931 (Washington, 1931).

REEVE, FRANK D. "The Federal Indian Policy in New Mexico, 1858–1880," in *New Mexico Historical Review,* XII, pp. 218–269; XIII, pp. 14–49, 146–191, 261–313.

SAUER, CARL O. "Land Resource and Land Use in Relation to Public Policy," in *Report of the Science Advisory Board, July 3, 1933, to September 1, 1934* (Washington, 1934).

SECRETARY OF THE INTERIOR. *Annual Report for the Fiscal Year Ended June 30, 1938* (Washington, 1938).

SECRETARY OF THE INTERIOR. *Annual Report for the Fiscal Year Ending June 30, 1940* (Washington, 1940).

STABLER, HERMAN. "Rise and Fall of the Public Domain," in *Civil Engineering,* II, pp. 541–545.

THORNBER, J. J. *Grazing Ranges of Arizona,* Arizona Agricultural Experiment Station, Bulletin No. 65 (Tucson, 1910).

UNITED STATES BUREAU OF THE CENSUS. *Eleventh Census, 1890,* Compendium, pt. 3 (Washington, 1897).

UNITED STATES CONGRESS. *Congressional Record,* LXXX, pt. 9 (Washington, 1936).

UNITED STATES CONGRESS. 58th Cong., 3d sess., Sen. Doc. 189, *Report of the Public Lands Commission* (Washington, 1905).

UNITED STATES CONGRESS. 73d Cong., 1st sess., Sen. Doc. 12, *A National Plan for American Forestry* (Washington, 1933).

UNITED STATES CONGRESS. 74th Cong., 2d sess., Sen. Doc. 199, *The Western Range* (Washington, 1936).

UNITED STATES CONGRESS. Subcommittee of Senate Committee on Indian Affairs, 71st Cong., 3d sess., *Survey of Conditions of the Indians in the United States*, pts. 17 and 18 (Washington, 1931–1932).

UNITED STATES CONGRESS. Subcommittee of Senate Committee on Indian Affairs, 75th Cong., 1st sess., *Survey of Conditions of the Indians in the United States*, pt. 34 (Washington, 1937).

UNITED STATES CONGRESS. Senate Committee on Public Lands and Surveys, 69th Cong., 1st sess., *Grazing Facilities on Public Lands* (Washington, 1926).

UNITED STATES CONGRESS. Subcommittee of Senate Committee on Public Lands and Surveys, 69th Cong., 1st sess., *National Forests and the Public Domain*, pt. 4; pt. 13 (Washington, 1926).

UNITED STATES CONGRESS. Senate Committee on Public Lands and Surveys, 72d Cong., 1st sess., *Granting Remaining Unreserved Public Lands to States* (Washington, 1932).

UNITED STATES CONGRESS. Senate Committee on Public Lands and Surveys, 76th Cong., 3d sess., *Amending the Taylor Grazing Act* (Washington, 1940).

UNITED STATES CONGRESS. Subcommittee of Senate Committee on Public Lands and Surveys, 77th Cong., 1st sess., *Adminstration and Use of Public Lands*, pt. 1 (Washington, 1941).

UNITED STATES DEPARTMENT OF THE INTERIOR. *Decisions*, LIII (Washington, 1933).

UNITED STATES DEPARTMENT OF THE INTERIOR, Grazing Service. *The Grazing Bulletin*, March, 1940; April, 1941.

UNITED STATES GENERAL LAND OFFICE. *Circular No. 850* (Washington, 1922).

UNITED STATES GENERAL LAND OFFICE. *Circular No. 1208* (Washington, 1930).

WOOTON, E. O. *Factors Affecting Range Management in New Mexico*, United States Department of Agriculture, *Bulletin* No. 211 (Washington, 1915).

WOOTON, E. O. *The Public Domain of Nevada and Factors Affecting Its Use*, United States Department of Agriculture, *Technical Bulletin*, No. 301 (Washington, 1932).

WOOTON, E. O. *The Relation of Land Tenure to the Use of the Arid Grazing Lands of the Southwestern States*, United States Department of Agriculture, *Bulletin* No. 1001 (Washington, 1922).

INDEX

Arizona State Land Commission, 15
Atchison, Topeka & Santa Fe Railroad Co.,
12
Atlantic & Pacific Railroad Co., 11
Aztec Land & Cattle Co., 12, 24, 25, 28

Barnes, Will C., 33 *n.*

Calkins, Hugh G., 54
"Checkerboard" tenure pattern, 8–9, 19, 21,
31; land-use problems, 33–43
Collier, John, 14, 16 *n.*, 20
Consolidation of holdings
desirability of, 59–60; exchanges, 45–48;
impediments to, 48–52; methods used,
45; under Arizona bill, 57; under Taylor
Act, 57, 58–59

Dry farming, 5–6

Exchange of holdings
authorized by Taylor Act, 53; impediments to, 48–52, 58–59; legislation, 45–46
Exchange-of-use agreements, 60

Gates, Paul W., 5, 39 *n.*, 42
Grazing districts, 53–56
Grazing Service
area under jurisdiction of, 53; established, 53; exchange program, 58; policies, 61; problems in "checkerboard"
areas, 9; records of ownership, 53

Hagerman, H. J., 14 *n.*, 46, 47, 50
Hibbard, B. H., 11 *n.*, 34
Homesteads
anticipation of Taylor Act, 30; "colonizing agents," 29–30; failures, 6; handicap
to use of area, 36; mingling with Navajo
allotments, 37; motives for filing, 29, 35,
50; stoppage of, 30, 50
Hualapai Reservation
controversy settled, 23; established, 20–
21; railroad holdings in, 21; segregation
of holdings, 22

Ickes, Harold L., 35 *n.*
Indian Appropriation Act (1921), 46
Indian Rights Association, 22

Land policy, national
critique of, 5; new policy under Taylor

Act, 52; objectives of, 4–5; relation to
range depletion, 5–9
Lee, Laurence F., 33
Lieu land scrip, 45

McKinley Land & Lumber Co., 27
Mexican land grants, 30–31
Mineral rights, 50–51

National forests
administration of private lands in, 28;
homesteads in, 28; railroad lands in, 27;
state lands in, 28
National Resources Board, 5 *n.*, 29 *n.*
Navajo allotments
Arizona bill, 57; handicap to use of area,
36–37; impediment to exchanges, 49;
Indian Office policy, 17, 18–20
Navajo Reservation
area of, 13; Arizona bill, 48, 51, 57;
boundaries poorly defined, 15; extension
of, 14–17, 45, 47–49, 54–55, 57; Hagerman report, 47; impediments to extension of, 47; New Mexico bill, 48, 53;
original area, 14
Navajo Reservation Act (1934), 16
Navajo tourist trade, 56–57
New Mexico & Arizona Land Co., 13, 24, 25
New Mexico Sheep and Wool Growers'
Association, 20

"Open range" tradition, 38

Pierce Act (1938), 53
Public domain
disposal of, 6–7; fencing of, 34–35, 38;
lack of regulation, 6–7, 31; leasing of,
53; nature of, 31; proposal to give public
domain to states, 51–52; report of President's Committee (1931), 52
Public Lands Commission (1905), 6–7

Railroad land grants, 11
Range depletion, 2–3, 38, 39, 42, 43
Reeve, Frank D., 14 *n.*
Regional land programs, need for, 60–61
Rutledge, R. H., 9, 56

St. Louis & San Francisco Railroad Co., 12
Santa Fe Pacific Railroad Co., 12, 21, 22,
28, 42
Sauer, Carl O., 61 *n.*

[65]

PUBLIC LANDS, POLITICS, AND PROGRESSIVES:

The Oregon Land Fraud Trials, 1903-1910

John Messing

Public Lands, Politics, and Progressives: The Oregon Land Fraud Trials, 1903–1910

JOHN MESSING

Now connected with the Stanford Law Review, *John Messing wrote this paper as a student at Princeton.*

IN OREGON AND CALIFORNIA in the last half of the nineteenth century swindlers and speculators found that government lands could be obtained by fraudulent operations, and that the sale of such lands for the timber or grazing areas which they possessed was highly profitable. In 1902 the government began to investigate the land frauds; in short order a series of prosecutions was instituted against the offending parties. In the course of the trials, numerous prominent political officials were exposed and tried. The trials, it should be noted, are not only interesting as a part of the history of conservation, but also as an example of the way in which the themes of conservation and progressivism were intertwined.[1]

Fraud was not unusual on the public domain. Ever since the Civil War, the government had given away vast tracts of land to settlers and railroads in the hope that these land grants would spark the development of regions of small farmers serviced by the intercontinental railroads. Settlers were promised land if they would homestead a tract for a certain period of time. The railroads were also promised alternate parcels of ten to twenty sections along the right of way of their lines.[2]

---

[1] I would like to thank both Professor Malcolm J. Rohrbough (formerly of Princeton University and now of the University of Iowa) and Mr. J. A. O'Callaghan (of the Bureau of Land Management, Department of the Interior, Washington, D.C.) for their assistance in the preparation of this paper.

[2] See the following materials issued by the Bureau of Land Management, Department of the Interior: *1862–1962: Trans-Continental Railroad Land Grants; 1862–1962: The*

The laws had not operated as intended. By the middle of the nineteenth century, the American farmer was normally a cash-crop farmer and a businessman. Few settlers wanted to establish subsistence farms as the early American colonists had done; instead, they wanted cash, and they often indulged in land speculation for their profits. Since the number of entries a single farmer could make under the homestead law was unlimited until 1888, many settlers made their livings by establishing claims, selling them to another farmer or a corporation, and moving on to establish another claim. From 1860 to 1900, it is estimated that for every entry made by a bona-fide farmer, nine bogus claims were filed.[3]

The topography of the Far West further complicated matters. Whereas the Middle West was suited for small farms, the regions of the Far West beyond the 100th Meridian were suited for commercial cattle-raising, lumbering, and mining ventures which necessitated greater capital than the average settler possessed. The scarcity of water in most regions precluded the possibility of widespread farming belts, and great numbers of honest homesteaders failed in their ventures. The "dummy" entryman, hired at the behest of the railroad, local cattleman, or lumbering company was the successful claimant.[4]

The conditions within the General Land Office facilitated the subversion of the land laws. With the passage of the Homestead Act and related legislation, the business of the office had greatly increased. From 1860 to 1900, the agency was in charge of the greater portion of the lands owned by the government. Yet the machinery of the office was too antiquated to perform the job efficiently. Crowded quarters, inadequate personnel, overburdened officials, low pay, and rapid turnover of clerks characterized the agency. Both in Washington and the District Land Offices, influence, friendship, family ties, and money were essential for the proper expediting of a claim. Under such condi-

---

Homestead Law; and *The Public Lands: A Brief Sketch in United States History.* These pamphlets contain a great deal of useful information on the history of the public lands. A good secondary source is Roy M. Robbins, *Our Landed Heritage,* (Princeton, 1942), chaps. 15 and 16.

[3] Richard Hofstadter, *The Age of Reform: From Bryan to F.D.R.* (New York, Vintage Books, 1960), 45, 55.

[4] See "Report of the Public Lands Commission Created by the Act of March 3, 1879: Relating to Public Lands in the Western Portion of the United States and to the Operation of Existing Land Laws," House Executive Document 46, 46th Cong., 2nd sess., for a complete discussion of these problems. An excellent analysis is Paul Wallace Gates, "The Homestead Law in an Incongruous Land System," *American Historical Review, XLI* (1935), 652–681.

tions, speculators and corporations desiring large tracts of valuable land at low prices had little difficulty in getting their share.[5]

Particularly relevant to the Pacific Northwest were the fraudulent transactions committed under the Timber and Stone Act and the Forest Reservation Act of 1897. The Timber and Stone Act had been passed to help the settler get timber and stone from lands contiguous to his claim. Specifically, it provided the lands not valuable for agriculture might be sold in tracts not exceeding 160 acres for $2.50 per acre. Under the system of "bogus" entries practiced in the West, the law had provided a convenient method whereby thousands of acres of valuable timber lands in the far Northwest had passed at a fraction of their value into the hands of corporations. Under one provision of the Forest Reservation Act of 1897 the so-called lieu land provision, persons settling or owning lands to be included in proposed forest reserves would have the option of retaining their lands or exchanging them for an equal amount of land on the remaining public domain. The exchanges were by acres and not value of the lands involved, so that ordinarily valuable lands were retained by the owners, while worthless ones were dumped upon the government. Moreover, speculators often invested in worthless lands near proposed forest reserves in anticipation of exchange. If they had political contacts, they frequently persuaded or bribed officials charged with creating the reserve to include their lands within the boundaries.[6]

By the turn of the century, government officials were ready to reevaluate the policies of the last forty years. In 1897, the President was given the power to make forest reservations, although as we have noted, the lieu land provisions of the Forest Reservation Act created the means for further abuses. At the same time, the Forestry Service was created in the Department of Agriculture,[7] and while the service had no control over the reserves (still managed by the Land Office in the Interior Department), foresters at least provided a measure of protection against fire and erosion within the forests.

The assassination of President McKinley brought Theodore Roosevelt to the White House, and the Roosevelt administration fostered

---

[5] See Harold H. Dunham, "Some Crucial Years of the General Land Office: 1875–1890," *Agricultural History*, XI (1937), 117–141, for further details.

[6] See "Report of the Public Lands Commission of 1903–1905," Senate Document 189, 58th Cong., 3rd sess., v–vii, xv–xvi. See also, House Report 445, 58th Cong., 2nd sess., 1–4.

[7] Bureau of Land Management pamphlet, *The Public Lands: A Brief Sketch in United States History*, 66.

the new movement. Gifford Pinchot, the chief forester, conducted a vigorous campaign to improve the public relations of the service. Eventually he hoped to wrest the forest reservations from the pernicious control of the General Land Office (located in a different department, the Interior Department).[8] The President supported conservationists like Pinchot. Secretary of the Interior Ethan A. Hitchcock, though reluctant to give the new forest reserves to the Agriculture Department, shared the President's views.[9]

If Hitchcock favored conservation, his Commissioner of the General Land Office, Binger Hermann, did not. In fact, Hermann strongly resented Hitchcock's active interest in the affairs of the Land Office, preferring his own control. Hermann's motives were two-fold. A great deal of evidence suggests that Hermann had participated in some of the land frauds (although he was never convicted for his activities) and feared exposure. His pride entered into his resistance as well, for he was a prominent Oregon politician—he had been the receiver of a local land office, a state senator, a representative to Congress from 1884 to 1897, commissioner of the General Land Office for years, and a close friend of President McKinley (to whom he owed his appointment).[10]

Hitchcock was not without allies in the General Land Office. Hermann had maintained a feud with Assistant Attorney General Van Deventer for years regarding some lands which were to be included in the early forest reserves. Hermann (as we have noted) was a prominent Oregon politician and had a great many friends who wanted their lands included within the reserves. Van Deventer was prominent in Wyoming and was similarly obliged to guard the interests of his constituents. Hermann's supporters had prospered from the creation of the reserves; Van Deventer's friends had suffered. The feud had raged between the two ever since. Assistant Commissioner of the General Land Office Richards, like Van Deventer, was from Wyoming. A former Governor of Wyoming, he was a close friend of Van Deventer and he generally opposed Hermann within the Land Office. Because of his extensive political influence he could not be removed. He was, moreover, ambitious, and he saw in Hitchcock's new activism

---

[8] Gifford Pinchot, *Breaking New Ground* (New York, 1947), 158, 160.
[9] *The Dictionary of American Biography*, IX, 74–75.
[10] From the testimony of Binger Hermann in *U.S. v. Binger Hermann* (for conspiracy to defraud the government) as quoted in the Portland *Oregonian*, Feb. 1, 1910, 1. Hereinafter cited as the *Oregonian*.

a means both of repaying Hermann for the Van Deventer affair and of getting Hermann's job.[11]

In 1902, Richards got his chance. The General Land Office had received several letters from Joost H. Schneider of Tucson, Arizona, who claimed to be the employee of a land fraud ring working on the Pacific Coast, principally northern California and Oregon.[12] The ring, Schneider claimed, was run by a pair of California real estate agents, John Benson and F. A. Hyde. The Benson-Hyde ring secured worthless school lands owned by the states by fraudulent means, and then bribed officials of the General Land Office to have these lands included in proposed forest reserves. The lands were then exchanged for valuable government lands under the lieu land provisions relating to the creation of forest reservations.[13] Schneider claimed that he was writing solely for revenge upon his former employers.[14]

Schneider's letter was ignored at the Land Office, and when he received no answer, he wrote again. As before, he received no reply. He then went to his attorney who wrote to Hermann directly. Hermann pocketed the letter and the correspondence, probably fearing that an investigation would expose his own activities.[15] One of the Schneider letters came while Hermann was on vacation and was referred to Assistant Commissioner Richards, who sent a special agent to investigate the charges according to the standard procedure of the Land Office. Hermann arrived back in time to intercept the agent, and sent

[11] New York *Times*, Dec. 30, 1902. This is an article written at the time of Hermann's resignation.

[12] Actually the Land Office had received a previous letter exposing the activities of the Benson-Hyde ring. The letter probably had been ignored because it had been signed "an American Citizen." *Oregonian*, Jan. 26, 1910, pp. 1 and 12.

[13] The conspiracy was exposed before the complicated transactions had been completed. Secretary Hitchcock ordered that all Benson-Hyde lieu selections be suspended pending investigation when the frauds were reported to him. At that time, only one-twelfth of the government lands applied for under the lieu land provisions had been patented. Commissioner of the General Land Office Ballinger to the Secretary of the Interior, Feb. (?), 1908, National Archives, General Land Office files, File 2-36 partl. In July, 1907, one employee of the Land Office estimated that if "the conspiracy had been entirely consummated, the sale of the lands selected in lieu of the school lands in forest reserves would have yielded the conspirators a profit of between $3.00 and $5.00 per acre, or a total of between $1,329,000 and $2,215,000." Also in File 2-36, part 1.

[14] See Lincoln Steffens, "The Taming of the West, Part I," *American Magazine*, LXIV (Sept., 1907), 493. Hereinafter cited as "Taming," I.

[15] Hermann later claimed (during one of the trials) that he had withdrawn the Benson-Hyde correspondence because he suspected that Hyde and Benson had hired agents within the Land Office. If the letters were left in the file, Hermann claimed, these agents would alert the ring. The government showed, however, that at the same time that Hermann withdrew these letters, he was urging that several other Hyde claims in Oregon be brought to patent. *Oregonian*, Jan. 26, 1910.

him on various errands. In September of 1902, despite Hermann's interference, the special agent finally interviewed Schneider.[16] Hermann filed the report when it arrived in November, hoping to avoid further action.[17] But Richards or one of his subordinates came across the report about six weeks later and he notified Secretary Hitchcock of its contents. Hitchcock sent his private secretary for Hermann, with an order that Hermann deliver the report. Livid with rage, he cross-examined Hermann about his activities,[18] and subsequently, with the permission of the President, he asked Hermann for his resignation.[19] Hermann begged to be allowed to remain until February, and Hitchcock agreed. The decision proved to be a mistake, for in the interim Hermann destroyed files and letterbooks which might have been used in evidence against him.

To investigate the conditions in the report thoroughly, agents were sent to California and Oregon. Special Agent Steece and Arthur Pugh (a clerk for Van Deventer in the Department of Justice) were sent to California. On the way, they stopped at Tucson to talk with Schneider. When they arrived, however, they found him uncooperative, and they had little luck in California as well. To assist the Interior Department, William J. Burns (later founder of the Burns Detective Agency and predecessor to J. Edgar Hoover in the F.B.I.), an agent in the Secret Service, was assigned to the case. Burns remained in Washington to study the operation of the Land Office, and then went to California to work exclusively on the Benson-Hyde cases.[20]

The agents assigned to Oregon, Special Agents Greene and Linnen, had better luck. While they found little evidence relating to the Benson-Hyde ring, they uncovered a second land fraud operation. The Oregon ring was much newer than the Benson-Hyde group and ran a smaller operation. At the head of the ring was Franklin P.

---

[16] Steffens, "Taming," I, 494–495.

[17] Chief Clerk of the Land Office Forestry Division McGee later testified that when he received the report, he took it directly to Hermann. Hermann, he claimed, asked him rather blandly what ought to be done. McGee replied that if the report were true, one of the most stupendous frauds ever committed had been revealed. Hermann said that he wished to keep the report confidential, for he wished to take care of the matter without the knowledge of the Secretary. *Oregonian*, Jan. 27, 1910.

[18] Hitchcock and his private secretary both claimed that Hermann was asked for the report; Hermann on the other hand maintained that he willingly delivered it. *Oregonian*, Feb. 8, 1910.

[19] Henry S. Brown, "Punishing the Land Looters," *The Outlook*, LXXXV (Feb. 23, 1907), 429.

[20] Steffens, "Taming," I, 497–500.

Mays, a prominent Portland attorney and state senator, Steven A. D. Puter, a lumber assessor (or cruiser), and Horace G. McKinley, a minor speculator in timber lands. The group worked together from the beginning of 1900.[21]

The exposure grew out of a private transaction between McKinley and a father and son who wanted to invest in timber lands. The son, Clyde D. Lloyd, commissioned McKinley to secure lands for him in western Oregon. McKinley had just taken a trip to the East, and he needed money desperately. He and Puter had just completed a fraud upon the government for lands to be included very shortly within a forest reserve. They had transferred the title to the lands to a third party pending sale, but had not yet recorded the deeds.

McKinley, however, could not wait for the sale of the lands. In a fit of desperation, he sold one of the unrecorded claims (to which he did not hold title either legally or fraudulently) to Lloyd, fully intending to buy back the claim when he had money once more. Soon he found that Puter was delaying his share of the proceeds from another transaction. Once he had sold one piece of property to Lloyd to which he did not hold title, McKinley found it easy to sell several others. In short order, he sold three more such pieces of property to Lloyd, collecting $1800 for all four claims. Puter learned of McKinley's activities, and he rushed to the recorder's office to file his own deeds in an attempt to stop Lloyd from successfully filing the McKinley deeds. When Lloyd tried to record his deeds, he naturally was unsuccessful. Not knowing of Puter's connection with McKinley, Lloyd went to Puter for advice. Puter sent him to Mays (the Portland attorney who was a member of the ring), and Mays advised Lloyd that he did not have a case against McKinley.

Matters became more complicated when the elder Lloyd, who had supplied the money, arrived on the scene. Lloyd likewise sought the advice of Puter and Mays, but he was not satisfied with their counsels. Unfortunately for the ring, Lloyd's visit coincided with the arrival of Greene and Linnen, sent to investigate the Benson-Hyde ring. The Lloyds revealed the whole story to Greene, and the special agents investigated the claims and found them indeed suspicious.[22]

---

[21] S. A. D. Puter and Horace Stevens, *Looters of the Public Domain* (Portland, 1908), 73–78. Puter wrote this book while in prison for the frauds with the help of Stevens, who was formerly a government employee.

[22] From testimony before the grand jury by Lloyd and others, quoted in the *Oregonian*, Dec. 22, 1904.

Greene and Linnen made a complete investigation of the Eugene Land Office (where the ring had operated) and found evidence that the United States Commissioner, Marie Ware, had been involved in some of the land frauds. Miss Ware resigned when confronted with the evidence, and three clerks in the office were removed.[23] In addition, the agents found that the ring had in the course of its operations fraudulently obtained two large tracts of government land. They felt that the evidence warranted prosecution of the ring.

The two cases are described by Puter in his book. The so-called "11-7" case started when the government opened the lands in Township 11 South, Range 7 East, for entry in 1900. These lands were soon to be incorporated within the Cascade Forest Reserve being formed for Oregon, and the ring realized that it might get valuable scrip if it could get title to the lands in the township. Since the homestead requirements were retroactive for those settlers in the township who had settled before the area had been surveyed and officially opened, the ring only had to hire persons to fraudulently claim that they had been living in the area for the required period of time. Once the claims of these fictitious settlers were patented, deeds would be made out to one of the settlers—Emma Watson, a local widow and an intimate acquaintance of Puter. The ring picked certain tracts on a remote peak of Mt. Jefferson in the Cascade Mountain Range for the operation in order to discourage investigation by the authorities. Dan Tarpley, a local attorney, was hired to keep track of the claims and to make the necessary arrangements to prevent any exposure of the ring. Clerk Montague of the local land office agreed to report developments within the land office which might affect the status of the claims.

Despite these careful preparations, there was a great deal of difficulty in getting the claims to patent. Puter was approached by a total stranger who demanded $50 to keep quiet about the operation. Someone filed a complaint against the entries, and Special Agent Loomis of the land office was sent to investigate. The ring gave him $1000 for his "expenses" for going out to examine the claims. Rather hypocritically, the ring supplied him with a guide who took him to a different area filled with bona-fide settlers. His favorable report was not enough for the General Land Office, and Superintendent of the

[23] Judge Bellinger to United States Attorney Hall, May 5, 1903, National Archives (hereinafter cited at NA), Department of Justice Central Files (hereinafter cited as DJ), 1903–6442.

Cascade Forest Reserve Ormsby was asked to look into the matter. Ormsby was paid $1000 as well, but still the claims were delayed. Puter and Mrs. Watson went to Washington to enlist the aid of Senator Mitchell of Oregon early in 1902, armed with a letter from Mays. Through Mitchell's influence with Binger Hermann, the claims were expedited immediately thereafter.[24]

Despite the difficulties that they had encountered, the ring members were heartened by their success, and when a second region was opened to entry, Township 24 South, Range 1 East, also within the proposed reserve, they repeated their operation. This time however, the ring decided to dispense with actual settlers, for McKinley's girl friend, Marie Ware, was the United States Commissioner for the Eugene Land Office. According to Puter, Miss Ware agreed to expedite the claims for $100 per claim. Again the deeds were transferred to Mrs. Watson. Six of the claims were patented, and three of them were disputed claims that McKinley sold in panic to Clyde Lloyd.[25]

The special agents of the land office, to whom the Lloyds had told their story, pieced together the activities of the ring, and by the end of April, 1903, they felt that they had enough evidence to warrant indictment. The case was turned over to the United States Attorney for Oregon, John Hall. On June 3, McKinley and Ware were arrested. By late October, Hall had prepared the cases, and on October 27, indictments were returned against Dan Tarpley, Ware, McKinley, Puter, and several lesser members of the ring for their parts in the "24-1" deal.[26]

Hall then wired Attorney General Knox asking for a special assistant attorney to help in the prosecution of the case, for Hall's calendar was crowded with a number of cases.[27] Hall named a local man, D. J. Malarkey, a prominent Oregon Republican whom he preferred, and Senators Mitchell and Fulton of Oregon urged Malarkey's appointment. Attorney General Knox chose to ignore such recommendations, and asked his good friend Francis J. Heney of San Francisco to take the case.[28]

---

[24] This episode is traced in detail in Puter, *op. cit.*, 46–65.

[25] *Ibid.*, 67–72.

[26] New York *Times*, Oct. 28, 1903. F. P. Mays was not indicted, nor was he mentioned in any of the indictments.

[27] Hall to Knox, Oct. 31, 1903, NA, DJ, 1903-6442.

[28] Attorney General Knox and Secretary of the Interior Hitchcock worked together on the fraud cases, and they distrusted the Oregon Senators. Hermann had returned to Oregon after his resignation and had successfully run for his old seat as U.S. Representative when the incumbent, Congressman Tongue, had died. Knox and Hitchcock believed

Heney's career prior to his appointment had been rather colorful. Heney's parents had moved to San Francisco while he was an infant and had settled in the city's immigrant section known as "South of the Slot." There Heney spent the remainder of his boyhood days. As a youth he regularly engaged in street fighting and he even joined a street gang. If he was wild he was also ambitious, and despite his father's insistence that he leave school to work in the family furniture store, he completed his education and became a schoolteacher. For one term he taught school in northern California; once he had saved enough money, he returned to San Francisco and enrolled in the University of California. In his freshman year he was expelled for fighting with another student and for several months thereafter he taught school, worked in mines and mills, and drank and gambled as he wandered through the Pacific Northwest. Eventually he drifted into Silver City, Idaho, where he worked as a law clerk. Convinced that he wanted to be a lawyer, he returned to San Francisco and enrolled in the Hastings School of Law. After graduation, he went to Arizona in an effort to cure chronic sciatica he had contracted in an Idaho mine. His brother, Ben, owned a ranch outside of Tucson and Frank worked on the ranch for the next several years, herding cattle, running a small Indian trading post that he owned with his brother, and participating in the final battles against the renegade Apache leader Geronimo. In 1888, he moved into Tucson to establish a law practice and his practice flourished. Taking advantage of a split in the local Democratic Party he became a prominent politician and was made Territorial Attorney General in 1892. A reformer, he created a great deal of opposition within the Administration, and when the split was healed within the party, he was forced to resign. Shortly thereafter he left Arizona and politics (disgusted with both) and returned to San Francisco to establish another law practice.[29] For seven

that an honest investigation would expose Hermann, and that the Oregon congressman would try to prevent such an exposure. The appointment of a fellow Republican to conduct the case might be the solution for Mitchell and Fulton. Knox's disregard of the Oregon Senators was highly unpopular in Oregon, and to make matters worse, he appointed C. A. S. Frost as Heney's assistant. Frost had been convicted and subsequently pardoned for his part in the Nome (Alaska) conspiracy in 1901. The reaction in Oregon to the Heney-Frost appointment was great. See the *Oregonian*, Nov. 30, 1903, and Dec. 7, 1903.

[29] Arizona *Daily Star*, 1888–1895 (inclusive dates); interview with Ruth Heney (Heney's niece) Tucson, Arizona, Dec. 28, 1963; Lincoln Steffens, "The Making of a Fighter," *American Magazine*, LXIV (Aug., 1907).

years he built up his practice and by 1903 he was making on the average $30,000.00 per year.[30] Heney was a good choice for the job. Blond, peppery, quick to take offense yet cautious if the situation demanded, Heney was a fighter. If the evidence was strong, Heney would properly present it. If it was not so strong, then he would argue brilliantly to make it appear conclusive. If it was weak, then he would argue at length until it seemed at least persuasive. Under no circumstance would he capitulate. He was, moreover, a devoted and honest man, and if the evidence led to Hermann, then Heney would doggedly pursue Hermann until he was convicted. Heney accepted Knox's offer on November 6, 1903, mainly because he envisioned a short trial of two to three weeks[31] and because he had recently refused an offer from Knox to become regular Assistant Attorney General and he regretted his decision. Hitchcock was immediately notified of the appointment[32] and Hall was requested to postpone the hearings on the demurrers of Puter, McKinley, *et al.* for a week until Heney arrived. Hall did not, claiming that the court refused to grant a postponement, but the demurrers were overruled anyway.[33]

Heney was prepared for trial when he arrived in Portland, but he found that the case had been postponed, for the defendant Emma Watson (to whom all the fraudulent claims had been transferred) had disappeared. Heney was not disturbed by the delay, for it gave him extra time to prepare the case. But when he conferred with Hall, he found Hall prepared to treat him as an assistant. Hall, moreover, refused to consider prosecution of the ring in the "11-7" case, preferring instead the much weaker "24-1" indictment. Hall might have been under pressure from the Oregon senators, for his appointment as United States Attorney had expired, and he needed Senatorial good-will for re-appointment. At the moment, Heney chalked Hall's behavior up to professional jealousy. When he went to talk with Greene, he found the special agent totally uncommunicative. Furious

---

[30] Heney to Attorney General Knox, telegram, June 28, 1906, NA, DJ, 1903-6442-S24. Heney had become friendly with Knox in 1901, when he had defended those accused in the Alaska Nome conspiracy mentioned earlier.

[31] Lincoln Steffens, "Taming of the West, Part II," *American Magazine*, LXIV (Oct., 1907), 586.

[32] Hitchcock to Knox, Nov. 7, 1903, NA, Land and Railroad Letterbook of the Interior, 1902–1903.

[33] Hall to Knox, telegram, Nov. 16, 1903, NA, DJ, 1903-6442-S1.

at the turn of events, Heney wired Knox for a personal interview in Washington, and since there was nothing for Heney to do in Oregon pending the arrest of Mrs. Watson, Knox agreed. At the meeting, Heney assured Knox that Hall seemed to be acting from professional jealousy only, and to clothe Heney with the necessary authority to command Hall's respect, Knox appointed him Special Assistant Attorney General and wired Hall that Heney was to be in charge of the cases. Heney also visited Secretary Hitchcock while in Washington, and Hitchcock sent a strong letter to Greene telling him to cooperate fully with Heney.[34]

At this conference with Hitchcock, Heney was first introduced to detective Burns, who was now making great progress in the Benson-Hyde cases. Burns' work, in fact, was nearing completion. After his initial observations of the Land Office (during which time he forced the confession of a clerk in the Land Office), Burns travelled to California. There his overwhelming evidence forced the confession of Forest Superintendent B. F. Allen, who admitted that he had adjusted the boundaries of the proposed reserves to include Benson-Hyde lands. Armed with this information, Burns went to Tucson to interview Schneider, whose original letter had started the investigations, but who had subsequently become uncommunicative. With the help of the local postmaster, Burns got Schneider to reveal what he knew.[35] By the time he returned to Washington, Burns had enough information in his possession to implicate the heads of Division P of the Land Office, Harlan and Valk, who were charged with making the lieu-land selections.[36] When exposed they confessed their parts in the scheme and offered their services to Burns.[37] This is what had occurred up to the time of the Heney-Hitchcock-Burns meeting.

About two weeks after the meeting Harlan accepted a bribe of $500 from the leader of the ring, Benson, who had come to Washington anxious to find information about the progress of the investigation. The bribe had been taken under Burns' close supervision in order to trap Benson, and immediately afterwards Benson was arrested. But Benson was clever and, disregarding his bond he fled

---

[34] Steffens, "Taming," II, 587–588.
[35] Tucson *Citizen*, June 20, 1908.
[36] Harlan and Valk, according to Valk's later testimony, worked together for Benson until Harlan (who was his superior) refused to divide the fees. Thereafter they individually worked to push the Benson-Hyde claims to patent. *Oregonian*, Jan. 26, 1910.
[37] Steffens, "Taming," II, 503–504.

to New York, where he hoped that he could not be removed to Washington. Upon his arrival in New York, he was held pending removal proceedings. Shortly afterwards, Hyde and Dimond (who was the attorney for the group) were arrested in San Francisco pending removal to Washington, where they had been charged with conspiracy to defraud the government.[38]

The scattered arrests of the defendants greatly complicated the task for the prosecution, for removal proceedings had to be completed before the actual trial of the cases could take place. The Benson removal proceeding was adjudicated first before Judge Lacombe, United States District Court Judge for the Southern District of New York. The United States Attorney for New York presented the government's case in a rather inept fashion, and Judge Lacombe denied the motion to remove Benson. According to Lacombe's opinion, the government had failed to prove conspiracy in the indictment filed in the District of Columbia court. It might be true, reasoned Lacombe, that the defendants had committed fraud upon the State of California when they hired persons to make fraudulent entries upon California school lands. But the exchange of these lands for the federal lieu lands was according to law, and the United States had no cause of action against Benson. Benson was freed on bail pending appeal by the government.[39]

The failure of the government in this first removal case jeopardized the entire conspiracy case, for the California courts might accept the Lacombe ruling and refuse to extradite Hyde and Dimond as well. In that case, the defendants would never be brought to trial in Washington before the District of Columbia Court. All the spare legal talent at the disposal of the Attorney General's office was committed to the impending California removal cases. Heney was still waiting for the start of the Oregon cases, for although Mrs. Watson had been found in Chicago, arrested, and removed to Oregon, an important witness, Hobson, had subsequently disappeared, and the cases had been postponed once more. He too was assigned to the Benson-Hyde removals.[40] Heney and Arthur Pugh argued the cases for the govern-

---

[38] New York *Times*, Dec. 19, 1903.
[39] Opinion of Judge Lacombe, transcript, NA, DJ, #25366, Box 6.
[40] See the following telegrams in the Justice Department files: Heney to Attorney General Moody, April 4, 1904; Heney to Moody, April 27, 1904; Heney to Moody, May 4, 1904; Hall to Moody, May 2, 1904; Hall to Moody, May 16, 1904; Hall to Moody, May 17, 1904: All are in NA, DJ, 1903-6442-S1. It is interesting to note the comment of the *Oregonian* as the date for the California removal hearings drew near: "This is conceded

ment before Judge DeHaven of the Northern California District Court. On September 2, 1904, Judge DeHaven ruled for the government notwithstanding the Lacombe decision. The next day, the Circuit Court of Appeals sustained DeHaven and overruled the Lacombe interpretation. The defendants had defrauded the United States, said the Circuit Court, because they had exchanged lands with imperfect titles (that is, those lands fraudulently obtained) for lands with valid titles. The United States had been robbed in the bargain.[41] The defendants were ordered to Washington pending appeal to the Supreme Court of the United States.

Heney, Pugh, and Oliver Pagin of the Justice Department travelled to New York to reargue the Benson case before Judge Lacombe. The United States Attorney for New York, Henry L. Burnett, whose blunders had caused the original unfavorable decision, convinced Judge Lacombe to reconsider the case in the light of the California Circuit Court decision. Lacombe however, refused to hear further oral argument. On October 10, 1904, after reading the supplementary briefs, Lacombe affirmed his previous decision. Rather than wasting further time by appealing the case to the New York Circuit Court of Appeals, the Justice Department decided to combine the Benson removal case with those for Hyde and Dimond, and to argue the three simultaneously before the Supreme Court, which had scheduled the Hyde and Dimond cases for February 21, 1905.[42]

With work finished on the Benson-Hyde cases for the present, Heney rushed back to Oregon to prosecute the "11-7" case, for the missing witness, Hobson, had been found. Burns was now finished with his work on the Benson-Hyde cases, and recognizing the detective's capabilities, Heney invited him to work on the Oregon cases. With Hitchcock's permission, Burns agreed. When they arrived in Oregon, the pair began to investigate the frauds thoroughly. From this investigation, two facts became apparent: that the Oregon congressional delegation was somehow involved in the frauds as Hitchcock and Knox had anticipated, and that United States Attorney Hall was reluctant to implicate any members of the delegation. Act-

---

to be the greatest Federal case ever conducted on the Pacific Coast, and attorneys will undoubtedly fondle it for many moons." May 14, 1904.

[41] Heney to Moody, Sept. 3, 1904; Heney to Moody, Sept. 4, 1904; Opinion of Judge Morrow (Circuit Court), transcript; all are in NA, DJ, #25344, Box 6.

[42] Burnett to Moody, Sept. 21, 1904; Pugh to Moody, Oct. 13, 1904; NA, DJ, #25366, Box 6.

ing upon the assumption that Hall feared that his commission would not be renewed, Heney persuaded the President to disregard the candidates proposed by the delegation and to renew Hall's commission without first consulting Senators Mitchell and Fulton.[43] According to the *Oregonian* the reappointment did not solve the problem, and Hall's suspect activities continued.[44] Heney and Burns began to gather evidence to implicate Hall in the frauds as well.

The "11-7" case came to trial about a week after Hall's reappointment, and although Hall was the central figure for the prosecution for the first few days, Heney took control shortly thereafter. Heney spent several days establishing that Puter and Mrs. Watson had lived together as man and wife and had traveled together under various assumed names in order to show that they had conspired together to defraud the government. Once this initial conspiracy was established, the other members of the ring (with the notable exception of Mays, who had been shielded by Hall) were connected to it by reliable testimony.[45] The case reached a climax when the guide who had conducted Ormsby on his trip to investigate the claims, but who had instead taken him to another area, was produced. Nervous, highly agitated, and sometimes close to hysteria, the guide related how he had become involved with the ring, how he had tried to quit but had not been permitted, and how he had been eventually exposed.[46] The defense presented no witnesses, and at the close of the case, one of the defendants changed his plea to guilty. At Heney's request, Miss Ware was released, for although she had been involved in the "24-1" transaction, she had little to do with the "11-7" case. On December 6, 1907, the remainder of the group was convicted by the jury.[47]

---

[43] *Oregonian*, Nov. 13, 1904.

[44] *Oregonian*, Jan. 2, 1905. According to Steffens, Heney was rather naive about Hall, while Burns suspected him all along. Supposedly, Hall revealed himself one day, when he called an important witness that Heney and Burns were investigating aside. Afterwards, the witness was uncommunicative. Though more dramatic than the *Oregonian* version, the Steffens account seems the less likely of the two. Steffens, "Taming," II, 588, 593–594. Hall was later removed from office upon Heney's recommendation.

[45] *Oregonian*, Nov. 26, 27, 29, Dec. 1, 1904. In this connection it is interesting to note that Binger Hermann, when called to the stand could not "remember" his own correspondence with Senator Mitchell relating to the Puter claims. Mitchell's response was interesting too—he refused to come to the trial or reveal Mays as the attorney who had recommended Puter to him. *Oregonian*, Nov. 24, 1904.

[46] *Oregonian*, Dec. 4, 1904.

[47] *Oregonian*, Dec. 7, 1904. The group was not sentenced so that the members of the ring could testify in subsequent cases. Before these cases could come to trial, the members

Plans were made immediately to prosecute the ring for the "24-1" transaction, but on December 15, this case was continued until the spring.[48] Events of the past several days had modified the plans of the prosecution greatly. Burns had been investigating the frauds thoroughly, and on December 15 and 16 he forced the confessions of several participants in the crimes. The first to confess was Forest Superintendent Ormsby. Ormsby revealed that he had been part of a conspiracy to create the Blue Mountain Forest Reserve for Oregon. Hermann had contacted him (while still commissioner of the General Land Office) and had directed him to meet with F. P. Mays (the attorney and state senator connected with the Puter ring). Mays had informed Ormsby that a great deal of money had been invested in the lands in the area, and had supplied Ormsby with the money, maps, and data needed to create the reserve. When Ormsby was nearly indicted, Senator Mitchell had contacted United States Attorney Hall and the case had been dropped. For his services, Ormsby had received two sections of land which he had later sold for one thousand dollars apiece.[49]

The following day, deserted by his former colleagues and angered because Mays had gone free, Puter likewise confessed.[50] He told Burns that when he had gone to Washington with Mrs. Watson in 1902 to see Senator Mitchell, he had bribed the senator, for the "11-7" claims had been so suspicious that the Land Office had refused to patent them. Panicked, Puter had rushed to the senator's office and had explained his problem to Mitchell, offering him two $1,000.00 bills to get the claims to patent. Mitchell had at first sym-

---

of the ring disappeared. Puter's fraudulent dealings in state lands were soon exposed, and he fled to escape trial by the state. He was nearly captured in Boston by Burns, but in a fashion reminiscent of the "old West," he drew a gun and escaped. He was later captured in California where he allegedly was trying to obtain an interview with Heney. He was returned to Oregon, where he was sentenced under the "11-7" conviction to the maximum that the law allowed. Later he was pardoned upon Heney's recommendation. *Oregonian*, Dec. 12, 13, 1905; March 27, May 21, June 8, and July 7, 1906. According to a correspondent from the *Oregonian*, McKinley married Miss Ware, but then left her in California and fled to the Orient to escape punishment in the company of the notorious belly dancer, "Little Egypt." *Oregonian*, April 13, 1906. He later returned to testify for the government.

   [48] *Oregonian*, Dec. 15, 1904.

   [49] Burns to Attorney General Moody, telegram, Dec. 15, 1904, NA, DJ, 1903-6442-S2.

   [50] The *Oregonian* of Dec. 20, 1904, claims that on the night of December 12 all the defendants convicted in the "11-7" case, joined by Miss Ware (about to be tried in the "24-1" case), met and decided to reveal everything in order to prevent further conviction in the "24-1" case. Evidently, the other defendants must have changed their minds, for Puter alone confessed to Burns.

pathized with Puter, offering to help him for nothing and saying, "Mr. Puter, you cannot afford to pay me such a sum as this." Puter, however, had wanted to take no chances with his claims, and had finally convinced the senator to take the money. Through Mitchell's influence with Binger Hermann, the claims had been patented shortly thereafter.[51]

With confessions of Ormsby and Puter and the evidence gathered by Burns, Heney felt that he could secure the conviction of the prominent individuals "higher-up" involved in the frauds. From the correspondence, it becomes obvious that Heney took the initiative in pressing prosecution of the group, while Burns and the Federal Judge Bellinger were reluctant to tackle the prominent citizens of Oregon.[52] On December 20, Heney wired the Department of Justice asking for permission to commence proceedings. The next day, the Attorney General wired back that Heney could proceed with the backing of the Interior and Justice Departments if he felt that he could secure convictions.[53]

The focus of interest now shifted to the grand jury which had been called originally to deal with the faulty indictments in the "24-1" case. This grand jury, perhaps conveniently entitled the "long grand jury," sat from December, 1904 to April, 1905 (except for a period in February and March while Heney was in the East to argue the Benson-Hyde cases before the Supreme Court). Numerous indictments returned by this long grand jury were to form the basis of the Oregon prosecutions as they progressed until 1910.[54]

Four cases of major importance were brought before the grand jury.[55] The first concerned Senator Mitchell. Mitchell had used his influence with Binger Hermann to expedite claims for Fredrick A. Kribs, an agent for an Eastern capitalist. Kribs had worked indirectly with Mitchell through Mitchell's law firm, Mitchell & Tanner. Kribs

---

[51] Burns to Moody, telegram, Dec. 16, 1904, NA, DJ, 1903-6442-S2; also Puter, *op. cit.*, 63–65.

[52] Burns to Moody, telegram, Dec. 18, 1904, NA, DJ, 1903-6442-S2.

[53] Heney to Moody, telegram, Dec. 21, 1904; Moody to Heney, Dec. 21, 1904, NA, DJ, 1903-6442-S2. According to Puter, Heney did not have sufficient evidence at the time. Puter claims that he finally gave Heney a substantial lead by revealing that an agent for an eastern capitalist had conducted systematic bribes with Mitchell by check. Puter, *op. cit.*, 184–186. Actually, Heney knew of Kribs' (the agent) activities, and Kribs was appearing before the grand jury.

[54] Puter, *op. cit.*, 442–454, contains a convenient summary of the work of the long grand jury.

[55] There were numerous indictments growing out of these investigations, but only the most significant will be related here.

had paid the firm for claims which Mitchell had guaranteed would be patented by the Land Office. He had, moreover, paid the firm by check, and the government had the checks as evidence against Mitchell. Mitchell's partner, Judge Tanner, appeared before the grand jury and testified that Kribs had paid the firm solely for work that Tanner had performed for him. He produced a partnership agreement, moreover, in which he and Mitchell had agreed that Mitchell should receive no funds paid to the firm for any representation by Tanner before any government agency in Washington. The agreement was dated 1901. Tanner's son (a stenographer for the firm) corroborated his father's testimony. Nonetheless, evidence presented before the grand jury pointed to Mitchell's guilt, and he was indicted on February 1, 1905, for accepting a bribe.[56]

The Tanner testimony had some interesting ramifications. Tanner and his son subsequently were indicted for perjury, but still they remained adamant.[57] They were exposed, however, when Mitchell's private secretary, Harry C. Robertson, arrived and testified that the partnership agreement reported by Tanner was false. Furthermore, Robertson revealed a letter from Mitchell that he was to deliver to Tanner but which had been intercepted by the government.[58] The letter essentially was a series of instructions relating to Tanner's testimony. At the end of the letter appeared the phrase "burn this without fail." [59] Tanner thereupon confessed all to save his son, and the "burn this" letter was entered into evidence.

[56] *Oregonian*, Feb. 2, 1905. Mitchell denied the accusations vehemently, and when the story of Puter's confession was first told, he appeared on the floor of the Senate to answer Puter's charges in person. See Congressional Record, XXXIX, 58th Cong., 3rd sess., 959–963.

[57] Under examination before the grand jury, Tanner's son denied that the 1901 agreement was fraudulent and that he had recently drawn it for use in the Mitchell case. Some shrewd detective work showed that the paper had not been manufactured in 1901 and that the ink had not been used by the firm at that time. Furthermore, the words "salary" and "constituent" were misspelled in the agreement, and Tanner's son misspelled these same words on the stand. The pair however refused to change their stories. *Oregonian*, Feb. 12, 1905.

[58] The government was informed of the letter by a disappointed office-seeker named Max Pracht. Pracht had relied upon Mitchell to get him a job, but arrived in Washington after Mitchell had been indicted. Mitchell had used him as a messenger to deliver the "burn this" letter to Robertson, and he had opened the letter to read it. He recognized its importance, and contacted the Treasury Department, telling them that it was on the way to Oregon. He later was hired by the Treasury Department as his reward. *Oregonian*, Feb. 22, 1905.

[59] The effect of the "burn this" letter and the Tanner confession upon Mitchell's standing with his fellow senators was disastrous. Few now believed his protestations of innocence.

The second case brought before the grand jury involved United States Representative John Williamson, Dr. Van Gesner (his partner in the sheep business), and United States Commissioner Biggs (of the land office at Prineville, Oregon). Williamson and Van Gesner, the government claimed, had induced settlers to enter valuable sheep lands under the Timber and Stone Act which they desired to use as summer grazing land for their sheep business. For years, the company had leased lands intermingled with these government lands from a wagon road company. Recently settlers had begun to settle on the government lands. To prevent the settlement of the range, Van Gesner and Williamson hired the United States Commissioner at the local land office, Biggs, to employ settlers to make fraudulent claims and to see that such claims were brought to patent. Van Gesner Williamson, and Biggs, were indicted for subordination of perjury on February 11, 1905.[60]

The third case involved the Blue Mountain conspiracy. According to the prosecution, several state senators—George Sorenson, Willard Jones, H. A. Smith (by that time deceased) and F. P. Mays (of the Puter group)—had purchased worthless school lands in the hopes that these lands would be included within a proposed forest reserve to be created by the federal government. When the group had found that the reserve might not be created, Mays had contacted Hermann, and Hermann had directed that Forest Superintendent Ormsby meet with Mays. Ormsby's son had learned of the proposed reserve, and had conspired with Dan Tarpley and Horace McKinley (both of the Puter ring) to purchase state school lands in the proposed reserve intermingled with those of Mays and his friends. He hoped that either Mays would pay outrageous prices for the lands, or the lands would be exchanged for valuable federal lieu-lands. At the same time, news that a railroad was going to build a line through the region had caused a general rush for the vacant lands. Convinced that their interests were threatened, Mays and his fellow conspirators used their influence as state senators with Williamson, Mitchell, and Hermann to get a temporary withdrawal of the lands from further homestead entry. For their parts in the conspiracy, Williamson, Mitchell, Hermann, Mays, Sorenson, and Jones were indicted on February 13, 1905.[61]

---

[60] *Oregonian*, Feb. 12, 1905. See also Puter, *op. cit.*, 339–342.
[61] *Oregonian*, Feb. 14, 1905. The plot was foiled by Forestry Service Chief Gifford

The fourth case involved the Butte Creek Land, Livestock, and Lumber Company in Wheeler County, Oregon. Like Williamson and Van Gesner, the officials of the company found that lands which customarily had been used for grazing purposes had recently been invaded by homesteaders. Like Van Gesner and Williamson, the officials of the company urged fictitious settlers to settle the land first. When the company realized that such tactics could not stem the tide of settlement, it hired a small army of armed guards to keep the settlers out.[62] One settler had written to the Land Office for years complaining about the activities of the company, but while Hermann had been commissioner nothing had been done. Once Hermann resigned the case came to the attention of Secretary Hitchcock and special agents assigned to the case found that indeed the complaints were justified. They discovered, moreover, that Hall had not prosecuted the officials of the company because of the political pressure placed upon him by the attorney for the company, F. P. Mays. On February 10, 1904, Mays, Hall, Hermann, and the officials of the company were indicted for conspiracy to defraud the government.[63]

The exposures and indictments of the high officials and prominent figures in Oregon brought retaliations and plots to discredit those associated with the prosecutions. The secretary of the grand jury disappeared in the midst of the proceedings, and according to the *Oregonian* his disappearance was related to the intrigue of the defense.[64] Hall and a private detective tried to arrange for Heney's indictment in a state court for alleged illicit relations with Miss Ware, but Miss Ware and others approached by the conspirators revealed what they knew to Burns.[65] The Republican Party of Oregon (to which most of the offenders belonged) tried to persuade President Roosevelt to remove Heney, claiming that he was a California Democrat trying to ruin Republicanism in Oregon, but Roosevelt, though afraid that Heney was somewhat imprudent and dangerous, was willing to give him a chance to prove his case.[66] Heney was opposed

---

Pinchot. He reported to Hitchcock that the lands to be included within the proposed reserve were worthless. Hitchcock thereupon withdrew the plans for the creation of the reserve, and the conspirators were left with worthless school lands. After the repeal of the lieu land provisions of the Forest Reservation Act, the reserve (containing bona-fide lands) was approved on July 15, 1906.

[62] *Oregonian*, Aug. 3, 1906. See also Puter, *op. cit.*, 357–367.

[63] *Oregonian*, Feb. 11, 1905.

[64] *Oregonian*, Jan. 24, 1905. Phelps later returned and was discharged.

[65] *Oregonian*, Feb. 13, 1905. The conspirators were indicted for attempting to intimidate a public officer, but were never tried.

[66] Elting E. Morison, ed., *The Letters of Theodore Roosevelt* (Cambridge 1951), IV,

by popular opinion, Inspecter Greene of the land office, and the friends of the conspirators and freely admitted that he had forced Robertson to testify about the "burn this" letter to improve the public relations of the prosecution.[67] The attempts to remove Heney, though annoying, proved unsuccessful, and the cases were scheduled for early trial.

With the work of the grand jury nearly completed, Heney went to Washington to argue the Benson-Hyde-Dimond removals before the Supreme Court with Solicitor General Hoyt and Arthur Pugh. The cases were argued on February 21 and 23. The Benson removal was argued first. Benson should be removed, the prosecution charged, because the indictment spelled out a proper charge of bribery of an official of the land office. The issue of the proper basis for a charge of conspiracy was carefully avoided. The Hyde-Dimond case was then argued, the government claiming that the California courts had properly decided the issue of conspiracy. On April 17, the Supreme Court upheld the government in the Benson case;[68] on May 29, the Court again upheld the government in the Hyde-Dimond case.[69] The ring would be brought to trial.

Heney then rushed back to Oregon to complete the grand jury investigations. After a recess for the summer, at the end of June, 1905, the first and most important of the land fraud trials, that of Senator Mitchell, commenced. Heney literally buried the defense under a mass of documentary evidence and corroborating testimony. Kribs took the stand first and identified checks and agreements between the firm of Mitchell & Tanner and himself. Tanner then took the stand and for three days related the particulars of his dealings with Kribs, and Mitchell's role in the transactions. Finally as the

---

1176–1177, Roosevelt to Senator Charles W. Fulton, May 13, 1905. Roosevelt's attitude towards Heney at this time is clearly shown in relation to the appointment of a federal district judge for Oregon. Roosevelt, writing to Hitchcock, said "It is very important that we should not get into an improper position by seeming to go to extremes in backing Heney. You doubtless remember the trouble that came in connection with Bristow's letting his zeal run away with his discretion. Heney will do us a like turn sure as fate if we get to following him." *Ibid.*, 1300–1302, Roosevelt to Hitchcock, August 14, 1905. Later, after the successful prosecution of the cases, Roosevelt was to change his mind about Heney, and for many years thereafter they were close friends.

[67] Heney to Attorney General Moody, telegram, Dec. 20, 1904, NA, DJ, 1903-6442-S2. Also, Heney interview in Washington, printed in the *Oregonian*, Feb. 20, 1905.

[68] *Oregonian*, April 18, 1905. The Benson case is reported as *Benson* v. *Henkel*, 198 *U.S.* 1.

[69] *Oregonian*, May 30, 1905. These cases are cited as *Hyde* v. *Shine*, 199 *U.S.* 63 and *Dimond* v. *Shine*, 199 *U.S.* 88.

last in the trio of witnesses, Mitchell's private secretary, Harry Robertson, testified, and he corroborated the points made by Kribs and Tanner. He also related the story of the "burn this" letter. The defense in reality had no defense and relied upon the specious point that Mitchell had dispensed numerous favors to other parties without pay. The closing arguments on both sides were superb[70] but the evidence favored the prosecution and on July 3, 1905, at 11:00 P.M. (after eight hours of deliberation) the jury returned the verdict of guilty with a recommendation for leniency.[71] Mitchell was sentenced on July 25 to six months in jail, a $1,000.00 fine, and complete disbarment from public office. An appeal was entered on the grounds that the conviction was unconstitutional. According to the defense, the crime was a misdemeanor and not a felony, and according to the Constitution, Section 6, Article 1, a United States Senator may not be prevented from attending to his duties except for conviction in a felony. Clearly the conviction and sentence were illegal.[72] On December 8, 1905, before the case could be heard by the Supreme Court, Mitchell died of complications following a tooth extraction.[73]

Mitchell seems to have been the victim of his times. "Mitchell belonged to a passing generation which did not comprehend the change in public temper. He was caught in a shift of public mores, which is a cruel thing." [74] He never seemed to understand why he was being

---

[70] The defense made repeated indirect appeals to Mitchell's old age and long record of public service. One of Mitchell's attorneys, ex-United States Senator Thurston nearly fouled the case for the prosecution when he asked Heney 1) why Kribs had not been indicted if his bribes were actually performed, and 2) why Mitchell had not been indicted for perjury for his testimony before the grand jury, subsequent to the confession of Tanner. Heney revealed the next day that Kribs's crimes were beyond the statute of limitations, and that Mitchell had been indicted for perjury but that the indictment had not been returned by the grand jury in the haste of the last few days. This was a close call for the prosecution according to the *Oregonian*.

[71] For the trial, see the *Oregonian*, June 22–July 4, 1905, which included complete stenographic accounts of the proceedings. One juror apparently held out for Mitchell for five ballots but was compromised by the plea for mercy. It is important to remember that Mitchell was tried for accepting a bribe from Kribs, not from Puter, whose confession had brought Mitchell under the close scrutiny of the government.

[72] *Oregonian*, July 25 and 26, 1905.

[73] *Oregonian*, Dec. 8 and 9, 1905. The Senate flew the flag at half-mast, but refused to adjourn out of respect for Mitchell. This was a new precedent, and probably was a reaction to the wave of convictions against senators that year. *Oregonian*, Dec. 12, 1905. The government was likely fortunate that the case never was heard by the Supreme Court. Mitchell attorneys raised some very sound points about the sufficiency of the indictment and the rulings of the trial judge, and the court might well have overturned the conviction.

[74] J. A. O'Callaghan, *The Disposition of the Public Domain* (Washington: Senate Committee on Interior and Insular Affairs), 1960, p. 92.

prosecuted and he allegedly cried to his private secretary, Harry Robertson, "Harry, you know they hadn't ought to prosecute me for that. All I ever got was some little checks." [75] The verdict was a shock to him, and according to contemporary observers nearly caused him to break down in court.[76]

The trial of Congressman Williamson, his partner Dr. Van Gesner, and ex-Commissioner Biggs followed immediately after the trial of Mitchell. The polish of the Mitchell trial was lacking: the first few witnesses could not "remember" key events, and the presentation of the case seemed faulty. Although subsequent witnesses proved more cooperative and a great deal of documentary evidence was entered in support of the charges, the prosecution was weak. The defense admitted that Williamson and Van Gesner had bought lands from settlers and had loaned money to them, but denied that any contract either implicit or express had been made before the patents for the lands had been issued. If the settlers had committed perjury, then they had done so without the knowledge of the defendants. The defense further maintained that the alleged connection of Biggs had not been proven. It was indeed a weak case, and after forty-two ballots, on July 20, 1905, the jury announced that it could not reach a verdict.[77]

The second trial started two days later. The case proceeded smoothly, but the contentions and evidence offered by both sides scarcely differed from the first trial. Under the strain of the summer heat and the first inconclusive verdict, the summations degenerated into a clash of personalities and a rash of accusations. Heney accused the defense of tampering with the witnesses; defense counsel Bennett likened Heney both to an old gossip ready to besmirch the virtue of his neighbors and to a modern Don Quixote slashing at windmills. Heney in turn called Bennett a coward and asserted that he ought to be disbarred. Again the jury could not reach a verdict, and after thirty ballots the jurors were dismissed by the court.[78]

The third trial started after the summer. Judge DeHaven (who had presided at the earlier proceedings) had been replaced by Judge Hunt, and Hunt started the proceedings with a ruling favorable to the prosecution. DeHaven had ruled that according to the indict-

---

[75] Testimony of Robertson, *Oregonian*, June 27, 1905.
[76] *Oregonian*, July 4, 1905.
[77] *Oregonian*, July 18–21, 1905.
[78] *Oregonian*, July 23–Aug. 5, 1905.

ment, only subordination of perjury relating to the filings of the claims, and not to the final proof and patent was relevant. This had seriously weakened the prosecution, for a great deal of evidence had been thereby excluded. Hunt ruled that evidence relating to the final proof was relevant. The witnesses gave stronger testimony than in the earlier trials, and one witness even admitted that he had given his earlier testimony in a fashion designed to favor the defendants. The defense, on the other hand, presented a much weaker case than in the earlier trials. One witness, called to show that Gesner had refused to enter into such transactions, was shown on cross-examination to be an unsavory character and the half-brother of a recently convicted murderer. Williamson changed parts of his testimony, and fearing that the end was near tried to shift all responsibility upon Gesner. The closing arguments avoided all traces of personality clashes and character assassinations, and on September 28, 1905, the defendants were convicted after six hours of deliberation.[79] On October 14 the sentences were delivered by the court: Williamson and Biggs were given jail sentences of ten months and fines of $500 apiece; Van Gesner was given only five months and $1000 fine because of his age and former reputation.[80] Williamson appealed, on the grounds that the conviction prevented his attendance in Congress, in much the same manner as had Mitchell.[81]

Heney left for Washington after the conviction of Williamson and his associates to try the land fraud cases pending in the District of Columbia courts—the Benson-Hyde cases and the case against Binger Hermann for his destruction of the letterbooks and the files of the Interior Department. In Washington, Heney was approached by a San Francisco editor, Fremont Older, who had for years opposed the corrupt rule of the Union-Labor government in San Francisco. Older had been greatly impressed by Heney's Oregon successes, and he remembered a speech that Heney had made lambasting the San Francisco Union-Labor party and its boss, Abraham Ruef, during the

[79] *Oregonian*, Sept. 7–Sept. 28, 1905.
[80] *Oregonian*, Oct. 15, 1905.
[81] The Supreme Court granted Williamson a new trial upon appeal. The case became a leading one in interpreting the Timber and Stone Act because the court invalidated the conviction on the grounds that contracts made by settlers to sell the claims before filing were illegal, while those made between filing and final proof were legitimate. See *Williamson* v. *U.S.*, 207 *U.S.* 425. Williamson was never retried, nor was he ever tried for his part in the Blue Mountain conspiracy.

recent municipal elections.[82] The Union-Labor party had smashed all opposition at the polls, and in December of 1905, Older went to Washington to talk with Heney about prosecuting the municipal officials for accepting graft. After getting provisional pledges of support from Heney and Burns, and a promise from Roosevelt to release the pair from their Oregon obligations when the time was right, Older returned to San Francisco to raise funds for the prosecution.[83] By February, 1906, Burns had begun to work on the case, and Heney had begun to conclude his immediate obligations to the government so that he might start the San Francisco prosecutions as soon as possible.

Prime among Heney's list of obligations was the trial of Binger Hermann for his destruction of the files and letterbooks. Hermann had repeatedly stalled the proceedings, threatening to invoke his congressional immunity (to which he was not entitled, for this crime was a felony, but which would have delayed trial while the matter was appealed through the courts). Provisionally the trial had been set for April 25. One week before the trial, on April 18, 1906, the San Francisco earthquake and fire struck.[84] Heney had three sisters in the city, and he wished to return to the Bay Area as soon as possible. Suddenly Hermann's attorneys pressed for an immediate trial. The court granted a delay, and Heney returned to San Francisco. Since the case was not to come to trial until June 11, Heney went to Arizona to complete some law business of this own. There he received a telegram that Hermann's attorneys had succeeded in getting the trial date pushed up to June 7. The change made it impossible for Heney to arrive in Washington in time, and if he was to try the case, he would have to get the agreement of Hermann's attorneys. They refused to agree to a delay unless Heney agreed to try Hermann in Washington for the letterbook charge before trying him in Oregon on the Blue Mountain indictment. Heney reluctantly consented, for he was planning to try the Blue Mountain conspiracy during the summer and now he would be forced to try Hermann at a later date.[85]

---

[82] Heney's speech is reported in the *Oregonian*, Nov. 5, 1905.

[83] Fremont Older, *My Own Story* (New York, 1926), 74–75.

[84] Heney's sisters were safe, but he lost his office and his rather extensive law library in the fire. Heney to Attorney General, April 20, 1906, NA, DJ, 1903-6442. A good account of the fire and earthquake is given in A. L. A. Himmelwright, *The San Francisco Earthquake and Fire* (New York, 1906).

[85] *Oregonian*, Heney interview, July 6, 1906.

He had little luck in getting the Benson-Hyde cases to trial as well, for the defense had interposed numerous technical objections to proceeding to trial, and had appealed the rulings of the courts when these motions had been denied.[86]

Anxious to finish at least a major portion of the untried cases, Heney rushed back to Oregon. There he tried several minor cases, principally those against the employees of the Butte Creek Company in an attempt to lay the foundation for the cases against the company officials.[87] In July, the Blue Mountain conspiracy trial of Mays, Jones, and Sorenson (all former state senators) began. For twenty-five days the opposing counsel battled. Finally on September 13, 1906, the jury brought in a verdict of guilty.[88] Anxious to begin the San Francisco prosecutions, Heney left the remainder of the trials to the newly appointed United States Attorney for Oregon, William Bristol.[89]

For the next few years, Heney had little to do with the land fraud cases. His San Francisco work consumed most of his time.[90] He maintained contact with his associates in Oregon, and occasionally advised them on pending cases, but the pressure of the municipal prosecutions eventually proved too much. In December, 1907, he went to Washington to confer with Attorney General Bonaparte. He asked for his release from his remaining obligations to the government, and Bonaparte agreed if Heney would promise to try the case against former United States Attorney Hall, who had been removed by the President on January 1, 1905, and who had later been indicted in the Butte Creek conspiracy. Heney agreed and went to Oregon with his newly appointed successor, Tracy C. Becker.[91]

---

[86] The defendants were finally tried in 1908 (not by Heney). The jury could not reach a verdict, and, according to the jurors' interviews with the press, was under the impression that a verdict had to be entered. In an attempt to escape the heat of the jury room, the jury split the verdict, acquitting Benson and Dimond and convicting Hyde and (curiously) Schneider. *Oregonian*, Jan. 22, 1910.

[87] *Oregonian*, Aug. 6, 7, 9, 17, 18, and 19, 1906.

[88] *Oregonian*, Nov. 20, 1909.

[89] Bristol in fact owed his appointment to Heney. Later he was accused of acting improperly in his official capacity, and the Senate refused to confirm his appointment. Nonetheless, he was repeatedly reappointed by the President at each congressional session because of Heney's support. *Oregonian*, July 6, 1906.

[90] There are several accounts of the San Francisco prosecutions. One especially well researched account is Walton Bean, *Boss Ruef's San Francisco: The Story of the Union Labor Party, Big Business, and the Graft Prosecution* (Berkeley, 1952). For a contemporary view written by a participating newsman, see Franklin Hichborn, *"The System" as Uncovered by the San Francisco Graft Prosecution* (San Francisco, 1915). A rather colorful historical novel has been written about the prosecutions; see Lately Thomas, *A Debonair Scoundrel: An Episode in the Moral History of San Francisco* (New York, 1962).

[91] Heney to Attorney General Wickersham, Sept. 16, 1909, NA, DJ, 1903-6442-S24.

The prosecution charged that Hall had not prosecuted the Butte Creek company for the illegal enclosure of the disputed range, but had instead instituted civil proceedings to recover the lands. His motives were political. Hall had been warned by F. P. Mays (then a state senator and prominent Republican) not to investigate the Butte Creek company too closely. Furthermore, Hall had found that he could use the collected yet undisclosed evidence to his own advantage. He had threatened George C. Brownell, an aspirant for his job, with exposure in order to get Brownell to withdraw from the race. Heney brought out similar examples of Hall's dereliction of duty, and on February 8, 1908, Hall was convicted for his part in the conspiracy.[92]

Heney was not discharged as promised, however, and at the height of the San Francisco prosecutions, while he was running for District Attorney of the city in 1909, he was forced to resign from his Oregon commission to avoid charges of conflict of interests.[93] With his defeat in the race the prosecutions terminated, for the opposition had declared that it was opposed to the continuance of the trials. Heney was now without employment. Since he had been a loyal Taftite in California in the election of 1908, and since several of the land fraud cases had never been brought to trial, Attorney General Wickersham decided to renew Heney's commission.[94]

Prime among the cases remaining to be tried was that against Binger Hermann for his part in the Blue Mountain conspiracy. Hermann was brought to trial in January, 1910. Although a great deal of evidence was introduced to establish the existence of the Blue Mountain conspiracy, the prosecution had difficulty in linking Hermann to the plot. According to Heney, Hermann had temporarily withdrawn lands to be included in the proposed Blue Mountain reserve because he desired the support of state Senators Mays, Sorenson, Jones (all convicted in earlier trials) and Smith (by that time deceased). Hermann's motives were political: he desired to run for the United States Senate, and according to the electoral laws of the period, he could be elected by the legislature. But even Heney admitted

---

[92] Puter, *op. cit.*, 357–367. The corporation officials were never tried.
[93] Heney to Wickersham, Sept. 16, 1909, NA, DJ, 1903-6442-S24.
[94] *Oregonian*, Nov. 16, 1909. Heney to Wickersham, Nov. 9, 1909, NA, DJ, 1903-6442-S24. Hermann had been brought to trial in Washington for his destruction of the letterbooks while Heney was working on the San Francisco prosecutions. On April 25, 1907, he had been acquitted on the grounds that the files were his own property and not that of the government. A. S. Worthington (Hermann's attorney) to Wickersham, Dec. 14, 1909, NA, DJ, 1903-6442.

that his evidence was inconclusive. Former United States Surveyor for Oregon Henry Meldrum provided the sole link. He claimed that Hermann advised him to invest in certain lands soon to be included within the reserve. But Meldrum's testimony was suspect, for he had been convicted in an earlier trial, and had been recently pardoned by Taft so that he could testify in the Hermann case. In the end, the prosecution was driven to presenting the records of the Benson-Hyde and letterbook trials in an effort to impeach Hermann's reputation. Fortunately for Heney, Hermann's attorneys allowed him to take the stand, and Heney managed to trap him several times on cross-examination. In the closing arguments Heney relied heavily upon Hermann's testimony in the present case and the evidence presented relating to the earlier ones. The defense, on the other hand, maintained that Heney had yet to prove his case. On February 14, the jury reported that it could not reach a verdict, eleven voting for conviction, one for acquittal.[95] Heney claimed that the lone juror (named Selkirk) was a friend of Hermann's son and "Binger's man" on the jury, and the *Oregonian* reported a similar story but claimed that Heney had not heard Selkirk reply "yes" to the question whether or not he had an opinion as to the guilt or innocence of Hermann.[96]

The Hermann case marked the end of the Oregon prosecutions. In September, 1910, Heney decided to drop the remaining charges against Hermann, who was old and ill. Furthermore, the law under which he had been indicted had since been repealed, and there was little to be gained by prosecuting him.[97] Soon thereafter the case against Congressman Williamson relating to the Blue Mountain conspiracy was discharged on Heney's recommendation.[98]

The fraud trials were important for the ending of the flagrant abuses of our public lands. Evidence suggests that the trials were responsible for the repeal of the lieu-land provisions of the Forest Reservation Act in 1905. Bills for the repeal of the provisions were first introduced in the 57th Congress (December, 1903–April 1904).

[95] For the Hermann trial see the *Oregonian*, Jan. 12–Feb. 15, 1910. Judge Wolverton probably allowed Heney so much latitude in the production of testimony from the earlier trials because he owed his appointment to Heney.

[96] Heney to Wickersham, telegram, Feb. 14, 1910, NA, DJ, 1903-6442-S6. *Oregonian*, Feb. 15, 1910. Evidence supports the *Oregonian*. Heney had been shot in the head by an emotionally disturbed person during the San Francisco prosecutions, and had lost his hearing in one ear. Furthermore, when Wickersham suggested that Selkirk be prosecuted for perjury on his *voir dire*, Heney wrote that such a trial would be "dangerous to the government." Heney to Wickersham, Feb. 24, 1910, NA, DJ, 1903-6442-S6.

[97] Heney to Wickersham, Sept. 28, 1910, NA, DJ, 1903-6442-S6.

[98] Heney to Wickersham, March 17, 1911, NA, DJ, 1903-6442-S24.

In its report on the repeal bill, the House Committee on Public Lands commented as one of the reasons for repeal that

Three hundred and forty-three thousand nine hundred and seven acres of the lands relinquished [under these provisions] were California and Oregon school lands, and the Interior Department is now investigating alleged frauds in connection with securing these lands for basis of lieu selections and other fraud and irregularities in connection with lieu lands.[99]

In the final debates on the repeal in the House, one of the sponsors of the bill, Representative Lacey, obliquely referred to the Blue Mountain reserve when he remarked that reserves in the Northwest were being held up in order to prevent frauds from occurring pursuant to the lieu land provisions.[100] Finally on March 3, 1905, the repeal was enacted into law.

The fraud trials also influenced the executive branch of the government. According to Theodore Roosevelt

Throughout the early part of my administration the public lands policy was chiefly directed to the defense of public lands against fraud and theft. Secretary Hitchcock's efforts along this line resulted in the Oregon land fraud cases, which led to the conviction of Senator Mitchell, and made Francis J. Heney known to the American people as one of their best and most effective servants. These land fraud prosecutions under Mr. Heney, together with the study of the public lands which preceded the passage of the Reclamation Act in 1902, and the investigation of the land titles in the National Forests by the Forest Service, all combined to create a clearer understanding of the need of land law reform, and thus led to the appointment of the Public Lands Commission.[101]

The prosecutions, then, helped to shape the active conservation policy of the Roosevelt Administration.

The Oregon trials had an impact upon national public opinion as well. As one of the pieces of mounting evidence, they were im-

---

[99] House Report 2233, 58th Cong., 2nd sess., 2. Heney believed that the trials had a great role in the repeal; Hermann did not. The following exchange between the two during the Hermann trial is illuminating:

‘ "Was it not true," asked Heney, "that no action was taken on the repeal of the bill until Congress heard of the conviction of Puter, McKinley and Tarpley in Oregon?"

‘ "Not one in 25 members of the Congress ever heard of Puter or McKinley," said Hermann.

‘ "Did not Mitchell denounce his own indictment on the floor of the Senate as being brought about by a bunch of land thieves, headed by S. A. D. Puter?" ’

From the *Oregonian*, Feb. 3, 1910.

In his summation, Heney again made the point that the "law was not repealed until the indictments had been returned against these defendants in 1905, resulting in a great clamor from the public." *Oregonian*, Feb. 10, 1910.

[100] Congressional Record, XXXIX, 58th Cong., 3rd sess., 4036.

[101] Theodore Roosevelt, *Theodore Roosevelt: An Autobiography* (New York, 1929), 411.

portant for the rise of conservation, for the old patterns of fraud on the remaining public domain were dramatically exposed, particularly in the sensational trial of Senator Mitchell. The amount and extent of the fraud revealed by the trials and by the subsequent investigation of the General Land Office by Secretary Hitchcock helped to convince the American public that some sort of conservation of our remaining resources was the only sane alternative to the grab-bag encouraged by the antiquated land laws. "The conviction of a patriarchical U.S. Senator from Oregon . . . was due notice that the 'great barbecue' was over." [102]

The trials were vitally important for Heney's later career. His role in the cases gave him nation-wide fame, and led to his employment in the San Francisco graft cases. In addition to his work in San Francisco, Heney later became an important Progressive both in California and national politics.[103] His San Francisco work (for which he received no compensation) and his early work in the progressive movement probably would have been impossible without the small fortune that he received from the government for his services. His time otherwise would have been used to support himself and his dependents, and his ability to devote himself to public service would have been severely curtailed.[104]

---

[102] J. A. O'Callaghan, *op. cit.*, 95. The investigation of the Land Office led to the exposure of frauds in coal lands in Utah, illegal fencings of public lands by cattlemen in Nebraska and Wyoming, and a host of other scandals. For an example of the indignation produced, see the Arizona *Citizen*, April 7, 1905, where the editor remarked "It looks like the Interior Department, of which Ethan Allen Hitchcock, of Missouri, is the head and front, has been so agreeble (*sic*) to the thieves as to call for an investigation of its methods and purposes." The role of the land trials in this respect was negative, for they merely revealed existing abuses and made the public suspicious of the present methods of utilizing our resources. From this aspect, the trials may be said to have laid the foundations of distrust of those in favor of disposition of our public lands, and paved the way for conservation.

[103] See George Mowry, *The California Progressives* (Berkeley, 1951), for a discussion of Heney's role in the progressive movement.

[104] The payments to Heney are recorded in the Justice Department files as follows:

DATE	AMOUNT	CASE
July 16, 1904	$5,000	Hyde-Dimond-Benson
March 10, 1905	7,500	McKinley-Puter
Aug. 10, 1905	5,000	Hyde-Dimond-Benson
Feb. 13, 1906	7,500	Hyde-Dimond-Benson
Aug. 24, 1906	7,000	McKinley-Puter
Aug. 9, 1907	5,000	McKinley-Puter
March 2, 1908	8,000	Hyde-Dimond-Benson
July 16, 1908	10,000	Hyde-Dimond-Benson
Jan. 21, 1909	5,000	Hermann
May 16, 1910	5,000	Hermann and Williamson
Late 1911	2,500	Hermann
Total	$67,500	

The Oregon trials had an impact upon Heney's ideas. The exposures of the Puter ring, the Benson-Hyde ring, and the Mitchell-Hermann group convinced him that the land laws were antiquated and that they should be replaced by laws providing for the conservation of these resources. For the remainder of his career, he was a staunch conservationist and advocated a strong Federal policy towards the nation's public lands.

Heney's Oregon experience had even deeper significance for his later career. The scale of fraud and the heights to which it reached were astounding. During the first days of the long grand jury Heney remarked that

> The extent of the land-fraud cases in Oregon is far greater than I imagined, even after I learned the extent of the Hyde-Benson frauds through my connection with the prosecution of that case. Oregon is under the domination of a corrupt political ring, which hesitates at nothing to achieve its ends.[105]

Six months later, he saw the issue clearly:

> I am after the big fish, and as long as there is a hook and a line or a bit of tackle in the Government box, I will keep after them. Graft is ruining Russia today; graft ruined Rome, the ancient empire of the world, and unless the juries of the Nation sustain the laws of the United States, graft will ruin this country. . . .
>
> One millionnaire in the penitentiary is worth one thousand poor devils he bought, as an example to the world.[106]

Heney in his later years became a radical progressive, espousing governmental ownership of railroads, insurance companies, and telephone and telegraph companies.[107] The seeds of his radicalism are to be found in the Oregon prosecutions. To one trained in the tradition of democracy, where the government works for the benefit of the people and not for the interests of the few, the exposures were disillusioning. To one trained in the law and imbued with a strong sense of professional duty, the willful and systematic violation of the land laws for private gain constituted a heinous crime. Heney nat-

---

This table has been arranged from a memorandum in the Justice Department files and a letter from Wickersham to Heney, March 14, 1911 (the last figure above). It is significant that Heney received these payments at a time when there was little income tax, and the value of the dollar was two or three its present rate. The sum paid to him by the government was sufficient income for many years. See NA, DJ, 1903-6442-S24.

[105] *Oregonian,* Jan. 3, 1905.

[106] *Oregonian,* Aug. 1, 1905.

[107] See Helene Hooker Brewer, "A Man and Two Books," *Pacific Historical Review,* **XXXII** (1963), 221–234.

urally favored strong government in his later years. In Oregon, the only check upon the grafters had been responsible and effective prosecution by the government. From prosecution, it was only a short step to regulation, and Heney took that step. The Oregon prosecutions were the making of a radical.

GEORGE W. JULIAN AND LAND REFORM
IN NEW MEXICO, 1885-1889

R. Hal Williams

R. HAL WILLIAMS

GEORGE W. JULIAN AND
LAND REFORM IN
NEW MEXICO, 1885-1889

On Sunday, August 18, 1889, George W. Julian entered in his journal a review of the results of his four years as Surveyor General of the territory of
New Mexico:

> I look back over my work here during the past four years with the most unqualified
> satisfaction. I can say truly that I have no fault to find with it. If what I have set
> on foot should be carried out it will work out the regeneration of New Mexico. If
> not, the credit of having attempted it will be my sufficient honor and reward. My
> record as Surveyor General ought to be, and I believe will be, historic. It is con-
> spicuously and honorably in contrast with that of every one of my predecessors.

Julian was certain that he had been "a real benefactor to the Territory." [1]
Julian's personal assessment of his "historic" role in New Mexican affairs
is belied by the hostile treatment he has received both from his contemporaries and in the standard histories of New Mexico. The territorial press
dubbed him "Old Malaria" [2] and "that antiquated combination of vinegar,
oil of vitrol and concentrated venom. . . . The damage he has done this territory is simply incalculable." [3] Helen Haines in her *History of New Mexico*
concluded that Julian's actions made matters "infinitely worse" in New
Mexico.[4] And Ralph E. Twitchell has described Julian as a "political
mountebank" whose policy was "a complete failure, owing to its virulence
and partisan political character." [5]
George W. Julian was accustomed to personal obloquy. In earlier years, he
had won national prominence as an abolitionist leader and, from 1848 to
1870, as a Free Soil and Republican Congressman from Indiana.[6] In 1852 he

R. HAL WILLIAMS is a graduate student at Yale University.
[1] Journal of George W. Julian, August 18, 1889, Indiana State Library, Indianapolis.
Hereafter cited as Journal.
[2] William A. Keleher, *Maxwell Land Grant* (Santa Fe, 1942), 125.
[3] San Marcial *Reporter*, quoted in the Santa Fe *Daily New Mexican*, August 21, 1889.
[4] Helen Haines, *History of New Mexico* (New York, 1891), 259.
[5] Ralph E. Twitchell, *The Leading Facts of New Mexican History* (Cedar Rapids, Iowa,
1912), II, 462–463.
[6] For a brief summary of Julian's life, see Paul L. Haworth, "George Washington
Julian," *Dictionary of American Biography*, X, 245–246. The years in Congress were not
continuous. The only scholarly biography of Julian is Patrick Williams Riddelberger's,

71

was selected as the Free Soil Party candidate for Vice President. Later, a position on the Committee on the Conduct of the War, speeches in behalf of
rebel land confiscation, and a prominent role in the attempted impeachment
of Andrew Johnson earned Julian a reputation as a leading Radical Republican.[7] Once his abolitionist goals were accomplished, however, Julian gradually lost sympathy with the party leadership, and in 1872, alienated by
the corruption of the Grant administration, he joined the Liberal Republican movement. Four years later he completed the break with his old party
and became an outspoken Democratic supporter. His appointment to territorial office by Grover Cleveland in 1885 was, in part, recognition for his
recent services to the Democratic party.

In a larger sense, Julian's appointment as Surveyor General of New Mexico
reflected the deep concern of the Cleveland administration over federal
land policy in the West. There was much evidence that, as a New York
Herald editorial expressed it, "Swindling cattle kings, surrounded by a
gang of swindling herders, all of whom are in collusion with swindling
surveyors, have swallowed our Western acres as a gourmand swallows oysters." [8] Determined to end the misappropriation of the public domain,
Cleveland appointed "a born crusader," [9] William Andrew Jackson Sparks,
as Commissioner of the General Land Office, and sent a number of federal
officials, among them George W. Julian, to the various territories with instructions to reform the administration of the federal land laws.

Commissioner Sparks immediately conducted an investigation which officially confirmed the reports of fraud in the land department:

I found that the magnificent estate of the nation in its public lands had been to a
wide extent wasted under defective and improvident laws and through a laxity of
public administration astonishing in a business sense if not culpable in recklessness of official responsibility.

The widespread belief of the people of this country that the land department
has been very largely conducted to the advantage of speculation and monopoly,
private and corporate, rather than in the public interest, I have found supported
by developments in every branch of the service.[10]

Sparks traced much of the "speculation" and "monopoly" to the territory
of New Mexico where, in the past, federal land policy had been "characterized by a prodigality of award even exceeding that bestowed upon grants to

---

"George W. Julian, Nineteenth Century Reformer as Politician" (unpublished Ph.D. dis-
sertation, University of California, Berkeley, 1953).

[7] Julian as a Radical Republican is treated in Eric L. McKitrick, *Andrew Johnson and
Reconstruction* (Chicago, 1960). Older treatments include: Howard K. Beale, *The Critical
Year: A Study of Andrew Johnson and Reconstruction* (New York, 1930); and T. Harry
Williams, *Lincoln and the Radicals* (Madison, Wisconsin, 1941).

[8] New York *Herald*, April 10, 1886.

[9] Allan Nevins, *Grover Cleveland, A Study in Courage* (New York, 1932), 216. According
to Nevins, "No early problem of his Administration worried Cleveland so much as this
wholesale spoliation of the West" (*ibid.*, 225).

[10] *Annual Report of the Commissioner of the General Land Office for the Year 1885*
(Washington, D.C., 1885), 3 (hereafter cited as *L.O.R.*).

railroad corporations." [11] A Congressional investigation had also just uncovered evidence of the illegal appropriation of large areas of New Mexican land.[12] On May 11, 1885, President Cleveland asked Julian to "break up the [land] rings in New Mexico." [13]

Two years later, in the *North American Review*, Julian gave a somewhat distorted version of the circumstances behind his appointment as Surveyor General. He stated that Cleveland's letter of May 11 had asked him to choose between the offices of Governor and Surveyor General, a request which "was a complete surprise to me," and that he had chosen the latter in compliance with the President's suggestion that it was "the more important of the two." [14] A far different story, however, is told in Julian's journal and in his letters in the Cleveland collection. Julian had been forced by financial necessity to request appointment to a position under the incoming Democratic administration: "Without some position now, I shall be obliged ... to end my life in a dismal scuffle for bread and butter for myself and children...." [15] Apparently, he expected to be appointed Commissioner of the General Land Office in Washington, having secured recommendations in his behalf from Samuel J. Tilden and Abram S. Hewitt.[16] The appointment of Sparks to this office left Julian unemployed and extremely discouraged: "My defeat is very vexatious and humiliating, and nothing but financial necessity could have induced me, at my time of life, to join the army of office-beggars in Washington. I am ashamed of it." [17] The arrival of Cleveland's offer of federal office in New Mexico found Julian still hoping for a Washington appointment. His reply, therefore, while specifying the Governorship as his preference, took the form of a reminder that, in applying for office, he had had "no thought of any position so far out on our frontiers and among so rough and miscellaneous a population." [18] However, when Cleveland selected Edmund G. Ross of Kansas as Governor of the territory, Julian became "quite uneasy" as to his prospects,[19] and he quickly sent the President an appeal that his previous "hasty and somewhat deprecatory letter" not exclude him from consideration for other appointments.[20] When once again the offer of the Surveyor Generalship came, Julian promptly accepted it.

[11] *Ibid.*, 17.

[12] "Title to Lands in New Mexico," *Sen. Exec. Doc. 106*, 48 Cong., 2 sess., 1–404.

[13] Journal, June 21, 1885. See also Julian, "Land-Stealing in New Mexico," *North American Review*, CXLV (July 1887), 17.

[14] Julian, "Land-Stealing in New Mexico," 17.

[15] Julian to ?, March 22, 1885, the Papers of Grover Cleveland (Library of Congress, Washington, D.C.). Hereafter cited as Cleveland Papers.

[16] *Ibid.;* Journal, 102. Tilden wrote Daniel Manning that "I think it would be a most admirable appointment." John Bigelow, *The Life of Samuel J. Tilden* (New York, 1895), II, 313. And Hewitt suggested that Julian "made great sacrifices when he left the Republican party and advocated the election of Tilden.... I do not know of anyone who has a better right to be expected to be taken care of in some way" (Hewitt to Cleveland, April 7, 1885, Cleveland Papers).

[17] Julian to ?, March 22, 1885, Cleveland Papers.

[18] Julian to Cleveland (undated), 1885, Cleveland Papers.

[19] Journal, June 21, 1885.

[20] Julian to Cleveland, May 27, 1885, Cleveland Papers.

To an administration concerned with land reform in the territories Julian must have appeared the ideal candidate for territorial office. His career in the House of Representatives, including a period as chairman of the Committee on Public Lands, had made him, both from necessity and inclination, a specialist in the public land question. His daughter later recalled: "Next to the abolition of slavery, the policy of the government in dealing with its unoccupied domain was the most engrossing interest of Julian's public life. . . ." [21] Indeed, for a man of his Free Soil background and convictions, a proper land policy formed the heart of the attack on all types of slavery; he believed with the Free Soilers that "Land monopoly is one form of slavery, and, indeed, the underlying foundation of all slavery, because freedom *must* have its roots in the soil." [22]

The laws regulating the ownership and disposition of landed property not only affect the well-being but frequently the destiny of a people. The system of primogeniture and entail adopted by the Southern States of our Union favored the policy of great estates, and the ruinous system of landlordism and slavery which finally laid waste the fairest and most fertile section of the Republic and threatened its life; while the New England States, in adopting a different system, laid the foundations of their prosperity in the soil itself, and "took a bond of fate" for the welfare of unborn generations. Their political institutions were the logical outcome of their laws respecting landed property, which favored a great subdivision of the land and great equality among the people, thus promoting prosperous cultivation, compact communities, general education, a healthy public opinion, democracy in managing the affairs of the church, and that system of local self-government which has since prevailed over so many States. So intimate and vital are the relations between a community and the soil it occupies that in the nomenclature of politics the word[s] "people" and "land" are convertible terms. . . .[23]

During his years in Congress, Julian implemented this philosophy by an uncompromising devotion to the homestead principle; as Paul W. Gates has concluded, "no one had the interests of the homesteader more at heart. . . ." [24] To New Mexicans, therefore, Julian's record left little doubt as to the land policy he would pursue as Surveyor General. His appointment was widely considered to be the initial phase in the prosecution of large numbers of New Mexicans for land frauds.[25]

Julian was understandably reluctant, at the age of sixty-eight, to be "sent into the worst den of thieves in the West." In his journal he confided that "I dread the undertaking, and greatly fear that I shall fail. I shall certainly

[21] Grace Julian Clarke, *George W. Julian* (Indianapolis, 1923), 252.

[22] Julian, *Later Speeches on Political Questions with Select Controversial Papers* (Indianapolis, 1889), 60. Italics in the original.

[23] Julian, *Political Recollections, 1840 to 1872* (Chicago, 1883), 296–297.

[24] Paul W. Gates, "The Homestead Law in an Incongruous Land System," *American Historical Review*, XLI (July 1936), 677.

[25] Ralph E. Twitchell, *Old Santa Fe* (Santa Fe, 1925), 411. Julian remarked in his journal that the position "has been given me because of my known hostility to land swindles, and the understanding of the public is that I am sent into the worst den of thieves in the West for the purpose of breaking it up" (Journal, June 21, 1885).

do so without vigorous backing from Washington and the zealous cooperation of the people of New Mexico." [26]
Unfortunately for Julian, in matters of land reform, the "zealous cooperation" of New Mexicans could not be reasonably expected. In the almost
forty years since the Treaty of Guadalupe Hidalgo had formally bound the
United States to respect Spanish and Mexican land grants, speculation in
these land grants had become the territory's largest "industry." [27] At the
center of this speculation was a group of lawyers, merchants, and large landowners, called the "Santa Fe Ring," which for years had controlled both
political and economic affairs in order to manipulate more profitably the
unsettled land grants.[28] Although nominally Republican, the "Ring" was
actually organized so that it included in its membership prominent figures
from both political parties, among them the chairman of the Democratic
Central Committee. As Julian was to remark ruefully, "The whole business
[of politics in New Mexico] is entirely subordinated to private gain. The
difference between a Democrat and a Republican is metaphysical rather
than real. . . ." [29] The "Santa Fe Ring" was so successful in dominating the
territory that, "From the late 1860s until 1885, nearly every governor appears to have been a member, as well as other federal officers." [30] In striking
a blow for land reform, it was clear, Julian would be threatening the profits
and power of New Mexico's most prominent and influential citizens.

Julian took formal possession of the Surveyor General's office in Santa Fe
on July 22, 1885. In combination with Governor Ross, a man whose views
on federal land policy in New Mexico were almost identical to his own,[31]
he proceeded at once to correct "the blunders and mistakes" of previous
surveyors general.[32] The land office itself he found to be "badly in arrears"
in its work, with everything done in "a helter-skelter and slipshod fashion." [33] In an attempt to end the confusion and laxity which normally characterized the administration of the New Mexico land office, he indexed the
documents relating to land claims and adopted a more rigorous system of
examining surveys.[34] At the end of two months in office, after a careful review of the records and decisions of his predecessors, Julian pronounced the
territorial land department "the centre of as atrocious a system of organized

[26] Journal, June 21, 1885.
[27] See, for example, Howard R. Lamar, The Far Southwest, 1846-1912: A Territorial
History (New Haven, 1966), 149.
[28] Twitchell, Old Santa Fe, 394; Julian, "Land-Stealing in New Mexico," 27-28.
[29] Journal, October 11, 1885. "The change in the administration did not bring the
expected relief, for the very simple reason that members of both parties are in the ring."
Raton Weekly Independent, December 17, 1887.
[30] Lamar, The Far Southwest, 147.
[31] Ross believed, with Julian, that "Cranks and isms do not thrive in the presence of a
population of rural freeholders" (Council Journal: Proceedings of the Legislative Council
of the Territory of New Mexico [Las Vegas, New Mexico, 1887], 19).
[32] Journal, October 11, 1885.
[33] L.O.R., 1886, p. 531. Journal, October 11, 1885.
[34] L.O.R., 1886, pp. 531-532.

rascality and mis-rule as ever defied the authority of the Government and the public opinion of the country." [35]

Julian soon had the entire territory in an uproar. With continual encouragement from Commissioner Sparks, he re-examined twenty land claims which had been confirmed as valid by his predecessors in office: he approved three, reduced the acreage granted in another three, and disapproved and invalidated fourteen, including several of the largest claims.[36] Five years later Frank Springer, lawyer for the Maxwell Land Grant Company, president of the New Mexico Bar Association, and no friend of Julian, still exhibited the anger and consternation aroused among the grant interests by the Surveyor General's findings: "Titles that have been confirmed by congress and patented, and even decided by the highest courts of the country to be good and valid, and free from fraud, were not safe from the venomous tongue of this official scandal monger." [37] In his first year as Surveyor General, Julian recommended the invalidation of claims to 1,600,208.71 acres of New Mexican land.[38] Even more disturbing to some New Mexicans, however, were the numerous indications that this was only the beginning of Julian's reform campaign in the territory. The Surveyor General surmised in his journal that "The aggregate of lands belonging to the United States which have been dishonestly appropriated by private roguery under invalid grants or fraudulent surveys, as shown by my investigations, is about four million acres." [39] His first annual report, which was serialized at his request in the local press,[40] placed the aggregate at "not far from 5,000,000 acres." [41]

Having thrown doubt on the validity of land grant titles throughout the territory, Julian proceeded to undermine existing homestead and pre-emption claims. He decided that "a very large proportion" of the surveys in New Mexico had been "fraudulently or inaccurately executed" and advised Commissioner Sparks that "the great body of the surveyed lands of the territory will have to be resurveyed. . . ." [42] Then, in a clean sweep, Julian announced that 90 percent of all the land entries in the territory were fraudulent.[43] As Howard R. Lamar has observed, "While this statistic was probably correct, it also struck at every citizen of means in New Mexico and at the livelihood of the entire legal profession there." [44]

The effects of Julian's charges soon began to appear. His findings led to the arrest and conviction for fraudulent land entry of former Land Register

[35] Journal, October 11, 1885.

[36] L.O.R., 1886, pp. 533–534.

[37] Quoted in Twitchell, Facts, II, 462 n.

[38] L.O.R., 1886, p. 534.

[39] Journal, December 7, 1886.

[40] Ibid., September 30, 1886.

[41] L.O.R., 1886, p. 534.

[42] Ibid., 532. Julian's assertion was verified by special agents from the General Land Office (ibid., 14).

[43] Julian, "Land-Stealing in New Mexico," 20–25; New York Herald, April 5, 1886; Santa Fe Daily New Mexican, December 27, 1888.

[44] Howard R. Lamar, "Edmund G. Ross as Governor of New Mexico Territory: A Reappraisal," New Mexico Historical Review, XXXVI (July 1961), 190.

Max Frost, a prominent Republican and member of the "Santa Fe Ring." [45] The fact that Frost was editor of the territory's most powerful newspaper, the Santa Fe *Daily New Mexican*, served to array much of the territorial press against the new Surveyor General. Julian also attacked the extensive landholdings of Stephen B. Elkins, Stephen W. Dorsey, and Thomas B. Catron, the latter "the one man who, more than any other, dominated New Mexican political and business affairs for fifty years." [46] Elkins and Dorsey were both prominent in territorial and national politics. Dorsey, who achieved notoriety through the "Star Route" mail frauds, had conducted Garfield's presidential campaign in 1880 and had earlier served as United States Senator from Arkansas.[47] Elkins, Catron's law partner, had been attorney general of the territory, United States district attorney, and founder-president of the Santa Fe First National Bank. A member of the Republican National Committee, he would later be Secretary of War under Benjamin Harrison and Senator from West Virginia.[48]

That Julian had little awareness of the possible effects of his actions, or of the realities of political and economic power in the territory, is demonstrated by a complacent entry in his journal:

I am now very busy in overhauling some old surveys involving the title to large areas of land claimed by T. B. Catron and S. B. Elkins, which I think will result in restoring to the public domain a large body of valuable land and stripping these rascals of their ill-gotten possessions to the same extent. I have also been setting on foot some important inquiries into the title of S. W. Dorsey and his confederates to large areas of land in Colfax County, and I hope for very important and valuable results. . . . In short, my work here is turning out to be more beneficial to the Territory than I ever expected. . . .[49]

In 1887, in an article in the *North American Review*, he publicly labelled Dorsey, Elkins, and Catron "land thieves" and pronounced C. H. Gildersleeve, the chairman of the Democratic Central Committee, a "trafficker" in land grants and a politician "for revenue only." [50] It is not surprising that the 1886 Democratic Territorial Convention, disgusted with Julian and with the Cleveland reform administration, unanimously resolved to play down land frauds. As Julian commented,

The leading politicians of the Territory are all interested in these old grants, and

[45] *Ibid.*, 190–191; Twitchell, *Old Santa Fe*, 411.
[46] William A. Keleher, *The Fabulous Frontier—Twelve New Mexico Items* (Albuquerque, 1945), 117. In 1896, Catron listed his landholdings as: an undivided one-half interest in the San Cristobal grant of 91,032 acres; the Tierra Amarilla grant of 584,515 acres; the north 240,000 acres of the Mora grant; the Espiritu Santo grant of 113,141 acres; Canon del Agua, 3,501 acres; Mesita de Juan Lopez, 42,022 acres; and Alamitos, 2,500 acres (*ibid.*, 130).
[47] David Y. Thomas, "Stephen Wallace Dorsey," *Dictionary of American Biography*, V, 387.
[48] James M. Callahan, "Stephen Benton Elkins," *ibid.*, VI, 83–84.
[49] Journal, December 7, 1886.
[50] Julian, "Land-Stealing in New Mexico," 27–28.

they all long to be rid of me. In the Territorial Convention this Fall ... no mention was made of my work, and the platform adopted was a sneaking and cowardly dodge of the whole question of land frauds, and a stab at Cleveland's administration.[51]

Much of the territory soon clamored for the dismissal of the Surveyor General. An occasional letter to the General Land Office endorsed Julian's policies—said one, "Thank God, day is breaking for the honest settlers"[52]— but Senator Preston B. Plumb of Kansas notified Governor Ross that complaints about Julian were pouring into Washington.[53] One letter to Plumb described the Surveyor General as a "monomaniac as to Spanish and Mexican titles" and accused him of being "exceedingly injurious to the Territory."[54] The Santa Fe *Daily New Mexican* suggested that Julian be appointed Ambassador to "Tierra del Fuego."[55] Charges were promptly filed before the Senate Public Lands Committee protesting his confirmation; indeed, Julian would be *de facto* Surveyor General for almost two years before the Senate confirmed his appointment.[56]

No matter how unsettling his methods, the nature of Julian's assault on land frauds in New Mexico demonstrated his deep concern for the future welfare of the territory and of the small settler. At the time of his appointment New Mexican land was being illegally appropriated in astonishing quantities. The limited supply of available water in the territory had produced what Ernest S. Osgood, in a study of Montana and Wyoming, has called "range control by ownership of water."[57] The Governor of New Mexico reported in 1883: "Locations are made which embrace springs, and the surrounding lands are valueless to any but the locators of the water. ... A cattle company, or individual, may, by owning a few acres, have the occupancy of a tract as large as some of the states of the union."[58]

Such reports were confirmed when, in the spring of 1887, Commissioner Sparks ordered an investigation into the practical results of the homestead and pre-emption laws. Inspectors and special agents examined the land systems in nine western states and territories. They reviewed 1,416 agricultural entries, embracing over 225,000 acres of land, and discovered that the federal land laws had been complied with in only 268 instances.[59] In New Mexico,

[51] Journal, December 7, 1886.
[52] *L.O.R.*, 1886, p. 67.
[53] Lamar, "Edmund G. Ross," 191.
[54] Julian somehow obtained (probably from Ross) excerpts from this letter and used them in an appeal to Cleveland for aid in obtaining his confirmation (Julian to Cleveland, July 15, 1886, New Mexico Surveyor General Charges File, Interior Department, National Archives [NA], RG 48). See also Julian to Benjamin Harrison, July 15, 1886, the Papers of Benjamin Harrison, Library of Congress, Washington, D.C.
[55] Santa Fe *Daily New Mexican*, March 12, 1889.
[56] He was finally confirmed February 28, 1887. *Cong. Record*, 49 Cong., 2 sess., XVIII, 2669.
[57] Ernest S. Osgood, *The Day of the Cattleman* (Minneapolis, 1929), 204–205, esp. map facing 204.
[58] Kelcher, *Fabulous Frontier*, 112.
[59] *L.O.R.*, 1887, p. 82. See also Harold H. Dunham, *Government Handout: A Study in the Administration of the Public Lands, 1875–1891* (New York, 1941), 210–211.

where two townships were selected at random for examination, the investigation revealed that the provisions of these laws "in respect to inhabitancy, improvement, and cultivation" had been completely ignored. No one resided on the land. The special agent in charge found one township controlled by the Cimarron Cattle Company and the other by the Dubuque Cattle Company. The latter held "every claim on the Tequiesquite arroyo for a distance of 17 miles . . . which gives them the control of several hundred thousand acres of the public domain, embracing the finest grass lands in New Mexico." [60]

Spanish and Mexican land grants provided even more opportunity for acquiring large areas of New Mexican land. In the Canada de Cochiti claim, for example, the original grant from Mexico was for 32 acres and "pasture enough for small stock and horse herd," but it was surveyed by a Surveyor General for 104,554.24 acres. The Canon de Chama grant claimants were still more successful, petitioning for 184,320 acres and being awarded 472,736.95 acres.[61] The Estancia grant, later found by Julian to be "fraudulent and void," was surveyed and approved for over 415,000 acres.[62] In 1887 Julian reported to the General Land Office an "approximate estimate" of "from 8,000,000 to 9,000,000 acres of the public domain which are now and for many years past have been in the grasp of men who have used and enjoyed the land for their own emolument, and whose earnest prayer is to be let alone in the possession of their ill-gotten gains." [63] A year later he raised the estimate to 10,000,000 acres.[64] The New Mexican experience confirms, for one region at least, Paul W. Gates' conclusion that "there were few obstacles in the way of speculation and land monopolization after 1862." [65]

Julian's findings convinced him that "The paramount need of New Mexico is a policy that will compel its public rogues to make restitution of their swag." [66] The adoption of such a policy, he argued, would effect a radical transformation in the economic and political destiny of the territory. Much as he had earlier proposed to reconstruct the South through rebel land confiscation, Julian now attempted to employ the federal land laws to "reconstruct" New Mexico.[67]

True to his Free Soil philosophy, the Surveyor General envisioned a New Mexico in which homesteads would supplant ranches as the basic pattern of settlement. In this way, he believed, a population of small settlers would rapidly displace the large landowners, and a new era would arrive for the territory. First, however, it was necessary to provide land for the fu-

[60] *L.O.R.*, 1887, pp. 77–78.

[61] *L.O.R.*, 1889, pp. 386–387. Julian believed the Canon de Chama grant to be between thirty and forty thousand acres.

[62] *L.O.R.*, 1887, p. 581. For the history of the most notorious of these land grants, the Maxwell Land Grant, see William A. Keleher, *Maxwell Land Grant* (Santa Fe, 1942) and Dunham, *Government Handout*, chap. XI.

[63] *L.O.R.*, 1887, p. 582.

[64] *L.O.R.*, 1888, p. 469.

[65] Gates, "The Homestead Law in an Incongruous Land System," 662.

[66] *L.O.R.*, 1887, p. 584.

[67] For similar conclusions regarding Ross, see Lamar, "Edmund G. Ross," 184.

ture homesteaders, and this requirement demanded a permanent solution to the tangle of New Mexican land claims.

The solution which Julian offered had several clearly defined phases. His initial step was to focus the attention of the public, in both New Mexico and the East, on the territory's land problems. This would arouse support for his policies and perhaps lead Congress to pass remedial legislation. As Julian put it, "The reform of great abuses is necessarily preceded by their exposure, and when the cry of danger needs to be sounded silence is a crime." [68] The Surveyor General did not remain silent, and by 1889, his annual reports, speeches, and magazine articles had made New Mexico "a by-word" for land law violations.[69]

Julian believed that with public attention centered on the territory frauds and speculation would cease. Then, an effective method could be found to clear land titles and thus attract settlers to the region. He rejected proposals that a land commission or the territorial courts, both of which he regarded as too susceptible to local influences, be empowered to adjudicate land claims. He argued instead that all claims should be referred to the Commissioner of the General Land Office for decision, with the right of appeal to the Secretary of the Interior. This Julian viewed as "the best and speediest method," for titles would be settled in three or four years and the territory placed "on the highway of prosperity and progress." [70] Once land claims were decided, and the public domain opened to an increasing number of homesteaders:

> The stream of settlers now crossing the Territory in search of homes on the Pacific will be arrested by the new order of things and poured into her valleys and plains. Small land-holdings, thrifty tillage, and compact settlements will supersede great monopolies, slovenly agriculture, and industrial stagnation.[71]

The nature of Julian's proposals reveals his failure to adjust his Free Soil convictions to the geographical realities of New Mexico. This was perhaps best expressed in Julian's heated exchange with Stephen W. Dorsey in the *North American Review*.[72] Aroused by the Surveyor General's July article, in the course of which the New Mexican had been bluntly labelled a "land thief," Dorsey accused Julian of attempting to translate his Free Soil views to New Mexico without reference to the vastly different physiographic conditions which might possibly affect their operation. The lands of the arid

---

[68] *L.O.R.*, 1886, p. 534.

[69] Dunham, *Government Handout*, 213. Julian, of course, was not alone in publicizing New Mexican land troubles: Governor Ross did his share, and the New York *Herald* had a special correspondent in New Mexico just for that purpose. See the New York *Herald*, April 5–10, 1886.

[70] Julian, "The Redemption of a Territory," *Magazine of Western History*, X (July 1889), 243. *L.O.R.*, 1886, p. 536.

[71] Julian, "Land-Stealing in New Mexico," 31.

[72] Julian, "Land-Stealing in New Mexico," 17–31; Stephen W. Dorsey, "Land-Stealing in New Mexico—A Rejoinder," *North American Review*, CXLV (October 1887), 396–409; Julian, "Land-Stealing in New Mexico," *ibid.*, CXLV (December 1887), 684–685.

region, he argued, require "a different system of disposal and settlement"
than the more fertile areas for which the homestead policy had been originally designed—"the practice is absurd which legally permits the occupation, settlement, and purchase of only 160 acres within the arid region."
Dorsey ridiculed the Surveyor General's notion of populating the territory
with "prosperous agriculturalists." [73] Significantly enough, Julian ignored
the New Mexican's charges in his reply in December, and a similar silence
in his journal and in his annual reports indicates a crucial lack of adjustment to the different requirements of subsistence agriculture on arid and
semi-arid lands. Whatever Dorsey's personal motivation in urging the distribution of larger areas of land, his argument has been endorsed by more recent, and more disinterested, authorities as basically sound. As Victor Westphall has commented, "The idea of small farms here was a tenacious eastern
dream and wholly untenable." [74]

The likelihood that Julian would ever realize his vision of a homesteaders' New Mexico was further weakened by his position as a nonresident
appointee. In New Mexico, as in the other territories, federal officials were
regarded as unwanted intruders, "carpetbaggers," who could not possibly
understand the real needs of the region.[75] Evidence that Grover Cleveland
was considering nonresident appointments, therefore, brought vigorous protests from territorial Democratic leaders. Conscious of the importance of
the "carpetbag" issue in New Mexico politics, they had hoped to use the
patronage to consolidate the party's position in the territory. Anthony Joseph, the Democratic delegate elect to Congress, and C. H. Gildersleeve,
chairman of the Democratic Central Committee, argued that "*None of them
have any claim to office, nor are they the choice of the Democrats of this
Territory.*" Cleveland's policy, if carried into effect, "will prove ruinous and
work us great injury." [76]

But the Cleveland administration sent George W. Julian and other non-
residents to New Mexico. Local Democrats were, as one wrote, "utterly disgusted"—"old and tried democrats that have suffered, and been persecuted
for the last twenty-five years, on account of their political principles, are
entirely ignored, and Strangers, and in some instances radical republicans
receive the preference in occupying positions...." [77] Resentment was intensified by the actions of the new Surveyor General. His methods threatened
to discredit the Democratic party in the territory and to jeopardize party
harmony. "Discontent, disharmony and dissension," complained a Demo-

[73] Dorsey, "Land-Stealing in New Mexico—A Rejoinder," 405–407.
[74] Victor Westphall, "The Public Domain in New Mexico, 1854–1891," *New Mexico
Historical Review*, XXXIII (January 1958), 39. See also, Jack Ellsworth Holmes, *The
Public Land Question in New Mexico* (Albuquerque, 1947), 18.
[75] Earl S. Pomeroy, *The Territories and the United States, 1861–1890* (Philadelphia,
1947), 101. See also Pomeroy, "Carpet-baggers in the Territories, 1861 to 1890," *The Historian*, II (Winter 1939), 53–64.
[76] Anthony Joseph and C. H. Gildersleeve to William C. Whitney, March 10, 1885, the
Papers of William Collins Whitney, Library of Congress, Washington. D.C. Italics in the
original.
[77] August Kirschener to Anthony Joseph, March 17, 1886, Cleveland Papers.

crat, "are spreading rapidly in our ranks," [78] and an attempt was made at the 1886 Territorial Convention to dissociate the party from the policies of its Surveyor General.

Moreover, Julian's uncompromising insistence that land claims be decided by the Commissioner of the General Land Office brought him into bitter conflict with Governor Ross. For a time the two men had worked harmoniously toward a solution to New Mexican land problems. Ross, like Julian, believed that "Great landed estates are a constant menace to popular government," [79] and he actively supported the Surveyor General's efforts to replace them with homesteads.

Soon, however, disagreement arose over the method to be used to settle private land claims. The Governor favored the McCreary bill in the House of Representatives which proposed the creation of a land commission of three persons.[80] Convinced that such a commission would soon be dominated by the "Santa Fe Ring," Julian regarded the bill as "utterly and absolutely preposterous." [81] In his annual messages, in magazine articles, and in numerous letters to friendly Congressmen, the Surveyor General continued to urge the adoption of his own policy.[82]

The disagreement between Ross and Julian need not have been serious except that the latter convinced himself that the Governor had somehow succumbed to the persuasions of the "Santa Fe Ring." "Wittingly or unwittingly, he has become their tool. . . ." [83] The unfavorable action of the 1886 Territorial Convention, he believed, "was brought about by a secret combination of the friends of Gov. Ross on the one side and of Mr. [Anthony] Joseph on the other, and inspired by the land thieves who ruled the Convention." [84] Julian publicly repeated these charges in his annual report in 1888 and further accused Ross of "opposing the policy of the administration." [85] Then, in a letter which revealed his blindness to his own position in New Mexico, he wrote President Cleveland that Ross "is exceedingly unpopular with men of all parties in every section of the Territory." [86] Thus, after only two years in office, Julian, with some provocation to be sure, had alienated territorial Democrats and Republicans and, finally, his fellow federal appointees as well.

Until the very end Julian was convinced that his record as Surveyor General would be regarded as "historic" by later generations. Meanwhile, "It is very pleasant to be able to render a real service to the public and to the land-

[78] *Ibid.*

[79] *Council Journal: Proceedings of the Legislative Council of the Territory of New Mexico* (Las Vegas, New Mexico, 1887), 16.

[80] *Report of the Governor of New Mexico to the Secretary of the Interior, 1888* (Washington, D.C., 1888), 4.

[81] Julian, "The Redemption of a Territory," 241.

[82] *Ibid.*, 243–244. *L.O.R.*, 1886, p. 26. *Cong. Record*, 49 Cong., 1 sess., XVII, 4377; *ibid.*, 50 Cong., 1 sess., XIX, 2597–2598.

[83] Journal, December 25, 1887.

[84] Journal, December 7, 1886.

[85] *L.O.R.*, 1888, p. 472.

[86] Julian to Cleveland, December 9, 1888, Cleveland Papers.

less poor through the machinery of a public office which has been so long prostituted to the base uses of roguery and plunder." [87] In truth, however, the "landless poor" made little progress under Julian's tutelage in New Mexico. The census reports of 1890 and 1900 reveal that the average size of New Mexican farms actually increased significantly during this period, and the territory's land system, contrary to Julian's intentions, continued to be dominated by large agricultural units. [88]

By 1889, moreover, the Surveyor General's actions, especially his charge that 90 percent of all land entries were fraudulent, had undermined homestead and pre-emption claims in the territory, and his methods and intentions had left most influential New Mexicans abnormally sensitive to suggestions of land reform. Governor Ross' plan, for example, to implement homestead principles by the establishment of government irrigation projects to supply water at cost to the small settler—a plan which has been called "a thorough and significant free soil theory of colonial maturation" [89]—clearly suffered by association with the schemes and public diatribes of the Surveyor General. It is true that Julian so publicized New Mexico's land problems that Congress soon legislated a remedy, but even this limited victory ironically came in the form of a Court of Private Land Claims which Julian had bitterly fought for four years. [90]

In large part, Julian's failure in New Mexico reflected his inability to adjust to the realities of a new era. For him, "stimulation often came more from hatred of his enemies, real or supposed, than from a recognition of social and economic needs." [91] The treasured concepts which he attempted to impose upon the territory—concepts such as "yeoman" and "homestead" —had little meaning for the region or, indeed, for an increasingly industrial and urban America. As Henry Nash Smith has suggested:

The impotence of the land reformers . . . was due at least in part to the fact that their social theory offered them no aid in analyzing the actual situation and displaying the real issues. The advocates of the homestead principle, especially its Western supporters like Julian . . . were employing ideas that had little relevance to the conditions of Western agriculture or American society in general in the late nineteenth century. [92]

Julian's mind lingered in his Free Soil past, and his "social theory," which included a blind faith in the regenerative potential of the Homestead Act, contributed significantly to his ineffectiveness as Surveyor General.

Julian's official career in New Mexico thus suggests certain conclusions

[87] Journal, August 21, 1887.

[88] *Abstract of the Eleventh Census: 1890* (Washington, D.C., 1896), 98; *Abstract of the Twelfth Census of the United States, 1900* (Washington, D.C., 1904), 289.

[89] Lamar, "Edmund G. Ross," 196.

[90] Created in 1891, the Court adjudicated all grant titles in the Southwest, confirming claims to about 2,000,000 acres and rejecting claims to nearly 33,500,000 acres (Dunham, *Government Handout*, 240).

[91] Riddleberger, "George W. Julian," 305.

[92] Henry Nash Smith, *Virgin Land, The American West as Symbol and Myth* (Cambridge, Mass., 1950), 191–192.

concerning the land reform policies of the Cleveland administration. For a time, the efforts of Ross, Julian, and other officials in the territories received vigorous support in Washington from Land Commissioner Sparks. "In the name of the homeseekers I thank you," Sparks wrote Ross. "Let the good work go on. The Land 'grabbing' rascals will die hard, but as sure as God is just we'll beat them." [93] But Sparks' actions, like Julian's, aroused strong protest against his "ecstatic and hysterical spirit of alleged reform." [94] Most Westerners were willing to accept a certain amount of fraud in return for a rapid and easy disposition of the public domain. Sparks increasingly lost influence in Washington, and in November 1887, he resigned after a quarrel with Secretary of the Interior Lamar.[95] His departure from office and the appointment of William F. Vilas to replace Lamar signified Cleveland's diminishing interest in land policy and the adoption of a more conservative approach to land reform.

In studying Sparks' attempts at reform, historians have neglected to investigate the execution of his policy on the local level. There, in the territories themselves, the success or failure of land reform hinged directly upon the capacity of the men who interpreted and carried out the Commissioner's orders. The actions of George W. Julian in New Mexico, therefore, help to explain the frustration, on the national level, of the administration's land policy. Julian's career, like Sparks', showed an unhappy reliance on panaceas, a failure to build a secure base of political support, and an unfortunate tendency to allow well-intentioned reform to become harsh and misdirected.

The defeat of Grover Cleveland in the election of 1888 left Julian "heartsick and soul-sick" [96]—and potentially unemployed. The territorial press, on the other hand, was jubilant at the prospective removal of the Surveyor General. Typical was the reaction of the Raton *Range:* "Title-tortured New Mexico will soon be rid of a man who has done more than all others combined to cloud land titles and retard the progress of our young commonwealth." [97] For his part, Julian was only slightly reluctant to leave New Mexico. He had never really grown accustomed to life in the land of *poco tiempo,* referring often to the stagnation of the natives and the "prevailing tendency here to degenerate into barbarism." Especially did he despise "the piles of mud in which the people of Santa Fe are domiciled." [98] When, in August 1889, his successor was finally announced, all were in some measure pleased. The *Daily New Mexican* commented: "Everybody wore a smile this morning. The sky, the lawyers and every good citizen. And all on account of the news of Julian's removal." [99] And as for Julian, he saw "the way open at last for a final escape from this God-forsaken land." [100]

[93] Lamar, "Edmund G. Ross," 190 n.
[94] Santa Fe *Daily New Mexican,* August 31, 1888.
[95] Roy M. Robbins, *Our Landed Heritage: The Public Domain, 1776–1936* (Princeton, New Jersey, 1942), 292–293.
[96] Julian to Cleveland, November (undated), 1888, Cleveland Papers.
[97] Quoted in the Santa Fe *Daily New Mexican,* February 9, 1889.
[98] Journal, August 2, 1885, October 11, 1885.
[99] Santa Fe *Daily New Mexican,* August 6, 1889.
[100] Journal, August 18, 1889.

VALENTINE SCRIP

The Saga of Land Locations
in Southern Dakota Territory
Originating from a Mexican Land Grant

Robert Lee

Valentine Scrip: The Saga of Land Locations in Southern Dakota Territory Originating From a Mexican Land Grant

ROBERT LEE

The Treaty of Guadalupe Hidalgo, concluded with Mexico on 2 February 1848 following the brief war between the two countries, greatly expanded the territorial domain of the victorious United States. It formally ceded the California and New Mexico territories, which would later form the states of California, Nevada, Utah, and New Mexico and large parts of Arizona and Colorado. One of the key provisions of this treaty was to prove extremely troublesome for it provided that all the Mexican land grants in the ceded territory would be "respected as valid" by the United States government.

The Mexican government had awarded over six hundred land grants in the California province alone as an inducement to colonization prior to the war. Many land grants had also been given during the earlier Spanish rule of the region. The Mexican government had authorized grants of up to eleven square leagues, about seventy-six square miles, but even larger grants were not uncommon. However, wholesale fraud was evident in many of these transactions. For example, General Manuel Micheltorna, the Mexican governor of California in 1842-45, issued a grant of California land in 1852, predating the documents to 1843. The falsification took place seven years after a political revolt had forced Micheltorna to return to Mexico and four years after the province had been ceded to the United States. Not surprisingly, Micheltorna was included among the high Mexican officials who were described as "professional forgers and perjurers" in the issuance of the fabricated land grant documents.[1]

As an implementation of the treaty, in 1851 Congress established a Board of Land Commissioners to judge the validity of the land grants. Its jurisdiction extended to all grants and not just the disputed claims. The Americans who had acquired title to Mexican land grants were affected along with the Mexican nationals who had colonized the ceded territory. The land involved in the rejected claims became a part of the public domain and available for settlement. Both the claimants and the government had the right to appeal the board's ruling to the federal district courts and to the United States Supreme Court. Mexico agreed to produce "any books, records or documents in its possession necessary for the Board to make a just decision of any claim."[2]

Many conflicting claims were presented to the board, which heard over eight hundred cases involving the old grants between January 1852 and March 1856. The claimants had two years to present their claims and almost all of the board's decisions were appealed; consequently, the litigation often dragged on for years. In fact, it took the landholders an average of seventeen years to prove their legal ownership. The procedure was particularly burdensome to the Mexican landowners in California. A sympathetic congressman described their plight on the floor of the House of Representatives saying that "persons who had been in possession of their lands for generations, who had their children born there, who had pastured there their flocks and herds on their old ranches, suddenly found themselves by this legislation of Congress required to come forward and prove that they had any right whatever to their lands. It must be admitted that it was a great hardship to require these persons, many of them unacquainted with our

1. Walton Bean, *California: An Interpretive History* (New York: McGraw-Hill Book Co., 1968), pp.,154, 159-60.

2. Ibid., p. 156; Nathan Covington Brooks, *A Complete History of the Mexican War: Its Causes, Conduct, and Consequences, Comprising an Account of the Various Military and Naval Operations from its Commencement to the Treaty of Peace* (1849; reprint ed., Chicago, Ill.: Rio Grande Press, 1965), p. 551.

laws and customs, to come forward under many disadvantages, the prey of lawyers, and at great expense, to show that they had any right to this land that they possessed."[3]

One of the most interesting cases to come before the Board of Land Commissioners involved a grant of three square leagues (about nine square miles) of land north of San Francisco to Juan Miranda. General Micheltorna awarded the land to Miranda on 8 October 1844, although Miranda had settled on the land, the Rancho Arroyo de San Antonio, in 1838. He had built a house, cultivated land, raised livestock, and lived there with his large family until his death. He died about a year after acquiring it and his family continued living on the grant until it was sold. The sale of this grant of land led to filings on public domain lands in the United States in seventeen states—including South Dakota.[4]

Miranda's heirs appeared in probate court in San Rafael, Marin County, on 19 August 1850 to ask disposition of the estate, two years after California had been ceded to the United States. The court appointed B.R. Buckelew and James Black as special administrators. One month later a public auction was held in San Rafael and Miranda's rancho was sold for $9,550, "which was the highest bid therefor." The successful bidder was Thomas B. Valentine of San Francisco. The sale was confirmed

3. Bean, *California: An Interpretive History*, p. 157; U.S., Congress,' House, *Congressional Globe*, 42nd Cong., 2nd sess., 1872, 45, pt.2:1186-87.

4. J.P. Munro-Fraser, *History of Sonoma County* (San Francisco, Calif.: Alley, Bowen and Co., 1880), pp. 154, 256-58; U.S., Department of the Interior, *Report of the Commissioner of the General Land Office to the Secretary of the Interior, 1874* (Washington, D.C.: Government Printing Office, 1874), pp. 21-22; U.S., Congress, *Congressional Globe*, Appendix, 42nd Cong., 2nd sess., 1872, 45, pt.4:824-25; Jacob N. Bowman, "Index of the Spanish-Mexican Private Land Grant Records and Cases of California" (1958), pp. 16-18, Manuscript Collection, Bancroft Library, University of California, Berkeley; W.W. Robinson, "The Strange Case of Thomas Valentine," *Westways Magazine* 38, no. 3 (March 1946):32-33; Bean, *California: An Interpretive History*, p. 70; Edwin R. Flatequal, Chief, Archives Branch, National Archives and Records Service, Washington National Records Center, General Services Administration, to Robert Lee, Sturgis, S. Dak., 7 Apr. 1970; Board of Commissioners to Ascertain and Settle the Private Land Claims in California, Case no. 812, deposition by Theodoro Miranda before Land Commissioner Harry I. Thornton, San Francisco, Calif., 5 Mar. 1853, Bancroft Library, University of California, Berkeley; William M. Roberts, Reference Librarian, Bancroft Library, University of California, Berkeley, to Robert Lee, 30 Mar. 1970, 28 Mar. 1972.

by the court on 20 September 1850 and Valentine received the deed to the property on 24 January 1851.[5]

It is not known exactly when or why Valentine, a former resident of New York, came to California. The new-found El Dorado attracted thousands of intrepid American argonauts following the gold strike at Sutter's Mill on 24 January 1848. California's population at that time, aside from the native Indians, was less than fifteen thousand. Four years later, however, when the new state took its first census, the population had swelled to over two hundred and thirty thousand. But, by the time the gold rush ended, few men had hit anything resembling a bonanza, although many remained and made their fortunes in ways other than mining. A fortunate few became wealthy speculating in land. Among them was Thomas B. Valentine.[6]

One report listed Valentine as a member of the California Company that left New York for California on 8 February 1849. John Woodhouse Audubon, a naturalist and artist like his famous father, was one of the leaders.[7] However, Valentine's obituary in the 28 October 1896 issue of the *San Francisco Call* reported that he first came to the land of gold in 1851.[8] In any event, he was around twenty when he joined the much-heralded

5. Judge James A. Shorb, order by probate court, Marin County, Calif., 19 Aug. 1850, 24 Jan. 1851, Bancroft Library, University of California, Berkeley.

6. Bean, *California: An Interpretive History*, p. 197; Ferol Egan, *The El Dorado Trail* (New York: McGraw-Hill Book Co., 1970), p. 281.

7. John W. Audubon, *Audubon's Western Journal, 1849-1850* (Cleveland, Ohio: Arthur H. Clark Co., 1905), pp. 195, 242-43. The *New York Evening Express* (New York City), 9 Feb. 1849, reported that there were seventy-five young men from New York and Philadelphia in the original California Company. The list of original members included three Valentines—Charles, Matthias B., and Thomas B.—although the article did not indicate whether or not they were related. The newspaper stated that the company would "take the land route via Corpus Christi, Monterey, etc., to the gold regions of California." After reaching Brownsville, Texas, the company traveled northwesterly across Mexico by wagon train. "Death [from cholera], desertion and disability" took a large toll and only about forty men reached San Francisco together.

8. *San Francisco Call*, 28 Oct. 1896, p. 14. The obituary report that Valentine came to California in 1851 is an apparent error since he purchased the Miranda grant at a public auction at San Rafael on 20 September 1850.

rush to the gold fields. After he arrived in California, "he branched forth in the real estate line, the venture being attended with uniform success." His purchase of the Miranda grant, while the most celebrated of his real estate dealings, was not the sole source of his eventual wealth, although he held vast landed interests in California at the time of his death. In the *San Francisco Directory of 1852*, he was listed as a printer. The directories from 1852 through 1860 identified him as a member of the firm of Monson, Valentine and Company. He was president of the company when it was incorporated, about a year prior to his death in 1896. [9]

Valentine filed his claim on the Miranda grant with the Board of Land Commissioners on 17 February 1852. However, two other claims covered the same grant. One of the other claims was filed on 7 February 1853 by Charles White of San Jose who contended that he had purchased the Rancho Arroyo de San Antonio from Antonio Ortega, Miranda's son-in-law. Ortega had married Francisca Miranda, and consequently, he claimed to be the real occupant of the rancho. Ortega's grant was purportedly awarded to him by General Alvarada, then Mexican governor of California, on 10 August 1840—four years earlier than Micheltorna's grant of the same land to Miranda. The third claim was filed a short time later on 3 March 1853 by James A. Short, address not given, who claimed two square leagues of the three granted by Micheltorna to Miranda in 1844. Valentine withdrew his claim on 6 February 1855 and Short followed suit two days later. [10]

There are two probable explanations for why Valentine mysteriously withdrew his claim, but none at all for Short. One explains that Valentine withdrew after entering into a pact with

9. *San Francisco Call*, 28 Oct. 1896, p. 14; Roberts to Lee, 30 Mar. 1970. Valentine's brother, S.D. Valentine (not listed as an original member of the California Company), became a partner in the printing company of Monson, Valentine and Company. Thomas sold his interest to D.B. Francis in 1863, but his brother remained with the firm and it became known as the Francis and Valentine Company. Thomas later rejoined the firm. He died of stomach cancer in his apartments at the Baldwin Hotel in San Francisco on 27 October 1896.

10. Bowman, "Spanish-Mexican Private Land Grant Records and Cases of California," pp. 16-18.

White to split the proceeds of the sale of the tract when the Ortega grant was confirmed.[11] Another contends that the hearings before the board appeared to be against Valentine's claim and he preferred to intervene against the Ortega claim in district court. The United States Supreme Court, however, ruled that Valentine had no right to intervene "since the claim he had was not under the same original grantor as that of Ortega's grantees." By the time this ruling was handed down, it was too late for Valentine to resubmit his claim before the board. He was, in fact, "out of court."[12]

Meanwhile, on 26 June 1855 the board confirmed the validity of the Ortega claim and the district court upheld the decision on 17 August 1857. But, upon appeal the United States Supreme Court remanded the case back to the lower court where it was rejected on 20 August 1862. This time the claimants appealed to the Supreme Court and on 18 April 1864 the claim was rejected "because the genuineness of the grant was not proven."[13] Thus, the old rancho became public domain land. The government surveyed the tract and sold part of it to settlers under the preemption laws. Petaluma, California, had been established on a portion of the old rancho. This sector was then ceded to the city by an act of Congress on 1 March 1867.[14]

Following the final rejection of the Ortega claim, Valentine realized that he had made a mistake in withdrawing his claim. Using his political influence, he besieged Congress for many years for special legislation that would permit him to prove his

11. Munro-Fraser, *History of Sonoma County*, pp. 154, 256-58.

12. U.S., Congress, House, *Congressional Globe*, 42nd Cong., 2nd sess., 1872, 45, pt.2:1186.

13. Bowman, "Spanish-Mexican Private Land Grant Records and Cases of California," pp. 16-18.

14. U.S., Congress, House, *Congressional Globe*, 42nd Cong., 2nd sess., 1872, 45, pt.2:1186-87; Munro-Fraser, *History of Sonoma County*, pp. 154, 256-58; Mrs. D.N. Craig, Secretary of the Petaluma, Calif., Historical Society, to Robert Lee, 7 Mar. 1970. Petaluma was settled in the early 1850s and was a port for a wide area for many years because of its location along the Petaluma River, which is an arm of San Pablo Bay. The traffic on the river gradually declined with the construction of railroads in the area.

claim in court. Private bills offering him this opportunity passed the House of Representatives in two different Congresses, but both times the Senate adjourned without taking action on the bills. The Senate passed a bill allowing him to take his case to court, but it failed in the House in 1871 "merely for want of time." [15]

In 1872 Congressman Sherman O. Houghton of California introduced House Resolution 1024 for "The Relief of Thomas B. Valentine." [16] House Resolution 1024 required the Ninth Circuit Court of California to "hear and decide upon the merits" of Valentine's claim and authorized the court to admit, as evidence, any testimony pertaining to the claim that had been presented to the Board of Land Commissioners prior to Valentine's voluntary withdrawal of his claim. In addition, it also provided that an appeal "may be taken" to the United States Supreme Court by either Valentine or the government' and stipulated that if the Court upheld Valentine's claim, he would be allowed to secure patents for acreage equal to that taken from him by the government. This "equal quantity," however, was restricted to "unoccupied and unappropriated lands of the United States, not mineral, and in tracts not less than the subdivisions provided for in the United States land laws." Finally, the bill authorized the commissioner of the General Land Office to issue scrip for whatever tracts Valentine selected, within the limitations of the bill and "in lieu" of the lands taken from him. The privileges extended to Valentine under the provisions of the bill also applied to his legal representatives, and thus were transferable. [17]

Congressman Washington Townsend of Pennsylvania reported the bill to the House with one amendment, which was accepted, for the Committee on Public Lands. The amendment

15. Munro-Fraser, *History of Sonoma County*, pp. 154, 256-58; U.S., Congress, House, *Congressional Globe*, 42nd Cong., 2nd sess., 1872, 45, pt.2:1186.

16. *Biographical Directory of the American Congress*, 1774-1961, s.v. "Houghton, Sherman O."

17. U.S., Congress, House, *Journal*, 42nd Cong., 2nd sess., 1872, pp. 395, 1185-87; U.S., Congress, *Congressional Globe*, Appendix, 42nd Cong., 2nd sess., 1872, 45, pt.4:824-25.

provided that any appeal from the circuit court's decision would have to be taken within six months. In the House floor debate, Congressman Townsend stated that "all we ask is that Valentine be allowed to go in court and prove his title if he can. If he can prove his title, then he is not to have the lands which were given by the Mexican grant to Miranda, because of the nation having taken possession of those lands and sold them—and there is a City erected upon those lands—but he is to be allowed, if he maintains his title, to have Scrip equivalent to the amount of land which he would have had under the Miranda title. Nobody's rights are infringed. Nobody is damaged. It is only a claim between him and the United States, and the bill merely permits him to come into the court and have an opportunity to be heard. This we think is a fair and honest bill." [18]

Congressman John Coghlan of California, aware of the bill's importance to his constituents, offered a second amendment that stated that no decree in favor of Valentine could be executed against any person. This prohibition was contained in the original bill, but the Californian obviously sought to cement this point with his amendment. In addition, the amendment prohibited the issuance of any scrip or patents to Valentine until he delivered a deed for the Miranda grant to the United States. Congressman Coghlan believed that the amendment would "sufficiently guard the interests of our constituents settled upon the land claimed by this grant. . . . If the amendment be adopted, no member of the California delegation will oppose the bill." [19]

The amendment was adopted, and Congressman Coghlan emphasized that "upon the land claimed by this grant there has grown up a good-sized City, and there is probably the amount of $2,000,000 worth of property upon these lands. It is a dark cloud hanging over the heads of those who have acquired the titles to these lands from the government to have this grant,

18. U.S., Congress, House, *Congressional Globe*, 42nd Cong., 2nd sess., 1872, 45, pt.2:1185-86.

19. Ibid., p. 1186.

whether good or bad, hanging over their heads, and at least one House of every Congress that meets passing a bill to allow the Miranda grant to go into the courts for adjudication. . . . The bill, as amended by me, gives Valentine the right to go into court and try the case, and if his claim proves to be just, under the grant from Miranda, a decree will be given in his favor, but shall amount to no more than waste paper until he shall have conveyed to the government, in trust for the settlers upon these lands, all his right, title, and interest to the lands. . . . This bill, as amended by me, will raise the cloud from the title of probably 2,000 persons who reside in and around the City of Petaluma." [20]

Congressman Aaron A. Sargent was another member of the California delegation who spoke out for the bill's passage. In the debate he indicated that he believed Valentine's claim to be just. He further explained that "there is a book called Tomas de Razon, a record of the titles granted by the Mexican government in Upper and Lower California. This book is kept with all the solemnity which pertains to any records of property. That book is a test or touch-stone by which bad claims can be sifted out from good claims. If those records contain the names of parties claiming the land, and also a description of the grant, that is taken by our courts as conclusive evidence in their favor. After the time for this intervention had passed, these books were brought from Mexico, and it was found, I am informed, that this Miranda grant was there named with all the solemnity that could attach to any grant.

"We, in California, feel a great interest in this matter, not so much on account of this claimant as upon account of the citizens of Petaluma. The government of the United States, on the rejection by the Supreme Court of the right of intervention and the rejection of the Ortega grant, proceeded to sell to parties in possession under its pre-emption and townsite laws this property upon which is now situated the City of Petaluma. But any man, I think, who examines the facts and ascertains the

20. Ibid.

origin of this title, must concede that the government had no right to sell that land; that the title was really in Miranda, and that some time or other justice must be done to the claimant.

"Now, if Miranda's successor is willing to accept other land instead of the specific property in question, the taking of which would dispossess 5,000 people of $2,000,000 worth of property, if he is willing to accept unoccupied land elsewhere, it seems to me it is undoubtedly the wisest policy for the government to accede to the proposition . . . in order to remove the cloud from the title which it has granted to these people whose money it has had for years in its treasury." [21]

Despite the strong support from the California delegation, the bill did not have easy sledding. Some congressmen questioned the wisdom of extending the statute of limitations on such claims, especially for one who had disbarred himself by voluntarily withdrawing his claim from the Board of Land Commissioners. Others confessed that they had difficulty grasping the legal ramifications. A third amendment was approved, which removed these objections; it substituted the word "shall" for "may" in the section authorizing an appeal—"so there shall be appeal, as a matter of course, to the Supreme Court." It was proposed that the complicated legal measure be referred to the Committee on the Judiciary, but Congressman Townsend moved the previous question, and the bill passed. [22]

Senator Eugene Casserly of California, a lawyer who had published newspapers in San Francisco and had served as the state printer prior to his election to the Senate, introduced Senate Resolution 416 as a companion measure to Congressman Houghton's bill. [23] But, since House Resolution 1024 had already passed the House, the Committee on Private Land Claims reported it out and onto the Senate floor rather than Senator Casserly's measure. Senator Thomas F. Bayard of Delaware asked for the immediate consideration of 1024,

21. Ibid.

22. Ibid.

23. *Biographical Directory of the American Congress, 1774-1961*, s.v. "Casserly, Eugene."

pointing out that "a bill more favorable in terms to the petitioner, has already passed the Senate and has twice been considered by the Committee on Private Claims"; he was apparently referring to the earlier bills without the House amendments. A single objection was voiced by Senator James Harlan of Iowa who complained that he had not had an opportunity to examine the bill. After examining the bill, Senator Harlan withdrew his objection and the measure passed the Senate and became law on 5 April 1872.[24]

Valentine filed his claim in the circuit court at San Francisco (Case 1053) on 5 June 1872, just two months after passage of the special legislation. The principal evidence supporting the claim was submitted by J.R. Hardenbergh, the United States surveyor general of California, who certified the authenticity of the deeds granted to Valentine. Hardenbergh had charge of "a portion of the Archives of the former Spanish and Mexican Territory, or Department of Upper California, as also the papers of the late Board of Commissioners to ascertain and settle the private land claims in California," and he certified that Valentine had been issued three deeds to the old rancho. One was from Theodoro and Francisca Miranda, another from Juan (probably a son of the original grantee), Sonfa, Luisa, and Magdaline Miranda, and the third from the administrators of the Miranda estate.[25]

The court also considered a deposition from Theodoro Miranda taken by Harry Thornton, land commissioner, on 5 March 1853. In it Miranda, then thirty-six, testified that he was a son of the original grantee and that the family had continued to occupy the rancho after his father's death (in about 1845) until 1850, "when it was sold to Mr. T.B. Valentine."[26] Judge Lorenzo Sawyer decreed on 6 January 1873 that Valentine's

24. U.S., Congress, Senate, *Journal*, 42nd Cong., 2nd sess., 1872, pp. 206, 1210, 1224, 1964, 1986-87; U.S., Congress, Senate, *Congressional Globe*, 42nd Cong., 2nd sess., 1872, 45, pt. 3:1963-64, 1986-87.

25. Bowman, "Spanish-Mexican Private Land Grant Records and Cases of California," p. 18; Roberts to Lee, 30 Mar. 1970; J. R. Hardenbergh, "Office of the Surveyor General of the United States, for California," 24 June 1872, Bancroft Library, University of California, Berkeley.

26. Board of Commissioners to Ascertain and Settle the Private Land Claims in California, Case no. 812, 5 Mar. 1853.

claim was valid. The case was then appealed to the United States Supreme Court, as required, and it was heard during the October term of 1873.[27] Valentine and his wife Maria signed a deed on 17 December 1873 conveying the title of the grant to the United States. The deed was delivered to Senator Sargent of California in Washington to be held in trust pending the Supreme Court's decision. On 6 January 1874, exactly one year after the lower court's decree in Valentine's favor, the long-disputed claim was affirmed.[28] The deed was presented to the commissioner of the General Land Office on that same date and it was filed on 24 January 1874 with the recorder of deeds for Sonoma County, California.[29] It had taken Valentine almost twenty-two years to prove his title to the grant that he had purchased in 1850.

Concern about the lengthy litigation was evident in Petaluma and the news that the case was finally settled was greeted with great elation. On 8 January an editorial in the *Petaluma Weekly Argus* pointed out that "when there is a shadow upon the title of our homes there is always an uneasiness that periodically breaks into downright fear and oftentimes panic. There seems to be no security. We build elegant residences and beautify our grounds, but so long as there is a question to the title of our lands, there is a lurking fear always that some day in our lifetime, or in the lifetime of our children, the lands may be wrested from us and we would have our 'trouble fore our pains.' Again, in event of a desire to sell our realty, the shadow comes up, and our property is depreciated thereby. And this has been the case with Petaluma from the very day of its settlement. . . . Many rumors have been rife that Mr. Valentine, having got into court and proven his claim, was not necessarily compelled by the terms of the Act to take lieu lands, but might, upon the affirmance of his case at Washington, come upon and dispossess the settlers here. A good

27. U.S., Department of the Interior, *Report of the Commissioner of the General Land Office to the Secretary of the Interior, 1874*, pp. 21-22.

28. *Petaluma Weekly Argus*, 5 Jan., 7 Jan. 1874.

29. W.W. Robinson, "The Strange Case of Thomas Valentine," pp. 32-33.

deal of talk had been made, and a great deal of fear endured by our people over these complications. Finally, however, like all our worldly troubles, this vexed and complicated question has been finally settled by Mr. Valentine giving a deed to government through our energetic and faithful Senator, Mr. Sargent." [30]

The *Petaluma Weekly Argus* also published two dispatches from Washington about the settlement of the case. One pointed out that Valentine was to receive "land Scrip to the same extent [as the Miranda grant] on unoccupied public lands. This quiets title in favor of purchases from the government on the grant." The other dispatch noted that "this action perfects the settlers title to all lands covered by the grant, including the town of Petaluma, and puts an end to all litigation and further uneasiness in the matter." [31]

After Valentine conveyed the deed to the United States, the commissioner of the General Land Office issued the required scrip to him in exchange for the lands illegally taken from him by the government. The scrip took the form of Special Certificates of Location and each of them followed the terminology stated in the act of 5 April 1872 which provided that "on surrender of this certificate to the register of any land office of the United States, the said Thomas B. Valentine, or his legal representative, shall be entitled to enter, in part satisfaction of said claim, the quantity of _____ acres of land upon any of the unoccupied and unappropriated public lands." The figure "40" was inserted in the blank space on most of the certificates, although lesser acreage was sometimes inscribed. It appears, however, that no more than forty acres were located on any one certificate. [32]

30. *Petaluma Weekly Argus*, 8 Jan. 1874.

31. Ibid.

32. U.S., Department of the Interior, *Report of the Commissioner of the General Land Office to the Secretary of the Interior, 1874*, pp. 21-22; *Selected Cases from the South Dakota Valentine Scrip Case Files*, NCWN 70-344, Records of the Bureau of Land Management, Record Group 49, National Archives and Records Service, Washington National Records Center (hereafter cited as *S.Dak.VSC Files*, NCWN 70-344). A copy of the microfilm is deposited in the Microfilm Collection of the South Dakota State Historical Society, Pierre.

The Miranda grant contained 13,316 acres, and with the grant divided into 40 acre tracts, Valentine was entitled to 332 certificates plus 36 acres. However, the National Archives and Records Service, which has custody of the old records of the General Land Office, could find case files on only 263 of the certificates. Of the 263 certificates, the largest single number, or 76, were redeemed in California. The certificates were also used to locate on land in 16 other states, including Arizona (46), South Dakota (34), North Dakota (28), Minnesota (25), New Mexico (12), Montana (11), Utah (8), Washington (6), Florida (5), Colorado (4), Nevada (3), Idaho, Illinois, Michigan, and Wisconsin (2), and Iowa (1).[33]

Although Valentine used few of the certificates to locate on land himself, the *San Francisco Call* reported that "the issuance of that Scrip to Valentine rendered his fame world-wide. A portion of it was sold to speculators, one of them creating a sensation about a year ago [1895] by locating on property in Chicago worth millions of dollars. The claim being contested is still in litigation."[34] Speculators who purchased the scrip from Valentine often resold the certificates for a considerable profit. The scrip reportedly brought nearly $1,000 an acre during Florida's land boom and was used to purchase islands and keys along the coastline. As late as 1928 it was used to acquire patent to the tiny White Rock Island off Catalina, which had escaped the attention of early-day government surveyors.[35]

Valentine received the scrip certificates from the commissioner of the General Land Office on 28 March 1874,

33. Bowman, "Spanish-Mexican Private Land Grant Records and Cases of California," pp. 16-18; Flatequal to Lee, 7 Apr., 24 Sept. 1970; James E. Sperry, Superintendent, State Historical Society of North Dakota, to Robert Lee, 16 Nov. 1970. Two of the twenty-eight certificates redeemed in North Dakota were used to locate on land at the site of Medora, the town established in territorial days by the ill-fated French entrepreneur, the Marquis de Mores. Certificate E 247 was used by Louis A. Hoffman on 20 April 1883 to locate forty acres in the northern half of the town, and E 73 was used by Frank B. Allen on 24 September 1883 to file on forty acres in the southern half. Louis Hoffman was undoubtedly the Marquis' father-in-law, the New York capitalist, and Frank Allen was a Bismarck attorney who did legal work for the Marquis. Nineteen of the certificates were used to locate on land at the site of Devils Lake, and the others that were redeemed were filed on land at Minot, Willow City, Port Emma, Rugby, Odessa, and Barton.

34. *San Francisco Call*, 28 Oct. 1896, p. 14.

35. W.W. Robinson, "The Strange Case of Thomas Valentine," pp. 32-33.

slightly more than two months after the commissioner had received his deed to the Miranda grant. He soon began selling the scrip and was relatively unconcerned about the identity of the persons who eventually used his scrip to locate on land, once he had collected his fee. The certificates contained Valentine's signature, the selling price, and the date. Valentine's signature was attested to by two witnesses, one of whom was frequently D.B. Francis, his partner in the printing firm. The name of the buyer was generally not listed at the time of the sale. Because it was not necessary for the buyer to be listed until the scrip was presented to land offices in exchange for locations, the scrip could, and often did, pass through several hands before actually being redeemed. The redemptions generally took place years after Valentine had sold the certificates. This procedure, while technically legal, invited misappropriation.[36]

Two procedures were followed to trace the circuitous paths of the scrip certificates redeemed in South Dakota, or more accurately, in Dakota Territory for South Dakota did not become .a state until 1889, and all the certificates redeemed in the territory were used prior to 1889. One procedure, based on the date that Valentine sold the certificate, established the date of each sale and the sale price but did not identify the buyer, since the assignments carried only the signatures of Valentine, the witnesses, and the notary public. The second procedure, based on the date that each certificate was actually presented to a land office in exchange for a location, established the identity of the user, since his name had to be on the assignment. It is questionable, however, whether the eventual user was the original buyer of the scrip. In addition, the case files at the National Archives contained no assignments from Valentine for certificates E47, E51, E104, E105, E316, E319, and E320, seven of the thirty-four redeemed in South Dakota, although there were subsequent assignments of these certificates. (For the following discussion, see Tables 1, 2, 3, and 4, pages 295-99.)

The first method of investigation established that four of the certificates sold by Valentine in 1874 were eventually redeemed in Dakota. They were E5, E23, E78, and E90, and E5 was the first certificate sold that was eventually redeemed in

36. *S.Dak. VSC Files*, NCWN 70-344.

Dakota. It was sold on 25 April 1874 to C. Underwood of Monterey, California, for $240. On 31 December 1881 A. Leon Cervantes "to whom the annexed Valentine Scrip E5 was assigned" sold it "for value received" to William T. Love of Beadle County in Dakota Territory. The case file on this certificate does not contain an assignment from Underwood to Cervantes, thus it is not known when Cervantes bought the certificate or what he paid for it. Love used the scrip to file on forty acres in Hand County on 4 March 1882. Valentine sold E23 on 21 July 1874 for $200 and it was redeemed for land in Dakota in 1881. Certificates E78 and E90 were sold by Valentine for $400 each on 12 August 1874 to Theodore Leroy of San Francisco. Leroy sold both of the certificates to William T. Coleman, also of San Francisco, on 6 January 1880 "for value received." Coleman sold E90 to Eugene S. Elliott on 1 August 1882, also "for value received," and Elliott used it to locate on forty acres in Walworth County on 14 April 1883. Coleman sold E78 to Henry P. Bolles for $700 (a $300 profit) on 10 August 1882, and Bolles used it to file on forty acres in Campbell County on 17 July 1883. While these certificates were among the first that Valentine sold, they were not the first to be used in Dakota.[37]

The second method of tracing the scrip's usage in Dakota produced the most reliable information. The first certificates filed in Dakota were E176 and E208. Valentine had sold E176 on 3 March 1875 and E208 on 24 June 1875, each for $480 and both to Henry McDaid, an attorney in Chicago, Illinois. On 11 December 1877 in Washington, D.C., McDaid sold the two certificates to Barney G. Caulfield for $640 apiece and realized a profit of $160 on each.[38] Caulfield redeemed both of the

37. Ibid.

38. *Biographical Directory of the American Congress, 1774-1961*, s.v. "Caulfield, Barney"; Larry A. Viskochil, Reference Librarian, Chicago Historical Society, to Robert Lee, 19 Feb. 1970; *Chicago Tribune*, 21 Dec. 1887; *Black Hills Daily Times* (Deadwood), 23 Dec. 1887; *Sturgis Weekly Record*, 23 Dec. 1887. Caulfield was an attorney and a congressman from Illinois and served in the House from 1874 until 1877. He was not a member of Congress when he purchased the two scrip certificates from McDaid, although the transaction took place in Washington. He moved to Deadwood and continued his law practice there. He was a prominent member of the community and he reportedly "owned considerable property in Sturgis, acquired when the city was first platted."

certificates at the United States Land Office in Deadwood on 25 October 1878 for two tracts of land "in the prospective townsite of Sturgis City," then in Lawrence County but subsequently the county seat of Meade County. Each of the two tracts were described as containing .36 acres in excess of the forty, and Caulfield paid the land office a total of ninety cents for the additional acreage.[39]

How Caulfield happened to participate in the establishment of Sturgis City was revealed in an article in the *Sturgis Weekly Record*, written by the man who actually laid out the town site, Jeremiah C. Wilcox, a major in the Civil War who had left the service to become a newspaper publisher in Omaha, Nebraska.[40] Wilcox told how he left Omaha to visit Colonel Samuel D. Sturgis, commander of the Seventh Cavalry at Bear Butte, in the fall of 1878. During the course of the visit, he proposed to Colonel Sturgis that a town site should be laid out near the new post. "The general [Colonel Sturgis' Civil War rank] seemed to regard the project favorably, and a few days later visited me in my cabin at Deadwood where I submitted to him definite plans and he consented to become a member of the company, rather, I think, to oblige me than from any prospect of gain for himself. On leaving he handed me a twenty dollar gold piece, remarking, 'I am tolerably short now, but you can give me credit for so much on the townsite account and draw on me for more at your pleasure.' About three o'clock on the morning of August 26, 1878, I staked the ground where Sturgis City now is. . . . That night I went to Deadwood for an assistant, as I had to get around and could not be in two places

39. *S.Dak. VSC Files*, NCWN 70-344.

40. Francis B. Heitman, *Historical Register and Dictionary of the United States Army, 1789-1903* (1903; reprinted ed., Urbana: University of Illinois Press, 1965), p. 934; Melbourne C. Chandler, *Of Garry Owen in Glory: The History of the Seventh United States Cavalry Regiment* (n.p., 1960), p. 77; Jerusha Wilcox Sturgis, "Biography of Sturgis and Wilcox Families" (unpublished manuscript, 1910), a copy in the private collection of Robert Lee, Sturgis. Wilcox was a cousin of Mrs. Jerusha Wilcox Sturgis whose husband Colonel Samuel D. Sturgis was commander of the Seventh Cavalry from May of 1868 until his retirement in June of 1886. Units of the Seventh Cavalry were sent to the Black Hills in the summer of 1878 to aid in establishing a military post near Bear Butte. White settlers who had swarmed into the Indian region during the gold boom demanded military protection from the Sioux who were disgruntled over the loss of their sacred Black Hills.

Ɛ 208

Department of the Interior,

GENERAL LAND OFFICE,

Washington, D.C., _March 28, 1874._

Whereas, by Act of Congress approved April 5, 1872, entitled "An Act for the relief of Thomas B. Valentine," it was enacted:

That the ninth circuit court of the United States, of California, be, and hereby is, authorized and required to hear, and decide upon the merits the claim of Thomas B. Valentine, claiming title, under a Mexican grant to Juan Miranda, to a place called the Rancho Arroyo de San Antonio, situate in the county of Sonoma and State of California, in the same manner, and with the same jurisdiction, as if the claim to the said tract of land had been duly presented to the board of land commissioners under the provisions of the act entitled "An act to ascertain and settle the private land claims in the State of California," approved March third, eighteen hundred and fifty-one, and an appeal had been duly taken from their decision to the district court of California by the said Thomas B. Valentine.

That on the said hearing any testimony heretofore taken before the said board of commissioners in relation to said claim on behalf of the said claimant, or of the United States, may be read, subject to all just exceptions to its competency; and additional testimony, on either part, may be taken, under the order and direction of said circuit court, as to the validity and extent of said claim.

That an appeal shall be taken from the final decision and decree of the said circuit court to the Supreme Court of the United States by either party, in accordance with the provisions of the tenth section of said act of March third, eighteen hundred and fifty-one, within six months after the rendition of such final decision; and a decree under the provisions of this act, in favor of said claim, shall not affect any adverse right or title to the lands described in said decree; but in lieu thereof, the claimant, or his legal representatives, may select, and shall be allowed, patents for an equal quantity of the unappropriated public lands of the United States, not mineral, and in tracts not less than the subdivisions provided for in the United States land laws, and, if unsurveyed when taken, to conform, when surveyed, to the general system of United States land surveys; and the Commissioner of the General Land Office, under the direction of the Secretary of the Interior, shall be authorized to issue scrip, in legal subdivisions, to the said Valentine, or his legal representatives, in accordance with the provisions of this act: _Provided_, That no decree in favor of said Valentine shall be executed nor be of any force or effect against any person or persons; nor shall land scrip or patents issue as hereinbefore provided, unless the said Valentine shall first execute and deliver to the Commissioner of the General Land Office a deed conveying to the United States all his right, title, and interest to the lands covered by said Miranda grant.

And whereas, the said Thomas B. Valentine did, on the 5th day of June, A. D. 1872, pursuant to the act aforesaid, file in the said Circuit Court of the United States, a petition praying the said court to hear and decide upon the merits of his claim to the said Rancho Arroyo de San Antonio, whereupon the said court, on the 6th day of January, A. D. 1873, in the cause entitled Thomas B. Valentine vs. The United States, rendered the following decree:

In this case, on hearing the proofs and allegations, it is ordered, adjudged, and decreed that the said claim of the petitioner is valid, and that the same be and hereby is confirmed; but this decree and confirmation are hereby made subject to the restrictions and limitations prescribed in the act of Congress entitled "An Act for the relief of Thomas B. Valentine," approved April 5, 1872.

The land ot which confirmation is made is the same which was granted by Manuel Micheltorena, in the name of the Mexican government, to Juan Miranda, on the 8th day of October, 1844, and on which he resided in his lifetime, and is known by the name of Rancho Arroyo de San Antonio, and bounded by the laguna and arroyo of the same name, and the pass and estero of Petaluma; and is in extent three square leagues, and no more; and if a less quantity is included in said boundaries, then said lesser

FOR AND IN CONSIDERATION of the sum of *Four Hundred*
Eighty ($480*)* _____ Dollars,
to me in hand paid, I, THOMAS B. VALENTINE, of the City and County of
San Francisco, and State of California, to whom the within Special Certificate of
Location E, No. *208* was issued, do hereby sell and assign unto
Henry O McDaid
of *Cook* _____ County and State of *Illinois* _____ and to
his heirs and assigns forever the said Special Certificate of Location E, No. *208.*
and I do hereby authorize him to locate the same and receive a Patent for the
land so located.

Witness my hand and seal this _____ *24th* _____ day of
June _____ A. D. 187*5*

Attest. *Henry S Tibbey*   *Thos B Valentine*
D B Francis

State of California,
City and County of San Francisco, $\}$ *ss* :

On this *Twenty fourth* _____ day of
June _____ A. D. eighteen hundred and seventy *five*
before me, *Henry S Tibbey* _____ a Notary Public in and for said City
and County, personally appeared THOMAS B. VALENTINE, known to me to be
the person whose name is subscribed to the within Instrument, and he duly
acknowledged to me that he executed the same.

IN WITNESS WHEREOF, I have hereunto
set my hand and affixed my Official Seal
at my office in the City and County of
San Francisco, the day and year in this
Certificate first above written.

Henry S Tibbey
Notary Public

Special Certificate of Location E208
and the first assignment of E208 from Thomas B. Valentine to Henry O. McDaid.

For and in consideration of the sum of Six Hundred and forty dollars to me in hand paid I Henry O. McDaid of the City of Chicago, County of Cook, State of Illinois to whom the within special certificate of Location "E," No. 208, has been assigned by Thomas B. Valentine of the City and County of San Francisco, and State of California, do hereby sell and assign unto Bernard G Caulfield of County of Laurence and Territory of Dakota and to his heirs and assigns for= ever the said special certificate of Location "E" No. 208, and I do hereby authorize him to locate the same and receive a patent for the land so located.

Witness my hand and seal this eleventh day of December A.D. 1877.

Henry O McDaid (seal)

Attest,
John T. Burch.
C A Tedder

Land Office at Deadwood Dakota

October 25 , 1878.

Mr. Bernard G. Caulfield ____ has this day paid

~~Application for~~ *Valentine Scrip E no 208* ____ dollars, the Register's and Receiver's fees,

to file an ~~Declaratory Statement~~, the receipt whereof is hereby acknowledged.

M McKenna

Receiver.

No. 4

Mr. Bernard G Caulfield ____, having paid the fees,

has this day filed in this Office his ~~Declaratory Statement~~ *application*, No. 4

~~for~~ *the* Locate Valentine Scrip E no 208

On unsurveyed *lands*, as described Section in diagram

~~Township~~ on file ____, of ~~Range~~ in this office, containing

~~Forty acres~~ 3 4/100 acres, ~~settled upon~~ _____, 18 ___, being

____ un offered.

A S Stewart

Register.

The second assignment of E208 from Henry
O. McDaid to Bernard G. Caulfield and
Caulfield's receipt from the Deadwood Land
Office, 25 October 1878. E 208 was used to
locate land on the Sturgis City town site.

at once, and I got Arthur Buckbee to join me next morning and hold the claim (promising him an interest which he got) while I went to Deadwood to talk up the scheme and organize the town company." Besides Wilcox, Colonel Sturgis, Buckbee, and others, Caulfield was also a member of the town company.[41]

Caulfield filed on 80.72 acres of the town site of Sturgis City for his two Valentine Scrip certificates permitted him to locate on the site without ready cash. Because he was an attorney, he may have been made a partner in the company in exchange for his legal services. On 2 November 1878, eight days after filing the scrip, Caulfield conveyed thirty-five lots in ten blocks to Wilcox for the consideration of "certain rights and interests claimed."[42] This was undoubtedly Wilcox's reward for staking out the site and forming the company.

Wilcox secured scrip certificate E228, the third one redeemed in the territory, and used it to locate forty acres on the eastern boundary of Sturgis City, in what became known as the Wilcox Addition. Valentine had sold E228 on 18 August 1875 for $420, but Wilcox did not file it at the land office in Deadwood until 22 July 1879, nine months after Caulfield had filed his scrip.[43] It is uncertain whether Wilcox purchased his certificate directly from Valentine in 1875, although there is no earlier assignment of it to anyone else, or whether Caulfield may have purchased this certificate with the other two in 1877 and left the assignment blank. In any event, Caulfield may have been an agent in Wilcox's procurement of the scrip.

The use of scrip to locate on the site of Sturgis City was contested by a group of the town's earliest settlers who claimed that the tract of land was neither unoccupied nor unappropriated as required at the time of filing.[44] The 1880 census reported that sixty people were living in Sturgis City and some of these early settlers claimed that they were there in

41. *Sturgis Weekly Record*, 8 May 1889.

42. Register of Deeds, Records of Meade County, Book 26, Document 152127, p. 405.

43. *S.Dak. VSC Files*, NCWN 70-344; Flatequal to Lee, 7 Apr. 1970.

44. *Sturgis Weekly Record*, 24 Aug. 1883.

1878 when the site was located on—with the Valentine Scrip.[45] These claims, however, were not substantiated at a hearing conducted by the land office in Deadwood, and the legality of the scrip locations was upheld by the commissioner of the General Land Office. Caulfield received patent to his tracts on 2 February and 17 February 1885, and Wilcox received his patent on 23 December 1883.[46]

Most of the certificates used in Dakota, however, were redeemed by two officials of the Chicago and North Western Railway Company, Albert Keep, president of the railroad from 19 June 1873 to 2 June 1887 and Charles E. Simmons, the land commissioner of the company from 1878 to 1897. Between them, they used nineteen scrip certificates to locate on land along the railroad's route in Dakota.[47] In 1880 the Dakota Central Railway Company, which was operated by the Chicago and North Western, was extending its tracks from Volga, on the territory's eastern border, to the Missouri River. Two years earlier Marvin Hughitt, the company's general manager, had made a personal tour of the Dakota prairies by buckboard and had concluded that to extend railroads across the Dakota prairies was an inducement to settlement, and therefore, good business.[48] The company's officials may have used scrip to file on land in other states, but only nineteen of the thirty-four certificates redeemed in Dakota can be traced directly to Keep and Simmons.

Valentine sold E103 on 17 September 1880 for $600 to Albert Keep. Keep also acquired E104 and E105, but because there are no assignments on record for them, the date that they were sold and their sale price is unknown. Keep may have

45. U.S., Department of Commerce, Bureau of the Census, *Tenth Census: Population, 1880*, Vol. 2, *Schedule I*, Lawrence County, C 595½, Microfilm Collection, South Dakota State Historical Society, Pierre.

46. *Sturgis Weekly Record*, 8 Sept. 1883; *S.Dak. VSC Files*, NCWN 70-344.

47. F.V. Koval, Director of Public Relations, Chicago and North Western Railway Company, to Dayton Canaday, Director, South Dakota State Historical Society, Pierre, 24 Sept. 1970; Flatequal to Lee, 5 June 1970. •

48. Herbert S. Schell, *History of South Dakota* (Lincoln: University of Nebraska Press, 1961), pp. 161-62.

bought them on the same date and for the same price as E103 since the certificates were consecutively numbered. He used all three certificates on 4 January 1881 to locate on tracts in Beadle County near Huron where the Dakota Central had established a construction camp the previous May.[49] Simmons, who had sixteen certificates, used all or portions of ten of them on 26 May 1881 to locate on 365.80 acres in Hughes County. He used his six remaining certificates, also on 26 May 1881, to locate on 236.90 acres across the river in Stanley County. Four of them were exchanged for 40 acre tracts and two were redeemed for tracts of 38.10 and 38.80 acres. While the sixteen certificates redeemed in the two counties were good for a total of 640 acres, they were exchanged for 37.30 fewer acres. [50]

The Chicago and North Western had visions of stretching its tracks, once it reached the Missouri River, westward across the Great Sioux Reservation to the Black Hills. Fort Pierre, on the river's west bank, was the freighting center for supplies to the booming mining camps in the Black Hills, which the Sioux had ceded in 1877. Only a few squatters were living east of the river, opposite Fort Pierre, and they were congregated around a small settlement called Matto. People speculated on where the railroad would cross the river and the squatters were naturally most anxious about it. Although the river was not bridged until 1907, the Chicago and North Western took steps early to avoid paying exorbitant prices for the land it needed for its river terminal. [51]

A party of men hired by the railroad and traveling in a covered wagon invaded the country around Matto in the summer of 1880, ostensibly looking for land for a cattle ranch. They succeeded in buying out a number of the squatters, especially after spreading the rumor that the railroad had picked Fort George, some twenty miles down river, as the river terminal. Joseph Kirley, a squatter who had located at Matto in

49. *S.Dak.VSC Files*, NCWN 70-344.

50. Ibid.

51. Will G. Robinson, "Waiting for a Railroad," *South Dakota Historical Collections* 24(1949):155.

1879 and who operated the ferry to Fort Pierre, also sold out. He and several others felt that they had been duped when they learned that the "cattlemen" who had bought them out were actually agents of the railroad. Kirley's daughter, Laura Kirley McAllister, wrote that "by using the ranch site hoax and the Fort George decoy, the railroad finally won out. And by raising the original cash offer to $1,500 and a small piece of ground, the railroad persuaded Joseph to sign away his home, his flatboat business, and his rights to the townsite of what was to become Pierre.... To ingratiate the couple [Kirley and his wife] further, he [the railway company agent] presented Joseph with a bonus of a shotgun." Laura McAllister also reported that the railroad acquired clear title to the Pierre town site through "Sioux Indian Scrip," writing that "as a rule, the early settlers were unaware of its existence or its purposes."[52] Actually, the land was acquired with Valentine Scrip.

The plat map of the original site of Pierre reveals that Thomas F. Nicholl, a surveyor, "at the instance of Charles E. Simmons of Chicago," staked out the town site in blocks, lots, streets, and alleys "on and prior to" 20 September 1880 "for the purpose of laying out a town to be called Pierre." The plat, covering fourteen blocks, is dated 27 September 1880.[53] Simmons had filed his scrip certificates for Pierre locations and other tracts in that region at the United States Land Office in Sioux Falls on 3 June 1880. The desired tracts were within the jurisdiction of the land office at Mitchell and the certificates were later refiled there.[54] By that time, two railway additions to the original site of Pierre had been platted—there were eventually to be five railway additions.[55]

On 4 November 1880 the first train arrived in Pierre, and on

52. Laura Kirley McAllister, *Gumbo Trails* (Pierre, S. Dak.: State Publishing Company, 1957), pp. 85-87.

53. Carl Fischer, Fort Pierre, to Robert Lee, 14 July 1970; Register of Deeds, Hughes County, Plat Book 1, pp. 1-2, Hughes County Courthouse, Pierre, S. Dak. (hereafter cited as Hughes County Plat Book 1).

54. *S.Dak. VSC Files*, NCWN 70-344.

55. Fischer to Lee, 5 Aug. 1970; Hughes County Plat Book 1, pp. 2-3.

1883 MAP OF SOUTHERI

DAKOTA TERRITORY

21 December 1880 the Western Town Lot Company was incorporated in Chicago by Keep, Simmons, Hughitt, N.M. Hubbard, and Joseph B. Redfield. The corporation, which began operations on 1 January 1881 with its principal office in Clinton, Iowa, was organized to "buy, improve, plat and lay out into town lots, and sell and deal in land and town lots in the States of Iowa and Minnesota and the Territory of Dakota." Its articles of incorporation also stated that the company was formed "to promote imigration [*sic*] and the settlement or occupation of lands in such States and Territories." The corportion had a capital stock of $100,000 divided into shares for $100, and the first officers were Keep, president; Hughitt, vice-president; Redfield, secretary; and M.M. Kirkman, treasurer. The company's principal office was later moved to Huron and Thomas J. Nicholl (or Nichol) served as resident agent there until 22 July 1886.[56]

Nicholl was undoubtedly the man who had laid out the town site of Pierre. Two days after the Western Town Lot Company was organized, Nicholl acquired E56 and the assignment from Valentine showed that it was sold to him for $1,040. Nicholl used E56 to locate on forty acres in Hyde County on 9 June 1882. On 23 December 1880, the same date that Nicholl received his certificate, Frederick H. Steigmeyer of Hughes County bought E123 from Valentine for $1,200. Steigmeyer used E123 to locate on forty acres in Sully County on 9 April 1883. On the first assignments, the certificates purchased by Nicholl and Steigmeyer sold for the highest prices of all thirty-four redeemed in Dakota. But another certificate sold for a higher price on the second assignment.[57]

Simmons, who redeemed the largest number of certificates in Dakota, appears to have acquired the scrip largely for himself rather than as an agent for the railroad since the first quit claim deeds filed in Pierre were sold by Simmons and his wife Lucy early in 1881. They first sold lots nineteen and twenty in block

56. Schell, *History of South Dakota*, p. 162; Articles of Incorporation, Western Town Lot Company, File Box 95, Document 10121, Office of the Secretary of State, Pierre, S. Dak.; Koval to Lee, 28 Oct. 1971; Flatequal to Lee, 5 June 1970.

57. *S.Dak. VSC Files*, NCWN 70-344.

seven to the American Express Company for $200 and the deed was dated 14 February 1881. On that same date, they also conveyed the deeds for eight lots in two blocks of the site to E.F. Warner of Saint Paul for $800. The third and fifth deeds filed in the Hughes County courthouse reveal that Simmons and his wife sold lots fifteen and sixteen in block seven to Henry C. Laferty and Joseph Kirley, respectively, for $1 each. Laferty, like Kirley, was among the early squatters on the town site. The sale to Kirley for the nominal fee was probably a fulfillment of the promise of "a small piece of ground" to be given to him when he sold out to the railroad. Some of the other first deeds for Pierre lots sold in 1881 reveal that the premises were contracted to be sold the previous fall when the site was being platted. These deeds were probably conveyed to former squatters too. Many of these early deeds were conveyed upon the express condition that "no spiritous liquor of any kind, except for medicinal purposes, shall ever be sold upon said premises." [58]

However, in 1881 Simmons also assigned "all my rights, title and interest" to all sixteen of his scrip certificates to Keep. Although he assigned only one certificate, E187, to Keep on 7 May, all of the other assignments were dated 7 November, or almost six months after he had used all sixteen scrip certificates to locate on tracts in Hughes and Stanley counties on 26 May. [59] The certificates, although filed in the land office in exchange for land, were undoubtedly transferrable prior to the issuance of the patents, which were not granted until late in 1882.

Included in the Simmons-Keep transaction were certificates E185 and E187, sold by Valentine on 3 April 1875 for $438. The buyer was listed as Edwin C. Peters "of Lawrence County, D.T.," although it is probable that his name was not written on the assignments until some time after the sale date. Peters could have been in Lawrence County as early as April of 1875, but, if so, he was there illegally. He may have been among the first

58. Ibid; Fischer to Lee, 14 July 1970; Quit Claim Deeds, Book A-15, pp. 1-5, Hughes County Courthouse, Pierre.

59. *S.Dak. VSC Files*, NCWN 70-344.

gold seekers that illegally invaded the Great Sioux Reservation during the initial stampede to the newly discovered gold fields. He was living, however, in Sioux City, Iowa, when he assigned both of his certificates to Simmons on 22 and 23 November 1878 for $440 each, thus realizing a profit of only $2 on each certificate.[60]

The most interesting of the scrip certificates that came into Simmons' possession, and subsequently into Keep's, is E23. Of all the certificates redeemed in Dakota, it carries the earliest assignment date from Valentine and also illustrates the danger inherent in Valentine's practice of selling the certificates without listing the buyers on the assignments. Valentine sold this certificate on 21 July 1874. Ten days later William L. Webber presented it to the land office at Ionia, Michigan, without attaching his name to the assignment. The tract of land Webber desired had not been surveyed (and was not until 1883) so he left the certificate and the blank assignment in that office until he could legally locate on the land he wanted. When he returned, he discovered that the documents he had left behind were missing. Meanwhile, the land office had been moved to Reed City, Michigan, and a clerk there confessed to carelessness "in keeping the safe open and sometimes leaving it unlocked."[61]

Further investigation by the land office revealed that E23 was one of the certificates that Simmons had used to file on the Pierre town site on 26 May 1881. It had been redeemed for twenty-one acres "and patent issued thereon," and the assignment carried Simmons' name and the sale price of $200, leaving the impression that Valentine had sold it directly to him. But, Simmons admitted to the land office officials that he had bought the scrip in April 1880 from D.H. Talbott of Sioux City, Iowa. Talbott, in his explanation, reported that he had purchased the document on 17 May 1879 from G.F.D. Wilson of Reed City. This was the name of the land office clerk who had earlier confessed to "carelessness" about the office safe. As

60. Ibid.; Mildred Fielder, ed., *Lawrence County: Dakota Territory Centennial, 1861-1961* (Lawrence County Centennial Committee, 1961), pp. 14-15.

61. *S.Dak. VSC Files*, NCWN 70-344.

several years had elapsed since Webber had left the documents in the office, perhaps Wilson believed it was safe to market them. The acting secretary of the interior, in commenting upon the case, pointed out that "the government does not guarantee the integrity of its officers. It prescribes rules for them, requires the oath of faithful discharge of duties, exacts a bond, and provides penalties for their misconduct or fraud, but there its responsibility ends." The patent for the twenty-one acres located on by Simmons, and assigned to Keep, was allowed to stand. [62]

Although all of his certificates had been assigned to Keep in 1881, Simmons appears to have retained an interest in four certificates, which had been redeemed for less than forty acres each. These four certificates were the stolen E23, and E316, E319, and E320; and they were used to locate on tracts of 21, 38.10, 38.30, and 24.80 acres, respectively, in Hughes and Stanley counties. After Simmons' death, his wife sold the unused portions of these certificates on 21 June 1904 to Hughitt, who had succeeded Keep as president of the Chicago and North Western. The commissioner of the General Land Office, however, rejected Hughitt's application for recertification of the "unexhausted quantity" of the ill-fated E23. The rejection was upheld by Acting Secretary of the Interior Thomas Ryan, who wrote on 4 August 1905 that "it is not pretended that there was any semblance of color for the clerk in the local land office [at Reed City, Michigan] to remove the Scrip from the files and reissue it. The Scrip was satisfied by location of the land and was no longer evidence of an existing right. Its larceny and reissue could give no new life to it, or recreate or resurrect an obligation which was paid and dead." Thus, Hughitt failed to acquire patent to the unused portion of E23. He may have been permitted to locate on land using the inexhausted quantity of the other three certificates, but, if so, they were not redeemed in South Dakota. [63]

Keep had used three certificates, not assigned to him by Simmons, to locate on tracts in Beadle County in 1881. Two of

62. Ibid.

63. Ibid.

them had been redeemed for less than forty acres each. In 1904 "for a valuable consideration," Keep assigned the unused portions of E104 (3.41 acres) and E105 (4.27 acres) to Hughitt. The commissioner of the General Land Office recertified the two certificates "as to the unused portions thereof" early in 1905, but the recertified scrip were not used in South Dakota. [64]

At this point, six of the thirty-four certificates used in Dakota are still to be accounted for. Certificate E5, the first sold by Valentine to be eventually redeemed in Dakota, became the possession of William T. Love of Beadle County, who had acquired it by assignment from C. Underwood and A. Leon Cervantes. Certificates E216 and E253 were sold by Valentine on 25 March 1882 and 4 October 1878, respectively, to George J. Love, also of Beadle County, who paid $1,000 for each of them. George Love used E216 and E253 to locate on two forty-acre tracts in Hand County on 10 July 1882. William Love had also redeemed his certificate in Hand County on 4 March 1882. George's application for a location under E253 was accompanied by a map of the tract he desired and the map was drawn on the letterhead stationery of the superintendent's office of the Dakota Central Railway and the Chicago and Dakota Railway companies at Huron, which were divisions of the Chicago and North Western. [65]

There is evidence linking the two Loves. On 25 March 1882, the same date that E216 was sold to George Love, Valentine sold E215 for $940 and the buyer was listed as Edson O. Parker of Hyde County. Parker used E215 to locate on forty acres in Hyde County on 20 September 1883. It is conceivable that George Love had acquired E215 at the same time as E216, left the assignment blank, and then conveyed it to Parker in a land exchange. In any case, Parker requested that the patent for the Hyde County tract be sent to William F. and George J. Love at Huron. Earlier, on 9 June 1882, Parker had signed a

64. Ibid.

65. Ibid.; Koval to Lee, 28 Oct. 1971. No information could be found to substantiate that William T. and George J. Love, Barney G. Caulfield, Eugene S. Elliott, Henry P. Bolles, Jeremiah C. Wilcox, Edson O. Parker, Christopher A. Bliss, Isahel Todd, F.A. Davis, and D.N. Hunt were agents of the Chicago and North Western Railway Company in the 1880s.

Relinquishment of Homestead and Timber entry to the tract and asked that the "application to put Valentine Scrip thereon be allowed. The relinquishment being made for that purpose only." The relinquishment was witnessed by William T. Love and was accompanied by a statement from Parker that stated that the tract was "unoccupied and unappropriated by any person or persons claiming the same under the pre-emption or homestead or other laws of the United States." Parker further certified that the tract was "now held by me as a squatter." The location was approved for patent on 20 January 1885.[66]

Fortunately, there were no complicating ties linking the three remaining certificates with certificates used by others to locate on land in the territory. The three are E51, E220, and E255. The case file shows no first assignment for E51, but, Christopher A. Bliss of Brown County used it to locate on forty acres in Edmunds County on 14 March 1883. Valentine sold E220 on 31 August 1881 for $600 and Reuben Richardson of Kankakee County, Illinois, was listed as the buyer. On 17 July 1882 in Chicago, Richardson sold the certificate for the same price he paid for it to Isahel Todd of Huron and Todd redeemed it for forty acres in Potter County on 13 September 1883. Valentine sold E255 on 10 October 1878 for $640 to Allen Macomber of Mantealin County, Michigan. On 15 July 1882 in Detroit, Macomber sold the certificate to Fredrick A. Davis and Daniel N. Hunt of Redfield. The assignment was made for $1,320, the highest sum paid for a second assignment. Davis and Hunt redeemed this certificate for forty acres in Faulk County on 7 December 1882. The previous day, Charles Varnam (or Nauman, the name is illegible on the document) had signed a relinquishment on part of the tract located on by Davis and Hunt; he certified that he was the only one living there and that he had a house ten by twelve feet on the site. He further testified that the relinquishment was granted so that Valentine Scrip could be used to locate on the tract. Patent for the tract was issued on 26 June 1891.[67]

Valentine was rather handsomely rewarded for the $9,550

66. *S.Dak. VSC Files*, NCWN 70-344.

67. Ibid.

he had spent in acquiring the title to the Miranda grant, although the expense of the lengthy litigation required to prove his title unquestionably cut deeply into his profits. The sale price on twenty-seven of the original assignments of the certificates redeemed in Dakota show that Valentine received a total of $13,716 for them, thus recovering $4,166 more than the price of the grant on the certificates used in Dakota alone. Valentine had sold these certificates for prices ranging from a low of $100 to a high of $1,200. Twenty certificates were sold a second time, but a sale price was listed on only six of them. These six certificates were originally purchased for a total of $3,076, for prices ranging from $438 to $640. They were assigned a second time for prices ranging from $440 to $1,320 and brought a total of $4,080, representing a $1,004 profit to the original purchasers. In addition, six certificates were assigned a third time, but a sale price was listed on only one of them. Certificate E78, originally sold by Valentine for $400, was sold a second time "for value received." But, on the third assignment, it sold for $700. Thus, what Valentine realized from the sale of his scrip in all of the states was likely more than enough to properly reward him for the long and costly effort he had expended in proving his title.[68]

The remarkable feature of the Valentine Scrip is not their monetary value but rather their appearance in many widely scattered sections of the country—where they were marketed with apparent ease. Their use in the procurement of public domain tracts has no special significance, although their existence exposes a little-known facet of land settlement. The town sites of Pierre and Sturgis, for example, would undoubtedly have been purchased by the conventional means of cash payments if the founders of the towns had not come into possession of Valentine Scrip.

68. Ibid. The figures are reached by totalling the prices on the certificates.

TABLE 1

VALENTINE SCRIP CERTIFICATES
USED TO LOCATE ON LAND IN DAKOTA TERRITORY

First Assignment

Certificate	Date	Price	Buyer
E5	25 Apr. 1874	$240	C. Underwood
			Monterey, Calif.
E23	21 July 1874	$200	C.E. Simmons
			Chicago, Ill.
E38	15 Sept. 1874	$100	C.E. Simmons
E56	23 Dec. 1880	$1,040	T. Nicholl
E78	12 Aug. 1874	$400	T. Leroy
			San Francisco, Calif.
E90	12 Aug. 1874	$400	T. Leroy
E97	29 Apr. 1880	$400	C.E. Simmons
E98	29 Apr. 1880	$400	C.E. Simmons
E103	17 Sept. 1880	$600	A. Keep
E123	23 Dec. 1880	$1,200	F.H. Steigmeyer
			Hughes County
E176	3 Mar. 1875	$480	H. McDaid
			Chicago, Ill.
E185	3 Apr. 1875	$438	E.C. Peters
			Lawrence County
E187	3 Apr. 1875	$438	E.C. Peters
E208	24 June 1875	$480	H. McDaid
E215	25 Mar. 1882	$940	E.O. Parker
			Hyde County
E216	25 Mar. 1882	$1,000	G. J. Love
			Beadle County
E220	31 Aug. 1881	$600	R. Richardson
			Kankakee County, Ill.
E228	18 Aug. 1875	$420	J.C. Wilcox
			Omaha, Nebr.
E237	9 Apr. 1880	$400	C.E. Simmons
E238	9 Apr. 1880	$400	C.E. Simmons
E239	21 Aug. 1879	$200	C.E. Simmons
E253	4 Oct. 1878	$1,000	G.J. Love
E255	10 Oct. 1878	$640	A. Macomber
			Mantealin County, Mich.
E269	9 Apr. 1880	$400	C.E. Simmons
E317	9 Apr. 1880	$400	C.E. Simmons
E318	9 Apr. 1880	$100	C.E. Simmons
E321	9 Apr. 1880	$400	C.E. Simmons

NOTE: These certificates are accompanied by assignments from Thomas B. Valentine to the above named buyers.

TABLE 2

VALENTINE SCRIP CERTIFICATES
USED TO LOCATE ON LAND IN DAKOTA TERRITORY

Second Assignments

Certificate	From	To	Date	Price
E5	C. Underwood	A. L. Cervantes	Unknown	Unknown
E23	C.E. Simmons	A. Keep	7 Nov. 1881	Unknown
E38	C.E. Simmons	A. Keep	8 Nov. 1881	Unknown
E78	T. Leroy	W. T. Coleman San Francisco	6 Jan. 1880	Value rec'd.
E90	T. Leroy	W.T. Coleman	6 Jan. 1880	Value rec'd.
E97	C.E. Simmons	A. Keep	8 Nov. 1881	Value rec'd.
E98	C.E. Simmons	A. Keep	7 Nov. 1881	Value rec'd.
E176	H. McDaid	B.G. Caulfield	11 Dec. 1877	$640
E185	E.C. Peters	C.E. Simmons	22 Nov. 1878	$440
E187	E.C. Peters	C.E. Simmons	23 Nov. 1878	$440
E208	H. McDaid	B.G. Caulfield	11 Dec. 1877	$640
E220	R. Richardson	I. Todd of Huron	17 July 1882	$600
E237	C.E. Simmons	A. Keep	7 Nov. 1881	Value rec'd.
E238	C.E. Simmons	A. Keep	7 Nov. 1881	Unknown
E239	C.E. Simmons	A. Keep	7 Nov. 1881	Unknown
E255	A. Macomber	F.A Davis and D.N. Hunt Redfield	15 July 1882	$1,320
E269	C.E. Simmons	A. Keep	7 Nov. 1881	Unknown
E317	C.E. Simmons	A. Keep	7 Nov. 1881	Unknown
E318	C.E. Simmons	A. Keep	7 Nov. 1881	Unknown
E321	C.E. Simmons	A. Keep	7 Nov. 1881	Unknown

TABLE 3

VALENTINE SCRIP CERTIFICATES
USED TO LOCATE ON LAND IN DAKOTA TERRITORY

Third Assignments

Certificate	From	To	Date	Price
E5	A.L. Cervantes	W. T. Love	31 Dec. 1881	Unknown
E78	W.T. Coleman	H.P. Bolles Brown County	10 Aug. 1882	$700
E90	W.T. Coleman	E.S. Elliott Milwaukee, Wis.	1 Aug. 1882	Value rec'd.
E185	C.E. Simmons	A. Keep	7 Nov. 1881	Value rec'd.
E187	C.E. Simmons	A. Keep	7 May 1881	Value rec'd.
E316	C.E. Simmons	A. Keep	7 Nov. 1881	Unknown

TABLE 4

VALENTINE SCRIP CERTIFICATES OF LOCATION
USED TO LOCATE ON LAND IN DAKOTA TERRITORY

Certificate	Locator	Location Date	Land Description
E5	William T. Love	4 Mar. 1882	SW¼SW¼, Sec.12, T112N, R70W (40 acres) Hand County
E23	Charles E. Simmons	26 May 1881	Lot 2, NW¼, Sec. 32, T11N, R79W (21 acres) Hughes County
E38	Charles E. Simmons	26 May 1881	NE¼NE¼, Sec. 5, T110N, R79W (40 acres) Hughes County
E47	Eugene S. Elliott	19 Apr. 1883	SW¼SW¼, Sec. 19, T123N, R70W (36.44 acres) Edmunds County
E51	Christopher Bliss	14 Mar. 1883	NW¼NW¼, Sec. 5, T122N, R68W (40 acres) Edmunds County, entry cancelled
E56	Thomas F. Nicholl	9 June 1882	NW¼SW¼, Sec. 12, T112N, R72W (40 acres) Hyde County
E78	Henry P. Bolles	17 July 1883	SE¼NE¼, Sec. 26, T128N, R79W (40 acres) Campbell County
E90	Eugene S. Elliott	14 Apr. 1883	NE¼NE¼, Sec. 14, T121N, R75W (40 acres) Walworth County
E97	Charles E. Simmons	26 May 1881	SW¼NW¼, Sec. 4, T110N, R79W (40 acres) Stanley County
E98	Charles E. Simmons	26 May 1881	NE¼SE¼, Sec. 32, T111N, R79W (40 acres) Hughes County
E103	Albert Keep	4 Jan. 1881	SE¼NE¼, Sec. 1, T110N, R62W (40 acres) Beadle County

TABLE 4 – *continued*

E104	Albert Keep	4 Jan. 1881	Lot 5, Sec. 6, T110N, R61W (36.59 acres) Beadle County
E105	Albert Keep	4 Jan. 1881	Lot 6, Sec. 6, T110N, R61W (35.73 acres) Beadle County
E123	Frederick H. Steigmeyer	9 Apr. 1883	SW¼NE¼, Sec. 25, T114N, R79W (40 acres) Sully County
E176	Barney G. Caulfield	25 Oct. 1878	NE¼NE¼, Sec. 9, T5N, R5E, BHM (40 acres) Lawrence County
E185	Charles E. Simmons	26 May 1881	NW¼NW¼, Sec. 4, T110N, R79W (40 acres) Stanley County
E187	Charles E. Simmons	26 May 1881	SE¼SE¼, Sec. 4, T111N, R79W (40 acres) Hughes County
E208	Barney G. Caulfield	25 Oct. 1878	NW¼NE¼, Sec. 9, T5N, R5E, BHM (40 acres) Lawrence County
E215	Edson O. Parker	20 Sept. 1883	NE¼SE¼, Sec. 11, T112N, R72W (40 acres) Hyde County
E216	George J. Love	10 July 1882	SE¼SW¼, Sec. 12, T112N, R70W (40 acres) Hand County
E220	Isahel Todd	13 Sept. 1883	SE¼SE¼, Sec. 23, T118N, R76W (40 acres) Potter County
E228	Jeremiah C. Wilcox	22 July 1879	NW¼NW¼, Sec. 10, T5N, R5E, BHM (40 acres) Lawrence County
E237	Charles E. Simmons	26 May 1881	SW¼SE¼, Sec. 32, T111N, R79W (40 acres) Hughes County

TABLE 4 – *continued*

E238	Charles E. Simmons	26 May 1881	NE¼NW¼, Sec. 4, T110N, R79W (40 acres) Stanley County
E239	Charles E. Simmons	26 May 1881	SE¼NW¼, Sec. 4, T110N, R79W (40 acres) Stanley County
E253	George J. Love	10 July 1882	NW¼NW¼, Sec. 24, T112N, R70W (40 acres) Hand County
E255	Fredrick A. Davis Daniel A. Hunt	7 Dec. 1882	NW¼NW¼, Sec. 15, T118N, R68W (40 acres) Faulk County
E269	Charles E. Simmons	26 May 1881	Lot 1, SW¼, Sec. 4, T110N, R79W (40 acres) Stanley County
E316	Charles E. Simmons	26 May 1881	Lot 2, NE¼, Sec. 5, T110N, R79W (38.10 acres) Stanley County
E317	Charles E. Simmons	26 May 1881	SW¼SW¼, Sec. 33, T11N, R79W (40 acres) Hughes County
E318	Charles E. Simmons	26 May 1881	Lot 3, SW¼, Sec. 32, T111N, R79W (40 acres) Hughes County
E319	Charles E. Simmons	26 May 1881	Lot 1, NE¼, Sec. 5, T110N, R79W (38.80 acres) Stanley County
E320	Charles E. Simmons	26 May 1881	Lot 4, SW¼, Sec. 32, T111N, R79W (24.80 acres) Hughes County
E321	Charles E. Simmons	26 May 1881	NW¼SE¼, Sec. 32, T111N, R79W (40 acres) Hughes County

SOURCE: *Selected Cases from the South Dakota Valentine Scrip Case Files*, NCWN 70-344, Records of the Bureau of Land Management, Record Group 49, National Archives and Records Service, Washington National Records Center.

THE DISPOSAL OF THE PUBLIC DOMAIN ON THE TRANS-MISSISSIPPI PLAINS:

Some Opportunities for Investigation

Thomas Le Duc

THE DISPOSAL OF THE PUBLIC DOMAIN ON THE TRANS-MISSISSIPPI PLAINS: SOME OPPORTUNITIES FOR INVESTIGATION

THOMAS LE DUC

Department of History, Oberlin College

Of all the peacetime activities of the Federal Government in the nineteenth century, none was more fateful than the transfer of three-quarters of a billion acres of natural resources from public to private ownership.* In the making and administering of policy, the government assumed no other responsibility so formidable in extent and so meaningful to posterity. What kind of job did democratic government do?

The history of the disposal of the public lands remains to be written. It may not be written in our generation. It will not be written unless we ask ourselves the right questions and then devise the methods that will enable us to answer them.

One wonders whether we have been asking the right questions and whether we have been making the correct assumptions. Have we, for example, escaped the great American fallacy that laws are self-enforcing? Historians have generally concentrated—although there is still much to be done—on the legislative and policy-making stages of land history. Should we not now try to emphasize not only the stated intent of the laws but also the actual operational behavior in the larger context of environment: economic, political, and physical? This is to say, simply, that the closing of the public domain is not an event but a process—indeed, a

* This article was presented at a session on opportunities for research at the annual meeting of the Mississippi Valley Historical Association at Oklahoma City, Oklahoma, on April 21, 1950.

complex of several interrelated processes. One is forced to ask whether the meaning and effect of public policy can be accurately judged from the course of political debate, or even from the tabulation of patents issued by the General Land Office. Do we not have to follow the process further, examining actual land use, and searching for the date when ownership became stabilized? Entry is only a step, never insignificant, but often false or tentative.

Public policy does not operate in a vacuum. Its operation is related to the operation of other strategic factors in the field. We have to note, at appropriate points, the significance, for a specific land policy, of the incidence of other land policies, of actual practices of administration, of dynamic factors in the total economy, of the physical environment, and of the character of private enterprise.

This complexity is real. We cannot escape the interplay of diverse elements. The central theme of this article is the need for developing, in studies of the agricultural lands of the trans-Mississippi plains, methods that will integrate the diversity in a credible way. To see the problem, however, it is necessary to pursue a few themes individually.

We might first reconsider the widespread assumption that 1862 is the great dividing line in federal land legislation. Scholars seem generally to have accepted the concept that the wartime land laws represent a distinct break with the ante-

bellum period. But would not 1846 be a better "year of decision"? In that year came the big river-improvement grants. From 1846 to 1856 came the vast land bonuses to military veterans. From 1845 to 1852 one notes the substantial canal grants. In 1848 the school-land donations were doubled. And in 1850 we see the Swamp Lands Act, the portentous grant to the Illinois Central Railroad, and the Oregon State donation, really the first homestead act.

The total acreage appropriated under these laws is small when compared with the amount transferred by the transcontinental railroad grants, the Homestead Act, and the Land-Grant College Act. But in these laws of the late forties we see the final degradation of the tradition of using public land to finance public beneficence. Here, more frankly than in the wartime legislation, is the practice of using purported public beneficence to justify what in fact was beneficence to speculators. If we are looking for legislation incongruous to the Homestead Act, we must look not only to the Civil War grants but back to the Polk and Pierce days. These laws, together with a number of others adopted before 1862, were activated to a very great extent in the corn-belt States and before the passage of the homestead law. They operated, as many of the Pacific railroad grants did not, to diminish homesteading in the humid areas. The strategic position of the military bounties, for instance, in closing high-grade lands to homesteading, can scarcely be exaggerated.

This theme of land quality suggests that we need to introduce into our land studies more precise differentiations of land types based on the findings of the geographers. Taking our cue from the estimable Thomas Donaldson and from the 1905 report of Theodore Roosevelt's Public Lands Commission, we have laid too much stress on mere quantity. This has led us to minimize corn-belt and cotton-belt transfers and to take an exaggerated view of the significance of the vast desert appropriations. Paul W. Gates, concentrating for twenty years on the history of the humid lands, and relating title turnover to crop practices, soil differences, and marketing structures, has led us toward more realistic and qualitative appraisals.

We need to apply the same kinds of discrimination to the trans-Missouri region. Here, indeed, there is an even greater need to apply the available knowledge of ecologic factors, for here the role of natural environment has been even more critical.

But historians have generally steered away from exploiting the extensive and useful work of the scientists. The natural environment has been viewed as static rather than dynamic. The total ecologic interplay of climate, soil mechanics, macroorganism, and microorganism as an ·elaborate and continuing process is noticed by James C. Malin of the University of Kansas but is generally ignored by other professional historians working on the trans-Missouri country.

We have used a few simple and almost meaningless concepts like average crude rainfall, without making adjustments for evaporation and transpiration rates. We have talked blandly about the boundary of 24-inch rainfall, without remembering that 17 inches on the Canadian boundary is probably the equivalent of 27 inches on the Rio Grande. And we have tried to write history, as some have tried to farm: by long-term averages. But the distinguishing element in trans-Missouri precipitation and the critical element in patterns of land use is not averages but year-to-year fluctuations. Earth may be the mother, but climate is the grandmother: nursing and controlling organic life and, by leaching, glaciation, and erosion of wind and water, working changes in terrain and in soil. If historians have emphasized legislative policy making and neglected the role of the physical environment in determining the patterns of adaptation and land use, it is possibly because they are not aware of the immense body of scientific learning now available. In fairness, however, it should be added that the perennial revisions of the ecologic sciences is to the layman perplexing if not indeed dismaying. C. Warren Thornthwaite's *Atlas of Climatic Types in the United States, 1900-1939*, published in 1941, is based on a formula that is now considered obsolete. Progress in soil science has been equally revolutionary. One may note, nonetheless, that the student of land history working with specific quarter-quarter-sections does not often find that revisions in climatology and pedology seriously disturb the description of particular farms. And he will be aware that rarely are the ecologic factors determining to the exclusion of human factors.

It is rather more difficult to evaluate human factors, both in land use and in public administration. But we have been slow to explore the actual administration of the General Land Office. We have long known that mass nullification and executive negligence combined to make many provisions

of the land laws largely inoperative. If this is true, then policy making is less relevant to land occupation than the normal practices of public administration. There is, curiously, no study of the administration of the regional land offices and only the sketchiest accounts of the work of the General Land Office. And this, I remind you, was the largest job of administration ever undertaken by the Federal Government in peacetime. In the fiscal year 1883, for example, the land offices processed 27 million acres. The executive, then and earlier, found it easier to issue patents to all comers than to make effective checks on the authenticity of the applications. That widespread fraud resulted from this negligence is well known. William A. J. Sparks, Commissioner of the General Land Office, estimated the percentage of fraud as something like this: Standard 5-year homesteads, 40 percent; Timber claims, 90 percent; Preemptions, 100 percent; and commuted homesteads, 100 percent. Historians have never discredited these estimates, nor, so far as I know, even challenged them. They have, rather, developed a curious bifocalism that identifies land fraud as a monopoly of the big, absentee operators. But perjury is not defined as a felony by the domicile of the affiant or by the size of the grab.

To correct this popular delusion that fraud was a monopoly of the monopolists we must analyze actual operations and occupancy under the land laws. We need to follow our petty entrymen from the tract books to the census rolls and the assessors' lists. How many of our sworn occupants and improvers of the soil shall we find in these records of reality?

One preliminary tool that we most urgently need in this connection is an index of entrymen. The General Land Office was required to administer laws that forbade repeat entries of various kinds. Under the Homestead Act, for instance, the original entry, even if not perfected to final patent, exhausted the applicant's rights under the law. How many persons homesteaded more than once? Don't ask the United States Government; the General Land Office never had any practicable way of determining the answer, and it appears never to have taken any effective steps to check the practice. Its files were a jumble of chronological records wholly lacking in alphabetical indexes.

The big frauds and the big investment operations and the big speculations have been made more conspicuous, but the aggregate acreage of high-quality land involved in the petty perjuries remains unknown. It would be interesting, incidentally, to know more about the attitudes of the churches toward individual and corporate land frauds.

But let us turn from these disagreeable reminders of the activities of the pioneers to the role of the real devils of land administration: the grantees and the speculators.

The relation of the land-grant railroads to the process of settlement is still imperfectly understood. The tendency has generally been to look at the gross acreage with a view to estimating the fairness of the contracts of subsidy. Few qualitative differentiations about the land actually alienated have been ventured. If anyone has made such a study for the Union Pacific Railroad, for example, I must confess ignorance of it. Investigations now under way seem to reveal that the U. P. secured only 40 percent of its nominal grant in the six most accessible counties of the most valuable humid lands in Nebraska. In those six counties land lost to the railroad by prior private entry totaled 400,000 acres.

We should ask, too, how the settlers brought in by the railroads compared in efficiency with the homesteaders. No opinion is here ventured except that the subject invites investigation. Admittedly, it will not be easy to reach conclusions that will be universally accepted. But one index of efficiency would be stability of ownership. What was the ratio of defaults on purchase contracts and how did these defaults affect actual land use? How much tenancy was there on railroad lands? A study of railroad lands in these respects should be made in comparison with patterns of default and lapse on public lands and on lands sold by entrepreneurs. Another significant aspect of the management of railroad lands is the question of idleness. Were the railroad lands kept idle as so many of the homesteads, scrip entries, and State lands?

We must keep our eyes focused on the process of settlement and land use. To understand it we must make comparative studies that will trace the simultaneous operation of varied and often contradictory land policies in an environment more diversified than some investigators seem to understand.

Of even greater significance than the railroad grants in the occupation of the arable lands was the management of land scrip issued to military veterans, to miscellaneous private claimants, and to the agricultural colleges of the Eastern States.

It is not only quantitatively significant—80 million acres—but qualitatively even more important. The scrip was issued and most of it located before the good lands were gone, and much of it, indeed, even before the Homestead Act was passed. Its value and its meaning in the closing of the public domain was further enhanced by the fact that the holders or assignees could choose their lands as the railroads normally could not.

We should like to know a lot more about the scrip brokers and about the ultimate use of the scrip. How far did these brokers influence legislation? What were their services in securing authentication of bounties for individual veterans and their heirs? How was the scrip marketed; who actually bought it, and in what amounts? What was the effect on land settlement and use if one broker secured, as he boasted, the control of 92 percent of all agricultural college scrip? Is it also true, as he asserted, that his congressional pals slipped into the Land-Grant College Act the joker requiring the Eastern States to sell their scrip rather than locate it themselves?

In a word, we must recognize frankly that much of the subsidy legislation for the aid of education, transportation, irrigation, and other public purposes used the purported benevolence merely as a guise for unloading the public land faster than the settlers could take it up. Acts to relieve the heirs of deceased veterans might better be termed acts to relieve the people of the United States of their public land.

Even more conspicuously neglected by historians is the role of the Western States as grantees and middlemen. Kansas, Iowa, Nebraska, the Dakotas, and Wyoming each took about 7 percent of the entire area of these States. Minnesota, like Wisconsin, took 15 percent. In Idaho grants to the State exceeded grants to the railroads. In Iowa the State lands comprised an area double the aggregate area of all the homesteads.

The disposition of these lands was wholly in the hands of the State legislatures. Did these farmer governments use these grants for public benefit and hold out for high prices, or did they respond to the demands of land-seeking farmers and speculators? What was the unit of sale and what was the progress of sales in relation to transfers of the public domain and railroad grants in adjacent sections? How, in a word, did the policies of the States interact with other policies of land disposition?

Here, certainly, is an opportunity for extensive and rewarding research in the State universities of the Plains States. Why it has been so long neglected is something of a mystery, related perhaps to the reluctance of some westerners to recognize that their own State governments were middlemen in land as big as some of the railroads and bigger than most of the individual speculators.

As to homesteads, we appear still to be suffering from the ambiguities of Frederick Jackson Turner. It is too little recognized even now that the homestead law was not enacted until most of the prairie land in the humid zone had been otherwise entered. In the band of States from Ohio to Iowa, the prize agricultural area of the United States, only 10,000 final-entry homesteads are recorded. Even in Iowa, the farthest west and the last settled, less than 3 percent of the land was homesteaded. Taking the second tier of States west of the Mississippi, Kansas, Nebraska, and the Dakotas—and including the homesteads fecklessly entered in the arid zones —less than 20 percent of the whole area was homesteaded. Systematic investigations, now in progress, seem to show that the actual number of stable homesteads in the humid belt of Nebraska is trifling.

We need a more realistic analysis of homesteading that will qualify the gross figures in a variety of ways. How many of the entries were made in soil and climatic areas where 160 acres was a dependable unit for the support of a farm family? What is the ratio of cancelled entries—abandonments and relinquishments—to sustained and purposeful entry? In Nebraska the ratio is 2.3 cancellations for each final entry; the ratio is slightly lower for Kansas and Minnesota; the ratio for these three States taken together is 2.1 to 1. How many of these cancellations represent abandonments by novices ill-suited to undertake farm enterprise? And how many of them represent the petty blackmail of roving opportunists who entered land and held it without cultivation or improvement until a bona fide settler came along and paid for a relinquishment? And how many of them were dummy entries for large investors? How do these negative entries correlate with the exhaustion of the supply of grant lands of the railroads and the State governments? These lapses of entry have been almost ignored by historians, perhaps because systematic analysis requires fairly elaborate detective work, but they will repay the effort by producing a more realistic picture of the operations of the individual entrepreneur.

Related in kind to the fraud of selling relinquishments are the practices, not always fraudulent, that arose in the commutation of homestead entries by cash payment or use of land scrip. Commutation, for practical purposes, was the equivalent of preemption, and its privileges remained available after the well-publicized repeal of preemption in 1891. Doubtless some bona fide entrymen used commutation as a way of securing an immediate title on which they could borrow money. But the evidence suggests that commutation was frequently used as a device by which a host of nonresident entrymen commuted their fake homesteads in cash advanced by investors with whom they had illegally contracted to sell their land.

The high ratio of commutations in prosperity and the comparatively low ratio in hard times and the high number of quick sales soon after commutation attract the attention of the investigator. But the General Land Office not only left the fraud unchecked during the nineteenth century but even failed before 1881 to tabulate the extent of commutation. For the subsequent twenty-three years, the official records show that the ratio of commuted homesteads to standard 5-year homesteads is 1 to 4. In some land offices commutation rose as high as 90 percent. The procedure was simplicity itself. Urban dwellers and members of farm families could enter a homestead and, thanks to a complaisant administration, ignore the residence and cultivation requirements. Fourteen months later they would find themselves owners of a property worth $1,500 to $2,000. The operation of the commutation provisions of the law demonstrates again the necessity of tracing landownership past the point of patent from the public domain.

We must do this also for the 5-year patents. If we are to understand the relation of the land laws to use and occupation, we should look at the subsequent history of homesteads and of other outright titles to see how long they remained unencumbered. There is great need for studying the growth of tenantry. Someone has said that tenancy is to agriculture what unemployment is to industry: the element that provides the needed elasticity in an enterprise with high fixed costs, substantial capital requirements, and wide fluctuations in the market.

Our understanding of the actual dynamics of tenantry on the plains is primitive. We must put aside the easy generalities about the diabolical forces that got the better of the honest farmer. It will be more helpful, perhaps, if we attempt to connect the growth of tenantry with the fundamental changes wrought in plains farming in the late nineteenth century. It should be obvious that the economic structure was transformed as the cost picture became more rigid and the fluctuations of income wider. The external rigidities bore more heavily where environmental factors dictated high specialization. When specialization took place in zones where the annual fluctuations of ecologic variables—climate, bugs, and blights—were most pronounced, we have to evaluate not merely extrinsic economic factors but also the effectiveness of adaptations.to an environment that was never static. We must, in summary, raise the question whether the basic explanation of tenantry lies in the activities of predatory interests so much as in the inherent weakness of the ecologic adjustment.

Environmental influences and unscientific use of the land, with resultant economic disaster, are more easily demonstrable in geographic belts of established aridity than in the transitional zones. Someone should get busy, therefore, with a systematic evaluation of the working of the Kinkaid Act and the Enlarged Homestead Act. These attempts to impose on the range lands the institution of small-scale owner operation may not have proven as intelligent a program of resources conservation as the publicity staff of Theodore Roosevelt would have us believe.

We must subject their assertions and the assertions of local optimists like Addison E. Sheldon of Nebraska to conscientious analysis. We must take our historical researches beyond the columns of the chauvinistic newspapers of the short-grass country. The real answers will be found in the census returns, in the original records of the land office, and in the county records of title and mortgage. These data must be interpreted in relation to the recent contributions of the soil and climate scientists and in relation to the economics of the range cattle industry.

From the foregoing mélange of comments about the state of historical research on the public lands of the trans-Mississippi west, we may suggest a few tentative conclusions:

1. The actual closing of the public domain by original entry is not as critical a factor as has been generally assumed. If our central theme is human occupation rather than the antiquarian quest for

"firsts," we must pursue our study beyond the original entry and indeed beyond the first patent. We cannot leave unnoticed the high turnover of title in early years or the high ratio of idle land in the hands of private entrymen.

2. We must give to small entries the same searching examination that has been bestowed on large grants and purchases.

3. We must employ more exact and elaborate differentiations of natural ecologic factors. As we cross the Missouri River and move into transitional zones and then move further into the distinctive high plains regions, our need to understand the physical and biologic factors is even greater.

4. We cannot understand the operation of a particular land policy without studying it in the total context of other policies, of administrative practices, and of the natural environment. We must learn how to process the mass of data in manageable chunks.

These simple conclusions seem to add up to a first-class problem of methods. If piecemeal, monographic study along traditional lines must be rejected in favor of a holistic and evolutionary approach, then how shall we go about organizing a more systematic and adequate operational analysis of the total process?

For historians, the practical problem is that of managing a vast quantity of records. It will be at once apparent that sampling methods will be of almost no use in these researches. Because the variables are so many the number of combinations and permutations would be so great that a sample would approach the universe. We may just as well do the whole field and avoid at once the inevitable errors of sampling and the inevitable challenge to the method.

Just as we must reject sampling, so must we reject a procedure that would accumulate a large number of intensive studies in small areas. Sound conclusions for the area cannot be drawn by such a myopic process, and sound generalizations cannot be drawn from an aggregation of such studies.

It is clear, however, that a geographic approach makes more sense than a purely topical one. The size of the unit to be studied must be established empirically. We must ignore arbitrary political boundaries and set up our units in functional relation to ecologic process, to the fundamental object of our study, namely the course of human settlement and adaptation in new environments. Instead of setting up regional boundaries a priori, why not let our findings draw them for us? Why not sort our data and see where the lines emerge?

This means work and a lot of it. We must process the data describing the resources and the data describing scores of thousands of transactions for millions of acres. No one man can do it.

One project, now at an experimental stage, is designed to develop and test methods for cooperative research in a coordinated program that will cover a large area intensively. We hope to assemble in one place, and indeed in a single series of summaries arranged geographically, the data relating to land use over a period of thirty-five years after the opening of the domain. We are experimenting with new-fangled techniques of mechanical sorting that are always suspect to the academic historian. We suspect them, but we propose to go forward with confidence that if they prove unworkable we can find other methods that will permit us to come closer to certainty than we have yet come in this particular field of research.

We have tried to put aside as many presuppositions as we can recognize. We make no assumptions about cultural faults, safety valves, or the glories of pioneer democracy. We think that just possibly what historical scholarship most needs in our time is a return to the scientific ideal of analyzing all the data. We are neither dismayed by the size of the job, nor distraught by the counsel of the relativists who tell us that our certainties are bound to be either pointless or poisoned. If they are correct we may as well merge the Mississippi Valley Historical Association with the nearest public-relations agency—public or private.

P9-ECZ-942

Don't Assume I don't Cook!

RECIPES FOR WOMEN'S LIVES

THE FIRST SUPPER

My sister Native American,
I reach out to you,
For yours is the way
of respect for the earth,
My sister Africa,
you I embrace,
For yours is a
compassionate race,
My sister Asia—I look
deep in your eyes,
Let us be strong together.
Yes, sisters Chicana,
Latina, Muslim and Jew
I am white and
I am woman
And I am tired of
watching for centuries
While my husbands, sons,
and fathers,
steal and pillage,
Here, I give back
what I can,
It is not too late
to make a new world
together.

—Jane Evershed

ABOUT THE ARTIST

Jane Evershed was born in England and grew up in South
Africa, moving to the United States in 1983 at age 25:
"Living in South Africa at the time that I did, during the
reign of the white supremacists, made me feel like a walking
symbol of oppression—unaligned with white policy, yet not
able to integrate with the African people because of the color
of my skin. This dilemma was the initial catalyst for my work
as an artist/communicator."

"The First Supper" is one of several works in Evershed's
Power of Woman series, in which she uses vibrant colors and
lush, tropical images to convey her political convictions. To
see and purchase works by Jane Evershed, including her Rights
of Children and Revisiting Our Souls series, connect to her
website at http://members.aol.com/evershed/jane/jane1.html.

Don't Assume I don't Cook!

RECIPES FOR WOMEN'S LIVES

National Organization for Women Cookbook

Don't Assume I ⟨don't⟩ Cook!

RECIPES FOR WOMEN'S LIVES

PHOTO CREDITS

Byron J. Cohen, page 11, 117, 139
Midland Daily News, page 19
Angie Dickson, page 53
Gina Kaysen, page 63
Michael Williams, page 71
Michelle McDonald,
Boston Globe, page 73
Phil Rosenberg, page 89
Jan B. Tucker, Los Angeles
Newspaper Guild, Local 69,
page 109
Faith Evans, page 155
Beth Corbin, page 163
Matt McVay, *Seattle Times*,
page 189 and back cover

This cookbook is a collection of favorite recipes, which are not necessarily all original recipes.

Library of Congress Catalog Number: 98-87611
ISBN: 0-9638563-4-0

Book Design: Starletta Polster

Manufactured in the United States of America
First Printing: 1998
10,000 copies

TABLE OF CONTENTS

INTRODUCTION

WHERE TO FIND US:

National Organization for Women
1000 16th St. NW, Suite 700
Washington, D.C. 20036
Phone: (202) 331-0066
Fax: (202) 785-8576
Email: now@now.org
Internet: www.now.org

The idea of publishing a NOW recipe book was approached with trepidation, mostly because there are so many stereo-types about the women's rights movement and our supporters. Would anyone buy a cookbook from folks who sport buttons like, "Don't Assume I Cook!" and "Women Make Policy, Not Coffee"?

But as our completely unscientific survey progressed, those concerns evaporated. Sure, whenever we raised the idea, people did a predictable double-take, "What? A NOW recipe book?"

Followed promptly by some version of: "Oh, wow— I have a great recipe for . . . (fill-in-the-blank)."

Among the women and men who represent NOW on the front lines of our movement, we found lots of gourmet cooks (and even more gourmet "eaters"), and a surprising number who just like to read cookbooks!

This book will satisfy both desires, as well as provide some "food for thought" and the inspiration of wonderful quotes from great women (and great quotes from wonderful women!)—use it as a cookbook, as well as a daybook of sorts. Read about some of "today's" courageous women while you whip up the Berry Clafouti. Or entertain your own resident "chef" with funny stories while the Cajun Seafood Gumbo bubbles. Or make "The Best Spaghetti Sauce I Ever Made" together and take turns picking out the quote that sounds most like you (or your mom . . .).

We regret that space prevented us from including all of the terrific recipes, quotes and anecdotes that were submitted. With the help of professional food editors, we chose a diverse array of recipes to suit gourmet tastes as well as busy lifestyles, and added a sampling of NOW issues and actions, quotes and anecdotes that many supporters found memorable. Some of their responses were memorable as well . . .

In our first call for submissions, we asked NOW activists and leaders to send a favorite recipe, anecdote or quote by April 1st. A few thought the request was an early April Fool's joke. One chapter wrote this note: "We in our Saratoga NOW chapter weren't sure if the call for recipes was a joke or not. In case it's real, we're sending a recipe full of virtues for busy feminists." In case you doubted, feminists *do* have a sense of humor! Thank you and Bon Appetit!

Sylvia by Nicole Hollander

7

CONTRIBUTORS

ACKNOWLEDGEMENTS

Special thanks to our team at Favorite Recipes® Press and to the NOW officers and staff, who contributed their time and expertise to make this book possible.

Susan Anderson, Blacksburg, VA
E.C. Antares, Edmond, WA
Pamela Aughe, Drexel Hill, PA
Baltimore NOW Chapter,
    Baltimore, MD
Dot and LeRoy Barnett,
    Lansing, MI
Amy Baronoff,
    Gaithersburg, MD
Joan Marsh Belles,
    Rochester, NY
Phyllis A. Benn, LaPorte, IN
Ann Blessing, Greenland, NH
Winnie Boal, Ashland, OR
Gary Bouquet, Arcadia, CA
Andrea Brancato, Lawrence, KS
Susan Bryson, New Orleans, LA
Janice Burns, Gansevoort, NY
Patrick Butler, Alexandria, VA
Twiss Butler, Alexandria, VA
Ambler Carter, West Chester, PA
Mary J. Case, Danville, CA
Alice Christensen, Edmond, OK
Jodane Christoffersen,
    Boise, ID
Alexandra Cless, Phoenix, AZ
Molly Cochran, Milton, MA
Ann Corcoran, Sarasota, FL
Lyn Crosby, St. Paul, MN
Dr. E. K. Daufin,
    Montgomery, AL
Robin Davis, Raleigh, NC

Deanna DellaVedova,
    Monroeville, PA
Joanie DiMartino,
    Barrington, NJ
Edna Marsh Dubois,
    Rochester, NY
Barbara Marsh Dvorozniak,
    Rochester, NY
Tammy Jo Eckhart,
    Bloomington, IN
Deb Ellis, Brooklyn, NY
April Emmert, Plano, TX
Ray Engelberg, Maywood, NJ
Jan Erickson, Washington, DC
Kara Erickson, Washington, DC
Mickey Esser, New Ulm, MN
Johanna Ettin,
    Winston-Salem, NC
Shirley Anne Evenson,
    Cumberland, WI
Nina Feldman, Oakland, CA
M. M. Filon, Laurel, MD
Grace K. Foster, Norris, TN
Gayle V. Gagliano,
    New Orleans, LA
Nancy Galloway,
    Washington, DC
Alfred K. Gandy,
    Bossier City, LA
Kellie Ann Gandy,
    Bossier City, LA
Kim Gandy, New Orleans, LA

Roma Young Gandy,
    Bossier City, LA
P. J. Glasser-Harris, Antioch, CA
Herman Grumbach,
    Spring Hill, FL
Merle Grumbach,
    Spring Hill, FL
Lisa Bennett Haigney,
    Kensington, MD
Cindy Hanford, Burlington, NC
Barbara Hays,
    Silver Spring, MD
Leslie Hurst, Palm Springs, CA
Linda Hutton, Decatur, IL
Patricia Ireland, Miami, FL
Karen L. Johnson,
    San Antonio, TX
Colleen Kelly Johnston,
    Wichita, KS
Margaret Kamp, Taos, NM
Paula Kassell, Dover, NJ
Doris Kravitz,
    Boynton Beach, FL
Linda Krinsky, Rochester, NY
Beth K. Labush, New York, NY
Kay Marsh Lochner,
    Rochester, NY
Pat Lochner, Rochester, NY
Betty Jane Lornell, Delmar, NY
Laura Lucero,
    Colorado Springs, CO
Lee Maassen, Springfield, VA

Susan Mackenzie, Memphis, TN
Kathy Marsh, Rochester, NY
Massachusetts NOW
Colline L. Mathews,
    Laguna Beach, CA
Kathy Mayer, Lafayette, IN
Maggie McAnaney,
    Sacramento, CA
Mary Melchior, Washington, DC
Casey Miller, East Haddam, CT
Carolyn Modeen, Sun City, AZ
AnitaMarie Murano,
    Washington, DC
Judy Murphy, Manchester, VT
Susannah Northart,
    Oxford, MS
Sheila Oddi, Niantic, CT
Linda Olson, Moline, IN
Sue O'Shaughnessy,
    Bolingbrook, IL
Palos Verdes/South Bay NOW
    Chapter, CA
Lucia Perri, Guthrie, OK
Deborah Blair Porter,
    Manhattan, CA
Josephine Powell, Detroit, MI
Robyn Robbins, Wichita, IL
Phyllis Rosner, New Paltz, NY
Arlene Ross, Green Bay, WI
Laurie Russell, Brooklyn, NY
Mary Scott, Washington, DC
South Orange County NOW, CA

Virginia Stallworth,
    Memphis, TN
Sarah Stapleton-Gray,
    Arlington, VA
Jacqueline Steingold, Detroit, MI
Hila Richards Stratton,
    Charlotte, NC
Kate Swift, East Haddam, CT
Barbara K. Thomas,
    Ballston Spa, NY
Elizabeth Toledo,
    San Francisco, CA
Linda Tosti-Lane, Brier, WA
Susan Webb Tregay, Snyder, NY
Brenda Turner, Randolph, NJ
Susan J. Waldman, Randolph, NJ
Margaret Waterstreet, Chicago, IL
Dimple Welch, Marlin, TX
Gracie Ripa Welch, Islandia, NY
Mira Weinstein, Washington, DC
Samuel Wetmore, Venice, FL
Sheila White, Riverview, MI
Lori Whitney, Madison, WI
Janet Whittington, Dixon, KY
Gail Ann Williams,
    San Francisco, CA
Lola Wolf, Kirkland, WA
C. M. McGarry Wood,
    Key Colony Beach, FL

9

Eating to be Healthy vs. Eating to be Thin

For more information about the impact of advertising on women's health, contact the NOW Foundation's Women's Health Project at (202) 331-0066. Ask about their video *Redefining Liberation*.

This collection includes delicious, low-fat recipes because trying to lower fat in our diets is the healthy way to eat. But there is a difference between striving to eat a healthy diet and dieting/dying to be thin. The difference can be fatal.

Consider this:

Eighty percent of 4th grade girls have already been on a diet. The societal obsession with thinness undermines self-esteem and leads thousands of women and girls into anorexia and bulimia.

Large-sized women also suffer as a result of risky, ineffective and costly operations, drugs and diets, even though most studies show that their weight is rarely within their control.

Advertising on television and in magazines focuses on extreme thinness, sending mixed messages to women as the principal buyers and preparers of food. The insidious message is that women are to feed their families, but starve themselves.

Whatever your size, we hope you will enjoy the low-fat recipes in this book as well as those that are more indulgent. Don't let society's obsession with thinness harm your body.

Eat to be healthy!

ON THE RISE
BREADS, BREAKFAST AND BRUNCH

Our foremothers started over 150 years ago with a

handful of activists, and the feminist movement now

involves millions of people every day.

Standing on their shoulders, we launched the National

Organization for Women in 1966, the largest and strongest

organization of feminists in the world today. A devoutly

grassroots, action-oriented organization, NOW has sued,

boycotted, picketed, lobbied, demonstrated, marched, and

engaged in non-violent civil disobedience. We have

won in the courts and in the legislatures; and we have

negotiated with the largest corporations in the world,

winning unparalled rights for women.

In the past 32 years, women have advanced farther

than in any previous generation. Yet we still do

not have full equality.

SUSAN B. ANTHONY'S CREAM BISCUITS

2 CUPS SIFTED FLOUR
1/2 TEASPOON SALT
1 TABLESPOON BAKING POWDER
1 CUP HEAVY CREAM, WHIPPED

♀ Preheat the oven to 450 degrees.
♀ Sift the flour, salt and baking powder into a medium bowl. Add the whipped cream to the flour mixture and fold gently until almost blended.
♀ Knead the mixture on a lightly floured surface for 1 minute. Pat the dough 1/2 inch thick. Cut with a biscuit cutter or knife and arrange on a lightly greased baking sheet.
♀ Bake for 12 minutes or until golden brown. Serve piping hot.

MAKES 12 BISCUITS

♀ *No self-respecting woman should wish or work for the success of a party that ignores her sex.*
Susan B. Anthony, 1872

IT DOESN'T ADD UP

Higher math was not taught to girls in school. Susan was very excited that her cousin, Moses Vail, a teacher, gave her instruction in algebra. When she visited her sister Guelma and her brother-in-law Aaron McLean she told of her great accomplishment. Later at supper she made the most delicious cream biscuits. Aaron said, "I'd rather see a woman make such biscuits as these than solve the knottiest problem in algebra." "There is no reason why she should not be able to do both," was the reply.

From *Life and Work of Susan B. Anthony*, Vol. I, by I. H. Harper.

REFORM

"Cautious, careful people,
Always casting about to preserve
Their reputation and social
    standing
Never can bring about a reform.
Those who are really in earnest
Must be willing to be anything or
    nothing
In the world's estimation –
And publicly and privately, in
    season and out,
Avow their sympathies with
    despised and persecuted ideas,
And their advocates,
And bear the consequences."

*Susan B. Anthony spoke these
words over a hundred years ago.
She was talking about that most
radical of reforms—the right to
vote for women.*

PASTEL DEL ELOTE

A meal in a bread. This is excellent served with a spicy chicken or vegetarian stew, or just with a salad. It can be made with fresh corn in the summer, or canned cream-style all year-round. It can also be made ahead of time and reheated.

1 CUP BUTTER OR MARGARINE, SOFTENED
1 CUP SUGAR
3 EGGS
1 (4-OUNCE) CAN CHOPPED GREEN CHILES
1 (16-OUNCE) CAN CREAMED CORN
1/2 CUP SHREDDED MONTEREY JACK CHEESE
1/2 CUP SHREDDED MILD CHEDDAR CHEESE
1 CUP FLOUR
1 CUP YELLOW CORNMEAL
4 TEASPOONS BAKING POWDER
1/4 TEASPOON SALT

♀ Preheat the oven to 350 degrees.
♀ Cream the butter and sugar in a large bowl until light and fluffy. Beat in the eggs 1 at a time. Add the green chiles, corn and cheeses and mix well.
♀ Mix the flour, cornmeal, baking powder and salt together in a small bowl. Add to the corn mixture and mix well. Pour into a greased and floured 8x12-inch baking pan.
♀ Place the pan in the preheated oven and reduce the temperature to 300 degrees. Bake for 1 hour or until golden brown and firm.

SERVES 10

ELLEN'S ROLLS

1 CAKE YEAST
2 TABLESPOONS LUKEWARM WATER
1/4 CUP BUTTER
1 CUP MILK, SCALDED
2 EGGS
1/2 CUP SUGAR
1 TEASPOON SALT
3 1/2 CUPS FLOUR

♀ Soften the yeast in the lukewarm water. Add the butter to the hot milk and stir until melted. Set the milk mixture aside to cool to lukewarm.
♀ Beat the eggs in a large bowl. Add the sugar and salt and mix well. Blend in the milk mixture and yeast.
♀ Add the flour 1 cup at a time, mixing well. Dough will be stiff.
♀ Knead the dough on a lightly floured surface until smooth and elastic. Place in a large greased bowl, turning to coat surface. Let rise, loosely covered, until doubled in bulk.
♀ Knead lightly, roll, cut and shape into rolls as desired. Place on a greased baking sheet. Let rise for 1 hour or until doubled in bulk.
♀ Preheat the oven to 450 degrees. Bake the rolls until lightly browned.

MAKES 3 DOZEN

12-YEAR-OLD MARCHES FOR 80-YEAR-OLD PIONEER

A "sea of suffragist white" converged on Chicago on Mother's Day, 1980, when over 90,000 people joined NOW's march to support the Equal Rights Amendment. Twelve-year-old Rachel Thompson of Flint, Michigan, marched wearing a sash that said "Olive." The sash was in honor of 80-year-old Olive Hurlburt, a pioneer for women's rights since 1930 when she joined the National Woman's Party. Olive, a NOW member since 1977, had been sidelined from the march with knee problems.

This yeast-raised bread requires an afternoon to make, but you are not involved during every minute. Fit it in around other things you are doing and it will be a lovely treat at the close of the day.

EASY HONEY WHEAT BREAD

$1/3$ CUP VERY WARM WATER
3 TABLESPOONS HONEY
2 (4-OUNCE) ENVELOPES DRY YEAST
$1^1/2$ CUPS ALL-PURPOSE FLOUR
$1^1/2$ CUPS WHOLE WHEAT FLOUR
1 TEASPOON SALT
$1/2$ CUP OLD-FASHIONED OATS
$1/2$ CUP STEEL-CUT OATS OR WHEAT GERM OR
    SUNFLOWER SEEDS
$1^1/2$ CUPS BUTTERMILK
1 TABLESPOON (APPROX.) VEGETABLE OIL

♀ Blend the water and honey in a small bowl. Sprinkle the yeast over the mixture and stir until dissolved.
♀ Combine the flours, salt and oats in a large bowl and mix well. Make a well in the center and mix. Add the buttermilk and mix until the mixture clings together.
♀ Knead on a lightly floured surface until smooth and elastic. Shape into a ball and place in a large greased bowl, turning to coat the surface.
♀ Let rise, loosely covered, for $1^1/2$ hours or until doubled in bulk and 2 fingers inserted in the center leave an imprint.
♀ Turn the dough onto a lightly floured surface, knead lightly and shape into 2 medium loaves or 1 large round loaf. Place in greased loaf pans or on greased baking sheet. Cut a large X in the round loaf. Brush lightly with vegetable oil or shortening. Let rise for 2 hours or until doubled in bulk.
♀ Preheat the oven to 375 degrees. Bake for 45 minutes or until the loaves sound hollow when tapped.

MAKES 1 LARGE OR 2 MEDIUM LOAVES

FORTY-DOLLAR BREAD

2 (4-OUNCE) ENVELOPES QUICK-RISING DRY YEAST
1/2 CUP WARM WATER
2 CUPS MILK, SCALDED
2/3 CUP BUTTER-FLAVOR SHORTENING
1/2 CUP SUGAR
1 TABLESPOON SALT
1 EGG
7 TO 9 CUPS BREAD FLOUR
1/2 CUP (APPROX.) MELTED BUTTER

National Board Member Linda Sievers made this bread for a Mid-South NOW Conference auction fundraiser in 1986. Three loaves sold for $40!

♀ Dissolve the yeast in the warm water. Combine the hot milk, shortening, sugar and salt in a large mixer bowl and stir until the shortening melts. Let stand until cooled to lukewarm. Add the yeast, egg and 2 to 3 cups flour. Beat until a soft dough forms. Stir in enough of the remaining flour to make a stiff dough.

♀ Knead the dough on a floured surface for 7 to 10 minutes or until smooth and elastic. Place in a greased bowl, turning to coat the surface. Punch 8 holes in the dough with a fork. Let rise, loosely covered, for 55 minutes or until doubled in bulk. Punch the dough down and let rest for 15 minutes.

♀ Shape the dough into 3 loaves and place in 3 greased 5x9-inch loaf pans. Brush the tops with a small amount of the melted butter. Let rise until doubled in bulk. Brush the tops with some remaining butter, slash the loaves lengthwise and pour some of the remaining butter into the slashes.

♀ Preheat the oven to 350 degrees. Bake for 35 minutes or until brown. Remove the loaves from the pans and place on wire racks. Brush on all sides with melted butter. Cover with paper towels. Let cool for about 5 minutes. Wrap in plastic wrap if bread is to be stored for longer than one day.

MAKES 3 LOAVES

LONGEST WALK FOR ERA!

To raise money to push for the ratification of the Equal Rights Amendment, NOW chapters held walk-a-thons. In 1980, while thousands of others did a weekend walk-a-thon, one determined, dedicated young woman spent 125 days walking 1,500 miles along the Appalachian Trail from Virginia to Maine for the Amendment.

Carol Marchel, a NOW member from La Crosse, Wisconsin, met many women along the trail who, when they found out her purpose, pledged money to her. And once, in New Hampshire, she was joined by a man who said he had heard rumors of a "radical feminist" walking the trail. Carol told him who she was and why she was walking, and he pledged, too.

PUMPKIN BREAD

$2/3$ CUPS SHORTENING OR VEGETABLE OIL
$2^2/3$ CUPS SUGAR
4 EGGS
1 (16-OUNCE) CAN SOLID-PACK PUMPKIN
$2/3$ CUP WATER
$3^1/3$ CUPS FLOUR
2 TEASPOONS BAKING SODA
$1^1/2$ TEASPOONS SALT
$1/2$ TEASPOON BAKING POWDER
1 TEASPOON CINNAMON
1 TEASPOON NUTMEG
$2/3$ CUP RAISINS
$2/3$ CUP CHOPPED PECANS

♀ Preheat the oven to 350 degrees.
♀ Cream the shortening and sugar in a large bowl until light and fluffy. Add the eggs, pumpkin and water and beat until smooth.
♀ Sift the flour, baking soda, salt, baking powder, cinnamon and nutmeg together in a large bowl. Add to the pumpkin mixture and mix until smooth. Stir in the raisins and pecans. Pour the mixture into 2 greased and floured loaf pans.
♀ Bake for 50 to 60 minutes or until a knife inserted in the center comes out clean. Cool in the pans for 5 minutes. Remove loaves to a wire rack to cool completely.

MAKES 3 LOAVES

RAISIN QUICK BREAD

1 1/2 CUPS SEEDLESS RAISINS
1 1/2 CUPS WATER
1 EGG
1 CUP PACKED BROWN SUGAR
2 TABLESPOONS VEGETABLE OIL
2 1/2 CUPS FLOUR
1 TEASPOON SALT
2 TEASPOONS BAKING POWDER
1/2 TEASPOON BAKING SODA

♀ Preheat the oven to 325 degrees.
♀ Combine the raisins and water in a saucepan. Bring to a boil and set aside to cool.
♀ Beat the egg, brown sugar and oil together in a large bowl. Add the raisin mixture and mix well.
♀ Sift the flour, salt, baking powder and baking soda together in a large bowl. Add to the raisin mixture and mix well. Pour into a greased 5x7-inch loaf pan.
♀ Bake for 60 minutes or until a knife inserted in the center comes out clean. Cool in the pan for 5 minutes. Remove loaf to a wire rack to cool completely.

MAKES 1 LOAF

Midland (MI) NOW raised $2500 for ERA with this 1977 walk-a-thon led by young chapter members Melissa and Julie Hamilton, daughters of Chapter President Barbara Hays. Their balloons read "Women Hold Up Half the Sky."

ZUCCHINI BREAD

3 CUPS FLOUR
2 TEASPOONS BAKING SODA
1/2 TEASPOON BAKING POWDER
1 TEASPOON SALT
1 1/2 TEASPOONS CINNAMON
3/4 TEASPOON NUTMEG
3 EGGS, BEATEN
1 CUP VEGETABLE OIL
2 CUPS SUGAR
2 TEASPOONS VANILLA EXTRACT
1 CUP CHOPPED NUTS
2 CUPS GRATED ZUCCHINI
1 CUP WHITE RAISINS
1 CUP CRUSHED PINEAPPLE

♀ Preheat the oven to 350 degrees.
♀ Combine the flour, baking soda, baking powder, salt,
cinnamon and nutmeg in a large bowl and set aside.
♀ Beat the eggs, oil, sugar and vanilla in a medium bowl
until thick and frothy. Add to the flour mixture and
mix well.
♀ Fold the nuts, zucchini, raisins and pineapple into the
mixture. Pour into 2 greased and floured 5x9-inch loaf pans
or 3 greased and floured 3x7-inch loaf pans.
♀ Bake for 55 minutes or until a knife inserted into the
center comes out clean. Cool in the pans for 5 minutes.
Remove loaves to wire racks to cool completely.

MAKES 2 OR 3 LOAVES

RHUBARB COFFEE CAKE

1 CUP CHOPPED PECANS, WALNUTS OR HAZELNUTS
1/2 CUP PACKED BROWN SUGAR
1 TEASPOON CINNAMON
1/4 CUP MARGARINE, SOFTENED
1 1/2 CUPS SUGAR
2 EGGS
1 TEASPOON VANILLA EXTRACT
2 1/2 CUPS FLOUR
1 TEASPOON BAKING POWDER
1 TEASPOON BAKING SODA
1/2 TEASPOON SALT
1 POUND RHUBARB, CUT INTO 1/2-INCH PIECES
   (APPROX. 4 CUPS)
1 CUP SOUR CREAM

♀ Preheat the oven to 350 degrees.
♀ Mix the pecans, brown sugar and cinnamon in a small bowl and set aside.
♀ Cream the margarine and sugar in a large bowl until light and fluffy. Add the eggs and vanilla and blend well. Add the flour, baking powder, baking soda and salt and mix until smooth.
♀ Fold in the rhubarb and sour cream.
♀ Sprinkle 1/3 of the pecan mixture in the bottom of a greased 10-inch tube pan. Add layers of half the batter and half the remaining pecan mixture. Repeat the layers.
♀ Bake for 50 to 55 minutes or until a toothpick inserted in the center comes out clean. Cool completely in the pan on a wire rack. Invert onto a serving plate.

SERVES 12 TO 16

GROWING-UP SKIPPER

Growing-Up Skipper, a doll that develops breasts and a tapered waist when her arm is twisted, first hit the toy stores in 1975. "When we first heard about Growing-Up Skipper, we thought it was nothing but a bad joke," said Allena Leonard, Coordinator of NOW's Subcommittee on Toys. "We thought no toy company could express such contempt for the female body and its processes of maturation as to market such a doll. We were wrong."

In a letter to Mattel Toy Company, Leonard expressed NOW's outrage and pointed out the obvious contrast to male dolls that lack genitals entirely: "We'll be happy when the development of a girl's mind receives as much attention as the development of her bosom."

Mattel stopped making the doll.

KEEPING THE DOORS OPEN...

In 1994, NOW helped push through the first major congressional victory for abortion rights in more than a decade, the Freedom of Access to Clinic Entrances (FACE) Act. FACE provided penalties for the use of force, threat of force or physical obstruction at facilities which provide abortion-related services.

The legislation, which had been in the works for several years, was motivated in part by one woman's ordeal. Six months pregnant, she had begun bleeding and went to her clinic for medical assistance.

Protesters outside assumed she was going in for an abortion and manhandled her, preventing her from entering. They delayed her care for so long that she miscarried. NOW advocated for the inclusion

OVERNIGHT FRENCH TOAST

1 LONG LOAF FRENCH BREAD
8 LARGE EGGS
3 CUPS MILK
1 TEASPOON SUGAR
1 TABLESPOON VANILLA EXTRACT OR
   2 TABLESPOONS RUM
2 TO 3 TABLESPOONS BUTTER

♀ Slice the bread into 1- to 1$1/2$-inch-thick slices and arrange snugly in a buttered 9x13-inch baking dish.
♀ Beat the eggs in a large bowl. Add the milk, sugar, and vanilla and blend well. Pour over the bread. Cover the dish tightly with foil or plastic wrap. Refrigerate for 4 hours. (May be refrigerated for up to 36 hours.)
♀ Preheat the oven to 350 degrees. Uncover the baking dish and dot with the butter.
♀ Bake, uncovered, for 50 minutes or until puffed and light golden brown. Serve with syrup, honey, jam or yogurt.

MAKES 6 TO 8 SERVINGS

♀ *Never doubt that a small group of committed people can change the world. Indeed, it's the only thing that ever has.*
Margaret Mead

LATKES (POTATO PANCAKES)

These wonderful latkes are great served with any number of things. It is traditional to serve them with applesauce and/or sour cream, but they are also good at dinner as a base for ratatouille or veal or mushroom stews.

5 OR 6 LARGE POTATOES, GRATED
1 LARGE YELLOW ONION, FINELY CHOPPED
1/2 CUP MATZO MEAL OR FLOUR
1/2 TEASPOON SEA SALT
1/2 TEASPOON FRESHLY GROUND PEPPER
PINCH OF GARLIC POWDER (OMIT IF SERVING WITH
    A SWEET ACCOMPANIMENT)
DASH OF NUTMEG
1 EGG, SLIGHTLY BEATEN
PEANUT OIL FOR FRYING

♀ Place the grated potatoes in a colander to drain well but do not allow the potatoes to discolor.

♀ Combine the potatoes, onion, matzo, salt, pepper, garlic powder and nutmeg in a large bowl and mix well. Add the egg and mix well. Add a small amount of additional matzo meal if mixture must be thickened.

♀ Heat 1/8-inch peanut oil in a large heavy skillet until very hot but not smoking. Drop the potato mixture by large spoonfuls into the hot oil and flatten with the back of the spoon.

♀ Fry until golden brown on both sides, turning once. Drain on paper towels and serve with your choice of toppings.

MAKES 10 TO 12 SERVINGS

(Keeping the Doors Open, continued)

of volunteer clinic escorts, but was unsuccessful.

The next year, Jim Barrett, a NOW escort, was murdered outside a clinic in Pensacola, Florida, along with the clinic's physician, Dr. Bayard Britton. June Barrett, also a volunteer escort, who was in the car with the two men, survived and continued to work for abortion rights by telling the story of her husband's tragic death.

NOW Drops a Dime on Ma Bell

NOW helped put a price tag on sex discrimination at the phone company. For years AT&T had rigidly segregated its workforce. 97 percent of the telephone operators were women, 86 percent of the plant workers were men. In all, 1,800 sex and race discrimination complaints had been filed against the company. Not much was being done about this until the day AT&T asked the Federal Communications Commission for a $500 million rate hike.

That's when NOW, the NAACP, and the Equal Employment Opportunity Commission jointly sued to have the FCC deny the increase, because of AT&T's employment practices. It took three years, but AT&T finally agreed to a legal settlement—to divide $38 million among 13,000 women and 2,000 minority men, in back pay and raises. With help from NOW and others the telephone company is learning that discrimination can be bad business.

from a 1975 NOW brochure

Fragrant Pancake Roll-Ups

2 CUPS FLOUR
1/3 CUP SUGAR
1 TABLESPOON BAKING POWDER
2 EGGS
1 1/2 CUPS SKIM MILK
1 TABLESPOON CANOLA OIL
2 TABLESPOONS UNSWEETENED APPLESAUCE
1 TABLESPOON VANILLA EXTRACT
1 TEASPOON ALMOND EXTRACT

♀ Preheat a nonstick griddle.
♀ Mix the flour, sugar and baking powder in a large bowl.
♀ Beat the eggs with the skim milk, canola oil, applesauce, vanilla and almond extract. Add to the flour mixture and mix well; the batter will be thin.
♀ Spoon the desired amount of batter onto the hot griddle. Turn the pancakes over when the tops begin to bubble. Cook until light brown on both sides.
♀ Roll-up plain or spread with a teaspoon of all-fruit jam, honey, sour cream or fresh fruit.

MAKES 8 TO 12 PANCAKES

♀ *If I didn't start painting, I would have raised chickens.*
Grandma Moses

FRUIT YOGURT PANCAKES

2 CUPS FLOUR
2 TEASPOONS BAKING POWDER
1 TEASPOON BAKING SODA
1 TEASPOON SALT
1/4 CUP MELTED BUTTER OR VEGETABLE OIL
1 CUP FRUIT YOGURT
2 EGGS
2 CUPS MILK
1 CUP FINELY CHOPPED PEACHES, APPLES OR BERRIES
    (OPTIONAL)

♀ Preheat a nonstick griddle.
♀ Mix the flour, baking powder, baking soda and salt in a bowl. Add the butter, yogurt and eggs and mix well.
♀ Blend in the milk 1/2 cup at a time, blending well after each addition. Stir in the fruit.
♀ Spoon the desired amount of batter onto the hot griddle. Turn the pancakes over when the tops appear bubbly and edges appear dry. Cool until brown on both sides.
♀ Serve with a warm fruit compote, or with yogurt and fresh fruit.

MAKES 8 TO 12 PANCAKES

SENATOR TURNS THE TABLES

In 1982, Florida state Senator Pat Frank, who described herself as a moderate Democrat with strong feelings about individuals' rights to privacy, came as close as anyone to giving the gentlemen in her statehouse an idea of what it would be like to have the shoe, as it were, on the other foot.

An opponent of gay rights had come up with a bill to increase penalties for fornication between members of the same sex, leaving a lower penalty for fornication between opposite sexes. "The chairman of the committee asked me what I was going to do. I said I was going to vote for it and was going to tack an amendment on." She told him she didn't believe in extra-marital relations, so would add an amendment requiring the removal from office of any state senator violating the fornication statute.

The bill was quickly withdrawn.

Frank had been elected with support from NOW's campaign to increase the number of ERA supporters in state legislatures.

STRIKE!

A Florida NOW member and historian, Betty Armistead, suggested to Betty Friedan that there be a nationwide strike on the 50th anniversary of women's suffrage in the United States. In her farewell speech as NOW's president in March 1970, Friedan took up the gauntlet and called for a nationwide general strike "by all women in America against their concrete conditions of oppression."

At that time, NOW was a tiny organization of 1500 members, but we cobbled together an impressive coalition of strike supporters. Still, no one really knew how many would support the strike on August 26, 1970.

CLUB SODA WAFFLES

2 CUPS BAKING MIX
1 EGG
1/2 CUP VEGETABLE OIL
1 1/3 CUPS CLUB SODA

♀ Preheat a nonstick waffle iron.
♀ Combine the baking mix, egg, oil and club soda in a bowl and mix well; batter may be slightly lumpy.
♀ Spoon the desired amount of batter onto the hot waffle grid, close the lid and bake until steaming stops and the waffle is crisp and golden brown.
♀ Serve with a warm fruit compote.

MAKES 6 TO 8 WAFFLES

♀ *There are no such things as women's issues! All issues are women's issues. The difference that we bring to the existing issues of our society . . . is that we are going to bring the full, loud, clear determined voice of women into deciding how those issues are going to be addressed.*
Aileen Hernandez, President of NOW, 1970–71

OH BOY WAFFLES

Lee Maassen named these waffles after the reaction of his children whenever he made them. Lee prefers the old-fashioned waffle iron that requires greasing.

2 1/4 CUPS FLOUR
4 TEASPOONS BAKING POWDER
3/4 TEASPOON SALT
1 1/2 TABLESPOONS SUGAR
2 EGGS
2 1/4 CUPS MILK
3/4 CUP VEGETABLE OIL

♀ Preheat and grease a waffle iron.
♀ Sift the flour, baking powder, salt and sugar together into a large bowl.
♀ Beat the eggs, milk and oil together. Add to the dry ingredients and mix just until moistened; the batter will be thin.
♀ Spoon the batter onto the hot waffle grid, close the lid and bake until steaming stops and the waffle is crisp and golden brown.

MAKES 10 TO 12 WAFFLES

(Strike, continued)

When the day came, 90 cities and towns across the country were affected by the strike; marches and rallies in the major cities drew thousands of people. It made the front pages of every major newspaper and led on TV and radio newscasts. The Women's Strike for Equality catapulted the movement into public awareness, making its potential power broadly apparent.

QUICK BREAKFAST CASSEROLE

6 THICK SLICES ITALIAN BREAD, CUT INTO CUBES
1/2 MEDIUM ONION, CHOPPED
4 SLICES CRISP-COOKED BACON, CRUMBLED
  (OPTIONAL)
1/2 CUP SHREDDED MOZZARELLA CHEESE
3 SLICES PROCESSED CHEESE, CUT INTO
  1-INCH PIECES
3 EGGS, LIGHTLY BEATEN
1 CUP MILK
SALT AND PEPPER TO TASTE

♀ Combine the bread cubes, onion, bacon and cheeses in a 2-quart baking dish.

♀ Beat the eggs lightly in a bowl. Add the milk, salt and pepper and beat thoroughly. Pour over the bread mixture and stir lightly to distribute the cheeses evenly. Add a small amount of additional milk if necessary to almost immerse the bread. Cover with plastic wrap and refrigerate overnight.

♀ Preheat the oven to 375 degrees. Bake, uncovered, for 30 minutes or until puffed and golden brown.

♀ May substitute other cheeses if desired.

SERVES 4 TO 6

♀ *If you're going to play the game properly, you'd better know every rule.*

Barbara Jordan, 1975

FRITTATA

9 EGGS, BEATEN
SALT AND PEPPER TO TASTE
6 TABLESPOONS OLIVE OIL
3 GREEN ONIONS, SLICED
6 CHERRY TOMATOES, SLICED
10 FRESH BASIL LEAVES, CHOPPED

♀ Beat the eggs in a large bowl. Add the salt and pepper.
♀ Preheat 3 tablespoons olive oil in a large nonstick skillet until a drop of water spurts when added. Pour the egg mixture into the skillet. Cook until the eggs are about half cooked, lifting the edge gently to allow the uncooked mixture to flow underneath.
♀ Begin heating a second nonstick skillet with the remaining olive oil. Sprinkle the partially cooked eggs with green onions, cherry tomatoes and basil leaves. Cook for 2 to 4 minutes or until oil in second skillet is hot.
♀ Flip the partially cooked frittata into the second skillet. Cook until the egg mixture is cooked through. Place on a serving platter to serve hot or let stand until cooled to room temperature.
♀ Serve with a dollop of sour cream or a spicy spinach or tomato sauce.

SERVES 6 TO 8

ONE RINGY-DINGY, TWO RINGY-DINGYS

A 1979 action by Pennsylvania NOW resulted in a standard of two separate telephone listings per household, free of charge. Previously, two separate listings for a single household had only been available at an additional charge of $0.50 per month. Bell of Pennsylvania had previously proposed a change to a single line, dual listing: Doe, John—Jane, but NOW petitioned for and won a double listing: Doe, Jane; Doe, John.

WE'VE GOT A FETISH ABOUT BAD ADS

Oklahoma NOW activists were horrified and outraged by a 1997 advertising campaign for Fetish perfume. Magazine ads depicted a teen-aged girl wearing a halter top, with the slogan: "Fetish #16: Apply generously to your neck so he can smell the scent as you shake your head 'no.'"

The ad was reprehensible on many levels, from associating young girls with the word "fetish" to implying that when a girl shakes her head "no," it is just a seductive ploy.

They started a letter-writing and petition campaign to pressure the manufacturer, Dana Perfumes, and enlisted the help of Elizabeth Toledo, who directs the NOW Foundation's Women's Health Project. Within weeks Dana notified them the ad would be removed.

With the *Redefining Liberation* campaign, the NOW Foundation continues to expose advertising that harms women.

RED LETTER EGGS

2 LARGE TOMATOES
1 SMALL ONION, MINCED
1 CLOVE OF GARLIC, MINCED
1 TO 2 TABLESPOONS BUTTER OR OLIVE OIL
SALT AND PEPPER TO TASTE
2 EGGS
GRATED PARMESAN OR ROMANO CHEESE TO TASTE (OPTIONAL)
CHOPPED FRESH PARSLEY TO TASTE (OPTIONAL)

♀ Cut a thick slice from the top of each tomato. Scoop the pulp from the bottoms to form cups. Chop the tops and scooped out pulp finely and set aside. Place the bottoms in individual gratin pans and set aside.

♀ Sauté the onion and garlic in butter in a skillet. Add the chopped tomato, salt and pepper. Cook over medium heat until the mixture has been reduced to a velvety sauce, stirring and mashing frequently. Place a spoonful in each tomato cup.

♀ Preheat the broiler. Poach or lightly fry the eggs. Place the eggs in the tomato cups and spoon the remaining sauce over the tops.

♀ Sprinkle with cheese and parsley. Broil for 3 to 4 minutes or just until the tomatoes are heated. Serve immediately.

SERVES 2

♀ *[W]e whose hands have rocked the cradle, are now using our heads to rock the boat . . .*
Wilma Scott Heide, President of NOW, 1971–74

IN THE FOREFRONT
APPETIZERS AND SOUPS

It all started when attorney Pauli Murray, who later

became the first African-American woman to be

ordained as an Episcopalian minister, suggested to *Feminine*

Mystique author Betty Friedan that women

needed a group to advocate on their behalf, much as the

NAACP advocated for African-Americans.

In June of 1966 at the National Conference of the Commissions

on the Status of Women, which was held in Washington, DC,

27 women and one man, including Friedan and Murray,

established the National Organization for Women.

PICTURED ON OVERLEAF: *Elizabeth Toledo (with bullhorn) leading 1992*
California NOW March for Women's Lives, San Francisco, CA.

BUSY WOMAN'S GUACAMOLE

1 RIPE AVOCADO
1/2 CUP SALSA
1/2 TO 1 TEASPOON FRESH LIME JUICE (OPTIONAL)

♀ Cut the avocado into halves. Discard the pit and scoop the pulp into a bowl or food processor.
♀ Add your favorite salsa and lime juice. Mash with a fork or process until smooth.
♀ Serve immediately, or place plastic wrap tightly over the surface to prevent browning and refrigerate.

SERVES 2 TO 4

♀ *We little dreamed when we began this contest [for woman suffrage], optimistic with the hope and buoyancy of youth, that half a century later we would be compelled to leave the finish of the battle to a younger generation of women. But our hearts are filled with joy to know that they enter upon this task equipped with a college education, with business experience, and . . . the right to speak in public—all of which were denied to women fifty years ago.*
Susan B. Anthony, in a letter to Elizabeth Cady Stanton on Stanton's 87th birthday, 1902

JUST ANOTHER WOMAN OF THE '90S

Alcohol is a main target of Lisa Tiger's campaign to aid Native Americans while she educates women on AIDS and HIV. Lisa, a Muscogee Indian from Oklahoma, lost both her father and brother to alcohol-related shootings, then discovered she was HIV positive.

"I was supposed to be low-risk; I was infected in a relationship I was in for three years," said Tiger. "I didn't know he was bisexual until a year after I had broken up with him. When the test came back positive, I knew I had to go out and tell other women about my situation, that I didn't think I was at risk. You may think you're not at risk. But if you're having unprotected sex . . . . you are at risk."

Tiger has been a featured speaker at several NOW rallies and conferences, and was the recipient of our Women of Courage award.

A Matter of Courage

Loretta Ross, NOW activist and former staff member, was invited to monitor the April 1994 elections in South Africa—the first in which all races participated. Ross told of one elderly black woman who was voting for the first time.

She couldn't walk and had no wheelchair, so her children carried her to the polling station. Once there, the woman needed assistance to stand and vote. But the white polling officer said it was not permitted for her to have someone in the booth with her—voting was supposed to be secret. Thus, she couldn't vote.

"Out jumped my NOW anger," said Ross (*photo opposite*). "And when I finished transforming myself from an observer into a facilitator, not only did she vote, but as she was leaving, she whispered to me, 'Mandela, Mandela.'"

Bleu Cheese Dip

16 OUNCES CREAM CHEESE, SOFTENED
8 OUNCES BLEU CHEESE, CRUMBLED
ITALIAN SALAD DRESSING

♀ Combine the cream cheese and bleu cheese in a bowl and mix well.
♀ Add enough salad dressing to make a dip of the desired consistency.
♀ Serve with bite-size fresh vegetables for dipping.

MAKES 1 1/2 CUPS

Feta Cheese Ball

8 OUNCES CREAM CHEESE, SOFTENED
4 OUNCES FETA CHEESE, CRUMBLED
2 TABLESPOONS CHOPPED GREEN ONIONS
2 TABLESPOONS SLICED BLACK OLIVES
1 TO 2 TABLESPOONS CHOPPED FRESH BASIL

♀ Combine the cream cheese, feta cheese, green onions, olives and basil in a bowl and mix well.
♀ Shape into a ball and wrap in plastic wrap. Refrigerate until serving time.
♀ Unwrap the cheese ball and place on a lettuce-lined serving plate. Garnish with grape clusters and serve with a basket of garlic-flavored bagel chips and pita bread triangles.

SERVES 6 TO 8

JALAPENO PIMENTO CHEESE

This has been enjoyed by many Tennessee NOW members at planning retreats and potlucks.

1 POUND COLBY JACK CHEESE, SHREDDED
1 POUND SHARP CHEDDAR CHEESE, SHREDDED
1 (4-OUNCE) JAR CHOPPED PIMENTOS, MASHED
4 TO 6 GREEN ONIONS, FINELY CHOPPED
2 OR 3 (OR MORE) JALAPENOS, SEEDED, MINCED
1/3 CUP MAYONNAISE
1/3 CUP SOUR CREAM

♀ Combine the cheeses, pimentos, green onions and jalapenos in a large bowl and mix well.
♀ Blend the mayonnaise and sour cream in a small bowl. Add to the cheese mixture and mix well.
♀ Use the cheese mixture as filling for finger sandwiches or serve with crackers as a spread.

SERVES 10 TO 12

Backstage at NOW's 1995 rally to call attention to violence against women, Loretta Ross (far left) hears from stage manager Jane Hickey that she is speaking next. Elizabeth Toledo is at right.

HELP WANTED

Employers still discriminate against women. But, thanks to NOW, they don't advertise it.

Remember when newspapers used to list job openings in separate columns, one marked Male, the other Female? You don't see that much anymore, because a NOW chapter got the Supreme Court to see things their way. And nearly every newspaper from the *New York Times* to *Rolling Stone* stopped listing jobs that way.

It all started when Pittsburgh NOW convinced the local human relations commission to order the *Pittsburgh Press* to stop segregating its help-wanted ads. It was helping employers illegally discriminate against women.

It all ended when the Supreme Court rejected the *Press'* freedom of press argument. On the grounds that the newspaper had no more right to advertise sex discrimination than to advertise illegal drugs.

By winning this case, NOW didn't open all jobs to women. But it did open a lot of women to jobs they never considered before.

from a 1975 NOW brochure

TUNA BALL

2 (6-OUNCE) CANS TUNA, DRAINED
8 OUNCES CREAM CHEESE, SOFTENED
2 TABLESPOONS MINCED ONION
1 TABLESPOON WORCESTERSHIRE SAUCE
1 TABLESPOON LEMON JUICE
1 TEASPOON PREPARED HORSERADISH
1/2 CUP CHOPPED FRESH PARSLEY
1/2 CUP CHOPPED WALNUTS

♀ Flake the tuna in a medium bowl. Add the cream cheese, onion, Worcestershire sauce, lemon juice and horseradish and mix well.

♀ Mix the parsley and walnuts on a plate. Shape the tuna mixture into a ball. Roll in the walnut mixture to coat. Wrap in plastic wrap and refrigerate until serving time.

♀ Unwrap and place on a serving plate. Serve with assorted crackers.

SERVES 6 TO 8

♀ *I'm not going to limit myself just because people won't accept the fact that I can do something else.*

Dolly Parton

CAPONATA

1 CUP CHOPPED ONION ·
1 CUP CHOPPED CELERY
2 MEDIUM EGGPLANT, CHOPPED
3 TABLESPOONS OLIVE OIL
1$^{1}/_{2}$ CUPS TOMATO SAUCE
$^{1}/_{2}$ TEASPOON OREGANO
2 TEASPOONS VINEGAR
1 TEASPOON SUGAR
$^{1}/_{4}$ CUP GREEN OLIVES, CHOPPED
$^{1}/_{4}$ CUP BLACK OLIVES, CHOPPED
1 TEASPOON CAPERS

♀ Sauté the onions, celery and eggplant in olive oil in a large skillet for 10 minutes.

♀ Add the tomato sauce, oregano, vinegar and sugar. Cook for 10 minutes, stirring occasionally. Let stand until cool. Stir in the olives and capers.

♀ Serve warm, cool, or at room temperature with pita triangles or crackers.

SERVES 6 TO 8

THESE ARE A FEW OF MY FAVORITE ZINGS

One of NOW's strongest allies in the U. S. House was Rep. Patricia Schroeder, D-Colo, who retired in 1996 after serving for almost a quarter century. In addition to her unfailing support of feminist issues, Rep. Schroeder could always be counted on for a good quip. It was she who coined the description of Ronald Reagan, "the Teflon president."
—In 1988, when Schroeder announced her candidacy for U.S. president, a reporter asked her: "Will you run as a woman?" A bit bemused, Schroeder inquired, "How would you have me run?"
—In a debate on sexual harassment, she pointed out that some men think "harass" is two words.
—When asked how she could combine the jobs of mother and legislator, Schroeder replied, "Because I have a brain and a uterus and they both work."

BLEU CHEESE PUFFS

3/4 CUP WATER
1/4 CUP BUTTER OR MARGARINE
3/4 CUP FLOUR
3 EGGS
2/3 CUP CRUMBLED BLEU CHEESE, SUCH AS ROQUEFORT, STILTON OR MAYTAG BLUE

♀ Bring the water and butter to a full rolling boil in a 2- or 3-quart saucepan over high heat. Remove from the heat. Add the flour all at once and stir until the mixture is smooth.
♀ Add the eggs 1 at a time and beat until smooth after each addition. Stir until the mixture loses its gloss.
♀ Stir in the cheese. Let the mixture stand for 15 minutes.
♀ Preheat the oven to 400 degrees. Grease and flour a baking sheet.
♀ Drop the dough by rounded tablespoonfuls onto the prepared baking sheet, leaving space between mounds.
♀ Bake for 30 minutes or until the puffs are a rich brown and appear dry. Loosen with a spatula and serve warm.
♀ May cool on a wire rack and wrap in plastic wrap to store for 1 day or freeze for up to 2 weeks.
♀ Reheat thawed puffs at 350 degrees for about 3 minutes.

MAKES 24 PUFFS

GOUDA EASY WEDGES

1 (8-COUNT) PACKAGE CRESCENT ROLL DOUGH
1 (4-OUNCE) ROUND GOUDA

♀ Preheat the oven to 350 degrees.

♀ Separate the dough into triangles. Arrange the triangles on a nonstick baking sheet with points toward the center to form a circle. Press the edges together to seal.

♀ Peel the wax from the cheese and discard. Place the cheese round on the dough circle. Fold the dough over the cheese and press the seams together to completely enclose the cheese.

♀ Bake for 20 to 30 minutes or until the cheese melts.

♀ Let stand at room temperature for 10 minutes before cutting into wedges and serve warm.

MAKES 10 TO 12 WEDGES

At a "No on 2" rally in 1992, Hon. Patricia Schroeder and Rosemary Dempsey, then NOW's Action Vice President, campaigned in Colorado against a right wing anti-lesbian and gay ballot measure.

JUST ANOTHER WOMAN OF THE '90S

Dolores Huerta, co-founder and First Vice President of the United Farm Workers of America, AFL-CIO, directs the UFW's Collective Bargaining Department. A graduate of Delta College in Stockton, California, she taught grammar school but quit because, "I couldn't stand seeing kids come to class hungry and needing shoes. I thought I could do more by organizing farm workers than by trying to teach their hungry children."

"Dolores is totally fearless, both mentally and physically," Cesar Chavez once remarked. "For more than 30 years, she has been one of the UFW's most visible symbols, repeatedly facing down burly goons on tense picket lines." Huerta is the mother of eleven children and is a staunch defender of women's reproductive rights.

SPINACH BALLS

A nice appetizer—crispy on the outside and soft on the inside.

2 (10-OUNCE) PACKAGES FROZEN CHOPPED SPINACH
2 CUPS HERB-SEASONED STUFFING MIX
1$^{1}/_{2}$ TEASPOONS DRIED ONION FLAKES
2 EXTRA-LARGE OR 3 MEDIUM EGGS, LIGHTLY BEATEN
$^{1}/_{2}$ TEASPOON GARLIC SALT
$^{1}/_{3}$ CUP MELTED BUTTER OR MARGARINE
$^{1}/_{3}$ CUP GRATED PARMESAN CHEESE
DASH OF RED OR BLACK PEPPER

♀ Cook the spinach using the package directions, drain and squeeze dry. Place in a large bowl.

♀ Add the stuffing mix, onion flakes, eggs, garlic salt, butter, Parmesan cheese and pepper and mix well. Chill the mixture for 2 hours or longer.

♀ Shape into 1$^{1}/_{2}$-inch balls and arrange on a lightly oiled baking sheet. Cover with plastic wrap. Refrigerate for several hours to overnight.

♀ Preheat the oven to 350 degrees. Bake the spinach balls, uncovered, for 20 to 25 minutes or until firm and light brown. Serve hot.

SERVES 8 TO 12

GRILLED HALIBUT SKEWERS

These skewers can be broiled, baked or barbecued. Alternate the fish with bite-size chunks of vegetables, such as zucchini, yellow squash, whole mushrooms and pearl onions, and serve on a bed of rice for a main course. Add skewers of cherry tomatoes only, cooked for half the time of the fish skewers.

2 POUNDS HALIBUT OR OTHER FIRM WHITE FISH
1/2 CUP ITALIAN OLIVE OIL VINAIGRETTE

♀ Cut the halibut into pieces about the size of golf balls. Place in a large dish or sealable plastic bag.

♀ Add the vinaigrette and mix gently. Seal tightly and marinate in the refrigerate for 30 minutes to overnight. (If adding vegetables, prepare enough vegetables to equal half the number of halibut pieces and marinate separately in 1/4 cup vinaigrette.)

♀ Drain the halibut (and vegetables) in a colander. Thread onto skewers.

♀ Preheat the broiler, oven or grill as desired. Cook just until the halibut flakes easily and any vegetables are tender-crisp. Serve hot.

SERVES 8 TO 12

Dolores Huerta joins Prema Mathai-Davis of the YWCA/USA and Gloria Steinem. All spoke at NOW's 1996 March to Fight the Right in San Francisco, CA.

AVOCADO MANGO SOUP

1 OVER-RIPE AVOCADO
1 OVER-RIPE MANGO
1 CUP PLAIN YOGURT
1 (6-OUNCE) CAN FROZEN APPLE JUICE
    CONCENTRATE
1/2 CUP COLD WATER
DASH OF FRESH LEMON OR LIME JUICE

♀ Peel and seed the avocado and mango. Cut the pulp into chunks and place in a blender or food processor container.
♀ Add the yogurt, apple juice concentrate, water and lemon juice. Process for 30 seconds or until smooth. Serve cold.

SERVES 4

♀ *Bea Farber is harness racing's most successful woman driver. When asked why she didn't stay in the kitchen where she belonged, Farber responded: "Honey, you show me how to earn over $600,000 a year in the kitchen, and I'm on my way."*

CURRIED BROCCOLI SOUP

This is a fat-free vegan recipe. Non-vegans can substitute ordinary milk for the soy milk.

1 LARGE ONION, CHOPPED
2 CLOVES OF GARLIC, CHOPPED
3 CUPS WATER
1 TABLESPOON CURRY POWDER
1 TEASPOON NUTMEG
SALT AND PEPPER TO TASTE
1 BUNCH BROCCOLI, CHOPPED
2 POTATOES, PEELED, CHOPPED
1 CUP SOY MILK

♀ Combine the onion, garlic and a few tablespoons of the water in a large saucepan. Cook for several minutes until the onion and garlic are translucent, stirring frequently.

♀ Stir in the remaining water, curry powder, nutmeg, salt and pepper. Bring to a boil.

♀ Add the broccoli and potato. Return to a boil and reduce the heat. Simmer for 20 minutes or until the vegetables are tender.

♀ Purée the mixture in several batches in a blender, adding a small amount of soy milk to each batch.

♀ Return the puréed mixture to the saucepan. Blend in the remaining soy milk. Cook over low heat until heated thoroughly, adjust seasonings and serve immediately.

SERVES 3 OR 4

A QUEEN FOR REAL

In 1994, New Mexico Highlands University crowned NOW activist Tobi Hale Homecoming Queen, blowing all the stereotypes out of the water. Hale was a 44-year-old, legally blind, openly lesbian wheelchair jockey.

Tobi's friends helped her gather the required signatures and put up campaign posters, and she met all the other requirements, including the pageant dance category, in which she wheeled around the stage while people danced around her. For the talent portion of the contest, Hale did a comedy routine she described as "precision wheelchair driving" to the Patsy Cline song *Stop the World*.

With her 4.0 grade point average and active participation in a number of organizations, Highlands was well-represented by Tobi Hale. In 1998, Hale was elected to NOW's National Board.

JUST ANOTHER WOMAN OF THE '90s

Attorney Fay Clayton, lead counsel on *NOW v. Scheidler*, won this 1998 case establishing that there is an organized conspiracy to stop abortion through fear, force, and violence.

Fay grew up on a farm in New Jersey, where she learned to drive a tractor by age 6. She married at 18, and soon had three children. While she liked motherhood, she didn't like staying home. She began teaching at a Montessori preschool, and while there decided to attend law school.

"I went to school nights, taught in the morning, and in the afternoon I played with my own kids and studied," said Clayton. "Was it hard? No, for a woman who is raising three kids and teaching preschool, going to law school was a piece of cake. You already know how to do 30 things at once."

BROCCOLI AND WATERCRESS SOUP

Upon learning of then-President George Bush's childish refusal to eat broccoli, Mary J. Case felt challenged— her creative juices began to flow—and this recipe was the result!

3 MEDIUM LEEKS
1 TABLESPOON VINEGAR
1 CUP FAT-FREE CHICKEN OR VEGETABLE STOCK
1 MEDIUM YELLOW ONION, COARSELY CHOPPED
1 TABLESPOON SALT
1 TEASPOON FRESHLY GROUND PEPPER
2 QUARTS FAT-FREE CHICKEN OR VEGETABLE STOCK
2 MEDIUM POTATOES
2 BUNCHES BROCCOLI, PEELED, CHOPPED
1 BUNCH WATERCRESS

♀ Cut off and discard the green tops and root ends from the leeks. Cut the leeks into halves lengthwise, place in a large deep container and add the vinegar and water to cover. Let stand for 15 minutes. Drain, rinse well and chop coarsely.
♀ Heat 1 cup stock in a large soup pot. Add the leeks, onion, salt and pepper. Cook over low heat for 10 minutes or until the vegetables are wilted.
♀ Add 2 quarts stock, potatoes and broccoli. Simmer, uncovered, for 20 to 25 minutes or until the vegetables are tender.
♀ Rinse the watercress, discard stems and pat dry. Add the watercress to the soup. Let the soup stand for 10 minutes.
♀ Process the soup in small batches in a blender or food processor. Return to the pot and reheat to serving temperature over low heat. May refrigerate up to 2 days or freeze for later use.

SERVES 8

GARLIC SOUP

What a great treatment for colds!

2 TABLESPOONS (OR MORE) MINCED GARLIC
2 TEASPOONS OLIVE OIL
4 CUPS CHICKEN BROTH
2 EGGS

♀ Sauté the garlic in olive oil in a 2-quart saucepan over low heat for 30 seconds or until pale gold and fragrant, stirring constantly. Do not burn or the garlic will have a bitter flavor.
♀ Add the broth. Simmer for 5 to 7 minutes.
♀ Beat the eggs in a small bowl. Add to the soup gradually, stirring gently.
♀ Cook for 1 minute longer. Serve immediately.

SERVES 2 TO 4

Fay Clayton responds to reporters after the 1993 Supreme Court argument in NOW vs. Scheidler.

LADIES LAST

I find some irony in the situation where women actually have to picket to demand their full legal status as a deprived minority. It is too well known that as a group women are the very last entitled to equal rights, much less equal opportunity; if we demand either, then of course we are no longer ladies and don't deserve anything at all.

If the price of being a lady is to earn 73 cents an hour less as a selector-packer than as a forklift truck operator, then we are going to take the 73 cents and the forklift. If having our cigarettes lighted and our doors opened means we earn half as much as the man who does those things for us, then we will open our own doors and carry our own matches, and lady be damned.

From *Feminism vs. The Feds* (1970)
by Ann London Scott

Scott was a Vice President of NOW from 1971 until she died of cancer in 1975.

HEARTY VEGETARIAN LEEK AND POTATO SOUP

3 LEEKS
$1/4$ CUP BUTTER
2 CLOVES OF GARLIC, CRUSHED
2 CUPS MUSHROOMS, QUARTERED
4 TO 5 CUPS WATER
6 MEDIUM POTATOES, PEELED, CHOPPED
2 CHICKEN OR VEGETARIAN BOUILLON CUBES
2 CUPS HEAVY WHIPPING CREAM OR LIGHT CREAM
$1/4$ TEASPOON NUTMEG
SALT AND PEPPER TO TASTE

♀ Clean the leeks well. Cut into thin cross-slices. Reserve some of the green tops for garnish.

♀ Sauté the remaining leeks in butter in a soup pot for several minutes. Add the garlic and mushrooms. Sauté for several minutes.

♀ Add the water, potatoes and bouillon cubes. Simmer, covered, for 2 to 3 hours or until the soup is somewhat reduced.

♀ Add the cream and nutmeg just before serving. Bring to serving temperature; do not boil. Adjust seasonings, adding salt and pepper.

♀ Ladle into soup bowls and garnish with slices of the reserved leek tops.

SERVES 8 TO 10

WILD RICE SOUP

A delicious, quick-to-fix soup, especially during crisp fall days.

1/2 MEDIUM ONION, CHOPPED
1 SMALL CARROT, CHOPPED
1 RIB CELERY, CHOPPED
2 TABLESPOONS BUTTER
3 TABLESPOONS FLOUR
5 CUPS CHICKEN OR VEGETABLE BROTH
2 CUPS COOKED WILD RICE
2 TABLESPOONS DRY SHERRY (OPTIONAL)
SALT AND PEPPER TO TASTE

♀ Sauté the onion, carrot and celery in butter in a 3-quart soup pot until the onion is translucent. Add the flour. Cook for several minutes, stirring constantly.

♀ Stir in 1 cup broth gradually. Stir in the remaining broth. Add the cooked wild rice. Simmer for 5 minutes.

♀ Add the sherry, salt and pepper. Ladle into bowls and garnish with a sprinkle of minced parsley and chives.

VARIATIONS:

♀ Substitute 1 cup cooked wild rice and 1 cup cooked long grain rice for the 2 cups wild rice.

♀ Substitute a prepared package of herb-flavored wild rice.

♀ Add 1/3 cup minced ham or chicken.

♀ Add 3 tablespoons slivered almonds just before serving.

SERVES 6

WOMEN IN THE SERVICE ACADEMIES

In 1974, NOW testified in hearings held by the House Armed Services Committee urging admittance of women to the service academies. The bill was defeated in the Committee's first vote, by 18-16.

NOW and other groups persisted, however, and in 1980 was proud to announce the first NOW member to graduate from a service academy. Melissa Harrington commanded the 4th Battalion in her last year at the Naval Academy, was Regimental Commander in her 2nd class year, and was elected to the Sigma Xi Honorary Scientific Fraternity.

Evaluated by her commander as the most outstanding Mid in her class, she was the first woman to be sent from Annapolis to the Royal British Naval Academy.

Melissa's mother, Roberta Harrington, had been president of Fayetteville (NY) NOW, and served on the New York State NOW Board for several years.

As-Good-As-It-Gets Vegetarian Vegetable Soup

Whip up a pot of soup on Sunday and you won't have to bother cooking dinner for the rest of the week. Just warm the soup a bit, add your favorite bread, and satisfy your soul.

INGREDIENTS:

1 GALLON DISTILLED WATER

KOMBU (A TYPE OF SEAWEED)
    TO TASTE

1 ONION, QUARTERED

2/3 CUP CHOPPED FRESH PARSLEY

12 WHOLE PEPPERCORNS

3 LARGE CLOVES OF GARLIC,
    COARSELY CHOPPED

1 CARROT, PEELED, CUT INTO
    3 OR 4 PIECES

1 RIB CELERY, CUT INTO 3 OR
    4 PIECES

1/2 TEASPOON SALT

WHITE OF 1 LARGE OR 2 SMALL
    LEEKS, WELL RINSED,
    CHOPPED

4 CARROTS, PEELED, CHOPPED

2/3 CUP PEARL BARLEY

12 WHOLE PEPPERCORNS

6 TURNIPS, PEELED, CHOPPED

1 (12-OUNCE) CAN CHOPPED
    TOMATOES

6 LARGE LEAVES COLLARD
    GREENS OR SWISS CHARD,
    CUT INTO 2-INCH STRIPS

1 CUP FROZEN PEAS

SALT TO TASTE

CHOPPED FRESH HERBS, SUCH AS
    MARJORAM, OREGANO AND
    THYME, TO TASTE

METHOD:

♀ Combine the water and rinsed kombu in a large soup pot. Boil for about 10 minutes and remove the kombu.

♀ Add the onion, parsley, 12 peppercorns, garlic, 1 carrot, 1 rib celery and salt. Simmer for about 30 minutes. Remove the peppercorns and vegetables with a slotted spoon or hand strainer and discard.

♀ Add the leeks, chopped carrots, barley and remaining 12 peppercorns to the broth. Simmer for 20 minutes.

♀ Add turnips, undrained tomatoes, and collard greens. (If using Swiss chard, delay adding until the turnips are tender.) Simmer until all vegetables are tender.

♀ Add the peas and salt. Add enough additional distilled water to make the soup of the desired consistency. Simmer for 3 minutes longer. Serve with crusty bread.

VARIATION:

♀ Increase the amount of barley or add potatoes, beans or pasta at times appropriate to their cooking needs.

    MAKES A LOT

♀ *Too much of a good thing can be wonderful.*

Mae West

FIVE-HOUR STEW

2 POUNDS STEW MEAT
6 CARROTS
2 CUPS CHOPPED ONIONS
1 CUP CHOPPED CELERY
1 CUP SLICED WATER CHESTNUTS
1 CUP SLICED MUSHROOMS
2 CUPS TOMATOES
1/4 CUP INSTANT TAPIOCA
1/2 TEASPOON THYME
1/2 TEASPOON ROSEMARY
3/4 TEASPOON SALT
GARLIC SALT TO TASTE

♀ Preheat the oven to 250 degrees.
♀ Cut the stew meat and carrots into bite-size pieces.
Combine with the remaining vegetables, tapioca and
seasonings in a large roasting pan. Cover tightly.
♀ Bake for 5 hours; do not peek.

SERVES 4 TO 6

♀ *Cleaning your house while your kids are still growing is
like shoveling the walk before it stops snowing.*

Phyllis Diller

NOW CHALLENGES LITTLE LEAGUE

Several NOW chapters set their sights on Little League in 1973, challenging their denial of equal admittance to girls. Among them was Pittsburgh NOW, which filed a charge of sex discrimination in public accommodations against the City of Pittsburgh because Little League games were scheduled in public parks.

Later that year, a Little League All-Star Team from Oakton, Illinois was defeated by another All-Star team from Mattoon, Illinois, with a score of 8-7. The winning team was all girls!

TRUE BELIEVER

San Francisco NOW received a phone call in 1984 from a beleaguered male basketball player in Cuyahoga Falls, Ohio, who explained that his team had played a women's team.

The stakes were that if the men lost, they would have to call NOW chapters all over the country telling of the women's victory.

Well, the women won—76-54! When asked if he believed women should have equal rights, he replied, "Now I do!"

RED KIDNEY BEAN SOUP

1 (16-OUNCE) CAN RED KIDNEY BEANS
1 1/2 CUPS CHOPPED ONIONS
1 CUP CHOPPED CELERY
1 TABLESPOON CHOPPED GARLIC
1 TABLESPOON BUTTER
1 1/4 POUNDS SMOKED HAM HOCKS
8 CUPS WATER
2 CUPS CHICKEN STOCK
1 TEASPOON GROUND CUMIN
1/4 TEASPOON FRESHLY GROUND PEPPER
1 TEASPOON CHILI POWDER
1/4 TEASPOON SALT
1 BAY LEAF
1/4 TEASPOON DRIED THYME
1 TABLESPOON FRESH LEMON JUICE
2 TABLESPOONS RED WINE VINEGAR

♀ Drain the beans and rinse with cold water.

♀ Sauté the onions, celery and garlic in the butter in a large soup pot until the onions are translucent.

♀ Add the beans, ham hocks, water, chicken stock, cumin, pepper, chili powder, salt and bay leaf. Simmer, covered, for 1 1/2 hours.

♀ Remove the ham hocks, cool and chop the ham; set aside. Discard the bay leaf.

♀ Purée the soup in batches in a blender and return to the soup pot. Add the thyme, lemon juice, vinegar and ham. Heat to serving temperature over low heat.

SERVES 10.

SOUTHWESTERN LOZA LUPA SOUPA

4 SKINLESS BONE-IN CHICKEN BREASTS
12 CLOVES OF GARLIC, CHOPPED
16 CUPS WATER
1 MEDIUM ONION, CHOPPED
2 TABLESPOONS OLIVE OIL
4 MEDIUM TOMATOES, CHOPPED
1 (29-OUNCE) CAN HOMINY, DRAINED
SALT AND PEPPER TO TASTE

♀ Combine the chicken, garlic and water in a large soup pot. Bring to a boil. Reduce heat and simmer for 1 hour.
♀ Skim the broth; remove the chicken and cool. Bone and shred the chicken and return to the pot.
♀ Sauté the onion in olive oil in a large skillet until translucent. Add the tomatoes. Cook for 2 minutes, stirring constantly. Add the hominy. Cook for 2 minutes.
♀ Stir the tomato mixture into the chicken mixture. Heat to serving temperature and adjust the seasonings.
♀ Ladle into soup bowls. Garnish with tortilla chips and shredded Monterey Jack cheese.

SERVES 10 TO 12.

IF THE SHOE FITS . . .

The Detroit Athletic Club, which had refused to admit women as members and required all women coming into the building to enter through a side door, got its come-uppance on Women's Equality Day, 1986.

Activists from the Metro Detroit NOW Chapter dumped 400 pairs of women's shoes on its doorstep, accompanied by a sign saying, "The Real Heels Are Inside."

A Homecoming

In October 1997, attending the dedication ceremony and festivities for the Women in the Military Service of America Memorial with about 30,000 U.S. women veterans, I felt that I had come home. This was more than a dedication—it was a family reunion. A veteran of the Vietnam and Persian Gulf Wars, I hugged sister veterans of World War II and the Korean War. We laughed, shared "war stories," sang songs and celebrated our history together. In the middle of this reunion, I encountered a group of female cadets from the Virginia Military Institute (VMI). These young women with buzz haircuts were the end of the 159-year-old all-male tradition at VMI. NOW had filed an *amicus* brief supporting the right of women to attend VMI and the Citadel, protesting the sex discrimination at these state-supported schools. These cadets were so thrilled to be among women veterans that they all decided to join the military after completing their VMI education. They and others like them are our future military leaders—awesome. *Karen Johnson (photo opposite) retired as a Lt. Colonel after 20 years in the Air Force. She was elected National NOW Membership Vice President in 1993.*

Cajun Seafood Gumbo

3/4 CUP OLIVE OIL
1 1/2 CUPS FLOUR
3 CUPS CHOPPED ONIONS
1 CUP COARSELY CHOPPED GREEN BELL PEPPER
1/2 CUP CHOPPED CELERY
1 CUP CHOPPED GREEN ONIONS
1 TABLESPOON CHOPPED GARLIC
6 CUPS (APPROX.) COLD WATER
1 (6-OUNCE) CAN TOMATO PASTE
1/2 TABLESPOON EACH DRIED BASIL, THYME AND OREGANO
4 BAY LEAVES
3 TABLESPOONS WORCESTERSHIRE SAUCE
1 TABLESPOON SALT
6 TO 8 CRABS WITH CLAWS, BODIES BROKEN INTO HALVES
2 POUNDS PEELED SHRIMP, HEADS REMOVED
1 POUND CRAWFISH TAILS, PEELED
12 OYSTERS
TABASCO SAUCE TO TASTE
FILÉ GUMBO (OPTIONAL)

♀ Heat the olive oil in a large heavy soup pot. Stir in the flour gradually. Cook until the flour begins to darken, stirring constantly. Add the chopped vegetables and cook until tender, stirring frequently.

♀ Stir in the water. Add the tomato paste, seasonings and seafood and mix well. Bring to a simmer. Cook until the seafood is cooked through.

♀ Serve the gumbo over beds of hot cooked rice in large bowls. Sprinkle each serving with a tablespoon of filé gumbo.

SERVES 6 TO 8

WITH GREAT ZEST
SALADS AND DRESSINGS

NOW envisions a world where:

♀ women's equality and women's empowerment to

determine our own destinies is a reality;

♀ women have equal representation in all decision-making

structures of our societies;

♀ social and economic justice exist, where all people have the

food, housing, clothing, health care and education they need;

♀ there is recognition and respect for each person's

intrinsic worth as well as the rich diversity of the

various groups among us;

♀ non-violence is the established order;

♀ patriarchal culture and male dominance no longer

oppress us or our earth;

♀ women and girls are heard, valued and respected.

from NOW's 1998 Declaration of Sentiments

PICTURED ON OVERLEAF: *Karen Johnson and VMI cadets after
1997 dedication ceremony and festivities for the "Women in the Military
Service of America Memorial," Arlington National Cemetery, VA.*

Fennel and Apple Salad

Fennel looks a bit like celery but the delicious licorice flavor makes for a real change of pace.

2 heads fennel, trimmed, chopped
4 medium Gala or other crisp sweet apples, cored, chopped
2 tablespoons lemon juice
3 tablespoons vegetable oil
2 teaspoons sugar
Salt and pepper to taste
1/4 cup sunflower kernels

♀ Place the chopped fennel and apples in a large bowl.
♀ Combine the lemon juice, oil, sugar, salt and pepper in a jar and shake vigorously to mix.
♀ Pour the dressing over the apple mixture and toss to mix.
♀ Sprinkle with the sunflower kernels and toss lightly. Garnish with watercress.

Serves 6

♀ *Feminism is not the opposite of misogyny, it is the antidote.*
Sheila Oddi

Anti-Victim Laws Overturned

Persistent lobbying by California NOW chapters in 1980 was instrumental in eliminating two of that state's most objectionable rape laws.

The first provision, which had been on the books for over 100 years, required that a rape victim prove "resistance" before the rapist could be prosecuted. This made convictions extremely difficult, and in some cases prosecutors simply wouldn't press charges if there was no *physical* evidence of resistance.

The second law, now repealed, permitted police to routinely administer lie detector tests to victims of rape but not to victims of other crimes.

BECAUSE

Because woman's work is never done and is underpaid or unpaid or boring or repetitious and we're the first to get the sack and what we look like is more important than what we do and if we get raped it's our fault and if we get beaten we must have provoked it and if we raise our voices we're nagging bitches and if we enjoy sex we're nymphos and if we don't we're frigid and if we love women it's because we can't get a "real" man and if we ask our doctor too many questions we're neurotic and/or pushy and if we expect child care we're selfish and if we stand up for our rights we're aggressive and "unfeminine" and if we don't we're typical weak females and if we want to get married we're out to trap a man and if we don't we're unnatural and because we still can't get an adequate safe contraceptive but men can walk on the moon and if we can't cope or don't want a pregnancy we're made to feel guilty about abortion and . . . for lots and lots of other reasons we are part of the women's liberation movement.

—NUS Women's Campaign
London

ACTIVIST SLAW

$1/2$ MEDIUM HEAD CABBAGE, SHREDDED
1 SMALL RED ONION, THINLY SLICED
2 CARROTS, PEELED, GRATED
$2/3$ CUP VINEGAR
$1/3$ CUP CANOLA OIL
$1/4$ CUP SUGAR
1 TEASPOON SALT
$1/4$ TEASPOON FRESHLY GROUND PEPPER

♀ Place the prepared cabbage, onion and carrots in a large bowl and toss to mix.
♀ Combine the vinegar, canola oil, sugar, salt and pepper in a jar and shake vigorously or process the mixture in a blender or food processor for 10 to 15 seconds.
♀ Pour the dressing over the cabbage mixture and toss to mix.
♀ Refrigerate, covered, for 8 hours or longer.
♀ Drain the salad before serving.

SERVES 8 TO 10

♀ *We are not interested in the possibilities of defeat.*
Queen Victoria, 1899

56

WISCONSIN COLESLAW

1 LARGE HEAD CABBAGE, SHREDDED
1 CUP WHITE VINEGAR
1/2 CUP SUGAR
3/4 CUP CORN OR CANOLA OIL
1 CLOVE OF GARLIC, MINCED
1 SMALL ONION, MINCED
SALT AND PEPPER TO TASTE

♀ Place the cabbage in a large bowl.
♀ Combine the vinegar, sugar, oil, garlic, onion, salt and pepper in a jar and shake vigorously to mix.
♀ Pour the dressing over the cabbage and toss to mix.
♀ Serve immediately or chill until serving time and toss before serving.

SERVES 10 TO 12

Anti-violence activists show solidarity at NOW's 1995 Rally for Women's Lives.

It's a Matter of Rights

The National Organization for Women is proud to have been a part of the 1993 March for Lesbian, Gay and Bi Equal Rights at a time when our nation is embroiled in a great battle for civil rights. Since 1971, NOW has asserted our commitment to securing lesbian rights, not as something separate, but inextricably connected with our demands for full reproductive freedom, equal pay for women's work, an end to racism, and freedom from violence and harassment.

We march because oppression is simply wrong, whether based on immutable characteristics like race or ethnicity, accidents of brith like class, or lifestyle choices like religion. Discrimination is wrong whether against people with disabilities, people with AIDS/HIV, women, lesbians, gays or bisexuals.

We march for lesbian, gay and bi rights for the same reasons we march for abortion rights and reproductive freedom: for our right to privacy in the most intimate areas of our lives, sexuality and reproduction; for our right to be free from the imposition of religious right-wing dogma, whether imposed

Salted Salad

1 (6-INCH) CUCUMBER
2 MEDIUM TOMATOES
1/2 GREEN BELL PEPPER
4 OR 5 GREEN ONIONS, CHOPPED
1 RIB CELERY, CHOPPED
3 TO 4 TABLESPOONS SALT
1 TABLESPOON CRACKED BLACK PEPPER
2 TABLESPOONS VEGETABLE OIL
3 TABLESPOONS WHITE VINEGAR

♀ Peel several strips lengthwise from the cucumber in a decorative peeled and unpeeled pattern. Slice the cucumber thinly.
♀ Cut the tomatoes and green pepper into bite-size chunks.
♀ Combine the cucumber, tomatoes, green pepper, onions and celery in a large bowl. Sprinkle with salt, pepper and oil.
♀ Add enough cold water to cover the vegetables completely. Taste the water. The taste should be almost as salty as sea water. Add additional salt if necessary. Add the vinegar, taste and adjust seasonings if necessary.
♀ Refrigerate, covered, for several hours.
♀ Serve the vegetables with a slotted spoon to permit draining.

SERVES 4 TO 6

Winter Salad

4 SMALL KOHLRABI, PEELED, GRATED
SALT TO TASTE
3 RIBS CELERY, CHOPPED OR 1 CUP CHOPPED
    CELERY ROOT
3 OR 4 GREEN ONIONS, CHOPPED
2 TABLESPOONS SOY SAUCE
1/2 TEASPOON SUGAR
1/2 TEASPOON (APPROX.) HOT PEPPER SAUCE
1 TO 2 TABLESPOONS TOASTED SESAME OIL

♀ Place the kohlrabi in a bowl and sprinkle generously with salt. Let stand for 30 minutes. Rinse and drain well.
♀ Add the celery and green onions.
♀ Combine the soy sauce, sugar, desired amounts of hot pepper sauce and sesame oil in a jar and shake vigorously to mix. Pour over the vegetables and toss to mix.
♀ Chill for 1 hour or longer. Toss before serving.

SERVES 4

♀ *If the world were a logical place, men would ride side-saddle.*

Rita Mae Brown

(It's a Matter of Rights, continued)

by the force of laws or direct force and violence.

We march because we know homophobia is a powerful weapon used to keep women—all women—in their place. Fear of being identified as lesbian is used to scare women away from the feminist movement.

Fear is used to keep women from fighting for our own equality and freedom, because being identified as a lesbian in this society can carry very real penalties. But we can overcome the fear, bigotry, hatred and ignorance.

You can make a difference and become part of this historic struggle, which is literally changing the course of our country. We need your money and your life. We need to incorporate this work against oppression into every part of our lives.

Get involved. Take the next step. Stand up. Speak out. Fighting together, we can succeed.

Excerpt from the speech given by NOW President Patricia Ireland at the 1993 March in Washington, DC.

IRAs FOR HOMEMAKERS

In 1994, in a refreshing display of bipartisanship, women senators united across party lines to introduce a bill to allow homemakers to take a full Individual Retirement Account deduction.

Under the 1986 tax code, women who worked in the home had not been able to have their own IRAs, even though they had their own retirement needs. Thus, the tax code perpetuated the myth that women who work in the home don't work, since they don't earn an income.

NOW had been lobbying for years to enhance the economic position of women working in the home, beginning with our Homemakers Bill of Rights in 1977, and winning this bill was a small step forward.

BONNIE'S LAYERED SALAD

1 LARGE HEAD ICEBERG LETTUCE, TORN
2 CUPS CHOPPED CELERY
6 GREEN ONIONS, DICED
1 (10-OUNCE) PACKAGE FROZEN PEAS, THAWED, DRAINED
2 CUPS MAYONNAISE
3 TABLESPOONS SUGAR
4 OUNCES SHREDDED CHEDDAR CHEESE
1 POUND BACON, CRISP-COOKED, CRUMBLED

♀ Layer the lettuce, celery, green onions and peas in a 9x13-inch dish.
♀ Blend the mayonnaise with the sugar in a small bowl. Spread over the vegetable layers, sealing to the edge of the dish.
♀ Sprinkle the cheese and bacon over the top. Chill, covered, overnight.

SERVES 16

♀ *[T]rue emancipation begins neither at the polls nor in courts. It begins in woman's soul.*

Emma Goldman

MARINATED BEAN SALAD

Try this updated version of an old favorite. Make the most of the confetti look by serving it in a clear glass bowl. Keep the black beans marinating separately until just before serving to keep the colors crisp and clear.

1 (16-OUNCE) CAN BLACK BEANS, DRAINED
1 (16-OUNCE) CAN WHITE NAVY BEANS, DRAINED
1 (16-OUNCE) CAN WHOLE KERNEL CORN, DRAINED
1/2 GREEN BELL PEPPER, FINELY CHOPPED
1/2 RED BELL PEPPER, FINELY CHOPPED
6 TO 8 GREEN ONIONS, CHOPPED
VINEGAR AND OIL-BASED ITALIAN SALAD DRESSING
    TO TASTE

♀ Place the black beans in a small bowl and set aside.
♀ Combine the white beans, corn, bell peppers and green onions in a large bowl.
♀ Pour a portion of the salad dressing over the black beans and a portion over the vegetable mixture and mix gently.
♀ Refrigerate for several hours.
♀ Add the black beans to the vegetable mixture just before serving and spoon into a glass serving bowl.

SERVES 6 TO 10

NOW SOCKS IT TO MAY COMPANY

"They marched. They sang liberation songs. They shook clenched fists. One of them climbed on a counter and tossed a handful of socks on the floor. Others stomped on the socks."

This is how the *Cleveland Plain Dealer* covered a noontime demonstration by 300 NOW members at the May Co. department store in 1977 in response to the sale of socks printed with "Help stamp out rape, say yes," accompanied by a caricature of an ape-like man with a long red tongue hanging out.

Wire service stories headlined: "Store thinks rape is funny; NOW doesn't."

A HARSH REALITY

"Every day, at least 20 million lesbians and gay men live with the harsh reality that they could lose their jobs, regardless of job performance, if their private sexual orientation becomes known; they could be discharged from the military regardless of the quality of their military service; they could be denied a security clearance or professional license critical to their economic survival . . . Essentially, lesbian and gay male citizens are required to give up their free speech and free association rights for their very economic survival."

This Congressional testimony by NOW on behalf of the Lesbian and Gay Civil Rights bill argued for extension of the 1964 Civil Rights Act to prohibit discrimination on the basis of affectional or sexual orientation in federally-assisted programs, employment or housing. That bill never became law, and NOW continues to pursue equal opportunity and an end to discrimination and intolerance.

TURKISH BEAN SALAD

1 (16-OUNCE) CAN WHITE BEANS, RINSED, DRAINED
1 CUP WHITE VINEGAR
SALT TO TASTE
1 MEDIUM ONION
2 OR 3 MEDIUM TOMATOES, SEEDED, CHOPPED
1 LARGE GREEN BELL PEPPER, CHOPPED
1/2 BUNCH PARSLEY, FINELY CHOPPED
15 BLACK MEDITERRANEAN OLIVES
1/4 CUP OLIVE OIL
BLACK PEPPER TO TASTE
3 HARD-BOILED EGGS

♀ Place the beans in a large bowl and add 3/4 cup of the vinegar and salt to taste. Marinate for 3 hours. Drain and discard the marinade.
♀ Cut the onion into halves lengthwise and slice into crescents. Add the onion, tomatoes, green pepper and parsley to the beans. Reserve several olives for garnish and add the remaining olives.
♀ Combine the remaining 1/4 cup vinegar, olive oil and salt and pepper to taste in a jar and shake vigorously to mix. Pour over the vegetable mixture and toss lightly to mix.
♀ Spoon into a serving dish. Sprinkle with the reserved olives. Cut the hard-boiled eggs lengthwise into quarters and arrange on top of the salad.

SERVES 6 TO 8

FLSP Corn and Bean Salad

2 (16-ounce) cans whole kernel corn,
    drained
1 (19-ounce) can black beans, drained
1 (14-ounce) can artichoke hearts, drained,
    chopped
1 green bell pepper, chopped
1 red bell pepper, chopped
1/2 teaspoon ground cumin
1/2 teaspoon curry powder
Salt and pepper to taste
1/4 cup plain yogurt or mayonnaise

♀ Combine the corn, beans, artichoke hearts and bell peppers in a bowl.
♀ Combine the cumin, curry powder, salt and pepper in a separate bowl. Add yogurt and mix well.
♀ Add to the vegetable mixture and mix lightly. Adjust seasonings before serving.

Serves 6 to 10

Participants at a rally commemorating the Stonewall rebellion. The sign says it all.

UNWED FATHERS

When I was in law school and
we were reading cases on unwed
mothers, I asked if there were
any cases on unwed fathers. The
professor just thought that was the
funniest thing he'd ever heard.
There *are* no cases on unwed
fathers. They go on and are
captains of the football team and
graduate and go to college.

I want to read one case . . . .
A young junior in high school
is being kicked out for being
pregnant. This is the judge's letter.
Just think about *The Scarlett Letter*.

"The court would like to
make it manifestly clear that lack
of moral character is certainly a
reason for excluding a child from
public education . . . . By analogy,

CARROT AND ORANGE SALAD

*Use flavorful oranges for this fresh surprise from sunny
Morocco. If the oranges taste a bit flat, perk them up
with a bit of fresh lemon juice.*

4 MEDIUM CARROTS, PEELED, GRATED
1/2 TEASPOON CINNAMON
1 TO 3 TEASPOONS SUGAR
2 LARGE NAVEL ORANGES (SEEDLESS)

♀ Combine the carrots, cinnamon and sugar in a bowl and
mix lightly.
♀ Peel the oranges over a bowl to catch all the juice. Use a
serrated knife and cut slightly into the flesh to remove all the
peel. Cut the orange segments from the membrane in rough
chunks. Squeeze the membranes for any remaining juice
and discard.
♀ Add the oranges and juice to the carrot mixture, mix
lightly and adjust the seasonings. Serve immediately.

SERVES 4

♀ *Remember, Ginger Rogers did everything Fred Astaire did,
but she did it backwards and in high heels.*

Faith Whittlesey

64

MARINATED CARROTS

2 POUNDS CARROTS, PEELED, SLICED
1 MEDIUM ONION, CHOPPED
1 GREEN BELL PEPPER, CHOPPED
3/4 CUP VINEGAR
1/2 CUP VEGETABLE OIL
1/2 CUP SUGAR
1 TABLESPOON PREPARED MUSTARD
1 TABLESPOON WORCESTERSHIRE SAUCE

♀ Mix the carrots, onion and green pepper in a large bowl.
♀ Combine the vinegar, oil, sugar, mustard and Worcestershire sauce in a saucepan. Bring to a boil, stirring until the sugar dissolves completely. Pour over the vegetables and mix well.
♀ Refrigerate, covered, overnight.

SERVES 6 TO 8

♀ *I do not want to be remembered as the first Black woman to be elected to the United States Congress, even though I am. I do not want to be remembered as the first woman who happened to be Black to make a serious bid for the presidency. I'd like to be known as a catalyst for change, a woman who had the determination and a woman who had the perserverance to fight on behalf of the female population, because I'm a product of both, being Black and a woman.*
Hon. Shirley Chisholm

(Unwed Fathers, continued)

· the plaintiff's situation could well be likened to that of a typhoid carrier, otherwise an acceptable student in every way. The only real difference is that the carrier is one who acquired that status without fault, while the plaintiff's status is the result of her own wrongdoing. Public opinion identifies an unwed mother of school age as a threat to moral health, particularly of all other teenage school girls."

—Excerpt from a 1976 speech by
Karen DeCrow
NOW President, 1974-77

Spicy Carrot Salad

Make this recipe well in advance as the flavor improves with standing. Cooked beets are delicious prepared this way, too.

1 POUND CARROTS, GRATED
2 OR 3 GREEN ONIONS, FINELY CHOPPED
1/4 CUP MINCED CILANTRO (CORIANDER)
1 CLOVE OF GARLIC, MINCED
2 TO 3 TABLESPOONS SUGAR
1/2 TEASPOON SALT
1/2 TEASPOON GROUND CUMIN
BLACK PEPPER AND CAYENNE TO TASTE
3 TABLESPOONS LEMON JUICE
1/4 CUP VEGETABLE OIL
1/4 CUP MINCED PARSLEY

♀ Combine the carrots, green onions, cilantro and garlic in a bowl and toss to mix.

♀ Mix the sugar, salt, cumin, pepper and cayenne. Sprinkle over the carrot mixture and toss to mix.

♀ Pour a mixture of lemon juice and oil over the mixture and toss lightly. Marinate for 1 hour or longer. Sprinkle with the parsley. Serve at room temperature.

SERVES 6

Zesty Jicama Salad

If you don't know jicama (pronounced hi´-ka-ma) this is a wonderful introduction. It may look like a cross between a russet potato and rutabaga but it more nearly resembles the crunch and delicate, sweet flavor of a water chestnut. Try this refreshing salad as an accompaniment to burgers or on those too-hot-to-cook days.

1 1/2 CUPS GRATED CARROTS
1 1/2 CUPS PEELED GRATED JICAMA
1/4 CUP FINELY CHOPPED FRESH PARSLEY
1 GREEN ONION, FINELY CHOPPED
1 TO 2 RIBS CELERY, FINELY CHOPPED
1/2 SMALL GREEN BELL PEPPER, FINELY CHOPPED
1/4 TO 1/3 CUP ZESTY FRENCH SALAD DRESSING

♀ Combine the carrots, jicama, parsley, green onion, celery and green pepper in a large bowl. Add the Zesty French Salad Dressing and toss lightly. Serve immediately or refrigerate, covered, until serving time.

SERVES 4

ZESTY FRENCH SALAD DRESSING

1 TABLESPOON HONEY
1/2 TEASPOON HOT HUNGARIAN-STYLE PAPRIKA
1/4 CUP CATSUP
1/4 TEASPOON CELERY SEED
1 TEASPOON MINCED ONION
2 TABLESPOONS APPLE CIDER VINEGAR
2 TABLESPOONS MILD-FLAVOR VEGETABLE OIL

♀ Combine all the ingredients in a blender container. Process for several seconds until well mixed. Store any unused dressing in the refrigerator.

♀ *Each woman is made to feel it is her own cross to bear if she can't be the perfect clone of the male superman and the perfect clone of the feminine mystique.*

Betty Friedan, 1964

CREDIT WHERE CREDIT IS DUE

In 1972 there was a heated exchange between member Doris Ingres, NOW Finance Vice-President Gene Boyer, and the president of Marine Bankcard Corp., Eugene Hart.

The subject was the issuing of credit cards in the husband's name only, even where the wife was the wage earner.

Ms. Boyer eventually got a card in her own name, but Hart's letter to Ingres said: "With the exception of you and Ms. Boyer, no other women have shown the slightest interest in having cards issued solely in their names." Doris said, "Let's quit wagging our tails and start barking," and NOW set to work passing the Equal Credit Opportunity Act.

Since it went into effect, a woman who can prove she was unfairly denied credit will not only get credit, she'll get something else: $10,000 in damages.

SWISS BEEF SALAD
A wonderful way to use leftover roast beef or steak.

8 OUNCES RARE BEEF, CUT INTO $1/4 \times 2$-INCH STRIPS
4 OUNCES SWISS CHEESE, CUT INTO STRIPS
3 TO 4 TABLESPOONS CAPERS
$1/2$ RED BELL PEPPER, CUT INTO CHUNKS
2 GREEN ONIONS, CHOPPED
1 (3-INCH) DILL PICKLE, CUT INTO CHUNKS
TARRAGON DRESSING
ROMAINE

♀ Combine the beef, cheese, capers, red pepper, green onions and pickle in a bowl. Add the Dressing and toss lightly.
♀ Line serving plates with the romaine. Spoon the salad onto the romaine. Serve immediately.

TARRAGON DRESSING

1 TEASPOON DRY MUSTARD OR 2 TEASPOONS
    PREPARED COARSE-GROUND MILD MUSTARD
$1/4$ TEASPOON DRIED TARRAGON OR 1 TEASPOON
    MINCED FRESH TARRAGON
3 TABLESPOONS TARRAGON VINEGAR
1 TABLESPOON WATER
$1/4$ CUP VEGETABLE OIL

♀ Combine the mustard, tarragon, vinegar, water and oil in a jar and shake vigorously to mix.

SERVES 2

HOT GERMAN POTATO SALAD

16 SMALL RED POTATOES (APPROX. 2 POUNDS),
     SCRUBBED
4 SLICES THICK BACON, CUT INTO $1/4$-INCH PIECES
2 MEDIUM ONIONS, CHOPPED
$1/2$ CUP CIDER VINEGAR
$1/2$ CUP WATER
1 TEASPOON SUGAR
1 TEASPOON SALT
$1/2$ TEASPOON PEPPER
2 TO 3 TABLESPOONS PREPARED COARSE-GROUND
     MUSTARD (NOT HOT OR HONEY-FLAVORED)
$1/3$ CUP CHOPPED FRESH PARSLEY

♀ Cut the potatoes into halves or quarters. Cook in boiling salted water just until fork-tender. Drain and set aside.

♀ Cook the bacon and onion in a skillet until the bacon begins to crisp, stirring frequently. Pour off all but 3 tablespoons of the drippings.

♀ Add the vinegar, water, sugar, salt, pepper and mustard and mix well. Bring the mixture to a simmer.

♀ Add the potatoes and mix gently until coated. Adjust the seasonings, add the parsley and toss gently.

♀ Serve hot or warm within an hour or two or the salad loses its zing. May serve as a main dish with a tossed salad and a fresh fruit dessert.

SERVES 4 OR 5

Two Women of Courage

In 1983, Sharon Kowalski was severely injured in an auto accident. The hospital notified her father, who, after the extent of Sharon's injuries were known, became her legal guardian. He immediately ordered that her lesbian partner of 9 years, Karen Thompson, not be allowed to visit, and placed Kowalski in a nursing home with a minimal rehabilitative program.

For five years, Thompson pursued legal avenues to get proper medical care for her partner, as well as for the right to care for and visit her. Finally, in 1988, Kowalski was tested for competency, and it was determined in 1989 that she would benefit from intensive rehabilitation and visits from Thompson. Guardianship, however, was retained by her father.

Thompson continued to fight. NOW supported her by filing an *amicus curiae* brief, written by NOW staff Linda Berg and legal intern Allison Strickland, arguing that the trial judges' decision had been based on sexist stereotypes.

Chicken Salad

1 (3-POUND) CHICKEN
3/4 CUP CHOPPED WALNUTS
1/2 CUP CHOPPED CELERY
1/2 CUP SOUR CREAM
1/3 CUP SHARP OR MILD DIJON MUSTARD
1/3 CUP ITALIAN SALAD DRESSING

♀ Cook the chicken in water to cover in a saucepan until tender. Drain and bone the chicken, discarding skin and bones.
♀ Shred or finely chop the chicken and place in a bowl. Add the walnuts and celery.
♀ Blend the sour cream, mustard and salad dressing in a small bowl. Adjust the seasonings and proportions to taste.
♀ Add the mixture to the chicken mixture and mix well. Chill until serving time.
♀ Serve the salad on lettuce-lined plates, in scooped out tomatoes, in pita bread, or as filling for regular or finger sandwiches.

SERVES 6 TO 8

Honey Mustard Salad Dressing

1/2 CUP HONEY
1/4 CUP PREPARED MILD MUSTARD
2 TABLESPOONS RED WINE VINEGAR
1/4 TO 1/2 TEASPOON GARLIC PURÉE

♀ Combine the honey, mustard, vinegar and garlic in a bowl and blend well. Store in the refrigerator for up to several weeks.

♀ May adjust all ingredients to taste such as substituting lemon juice for all or part of the vinegar; using almost any mustard except harsh mustards; or omitting the garlic.

MAKES 3/4 CUP

(Two Women of Courage, continued)

Finally on December 17, 1991 a Minnesota appellate court named Thompson as Kowalski's guardian, culminating her 8-year battle to care for her life partner.

Sharon Kowalski and Karen Thompson accept NOW's 1990 Woman of Courage Awards from NOW President Molly Yard.

HEAD AND MASTER

"I was a new employee at South Central Bell, and excitedly filled out the form to participate in the company's Stock Option Plan. When I reached the bottom, it said IF A MARRIED WOMAN, HUSBAND MUST SIGN HERE: My boss explained that Louisiana's head and master law put the husband in charge of all the family money, even the wife's paycheck."

That was 1973. Her husband signed, but Kim Gandy tracked down the New Orleans NOW chapter anyway. They were hard at work on the issue and had filed several lawsuits—challenging this law that had bankrupted many women and left others homeless. Supporters educated, agitated, lobbied (and replaced) legislators, eventually passing an Equal Management law that took effect in 1980.

Gandy (photo opposite, at right) remained active in NOW and has been a national officer since 1987. She was elected Executive Vice President in 1991.

SPICY PEANUT DRESSING

1 1/2 TABLESPOONS CREAMY PEANUT BUTTER
2 1/2 TABLESPOONS SALAD OIL
2 TABLESPOONS SOY SAUCE
2 TABLESPOONS SUGAR
2 TEASPOONS WHITE VINEGAR
1/2 TEASPOON SESAME OIL
1/4 TO 1/2 TEASPOON CAYENNE
1 TABLESPOON MINCED GREEN ONION
1 TABLESPOON CHOPPED FRESH CILANTRO
  (OPTIONAL)

♀ Blend the peanut butter and oil in a small bowl. Add the remaining ingredients 1 at a time, blending well after each addition.
♀ Serve as a dressing over a salad of cooked rice mixed with chopped lettuce and bean sprouts; or as a dip for chicken or pork skewers.

MAKES 1/2 CUP

♀ *Men their rights and nothing more; women their rights and nothing less.*
  Susan B. Anthony, motto of *The Revolution*, 1868

72

SIDE BY SIDE
VEGETABLES AND SIDE DISHES

NOW has moved more feminists than ever into positions of

power in all of the institutions that shape our society.

We have achieved some measure of power to effect change in

these institutions from within; yet still we are far from

full equality in decision-making.

We demand an equal share of power in our families and

religions, in law, science and technology, the arts and humanities,

sports, education, the trades and professions, labor and

management, the media, corporations and small businesses

as well as government.

In no sphere of life should women be silenced,

underrepresented, or devalued.

PICTURED ON OVERLEAF: *1993 National NOW Conference, Boston, MA; Geraldine Miller and Kim Gandy holding Elizabeth Cady Lornell.*

KELLIE'S SAUSAGE AND PECAN DRESSING

2 (7-OUNCE) PACKAGES CORN MUFFIN MIX
4 TO 6 OUNCES BULK PORK SAUSAGE WITH SAGE
1/2 CUP EACH CHOPPED GREEN ONIONS, GREEN BELL
    PEPPERS, YELLOW ONION AND CELERY
3 SMALL CLOVES OF GARLIC, MINCED
1 TEASPOON (APPROX.) VEGETABLE OIL
1 LARGE RED APPLE, CORED, CHOPPED
1 CUP CHOPPED PECANS
3 OR 4 HARD-BOILED EGGS, CHOPPED
1 CUP TURKEY BROTH
SALT, PEPPER, POULTRY SEASONING, RUBBED SAGE,
    DRIED BASIL AND GROUND GINGER TO TASTE
2 EGGS, BEATEN
1/2 CUP MILK
1/2 CUP MELTED BUTTER

♀ Prepare and bake the corn muffin mix using the package directions for corn bread. Cool.
♀ Cook the sausage in a skillet until brown and crumbly, stirring frequently; drain and cool.
♀ Preheat the oven to 325 degrees.
♀ Sauté the green onions, green peppers, onion, celery and garlic in vegetable oil in a skillet until tender.
♀ Crumble the corn bread into a large bowl. Add the sautéed vegetables, apple, pecans, hard-boiled eggs, cooked sausage and broth and mix well. Add the seasonings.
♀ Beat the eggs with milk and melted butter. Add to the corn bread mixture gradually until of the desired consistency. If the mixture is too moist, do not add all of the egg mixture; if too dry, add additional broth. Adjust the seasonings.
♀ Pour into a greased baking pan. Bake until brown and crisp.

SERVES 10

LOVE, HONOR AND OBEY

Louisiana NOW helped defeat a state bill that would have given automatic grounds for divorce to any man whose wife had an abortion without his permission. Even abortions for health reasons would have put the wife at fault, and alimony would have been permanently denied regardless of circumstances.

The all-male state Senate passed the bill, but when it went to the House in 1980, the only three female representatives out of 105 House members, Diana Bajoie, Mary Landrieu and Margaret Lowenthal led the fight to defeat it. Landrieu was elected to the U.S. Senate in 1996.

NOW
SPEARHEADS ERA EXTENSION DRIVE

When Congress passed the ERA in 1972 and sent it on to the states for ratification, they set a time limit of seven years for the states to act. In 1977, with ratification still three states short, two California law students (and active NOW members) had a class project researching the question of the time limit.

They found that time limits on ratification were a rather recent development; the Constitution only specified amendments be ratified "within some reasonable time." Furthermore, the ERA's time limit appeared not in the body of the Amendment, but in the preamble. States had only been asked to ratify the Amendment; the preamble was just a "matter of detail."

Thrilled with their findings, the two students, Catherine Timlin and Alice Bennett, brought them to Toni Carabillo and Judith Meuli, both NOW National board members. Neither could see any holes in the reasoning. They called Ellie Smeal, NOW President, and told her the news.

FETTUCINI ALFREDO

1 (12-OUNCE) PACKAGE FETTUCINI
8 OUNCES CREAM CHEESE, CUT INTO CHUNKS
1/4 TO 1/2 CUP MARGARINE, CUT INTO CHUNKS
1/2 CUP MILK
3/4 CUP GRATED PARMESAN CHEESE
PEPPER TO TASTE

♀ Bring a large pot of water to a boil. Add the fettucini and start the sauce.

♀ Combine the cream cheese, margarine and milk in a saucepan over low heat. Cook until well blended, stirring constantly. Stir in the Parmesan cheese and pepper. Keep warm until the fettucini is cooked.

♀ Drain the fettucini; do not rinse. Place in a large heated bowl. Add the sauce, toss lightly to coat and serve immediately.

SERVES 3 OR 4

♀ *I had reasoned this out in my mind, there were two things I had a right to do, liberty and death. If I could not have one, I would have the other, for no man would take me alive.*
Harriet Tubman

LOW-FAT MACARONI AND CHEESE

1 (16-OUNCE) PACKAGE ELBOW MACARONI
1 SMALL ONION, FINELY CHOPPED
1/4 CUP LOW-FAT MARGARINE
1/4 CUP FLOUR
1 3/4 CUPS SKIM MILK
1/2 TEASPOON SALT
1/4 TEASPOON PEPPER
10 OUNCES LOW-FAT CHEDDAR, AMERICAN OR
    MOZZARELLA CHEESE, SHREDDED

♀ Preheat the oven to 375 degrees.
♀ Cook the macaroni according to the package directions, drain well and place in an ungreased 1 1/2-quart baking dish.
♀ Sauté the onion in the margarine in a large saucepan until translucent. Reduce to low heat; add the flour and mix well.
♀ Stir in 1/4 cup milk and mix well. Add the remaining milk gradually, mixing well. Stir in the salt and pepper. Boil for 1 minute, stirring constantly.
♀ Add the cheese gradually. Cook over medium heat until the cheese melts, stirring constantly.
♀ Pour the cheese sauce over the macaroni and mix gently. Bake for 30 minutes.

SERVES 4 TO 6

(NOW Spearheads ERA Extension Drive, continued)

Armed with the documentation, Smeal approached Rep. Elizabeth Holtzman (D-NY), who sat on the House Judiciary Committee; she agreed to push it forward.

The idea conceived by two law students in California was validated by a succession of Constitutional authorities, and went on to extend the time limit for ERA ratification three years, to June 30th, 1982.

HIGH-KICKER WINS CROWN

Cindy Judd Hill (Gams to her grandchildren) was crowned Ms. National Senior Citizen in 1993 at the age of 67.

Hill joined NOW in 1966 after being fired from her teaching job because she became pregnant. With NOW's help she got her job back, and she has been active with South Hills NOW in the Pittsburgh area for more than 30 years.

Her high-kicking dance routine and her feminist philosophy both contributed to her win: "We care for the home and the world is our home. It needs our compassion, our intelligence and our leadership. This is the true philosophy of Feminism, and we need to speak it to the world."

ITALIAN BROCCOLI

FLORETS OF 1 BUNCH BROCCOLI
1 TABLESPOON WATER
1/2 CUP FRESHLY GRATED PARMESAN CHEESE
OIL-BASED ITALIAN SALAD DRESSING

♀ Cut the broccoli into the same-size florets and place in a small microwave-safe baking dish. Add the water.
♀ Microwave, tightly covered, on high for 2 minutes. Drain well.
♀ Sprinkle with Parmesan cheese. Microwave, covered, for 1 minute longer.
♀ Pour the desired amount of dressing over the broccoli and serve immediately.

SERVES 2 TO 4

♀ *Feminism is the radical notion that women are people.*
Cheris Kramerae and Paula Treichler

CORN MAQUECHOU

KERNELS OF 4 EARS FRESH CORN
2 TABLESPOONS UNSALTED BUTTER
1 LARGE ONION, THINLY SLICED
1/2 GREEN BELL PEPPER, FINELY CHOPPED
1/8 TEASPOON CAYENNE
1 EGG YOLK
6 TABLESPOONS LOW-FAT MILK
SALT, BLACK PEPPER AND SUGAR TO TASTE

♀ Sauté the corn in butter in a large skillet for 2 minutes.
♀ Add the onion and green pepper. Cook over medium-high heat until the onion is tender, stirring constantly. Season with cayenne.
♀ Beat the egg yolk with the milk, salt, black pepper and sugar. Stir into the corn mixture.
♀ Cook for 2 to 3 minutes or until slightly thickened. Serve immediately.

SERVES 4

Cindy Judd Hill as Ms. National Senior Citizen, 1993.

Kate Swift submits this recipe from the late Casey Miller, her friend and writing partner. Together, beginning in the early 70s, they wrote numerous books and articles about English usage and its relationship to the status of women, thus waging a forceful campaign against sexist language. Kate says, "Neither of us was ever much of a cook, but since we both liked to eat, we had a few easy recipes. This most memorable one is great with crusty bread (to mop it up) and a green salad. It can easily be doubled or tripled."

CASEY'S KIDNEY BEANS IN SOUR CREAM

1 (16-OUNCE) CAN KIDNEY BEANS
3 LARGE YELLOW ONIONS, THICKLY SLICED
3 TABLESPOONS BUTTER OR MARGARINE
1 CUP SOUR CREAM
1/4 TEASPOON PEPPER
1 TEASPOON DRIED PARSLEY

♀ Preheat the oven to 325 degrees.
♀ Drain the beans and place in a 1¹/₂-quart baking dish.
♀ Sauté the onion in butter in a large skillet just until tender. Remove from the heat.
♀ Add the sour cream and pepper and mix well. Pour into the baking dish and mix with the beans. Sprinkle with parsley.
♀ Bake, covered, for 30 minutes.

SERVES 3 OR 4

♀ *We are truly indefatigable in providing for the needs of the body, but we starve the soul.*

Ellen Wood

Bombay Potatoes and Peas

1/2 teaspoon cumin seeds
2 tablespoons vegetable oil
2 large cloves of garlic, minced
1/2-inch fresh gingerroot, peeled, minced
1/4 teaspoon salt
1/4 teaspoon turmeric
Pinch of cayenne
3 large red potatoes, scrubbed, cut into
    1-inch pieces
1 cup chicken or vegetable broth
1 (10-ounce) package frozen tiny peas, thawed
2 tablespoons minced fresh cilantro
    (coriander)
2 to 3 teaspoons lemon juice

♀ Toast the cumin seeds in a small dry skillet over medium heat for 3 minutes or until brown and fragrant and set aside.
♀ Heat the oil in a nonstick skillet over medium heat. Add the garlic, gingerroot, salt, turmeric and cayenne. Cook for 2 minutes or until heated through, stirring gently.
♀ Add the potatoes and mix until the potatoes are coated. Cook for about 5 minutes. Stir in the broth. Bring to a boil and reduce the heat.
♀ Simmer, covered, for about 10 minutes or until the potatoes are tender. (Dish may be prepared to this point and held at room temperature for several hours.)
♀ Add the peas and toasted cumin seeds. Cook, uncovered, over medium heat for about 4 minutes or until heated through and sauce has thickened, stirring gently.
♀ Mix in the cilantro and lemon juice. Adjust the seasonings and serve hot.

Serves 3 or 4

Stop the Rescue Racket

NOW first sued Joseph Scheidler in 1986, accusing him of masterminding an organized, nationwide conspiracy to use fear, force and violence to deprive women of their constitutional rights and to close down clinics that perform abortions.

In 1994, the Supreme Court heard the case, *NOW v. Scheidler*, and gave NOW the go-ahead for this class-action suit against Joseph Scheidler, the Pro-Life Action Network, Operation Rescue, Randall Terry and others under the Racketeer-Influenced and Corrupt Organizations (RICO) law.

After 12 years of litigation, the case finally reached the jury in April, 1998. Four women and two men found in favor of NOW and the plaintiff clinics on all of the racketeering charges.

Even though NOW won't benefit financially, hundreds of clinics are now entitled to triple damages for all of the injuries and damage caused by these thugs. And, we won a nationwide injunction barring the defendants' illegal activities.

UNION OIL FOILED

When Union Oil told Janet Markusic this was no place for a woman, NOW put Union Oil in its place. When Janet Markusic's husband died, he left her with 5 children and a gas station. She ran the station for two months, just as she had helped her husband do for 14 years. Then Union Oil decided her franchise had expired with her husband. "Why don't you stay home with your family?" the man from Union Oil said.

Ms. Markusic took her case to NOW and the Columbus chapter organized a picket in front of the local Union 76 headquarters. Then Columbus NOW called Los Angeles NOW which put the heat on Union's corporate headquarters.

At stake was the issue of a woman's right to hold a franchise or dealership. When Ohio Senator Howard Metzenbaum heard about Ms. Markusic from NOW, he fired some tough questions at a Union Oil vice president in congressional hearings. Today Janet Markusic is back at the pumps, the proud owner of her gas station. Of course, the whole thing took a while for NOW to resolve—two weeks.

from a 1975 NOW brochure

BISTRO POTATOES

This absolutely wonderful way to prepare potatoes is perfect with a very plain roast chicken and a salad.

6 LARGE RED POTATOES (1 1/2 POUNDS)
5 LARGE CLOVES OF GARLIC, MINCED
4 OR 5 GREEN ONIONS, MINCED
1/4 CUP MILD OLIVE OIL
1 1/4 TEASPOON SALT
2 TO 3 TEASPOONS FRESHLY GROUND PEPPER
1/2 CUP GRATED IMPORTED PARMESAN CHEESE (OPTIONAL)

♀ Scrub the potatoes and slice thinly into rounds. Place the potato rounds as sliced into a large bowl of cold water to keep crisp. This step can be done a day ahead.

♀ Drain the potato slices, pat dry with paper towels, wipe out bowl and return the potato slices to the bowl. Add the garlic, green onions, 3 tablespoons of the olive oil, salt and pepper. Toss the potato slices by hand until the slices are evenly coated.

♀ Preheat the oven to 450 degrees. Place the oven rack in the upper third of the oven.

♀ Grease a shallow 7-inch round baking dish. Arrange the potato slices in overlapping layers in the baking dish. Cover with foil.

♀ Bake for 20 minutes. Remove the foil and press the potato layers with a spatula. Sprinkle with the cheese and drizzle the remaining tablespoon olive oil over the top.

♀ Bake for 20 minutes or until brown and crusty. Cut into wedges and serve hot.

SERVES 4 TO 6

SCALLOPED POTATOES

5 LARGE POTATOES, PEELED, THINLY SLICED
4 TO 5 TABLESPOONS FLOUR
SALT AND PEPPER TO TASTE
1/2 STICK COLD BUTTER, CUT INTO RAISIN-SIZE
    PIECES
2 TO 2 1/2 CUPS MILK

♀ Arrange a layer of potato slices in a 6-quart microwave-safe and ovenproof baking dish. Sprinkle with 1 tablespoon flour, salt and pepper and dot with 1 tablespoon butter.

♀ Repeat the potato layers adding flour, salt, pepper and butter until all the potatoes are used and the last layer is 1 to 2 inches below the rim of the baking dish.

♀ Pour the milk down the side of the baking dish until the potatoes are just covered. Cover the baking dish.

♀ Microwave on High for 10 to 12 minutes. Uncover and preheat the oven to 350 degrees.

♀ Bake the potatoes for 1 hour. Place foil under the baking dish to catch drips. P.J.'s mother says that if it cooks over, it is guaranteed to be good.

SERVES 6 TO 8

P.J. Glasser-Harris of Antioch, California, contributed this family recipe which came from her grandmother. Her grandparents arrived in the United States from Denmark on the Lusitania in 1906 and settled in upstate New York.

One morning when P.J.'s mother was small, her mother dressed in her "Sunday" clothes on a weekday. This made a strong impression on the little girl, as "good" clothes were never worn during the week.

P.J.'s grandmother was on her way to vote for the first time in her life.

EXCERPTS FROM AN OPEN LETTER

From: A Volunteer, 1982
To: Ms. Ellie Smeal, President
National Organization for Women

Dear Ellie:

Now you may think I helped you and NOW by coming to Illinois to work with the ERA Ratification Project. You may think that *you* owe *me* a thank-you note for spending seven days a week on the job, on the phone, on the road, on the speaking platform, on the firing line, on the legislators' "case."

I want you to know that it is we [volunteers] who are grateful for the opportunity . . . . We have participated in the historical struggle for equality in a way we shall never forget. I appreciate:

—NOW's leadership, especially yours, as you urged us to work harder, even when we were tired and discouraged, and reminded us that we would never give up.

—Our national, state and city NOW officers who were everywhere—rallying, speaking, strategizing, encouraging, phoning, marching, buttonholing, worrying, singing, sharing—trying to catch an

BAKED YAM WEDGES

2 MEDIUM YAMS
1 TABLESPOON LIGHT MARGARINE
1/4 TEASPOON CINNAMON
1/4 TEASPOON SUGAR

♀ Peel the yams and cut into 8 to 12 wedges. Soak the wedges in a bowl of cold water for 15 minutes.
♀ Preheat the oven to 425 degrees.
♀ Drain the yam wedges and pat dry. Arrange on a nonstick baking sheet.
♀ Melt the margarine in a small saucepan or in a small bowl in the microwave. Stir in the cinnamon and sugar. Drizzle over the yam wedges.
♀ Bake for 20 minutes. Turn the wedges over and bake for 20 minutes longer.
♀ Cool for 5 minutes before serving.

SERVES 2 TO 4

♀ *The single most impressive fact about the attempt by American women to obtain the right to vote is how long it took.*

Alice Rossi, *The Feminist Papers*, 1973

VEGETABLE CUSTARD

4 (APPROX.) NEW POTATOES, THINLY SLICED
3 EGGS
16 OUNCES COTTAGE CHEESE
1/2 CUP CHOPPED ONION
1 (10-OUNCE) PACKAGE FROZEN CHOPPED
    BROCCOLI, THAWED, DRAINED
1 CUP GRATED PEELED CARROTS
1/4 TEASPOON TABASCO SAUCE
SALT TO TASTE
1 TOMATO, THINLY SLICED
1/2 CUP SHREDDED MOZZARELLA CHEESE

♀ Preheat the oven to 350 degrees.
♀ Grease a 9-inch pie plate. Line the bottom and side of the pie plate with potato slices, overlapping slightly.
♀ Beat the eggs in a large bowl. Add the cottage cheese, onion, broccoli, carrots, Tabasco sauce and salt and mix well. Spoon into the prepared pie plate.
♀ Bake for 35 minutes. Arrange the tomato slices on top and sprinkle with the mozzarella cheese.
♀ Bake for 10 minutes longer or until a knife inserted in the center comes out clean.

SERVES 4 TO 6

(*Excerpts From an Open Letter, continued*)

hour's sleep or a quick lunch.
    —The NOW staff members, people whose lives are dedicated to our causes. People like Molly who has worked for civil rights since the 1930's [Ed. note: Molly Yard became president of NOW from 1987-1991] and Ruth, who resigned a professorship to work for the ERA and who has spent the past 14 months organizing the legislative districts of Illinois.

    And there I was too, in the midst of the most highly organized operation I could imagine (and as an administrator, I recognize good management), working as a field organizer, giving everything I had for our cause, for women, for equal rights.

    And so it has been for me an experience of a lifetime, an experience filled with people of all kinds who are dedicated to one goal—equality.

Sincerely yours,
Diane Marek Yerkes, President
North San Diego County NOW
1982

INFORMED CONSENT

In a 1982 column, writer Ellen Goodman considered an Akron, Ohio, law (now widespread) that requires doctors to present patients with so-called facts about abortion.

Goodman found the thought of legislating information perversely appealing:

"What if we decided that no citizen should consent to sex without being properly informed about the risks? . . .

The patient might, for example, like to know that the risk of death from childbirth is about ten times higher than the risk of death from a legal abortion . . . .

In the spirit of financial information, someone should also mention that a female-headed household has less than four-tenths the income of a two-parent household . . . .

None of these facts would be presented to frighten the patient. I merely offer them in the spirit of knowledge. After all, there appear to be a great many citizens who consent to harassing pregnant women without being informed about post-partum realities."

RUTH'S ZUCCHINI BOATS

4 MEDIUM ZUCCHINI
1 1/2 CUPS SOFT BREAD CRUMBS
1/2 CUP SHREDDED CHEDDAR CHEESE
2 TABLESPOONS BUTTER
2 EGGS, BEATEN
1/4 CUP MINCED ONION
2 TABLESPOONS MINCED PARSLEY
1 TEASPOON SALT
1/8 TEASPOON PEPPER
1/4 CUP GRATED PARMESAN CHEESE

♀ Cut the ends from the zucchini and cut into halves lengthwise. Parboil the zucchini until slightly tender. Drain, scoop out and reserve the pulp and shells.
♀ Preheat the oven to 350 degrees.
♀ Combine the zucchini pulp with the bread crumbs, Cheddar cheese, butter, eggs, onion, parsley, salt and pepper in a bowl and mix well.
♀ Spoon the mixture into the zucchini shells and place on a baking sheet. Sprinkle with Parmesan cheese.
♀ Bake for 30 minutes.

SERVES 4 TO 8

♀ *I never felt more keenly the degradation of my sex. To think that all in me of which my father would have felt a proper pride had I been a man, is deeply mortifying to him because I am a woman.*

Elizabeth Cady Stanton, 1922

ZUCCHINI BAKE

4 EGGS, BEATEN
1/2 CUP VEGETABLE OIL
1 TEASPOON SALT
1/2 TEASPOON CHOPPED PARSLEY
1/2 TEASPOON OREGANO
1 1/2 CUPS FINELY CHOPPED ONIONS
4 CUPS GRATED ZUCCHINI
5 OUNCES GRATED PARMESAN CHEESE
2 CUPS BAKING MIX

♀ Preheat the oven to 350 degrees.
♀ Combine the eggs, oil, salt, parsley and oregano in a large bowl and mix well. Stir in the onion and zucchini. Add the Parmesan cheese and mix well. Stir in the baking mix.
♀ Pour the mixture into a greased 9x12-inch baking dish.
♀ Bake for 40 to 45 minutes or until a knife inserted in the center comes out clean.

SERVES 8 TO 10

Homemade signs abounded in Washington, D.C. during NOW's November 1989 Mobilization for Women's Lives. Over 350,000 people came to support reproductive freedom.

A MATTER OF COURAGE

During NOW's 1989 national rally, Mobilize for Women's Lives, President Molly Yard asked participants to think how they could "do more." Dr. Susan Wicklund of Bozeman, Montana, answered with emphatic action recalling the condescending and dehumanizing treatment she received from a doctor when, in her early 20s, she sought an abortion.

Today Dr. Wicklund braves right-wing death threats to provide abortion services to rural women. For years, she shuttled between five clinics in three states, serving as the only doctor in three of the clinics, and the only abortion provider in all of North Dakota. She says, remembering her early experience, "Every patient who comes into my clinic is treated with respect, honor and dignity."

She was a key witness for NOW in 1998, when a Chicago jury returned a unanimous verdict for NOW in a racketeering lawsuit against Operation Rescue and leaders of an anti-abortion terrorist network. She is a recipient of NOW's Woman of Courage Award.

KUGEL

Pamela Aughe of Drexel Hill, Pennsylvania, submitted this recipe that she classifies as "pure comfort food." She notes that, as a nutritionist, it was a challenge to make kugel heart-healthy (or to even want to make this reminder of home heart-healthy!)

$1/3$ CUP SUGAR
$1/4$ CUP RAISINS
1 CUP 1% COTTAGE CHEESE
1 CUP NONFAT SOUR CREAM
$1/4$ CUP SKIM MILK
1 TABLESPOON MELTED MARGARINE
1 TEASPOON VANILLA EXTRACT
2 EGGS, LIGHTLY BEATEN OR $1/2$ CUP EGG
    SUBSTITUTE
3 CUPS COOKED NO-YOLK EGG NOODLES
$3/4$ CUP COARSELY CRUSHED CORNFLAKES
2 TABLESPOONS BROWN SUGAR
$1/4$ TEASPOON GROUND CINNAMON

♀ Preheat the oven to 350 degrees.
♀ Combine the sugar, raisins, cottage cheese, sour cream, skim milk, margarine, vanilla and eggs in a bowl and mix well.
♀ Stir in the noodles gently. Spoon the mixture into a 7x11-inch baking dish sprayed with nonstick cooking spray.
♀ Mix the cornflakes, brown sugar and cinnamon in a small bowl. Sprinkle over the noodle mixture.
♀ Bake, uncovered, for 1 hour or until set. Let stand for 10 minutes before serving.

SERVES 8

HERE TO STAY
MEATS AND MAINSTAYS

NOW is deeply committed to building a mass movement where

we are leaders, not followers, of public opinion.

More than 500 local NOW chapters exist across the country where

volunteers take the lead in forging change. NOW leaders represent

the full range of diversity in our communities, including race,

ethnicity, age, education, economic means, religion, sexual

orientation, physical ability and parental status. NOW leaders

bring many talents to the movement, turning the anger

spawned by oppression into action, turning personal experience

into expertise, and taking the lessons of the classroom into

the battle for social change.

PICTURED ON OVERLEAF: *April 5, 1992 NOW National March for
Women's Lives, Washington, DC.*

TERIYAKI FLANK STEAK

1/4 CUP LIGHT SOY SAUCE

3 TABLESPOONS HONEY

1/3 CUP VEGETABLE OIL

1 TABLESPOON FRESH CHOPPED GARLIC OR
   1 1/2 TEASPOONS GARLIC POWDER

1 1/2 INCHES FRESH GINGERROOT, PEELED, MINCED
   OR 1 1/4 TEASPOONS GROUND GINGER

2 TABLESPOONS RICE OR WHITE VINEGAR

1 (2-POUND) FLANK STEAK

♀ Combine the soy sauce, honey, oil, garlic, gingerroot and vinegar in a blender container. Process until very thick and lighter in color.

♀ Pour 1/3 of the marinade into a shallow dish. Place the steak in the marinade and pour the remaining marinade over the top.

♀ Marinate, covered, in the refrigerator for 8 hours to overnight, turning once.

♀ Drain the steak and grill or broil as desired. Slice the steak diagonally.

SERVES 6 TO 8

EVERY MOTHER DESERVES . . .

. . . . A Happy Mother's Day—Stop the War on Poor Women.

In May, 1995, NOW went to the Dirksen Senate Office Building to protest congressionally mandated cuts in welfare, AFDC, childcare and nutrition programs.

"The national holiday honoring our mothers dramatically conflicts with the message being sent to women and their children by politicians," said NOW President Patricia Ireland. "Instead of a heartfelt message of love and support, poor women are being handed an eviction notice."

Betty Freidan answers questions.

ASBESTOS NAPKIN CHILI

Truly, never was a dish so well-named! This recipe was submitted with a skull-and-crossbones warning label: "WARNING! The Surgeon General has determined that this recipe can be hazardous to your internal organs. Acceptance of either this formula for nuclear waste or the substance itself constitutes full responsibility on the part of the recipient of same, and absolves the supplier from all responsibility, legal, medical and otherwise." Forewarned is Forearmed!

1¹/₂ POUNDS BEEF CHUCK ROAST, PARTIALLY FROZEN
DASH OF PAPRIKA
1¹/₂ TABLESPOONS DRIED RED PEPPERS
3 CLOVES OF GARLIC, CRUSHED
1 TEASPOON GROUND CUMIN
3 TABLESPOONS CHILI POWDER
DASH EACH OF TABASCO SAUCE AND CAYENNE
2 MEDIUM ONIONS, CHOPPED
2 TABLESPOONS BACON DRIPPINGS
2 TABLESPOONS CORNMEAL
1¹/₂ CUPS BEEF BROTH
3 TABLESPOONS TOMATO PASTE
1 TEASPOON SUGAR
1 (15-OUNCE) CAN PINTO BEANS, DRAINED
SHREDDED MONTEREY JACK AND CHEDDAR CHEESE

TO AVOID SLIVERING BEEF:

♀ Cut the chuck roast with the grain into ¹/₂- to ³/₄-inch slices. Place in a large heavy Dutch oven. Add the bacon drippings, onions, all the seasonings, tomato paste, broth and sugar and mix well. Bake, tightly covered, at 250 degrees for 8 hours without uncovering. The beef will fall apart at the touch of a fork. Stir in the beans, heat for several minutes and ladle into bowls. Top with the cheese.

♀ Cut the partially frozen roast into fine slivers and place in a large bowl. Sprinkle with the seasonings. Work the spices into the beef while wearing rubber gloves. (Gloves are necessary; do not touch your eyes!) Marinate in the refrigerator overnight.

♀ Sauté the onions in the bacon drippings in a soup pot until brown. Sprinkle with cornmeal and mix well.

♀ Add the seasoned beef and cook until brown on all sides, stirring frequently. (You will probably want the kitchen exhaust fan on and the window open to avoid toxic chili fumes.)

♀ Blend the broth, tomato paste and sugar in a bowl. Stir into the soup pot. Simmer, covered, until the beef is tender.

♀ Add the beans. Heat to serving temperature. Ladle into bowls and top with some cheese.

SERVES 6 TO 8

BARBECUED HAMBURGERS

1 POUND LEAN GROUND BEEF
1 CUP DAY-OLD BREAD CRUMBS
1 MEDIUM ONION, MINCED
1/2 CUP MILK
1 TEASPOON SALT
BARBECUE SAUCE
4 TO 6 HAMBURGER BUNS

♀ Combine the ground beef, bread crumbs, onion, milk and salt in a bowl and mix well.
♀ Shape into the desired number of patties. Brown the patties on both sides in a large skillet. Cook until almost cooked through.
♀ Pour the Barbecue Sauce over the patties. Simmer for 10 minutes or longer. Serve the patties on the buns.

BARBECUE SAUCE

1 CUP CATSUP
1/4 CUP WORCESTERSHIRE SAUCE
2 TABLESPOONS APPLE CIDER VINEGAR
1/4 CUP PACKED BROWN SUGAR OR GRANULATED
    SUGAR

♀ Blend the catsup, Worcestershire sauce and vinegar in a small bowl. Add the sugar and stir until dissolved.

SERVES 4 TO 6

NOW Rallies Against Violence

More than 200,000 people turned out April 9th, 1995, in Washington, D.C. for the Rally for Women's Lives—the first massive action on violence against women. Organized by NOW and endorsed by a record 702 groups, the rally brought in many new young activists from over 200 college campuses.

Elizabeth Toledo, then President of California NOW, spoke of violence against women of color, especially immigrants: "In my state of California, when you have brown skin like mine and you go to certain neighborhoods, you

Marsala Meatballs

2 POUNDS GROUND CHUCK
2 EGGS
2 TABLESPOONS MARSALA
1/4 TEASPOON PEPPER
RIND AND JUICE OF 1 LEMON
3 TABLESPOONS FINELY CHOPPED PARSLEY
3 TABLESPOONS DRIED ONION FLAKES
1 CUP BREAD CRUMBS
1/2 CUP SHREDDED MOZZARELLA CHEESE
1/4 CUP OLIVE OIL
2 CUPS BEEF BROTH
1 CUP MARSALA
2 TABLESPOONS MELTED BUTTER
3 TABLESPOONS CORNSTARCH

♀ Combine the ground chuck, eggs, 2 tablespoons Marsala, pepper, lemon rind and juice, parsley, onion flakes, bread crumbs and cheese in a large bowl and mix well. Shape into walnut-size meatballs.

♀ Cook the meatballs in small batches in the olive oil in a large skillet until brown on all sides and drain well.

♀ Combine the broth with 1 cup Marsala in a large saucepan. Remove 1/2 cup of the mixture and set aside.

♀ Bring the mixture in the saucepan to a boil. Add the meatballs. Simmer, covered, for 30 minutes, stirring occasionally.

♀ Blend the melted butter with the cornstarch in a small bowl. Blend in the reserved broth mixture. Stir into the saucepan with the meatballs.

♀ Cook until clear and thickened, stirring constantly. Serve plain or over hot cooked fettucini.

SERVES 4 TO 6

E.T.'s Tacos

1 POUND GROUND BEEF
1/4 TEASPOON GROUND CUMIN
SALT AND PEPPER TO TASTE
4 TO 6 CORN OR FLOUR TORTILLAS
2 TABLESPOONS (APPROX.) VEGETABLE OIL
1 CUP SHREDDED MONTEREY JACK CHEESE
OPTIONAL TOPPINGS:
    SALSA
    SHREDDED LETTUCE
    CHOPPED TOMATOES
    CHOPPED ONIONS
    PEAS

♀ Combine the ground beef, cumin, salt and pepper in a bowl and mix well.

♀ Wrap the tortillas in a damp towel and heat in a dry skillet or a 200-degree oven until warm and pliable.

♀ Pat the ground beef mixture over half of each tortilla and fold the tortilla over to enclose the filling.

♀ Pour the oil into a large skillet and heat over medium heat. Place the folded tortillas in the skillet. Fry until the ground beef is cooked through, turning to cook on both sides. Drain on paper towels.

♀ Sprinkle some cheese inside each taco and add toppings to individual tastes.

MAKES 4 TO 6 TACOS

(NOW Rallies Against Violence, continued)

are expected to carry proof of your citizenship. Well, I know that a citizenship card does not guarantee me, as a woman, my rights, because we have been left out of the Constitution. I know that the Constitution has ignored my rights as a woman of color again and again, and so, instead of carrying my citizenship card, I carry my NOW card."

Toledo was elected national Action Vice President of NOW in 1997 and is the first Latina to hold that position.

THE BEST SPAGHETTI SAUCE
I EVER MADE

INGREDIENTS:

6 LINKS SWEET ITALIAN SAUSAGE
1¼ TO 1½ POUNDS GROUND
    BEEF
1¼ POUNDS GROUND TURKEY
6 TABLESPOONS OLIVE OIL
2 OR 3 RIBS CELERY, CHOPPED
1 LARGE ONION, CHOPPED
4 OR 5 FRESH MUSHROOMS,
    SLICED
2 CLOVES OF GARLIC, MINCED
1 (28-OUNCE) CAN WHOLE
    TOMATOES
½ (6-OUNCE) CAN TOMATO
    PASTE
1 (28-OUNCE) CAN CRUSHED
    TOMATOES
1 (15-OUNCE) CAN TOMATO
    SAUCE
1½ CUPS DRY RED WINE
1 TEASPOON EACH DRIED BASIL,
    ITALIAN SEASONINGS,
    ROSEMARY AND DILLWEED
2 FRESH TOMATOES, CHOPPED

METHOD:

♀ Remove the casings from the sausage and cut into pieces. Cook the sausage, ground beef and ground turkey in 3 tablespoons olive oil in a large skillet until brown and crumbly, stirring frequently; drain well and place in a large stockpot.

♀ Add the remaining 3 tablespoons olive oil to the skillet and add the celery, onion, mushrooms and garlic. Sauté until tender.

♀ Pour the whole tomatoes into a blender or food processor. Add the sautéed vegetables and tomato paste. Process until well mixed and pour into the stockpot.

♀ Add the crushed tomatoes and tomato sauce. Rinse the cans with a small amount of water and add to the stockpot.

♀ Bring to a simmer over medium-low heat. Stir in the wine and herbs. Simmer for 30 to 60 minutes.

♀ Add the fresh tomatoes. Simmer for 1 hour longer, stirring occasionally.

♀ Serve over your choice of hot cooked pasta.

SERVES 12 TO 16

♀ *I refuse to believe that trading recipes is silly. Tuna-fish casserole is at least as real as corporate stock.*
               Barbara Grizzutti Harrison, 1975

SPAGHETTI ALLA CARBONARA

6 TO 8 QUARTS WATER
1 TEASPOON SALT
1 POUND SPAGHETTI OR LINGUINI
1/4 CUP BUTTER, SOFTENED
2 WHOLE EGGS
2 EGG YOLKS
1/2 CUP GRATED PARMESAN CHEESE
8 SLICES BACON, CUT INTO 1/4-INCH PIECES
1/2 TEASPOON DRIED RED PEPPER FLAKES
1/2 CUP HEAVY CREAM
FRESHLY GROUND PEPPER TO TASTE
1/2 CUP GRATED PARMESAN CHEESE

♀ Bring the water with salt to a boil in a large stockpot.
Cook the pasta al dente according to the package directions,
timing the pasta and sauce to be finished within a minute or
two of each other.

♀ Cream the butter in a small bowl until light and fluffy.

♀ Beat the eggs and egg yolks in a small bowl. Stir in 1/2 cup
Parmesan cheese.

♀ Fry the bacon in a skillet until crisp. Pour off about half
the drippings. Add the red pepper and cream and mix well.
Keep warm over very low heat.

♀ Drain the pasta; do not rinse. Place in a warm serving
bowl. Add the butter and toss until butter melts. Add the
bacon mixture and toss. Add the egg mixture and toss
thoroughly; the heat of the pasta will cook the eggs.

♀ Top with black pepper and remaining 1/2 cup Parmesan
cheese. Serve immediately.

SERVES 4 TO 6

BOBOTI

This traditional South African casserole should be served with Mango Chutney (page 99) on the side and an additional side dish of rice cooked with turmeric and raisins.

2 ONIONS, CHOPPED
1/4 CUP BUTTER OR VEGETABLE OIL
2 POUNDS GROUND BEEF OR GROUND LAMB
1 THICK BREAD SLICE
1/2 CUP MILK
1/4 CUP (SCANT) VINEGAR OR LEMON JUICE
1/4 CUP SUGAR OR APRICOT JAM
1 TABLESPOON TURMERIC
2 TEASPOONS SALT
1 TEASPOON PEPPER
1/2 CUP SEEDLESS RAISINS
1 TART APPLE, COARSELY CHOPPED OR
    10 DRIED APRICOTS, SOAKED AND CUT UP
BAY LEAVES
2 EGGS
1/2 CUP MILK
1/4 CUP SLIVERED ALMONDS

♀ Preheat the oven to 350 degrees.
♀ Sauté the onions in butter in a large skillet until brown. Add the ground beef and cook until brown and crumbly, stirring frequently. Remove from the heat.
♀ Soak the bread in 1/2 cup milk and mash with a fork. Add to the ground beef mixture with the vinegar, sugar, turmeric, salt, pepper, raisins and apple and mix well.
♀ Spoon the mixture loosely into a large greased casserole. Insert the bay leaves randomly. Bake, covered, for 1 hour.
♀ Beat the eggs with 1/2 cup milk. Pour over the mixture, lifting the edges lightly to allow the mixture to penetrate.
♀ Bake, uncovered, for 10 to 15 minutes or until brown. Discard the bay leaves and sprinkle with slivered almonds.
♀ Serve with Mango Chutney and yellow rice.

SERVES 6 TO 8

MANGO CHUTNEY

For long-term storage, this must be canned properly using a water bath. For immediate use, the chutney can be stored briefly in the refrigerator.

3 POUNDS GREEN MANGOES
1/3 CUP SALT
2 CUPS PACKED DARK BROWN SUGAR
2 CUPS DRY WHITE WINE OR CIDER VINEGAR
2-INCH PIECE FRESH GINGERROOT, PEELED,
    CHOPPED
2 TEASPOONS HOT CHILI POWDER OR CHILI PASTE
2 CINNAMON STICKS
3/4 CUP CHOPPED DATES
3/4 CUP SEEDLESS RAISINS

♀ Peel and chop the mangoes and place in a large bowl. Add the salt and about 2 quarts water. Let soak for 24 hours
♀ Combine the brown sugar and wine in a large saucepan. Bring to a boil, stirring until the brown sugar dissolves.
♀ Drain the mangoes. Stir the mangoes into the brown sugar mixture. Add the gingerroot, chili powder, cinnamon sticks, dates and raisins and mix well.
♀ Boil until the mixture is thick, stirring occasionally. Discard the cinnamon sticks.
♀ Ladle the boiling mixture into hot sterilized jars, leaving 1/2-inch headspace. Seal with 2-piece lids.

MAKES 2 TO 4 PINTS

THOUGHTS ON ECONOMIC JUSTICE

In 1955, Congresswoman Edith Green of Oregon introduced legislation requiring equal pay for equivalent work. President Dwight D. Eisenhower urged passage of equal pay bills as a matter of simple justice. No Congressional action was taken on this bill, but Green and her colleague, Congresswoman Edith Rogers of Massachusetts, introduced the bill every session until 1963, when the Equal Pay Act was finally passed.

Reality always takes a little longer, however, and in 1985, NOW launched its Fair Share Campaign for Economic Justice to make the gears of justice grind faster: "It's time we moved out of the 1950's and got past the idea that women are just working for money to buy nylons."

Algerian Sweet Lamb with Prunes (Lahm Lhalou)

2 POUNDS BONELESS LAMB, CUT INTO 3/4-INCH
    CUBES
1/2 TEASPOON SALT
2 TABLESPOONS VEGETABLE OIL
1/3 CUP BLANCHED WHOLE ALMONDS
2/3 CUP SUGAR
1 (3-INCH) CINNAMON STICK
2 TABLESPOONS ORANGE JUICE OR ORANGE LIQUEUR
1 CUP WATER
1 1/2 CUPS PITTED PRUNES

♀ Sprinkle the lamb with salt. Heat the oil in a heavy Dutch
oven. Add the lamb about half at a time. Cook until lightly
browned on all sides and remove to a bowl.
♀ Add the almonds, sugar and cinnamon stick to the
drippings and mix well. Add the orange juice and water.
Bring to boil, stirring constantly.
♀ Return the lamb and any lamb juices to the Dutch oven
and mix well. Simmer, covered, for 1 hour.
♀ Discard the cinnamon stick. Mix in the prunes. Simmer
for 15 minutes.
♀ Serve with hot cooked rice, bulgur or couscous.

SERVES 6 TO 8

MALAYSIAN COCONUT PORK

1 1/2 POUNDS PORK, CUT INTO 1-INCH CUBES
3 TABLESPOONS VEGETABLE OIL
2 LARGE ONIONS
CRUSHED DRIED RED CHILES TO TASTE
2 TEASPOONS SHRIMP PASTE (OPTIONAL)
1/4 TEASPOON GROUND GINGER OR 1/2-INCH FRESH
    GINGERROOT, GRATED
1 TEASPOON CRUSHED GARLIC
1 TEASPOON SALT
2 TABLESPOONS BROWN SUGAR
1/2 CUP WATER
3 TABLESPOONS LIME JUICE
1 (14-OUNCE) CAN COCONUT MILK

♀ Sauté the pork in oil in a large heavy pan until well browned on all sides.

♀ Cut the onions into pieces and process in a food processor or blender until puréed. Add to the browned pork. Sauté until the onions begin to brown.

♀ Mix the chiles, shrimp paste, ginger, garlic, salt and brown sugar together, add to the pork mixture and mix well. Add the water if the mixture is dry. Cook, covered, over low heat for 45 minutes or until the pork is tender.

♀ Stir in the lime juice and coconut milk. Heat to serving temperature.

♀ Spoon into a serving dish. Garnish with additional chiles, fresh mint leaves or cilantro.

SERVES 4 TO 6

SUGAR BOWL COMMITTEE MELTS UNDER PRESSURE

Women scored a sweet victory in mid-September 1995 when the prestigious Sugar Bowl Committee in New Orleans succumbed to pressure and agreed to elect its first women members.

"It took pressure from NOW and other groups to make the committee members realize their 61 years of sexism, cronyism and bigotry are up," said Greater New Orleans NOW President Ivory Madison.

Much was at stake: "Having locked out more than half the population, rich and powerful men on the committee maintain control over the multi-million dollar Sugar Bowl events," said NOW President Patricia Ireland, who went to New Orleans to support the effort.

"Sugar Bowl committee members broker vendor deals, television coverage and advertising, hotel and travel packages—all generating an estimated $100 million into the New Orleans economy."

How sweet it is!

WELFARE

Sixty-eight percent of the recipients of welfare are children. Welfare should thus be viewed as an investment in our children and in our future.

While CEOs of today's Fortune 500 companies are making 185 times more money then their average employee, a mother and her two kids are receiving $434 per month in welfare support. What's wrong with that picture?

The applause lines of politicians who rail against "welfare cheats" and want to "end welfare as we know it" should remind us that the powers-that-be find it easier to place blame than to share resources. The opponents of welfare should be challenged to end poverty as we know it.

COUNTRY FRENCH CHICKEN

For a really quick meal, this recipe requires only 20 minutes to prepare. Serve with steamed asparagus and brown rice.

1 1/2 POUNDS BONELESS, SKINLESS CHICKEN BREASTS
2 TABLESPOONS BUTTER OR MARGARINE
1 ENVELOPE SPRING VEGETABLE SOUP MIX
2 TABLESPOONS FLOUR
3/4 CUP WATER
3/4 CUP WHITE WINE
1/2 CUP LIGHT SOUR CREAM

♀ Cook the chicken in butter in a large heavy skillet over medium-high heat until light brown on both sides, turning frequently.

♀ Mix the soup mix and flour in a bowl. Stir in the water and wine. Pour the mixture into the skillet and mix well.

♀ Bring to a boil and reduce the heat. Simmer, covered, for 10 minutes or until the chicken is tender. Remove the chicken to a warm serving platter.

♀ Add the sour cream to the sauce in the skillet and mix well. Heat to serving temperature; do not boil. Pour over the chicken.

SERVES 4 TO 6

APRICOT MUSTARD SKILLET CHICKEN

4 BONELESS, SKINLESS CHICKEN BREASTS
1 TABLESPOON VEGETABLE OIL
1 MEDIUM GREEN BELL PEPPER, CHOPPED
1 MEDIUM RED BELL PEPPER, CHOPPED
4 GREEN ONIONS, CHOPPED
1 (12-OUNCE) CAN APRICOT NECTAR
2 TABLESPOONS DIJON MUSTARD
1/4 CUP WATER
1 3/4 CUPS QUICK-COOKING BROWN RICE
1/2 CUP CHOPPED DRIED APRICOTS
4 OUNCES FRESH GREEN BEANS, CUT INTO
   1/2-INCH PIECES (OPTIONAL)

♀ Sear the chicken on both sides in oil in a large heavy skillet over high heat. Reduce the heat and cook for 10 minutes or until golden brown on both sides, turning occasionally. Remove to plate.

♀ Add the peppers and green onions to the skillet. Sauté for 5 minutes or until tender.

♀ Stir in the apricot nectar, mustard and water. Bring to boil. Add the rice, apricots and green beans and mix well.

♀ Return the chicken to the skillet. Return the mixture to a boil and reduce the heat to low. Simmer, covered, for 20 to 25 minutes or until the rice is tender.

SERVES 4

(Welfare, continued)

The national policy debate thus far is mired in racism, sexism and myths. Too many in power have short-sighted goals and too little compassion. Fundamental reform must begin by removing the stigmas and exploding the myths.

There is no shame in being poor—welfare cheats are rare—millions upon millions of children grew up and became productive adults with the financial aid of our government.

The real cheat is an economic, social and political system which condemns so many women to a life of dead-end poverty.

—by Karen Johnson, a NOW Vice President since 1993, whose family received welfare when she was growing up. She retired as a Lt. Colonel in the U.S. Air Force.

CHICKEN WITH OLIVES AND LEMONS

2 POUNDS BONED CHICKEN, CUT INTO BITE-SIZE
    PIECES
1/2 TEASPOON SALT
1/4 CUP VEGETABLE OIL
1 TABLESPOON MELTED BUTTER
1 CLOVE OF GARLIC, CRUSHED
1 TEASPOON GROUND GINGER
1/4 TEASPOON SAFFRON OR 1 TEASPOON TURMERIC
1 1/2 CUPS WATER
10 GREEN OR BLACK OLIVES
1 OR 2 LEMONS, SLICED OR QUARTERED

♀ Preheat the oven to 350 degrees.

♀ Sprinkle the chicken with salt and place in a heavy Dutch oven. Add the oil, butter, garlic, ginger and saffron and stir until the chicken is coated. Drizzle the water over the chicken.

♀ Bake, covered, for 30 minutes. Turn the chicken pieces over. Bake for 30 minutes longer.

♀ Add the olives and lemons and stir until well mixed. Bake for 10 minutes longer.

SERVES 4

♀ *I have a simple philosophy. Fill what's empty. Empty what's full. And scratch where it itches.*

Alice Roosevelt Longworth

LEBANESE CHICKEN DINNER

1 (4-POUND) CHICKEN
SALT AND PEPPER TO TASTE
3 TABLESPOONS CHOPPED RED ONION
3 TABLESPOONS CHOPPED GARLIC
4 TABLESPOONS BUTTER, CHOPPED
1/2 CUP OLIVE OIL
2 CUPS WHITE RICE
1/4 CUP ORZO

♀ Preheat the oven to 375 degrees.
♀ Rinse the chicken and pat dry inside and out. Rub the cavity with salt and pepper.
♀ Cut 1/4-inch slits all over the chicken using a sharp knife. Insert onion and garlic pieces alternately into the slits and add a bit of butter to each slit.
♀ Place the chicken in a baking dish. Sprinkle with salt and pepper. Drizzle the olive oil over the chicken.
♀ Bake for 1 to 1 1/2 hours or until the chicken is tender and golden brown, basting occasionally.
♀ Cook the rice and orzo according to the package directions for cooking the rice. Continue cooking over low heat until the mixture browns slightly on the bottom.
♀ Serve the rice mixture on the same plate with the chicken and add a green salad and red wine.

SERVES 6

OPPORTUNITIES FOR WOMEN

Presidents Roosevelt, Truman, Eisenhower, Kennedy and Johnson all signed executive orders aimed at ending job discrimination by employers doing business with the Federal government. These orders outlawed discrimination based on race, color, creed or national origin, but none addressed sex discrimination.

NOW was prominent among those protesting the omission. Almost immediately after our founding in October, 1966, NOW initiated a campaign to persuade President Johnson to extend his order to include gender.

Victory! On October 13, 1967, President Johnson signed Executive Order 11375, which prohibited sex discrimination.

In a 30th Anniversary celebration of E.O. 11375, Secretary of Labor Alexis Herman acknowledged NOW's leading role, and introduced founding president Betty Friedan to tell the story of its passage.

SELF-EMPLOYED FREELANCE AGITATOR

This is how Tish Sommers, co-ordinator of NOW's Task Force on Older Women (with Laurie Shields) identified herself on her business cards in 1975. A divorce after 23 years of marriage was a defining step for her, launching her into a totally new lifestyle that included collective living.

Her humor set her apart as a spokesperson for older women: "I look forward to the time when we can merchandise a cosmetic line to make youth look older—a special crow's foot pencil, the silver bleaches, the stick to make those delicious brown spots on the hands, eyeliner under the eye for that sexy mature look."

"Telling your age is very important," Tish said. "I came out on my 59th birthday. Let's celebrate age rather than deny it."

The NOW Task Force became the Older Women's League, under Tish and Laurie's leadership.

DELUXE CHICKEN BREAST

Use the same treatment for cooking pork, veal or fish. What a great recipe—increase it as much as you want and, best of all, no clean up!

1 BONELESS, SKINLESS CHICKEN BREAST
GARLIC POWDER, SALT AND PEPPER TO TASTE
1/4 CUP CHOPPED BABY CARROTS
1/4 CUP CHOPPED PEELED POTATOES
1/4 CUP CHOPPED GREEN BELL PEPPER
1/4 CUP CHOPPED TOMATO
1/4 CUP CHOPPED ONION
1/4 CUP QUARTERED FRESH MUSHROOMS
1/4 CUP WATER

♀ Preheat the oven to 375 degrees.

♀ Use a large square of heavy duty foil. Place the chicken in the center of the foil. Sprinkle with the garlic powder, salt and pepper. Remember that the seasonings are for the chicken and all the vegetables.

♀ Mound the vegetables over and around the chicken. Fold the foil around the vegetables to form a shallow dish. Drizzle the water over the vegetables. Fold the foil over the top and seal tightly.

♀ Place the packet on a baking sheet for easy handling and to catch leaks. Bake for 45 to 60 minutes.

♀ Open the packet carefully to avoid the steam. Slip the chicken and vegetables onto a plate or eat from the packet as desired.

SERVES 1

BETTYLEE'S CHICKEN POTPIE

This is really a delicious old-fashioned chicken and dumpling recipe that is very easy to make.

1 LARGE STEWING CHICKEN
1/2 TO 1 TEASPOON SALT
3 MEDIUM POTATOES, PEELED, CUT INTO CHUNKS
2 CARROTS, CUT INTO 1-INCH PIECES
1 MEDIUM-LARGE ONION, CUT INTO EIGHTHS
SALT AND PEPPER TO TASTE
CHICKEN BOUILLON CUBES (OPTIONAL)
DUMPLINGS (AT RIGHT)

♀ Cut the chicken into pieces and remove and discard the skin. Place the chicken in a stockpot, add the salt and cover with water.

♀ Bring to a boil, reduce heat and simmer for 10 minutes. Add the potatoes, carrots and onion. Simmer until the chicken is tender and the vegetables are almost tender.

♀ Remove the chicken from the broth and set aside to cool. Skim the broth and set aside.

♀ Bone the chicken and cut into bite-size pieces. Return the chicken to the stockpot. Adjust the seasoning of the broth, adding bouillon to enrich the broth if desired.

♀ Bring the broth to a simmer. Cook until the vegetables are almost tender. Bring to a full rolling boil. Add the dumplings 1 at a time, turning to moisten on all sides to prevent sticking before adding the next dumpling. Cook for 4 to 5 minutes or until cooked through. Serve immediately.

DUMPLINGS

2 EGGS
WATER
1 CUP FLOUR
1 TEASPOON BAKING POWDER
DASH OF SALT

♀ Crack the eggs into a bowl. Fill one of the eggshell halves with water 2 times and add to the eggs in the bowl. Beat the eggs and water until frothy.

♀ Combine flour, baking powder and salt in a bowl; add to egg mixture and mix well. Add a small amount of additional flour if the dough is sticky.

♀ Knead the dough several times on a lightly floured surface. Roll or pat to 1/4-inch thickness and cut into 2-inch squares.

SERVES 4 TO 6

AFFIRMATIVE EXCLUSION

Syracuse University hosted a nationwide affirmative action conference in November 1972. NOW representatives approached the conference planners, offering their expertise and were turned down—on the grounds that if NOW participated, they would have to contend with the NAACP, the Indians, who knows what else.

Women from Syracuse NOW, the Syracuse University Women's Faculty Caucus and the ACLU picketed the conference so successfully that many attendees refused to cross the picket line, and the press coverage consisted of NOW's demonstration and conference planners' reaction to it.

CHICKEN FAJITAS

2 POUNDS BONELESS, SKINLESS CHICKEN BREASTS
1/4 CUP VINEGAR
1/4 CUP LEMON OR LIME JUICE
2 TABLESPOONS WORCESTERSHIRE SAUCE
2 TABLESPOONS CHOPPED ONION
1 TEASPOON DRIED OREGANO
1/4 TEASPOON GROUND CUMIN
8 FLOUR TORTILLAS, WARMED
TOPPINGS:
    SOUR CREAM
    AVOCADO OR GUACAMOLE
    SALSA
    CHOPPED ONION
    CHOPPED TOMATOES

♀ Trim any fat from the chicken and pound the chicken with a meat mallet to flatten. Arrange the chicken in a shallow dish.

♀ Combine the vinegar, lemon juice, Worcestershire sauce, onion, oregano and cumin in a bowl, mix well and pour over the chicken.

♀ Marinate, covered, in the refrigerator for 30 minutes.

♀ Preheat the grill.

♀ Drain the chicken and arrange on a well-oiled grill over hot coals. Grill for 8 to 10 minutes or until cooked through but still moist, turning once. Remove to a plate.

♀ Let stand for 3 to 5 minutes. Cut into strips.

♀ Place the chicken on the warm tortillas, add the toppings to individual tastes, roll up and serve immediately.

SERVES 6 TO 8

TURKEY BURGER-ON-A-STICK

Children love to mix these with their hands.

1 POUND GROUND TURKEY
2 EGGS
$1/2$ TO $2/3$ CUP ROLLED OATS
1 TABLESPOON STEAK SAUCE
1 TABLESPOON CATSUP
PEPPER TO TASTE
$1/2$ CUP CORNFLAKE CRUMBS
4 HOT DOG BUNS

♀ Combine the turkey, eggs, oats, steak sauce, catsup and pepper in a bowl and mix well. Divide into 4 portions and shape each into a 5-inch long loaf. Roll in cornflake crumbs to coat well. Chill for 1 hour or longer.

♀ Preheat the grill.

♀ Skewer each of the loaves from end to end on a metal skewer at least 7 inches long. Place on the grill over hot coals. Grill for about 8 minutes or until cooked through and brown, turning as necessary.

♀ Place on hot dog buns and remove the skewers. Top with any desired toppings and serve immediately.

SERVES 4

Elizabeth Toledo leads a California rally in 1995 against Proposition 209, an anti-affirmative action ballot initiative that threatened 30 years of progress for women and people of color.

With bread and a salad, this dinner can be ready in 10 minutes.

VARIATION:
Substitute 3 dozen small shucked clams for the canned clams. Add to the sauce and cook for 1 to 2 minutes just before adding the sauce to the pasta.

SPAGHETTI WITH CLAM SAUCE

6 TO 8 QUARTS WATER
1 TABLESPOON SALT
1 POUND SPAGHETTI OR LINGUINI
1 TEASPOON (OR MORE) MINCED GARLIC
6 TABLESPOONS OLIVE OIL
2 (6-OUNCE) CANS CHOPPED CLAMS
BOTTLED CLAM JUICE
1/4 CUP DRY WHITE WINE
2 TABLESPOONS BUTTER, SOFTENED
2 TABLESPOONS CHOPPED FRESH PARSLEY
SALT AND WHITE PEPPER TO TASTE

♀ Bring the water with the 1 tablespoon salt to a boil in a large saucepan. Add the pasta to match the cooking time with the preparation of the sauce.

♀ Sauté the garlic in olive oil in a large skillet over medium heat for 30 seconds.

♀ Drain the clams, reserving the juice. Add enough bottled clam juice to the reserved juice to measure 1 cup.

♀ Add the clam juice and wine to the skillet. Boil until the mixture is reduced to about 3/4 cup. Add the clams to the skillet and bring to a boil.

♀ Drain the pasta; do not rinse. Place in a large warm serving bowl. Add the butter and toss to coat. Add the clam sauce and toss lightly. Add the parsley, salt and pepper, toss lightly and serve immediately.

SERVES 4 TO 6

Quickie Shrimp Curry for Company

2 MEDIUM ONIONS, CHOPPED
2 TABLESPOONS BUTTER OR VEGETABLE OIL
2 TABLESPOONS FLOUR
2 TEASPOONS CURRY POWDER
3/4 TEASPOON SALT
1/4 TEASPOON PEPPER
1 CUP WATER
1/2 CUP GOLDEN RAISINS
2 WHOLE CLOVES
GRATED RIND AND JUICE OF 1/2 LARGE LEMON
1 POUND PEELED, DEVEINED FRESH SHRIMP
TOPPINGS:
    CHOPPED WATER CHESTNUTS
    SHREDDED CABBAGE
    SHREDDED CARROTS
    CHOPPED BELL PEPPERS
    GRATED ORANGE RIND
    CHUTNEY

♀ Sauté the onions in the butter in a large skillet for 5 minutes. Mix the flour, curry powder, salt and pepper together and stir into the onion mixture.

♀ Stir in the water gradually. Add the raisins, cloves and lemon rind and juice. Cook until slightly thickened, stirring constantly.

♀ Add the shrimp. Cook, covered, over low heat for 15 to 20 minutes or until the shrimp turn pink, stirring occasionally.

♀ Serve over hot cooked rice. Add the toppings to individual tastes.

SERVES 4

LINKING ARMS IN DANGEROUS TIMES

NOW organized the historic "Women of Color & Allies Summit" in 1998 which brought together nearly 700 participants from across the country to work together on issues of race, class, gender and feminism. More than 165 organizations co-sponsored.

In addition to sharing information, strategizing and coalition-building, attendees participated in a protest on Capitol Hill in Washington, D.C. On behalf of the women custodial workers who clean the halls and offices of Congress, more than 200 picketers marched and rallied in front of the Rayburn Senate Office Building.

These women workers had filed a class action lawsuit asking for the same pay as the male laborers who perform equivalent duties. "This inequity exists right under the noses of some of the most powerful people in the country," said NOW President Patricia Ireland.

Hazel Dews, a custodian and organizer, spoke alongside Ireland at the rally: "We perform the same tasks under the same conditions as the [men] laborers and therefore we are entitled to the same pay."

INCREDIBLY FAST FISH

If you are looking for something that looks nice, tastes better and takes almost zero time and ingredients, this is it—and infinitely expandable, too. The scent that rolls out of the oven is extraordinary!

1 CATFISH FILLET
1 TO 2 TABLESPOONS COARSE-GROUND MUSTARD

♀ Preheat the oven to 350 degrees.
♀ Place the fillet on a lightly oiled or nonstick baking pan. Coat with the mustard.
♀ Bake thawed fillets for 12 to 18 minutes or frozen fillets for 20 to 30 minutes or until the fish flakes easily.

SERVES 1

♀ *I myself have never been able to find out precisely what feminism is. I only know that people call me a feminist whenever I express sentiments that distinguish me from a doormat.*

Rebecca West, age 21, 1913

SICILIAN FISH FILLETS

1/4 CUP BUTTER OR MARGARINE
1 1/2 POUNDS FISH FILLETS
1 TEASPOON JANE'S CRAZY SALT
1/2 TEASPOON DRIED BASIL
1/4 TEASPOON GARLIC POWDER
1/4 TEASPOON LEMON PEPPER
1/4 CUP FRESHLY GRATED PARMESAN CHEESE
2 TABLESPOONS MINCED FRESH PARSLEY
PAPRIKA TO TASTE

♀ Melt the butter in a skillet. Sprinkle the fish with the seasonings and place in the skillet, turning to coat with the butter.
♀ Sprinkle with the Parmesan cheese, parsley and paprika.
♀ Cook, covered, over medium-low heat for 10 to 12 minutes or until the fish flakes easily. Serve immediately.

SERVES 1

In 1992, NOW activists Boden Sandstrom, Marquita Sykes and Dixie Johnson (far right) demonstrated against delays and backlogs at the Equal Employment Opportunity Commission.

RICE NOODLE AND VEGETABLE STIR-FRY

The secret to this very attractive, flavorful and healthy dish is to have everything ready to go before you start the stir-frying.

INGREDIENTS:

1 (8-OUNCE) PACKAGE RICE OR
  CELLOPHANE NOODLES
3/4 CUP BELL PEPPER STRIPS
3/4 CUP SLICED CARROTS
3/4 CUP FRESH ASPARAGUS TIPS
3/4 CUP SUGAR SNAP PEAS
1 POUND FRESH TOMATOES
1 TO 3 TABLESPOONS OLIVE OIL
2 CLOVES OF GARLIC, CHOPPED
1 TABLESPOON CHOPPED FRESH
  GINGERROOT
2 GREEN ONIONS, CHOPPED
1 TABLESPOON SOY SAUCE
  (OPTIONAL)
3/4 CUP DRAINED BABY CORN
SALT AND PEPPER TO TASTE

METHOD:

♀ Soak the noodles in hot water to cover for 30 minutes to soften.

♀ Blanch the bell peppers, carrot slices, asparagus tips and snap peas in boiling water for 45 to 60 seconds, plunge into ice water, drain well and set aside.

♀ Dip the tomatoes in boiling water for 30 to 45 seconds, remove with a slotted spoon, remove the skins and chop the tomatoes.

♀ Drain the noodles. Heat the olive oil in a wok or skillet. Add the garlic, gingerroot and green onions. Stir-fry for 30 seconds. Add the tomatoes. Stir-fry for 2 to 3 minutes. Stir in the soy sauce.

♀ Add the drained noodles. Cook for 3 minutes, tossing lightly.

♀ Add the blanched vegetables and baby corn. Sprinkle with salt and pepper. Stir-fry until the vegetables are tender-crisp. Serve immediately.

SERVES 4 TO 6

♀ *You were once wild here. Don't let them tame you!*

Isadora Duncan

SOUTHWESTERN STUFFED SHELLS

18 JUMBO PASTA SHELLS
1 (16-OUNCE) CAN PUMPKIN
1 EGG
1/2 CUP ITALIAN-SEASONED BREAD CRUMBS
1/2 CUP GRATED PARMESAN CHEESE
1/2 TEASPOON GROUND NUTMEG
1 (16-OUNCE) JAR PICANTE SAUCE OR SALSA
1 CUP SHREDDED MONTEREY JACK CHEESE WITH
    JALAPEÑOS
2 TABLESPOONS CHOPPED FRESH PARSLEY

♀ Preheat the oven to 350 degrees.
♀ Cook the shells according to package directions, rinse with cold water, drain and set aside.
♀ Combine the pumpkin, egg, bread crumbs, Parmesan cheese and nutmeg in a bowl and mix well.
♀ Spoon about 1 cup of the picante sauce into a 9x13-inch baking dish. Fill the pasta shells with the pumpkin mixture and arrange in the prepared baking dish. Top with the remaining picante sauce.
♀ Bake, covered, for 30 to 35 minutes.
♀ Sprinkle with the Monterey Jack cheese and parsley. Serve immediately.

SERVES 4 TO 6

RATATOUILLE LA PETITE PARIS

Serve with omelets, crepes, pasta or brown rice.

1 (1½-POUND) EGGPLANT, PEELED, CUBED
½ CUP VEGETABLE OR OLIVE OIL
1 CUP CHOPPED GREEN BELL PEPPER
1 CLOVE OF GARLIC, CRUSHED
2 SMALL ZUCCHINI, SLICED
4 MEDIUM TOMATOES, PEELED, QUARTERED
1 TO 2 TEASPOONS SALT
¼ TEASPOON PEPPER
1 TEASPOON DRIED OREGANO, BASIL OR
    HERBES DE PROVENCE

♀ Sauté the eggplant in the oil in a large skillet; the eggplant will absorb a great deal of the oil.

♀ Add the green pepper and garlic. Sauté for several minutes.

♀ Add the zucchini and sauté for several minutes. Stir in the tomatoes, salt, pepper and oregano.

♀ Cook, covered, over low heat for 10 minutes or until the vegetables are tender-crisp, stirring occasionally. Correct the seasonings.

SERVES 6 TO 8

♀ *With women such as these consecrating their lives, failure is impossible.*

Susan B. Anthony's final public words

In Good Company
POTLUCK & PORTABLE DISHES

Over half a million people have joined the rolls as NOW

members and supporters, ensuring that the organization has a

voice strong enough to be heard around the world.

Members of NOW elect our leadership. NOW policy is

established and national officers are elected by its members at

annual conferences and by the board of directors, which is

elected by NOW members in the nine geographic regions.

Membership in NOW gives feminists a voice in the organization's

direction, and gives the organization a voice in the world's politics.

We don't expect every woman in this country to be a NOW

member. Just the millions who are discriminated against.

PICTURED ON OVERLEAF: *1992 Pride Parade, Chicago, IL; Leading*
NOW delegation: Loretta Kane, Patricia Ireland, Kim Gandy,
Virginia Montes, Rosemary Dempsey.

POTLUCK BROCCOLI AND SPINACH

2 (10-OUNCE) PACKAGES FROZEN CHOPPED
    BROCCOLI, THAWED, DRAINED
2 (10-OUNCE) PACKAGES FROZEN CHOPPED
    SPINACH, THAWED, DRAINED
2 CUPS SOUR CREAM
1 ENVELOPE DRY ONION SOUP MIX
4 TO 6 OUNCES GRATED PARMESAN CHEESE

♀ Preheat the oven to 325 degrees.
♀ Combine the broccoli and spinach in a bowl and mix well.
♀ Fold in the sour cream and soup mix. Spoon into a lightly greased 4-quart casserole.
♀ Sprinkle the cheese on top.
♀ Bake for 40 minutes. Serve immediately.

SERVES 16

♀ *Those who profess to love freedom and yet deprecate agitation are men who want crops without plowing. This struggle may be a moral one, or it may be physical, but it must be a struggle. Power concedes nothing without a demand. It never did and it never will.*
    Frederick Douglass, abolitionist and suffragist, 1857
Douglass was one of the few men to participate in the 1848 Women's Rights Convention in Seneca Falls, New York.

MOTHERHOOD AND APPLE PIE

In our Union today, we are taught from childhood on that our highest mission is that of wife and mother. Yet, should we follow this destiny, we are afforded not only economic disadvantage, but lack of respect.

The *Dictionary of Occupational Titles*, published by the Department of Labor, classifies mothering and homemaking skills in the lowest possible skill code; the occupation of dog trainer is given a higher rating!

We must work to change society's attitudes in regard to homemakers. Homemaking is work, and the fact that it is not salaried must not keep us from moving towards benefits enjoyed by other workers—social security, pensions, unemployment benefits, and disability and health insurance.

—Karen DeCrow,
NOW President, 1974-77

FLORIDA FLIPS

In response to a 1974 meeting with members of the Los Angeles chapter of NOW, producer Norman Lear made some changes in one of his sitcoms, *Good Times,* in order to better reflect feminist goals. The character of the mother, Florida, had become little more than a housekeeper picking up after her three teenagers while her husband worked long hours.

The first of the changes was an episode called "Florida Flips," where a discontented Florida goes to a consciousness-raising session with a friend. Skeptical about what she heard, she returns home only to discover her husband saying the things the group had portrayed as men's attitudes.

SAM'S ZUCCHINI FOR A POTLUCK

2 MEDIUM POTATOES, PEELED, CUBED
2 MEDIUM-LARGE ZUCCHINI, SLICED
1 MEDIUM ONION, CHOPPED
1 (4-OUNCE) CAN MUSHROOMS, DRAINED
2 (8-OUNCE) CANS TOMATO SAUCE
2 TO 4 TABLESPOONS OF A MIXTURE OF ANY OF THE
   FOLLOWING SEASONINGS: ANISEED, MARJORAM,
   OREGANO, CHERVIL, BASIL, SUMMER SAVORY,
   ROSEMARY, TARRAGON, THYME
SALT AND PEPPER TO TASTE

♀ Preheat the oven to 350 degrees.
♀ Cook the potatoes in a small amount of boiling water for 5 minutes; drain.
♀ Combine the partially cooked potatoes with zucchini, onion and mushrooms in a 9x12-inch baking dish and mix the vegetables lightly.
♀ Mix the tomato sauce with the desired seasonings and add salt and pepper to taste. Pour the tomato mixture over the zucchini mixture.
♀ Bake for 1 hour or until the vegetables are tender.

SERVES 6

ZUCCHINI CASSEROLE

2 ZUCCHINI
2 YELLOW SQUASH
2 (16-OUNCE) JARS FAVORITE SPAGHETTI SAUCE
2 CUPS SHREDDED MOZZARELLA CHEESE
GRATED PARMESAN CHEESE TO TASTE

♀ Preheat the oven to 350 degrees.
♀ Grease a large casserole lightly. Slice the zucchini and yellow squash no more than 1/4 inch thick.
♀ Layer a small amount of spaghetti sauce, some of the zucchini slices, spaghetti sauce, a sprinkle of mozzarella, some of the yellow squash, spaghetti sauce, and a sprinkle of mozzarella in the prepared casserole.
♀ Repeat the layers, alternating the zucchini and yellow squash until all the ingredients are used.
♀ Sprinkle with the desired amount of Parmesan cheese. Bake, covered, for 1 hour or until the squash is tender.

SERVES 16

(Florida Flips, continued)

Florida, played by Esther Rolle, ends by saying to her husband, "I don't want to walk ahead of you, I don't want to walk behind you. Take my hand and walk beside me."

Esther Rolle speaks at a NOW National march for the Equal Rights Amendment.

No Rest for the Battered

Asked at her press conference during the 1977 International Women's Year Conference in Houston why she and her followers opposed shelters for battered women, the head of Stop ERA, Phyllis Schlafly, replied, "It is just simply beyond me how giving a wife who's been beaten an R&R rest tour or vacation at taxpayers' expense is going to solve her problem."

The modern-day successor to Schlafly's indifference, the so-called Independent Women's Forum, continues to attack NOW's work on domestic violence, insisting that the problem is not widespread.

Brazilian-Style Black Beans and Rice

1 POUND DRIED BLACK BEANS
2 ONIONS, CHOPPED
4 TABLESPOONS OLIVE OIL
1 RED BELL PEPPER, CHOPPED (OPTIONAL)
6 CLOVES OF GARLIC, MINCED
4 TEASPOONS GROUND CUMIN
1 TEASPOON DRY MUSTARD
1 TEASPOON SALT
1/4 TEASPOON PEPPER
CAYENNE TO TASTE
4 FRESH TOMATOES, CHOPPED
4 FRESH JALAPEÑO PEPPERS, CHOPPED
3 CUPS UNCOOKED WHITE RICE
LEMON JUICE AND CHOPPED CILANTRO TO TASTE

♀ Sort and rinse the beans. Soak in water to cover for several hours to overnight, changing the water several times.
♀ Place the beans in a large stock pot. Add water to cover 2 inches above the beans. Add half the onion and 1 tablespoon olive oil. Simmer for 2 hours or until tender, stirring several times and adding water as necessary.
♀ Sauté the remaining onions in the remaining 3 tablespoons olive oil for several minutes. Add the bell pepper and the garlic. Sauté for several minutes. Stir in the cumin, mustard and cayenne. Cook for 1 minute longer.
♀ Mix the sautéed mixture, salt, pepper, tomatoes, jalapeños and water if necessary to the beans. Simmer for 15 minutes.
♀ Cook the rice according to the package directions. Stir the lemon juice and cilantro into the beans. Serve the beans over a mound of the hot cooked rice.

SERVES 12 TO 15

Kim's Red Beans and Rice

2 POUNDS DRIED KIDNEY BEANS
1 1/2 POUNDS SMOKED HAM HOCKS OR SMOKED
    TURKEY LEGS
4 LARGE ONIONS, CHOPPED
1 CUP CHOPPED CELERY WITH LEAVES
6 CLOVES OF GARLIC, MINCED
3 LARGE BAY LEAVES
2 TABLESPOONS MIXED ITALIAN HERBS
1 TABLESPOON GROUND CUMIN
1 TEASPOON DRIED THYME
CAYENNE TO TASTE
2 CUPS UNCOOKED WHITE RICE

♀ Sort and rinse the beans. Soak in water to cover generously in a stockpot overnight.

♀ Drain and add the ham hocks to the beans. Add water to cover generously. Simmer, covered, for 1 hour.

♀ Add the onions, celery, garlic, bay leaves, Italian herbs, cumin, thyme and cayenne. Simmer, covered, for several hours until the beans are tender.

♀ Remove several cups of the beans, mash lightly and return to the pot. Remove the ham hocks, cut the meat from the bones, discard the bones, and return the ham to the pot. Discard the bay leaves.

♀ Cook the rice according to the package directions. Mound the rice in large bowls. Ladle the bean mixture on top.

VARIATION:

♀ Cook 2 pounds of smoked sausage in a large skillet until brown and crumbly. Add to the bean mixture during the last 30 minutes of the cooking time.

SERVES 8 TO 10

A Woman's Place Is in the House . . .

Louisiana's nearly all-male legislature often treated women's rights as a joke. Rep. Carl Gunter questioned all the fuss about incest, saying that "inbreeding is the way we get thoroughbred race horses."

But the final straw was in 1990, when they passed the country's most punitive anti-abortion law—making the procedure virtually unavailable even in cases of rape or incest. No wonder...the legislature had only two women out of 141!

So NOW's political action committee took action. Kim Gandy and Harriet Trudell set up candidate searches, organized events and taught campaign techniques. With six interns, they set up phone banks and canvasses, designed ads, and wrote letters for candidates. After nine months, two women had become ten—two of them senators—and six of the most noxious men were defeated, including Gunter!

As a bonus, we turned out the women's vote to narrowly defeat David Duke, the Republican candidate for governor *and* to elect the first woman Lt. Governor.

This recipe came with the following note: "We in our Saratoga NOW Chapter couldn't be sure if the call for recipes was a joke or not. In case it is real, I'm sending a recipe full of virtues for busy feminists. It is quick to make, simple to serve, easy to store, vegetarian, low-fat, and low-cal."

SZECHUAN NOODLES

1/2 CUP SOY SAUCE
2 TABLESPOONS SESAME OIL
2 TABLESPOONS VEGETABLE OIL
6 TABLESPOONS RICE VINEGAR
2 CLOVES OF GARLIC, CRUSHED
4 TEASPOONS MINCED FRESH GINGERROOT
1/2 TEASPOON (APPROX.) CAYENNE
1 POUND LINGUINI
1/2 CUP COARSELY CHOPPED PEANUTS
1 CUCUMBER, PEELED, SEEDED, CHOPPED
1 (10-OUNCE) CAN BABY CORN
1 CUP BROCCOLI FLORETS
2 GREEN BELL PEPPERS, CHOPPED

♀ Combine the soy sauce, sesame oil, vegetable oil, vinegar, garlic, gingerroot, and cayenne in a bowl and mix well.
♀ Cook the linguini according to the package directions. Drain and place in a large bowl. Pour the soy sauce mixture over the noodles and toss until coated.
♀ Add the peanuts and all the vegetables and toss to mix.
♀ Serve hot, at room temperature, or cold.

SERVES 8

BEER BRAISED BEEF

3 POUNDS LEAN BEEF
1/4 CUP FLOUR
2 TEASPOONS SALT
1 TEASPOON PEPPER
3 TABLESPOONS VEGETABLE OIL
2 ONIONS, SLICED
8 OUNCES FRESH MUSHROOMS, QUARTERED
1 TABLESPOONS VINEGAR
2 TABLESPOONS SUGAR
2 CLOVES OF GARLIC, MINCED
1 TEASPOON THYME
1 BAY LEAF
1 (14-OUNCE) CAN BEEF BROTH
1 (12-OUNCE) CAN BEER

♀ Cut the beef into cubes. Mix the flour, salt and pepper in a large plastic bag. Add the beef cubes in batches and shake until coated with the flour mixture.
♀ Brown the beef on all sides in oil in a skillet. Place in a slow cooker.
♀ Add the onions, mushrooms, vinegar, sugar, garlic, thyme, bay leaf, broth and beer and mix well.
♀ Cook on Low for several hours until the beef is tender.
♀ Serve over hot cooked noodles.

SERVES 10

TACIT APPROVAL OF ANTI-CHOICE TERRORISM

In 1984, in response to a dramatic upsurge in violence against abortion clinics nationwide, NOW's President Judy Goldsmith met with Justice Department officials from the criminal and civil rights divisions. These officials, however, claimed they were powerless to stop the civil rights violations against women exercising their right to choose abortion.

NOW also sent telegrams to President Reagan, Attorney General William French Smith, and FBI Director William Webster warning of the "campaign of terrorism and intimidation," but it was clear we could not depend on them to protect clinic staff and patients from attack. In 1986, NOW filed its own suit against the ringleaders of the anti-abortion violence. After innumerable delays and a successful trip to the Supreme Court, NOW convinced a Chicago jury in 1998 to unanimously find Joe Scheidler, Operation Rescue, and other groups guilty of racketeering.

HERM'S FAMOUS BARBECUE

5 TO 6 POUNDS CHUCK ROAST, LEAN PORK OR CHICKEN
1/2 CUP BREWED COFFEE
SALT AND PEPPER TO TASTE
3 LARGE ONIONS, CHOPPED
3 OR 4 RIBS CELERY, CHOPPED
1 (20-OUNCE) BOTTLE FAVORITE BARBECUE SAUCE

♀ Preheat the oven to 300 degrees.
♀ Cut the roast into 1 1/2-inch-thick slices and place in an ovenproof Dutch oven. Add the coffee, salt and pepper. Cover tightly with foil and add the lid.
♀ Bake for 2 1/2 to 3 hours or until the roast is tender enough to be pulled apart with a fork. Remove the roast from the Dutch oven, reserving the pan juices.
♀ Cool the roast, shred and return with any juices to the Dutch oven. Add the onions, celery and barbecue sauce and mix well.
♀ Bake, covered, for 45 to 60 minutes or until the onions and celery are tender.
♀ Serve on toasted buns or bread.

SERVES 15

♀ *You cannot shake hands with a clenched fist.*
Indira Gandhi, 1971

BEAGLE'S HOBO BEANS

8 OUNCES LEAN BACON
8 OUNCES GROUND ROUND
1 MILD ONION, CHOPPED
6 CUPS DRAINED MIXED COOKED OR CANNED
    KIDNEY, GREAT NORTHERN, BAKED, PINTO,
    LIMA OR OTHER BEANS
3/4 CUP PACKED BROWN SUGAR
2 TEASPOONS VINEGAR
1 TEASPOON DRY OR YELLOW PREPARED MUSTARD
1/4 CUP CATSUP
1 TABLESPOON WORCESTERSHIRE SAUCE

♀ Cook the bacon in a skillet until brown and crisp; drain and crumble. Brown the ground round with the onion in a skillet, stirring until crumbly and drain well.

♀ Combine the bacon, ground round mixture, beans, brown sugar, vinegar, mustard, catsup and Worcestershire sauce in a slow cooker or large baking dish and mix well.

♀ Cook in the slow cooker on Low for 4 hours or bake at 350 degrees for 40 minutes, stirring several times.

SERVES 12 TO 16

1994 NOW protest at the Justice Department demands intervention after the murder of clinic doctors: (L to R) Karen Johnson, Kim Gandy, Kathy Spillar, Wanda Alston.

VEGETARIAN LASAGNA

While this recipe takes part of a Sunday afternoon to make, you will get ten meals out of it and it freezes well. The noodles do not need to be cooked in advance, which speeds the preparation immensely. This version is vegetarian (add any other vegetables, such as thinly sliced red bell pepper or carrots, too) but the non-vegetarian can add cooked ground beef or Italian sausage to the marinara. This makes enough to fill an 11x15-inch baking pan and also a 9x9-inch pan.

2 LARGE ONIONS, CHOPPED
4 CLOVES OF GARLIC, CHOPPED
2 TABLESPOONS OLIVE OIL
1 CUP DRY RED WINE OR WATER
1 POUND RICOTTA CHEESE
3 EGGS, LIGHTLY BEATEN
3 CUPS FINELY CHOPPED FRESH SPINACH OR
    2 CUPS SPINACH AND 1 CUP PARSLEY
1/4 CUP GRATED ROMANO CHEESE
PEPPER TO TASTE
4 CUPS MARINARA SAUCE
1 POUND UNCOOKED LASAGNA NOODLES
2 CUPS CHOPPED MUSHROOMS OR BROCCOLI
1 1/2 CUPS SHREDDED MOZZARELLA CHEESE
GRATED PARMESAN CHEESE TO TASTE

♀ Preheat the oven to 350 degrees.
♀ Sauté the onions and garlic in olive oil in a large skillet until tender. Add a small amount of the red wine if desired.
♀ Mix the ricotta cheese with the eggs in a bowl. Add the spinach, Romano cheese and pepper and mix well.
♀ Blend the remaining red wine with the marinara sauce.

♀ Spread a thin layer of the marinara mixture in the bottoms of the lightly greased baking pans. Arrange a layer of uncooked noodles in the pans, overlapping the noodles slightly.

♀ Add layers of the sautéed onions, $1/3$ of the ricotta mixture and $1/4$ of the remaining marinara sauce.

♀ Arrange a second layer of the noodles perpendicular to the first layer. Add layers of the spinach, half the remaining ricotta mixture and $1/3$ of the remaining marinara sauce.

♀ Repeat the layers with noodles, mushrooms, half the remaining marinara sauce, noodles and remaining sauce.

♀ Add water to the pans by pouring slowly around the edges of the pans until the water reaches the level of the top noodles. (The water is necessary because the noodles are uncooked.)

♀ Cover the pans tightly with foil. Bake for about 45 minutes or until the noodles are almost tender.

♀ Sprinkle the mozzarella cheese on top and add a sprinkle

♀ the desired amount of Parmesan cheese.

♀ Bake for about 20 minutes longer or until the noodles are tender.

♀ Let stand for 10 to 15 minutes before cutting the lasagna into servings.

SERVES 12 TO 15

♀ *Those who lose dreaming are lost.*
Australian Aboriginal proverb

SO SHE WANTS TO BE AN ARCHITECT

Seldom at a social event have I failed to meet someone who says, "You're an architect? I always wanted to be an architect!" If it is a man, I think he made another choice. If it is a woman, which is often, I think, "another opportunity lost."

I know that woman is not an architect today because: no one encouraged her to take math and physics in high school; no one suggested she take mechanical drawing or shop classes; she helped her mother paint the kitchen instead of helping dad build the fence and carport; she worked as a carhop instead of a go-fer on a construction crew during high school; she never saw or heard of a woman architect; her high school counselor told her architecture was a tough field for women and it would really be more practical if she learned to teach art.

Elaine Day Latourell, 1976 (former national officer of NOW)

This dish has about the same consistency as enchiladas but using the layering technique of lasagna with the tortillas instead of rolling them individually makes the preparation a snap, especially if the refried beans are heated for easier spreading. Do not use instant rice.

QUICK AND EASY VEGETARIAN MEXICAN LASAGNA

3 (8-OUNCE) CANS TOMATO SAUCE
1/2 MEDIUM ONION, FINELY CHOPPED
1 LARGE CLOVE OF GARLIC, CRUSHED, MINCED
1 TEASPOON CHILI POWDER
HOT SAUCE OR CRUSHED RED PEPPER TO TASTE
1 1/2 CUPS LONG GRAIN OR OTHER FAVORITE RICE
2 TABLESPOONS SALSA
1/3 CUP MIXED SHREDDED MONTEREY JACK CHEESE
    WITH JALAPEÑOS AND CHEDDAR CHEESE
1 (20-OUNCE) CAN VEGETARIAN REFRIED BEANS
8 FLOUR TORTILLAS

♀ Preheat the oven to 350 degrees.
♀ Combine the tomato sauce, onion, garlic, half the chili powder and hot sauce to taste in a saucepan and mix well. Simmer for 30 minutes.
♀ Measure the water according to package direction for the rice. Discard 1 tablespoon of the water. Add the rice, salsa, remaining chili powder and hot sauce to taste. Cook the rice until tender. Spoon into a large bowl; cool. Mix in the cheese.
♀ Spread about 3 tablespoons of the sauce on a tortilla and place in the casserole with the sauce side down in a greased 8- or 9-inch casserole. Add a second tortilla spread with sauce on both sides.
♀ Add 3 tortillas each spread with sauce and refried beans and 3 tortillas each spread with sauce and the rice mixture.
♀ Top with the remaining sauce and additional shredded cheese. Bake, covered, for 20 to 25 minutes. Let stand for 10 to 15 minutes before cutting into wedges like a pie.

SERVES 4 OR 5

Italian Sausage Lasagna

4 or 5 links sweet Italian sausage with fennel
1 1/2 pounds ground beef
2 large onions, chopped
4 cloves of garlic, minced
3/4 cup olive oil
2 (6-ounce) cans tomato paste
2 (8-ounce) cans tomato sauce
Salt and pepper to taste
1 pound uncooked lasagna noodles
2 pounds mozzarella cheese, cut into strips
1 pound ricotta cheese
1 cup grated Parmesan cheese

♀ Preheat the oven to 350 degrees.

♀ Broil the sausages until cooked through; drain and crumble.

♀ Cook the ground beef with onions and garlic in olive oil in a large skillet until brown and crumbly, stirring frequently. Drain well and combine with the tomato paste and tomato sauce in the skillet. Simmer for several minutes. Add the sausage, salt and pepper. Simmer until of the desired consistency. Spread a small amount of the sauce mixed with a small amount of water to cover the bottom of a lightly greased large baking pan.

♀ Arrange a layer of the uncooked noodles in the baking pan. Add layers of the sauce, mozzarella cheese and ricotta cheese. Repeat the layers with the remaining noodles, sauce, mozzarella cheese and ricotta cheese, ending with layers of ricotta and sauce.

♀ Sprinkle with the Parmesan cheese. Bake for 1 1/2 hours or until the noodles are cooked through.

♀ Let stand for 15 minutes before cutting.

Serves 12

FRIAR CLUCK

This dish can be frozen and reheated. It makes a great buffet dish as it is, or the chicken can be boned and cut into bite-size pieces.

8 CHICKEN THIGHS
1/3 CUP HONEY
1/3 CUP RED CURRANT JELLY
2 TABLESPOONS LEMON JUICE
2 TABLESPOONS PREPARED YELLOW MUSTARD
1/4 TEASPOON GROUND GINGER
1/2 TEASPOON SALT

♀ Preheat the oven to 325 degrees.
♀ Line a baking pan with foil and spray with nonstick cooking spray. Arrange the chicken in a single layer in the prepared baking pan.
♀ Combine the honey, jelly, lemon juice, mustard, ginger and salt in a small bowl and blend well. Pour over the chicken.
♀ Bake for 2 hours, turning and basting the chicken every 30 minutes. The color will darken as cooking progresses; check frequently to prevent burning.

SERVES 4 TO 8

♀ *Cooking is like love. It should be entered with abandon or not at all.*

Harriet Van Horne, 1956

HONEY MUSTARD CHICKEN WINGS

2 1/2 POUNDS CHICKEN WINGS OR OTHER FAVORITE
    CHICKEN PARTS
SPICY SEASONED SALT TO TASTE
1/4 CUP BUTTER OR MARGARINE
1/2 CUP HONEY
1/4 CUP PREPARED YELLOW MUSTARD
1 TEASPOON CURRY POWDER
JUICE OF 1 LEMON

♀ Preheat the oven to 350 degrees.
♀ Separate the chicken wings at the joints and discard the tips. Sprinkle with the seasoned salt and arrange in a single layer in a large greased baking pan; do not overcrowd.
♀ Combine the butter, honey, mustard, curry powder and lemon juice in a small saucepan. Cook over low heat until the butter melts and the mixture is well blended, stirring frequently. Pour over the chicken.
♀ Bake for 45 to 60 minutes, basting occasionally.

SERVES 2 TO 4

♀ *In general my children refuse to eat anything that hasn't danced on TV.*

Erma Bombeck

HEAVY LIFTING

When Lorena Weeks left the switchboard, she opened up more than one new job.

Lorena Weeks used to be a telephone operator who bid on a job Southern Bell sincerely titled "switchman." No woman was allowed to be a switchman.

Although she had more seniority, a man was given the job. And Lorena Weeks was given an excuse: "You're a woman, you shouldn't do lifting."

She was strong enough to take her case to NOW, and NOW took her case to the federal courts.

When the dust settled, NOW succeeded in winning her full relief: The job, back pay, over-time, plus interest . . . $30,000 in all.

But the biggest relief came when the court breathed life into the sex discrimination provisions of the 1964 Civil Rights Act.

The court also told employers if they wanted to "protect" women from certain jobs, they had to prove *all* women were unfit to handle them. Because Lorena Weeks had the courage to fight for her job, a lot of other women didn't have to fight for theirs.

from a 1975 NOW brochure

FOURTH WORLD CONFERENCE EMPOWERS WOMEN

More than 200 NOW members traveled to China for the unprecedented U.N. Fourth World Conference on Women, held in 1995 in Beijing. More than 30,000 women and men from over 180 countries attended the Forum for Non-Governmental Organizations, held just outside Beijing.

"The experience was very powerful, very uplifting," said Karen Johnson, NOW Membership VP. "Women, no matter what their circumstances, came with a lot of hope and excitement." Johnson came away impressed by women fighting for their lives in war-torn countries; women struggling with AIDS in Africa, where it is considered a woman's disease; and the Chinese women who are optimistic that their lot will improve.

NOW activists ran several workshops on Consciousness-Raising and grassroots organizing, giving other women the tools they need for their national feminist movements.

CHICKEN POCKETS

These neat little pockets are good for picnics, carry-along lunches, or a light supper.

3 OUNCES CREAM CHEESE, SOFTENED
2 TABLESPOONS BUTTER, SOFTENED
1/2 TEASPOON SALT
1/4 TEASPOON PEPPER
1 TABLESPOONS CHOPPED CHIVES
1 TABLESPOON MINCED PIMENTO OR
    RED BELL PEPPER
2 TABLESPOONS MILK
2 CUPS CHOPPED COOKED CHICKEN
1 (8-COUNT) PACKAGE REFRIGERATOR
    CRESCENT ROLLS

♀ Preheat the oven to 375 degrees.
♀ Blend the cream cheese and butter in a bowl. Add the salt, pepper, chives, pimento and milk and mix well. Stir in the chicken.
♀ Separate the crescent roll dough into 4 rectangles and press the perforations together to seal.
♀ Spoon the chicken mixture into the center of each rectangle. Fold the corners of the dough to the center and pinch the edges together to enclose the filling. Place on a lightly greased baking sheet.
♀ Bake for 10 to 15 minutes or until golden brown. Serve hot or at room temperature.

MAKES 4

WAY-COOL CHICKEN TACOS

1 (3-POUND) CHICKEN
6 SCALLIONS, CHOPPED
2 CUPS SHREDDED CHEDDAR CHEESE
2 LARGE AVOCADOS, PEELED, CHOPPED
2 LARGE TOMATOES, CHOPPED
3/4 CUP SOUR CREAM
2 CUPS SHREDDED LETTUCE
SALT AND PEPPER TO TASTE
TACO SHELLS OR TORTILLA CHIPS

♀ Cook the chicken in water to cover until tender. Cool, discard the skin and bones and chop into small pieces.
♀ Combine the chicken, scallions, cheese, avocados, tomatoes and sour cream in a bowl and mix well.
♀ Add the lettuce, salt and pepper just before serving and mix lightly.
♀ Serve in taco shells or on tortilla-lined plates. Serve with salsa.

SERVES 6

NOW *legal intern Elena Dimopoulos (front) and others protesting the threatened jailing of Bangladeshi feminist Taslima Nasrin in 1994. Dimopoulos went on to serve as plaintiff's counsel in a landmark 1998 Supreme Court case on sexual harassment,* Ellerth v. Burlington Industries.

SOCIAL SECURITY BENEFITS FOR DIVORCED WOMEN

NOW targeted two Social Security restrictions for elimination in 1971: 1) A divorced wife must have been married for 20 years to receive benefits (NOW sought and won a reduction to 10 years); and 2) A divorced woman is ineligible for Social Security if she doesn't receive alimony or can't prove that she receives substantial support from her husband. More than 10,000 older women were deprived of this tax-free pension by such provisions.

Since then, hundreds of thousands of older women have been prevented from falling into poverty by the elimination of these provisions.

BAKED HALIBUT FANTASTIC

Serve many or just a few but maintain the same proportions. It is a good choice for a casual dinner party—it is hard to overcook fish covered with a sauce, and it won't dry out or cool off quickly at the table. Use any sturdy, large-grained whitefish, such as flounder or orange roughy, if the fillets are at least 1 inch thick or can be overlapped to that thickness. Do not use low-fat mayonnaise or sour cream.

1 1/2 POUNDS HALIBUT OR OTHER WHITEFISH
1 SMALL YELLOW ONION, THINLY SLICED
1 LARGE CLOVE OF GARLIC, MINCED
1/4 TEASPOON SALT
1/4 TEASPOON WHITE PEPPER
1/2 CUP MAYONNAISE
1/2 CUP SOUR CREAM
1/2 SHREDDED MOZZARELLA CHEESE
2 TABLESPOONS GRATED PARMESAN CHEESE

♀ Preheat the oven to 350 degrees.
♀ Arrange the halibut in a buttered baking dish just large enough to hold the fillets without touching the sides. Cover with onion and garlic and sprinkle with salt and pepper.
♀ Whisk the mayonnaise and sour cream together in a small bowl. Spread evenly over the halibut and the exposed bottom of the baking dish. Prepare additional sauce if necessary.
♀ Sprinkle with the mozzarella and Parmesan cheeses.
♀ Bake, uncovered, for 12 minutes per pound. Remove from the oven, cover with foil and let stand for 10 minutes before serving.
♀ Serve with boiled red or white potatoes topped with the sour cream sauce.

SERVES 4

BAKED FISH A LA FATNA

1 (4-POUND) RED SNAPPER
1/4 CUP VINEGAR
1 TABLESPOON SALT
GRATED RIND AND JUICE OF 1 LEMON
3 OR 4 CLOVES OF GARLIC, CHOPPED
1/2 CUP FINELY CHOPPED FRESH PARSLEY
1 TEASPOON EACH CUMIN AND PAPRIKA
1/2 TO 1 TEASPOON FRESHLY GROUND PEPPER
4 MEDIUM TOMATOES, PEELED, CHOPPED
1/2 CUP OLIVE OIL OR VEGETABLE OIL
1 TEASPOON SALT
4 ONIONS, SLICED
3 MEDIUM TOMATOES, SLICED
1 LEMON, SLICED
1/2 CUP (APPROX.) WATER
JUICE OF 1/2 LEMON

This really beautiful Moroccan dish is surprisingly easy to make. The fish should be cleaned and scaled but otherwise remain whole. Any light-fleshed fish (such as sea bass) that has only a few small bones can be substituted for snapper. Do not attempt to turn the fish or even remove it from the baking dish before serving.

♀ Preheat the oven to 350 degrees.

♀ Rinse the fish well and soak in cold water to cover mixed with vinegar and 1 tablespoon salt for 10 minutes.

♀ Mix the next 9 ingredients in a bowl. Drain the fish and pat dry. Place the fish on a bed of onion slices in a baking dish. Spoon the tomato mixture into the fish cavity and over the top and sides. Arrange the tomato and lemon slices over and around the fish in a decorative manner. Add enough water to just cover bottom of the baking dish and drizzle with the remaining lemon juice.

♀ Bake, covered, with foil for 30 minutes. Bake, uncovered, for 30 minutes or until the fish is cooked through but not dry. The water should have been absorbed but the dish should not appear brown. Serve immediately.

SERVES 6

NOW ORGANIZING KEY TO ELECTION WINS

Aggressive field organizing was just one of the field-tested strategies which were replicated across the country in the critical election years of 1992 and 1996 when women voters made a difference.

"No matter how much money candidates have to spend on advertising or high-dollar political consultants," said NOW President Patricia Ireland, who also chairs NOW/PAC, "grassroots organizing is an absolute survival tool."

Senator Carol Moseley Braun (D-Illinois), (*photo opposite*), praised NOW's support as "key to my decision to run" in 1992 and said NOW/PAC campaign expertise was "a strong foundation for my campaign."

Her remarks were a tribute to NOW's steadfastness: "It was NOW members that I often turned to during the hard times of the campaign when I needed to feel the unconditional, understanding support that only sisters can give."

CORN BREAD CASSEROLE

1 POUND GROUND BEEF
1 ONION, CHOPPED
2 TABLESPOONS BUTTER
1 (8-OUNCE) CAN CREAM-STYLE CORN
3/4 CUP MILK
1/3 CUP MELTED BUTTER OR MARGARINE
2 EGGS, LIGHTLY BEATEN
1 CUP YELLOW CORNMEAL
1/2 TEASPOON BAKING SODA
1 TEASPOON SALT
1 TEASPOON SUGAR
3/4 CUP PICANTE SAUCE
1 1/2 CUPS SHREDDED CHEDDAR CHEESE

♀ Preheat the oven to 375 degrees.
♀ Cook the ground beef with the onion in butter in a skillet until brown and crumbly, stirring frequently and drain well.
♀ Combine the corn, milk, butter and eggs in a bowl and mix well. Mix the cornmeal, baking soda, salt and sugar together. Add to the corn mixture and stir just until mixed.
♀ Pour half the mixture into a greased 8x8-inch baking pan. Add layers of the ground beef mixture, picante sauce and half the cheese.
♀ Spoon the remaining cornmeal mixture over the layers and top with the remaining cheese.
♀ Bake for 40 minutes or until golden brown.

SERVES 4 TO 6

TO SWEET VICTORY
CAKES, COOKIES AND PIES

NOW invites all feminists to our annual summer conference,

to engage each other on current political issues, strategies,

and concerns. Tens of thousands of feminists have participated in

NOW conferences over our 32 year history. In addition to

shaping the organization's philosophy and priorities,

conference delegates create lasting friendships, embrace a

feminist-friendly environment, and learn from each

other's skills and experience.

NOW also organizes summits that call feminists together on

specific topics; recent summits have focused on racism, lesbian

rights, young feminism and global feminism. NOW state

organizations host an annual conference, and each region

hosts a bi-annual regional conference.

PICTURED ON OVERLEAF: *1992 national NOW March for Women's Lives,*
Washington, DC, Carol Moseley Braun and Patricia Ireland.

BERRY UPSIDE-DOWN ANGEL CAKE

1 ANGEL FOOD CAKE MIX
2 CUPS FRESH OR FROZEN BLUEBERRIES OR
  CURRANTS
1/2 CUP (APPROX.) SUGAR
1/2 CUP APRICOT JAM

♀ Preheat the oven to the temperature specified in the angel food cake mix.

♀ Place the blueberries in an ungreased large springform tube pan. Sprinkle with enough sugar to make of the desired sweetness. Bake for 10 to 15 minutes or until the sugar is dissolved. Set the pan aside to cool for 10 to 15 minutes.

♀ Prepare the angel food cake mix according to the package directions using completely grease-free metal or glass bowls.

♀ Spoon the prepared cake batter over the berries. Bake the cake according to the package directions. Place on a wire rack to cool completely.

♀ Loosen the cake from the side of the pan and remove the side. Place the serving plate upside-down on the cake and carefully invert the cake and plate. Remove the pan carefully. Heat the apricot jam in a small saucepan just until the jam comes to a simmer. Add a small amount of water if necessary to thin the jam to glazing consistency.

♀ Brush the glaze over the top of the cake. Serve at room temperature with whipped cream or ice cream.

SERVES 12

TURNING FEAR INTO ACTION

Massachusetts area NOW activists gave new meaning to the word courage on January 30th, 1995. That's the day an anti-abortion extremist gunned down two people and injured five others at two Brookline, Massachusetts, women's health clinics.

With the killer still on the loose, in a matter of hours NOW organized 1,000 people for a vigil at one of the clinics, followed by a service at a synagogue.

"It was the only time in my life I've been afraid to do something," said then-National NOW Board member Ellen Zucker. "It was the first time that people I love have said to me, 'Do you have to do this?'"

The next day, with the accused killer apprehended, 4,000 people turned out at 4 p.m. on New Year's Eve for a second NOW-organized protest at the Statehouse in downtown Boston. "We all have to turn our shock and mourning and fear into bold action," said NOW President Patricia Ireland.

GIRLS ARE STRONG!

Two sisters and NOW members, Rachel and Joanna Moresky, were the youngest girls in the U.S. to become black belts in Tae Kwon Do. They both won their black belts when they were ten years old. Rachel was the first, getting her picture in Sports Illustrated in January, 1980.

Their mother, former NOW National Board member Lana Moresky, said "We want our children to be able to take care of themselves, and not just physically. Their training is mental as well; it teaches discipline, control and respect."

This discipline certainly paid off: In 1998, Rachel finished medical school in Haifa, Israel, and after getting married, was starting her residency in Chicago. Joanna graduated from Cornell University and was working at the Center for Economic Priorities in New York City.

BROWN SUGAR CAKE

1 CUP MARGARINE, SOFTENED
1/2 CUP VEGETABLE SHORTENING
1 CUP GRANULATED SUGAR
1 (1-POUND) PACKAGE BROWN SUGAR
5 EGGS
1 CUP MILK
1 TEASPOON VANILLA EXTRACT
3 CUPS FLOUR
1 TEASPOON BAKING POWDER
1 CUP GROUND PECANS OR WALNUTS
1 CUP CONFECTIONERS' SUGAR
6 TABLESPOONS MILK OR CREAM
1/2 CUP CHOPPED PECANS OR WALNUTS

♀ Preheat the oven to 350 degrees.

♀ Cream the margarine and shortening in a large bowl. Add the granulated and brown sugars and beat until light and fluffy.

♀ Add the eggs 1 at a time, beating well after each addition. Add the milk and vanilla and beat until smooth.

♀ Sift the flour and baking powder. Toss in the ground pecans. Add to the sugar mixture 1/3 at a time, beating well after each addition. Beat for 2 minutes.

♀ Pour into a greased and floured large loaf pan. Bake for 1 1/4 hours or until a toothpick inserted in the center comes out clean.

♀ Cool in the pan on a wire rack for 5 to 10 minutes. Remove to a wire rack to cool completely.

♀ Blend the confectioners' sugar with the milk in a small bowl. Drizzle over the top of the cake. Sprinkle with the chopped nuts.

MAKES 1 CAKE

BURNT SUGAR CAKE

1/2 CUP SHORTENING, BUTTER OR MARGARINE,
    SOFTENED
1 1/2 CUPS SUGAR
2 EGGS
1 TEASPOON VANILLA EXTRACT
2 1/2 CUPS FLOUR
2 1/2 TEASPOONS BAKING POWDER
1/4 TEASPOON SALT
1 CUP MILK
1 CUP CARAMEL SYRUP (AT RIGHT)
CARAMEL ICING (AT RIGHT)

♀ Preheat the oven to 350 degrees.

♀ Cream the shortening and sugar in a large bowl until light and fluffy. Add the eggs 1 at a time beating well after each addition. Beat in the vanilla.

♀ Sift the flour, baking powder and salt together. Add to the creamed mixture alternately with the milk, beating well after each addition.

♀ Add the Caramel Syrup. Beat for 2 minutes. Pour into 2 greased and floured layer cake pans.

♀ Bake for 30 to 40 minutes or until the cakes test done. Cool in the pans on wire racks for 5 to 10 minutes. Turn onto the wire racks to cool completely.

♀ Spread the Caramel Icing between the layers and over the top and side of the cake.

MAKES 1 CAKE

CARAMEL SYRUP

♀ Pour 1 cup sugar into a nonstick skillet. Heat over medium-high heat until the sugar melts and becomes a rich golden brown color, stirring constantly. Stir in 1 cup boiling water gradually. Heat until the sugar dissolves completely, stirring constantly. Set aside to cool.

♀

CARAMEL ICING

1 CUP MILK
2 CUPS SUGAR
1 TEASPOON BAKING SODA
1 TEASPOON VANILLA
    EXTRACT
2 TABLESPOONS (APPROX.)
    BUTTER
1 CUP (APPROX.) CARAMEL
    SYRUP

♀ Combine the milk and sugar in a large saucepan. Cook to 234 degrees on a candy thermometer, soft-ball stage. Remove from the heat. Add the baking soda, vanilla and butter and mix well. Stir in the remaining Caramel Syrup. Let stand until slightly cooled. Beat until of spreading consistency.

HONEY PECAN CAKE

1 CUP MILK
1 TABLESPOON VINEGAR
1 1/2 CUPS SUGAR
1 CUP VEGETABLE OIL
3 EGGS
1 TEASPOON VANILLA EXTRACT
2 CUPS FLOUR
1 TABLESPOON BAKING POWDER
4 TEASPOONS CINNAMON
2 TEASPOONS GROUND CLOVES
1 1/2 CUPS CHOPPED PECANS
1/4 CUP HONEY
1 TABLESPOON WATER
1 TABLESPOON LEMON JUICE

♀ Preheat the oven to 350 degrees.
♀ Blend the milk with the vinegar and set aside for several minutes.
♀ Beat the sugar and oil together in a large bowl. Add the eggs and vanilla. Beat at medium speed for 1 minute.
♀ Sift the flour, baking powder, cinnamon and cloves together. Add to the sugar mixture alternately with the milk mixture, mixing after each addition. Beat at medium speed for 1 minute. Stir in the pecans.
♀ Pour into a greased and floured 10-inch tube pan. Bake for 40 minutes or until the cake tests done.
♀ Cool the cake in the pan on a wire rack for 10 minutes. Invert the cake onto a serving plate. Pierce holes in the cake using a skewer or long slender knife.
♀ Blend the honey, water and lemon juice in a small bowl. Drizzle the honey mixture over the cake.

MAKES 1 CAKE

POUND CAKE

1 CUP BUTTER, SOFTENED
1/2 CUP SHORTENING OR ADDITIONAL BUTTER
3 CUPS SUGAR
5 EGGS
1 TEASPOON VANILLA EXTRACT
1/2 TEASPOON LEMON JUICE OR GRATED LEMON
    RIND
1/2 TEASPOON BAKING POWDER
1/8 TEASPOON SALT
1 CUP MILK
3 CUPS FLOUR, SIFTED 2 TIMES
1 CUP CHOPPED PECANS (OPTIONAL)

♀ Preheat the oven to 350 degrees.
♀ Cream the butter, shortening and sugar in a large bowl until light and fluffy.
♀ Add the eggs 1 at a time, beating well after each addition. Add the vanilla, lemon juice, baking powder and salt and beat until blended.
♀ Add the milk and flour 1/3 at a time, beating well after each addition. Fold in the pecans.
♀ Pour into greased and floured large loaf pan. Bake for 1 1/4 hours or until golden brown and a toothpick inserted in the center comes out clean.
♀ Cool in the pan on a wire rack for about 10 minutes. Remove to the wire rack to cool completely before cutting.

MAKES 1 CAKE

PUT GIRLS IN THE GAME

In 1972, Rep. Patsy Mink sponsored and NOW pressured Congress to pass Title IX—to prohibit sex discrimination and guarantee equal educational opportunities. At that time, very few opportunities existed for girls and women to participate in high school or college athletics.

Title IX has had a dramatic impact on women's athletics. More U.S. women, both individuals and teams, are competing in the Olympics and more are winning medals. Professional women's sports leagues are gaining in popularity. However, despite gains in participation, athletic equity is not a reality. As of 1997, the 25th anniversary of Title IX, for every $1 spent on women's college sports, $3 are spent on men's.

California NOW has filed suit several times at the state level to correct inequities in women's sports and won each time, broadening athletic opportunities for girls and women and ensuring that funding and scholarships are distributed equitably.

NIGHT OF JOY AND TEARS

A tidal wave of emotion had swept the cavernous interior of the Moscone Center. Congresswoman Barbara Kennelly, her face alight with a radiance and pride unparalleled in the history of nominating speeches, fairly shouted into the microphone, "I nominate! Geraldine Ferraro for Vice-President of the United States!"

The band was playing, and smiles and tears intermingled on people's faces as they kept up the jubilant chant, "We want Gerry! We want Gerry!"

It is the faces that are most memorable. The hundreds, thousands of faces, upturned toward the podium, shining with the joyous disbelief we had felt since Walter Mondale had made his historic choice one week before.

On that day—July 12, 1984—he had stood in the rotunda of the Minnesota state capitol and said, "I searched for the best vice-president, and I found her in Gerry Ferraro." The word "her" hung in the air like a new word, one we had never heard before.

We are prouder now of our endorsed candidate, Walter Mondale, than we have ever been, and of his extraordinary leadership

MOM'S DARK FRUITCAKE

1 POUND CANDIED FRUIT
1 (12-OUNCE) JAR MINCEMEAT
5 CUPS CHOPPED WALNUTS
3/4 CUP FLOUR
1 CUP SUGAR
1 TEASPOON SALT
3 EGGS
3/4 CUP PLUS 2 TEASPOONS VEGETABLE OIL
1 1/2 TEASPOONS BAKING SODA
2 TABLESPOONS BOILING WATER

♀ Preheat the oven to 300 degrees.
♀ Combine the candied fruit, mincemeat and walnuts in a large bowl and mix well.
♀ Sift the flour, sugar and salt together, add to the mincemeat mixture and mix well. Blend the eggs and oil together and stir into the mincemeat mixture.
♀ Dissolve the baking soda in boiling water and stir into the mincemeat mixture immediately. Pour into a waxed or parchment paper-lined tube pan.
♀ Bake at 300 degrees for 2 1/2 to 3 hours or until firm. Cool in the pan for about 10 minutes. Invert onto a wire rack, peel off the paper and let stand until completely cooled. Store in an airtight container.

MAKES 1 FRUITCAKE

AWAKENING CENTER CHICAGO CAKE

Margaret Waterstreet of the feminist center that deals with eating disorders submits this flourless, fudgy brownie-like cake that is especially appreciated by those allergic to gluten. It can be prepared up to a week in advance.

1 POUND UNSALTED BUTTER
18 OUNCES SEMISWEET CHOCOLATE
2¼ CUPS SUGAR
1 CUP STRONG BREWED COFFEE
9 EGGS

♀ Preheat the oven to 250 degrees.
♀ Melt the butter and chocolate in a large saucepan over medium heat, stirring constantly.
♀ Add the sugar and coffee and mix well. Heat until the sugar dissolves, stirring constantly. Remove from the heat.
♀ Whisk the eggs in a bowl until frothy. Stir a small amount of the hot mixture into the eggs; whisk the eggs into the hot mixture. Pour the mixture into a buttered 10-inch round cake pan. Bake for 2 hours or until firm.

MAKES 1 CAKE

(Night of Joy and Tears, continued)

in taking this bold and precedent-shattering step into the future.

For one glorious night, we celebrated. An all-out, joyful, exuberant, stomping, clapping, singing celebration. We let it sweep over us and we reveled in it. Victories like this one are few and far between in the fight for justice and equality.

NOW editorial, August 1984

NOW President Judy Goldsmith (far right) welcomes elected feminists to the 1984 NOW conference: (L to R) Irma Hunter Brown, Mary-Rose Oakar, Barbara Kennelly and Geraldine Ferraro.

ASKING THE HARD QUESTIONS

When conservatives were pushing for a Human Life Amendment prohibiting abortion, NOW pushed for answers on the effect of "life begins at conception"—

Taxes: When would the fetus be counted as a dependent for tax purposes—from the moment of conception? How far could and would the IRS go to verify the pregnancy? Would Medicaid be available to fetuses? And child support?

Immigration Laws: What would be the citizenship status of a fetus? Could the fetus be a person and not a citizen? Would all children conceived by non-citizens in the U.S. be citizens? Could a pregnant woman who is not a citizen be deported when she is carrying a citizen fetus?

Child Neglect: Could the state force the mother to comply with certain standards of care and activity for the protection of the fetus? Could a pregnant woman be jailed for smoking? For drinking coffee?

CHOCOLATE FUDGE UPSIDE-DOWN CAKE

This kids-delight cake magically ends up with cake on the top and makes its own sauce on the bottom.

1/2 CUP SUGAR
1 TABLESPOON BUTTER, SOFTENED
1/2 CUP MILK
1 CUP FLOUR
1/4 TEASPOON SALT
1 TEASPOON BAKING POWDER
2 TABLESPOONS BAKING COCOA
1/2 CUP CHOPPED WALNUTS (OPTIONAL)
1/2 CUP SUGAR
1/2 CUP PACKED BROWN SUGAR
1/4 CUP BAKING COCOA
1 1/4 CUPS BOILING WATER

♀ Preheat the oven to 350 degrees.
♀ Cream 1/2 cup sugar with butter in a bowl. Blend in the milk.
♀ Sift the flour, salt, baking powder and 2 tablespoons baking cocoa together. Add to the milk mixture and mix well. Spread the mixture evenly in a buttered 9x9-inch baking pan.
♀ Sprinkle the walnuts over the batter. Mix the remaining 1/2 cup sugar, brown sugar and 1/4 cup cocoa in a bowl and sprinkle over the batter. Drizzle the boiling water over all.
♀ Bake for 30 minutes. Cool in the pan.

MAKES 6 KID-SIZE PORTIONS

WALNUT TORTE

8 OUNCES WALNUTS, FINELY GROUND
2 TABLESPOONS FINE DRY BREAD CRUMBS OR FLOUR
1/2 OUNCE UNSWEETENED BAKING CHOCOLATE,
    GRATED OR 1 TABLESPOON (HEAPING)
    BAKING COCOA
1 TABLESPOON INSTANT COFFEE POWDER
1 CUP SUGAR
6 EGGS, SEPARATED
SWEETENED WHIPPED CREAM
WALNUT HALVES

♀ Preheat the oven to 350 degrees.

♀ Combine the walnuts, bread crumbs, baking chocolate and coffee powder in a bowl and mix well.

♀ Beat the sugar and egg yolks together in a bowl until thick and lemon-colored. Beat the egg whites in a large bowl until stiff peaks form.

♀ Fold the egg yolk mixture and the walnut mixture into the stiffly beaten egg whites gently. Pour the mixture into 2 greased layer cake pans.

♀ Bake for 25 minutes or until the layers are golden brown and spring back when lightly touched. Cool in the pans on wire racks for several minutes. Remove to wire racks to cool completely.

♀ Spread the whipped cream between the layers and over the top and side of the torte just before serving. Garnish with walnut halves.

MAKES 1 TORTE

WHAT DO THESE HAVE IN COMMON?

The Fair Labor Standards Act
The G.I. Bill (1944)
The Equal Pay Act
The bill that created the Fair Employment Practices Commission
Tax deductions for child care expenses
Federal aid to education
The national network of veterans hospitals
Title IX, the law against sex discrimination in education
Federal Funds for the education of children with disabilities
The School Lunch Program
The Fair Credit Protection Act

These are just a few examples of the important social legislation that came from the few women who have served in Congress. If women did all this with less than 5% of Congress, think what we could do with 50%

—from the Feminist Majority's 1991 publication *Feminization of Power*

YOU GOTTA LAUGH

Ohio NOW chapter members transformed themselves into "Ladies Against Women" (LAW) and organized a rally when arch conservative Phyllis Schlafly spoke in Cleveland in 1982.

Sporting hats and white gloves for the occasion, about 75 women gathered at the club where Schlafly was speaking. They waved signs reading, "Suffering Not Suffrage," "Sperm Are People Too," "You're Nobody Till You're Mrs. Somebody," and "Fifty-Nine Cents Is Too Damn Much."

The liberal spoof of the conservative women's organizations continued its activities in 1984, with white-gloved, be-hatted members holding a bake sale outside the Republican Convention which nominated Reagan for his second term. The ladies sold Twinkies for $9 million apiece, with proceeds going to retire the national debt.

YUM YUM CAKE

During the food-rationing days of World War II, this was a popular cake because it was butterless and eggless. It is returning to popularity today because it is cholesterol-free and considered healthy.

2 CUPS WATER
1 (15-OUNCE) PACKAGE RAISINS
1 TABLESPOON BAKING SODA
2 CUPS SUGAR
1 TEASPOON GROUND CINNAMON
1 TEASPOON GROUND CLOVES
1 TEASPOON GROUND NUTMEG
1/2 CUP SHORTENING (CAN USE BUTTER OR MARGARINE)
1 CUP COLD WATER
4 CUPS FLOUR

♀ Preheat the oven to 350 degrees.

♀ Bring the water to a boil in a saucepan. Add the raisins. Simmer for 10 minutes, stirring occasionally. Remove from the heat and stir in the baking soda. Let stand until cool.

♀ Combine the sugar, spices and shortening in a bowl and mix well. Stir in the raisins. Add the cold water and mix well.

♀ Add the flour 1 cup at time, mixing well after each addition. Pour into greased and floured tube pan. Bake for 1 hour and 25 minutes or until the cake tests done.

♀ Cool in the pan on a wire rack for about 10 minutes. Invert onto the wire rack to cool completely.

MAKES 1 CAKE

THE LADIES AGAINST WOMEN TWINKOID RECIPE

Gail Ann Williams, who sent this recipe, reminded us to "always dedicate your recipes. This one is to the health and values of the Reagan Revolution." You can tell because of those ingredients: "white sugar, white flour, white power."

1 GENERIC RECTANGULAR SUPERMARKET
   ANGELFOOD CAKE
1 TUB ARTIFICIAL TOPPING MIX
1/4 JAR POWDERED NON-DAIRY COFFEE WHITENER
   (OR CORN STARCH—EASIER TO CLEAN UP)

♀ Take one generic rectangular angel food cake, remove wrapper. Using kitchen shears, trim off the crust and discard. You probably know the approximate dimensions of a Twinkie, so this may be done by eye. Open it up and lob in some quality whipped topping substance. You already have a reasonable treat, but you may find there is something missing. For that inimitable metallic sensation on the palate, dust with a healthy dash of non-dairy latex coffee whitener. If you coat it with a brand name spray disinfectant, it may be able to rival the shelf life of the original. Wrap in clingy plastic, and finally, avoid the microwave and place in a conventional oven, so it can be self-sealing as it bakes.

(You Gotta Laugh, continued)

LAW also promoted sexual inequality, with a *Bench Your Daughter Award* to President Reagan for his success in increasing sex discrimination in school athletic programs. Slogans of LAW ladies: "Gold Rings, Not Gold Medals," "Pump Iron, Do His Shirts," and "Brooms, Not Basketballs."

Ladies Against Women strike again.

LADIES AND GENTLEMEN OF THE JURY . . .

In 1989, the Supreme Court handed down a series of decisions that virtually gutted Title VII, the law that prohibits discrimination in employment. NOW saw an opportunity to make a breakthrough for women in the coalition effort to put teeth back into the law.

NOW demanded and won the inclusion of two key items for sex discrimination and sexual harassment cases: (1) a trial by jury and (2) compensation for damages—remedies that were already available for race discrimination. Although Congress reinforced our second-class status by capping punitive damages at $300,000, these changes in the Civil Rights Act of 1991 forced employers to take women's cases seriously—or pay the price.

CHOCOLATE CHERRY NUGGETS

MARASCHINO CHERRIES
2 CUPS MARGARINE, SOFTENED
2 CUPS CONFECTIONERS' SUGAR
2 TEASPOONS VANILLA OR ALMOND EXTRACT
1/2 TEASPOON SALT
4 1/2 CUPS FLOUR
2 CUPS SEMISWEET CHOCOLATE CHIPS
1/2 CUP CHOPPED PECANS

♀ Preheat the oven to 350 degrees.
♀ Drain and chop enough maraschino cherries to yield 1/2 cup, reserving the cherry juice. Set the cherries aside.
♀ Cream the margarine in a large bowl. Add the confectioners' sugar gradually, creaming well. Beat in the vanilla or almond extract, salt and enough of the reserved cherry juice to tint the dough as desired.
♀ Add the flour gradually, mixing well; the dough will be stiff. Mix in the chocolate chips, pecans and chopped cherries.
♀ Drop the dough by rounded teaspoonfuls about 2 inches apart on ungreased cookie sheets and flatten slightly with fingertips.
♀ Bake for 15 minutes or until light golden brown. Cool on the cookie sheets for 1 minute and remove to wire racks to cool completely.

MAKES 3 TO 4 DOZEN

Choco Chip Squares

1 (1-POUND) PACKAGE LIGHT BROWN SUGAR
$3/4$ CUP MELTED MARGARINE
$2^3/4$ CUPS FLOUR
$1/4$ TEASPOON SALT
4 EGGS
1 TEASPOON VANILLA EXTRACT
1 TABLESPOON LIGHT CORN SYRUP
1 CUP CHOCOLATE CHIPS

♀ Preheat the oven to 350 degrees.
♀ Blend the brown sugar and melted butter in a large bowl.
♀ Mix the flour and salt together in a bowl. Add to the brown sugar mixture 1 cup at a time, alternating with the eggs; mix well. Add in the vanilla and corn syrup. Stir in the chocolate chips.
♀ Spread the mixture in a greased 9x13-inch baking pan. Bake for 40 minutes. Cool in the pan on a wire rack. Cut into squares

MAKES 2 DOZEN

♀ *Eating is not merely a material pleasure. Eating well gives a spectacular joy to life and contributes immensely to goodwill and happy companionship. It is of great importance to the morale.*

Elsa Schiaparelli, 1954

Not Just Sticks and Stones . . .

Despite an increase in bias-motivated crimes, including the 1997 bombing of a lesbian bar in Atlanta, the federal government does not have jurisdiction to investigate or prosecute offenses motivated by a person's real or perceived sex or sexual orientation. NOW has been working for years to change this situation.

In coalition with other civil rights organizations, NOW urged Congress to amend section 245 of Title 18 of the U.S. Criminal Code to include prosecution of hate crimes motivated by gender, sexual orientation or disability. This has been NOW's position since 1989 but was only adopted by the coalition in 1997, in part because of the Atlanta bombing.

An engineering school in Montreal was the site of a heavily-reported hate crime in 1989 when a gunman shouting epithets against women moved the men and women into separate corners of a room, and murdered all 14 women. In 1998 in Jonesboro, Arkansas, a jilted middle-schooler and his friend targeted girls on the playground, killing four girls and a female teacher, and injuring 10 others.

CHANGING TIMES

In 1964, Maine Senator Margaret Chase Smith announced herself as a serious candidate for president, and even the women in the audience at the Women's National Press Club chuckled. The response was quite different in 1984, when Geraldine Ferraro ran as the vice presidential candidate with Walter Mondale.

NOW's political action committee (NOW/PAC), formed in 1976 to raise funds and support feminist candidates, has helped change the political landscape. As we advocate for women's rights, electing feminists is a crucial part of our strategy.

NOW/PAC's 1992 "Elect Women for a Change" coordinated campaign helped double the representation of women in Congress from five to ten percent.

It was a direct result of our ten-year commitment, after the failure of the ERA ratification drive, to fill the pipeline with feminists at the state and local level.

GRANDMA FRAHM'S HAYSTACKS

The original recipe for this no-bake cookie is from the great grandmother of Shirley Anne Evenson of Cumberland, Wisconsin. Shirley has vivid memories of Great Grandma Frahm, 93 years young, up fixing her roof because the "repairmen didn't do a good job!" The variation is Shirley's adaptation for her daughter who is allergic to dairy products and chocolate.

2 CUPS SUGAR
1/2 CUP MARGARINE
1/2 CUP EVAPORATED MILK
6 TABLESPOONS BAKING COCOA
1 TEASPOON VANILLA EXTRACT
3 CUPS ROLLED OATS
1 CUP COCONUT

♀ Combine the sugar, margarine and evaporated milk in a large saucepan. Bring to a boil, stirring constantly. Boil for 3 minutes, stirring constantly.

♀ Remove from the heat. Add the cocoa, vanilla, oats and coconut and mix well. Drop by spoonfuls onto a greased surface. Let stand until firm.

VARIATION:

♀ Substitute condensed soy milk for the evaporated milk and carob powder for the cocoa.

MAKES 3 TO 4 DOZEN

AUNT EXA'S PRALINE BARS

3 EGGS
1 (1-POUND) PACKAGE LIGHT BROWN SUGAR
1 TABLESPOON VANILLA EXTRACT
2 CUPS GROUND PECANS OR WALNUTS
1 1/2 CUPS FLOUR
3/8 TEASPOON BAKING SODA
3/8 TEASPOON SALT

♀ Preheat the oven to 375 degrees.
♀ Beat the eggs in a large bowl. Add the brown sugar and beat until smooth. Add the vanilla and pecans and mix well.
♀ Sift the flour, baking soda and salt together. Add to the brown sugar mixture and mix well.
♀ Spread the mixture evenly in a greased and floured 10x15-inch baking pan. Bake for 18 to 20 minutes or until golden brown.
♀ Cool in the pan on a wire rack. Cut into bars.

MAKES 3 TO 4 DOZEN

(Changing Times, continued)

In 1997, NOW/PAC launched the "Victory 2000" campaign to elect 2000 feminists at all levels by the year 2000, positioning our candidates for another breakthrough in the next post-reapportionment/ redistricting elections in 2002.

Diane Feinstein and Barbara Boxer campaigning in 1992 to become the two senators from California. NOW signs read "Yes, you can vote for both." They were both elected.

"THERE HE IS... MISTER E.R.A."

This fun fundraiser by the Jefferson (Louisiana) NOW chapter was also a consciousness-raiser. The 1979 tongue-in-cheek program read:

"The winner, Mr. ERA America, *may* get by on his good looks. Yet . . . the lack of women in political office means that he can't count on marrying a rich Senator as Miss Georgia of 1970 did; and, with female corporation presidents so scarce, the poise and grooming that would make him the perfect corporate husband will likely be wasted. In addition, the low salaries women earn mean he may have to use his other talents to earn a living, even if his good looks DO catch him a wife."

The beauty pageant spoof raised awareness as well as funds for ERA ratification efforts.

AVOCADO LIME CHIFFON PIE

The pie is especially attractive in a flat French-style pie plate with a fluted edge but it is just as delicious in an American-style pie shell.

3 TABLESPOONS CORNSTARCH
3 TABLESPOONS LIGHT BROWN SUGAR
1/2 CUP MILK OR WATER
GRATED RIND AND JUICE OF 3 LIMES
4 EGG YOLKS, BEATEN
1 TABLESPOON UNFLAVORED GELATIN (OR AGAR IF VEGETARIAN)
1/4 CUP COLD WATER
1 MEDIUM AVOCADO, MASHED
2 EGG WHITES
3 TABLESPOONS LIGHT BROWN SUGAR
1 BAKED PIE SHELL

♀ Mix the cornstarch and 3 tablespoons brown sugar in a heavy saucepan. Add the milk and mix well. Blend in the lime rind, lime juice and egg yolks. Cook over medium heat until thickened, stirring constantly. Pour into a bowl to cool slightly.

♀ Soften the gelatin in the cold water. Combine with the mashed avocado and lime custard in a blender and process until smooth and creamy.

♀ Beat the egg whites until soft peaks form. Add the remaining brown sugar and whisk until well blended. Fold the avocado mixture into the egg white mixture gently. Pour into the cooled pie shell.

♀ Chill the pie until serving time. Garnish with whipped cream and lime slices.

MAKES 1 PIE

BRANDY PIE

1 TABLESPOON UNFLAVORED GELATIN
1/4 CUP COLD MILK
3 EGG YOLKS, SEPARATED
1/2 CUP SUGAR
1/3 CUP BRANDY
1/2 CUP HEAVY CREAM
1/8 TEASPOON SALT
1/4 TEASPOON GROUND NUTMEG
1/8 TEASPOON GROUND ALLSPICE
1/8 TEASPOON CINNAMON
1/3 CUP BRANDY OR MILK
3 EGG WHITES
1/4 CUP SUGAR
1 GINGERSNAP PIE SHELL (AT RIGHT)
1/2 CUP SEEDLESS RAISINS

♀ Soften the gelatin in 1/4 cup cold milk. Beat the egg yolks in a double boiler. Add 1/2 cup sugar, 1/3 cup brandy, cream, salt, spices and softened gelatin and mix well.

♀ Cook the mixture over hot (not boiling) water until the mixture thickens and coats the spoon, stirring constantly. Remove from the heat and blend in the additional 1/3 cup brandy or milk. Set aside to cool and thicken slightly.

♀ Beat the egg whites in a bowl until frothy. Add 1/4 cup sugar gradually, beating constantly until stiff but not dry peaks form. Fold the egg whites into the custard gently.

♀ Pour the mixture into the Gingersnap Pie Shell. Sprinkle the raisins on top. Chill until firm.

MAKES 1 PIE

GINGERSNAP PIE SHELL

4 CUPS GINGERSNAP CRUMBS (APPROX. 36 COOKIES)
1/4 CUP PACKED BROWN SUGAR
1/4 CUP BUTTER, SOFTENED
1/4 CUP BRANDY

♀ Preheat the oven to 375 degrees.
♀ Mix the gingersnap crumbs and brown sugar in a bowl. Cut in the butter until crumbly. Press over the bottom and side of a 9-inch pie plate, shaping a small rim.
♀ Sprinkle the brandy over the crumb mixture. Bake for 10 minutes. Let stand until completely cooled.

AUNT LOUELLA'S EGG CUSTARD PIE

1 1/2 CUPS SUGAR
1/4 CUP MELTED BUTTER OR MARGARINE
1 TEASPOON VANILLA EXTRACT
1 TABLESPOON FLOUR
5 EGGS
2 CUPS WHOLE MILK (SKIM MILK IS NOT AN
    ACCEPTABLE SUBSTITUTE)
2 UNBAKED PIE SHELLS
1 TEASPOON NUTMEG

♀ Preheat the oven to 450 degrees.

♀ Blend the sugar, butter and vanilla in bowl. Add the flour and mix well. Beat in the eggs 1 at a time. Blend in the milk gradually.

♀ Pour the mixture into the pie shells. Dust with the nutmeg. Bake at 450 degrees for 15 minutes. Reduce the temperature to 300 degrees. Bake for 30 minutes longer or until set.

♀ May omit the pie shells and bake the custard in a greased ovenproof dish.

MAKES 2 PIES

♀ *Whenever I have two evils to choose between, I always like to choose the one I've never tried before.*

Mae West

IMPOSSIBLE COCONUT TART

4 EGGS
1 CUP SUGAR
1/2 CUP FLOUR
1/4 TEASPOON SALT
1/4 TO 1/2 CUP MARGARINE, SOFTENED
2 CUPS MILK
1 TEASPOON ALMOND OR VANILLA EXTRACT
1 CUP FLAKED DRIED COCONUT

♀ Preheat the oven to 350 degrees.
♀ Combine the eggs, sugar, flour, salt, margarine, milk, almond extract and coconut in a blender container and process until well mixed.
♀ Pour the mixture into a buttered 10-inch pie plate. Bake for 1 hour or until firm.
VARIATION:
♀ Prepare as above adding 1/4 cup fresh lemon juice and the grated rind of 1 lemon.

MAKES 1 LARGE TART

FEMINISTS DISPLAY POLITICAL CLOUT

After a concerted effort by NOW and other women's organizations, the Democratic National Committee was forced to accede to our demand for equal representation. In 1980, for the first time ever, women composed 50% of the Democratic Convention's voting delegates. Despite heavy opposition, we made ourselves heard, supporting issues over candidates to pass the strongest Equal Rights Amendment and reproductive rights planks in political history.

NEW REPUBLICAN SYMBOL

Cincinnati NOW unveiled a new symbol for the Republican Party at a 1980 event. "Ron," a foot-long gopher tortoise, represented the regression of the Republican Party's platform after 40 years of supporting the Equal Rights Amendment.

Chapter President Elizabeth Richardson said, "The tortoise has remained in its present evolutionary state for millions of years, unable to change, just like the right-wing branch of the GOP. They pull their heads into their shells and refuse to recognize that a strong majority of Americans support the Equal Rights Amendment."

ALICE'S COOL DELIGHT FRUIT PIE

1 1/2 CUPS CUT UP FRESH FRUIT SUCH AS PEACHES, STRAWBERRIES OR BANANAS OR WELL-DRAINED CANNED CRUSHED PINEAPPLE
12 OUNCES WHIPPED TOPPING
1 GRAHAM CRACKER PIE SHELL
CINNAMON AND NUTMEG TO TASTE

♀ Fold the fruit and whipped topping together. Spoon into the pie shell. Sprinkle with cinnamon and nutmeg.
♀ Chill until serving time. Garnish with mint leaves or additional fruit.

MAKES 1 PIE

♀ *"How'd you become a homosexual?*
"First there's the talent competition, then the interview—swimsuit and evening gown pretty much get rid of the undesirables."
"Did you choose to be a homosexual?"
"No, I was chosen."

Suzanne Westenhoefer, feminist comic
headliner for NOW/PACs Party with a Purpose

FROZEN RASPBERRY PIE

2 EGG WHITES
1 (10-OUNCE) PACKAGE FROZEN RASPBERRIES,
   THAWED
1 TABLESPOON LEMON JUICE
3/4 CUP SUGAR
1/2 TEASPOON ALMOND EXTRACT
1 CUP WHIPPING CREAM, WHIPPED
1 COOKIE CRUMB PIE SHELL (AT RIGHT)

♀ Combine the egg whites, raspberries, lemon juice, sugar and almond extract in a large mixer bowl. Beat at medium speed for 5 minutes or until stiff peaks form. Fold in the whipped cream gently. Spoon into the cooled pie shell.
♀ Freeze for 4 hours or until firm. Let the pie stand at room temperature for 10 minutes before serving for easier cutting.

MAKES 1 PIE

♀ *We specialize in the wholly impossible.*
Nannie Helen Burroughs
Motto, National Training School for Girls,
Washington, DC (1909)

COOKIE CRUMB CRUST

1 1/4 CUPS FLOUR
3 TABLESPOONS SUGAR
1/4 TEASPOON SALT
1/4 CUP CHOPPED TOASTED
   ALMONDS OR UNSALTED
   SUNFLOWER KERNELS
1/2 CUP BUTTER, SOFTENED

♀ Preheat the oven to 400 degrees.
♀ Mix the flour, sugar, salt and almonds in a bowl. Add the butter and mix well. Press over the bottom and side of a 10-inch pie plate. Prick with a fork.
♀ Bake for 10 to 12 minutes. Let stand until completely cool.

SNAKES DON'T HAVE LEGS

When I was five and living in Indianapolis, Indiana, I got into a fight with a neighborhood girl named Cynthia Kay Locke. I was passionately defending the status quo.

"Mommy is a doctor!" she shrieked, indignantly. "She is!"

"Liar!"

"Am not!"

I could be perfectly reasonable up to a point, but Cynthia Kay had gone too far . . . Daddies could be doctors, mommies had to be nurses—everyone knew that. Snakes don't have legs . . . . I gave her a good shove, and she sprawled into the muddy water.

Cynthia Kay started crying. I ran for home. I didn't want to be there when her mother—who, I later learned, was indeed an M.D.—came out to see what all the fuss was about . . . .

I am still a fierce fighter for truth and justice, but I no longer · believe in shoving—and some of my ideas about women have changed.

Excerpt from *What Women Want* by Patricia Ireland (*photo opposite*), President of NOW (Dutton, 1996)

PECAN PIE

3 EGGS, LIGHTLY BEATEN
1 CUP DARK OR LIGHT CORN SYRUP
1 CUP SUGAR
1 TEASPOON VANILLA EXTRACT
2 TABLESPOON MELTED BUTTER
1 1/2 CUPS PECAN HALVES
1 UNBAKED (9-INCH) PIE SHELL

♀ Preheat the oven to 350 degrees.
♀ Combine the eggs, corn syrup, sugar and vanilla, mix well and let stand for 5 minutes. Blend in the melted butter.
♀ Arrange the pecan halves in the pie shell. Pour the egg mixture over the pecans. The pecans will rise to the top.
♀ Bake for 50 to 60 minutes or until almost firm.

VARIATIONS:
♀ Chocolate Pecan Pie: Decrease the sugar to 1/3 cup and add 4 ounces melted semisweet chocolate to the egg mixture. Bake as above.
♀ Two-Layer Pumpkin Pecan Pie: Mix 1 egg, 1 cup canned pumpkin, 1/3 cup sugar and a dash each of cinnamon, ginger and cloves and bake as above until firm.
♀ Blend 2 eggs, 2/3 cup dark or light corn syrup, 2/3 cup sugar, 2 tablespoons softened butter and 1/2 teaspoon vanilla in a bowl. Stir in 1 cup pecan halves. Spoon over the pumpkin layer. Bake as above.

MAKES 1 PIE

♀ *I am not afraid to trust my sisters—not I.*

Angelina Grimke

JUST DESSERTS
COBBLERS, PUDDINGS AND MORE

Those who carried the struggle for women's suffrage through to

its end were not there at the start; those who started the

struggle did not live to see the victory. Like those strong feminist

activists, we will not let ourselves be dispirited or discouraged.

Even when progress seems most elusive, we will maintain

our conviction that the work itself is important. For it is the

work that enriches our lives; it is the work that unites us;

it is the work that will propel us into the next century. We

know that our struggle has made a difference, and we

reaffirm our faith that it will continue to make a difference

for women's lives. We dedicate ourselves to the sheer

joy of moving forward and fighting back.

PICTURED ON OVERLEAF: *NOW President Patricia Ireland in
front of the United States Supreme Court in 1993, protesting the
Court's judgment in a case brought by NOW. That decision
refused to allow the use of civil rights laws to protect against
anti-abortion terrorism. Two months after the decision, Dr. David
Gunn was murdered outside of a Pensacola, Florida, clinic.*

JOSEPHINE'S CHOCOLATE CHEESECAKE

24 OUNCES CREAM CHEESE, SOFTENED
3/4 CUP SUGAR
3 EGGS
4 OUNCES GERMAN'S SWEET CHOCOLATE
2 TABLESPOONS HEAVY CREAM
1 CUP SOUR CREAM
1/4 CUP STRONG BLACK COFFEE, COOLED
1/4 CUP ALMOND LIQUEUR
2 TEASPOONS. VANILLA EXTRACT
CHOCOLATE CRUMB CRUST (AT RIGHT)

♀ Preheat the oven to 350 degrees.
♀ Beat the cream cheese in a bowl until fluffy. Add the sugar gradually, beating constantly. Add the eggs 1 at a time, beating well after each addition.
♀ Melt the chocolate with the heavy cream in a small saucepan over low heat, stirring constantly. Cool slightly and blend into the cream cheese mixture. Add the sour cream, coffee, liqueur and vanilla and beat until smooth and creamy. Pour the mixture into the Chocolate Crumb Crust. Bake for 45 to 55 minutes or until the edges are set. Let stand at room temperature until cool.
♀ Chill for 12 hours to overnight. Place on a serving plate and remove the side of the pan. Garnish with chocolate curls and whipped cream.

MAKES 1 LARGE CHEESECAKE

CHOCOLATE CRUMB CRUST

1 (8-OUNCE) CHOCOLATE
   WAFER COOKIES,
   CRUSHED
2 TABLESPOONS SUGAR
1/2 TEASPOON CINNAMON
1/4 CUP MELTED BUTTER

♀ Mix the cookie crumbs, sugar and cinnamon in a bowl. Add the butter and mix until the mixture clings together. Press over the bottom and side of a buttered 9-inch springform pan. Chill until firm.

2000 Pray for ERA

The New York Avenue Presbyterian Church overflowed with participants in the National Prayer Vigil sponsored by the Religious Committee for the Equal Rights Amendment. The congregation, many in Suffragist white, joined religious and lay leaders of many denominations in a Litany of Struggle, a Litany of Liberation, and a rededication to working for the ERA.

The first text was from Exodus 13:14: "By sheer power, God delivered us."

Then a tie to the movement for equality: "Because women's anger and disappointment have been transformed into productive energy, the light of liberation rises," followed by the lighting of candles held by each person in the congregation.

The call to commitment was issued by the Reverend Delores J. Moss, "We have heard the call to justice and equality, and we will never back down!" "Amen!" came the response.

Amaretto Mousse Cheesecake

2 CUPS GRAHAM CRACKER CRUMBS
1/2 CUP MELTED BUTTER
1 ENVELOPE UNFLAVORED GELATIN
1/2 CUP COLD WATER
24 OUNCES CREAM CHEESE, SOFTENED
1 1/4 CUPS SUGAR
1 CUP EVAPORATED MILK
1 TEASPOON LEMON JUICE
1/3 CUP AMARETTO
1 TEASPOON VANILLA EXTRACT
3/4 CUP WHIPPING CREAM, WHIPPED

♀ Mix the crumbs with melted butter in a bowl. Press over the bottom and up the side of a 9-inch springform pan. Chill until firm.

♀ Soften the gelatin in the cold water in a small saucepan for 1 minute. Heat over low heat until the gelatin dissolves completely, stirring constantly. Remove from the heat.

♀ Beat the cream cheese and sugar in a large bowl for 2 minutes or until light and fluffy. Beat in the evaporated milk and lemon juice. Beat at medium-high speed for 2 minutes or until very light and fluffy.

♀ Add the gelatin mixture, amaretto and vanilla gradually, beating until well blended. Fold in the whipped cream gently. Pour into the prepared springform pan. Chill for 8 hours to overnight.

♀ Place on a serving plate and remove the side of the pan. Serve with chocolate sauce and/or fresh berries.

MAKES 1 LARGE CHEESECAKE

LEMON CHEESECAKES

32 OUNCES CREAM CHEESE, SOFTENED
3 EGGS
1 CUP (OR LESS) SUGAR
JUICE AND GRATED RIND OF 1/2 LEMON
2 GRAHAM CRACKER PIE SHELLS
2 CUPS SOUR CREAM
2 TABLESPOONS SUGAR
1 TEASPOON VANILLA EXTRACT

♀ Preheat the oven to 350 degrees.
♀ Beat the cream cheese in a bowl until fluffy. Add the eggs and sugar and beat until smooth and creamy. Blend in the lemon juice and rind. Divide the batter between the graham cracker pie shells.
♀ Bake for 30 to 40 minutes or until almost firm.
♀ Blend the sour cream, 2 tablespoons sugar and vanilla in a bowl. Pour over the partially baked cheesecakes.
♀ Increase the oven temperature to 425 degrees. Bake for 10 minutes longer.
♀ Cool the cheesecakes on wire racks. Refrigerate until serving time.

MAKES 2 MEDIUM CHEESECAKES

Ellie Smeal, NOW President, fires up the crowd at the 1978 National March for the ERA. Nancy Klimas (FL) and Donna Miller (NJ) hold banners.

SYRUP

1 CUP SUGAR
2 CUPS WATER
1/4 CUP BUTTER
1/4 TEASPOON GROUND
    CINNAMON

♀ Combine the sugar, water, butter and cinnamon in a saucepan. Bring to a boil, stirring until the sugar dissolves, stirring constantly. Boil for 3 minutes.

PENNSYLVANIA APPLE DUMPLING

2 1/4 CUPS FLOUR
3/4 TEASPOON SALT
3/4 CUP SHORTENING
5 TABLESPOONS WATER
6 APPLES, PEELED, CORED
1 1/2 CUPS SUGAR
3 TABLESPOONS GROUND CINNAMON
6 TABLESPOONS BUTTER
SYRUP (AT LEFT)

♀ Preheat the oven to 375 degrees.
♀ Sift the flour and salt into a bowl. Cut in the shortening until crumbly. Sprinkle with the water and mix with a fork until the mixture clings together. Divide into 6 portions.
♀ Cover with plastic wrap and let rest for 30 minutes or longer. Roll each portion into a rectangle. Place an apple in the center and fill the core with 1/4 cup sugar and 1 1/2 teaspoons cinnamon. Add 1 tablespoon butter, moisten the pastry edges with a small amount of water and press the edges together to enclose the apple.
♀ Arrange the wrapped apples 2 inches apart in a baking pan. Pour the Syrup over the dumplings. Bake for 30 minutes or until brown and bubbling.

MAKES 6 DUMPLINGS

MICROWAVE APPLE CRISP

6 CUPS SLICED PEELED APPLES
1/4 CUP APPLE JUICE OR WATER
1/2 CUP SUGAR
1/2 CUP PACKED BROWN SUGAR
1/2 CUP FLOUR
1/2 CUP QUICK-COOKING OATS
1/2 TEASPOON GROUND NUTMEG
1 TEASPOON GROUND CINNAMON
1/4 CUP BUTTER OR MARGARINE

♀ Butter a round microwave-safe tube pan. Place the apples in the pan and drizzle with the apple juice.
♀ Combine the sugars, flour, oats and spices in a bowl. Cut in the butter until crumbly. Sprinkle the oats mixture over the apples.
♀ Microwave, uncovered, on High for 14 to 16 minutes or until the apples are tender, rotating the pan once.
♀ Serve with ice cream or whipped cream.

SERVES 10 TO 12

♀ *In education, in marriage, in religion, in everything, disappointment is the lot of women. It shall be the business of my life to deepen this disappointment in every woman's heart until she bows down to it no longer.*

Lucy Stone, suffragist

CHURCH SURRENDERS

Liberating itself from hundreds of years of clerical sexism, in September, 1976, the Episcopal Church General Convention cleared the way for ordination of women to the priesthood. Members of NOW's Women and Religion Task Force had come from across the country to celebrate street liturgies outside the doors of the Minneapolis meeting.

The vote to permit ordination of women as priests was precipitated by the earlier irregular ordination of 15 women priests, among them the Rev. Betty Bone Schiess, former National Coordinator of the NOW Task Force, and the Rev. Alison Cheek, who had blessed the NOW 100 Mile Walk for Equality from Alexandria to Richmond, Virginia in 1975.

Rev. Pauli Murray, a NOW founder and co-author of NOW's Statement of Purpose, was the first African-American woman to be ordained an Episcopal priest.

BERRY BOMBE

Use a narrow bowl with high sloping sides for this attractive dessert. It is best made during the height of the summer fresh berry season but failing that, frozen berries will do.

30 LADYFINGERS
2 POUNDS MIXED BLACKBERRIES, RASPBERRIES,
    STRAWBERRIES, BLUEBERRIES, CHOPPED PLUMS,
    CRANBERRIES, RED OR BLACK GRAPES
1/2 CUP (APPROX.) PACKED LIGHT BROWN SUGAR
1 TABLESPOON UNFLAVORED GELATIN OR AGAR

♀ Use about 24 of the ladyfingers to line the bottom and side of the bowl, cutting and fitting as necessary and reserve any trimmings.

♀ Combine the fruit, brown sugar and gelatin in a large saucepan. Crush the fruit lightly and let stand until the gelatin softens. Bring the fruit mixture to a simmer over medium heat and simmer for about 10 minutes. Cool slightly and spoon into the ladyfinger-lined bowl.

♀ Arrange the remaining ladyfingers and trimmings over the top to cover the fruit. Add a cover of waxed paper and weight with a plate. Chill overnight.

♀ Remove the weight and waxed paper. Place a serving plate upside down on top, hold plate and bowl together firmly and invert, allowing the bombe to unmold from the bowl.

♀ Garnish with additional fruit and serve with whipped cream.

SERVES 12 TO 16

BERRY CLAFOUTI
Raspberries make it the berry, berry best.

3 EGGS
1¼ CUPS MILK
²⁄₃ CUP FLOUR
¹⁄₃ CUP SUGAR
2 TEASPOONS VANILLA EXTRACT
¼ TEASPOON GROUND NUTMEG
⅛ TEASPOON SALT
1½ CUPS FAVORITE BERRIES

♀ Preheat the oven to 350 degrees.
♀ Beat the eggs in a bowl until frothy. Add the milk, flour, sugar, vanilla, nutmeg and salt and beat at low speed until smooth.
♀ Pour into a buttered 9-inch quiche pan or pie plate. Spoon the berries on top.
♀ Bake for 45 minutes or until a knife inserted in the center comes out clean.
♀ Serve hot, cold or at room temperature.

SERVES 6 TO 8

♀ *One can never consent to creep when one feels an impulse to soar.*

Helen Keller

THE GENDER BIAS BAKERY

Pastrie$ with a Point

The Palos Verdes/South Bay (CA) Chapter of NOW held a bake sale to illustrate the issue of gender-based pay inequities. They offered brownies, cookies, muffins and tarts with a built-in price differential: Women paid only $0.75 each, but men paid $1.00— reflecting the amount of money a woman working full-time receives for every dollar earned by a man, according to recent statistics from the Department of Labor.

The aim of the Gender Bias Bakery was not to penalize men who make more than women, but to stimulate discussion about the demonstrated unfairness of this current method of doing business, while pointing out that it contributes to a general devaluation of women by society. The action was not about men and their wages, but rather about women and their *lack* of wages.

MAD COW DISEASE STRIKES MISSOURI

Missouri NOW leaders held an emergency meeting in 1997 to draft a response to COW, the Conservative Organization for Women, a newly formed legislative caucus of the Missouri House of Representatives. COW founders described it as a semi-serious spoof of NOW, that ultraliberal National Organization for Women.

Missouri NOW leaders responded: "Hey! We think COW is udderly ridiculous," said Karen Johnson, Communications Director of Missouri NOW.

COW founder, Representative LuAnn Ridgeway, reportedly stated that COWs are secure in their femininity, yet 18 of the 28 are men. NOW members wondered if this was an early sign of hoof and mouth disease.

"We noted with interest that there are more men than women in the group," said Legislative Coordinator Mary Mosley. "Have these men been cowed or is this organization just a bunch of bull?"

CHERRY CRUMBLE

1 (21-OUNCE) CAN CHERRY PIE FILLING
LEMON JUICE TO TASTE
1/4 TEASPOON GROUND CINNAMON
3/4 CUP FLOUR
1/2 TEASPOON SALT
6 TABLESPOONS SUGAR
6 TABLESPOONS UNSALTED BUTTER

♀ Preheat the oven to 350 degrees.
♀ Pour the pie filling into a buttered 8-inch square baking pan. Sprinkle with lemon juice and cinnamon.
♀ Combine the flour, salt, sugar and butter in a bowl and mix until crumbly. Sprinkle over the pie filling.
♀ Bake for 40 minutes. Serve warm with a scoop of vanilla ice cream or frozen yogurt.

SERVES 9 TO 12

♀ *There are two kinds of people, those who do the work and those who take the credit. Try to be in the first group; there is less competition there.*

Indira Gandhi

MICKEY'S RHUBARB COBBLER

4 CUPS 1/2-INCH PIECES RHUBARB
1 CUP (APPROX.) SUGAR
1/3 CUP BAKING MIX OR PANCAKE MIX
1 TEASPOON GRATED LEMON RIND
STRAWBERRIES OR BLUEBERRIES (OPTIONAL)
3/4 CUP BAKING MIX OR PANCAKE MIX
2/3 CUP SUGAR
1 EGG, BEATEN
1/4 CUP MELTED BUTTER OR MARGARINE

♀ Preheat the oven to 350 degrees.
♀ Combine the rhubarb, 1 cup sugar, 1/3 cup baking mix and lemon rind in a bowl and mix well. Stir in the berries. Place in a 9-inch square baking pan.
♀ Combine the 3/4 cup baking mix, 2/3 cup sugar and egg in a bowl and mix until crumbly. Sprinkle over the rhubarb mixture. Drizzle the butter over the top.
♀ Bake for 35 minutes or until golden brown and the rhubarb is tender. Serve with cream or ice cream.

SERVES 6

♀ *We don't need to have someone else represent us. We can represent outselves.*

Hon. Shirley Chisholm

(Mad Cow Disease Strikes Missouri, continued)

"Are these men riding herd on the women?" asked State Coordinator Minerva Glidden. "Are these women cowards? Perhaps they could be steered in a different direction."

COW did not announce its agenda, but NOW hopes it will support legislation requiring insurance coverage for mastectomies and permitting breastfeeding in public.

However, NOW does not wish to leave the impression that it is not taking COW seriously. Remembering the damage done by Mrs. O'Leary's cow, NOW hopes these COWs will watch their step lest their actions have unintended consequences.

For the present, NOW has no beef with COW. But if COW becomes a threat to the rights of Missouri women, NOW members may become cowpunchers. NOW has been in existence for over 30 years and we expect to be here at least until the COWs come home.

BREAD PUDDING

3 TABLESPOONS MELTED MARGARINE
1 LOAF STALE FRENCH BREAD, CUBED OR BROKEN
   INTO PIECES
1 CUP RAISINS
4 CUPS MILK
2 CUPS SUGAR
3 EGGS, BEATEN
2 TABLESPOONS VANILLA EXTRACT
1/2 TEASPOON SALT
BOURBON SAUCE

♀ Preheat the oven to 350 degrees.
♀ Butter a large casserole generously with the melted butter. Place the bread and raisins in the prepared casserole.
♀ Mix the milk, sugar, eggs, vanilla and salt in a large bowl. Pour over the bread and raisins and mix lightly.
♀ Bake for 45 minutes or until a knife inserted in the center comes out clean. Serve hot or warm with the Bourbon Sauce.

BOURBON SAUCE

1/2 CUP BUTTER
1 EGG YOLK
1 CUP SUGAR
1 (12-OUNCE) CAN SWEETENED CONDENSED MILK
3 JIGGERS BOURBON

♀ Combine the butter, egg yolk, sugar and condensed milk in a double boiler over hot water. Mix well and cook until thickened, stirring constantly. Stir in the bourbon.
♀ Serve warm over any plain cake or pudding.

SERVES 6 TO 8

FAILURE-IS-IMPOSSIBLE CREAM PUFFS

1 CUP WATER
$^{1}/_{2}$ CUP BUTTER
1 CUP FLOUR
4 EGGS, AT ROOM TEMPERATURE
1 (4-OUNCE) PACKAGE INSTANT PUDDING

♀ Preheat the oven to 400 degrees.
♀ Bring the water and butter to a boil in a 2-quart saucepan. Remove from the heat. Add the flour all at once and stir for 1 minute or until the mixture forms a ball. Add the eggs 1 at a time, beating well after each addition. Beat until smooth and glossy. Drop by walnut-size balls onto an ungreased baking sheet, leaving space between. Bake for 45 minutes or until golden brown and dry to the touch. Remove from the baking sheet to a wire rack to cool completely. Cut off the tops with a sharp knife. Scoop out and discard any soggy centers.
♀ Prepare the pudding according to package directions; may substitute sugar-free instant pudding. Spoon into the puffs, replace the tops and serve immediately.

MAKES 12 TO 20

This Body Shop campaign focused attention on the size difference between models and the rest of us.

There are 3 billion women who don't look like supermodels and only 8 who do.

THE BODY SHOP

LET THE WOMAN SPEAK!

Following 1975 news reports that First Lady Betty Ford and Happy Rockefeller, wife of former New York Governor Nelson Rockefeller, had both had radical mastectomies, NOW President Karen DeCrow wrote the following editorial:

"It is time for some feminist (indeed, human) protest about what is happening to Betty Ford and Happy Rockefeller.

"How do we know that these women consented to having their private medical histories announced on TV? In Ms. Rockefeller's case, her husband was holding a news conference before she came out of post-op. It is possible we knew she had cancer before she did. When she emerged from the hospital, it was her husband who told the cameras: Happy is a wonderful woman; she is doing fine. She never said a word.

CHOCOLATE CREME BRULEE

1 TABLESPOON UNSALTED BUTTER, MELTED
2 OUNCES SEMISWEET CHOCOLATE, CHOPPED
5 EGG YOLKS
1/2 CUP SUGAR
2 CUPS WHIPPING CREAM
1 TABLESPOON VANILLA EXTRACT (OPTIONAL)
1/4 CUP PACKED BROWN SUGAR

♀ Preheat the oven to 275 degrees.

♀ Brush 6 ramekins or custard cups generously with the melted butter. Place the ramekins in a glass baking dish. Sprinkle the chocolate evenly in the ramekins.

♀ Whisk the egg yolks in a bowl until thick and lemon-colored. Add the sugar and whisk until dissolved. Add the whipping cream and vanilla and whisk until well blended. Pour the mixture carefully into the prepared ramekins.

♀ Pour warm water into the baking dish to half the depth of the ramekins. Bake, uncovered, for 40 to 45 minutes or until barely set. Remove from the oven and let the ramekins stand in the water until cooled to room temperature. Cover the ramekins with plastic wrap and chill for 2 hours or longer.

♀ Spread the brown sugar in a small baking pan and place in the warm, but turned off, oven for 20 minutes or until the brown sugar is dry. Place the brown sugar in a plastic bag and crush very fine with a rolling pin.

♀ Preheat the broiler and place an oven rack at the second highest position. Place the ramekins in a baking pan, sprinkle each with 2 teaspoons of the dry brown sugar and broil for 2 to 3 minutes or until the brown sugar is brittle.

♀ Cool for 5 minutes or chill for 30 minutes. Do not refrigerate for more than 1 hour after adding the topping.

SERVES 6

ORANGE FLAN

1¹/₄ CUPS SUGAR
¹/₈ TEASPOON SALT
2 TEASPOONS VANILLA EXTRACT
FINELY GRATED RIND OF 1 ORANGE
7 EGGS
¹/₂ CUP COLD MILK
1 (12-OUNCE) CAN EVAPORATED MILK
1¹/₂ CUPS HOT WATER

♀ Preheat the oven to 325 degrees.
♀ Caramelize ³/₄ cup sugar in a small nonstick skillet. Pour the caramelized sugar into bottom of a baking dish or bundt pan and rotate to coat the bottom.
♀ Combine the remaining ¹/₂ cup sugar, salt, vanilla, orange rind and eggs in a bowl and beat until well blended. Blend in the cold milk, evaporated milk and hot water. Pour into the prepared baking dish carefully.
♀ Place the baking dish in a larger pan and add an inch or two of warm water to the pan.
♀ Bake for 1 hour and 20 minutes or until a knife inserted in the center comes out clean.
♀ Let stand at room temperature until completely cooled. Refrigerate until completely chilled.
♀ Set the casserole in a pan of hot water for 20 to 30 seconds to loosen. Place a serving plate upside down on the casserole, hold both plate and casserole together firmly and invert quickly. Remove the casserole carefully.

SERVES 12

(Let the Woman Speak, continued)

"Can you imagine Bella Abzug leading Martin out of the hospital, announcing he had his left testicle removed, but that he was a wonderful man and doing fine? (It would never happen; she is too much the civil libertarian.)"

In 1986 Betty Ford served as honorary co-chair of NOW's 20th Anniversary celebration, along with Pat Nixon, Rosalyn Carter, and Lady Bird Johnson.

Boys Will Be Boys? Not!

During 1997, many reports affirmed the toughness of military service. Not only is it a demanding job, but military women were coming forward in record numbers with serious allegations of sexual misconduct.

NOW demanded an outside investigation and enforcement of "zero tolerance" for harassment and discrimination. NOW Vice President Karen Johnson, a retired Air Force Lieutenant Colonel, spoke out against the sleazy tactics that further victimize women who file complaints:

"Lesbian-baiting is often used to portray women as man-haters who make up stories," Johnson said. "It is used to discredit the

Rice Custard

1 CUP SUGAR
2 TABLESPOONS FLOUR
1/8 TEASPOON SALT
4 EGGS
2 CUPS MILK
1 TO 2 CUPS COOKED RICE
1/2 CUP RAISINS (OPTIONAL)
1/2 TEASPOON NUTMEG

♀ Preheat the oven to 350 degrees. Butter a 1-quart casserole.
♀ Mix the sugar, flour and salt in a bowl. Add the eggs and mix well. Blend in the milk gradually.
♀ Add the rice and raisins and mix well. Pour into the casserole. Sprinkle with nutmeg.
♀ Bake for 45 to 60 minutes or until a knife inserted in the center comes out clean.

SERVES 4 TO 6

♀ *If I can't dance, I don't want to be part of your revolution.*
Emma Goldman

CHOCOLATE FUDGE

1 1/2 CUPS CHOPPED WALNUTS
4 OUNCES UNSWEETENED BAKING CHOCOLATE
4 CUPS SUGAR
1 1/2 CUPS MILK
1/4 CUP BUTTER
2 TEASPOONS PURE VANILLA EXTRACT

♀ Butter two 8-inch square pans. Sprinkle with the walnuts.
♀ Combine the chocolate, sugar and milk in a deep heavy saucepan. Cook over low heat until the chocolate melts and the sugar dissolves, stirring constantly. Increase the heat to medium. Cook to 234 degrees on a candy thermometer, stirring constantly.
♀ Remove from the heat. Add the butter and vanilla; do not stir. Place in a larger pan of ice water. Let stand until mixture is cooled to 110 degrees.
♀ Beat until the mixture loses its gloss. Spread the fudge in the prepared pans. Beat in a small amount of milk or cream if the fudge stiffens too quickly. Cut into squares.

MAKES 2 PANS

(Boys Will Be Boys? Not!, continued)

woman's testimony and scare away other women from reporting abuse. In the military, this threat has extra ammunition, because it can also mean losing your job, your career, your pension."

An unprecedented study by the Department of Defense in 1995 revealed that 78% of Army women experienced offensive sexual behavior, coercion, or assault. Another 51% said they faced job discrimination because of their sex.

ALICE PAUL: COURAGE AND DETERMINATION

Before Betty Friedan stopped waxing her kitchen floor, before Gloria Steinem went undercover as a Playboy bunny, even before Shirley Chisholm decided to run for President, there was Alice Paul. When she died in 1977 at 92, this indomitable woman had been fighting for women's rights for more than 70 years.

Alice Paul got her first exposure to militant feminism in England around the turn of the century, as a follower of Emmeline Pankhurst. She exposed herself to all the hazards and penalties, jail included, in the fight for woman's suffrage.

Back in the United States, she added D.C. jail and the Occoquan workhouse to her jail experience. She also had a taste of life in the psychiatric ward of a hospital where she was taken after her prison hunger strike had weakened her to the point where she needed medical care.

SUFFRAGE CANDY

Joanie DiMartino of Alice Paul (NJ) NOW explained the name of this candy: In 1911 the Pennsylvania Woman Suffrage Association needed to buy a telephone, so they sold postcards, buttons, stickers, notecards, and peanut brittle they called "Suffrage Candy."

Innumerable notecards and two hundred pounds of candy later, the telephone was purchased.

1 1/2 CUPS ROASTED PEANUTS
1/4 TEASPOON SALT
1 CUP SUGAR
1/2 CUP LIGHT CORN SYRUP
1/2 CUP WATER
1 1/2 TABLESPOONS BUTTER OR MARGARINE
1/2 TEASPOON VANILLA EXTRACT

♀ Preheat the oven to 325 to 350 degrees.

♀ Chop the peanuts, place evenly on a lightly greased baking sheet and sprinkle with salt. Place in the oven to warm.

♀ Mix the sugar, corn syrup and water in a large heavy saucepan. Heat over low heat until the sugar dissolves, stirring constantly. Cook over medium heat to 265 degrees on a candy thermometer, hard-ball stage.

♀ Add the butter. Cook over low heat to 290 degrees on the candy thermometer, brittle thread stage.

♀ Remove from the heat. Stir in the vanilla and the warmed peanuts. Pour into large lightly greased baking pan. Let stand until cool. Break into pieces.

MAKES 1 POUND

FEMINIST TEA PARTY

A natural way for busy activists to raise money! Mail an enticing tea bag (orange and spice smells great through the envelope) to supporters with the following recipe:

THE ENCLOSED TEA BAG
1 CUP WATER
MILK (OPTIONAL)
SUGAR (OPTIONAL)

♀ Find clean cup, and put teabag in it. Clear stove of paper and other NOW work. Dust stove burner. Put water into tea kettle or pan. Boil water; pour over tea bag. Add optional milk and sugar. Put feet up, stay home, write check to NOW for encouraging you to stay home and rest for one night.

(Alice Paul: Courage and Determination, continued)

It worked, of course. The 19th Amendment passed, and women had the vote. Three years later, in 1923, she wrote the Equal Rights Amendment, and worked unceasingly to see it accepted and ratified. Her dream remains unfulfilled.

Alice Paul is second from right.

RECIPE INDEX

SUBJECT INDEX

This index contains selected issues, events and people featured in the book. A page number in *italics* indicates that a related photograph appears on that page.

Six-year-old Alicia Jacot of Tacoma, Washington,
demonstrated her commitment to equality during an International
Women's Day March on March 6, 1982 in Seattle.

MEMBERSHIP APPLICATION

COUNT ME IN! I wish to join NOW and commit myself to take action to bring women into full participation in the mainstream of American society now, exercising all privileges and responsibilities thereof in truly equal partnership with men.

Name

Address   Phone

City   State   Zip

Daytime Phone   FAX

Evening Phone   E-Mail

Check one:

_____ Regular Dues. $35 covers national, state and local dues; $40 for residents of AZ, CA, IL, IN, MI and NY.

_____ Reduced Dues. A sliding scale available from $15 to $34.

♀

A FEMINIST CLASSIC

"The perfect gift for a young woman . . . who does not yet realize what Patricia Ireland . . . won for her, and at what price."
                       —*New York Times Book Review*

"Part memoir, part history, part call to action, *What Women Want* covers considerable ground."   —*Miami Herald*

"A blueprint of how to live a life of social and political activism. Ireland is an expert architect."   —*Bookpage*

Order by calling (202) 331-0066 or through the NOW online catalog at http://www.now.org

National Organization for Women
1000 16th Street NW, Suite 700
Washington, D.C. 20036
Phone: (202) 331-0066
Fax: (202) 785-8576
Internet: www.now.org/
catalogfiles/catalog.html

Don't Assume I don't Cook!

RECIPES FOR WOMEN'S LIVES

Name
_____

Street Address
_____

City   State   Zip
_____

Telephone

Your Order	Qty	Total
Don't Assume I don't Cook @ $18.95 ea.		$
Shipping and Handling (*see below*)		$
Total		$

Shipping/Handling: $4.00 for 1 to 2 books
$5.00 for 3 to 4 books
$6.00 for 5 or more books

[   ] MasterCard   [   ] VISA   [   ] AMEX
[   ] Check enclosed payable to NOW Cookbook

Account Number   Expiration Date
_____

Cardholder Name
_____

Signature

Photocopies accepted.